ELEMENTS OF
PHYSIOLOGICAL
PSYCHOLOGY

ELEMENTS OF PHYSIOLOGICAL PSYCHOLOGY

Allen M. Schneider
Swarthmore College

Barry Tarshis

McGraw-Hill, Inc.
New York   St. Louis   San Francisco   Auckland   Bogotá
Caracas   Lisbon   London   Madrid   Mexico City   Milan   Montreal
New Delhi   San Juan   Singapore   Sydney   Tokyo   Toronto

This book was set in New Aster by CRWaldman Graphic
Communications.
The editors were Jane Vaicunas, Beth Kaufman, and Tom Holton;
the designer was Karen K. Quigley;
the production supervisor was Elizabeth J. Strange.
The photo editor was Anne Manning.
Von Hoffmann Press, Inc., was printer and binder.

Cover Photo: André Baranowski

ELEMENTS OF PHYSIOLOGICAL PSYCHOLOGY

This book is printed on acid-free paper.

1234567890   VNH   VNH   9098765

P/N 055569-9
PART OF
ISBN 0-07-911488-1

Library of Congress Cataloging-in-Publication Data

Schneider, Allen M.
     Elements of physiological psychology / Allen M. Schneider, Barry
  Tarshis
          p.   cm.
     Includes bibliographical references and index.
     ISBN 0-07-911488-1 (set)
     1. Psychophysiology.   I. Tarshis, Barry.   II. Title.
QP360.S35   1995
612.8—dc20   94-21354

For my wife, Naomi, with gratitude and love.
—A.M.S.

CHAPTER 4

THE ELECTROCHEMICAL BASIS OF BEHAVIOR 105

CHAPTER 5

THE NEUROCHEMICAL BASIS OF BEHAVIOR 143

CHAPTER 6

SENSORY PROCESSING 186

CHAPTER 7

THE VISUAL SYSTEM 207

LEARNING 551

MEMORY 592

LOCALIZATION OF HIGHER-ORDER FUNCTION 632

When Barry Tarshis and I first decided in the early 1970s to collaborate on a textbook in physiological psychology, we had a clearly defined goal: to produce a textbook that would not only give undergraduate students a solid foundation in this dynamic science but would also prove to be more accessible and more enjoyable to read than other textbooks in the field. Our conviction at the time was that it was possible to present complex concepts clearly, coherently, and engagingly without oversimplifying, without talking down to students, and without sacrificing either the quality or the amount of information contained in the book.

Physiological psychology itself, of course, has changed dramatically since the first textbook was published a little more than 20 years ago, and the concepts, if anything, have become more complex than ever. What has *not* changed, however, is our conviction that the complexity of subject matter and the readability of a textbook covering this subject are not incompatible. So once again, as we have done in our previous work, we have shown equal concern for both the information we present and the manner in which we present it.

Instructors familiar with our earlier textbook—*An Introduction to Physiological Psychology*—will notice immediately that we have made a number of significant changes in our newest work, which is not simply a revision of our earlier textbook but is, in fact, a new and much more comprehensive book.

The most obvious difference between this book and our previous book, one that we made at the request of many instructors who have used our book in the past, is that we have reduced the number of chapters from 26 to 18—without, however, cutting down on the topics we cover or the depth with which we cover these topics. The reason behind this change was to make the organization of the book conform more smoothly to the typical school calendar.

In spite of the reduced number of chapters, *Elements of Physiological Psychology* is more comprehensive than its predecessor and, as such, is geared to a larger audience. Of course, expanding the scope of the book while cutting back on the number of chapters was a difficult challenge, but we think we have met that challenge, and we have done so by relying on many of the same techniques that we used successfully in our previous book. Because we have always operated under the assumption that many of your students do not have strong backgrounds in the physical and biological sciences, we have kept the language simple and direct and have avoided the all too common tendency in scientific textbooks to explain complicated technical concepts with equally complicated technical jargon. We have also tried to link every concept we introduce not only with concepts encountered earlier in the same chapter but earlier in the book as well. Indeed, we have taken special pains to ensure that students see the continuity of the principles that underlie physiological psychology.

As we did in our previous book, we have tried to strike a productive balance between information about experimental developments and information about clinical applications. And even more than we did in our previous book, we have gone out of our way to relate the concepts and processes we describe to issues and ideas that your students can recognize and identify with. Finally, we have tried to be highly selective about the experiments we've cited, describing only those of special significance or interest.

The change in the number of chapters notwithstanding, the basic structure of this textbook is essentially the same as it has always been. We begin by giving students a historical perspective of physiological psychology, and we devote the next several chapters (Chapters 2–5) to the nervous system, beginning with the neuron (2), then the structure (3) and function (4) of the nervous system, and ending with a close look at the neurochemical basis of behavior, including psychopharmacology (5). Sensory and motor processes are covered in the next five chapters (6–10): one devoted to vision (7); one combining audition, smell, and taste (8); one devoted to the cutaneous senses (including pain); and one devoted to the mechanics of movement. Eating and drinking have been combined into a single chapter (11), followed by chapters on sleep (12), and sex (13).

As we did in our last book, we have divided emotion into two chapters. The first (14) deals with the neural basis of emotion; the second (15) deals with the neural basis of psychological disorder including the anxiety disorders, depression, and schizophrenia. The three final chapters deal with learning, memory, and the localization of higher-order functions such as language. We've been careful, however, to keep the organization of the book as flexible as possible. Thus you can follow the order of chapters as presented or, within reason, alter it to your preference.

Two other key differences between this book and our earlier book are worth noting. The first is that we have put more emphasis than ever on the figures used throughout the book, many of which are now in color. The second is the addition at the end of each chapter of not only a summary of key points and suggested readings but a list of key terms as well. You will notice, finally, that references come at the end of the book, rather than the end of each chapter.

ACKNOWLEDGMENTS

There are a great many people without whose help, advice, and support this book could never have been written, and I want to offer my heartfelt thanks to all of them. Among those I want to single out in particular are a group of my colleagues, all of them dedicated teachers and scientists. This very special group of people includes the following:

Bruce Kapp, whose insights and critiques contributed immeasurably to the new developments covered in the chapters on learning and memory;

Earl Thomas, who provided unfailingly good advice in the areas of pharmacology, sleep, sex, and emotion, and who helped sharpen my thinking in so many different ways;

Jeanne Marecek, whose discussions and comments on the neural basis of psychological disorder gave me new insights and a new perspective of abnormal psychology and its connection to physiological psychology;

Myrna Schwartz, who generously shared with me her scholarly perspectives of language and neurodegenerative diseases;

Barry Schwartz, whose incisive comments and points of clarification gave critical focus to the learning chapter;

Peter Simson, whose comments and advice on the chemical basis of behavior were indispensable;

Glenn Rosen, who helped to clarify my understanding of language and dyslexia;

Andrew Garner and *Scott Gilbert*, who shared with me their expertise on neural development.

What pleases me in particular about this group of people, apart from the invaluable help they gave me, is that six of the nine are former students. There are few rewards in teaching greater than that of watching former students achieve success in their chosen fields; and so it is with an added measure of pride and pleasure that I ponder the irony of this switching of roles: I the student; they the teachers.

I would also like to thank Joanne Bramley, Julia Welbon, Dorthea Beebe, and Hattie Green, each of whom in her own way was a constant source of support and inspiration thoughout this project. And I owe a special debt of gratitude to everyone I worked with at McGraw-Hill, in particular, Jane Vaicunas, Beth Kaufman, Tom Holton, Elizabeth Strange, and Anne Manning. Each of them was involved in the book in a different and critical way but their collective contribution was monumental. Indeed, if it weren't for the patience, the encouragement, and the determination of Tom, Beth, and Elizabeth, in particular, this book might never have been written.

For their generous and valuable efforts in reading and evaluating many parts of the manuscript, I want to thank: Carol Mohr Batt, Sacred Heart University; Terry Blumenthal, Wake Forest University; Terry

Fetterman, Cabrillo College; Robert Frank, University of Cincinnati; Edward Holmes, Hampton University; Dianne Irwin, Glendale Community College; Yoshito Kawahara, San Diego Mesa College; Charles Kutscher, Syracuse University; Richard Lewis, Pomona College; Bruce McCutcheon, State University of New York at Albany; Charles Noble, North Georgia College; Carol Pandey, Los Angeles Pierce College; Ina Samuels, University of Massachusetts–Boston; Paul Wellman, Texas A & M University; Neil Wollman, Manchester College; and Betty Zimmerberg-Glick, Williams College.

The greatest debt, however, is the one I owe to my wife, Naomi, whose patience and support throughout this project went far beyond what any husband might reasonably expect.

Allen M. Schneider

As you will quickly discover, the subject you are about to study—physiological psychology—is a fascinating science, and largely because it incorporates elements from so many other sciences, including biochemistry, biology, endocrinology, neuroanatomy, and psychopharmacology. Unfortunately, however, this aspect of physiological psychology—its breadth—can be a source of concern and intimidation to some students, particularly students who lack a background in some of these sciences.

If you are feeling the least bit intimidated by what you need to learn in physiological psychology, our advice to you is to relax. That is because one of our main objectives in this book is to make sure that the concepts and the information we present are accessible. This is not to underestimate the complexity of this science but rather to emphasize our strong belief that it is possible to explain even highly complex concepts in ways that are relatively easy for students to understand and relate to.

HOW THE BOOK IS ORGANIZED

The book is divided among 18 chapters, and what follows is a brief look at each of these chapters:

Chapter 1 gives a historical perspective of physiological psychology that will make it all the easier for you to understand and appreciate the logic of the information you'll be encountering throughout the rest of the book.

Chapters 2 through 5 examine the nervous system, the vast network of cells without whose involvement no behavior could take place. You'll start (Chapter 2) by looking at the basic component of this system—the neuron. You will focus on what the neuron is, how it develops, how it ages, and two diseases, Alzheimer's and Parkinson's, associated with aging. In Chapter 3 you will read about the structure of the nervous system—the peripheral nervous system, the spinal cord, and the brain—and in Chapters 4 and 5 about the function of the nervous system—its electrical and chemical properties, including their implications for the area of psychopharmacology.

Chapters 6 through 9 focus on how the structure and function of the nervous system you've learned about in the first five chapters produces the kaleidoscope of sights, sounds, smells, tastes, and tactile sensations that you experience as part of your daily existence. Much of what we cover in these chapters involves a neurophysiological process known as sensory coding, the term used to describe how the brain "translates" the language of the nervous system into familiar sensations. Chapter 10 examines the physiological basis of movement.

The next set of chapters will introduce you to the physiological foundations of such basic behaviors as eating and drinking (Chapter 11), sleeping (Chapter 12), and sex (Chapter 13), and will broaden your understanding of many of the problems often associated with these behaviors, among them obesity and insomnia. You will then read two chapters (Chapters 14 and 15) that will examine the physiological basis of such common emotions as fear, aggression, and pleasure, and will give you a broad picture of the fascinating work being done today to solve the riddle of schizophrenia, depression, and other psychological disorders.

The book concludes with three chapters (Chapters 16 through 18) that focus on the higher-order behavioral processes—learning, memory, and language—that make humans so unique a species.

Each chapter begins with an outline of the topics to be covered and a brief introduction. At the end of each chapter you'll find a summary that capsulizes the key points of the chapter, along with a list of key terms and a list of suggested readings. References to journals and scholarly works appear at the back of the book. The references along with the suggested readings provide a basis for our conclusions and direct you to more complete information. Finally, the figures throughout the book should go a long way to enhance your understanding of important concepts.

We think you will enjoy reading this book. It will give you a solid foundation in what may well be the most important branch of the behavioral sciences today. It should also give you new insights into behavior in general and, we hope, into yourself.

Allen M. Schneider
Barry Tarshis

1

HISTORY OF PHYSIOLOGICAL PSYCHOLOGY

INTRODUCTION

On the evening of July 17, 1974, while driving home from work in his sports car, a 23-year-old man from Rehoboth, Rhode Island, picked up two teenage girls who were hitchhiking their way to a nearby amusement park. As soon as the girls climbed into the car, the young man offered to share a bottle of beer he was drinking. He then suggested that instead of going to the amusement park, the girls take a drive with him through the back roads outside Rehoboth. Because he seemed like a "nice guy," the girls went along with the idea. Three hours later, semiconscious and bleeding profusely, the two girls were rushed by ambulance to Union Hospital in Fall River, Massachusetts. At roughly the same time, the young man was making a phone call to his father, an endocrinologist. "Dad," he said, "I think I may have just killed two girls."

Fortunately for everybody concerned, the young man had not killed the girls, but he had come perilously close, for he had attacked both of them with a short-handled stonemason's hammer. "We asked him if he would drive us home," one of the girls testified 2 years later when the young man went on trial, "and all of a sudden he just hit me with a hammer."

When the time came to defend himself, the young man contended that the girls had been teasing him. Even so, he had no way of explaining why the teasing had goaded him to such violence. As he told his father on the night of the attack, "I simply went ape" (Mayer, 1982).

In Search of Answers

How does one explain the behavior that led to so senseless and violent a crime? If you know anything about psychology, you know, of course, that such questions do not lend themselves to easy answers. It is often suggested, for example, that random, violent behavior is a "conditioned" or learned behavior. The argument cited for this view is that people who commit violent crimes have often grown up in environments in which violence is commonplace. This explanation is plausible, except for one thing: not everyone who grows up in a violent environment becomes a violent adult, and violence is often committed by people who grew up in seemingly normal homes and in the best of neighborhoods. This is why violent behavior, in many cases, is seen as an emotional disorder, traceable to such factors as unresolved childhood conflicts.

None of these explanations, however, was put forward by the lawyer who defended the Rehoboth man when the case came to trial. Neither did he claim, as might have been expected, that the young man was "insane" at the time of the crime and therefore could not be held accountable for his actions.

What the lawyer did instead was to offer a defense that symbolizes the rationale behind this book—a defense rooted in the physiological basis of behavior. The young man's metabolism, his lawyer claimed, was different from that of most people: for whenever the young man consumed alcohol, the alcohol was not metabolized normally. Instead, traces of alcoholic residue remained in the man's system, profoundly affecting a portion of the brain, known as the limbic system, that appears to control emotional behavior. The result: whenever the young man drank too much, he was simply incapable of controlling any violent impulse.

The jury in this case found the young man from Rehoboth guilty. Importantly, though, the judge accepted the lawyer's argument. Citing "convincing medical evidence," the judge acknowledged that the young man was suffering from a "serious problem." And assured that the young man was receiving the proper therapy, he converted the 18-year sentence to 6 years of probation.

What makes this ruling so significant? Simply that this trial may have marked the first time in history that a criminal action had been defended on the basis of a brain disorder. Similar defenses, however, are becoming more and more routine, and largely because of the science you will be learning about in this book. The science is called physiological psychology.

PHYSIOLOGICAL PSYCHOLOGY DEFINED

Physiological psychology is a branch of psychology that seeks to explain behavior in physiological terms—that is, in terms of the electrochemical events that take place inside the body whenever behavior occurs. As the term implies, this science combines elements of physiology (the study of the vital processes of animal organisms) with elements of psychology (the study of behavior). The science is often referred to as *psychobiology*.

The basic assumption of physiological psychology is this: *all* behavior—whether it is as extreme as attacking two young women with a hammer or as routine as eating a hamburger—can ultimately be traced to physical events taking place inside the body and, in particular, inside the brain. To put the same thought another way, for every behavioral event—every action, every thought, every feeling—there is a corresponding physical event or series of physical events taking place in the body. These events, moreover, involve the chemical and electrical properties of the nervous system. The goal of this science is to discover the precise relationship between these events and behavior.

It is important to stress that physiological psychology is a *behavioral* science. The emphasis on behavior is important because it differentiates physiological psychologists from scientists working in such related fields as neurophysiology, neuroanatomy, and biochemistry. The specialists in these other life sciences focus on the vital processes of living organisms: studying how the enormously varied cellular components in animals are structured and how they function. Physiological psychologists are interested in these processes, too, but their focus is on the *behavioral implications* of these processes—how they control what we do, what we think, and what we feel.

The Behavioral Factor

To be sure, the idea that all behavior is, at root, biologically controlled is a sweeping premise, and we need to place the idea in proper perspective. For if it is indeed true, as physiological psychologists maintain, that all behavior can be traced to physical events taking place inside the body, it is fair to ask how and where other approaches to understanding behavior fit into the picture? How do you reconcile the premises of physiological psychology with, say, the behavioral theories of B. F. Skinner, the social theories of Emile Durkheim, or the personality theories of Sigmund Freud, Carl Jung, and Abraham Maslow?

The answer, in brief, is that explaining behavior within the context of physiological events doesn't necessarily refute or preclude other explanations of behavior or other therapeutic approaches. Findings in physiological psychology over the past 30 years, for instance, have led to the development of drugs that are now being used to treat a broad range of behavioral disorders that include anxiety, depression, alcoholism—even drug addiction. But their development doesn't mean nonchemical approaches to these disorders are outdated. The drug known as methadone has proven to be a reasonably effective way to wean drug addicts away from heroin. But no chemical therapy can do anything about the feelings of alienation and low self-esteem that may have led to the addiction in the first place. It is important to remember, then, that physiological psychology is simply one of many approaches to understanding behavior. And as psychologist Henry Gleitman reminds us, "psychology is a field of many faces, and to see it fully we must look at them all" (Gleitman, 1991).

LOOKING BACK: HOW PHYSIOLOGICAL PSYCHOLOGY EVOLVED

Physiological psychology is a young science. True, research into many of the areas now embodied by physiological psychology has been going on since the early part of the nineteenth century, but it has been only within the past 60 years or so that scientists have developed theories and conducted experiments aimed specifically at discovering the physical relationships between brain function and behavior. It wasn't until the 1930s, for instance, that researchers first began to see how the brain communicates with—and thus controls—the various muscles and organs throughout the body. It wasn't until the 1950s that researchers began to understand how the brain processes external stimuli into the sensory experiences we know as sight, hearing, smell, touch, and taste. And it has been only within the past decade or so that researchers have been able to isolate the cellular mechanisms now believed to control such higher-order psychological processes as learning and memory.

It is no accident that much of what we know about the physiological basis of behavior is of relatively recent vintage. For one thing, it has been only within the past 100 years or so that more than a handful of people, even in the scientific community, have been prepared to accept the fundamental notion of physiological psychology—that behaviors normally associated with the mind, such as thoughts, emotions, and dreams, can be explained in physical terms. Furthermore, the studies that underlie our understanding of the relationship between physiology and behavior simply could not have taken place without the technological advances that now enable researchers to study the brain with a degree of precision that would have been deemed impossible as recently as 50 years ago. In short, before physiological psychology could gain a foothold as a genuine science, two things had to happen: first, attitudes having to do with behavior itself had to change; second, methods had to emerge that would enable scientists to study the workings of the brain. It is against this backdrop that we will now present a brief history of the science you will be studying in this book.

Setting the Philosophical Framework

The roots of physiological psychology, like the roots of psychology itself, can be found in the works of the early Greek philosophers, Plato in particular. Like most early philosophers, Plato was intensely interested in the mind, but he viewed the world in *dualistic* terms. He saw the physical world—everything that could be seen, touched, or felt—as an entity separate from the "mind," and he contended that the mind, because of its "spiritual" nature, not only was superior to the physical body but also was beyond understanding. In Plato's view, no amount of analysis or reasoning could reveal how the mind works.

Few psychologists today, of course, take this view seriously. It is now generally accepted that the laws that govern the workings of the mind are no different, at root, from the laws that govern physical events—a philosophical view known as *monism*. But let us not condemn Plato. Among the many intriguing conjectures that can be made about the intellectual development of Western civilization in general is whether Platonic philosophy, on which so much of early Western thought was based, would have been quite the same if Plato had been able to witness the physiological psychology experiments now taking place in research laboratories.

The Pneuma Theory

The first real "theory" of how mind operates, initially advanced during the era of the Athenian Empire, was called the "pneuma theory," and it was based on the belief that the mind was controlled by invisible spirits known as pneuma. What is most interesting about the pneuma theory is that it went virtually unchallenged for centuries, even though anatomists and physiologists had long been aware of the brain and its relationship to behavior. As early as the fifth century B.C., for instance, the Greek physician Hippocrates theorized that the brain was the controlling mechanism of all mental and emotional faculties. Six centuries later, the Greek physician Galen severed the nerves leading to a pig's larynx and correctly offered the pig's inability to vocalize as proof of a relationship between the nervous system and behavior. But neither Hippocrates nor Galen used these findings to challenge the pneuma theory. Galen, in fact, merely embellished the theory. He explained that the function of the brain was to refine the pneuma and redirect it through the nerves to the muscles.

An even more telling example of how deeply the pneuma theory was embedded in Western thought is found in the case of the Italian physician and physicist Luigi Galvani. In the early 1790s Galvani discovered that electric current applied to a frog's nerves produced muscle movement, and he correctly theorized that nerves are capable of conducting electricity. Like Galen, however, Galvani did not challenge the pneuma theory. Instead, he attempted to fit his discovery into the pneuma mold, claiming that he had identified the nature of the pneuma: a unique substance—he called it "animal electricity"—that moves from nerve to muscle in the form of a fluid.

Why the Pneuma Theory Persisted

In view of the many discoveries that seemed to refute its validity, it is logical to question why it took so long for the pneuma theory to die.

There are two explanations. The first is that until the nineteenth century there was no experimental evidence to *disprove* the existence and impact of invisible spirits. After all, no one until the latter part of the nineteenth century had ever actually seen the internal functions of the nervous system that we can now observe and record in a laboratory.

The second and perhaps more important reason is that until the nineteenth century any challenge to the pneuma theory was considered a challenge to the religious dogma that dominated scientific thought throughout the Middle Ages and to only a slightly lesser extent for several centuries beyond. Whatever the reason, the pneuma theory was so deeply rooted in Western thought that, according to B. F. Skinner, it even influences the way some people think today. "Unable to understand how or why the person we see behaves as he does," Skinner has said, "we attribute his behavior to a person we cannot see, whose behavior we cannot explain either but about whom we are not inclined to ask questions. We probably adopt this strategy not so much because of any lack of interest or power but because of a long-standing conviction that for much of human behavior there are no relevant antecedents" (Skinner, 1970).

The Ascent of Monism

As long as students of human behavior were forced to limit their studies to a framework that attributed the mind to invisible spirits, there was little way for the pneuma theory to be challenged and little chance for progress in the search for the physiological bases of behavior. This is why the man sometimes referred to as the "father of physiological psychology" was neither a physiologist nor a psychologist. He was the seventeenth-century philosopher and mathematician René Descartes.

Though deeply religious, Descartes questioned the long-accepted notion that human fate is subject to the whim of invisible and unknowable forces. He argued instead that humans can become "masters and possessors of nature," and he insisted that the study of human behavior could be approached mechanistically—in much the same way that Kepler, Galileo, Newton, and other scientists were attempting to explain purely physical phenomena. Descartes also took issue with those medieval scientists and philosophers who sought to provide logical "proofs" for the "absolute truths" found in the Scriptures and in the writings of Plato. Descartes contended that the search for true knowledge begins with the willingness to doubt everything that has been presented as "truth." In Descartes's view, nothing is beyond human comprehension, so long as phenomena are studied without dogmatic adherence to past knowledge.

René Descartes.

Descartes was arguably the first person to propose a philosophy of mind rooted, in part at least, in physiology. He rejected the notion that the body and mind operated in separate, unrelated spheres, and he maintained that many behaviors formerly thought to be beyond the scope of conventional scientific investigation—basic sensory experiences, for instance—could be explained the same way you might explain the workings of a machine.

Descartes thus made the first true break from dualism, but it was a modest break at best. Iconoclast though he was, Descartes never rejected the pneuma theory; nor did he ever propose, probably because of his religious beliefs, that *all* human behavior could be reduced entirely to mechanics. He made no attempt, for instance, to apply the mechanistic view of behavior to the higher-order rational behaviors—thinking, learning, and language—that distinguish humans from lower animals. Rooted in dualistic thinking, he proposed the existence of a rational "soul" (i.e., mind), an entity that did not lend itself to a mechanistic explanation but that constituted, in fact, the difference between humans and other animal species.

Descartes ushered in a new way of thinking about many aspects of behavior, but his refusal to extend the mechanistic view to higher-order behaviors reinforced the notion that the mind was beyond the scope of scientific inquiry. He had good reason for doing this. For when one of Descartes's followers, the French physician and philosopher Julien Offray de La Mettrie, dared to extend the mechanistic view to the mind in a book entitled *The Human Machine*, published in 1748, he was banished from France for what were considered heretical views.

The British Empiricists: From Intuition to Observation

If we can thank Descartes, and later La Mettrie, for establishing and extending the philosophical framework that underlies physiological psychology, we can thank another group of philosophers, the British empiricists, for establishing the method of inquiry that is now at the very core of this science. More than any other group, the British empiricists—John Locke, George Berkeley, and David Hume, in particular—were responsible for taking the study of mind-body relations out of the realm of the metaphysical and the religious and into the mainstream of experimental scientific inquiry.

At the risk of oversimplifying, British empiricism was based on the idea that the only valid path to knowledge and wisdom was that of experience itself, not logic or intuition. Given this view, the empiricists rejected explanations of behavior that had been arrived at the way the Greeks had done it—through speculation and logic. Drawing their intellectual fuel from the writings of Thomas Hobbes and Francis Bacon, the empiricists agreed with Descartes that the search for true knowledge begins with the willingness to doubt everything in the past that has been presented as truth, but they added another ingredient to the search for knowledge: observation. According to the empirical way of thinking, if you want to know something about the workings of the mind, you do not sit back to ponder, speculate, and debate it the way Plato and Socrates might have done. You set up experiments in which the impact of these workings can be seen, studied, and measured.

Putting Empiricism to Practical Use

Empiricism established a philosophical framework for the scientific study of behavior and of the mind, but before physiological psychology could emerge as a true science, it needed a methodology, that is, a means of studying the workings of the brain and the impact these workings have on behavior. In the physical sciences—physics and chemistry, in particular—methodology is rarely an issue of controversy. Psychology, though, is different, and physiological psychology is more different still. Psychology deals with *people*, not chemicals. And physiological psychology deals specifically with the one organ—the brain—that defines who we are as human beings.

So even though the scientific world was willing to accept the notion that human behavior could be studied scientifically, obstacles still remained. The first obstacle was establishing the validity of using lower animals as subjects of experiments designed to produce an understanding of the physiological basis of human behavior. The second obstacle had to do with technology: developing tools and methods that would make experimentation possible. We will now look briefly at how each of these obstacles was overcome.

BEHAVIOR AND EXPERIMENTATION

We take it for granted today that one way to study psychological processes is to conduct experiments on lower animals. But the idea that you can learn something about human behavior by studying lower animals is relatively new. The person most responsible for fostering this view was Charles Darwin.

Darwin, of course, advanced the theory known as evolution, and while his name is not normally associated with psychology, his theory—the idea of a physiological and behavioral link between lower animals and humans—helped create the foundation of experimental psychology. Much of what we know today about the human brain and the role it plays in controlling behavior is the result of experiments involving lower animals. But none of these data would be valid were it not for the general belief that for all the differences that separate one species from another, there are nonetheless fundamental similarities. As you will see, much of what we know about the most basic neurobehavioral event—the neural impulse—is the result of experiments on the squid. And much of what we are beginning to learn today about the physiological basis of eating, drinking, sleep, sex, aggression, learning, and memory is based on studies involving rats and monkeys.

This is not to say that behavioral research should be done exclusively on lower animals, nor is it to say that we can learn about the brain and behavior only from lower-animal research. What it does say, as we will discover throughout the book, is that when research on humans, because of physical risk or ethical reasons, becomes impractical, researchers believe that lower-animal research, especially on behaviors that lower animals and humans share, is a perfectly legitimate approach to the study of the physiological basis of behavior.

Charles Darwin.

Watson and Behaviorism

Darwin published his most famous work, *The Origin of Species by Means of Natural Selection*, in 1859, but it wasn't until well after the turn of the century that experimentation with lower animals became recognized as a valid research tool in psychology and that John Watson, inspired by animal research, founded the school of psychological thought known today as *behaviorism.*

The behaviorist view advanced by Watson was based on the idea that "mind," because it cannot be seen, should be purged from the experimental psychologist's working vocabulary. This is not to say (as some writers have mistakenly maintained) that Watson disparaged the significance of the unseen mind in the shaping of behavior. He simply questioned the validity of something unseen as a suitable subject of scientific investigation.

Watson's views have had tremendous influence on the development of physiological psychology. Largely because of these views, physiological psychologists today are careful to differentiate between behavioral phenomena that can be observed and mental states that can only be inferred. You will rarely hear a physiological psychologist, or for that matter any experimental psychologist, report that a certain pattern of neuroelectrical activity is taking place in an experimental animal's brain because the animal at that moment is "afraid"—not unless the researcher can also define "afraid" in behavioral terms. Instead, a physiological psychologist may report that the animal is exhibiting certain overt behavioral patterns, such as pressing a lever to avoid shock, which may be taken as an indicator of fear.

The important point here is that fear—or, for that matter, any internal psychological state—is only *inferred* from behavioral indexes and is defined in terms of overt behavior used to measure it. These indexes of behavior, commonly referred to as *operational definitions*, represent one of the major legacies of Watson's behaviorism.

PHYSIOLOGICAL PSYCHOLOGY: ITS BIOLOGICAL ROOTS

Up to now we have seen that physiological psychology owes its philosophical roots to the break that Descartes made with traditional dualistic thinking and owes its methodological roots to the theory of Darwin and to the work of those early psychologists who established lower-animal experimentation as a valid means of studying behavior and established specific scientific criteria as the basis of these studies.

We now turn our attention to a third obstacle that needed to be overcome before physiological psychology, as we know it today, could emerge as a true science. This area involves physiology itself and, in particular, the structure and function of the nervous system.

Before the nineteenth century, physiologists and anatomists theorized that the nervous system differed little in its basic structure from the circulatory system—that it was simply a network of continuous "tubes" through which "fluids" might flow. Today we know that the nervous system is not made of tubes but of special cells known as *neurons*. We also know that the neurons themselves do not function by conducting fluids; they function by conducting electrochemical signals known as *neural impulses*.

The scientists who developed these early theories of the nervous system were no less creative than modern-day physiologists and anatomists. They simply lacked the tools needed to go beyond these early theories. This is a point worth stressing. However brilliant and visionary a scientist may be—and this is as true today as it was in the nineteenth century—without the technology and knowledge to carry out experiments in the field, the work produced will be of little scientific value. In the words of the great physiologist Pierre Flourens, "Everything in experimental research depends on the method, for it is the method which gives the results. A new method leads to new results; a rigorous method to precise results; a vague method has never led to anything but confused results" (Teitelbaum, 1967).

Pierre Flourens.

With these considerations in mind, let us trace briefly the sequence of events and discoveries that brought us from those early theories of tubes and fluids to the rapidly evolving picture we now have of the nervous system. Our survey will be shaped by the manner in which scientists were able to learn about two features of the nervous system: its structure (what it is) and its function (how it works).

Neuroanatomy: From Tube to Neuron

Two breakthroughs marked the transition from the idea that nerves were nothing more than tubes to the view that holds true today. One was the improvement in the magnifying powers of the microscope, which occurred around 1830. This breakthrough enabled neuroanatomists to see and describe the nerve cells (neurons) in the brain. The other was the development of a chemical technique known as *staining* which enabled neuroanatomists to see certain features of nerve cells that, even under the microscope, were not otherwise visible.

Several staining procedures were developed in the 1800s, but the one that produced the best results was introduced by Camillo Golgi in 1875. Golgi found, apparently by accident, that exposing neural tissue to a chemical called *silver nitrate* stained some of the neurons black with the result that different parts of the neuron—its cell body and extensions arising from the cell body known as dendrites and axons—stood out in bold relief when viewed under the microscope. Using Golgi's staining procedure, Santiago Ramón y Cajal was able to identify the neuron as the basic unit of the nervous system. He also showed, for the first time, that what appeared to be a gelatinous mass of fused cells was in fact a highly intricate collection of discrete cells. A historical footnote to these discoveries is that Golgi and Ramón y Cajal shared the Nobel Prize in 1906, but they engaged in bitter disputes throughout their careers as to whose discovery was the more significant.

The Synapse

The work of Ramón y Cajal and Golgi left open a key question: How are neurons interconnected? Do they physically touch, as Golgi proposed, or are they separated by microscopic gaps, spaces too small to be seen under the microscope, as Ramón y Cajal theorized?

The consensus from the very beginning favored the gap theory, and in 1906 a British researcher named Charles Sherrington dubbed this gap—as yet unseen—the "synapse," which is derived from a Greek word meaning "to clasp." Fifty years later, with the invention of the electron microscope and its extraordinary magnifying powers, Sherrington's suspicions proved correct and the hypothetical synapse became a reality.

Sherrington also speculated, and again correctly, that the form of communication across the synapse was not electrical but actually chemical. As we will discover in Chapter 5, no neural process is more critical to behavior than the chemical events that take place across the synaptic gap. They govern not only normal behavior but abnormal behavior as well, and they even govern the effects of drugs that are used to alter behavior.

Neurophysiology: From Fluid to Neural Impulse

While some scientists were concerned with the structure of the nervous system, others were focusing on function. And while the view of structure was changing from hollow tubes to discrete neural cells, the view of function was changing from fluids to electrochemical signals.

The initial discovery that neurons conduct not by fluid but by electrochemical signals was made, as we have already noted, by Luigi Galvani in the late 1700s. But Galvani, remember, tried to shoehorn his findings into the prevailing pneuma theory, using his observations as evidence for a unique substance—he called it "animal electricity"—transported from nerve to muscle in the form of a fluid. It wasn't until 50 years later that Emil Du Bois-Reymond broke with the pneuma tradition and began to describe activity in the nervous system for what it really was: a purely physical, electrical phenomenon governed by the basic laws of physics and chemistry. In contrast to Galvani, who electrically stimulated a frog's nerve, observed muscle contraction, and inferred the presence of an electric signal, Du Bois-Reymond used a device known as a galvanometer to measure the electric signal and correctly attributed that signal to the movement of electrically charged particles along the surface of the neuron.

Shortly after Du Bois-Reymond reported his findings, another researcher, Julius Bernstein, studied the nature of the electric signal and confirmed that it was indeed a result of the movement of electrically charged particles called ions. Based on this observation, Bernstein formulated the *membrane theory* of neural conduction as an explanation of why and how these charges move. In Bernstein's view (which since has proved to be correct), the neuron has two electrical states. One is a resting state in which the charges are separated across the neural membrane; the other is an excitation state in which charges move in and out of the neuron across the membrane to produce the neuroelectric signal. We will consider the electrochemical properties of the neuron in detail in Chapter 4.

All this work and theorizing was done within a span of roughly 50 years—between 1800 and 1850. Curiously, however, very little was added to this body of knowledge for more than 100 years. The next breakthrough didn't occur until the 1960s, when Alan Hodgkin and Andrew Huxley, using a highly sophisticated radioactive-chemical procedure, confirmed Bernstein's membrane theory by actually observing the movement of electrically charged ions in and around the membrane.

Why was there so great a time span between the work of Bernstein and the work of Hodgkin and Huxley? In a word, technology. Hodgkin and Huxley could not have conducted their experiments had it not been for the advent of radioactive-chemical technology. But in addition to technology there was one other limiting factor. The sequence (the order) of the discoveries was just as important as the methods used to make them. Steps could not be skipped. For Hodgkin and Huxley to make their discoveries, Bernstein had to first make his, but for Bernstein to make his discovery Du Bois-Reymond had to first make his. This point is worth dwelling upon. If there is one lesson to be learned from the history of neurophysiology—a lesson that applies to all science—it is that science cannot be rushed. Discoveries (and the techniques that produce them) must unfold naturally in an orderly, systematic way. When the state of knowledge is right and when the technology is present, then and only then can the next step be taken.

Summing Up

To sum up, there are striking parallels between the history of neuroanatomy and the history of neurophysiology. In neuroanatomy, we moved from a crude to a more precise view of structure—from a tube to the neuron to the structure of the neuron. In neurophysiology, we moved from a crude to a more precise view of function—from fluid to the electrochemical signal to the movement of ions that produce the signal. In both cases precision is keyed to the development of instrumentation: in the case of neuroanatomy, to staining techniques and the microscope, and in the case of neurophysiology, to neuroelectrical recording and radioactive-chemical techniques.

MAKING THE BRAIN-BEHAVIOR CONNECTION

Physiological psychology, as you should appreciate by now, represents the intersection of three disciplines: neuroanatomy, neurophysiology, and the experimental analysis of behavior. Each area, as we've just seen, has its own body of knowledge, its own methodology, its own history. But each, in its own way, involves the same organ in the body: the brain.

Descartes was among the first to see the human brain as the true source of psychological processes, even though his view of the brain was a curious mix of matter and spirit. Believing that the brain controlled basic sensory and motor processes but not higher-order psychological processes such as thinking and reasoning, he developed a view of how these two separate processes were coordinated. He theorized that a small gland in the center of the brain known as the *pineal gland* served as the intermediary between mind and body: a place where the mind, and the thinking and reasoning that it produced, interacted with and exerted control over the body.

At the time, Descartes could not have realized what his theory of brain function would lead to. For even though the details of his theory were incorrect, the impact it has had on modern-day physiological psychology has been monumental. By placing the control of psychological functions (with the exception of thinking) in the brain and not the mind and by attributing those functions to different parts of the brain, Descartes raised questions that have intrigued students of brain function for the past 200 years. The basic question is, Where and how are the psychological processes represented in the brain? A related question is whether specific psychological processes are controlled by structures located in specific parts of the brain—the so-called localization-of-function theory—or whether the brain operates to control the processes, more or less, as a whole.

This question will shape our concerns throughout the remainder of the chapter. We will be looking at both points of view and at the people and the studies that have influenced the view that guides physiological psychology research today.

Localization-of-Function Doctrine

Franz Joseph Gall.

The first proponent of what has since become known as the *localization-of-function doctrine* was Franz Joseph Gall, a nineteenth-century anatomist. Through careful comparative studies on the brains of different kinds of animals, Gall was able to show that behavioral differences among species correlated closely with anatomical differences in brain structure. He discovered, for example, that the ability of a species to engage in complex behavior correlated with the size of the cortex (the outer gray covering of the brain) in the species. The larger the cortex, Gall observed, the greater the ability.

Gall was also among the first to point out that the cortex of the human brain occupies a much larger portion of brain mass in general than the cortex of other animals, and he used this observation to explain the difference between human and lower-animal behavior, a fact that few people would dispute. The problem, though, is that Gall wasn't content to speculate solely about the differences between human beings and lower animals. He also sought to explain differences *among* humans. Why are some people more intelligent, more aggressive, or more cautious than others? Gall's answer was that different personality traits are localized in different areas of the cortex. He reasoned, too, that if personality traits varied among people, the cortex—the size of the specific areas controlling the traits—must vary as well. The more dominant the trait, he reasoned, the larger the area of the cortex; the less dominant the trait, the smaller the area of the cortex.

Gall and Phrenology

Assuming for the moment that Gall was correct—that different personality traits are controlled by different areas of the cortex—it should be possible to predict the strength of various personality traits by simply measuring the size of their corresponding cortical sites. Such was Gall's thinking. Along with his pupil, Johann Kaspar Spurzheim, he compiled a vast amount of clinical and anecdotal data on schoolmates and patients. He linked the sizes of different parts of their brains (which he determined by measuring bumps and indentations along the surface of the skull) with their personality traits.

This practice of linking the shape of the skull to personality traits is known as *phrenology*, and no scientist today takes it very seriously. Bumps and indentations of the skull, as it turns out, are unrelated to the size of areas in the underlying cortex. Consequently, measuring these bumps and indentations with an eye toward learning something about behavior falls into the same dubious category as astrology or palmistry. Even so, Gall's work kindled interest in the notion that different parts of the brain control different behaviors. His method of testing his theory (phrenology) was off-target, but his fundamental view—the idea of localization of function—was an important contribution to scientific thought.

Flourens and Ablation

One of the first scientists to follow up on Gall's localization-of-function theory was Pierre Flourens. Like Gall, Flourens was interested in testing the localization-of-function doctrine, but in contrast to Gall's anecdotal observations on humans, Flourens conducted experiments on lower animals (birds, rabbits, and dogs). In the 1820s he developed a surgical technique, known as *ablation*, which enabled him to remove sections of the brain of experimental animals without killing the animals. He reasoned that if a specific area of the brain indeed controls a specific behavior, as the localization-of-function view claims, then ablation of that area should *abolish* that behavior.

On the surface, Flourens's findings appeared to refute the localization-of-function theory. He found that ablation of certain areas of the brain—the cerebellum and the medulla, for instance—resulted in very specific behavioral losses: a loss of balance in the case of the cerebellum and a loss of respiration in the case of the medulla. And he correctly concluded that each area is involved in the control of different behavior. But when he performed ablations on areas in the cortex, a different picture emerged. The ablations produced behavioral losses—loss of the ability to see and to hear and to move voluntarily—but the losses were virtually the same regardless of *which* area in the cortex he removed.

Flourens's conclusion: the localization-of-function principle holds but in only a very limited way. It accounts for the difference in behaviors controlled by certain areas of the brain (the cerebellum and medulla) but not in other areas (the cortex).

Given the fact that he based his findings on experiments, as opposed to anecdotal data, Flourens's views concerning localization of function held sway for more than 40 years. As ablation techniques became more precise, however, it became apparent that Flourens, like Gall, had been limited by the technology he had at his disposal. Skilled surgeon though he was, he had relatively crude tools to work with and was not nearly as precise in his ablation technique as he believed. As later ablation studies would reveal, Flourens's ablation procedure damaged several areas at once. Thus there was no way of knowing whether the behavior that resulted from the procedure was linked to the specific site he thought he had removed or to the damage of other sites he had inadvertently removed.

Broca and Brain-Damaged Patients

We now come to a major juncture in the history of physiological psychology—a discovery made in 1861 that resurrected the localization-of-

Pierre Broca.

function doctrine. The discovery was made by a French physician named Pierre Broca who, for many years, had treated a patient who had lost the ability to speak—a condition known as *aphasia*. What made this patient unique was that the behavioral loss was selective. The patient could understand language and he could even communicate with motor gestures. What he could not do, with the exception of one or two expressions, was speak.

When the patient died, Broca performed an autopsy to verify or refute the localization-of-function theory. Broca reasoned that if the localization-of-function theory were correct—if specific behaviors, speech, in this instance, were indeed controlled by specific areas of the brain—his patient should have very *specific* brain damage. This is precisely what the autopsy revealed: damage in the third convolution of the frontal cortex on the left side of the brain.

Not one to trust results from a single patient, Broca performed autopsies on other former patients who suffered from aphasia. His findings confirmed his initial hypothesis. They represented the first serious challenge in over 40 years to Flourens's antilocalization view of the cortex. And for those skeptics who questioned the validity of Broca's findings because they lacked the rigor of lower-animal experimentation, even their misgivings were soon assuaged.

Fritsch and Hitzig and Electrical Brain Stimulation

Further support for the localization-of-function theory was furnished in 1870 by two German physiologists, Gustav Fritsch and Eduard Hitzig, who devised a new experimental method for studying brain-behavior relations in lower animals. Instead of *removing* areas of the brain as Flourens had done, Fritsch and Hitzig used small pulses of electric current to *stimulate* areas of the brain in experimental animals. Although this type of electrical stimulation did not precisely duplicate the normal electrochemical activity in the brain, it was a very close approximation—at least as judged by the behavior that it elicited. Fritsch and Hitzig surgically implanted very thin wires, known as *electrodes*, in the cortices of dogs. By systematically stimulating different areas of the cortex and observing the behavioral consequences, they were actually able to construct a crude "motor map" of the dog's cortex, relating the stimulation of five distinct areas to five different motor responses.

Not long after Fritsch and Hitzig's work on the motor cortex, David Ferrier found a similar result for the sensory cortex. Using an ablation procedure patterned after Flourens's but redesigned to remove very discrete areas of the brain, Ferrier found evidence for a "sensory map" of the cortex which consisted of a visual area, an auditory area, and an olfactory area—areas which, when removed, produced very specific yet different sensory losses.

All told, then, within a matter of roughly 10 years, the view of the brain, specifically of the cortex and its relation to behavior, changed dramatically. It went from that of an undifferentiated structure with higher-order behavior distributed homogeneously throughout the cortex to a highly differentiated structure with different areas controlling different psychological functions. Ironically, the view that emerged looked very much like the one originally proposed by the phrenologists—excluding, of course, the silly assumption about bumps on the skull reflecting the size and shape of the underlying cortex.

Wernicke: Fine-Tuning Localization of Function

These findings notwithstanding, it didn't take long for the localization-of-function view to come under attack once again—not for its broad outline but for its overly simplistic detail.

The assault began in 1876 when Carl Wernicke published a paper describing a new type of aphasia, one that called into question the basic assumption of the localization-of-function view without refuting the theory as a whole. Wernicke reported that, in contrast to Broca's patients who could understand what was said but could not speak, his own patients could speak but could not understand. He also reported that these patients, in contrast to Broca's, had damage in a different part of the cortex—the left temporal cortex rather than the left frontal cortex.

Localization-of-function theorists would argue that Wernicke's findings support the view that specific behaviors are controlled by specific sites in the brain. But the findings also pose a problem for the theory. The original localization-of-function view, the one that prevailed before Wernicke's discovery, argued that psychological functions—even the most complex and abstract functions such as language—are confined to *single* areas in the cortex; Wernicke disagreed. What is confined to a specific area, in his view, is not so much a complex psychological function—not language, not memory, not vision—but a component part of that function, such as the ability to articulate or to comprehend. And because there are several component parts that coalesce to produce any given psychological function, Wernicke theorized that there are several brain areas involved in the control of any single psychological function.

Wernicke's theory is now referred to as the *component view* of localization-of-function, and he used it to explain why Broca's patients lost speech while his own patients lost comprehension. His key point was that each patient suffered damage in an area controlling a *different* component of language: Broca's in the area controlling articulation, his in the area controlling comprehension. Wernicke also used his theory to explain why, with very extensive damage, a patient may lose both speech and comprehension. The reason: with extensive damage in two different areas of the cortex—the frontal and temporal cortex—both components are lost.

Wernicke went further. Based on his knowledge of neuroanatomy (Ramón y Cajal had just reported that neurons have long extensions that interconnect different parts of the nervous system) and drawing on the neurological studies that he had just conducted, he formulated an anatomical theory of language that has a remarkably modern-day ring to it. We will consider the theory in detail in Chapter 18. But it is enough to say at this time that Wernicke, by underscoring the importance of the interconnections between brain areas as well as the areas themselves, introduced to neurological study a new feature of behavior: *the relationship among behavioral components*. In doing so, he introduced a new way of looking at abnormal behavior—the loss of those relationships. Wernicke warned his fellow neurologists that some brain-damaged patients—those suffering damage in the interconnections *between* areas and not in the areas themselves—will *seem* perfectly normal in every respect. They will be able to hear and to see and to move and to speak, but they may not be able to read. Others will be unable to write. Still others will be unable to carry out motor instructions. In other words, they may not be able to *connect* the image of the sound of a word with the ability to comprehend or to speak or to write the word. The behavioral components (hearing, seeing, moving, language) will be intact, but the ability to interconnect the components may be missing. Wernicke predicted these behavioral abnormalities, and neurologists, now prepared to look for these subtle yet devastating losses in their brain-damaged patients, indeed found them and continue to find them today.

The Skeptics: Recovery from Brain Damage

On the surface, Wernicke's theory seems to represent an ideal compromise in the localization-of-function debate. It tempers the localization-of-function position by recognizing that what is localized to specific areas of the brain are not abstract psychological functions but rather components which collectively make up those complex functions.

Still and all, the prevailing view at the beginning of the twentieth century, despite Wernicke's theory, favored the antilocalization side of the debate. Scientists were willing to concede that sensory and motor processes are governed by localization of function but were not willing to yield when it came to the higher-order psychological processes, language, learning, and memory. Two renowned neurologists in particular, Henry Head and Kurt Goldstein, refused to accept the notion that Wernicke's component theory could be applied to higher-order processes.

Here, in brief, is their argument. It is true that both Broca and Wernicke found that damage to the cortex abolished different components of language—articulation, and comprehension. What both men failed to note, though, is that on occasion, particularly in children, the seemingly lost components recover. If behavior is localized to an area, it is easy to see why damage to that area will abolish that behavior. But why, if the damage is permanent, should that behavior recover? On the other hand, it is precisely this effect—recovery from brain damage—that one would expect if the brain were indeed undifferentiated, if language were controlled by the entire brain and the uninjured areas, because of their plasticity, took over the function of the missing areas.

Influenced by these observations, most neuroscientists, despite Wernicke's component theory, held fast to the notion that the brain operated more or less as a whole, particularly in its control of higher-order psychological processes such as language, learning, and memory. But it was not until the work of Karl Lashley, who in the 1920s took the problem into the laboratory and studied it with rigor and precision in lower animals, that the antilocalization position really took hold.

Lashley: The Last Challenge

Lashley based his antilocalization view on data that were undeniably valid but misleading as well. His procedure, in general, was to train rats to learn a maze, to subject specific areas of the rats' brains (the cortex) to damage, and then to observe the behavioral consequences.

Karl Lashley.

Lashley found that as long as the motor or sensory areas of a rat's cortex were undamaged, the rat's ability to learn and remember depended on how *large* an area was damaged and not on *where* that area was located. He concluded that while sensory and motor processes are localized—that is, controlled by specific areas of the brain—the higher-order processes, such as learning and memory, are controlled by the brain as a whole. When the brain is damaged, Lashley argued, the remaining intact tissue carries on the function of the damaged areas. Because of Lashley's stature and because of the time and care he devoted to his studies, his view regarding the physiological basis of learning and memory dominated the field for the next 50 years. In recent years, however, it has become increasingly clear that Lashley's view—that learning and memory are distributed homogeneously throughout the brain—is essentially incorrect, and that Lashley (much like his predecessor Flourens), for all his brilliance as a scientist, was simply a victim of a technology that was unequal to the task. He simply did not know—and could not have known, given the limitations of the surgical and behavioral techniques available to him at the time—that what held true for his surgical technique (ablation) and for his behavioral procedure (maze learning) would not hold true for other surgical techniques or other behavioral procedures.

A Glimpse at the Modern-Day View of Localization

Today we know that learning and memory are indeed localized in specific areas of the brain, but not as the strict localizationists envisioned. The findings are more in keeping with what Wernicke may have imagined—different brain areas controlling different behavioral components. Indeed the modern-day view of how the brain operates in general to control behavior favors the component view, and for good reason.

Advances in technology have made it possible to study the human brain while a person is engaged in different activities or mental functions. Thus, it has become possible to identify which areas of the brain become most active during a specific behavior or mental function. The results of one such study using a brain-imaging technique known as a *positron emission tomography* (PET) scan is shown in Figure 1.1. By monitoring cerebral blood flow (see details in Chapter 3), PET scans enable researchers to visualize directly the areas of the brain that are most active—and presumably most involved—in controlling a particular behavior or mental function.

In the study presented in Figure 1.1, PET scans were taken while subjects viewed different visual displays, in one case a Mondrian (an abstract painting containing different colors) and in the other case black-and-white moving images (Zeki et al., 1991). Consistent with Wernicke's component theory, you can see that different areas of the brain are activated by different features or components (color or motion) of the visual stimulus. When the subjects view the Mondrian, activity increases in a specific visual area referred to as V4; when the subjects view black-and-white moving images, activity increases in a specific visual area known as V5.

Evidence for specificity of localization in function also comes from modern-day studies on brain-damaged patients. Significantly, though, it

Figure 1.1 *Evidence for Localization of Function*
Different areas of the brain (V4 and V5) are activated by different features (color or motion) of a visual stimulus. Dark blue indicates the areas of the brain that are most active.

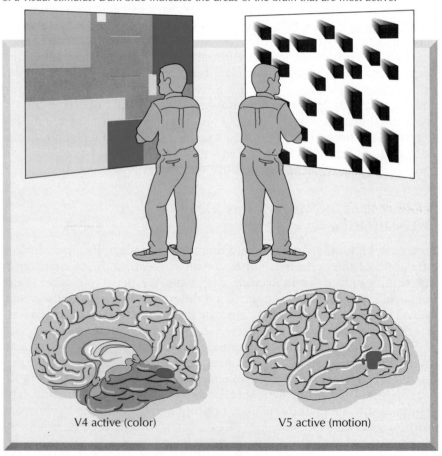

V4 active (color)   V5 active (motion)

is not that brain damage in these patients produces loss of behavior—that is to be expected. It is rather that the brain damage produces loss of components of behavior. In vision, for example, patients with selective damage in the V4 area see very well, except they see only in shades of gray; color vision is missing. The same holds for patients with selective damage in the V5 area, except that they can see only objects at rest; when the objects begin to move, they disappear.

LOOKING AHEAD: THE NEW DIRECTIONS

As naive as it was to think that psychological functions—language, memory, vision, and so on—can be localized in specific areas of the brain, it is equally naive to think that psychological functions can be understood purely from an anatomical perspective. What the brain *is* determines what the brain *does*, and what the brain does—its electrical and chemical activity—determines behavior. Historically, physiological psychology has focused on neuroanatomy (structure) not because neuroanatomy was necessarily seen as any more important than neurophysiology (function) but because neuroanatomy and the tools for studying it were better understood than neurophysiology. Today a shift has occurred, not in position but in emphasis. Physiological psychology is still—and always will be—concerned with understanding the relationship between the brain and behavior. Today, however, because of advances in technology, scientists have been able to examine brain *function* as well as brain *structure* and have been able to explore not only *where* behavior is represented in the brain but *how* behavior is represented as well.

What held in the eighteenth and nineteenth centuries holds today. However innovative a scientist may be, without the technology and knowledge to carry out experiments in the field, the work produced will be of little scientific value. Today our technology is far more advanced than it was in the eighteenth and nineteenth centuries, and we are able to look at the brain and its relation to behavior in new ways and to ask questions that even 10 years ago we could not have imagined.

Consider just one of the issues currently under vigorous study: the physiological basis of learning and memory. Not very long ago, as we've just seen, physiological psychologists believed that learning and memory could not be localized in specific areas of the brain. Today we not only know where these processes are localized but we are beginning to understand how they are actually produced as well. Recent research has shown, for instance, that learning and memory are related to neuroelectrical and neurochemical events that take place in the synapses, the myriad points at which neurons interact and transmit chemical signals to one another. Some researchers, in fact, have even been able to isolate some of the special chemical substances involved in producing learning and memory and, as you will see in Chapter 17, have been able to actually gain control of the processes, impeding or accelerating learning and memory through such techniques as electrical and chemical stimulation.

The discoveries being made today in such areas as learning and memory are being paralleled in virtually every area of behavior—from sleep to eating to sexual to emotional behavior. And while we are far from having a "cure" for such mental illnesses as depression and schizophrenia, we certainly understand these illnesses far better than we have understood them in the past. As you will see throughout the book, research has begun to yield data with extremely promising implications for treating people who suffer from these illnesses.

It goes without saying, of course, that experimental work of this nature raises crucial ethical, moral, and social questions, and such questions will undoubtedly assume increased importance as work in physiological psychology continues to move forward and as more is learned about the relationship between brain function and behavior. To many people the very idea of inducing or suppressing behavior through neural manipulation—whether the manipulation is chemical, electrical, or surgical—carries with it harrowing overtones of a "brave new world" of robots and automatons, a world devoid of feeling, emotion, and everything thought of as intrinsically human. Such a view is, of course, more philosophical than scientific, and it is not the purpose of this book to comment one way or the other on the philosophical or moral implications of current or future research in physiological psychology. What we have tried to do is to assemble, in a logical and comprehensible manner, the basic concepts, terminology, and methodology that constitute the science of physiological psychology as it stands today and to make you, the student, aware of what progress in this science may mean to the human species. The ultimate goal of this science is not merely to understand the physiological bases of behavior but also to use this knowledge to help people afflicted with behavioral disorders. Today, as we will see in Chapter 5, with the development of such fields as psychopharmacology, this goal is becoming a reality.

SUMMARY

1. *Physiological psychology defined.* Physiological psychology is a branch of psychology that seeks to isolate the physiological processes that take place inside the body whenever behavior occurs. The assumption underlying this science is that for every behavioral event—every action, thought, or feeling—there is a corresponding physical event or series of events taking place in the body. The principal difference between physiological psychology and other sciences that involve biological processes is that physiological psychology focuses on the behavioral implications of internal processes—how these processes control what we do, what we think, and what we feel.

2. *Philosophical roots.* Physiological psychology, like psychology itself, has its roots in the philosophical speculations of the ancient Greeks, whose philosophy was built around the idea of dualism—a clear distinction between the physical world and the mind. In Plato's view, for example, the mind was a spiritual force, beyond understanding. Dualism held sway until the late nineteenth century, which helps to explain why scientists operated for centuries on the assumption that the forces behind mental processes were beyond human comprehension.

3. *The pneuma theory.* The first real theory of how the mind works was known as the "pneuma theory" and was based on the belief that the mind was controlled by invisible spirits known as pneuma. This theory persisted for more than 2000 years—and for two reasons. The first is that until the nineteenth century there was no experimental evidence to disprove the existence and impact of invisible spirits. The second and perhaps more important reason is that until the nineteenth century any challenge to the pneuma theory was considered a challenge to the religious dogma that dominated scientific thought throughout the Middle Ages.

4. *The mind as an object of study.* One turning point in the history of psychology came in the seventeenth century when the philosopher René Descartes advanced the idea that the mental or spiritual side of human behavior, far from being beyond understanding, could be studied mechanistically, as with any physical science. A deeply religious man, Descartes retained an essentially dualistic view of human beings, depicting the "mind" as a rational "soul," an entity that did not lend itself to mechanistic interpretation.

5. *British empiricism.* The advent of British empiricism in the late seventeenth century went a long way to bring the study of human and animal behavior out of the realm of metaphysics and into the realm of disciplined scientific thought. Best represented in the writings of John Locke, George Berkeley, and David Hume, the empiricist view, roughly speaking, is that the true path to knowledge about the human mind is not speculation or deduction but actual (sensory) experience.

6. *Darwin and the advent of experimental psychology.* Empiricism provided a philosophical framework for the scientific study of behavior and of the mind, but it wasn't until more than two centuries later that psychology in general emerged as a true experimental science. The writings of Charles Darwin in the mid-1800s established a behavioral link between humans and lower animals, paving the route for animal experimentation as a valid research tool in psychology. Darwin's work also set the stage for the writings of John Watson, who founded the school of psychology known as behaviorism. All experimental psychologists adhere to Watson's position that behavior, because it is observable and measurable, is the only legitimate subject matter for analysis. But not all experimental psychologists are willing to ignore the importance of internal processes that are not directly observable. The compromise usually arrived at is the view that such internal processes as fear and anger are legitimate subjects for analysis so long as they are operationally defined in terms of their behavioral consequences.

7. *Technological advancements.* The invention of the microscope (roughly 1830), coupled with the development of a research technique known as staining, enabled several researchers in the mid- to late 1800s to conduct studies that changed the prevailing conception of the nervous system. Staining procedures pioneered by Camillo Golgi in 1875 produced an early glimpse of how neurons are structured, and the work of Ramón y Cajal helped to identify the neuron as the basic cellular unit in the nervous system. The discovery that neurons are not physically connected but separated by microscopic gaps came in the early 1900s, by which time it was recognized that activity in the nervous system was a neuroelectrical phenomenon governed by basic laws of physics and chemistry and linked somehow to the properties of the neural membrane. Even so, it wasn't until the 1960s, with the work of Alan Hodgkin and Andrew Huxley, that anyone was able to observe the electrochemical activity taking place in and around the membrane.

8. *The localization-of-function issue.* No question in physiological psychology is more fundamental than the question of whether specific behaviors are under the control of specific areas of the brain (generally referred to as the localization-of-function theory) or whether the brain functions more or less as a single unit in its control of behavior. Early experimental work, most notably by Pierre Flourens, appeared to weaken the localization-of-function position. Using a technique known as ablation—removing certain areas of the brain and observing the behavioral effects—Flourens found that while certain behavioral losses could be traced to the destruction of specific areas of the brain, other behavioral losses occurred regardless of where in the cortex the damage occurred. As research methodology improved, however, it became clear that Flourens had been limited by the technology at his disposal and there was no way of knowing whether the behavior that resulted from the ablation procedure was linked to the specific site he thought he had removed or to the damage of other sites he had inadvertently removed. At roughly the same time, Pierre Broca's work with speech-impaired patients, coupled with the brain stimulation work in dogs of Gustav Fritsch and Eduard Hitzig, made a strong case—with certain behaviors, at any rate—for a localization-of-function point of view.

9. *Reconciling the positions.* A paper published in 1876 by Carl Wernicke proposed what appeared at the time to be a logical compromise between the localization-of-function and the antilocalization-of-function theories. Wernicke agreed that there is a relationship between certain behaviors and certain areas of the brain, but theorized a "component" viewpoint, proposing that specific behavioral components (for example, articulation and comprehension) are controlled by specific areas of the brain and other more complex behaviors (for example, language) are controlled by the combined activity of those areas. Logical as that compromise may have seemed, it was overshadowed for nearly 50 years by the much more antilocalization views of Karl Lashley, whose work with rats seemed to suggest that higher-order behaviors (learning and memory) were controlled by the brain as a whole, rather than by specific areas.

10. *The modern view of how the brain operates.* The modern-day view of how the brain operates in general has been shaped largely by technological advances, such as PET scans, that make it possible to study the human brain while people are engaged in different activities or mental functions. This view suggests that higher-order behaviors are localized in specific areas of the brain, not as the strict localizationists originally envisioned but rather as Wernicke may have imagined—different brain areas controlling different behavioral components. The important point is that physiological psychology is still—and always will be—concerned with understanding the relationship between brain and behavior. Today, however, with advances in technology, scientists have been able to examine brain function as well as brain structure and have been able to explore not only *where* behavior is represented in the brain, but *how* behavior is represented as well.

KEY TERMS

ablation
aphasia
behaviorism
British empiricism
component view
Darwinism
dualism

localization-of-function doctrine
PET scan
phrenology
pneuma theory
staining
stimulation
synapse

SUGGESTED READINGS

Fancher, R. E. *Pioneers of Psychology*. New York: Norton, 1979.

Gardner, H. *The Mind's New Science: A History of the Cognitive Revolution*. New York: Basic Books, 1985.

Leahy, T. H. *A History of Psychology: Main Currents in Psychological Thought*, 3rd ed., Englewood Cliffs, NJ: Prentice Hall, 1992.

Two of the principal sources for this chapter were Fancher (1979) and Gardner (1985).

2

THE NEURON

INTRODUCTION

There are any number of animals on earth that are stronger and quicker than humans, that can see farther, hear better, and smell more keenly. No species, however, brings to the life process as varied and as adaptive a behavioral repertoire as human beings. And no animal comes even close to us in one crucial attribute: the ability to transcend our genetic blueprints. True, humans, like all animals, are born with sets of genes whose chemical makeup cannot be changed except through random mutations. But far more so than other animals, we have a highly developed capacity to learn, to remember, and to communicate what we learn to our children from generation to generation. Concepts, laws, theories, technology—none of these hallmarks of the human experience can be transmitted through the genes. Yet they are the very qualities that distinguish humans from all other animals.

Much of what you will be studying throughout this chapter and the next focuses on the structures that account for the sophistication and efficiency of our behavioral repertoire. These structures are the nervous system and the cells that constitute the nervous system. The cells are known as neurons and, as you will learn in this chapter, they have different specialties. Some neurons gather information from the environment and communicate that information to the brain. Others process that information once it reaches the brain. Still other neurons communicate information to those various parts of the body, the muscles and glands, that produce what we normally think of as behavior.

The key word in all of this is *communication*. Indeed the nervous system itself can be best understood if you view it as a vast communication network, albeit a network that is infinitely more complex than any structure that humans are capable of creating. In humans and other higher animals, the nervous system is divided into two major parts, the peripheral nervous system and the central nervous system, each of which has a specific function. The peripheral nervous system is essentially an input-output system, whose neurons do one of two things: one, gather information from the environment, and two, deliver information to muscles and glands. The central nervous system, consisting of neurons found in the brain and spinal cord, is essentially a decision maker: it processes the incoming information and issues the instructions that underlie the way we respond. The peripheral and central nervous systems will be considered in detail in the next chapter. The components of each system will be considered in this chapter.

We shall begin with the neuron, the basic building block of the nervous system. We will look briefly at the connections between neurons, the synapses. We will explore how neurons develop into the nervous system. And we will look finally at what happens when neurons age and at two diseases—Alzheimer's disease and Parkinson's disease—that may occur during this aging process.

THE NEURON

The basic operating unit of the nervous system is the nerve cell, or as it is usually called, the *neuron*. The number of neurons in the nervous system is estimated to be in excess of 100 billion, with the vast majority of them located in the brain and the rest distributed throughout the spinal cord and peripheral nervous system. Each neuron, moreover, is connected with other neurons—often with thousands of others—making the scope and complexity of the network of neural connections something that is almost beyond human comprehension. Yet it is the very scope and complexity of this network that make possible the incredibly varied repertoire of responses that constitute human behavior.

Differentiating Neurons from Other Cells

Although our primary focus when we examine the structure and function of the nervous system is the neuron, other cellular material deserves our attention, too. Numerous as neurons are, they are far outnumbered in the nervous system by nonneural cells, known as *neuroglial cells*. Nonneural cells are not directly involved in the transmission of information, but they nonetheless fulfill several indispensable functions in the nervous system. They hold neurons in place. They regulate the flow of energy-related material to the neural cells and of waste matter out of them. They insulate neurons from one another. They remove dead or damaged cells from the nervous system. They also play a crucial role in guiding the growth of neurons during embryonic development and during their regeneration after they have been damaged. These nonneural cells have their debit side as well: they are the chief source of tumors and other forms of disease in the nervous system.

In general, nonneural cells can be divided into two major groups. Those found in the central nervous system—*oligodendrocytes*, *astrocytes*, and *microglia*—are involved collectively in all the functions just mentioned. Those found in the peripheral nervous system—*Schwann cells* and *satellite cells*—are involved primarily in mechanical support and insulation of neurons. We shall encounter some of these nonneural cells shortly. First, however, let us consider the chief character in our plot, the neuron.

The Structure of the Neuron

As the basic operating unit of the nervous system, the neuron has one specialty—communication. Its function, in short, is to transmit information from one part of the body to another. This information takes the form of an electrochemical signal known as a neural impulse, a subject we will examine in detail in Chapter 4.

A close look at Figure 2.1 should give you an idea of why a typical neuron (and we use the word "typical" advisedly, because neurons are quite varied in appearance) is so well suited to its specialty. Like other cells, a neuron requires energy to function. Like other cells it has a cell body—the *soma*—where it processes (i.e., metabolizes) nutrients into energy. What distinguishes a neuron from other kinds of cells is its structure, in particular the extensions that branch out from its cell body. These extensions are of two types—*dendrites* and *axons*. Both are unique to neurons, and both account for the neuron's capacity to transmit information over long distances.

Dendrites and Axons: A Comparison

Dendrites and axons differ in two crucial respects: in function and in structure. The functional differences lie in the fact that dendrites are the "antennae" of the neuron—the parts that receive information from other cells. Dendrites, you might say, "listen" to other cells. Axons, on the other hand, form the "communication line" of the neuron. They generally "talk" to other cells. Dendrites and axons also differ in structure. Let us look at some of these differences.

Multibranching

In a typical neuron, the axon is the long single extension at one end of the cell body, and dendrites are the cluster of small multibranching extensions at the other end. At the end of the axon are other branches

Figure 2.1 *A Neural Cell*
(a) The main divisions of the neuron consist of a cell body and extensions: the multibranching dendrites and the single axon. A fatty sheath, myelin, encases the axon. (b) An electron micrograph showing neurons from the cortex of a monkey.

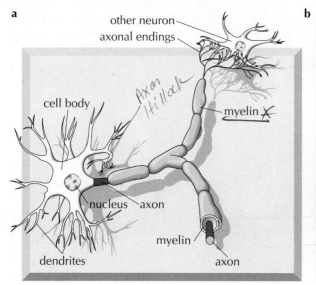

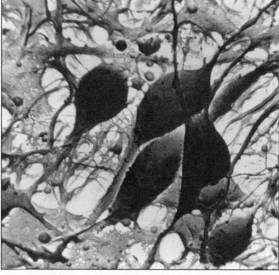

known as *axonal endings*. The branching itself, whether it occurs in dendrites or in axons, is significant: it enables a single neuron to connect with a huge number of receptors, muscles, or other neurons. This capacity for making connections establishes the cellular basis for the behavioral flexibility that characterizes animals with complex nervous systems.

Myelin

Yet another difference between axons and dendrites lies in the material surrounding them. Most axons are covered with a whitish fatty sheath known as the *myelin sheath*. No such sheath surrounds dendrites.

Figure 2.2   *Two Views of Myelin*
A lengthwise view and a magnified cross section. The cross section shows the formation of myelin by a Schwann cell.

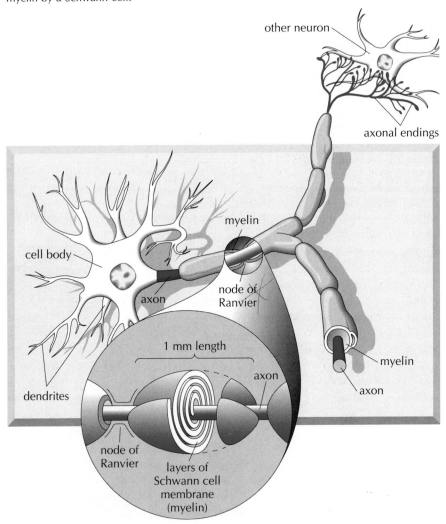

Myelin, as you can see in Figure 2.2, is composed of the membranes of special nonneural cells that wrap around the axon in layers. These non-neural cells have different names depending upon where they are located. In the peripheral nervous system these cells are called *Schwann cells*. In the central nervous system they are called *oligodendrocytes*; both are types of neuroglial cells.

Myelin serves a critical function: it prevents signals carried by adjacent neurons from interfering with one another. The myelin sheath itself is divided into segments that leave points along the axonal surface bare, or unmyelinated. These points are known as *nodes of Ranvier*, and as you will see in Chapter 4, they combine with the myelin sheath to speed the process of conduction through the nervous system.

The importance of myelin becomes apparent when you consider the impact of diseases that cause myelin to disintegrate. One such disease, *multiple sclerosis*, attacks areas of the brain related to motor control, producing tremors and postural rigidity. In multiple sclerosis, the neurons themselves are not destroyed initially; only the myelin is affected. Myelin depletion eliminates the insulation between adjacent neurons and results in the scrambling of neural messages. This scrambling in turn produces a loss of motor control. If researchers could devise a way to prevent the myelin from degenerating, this disease, now considered incurable, might be treatable, but only if detected at an early stage. For as the disease progresses, the neurons themselves degenerate.

Nissl Substance

Axons and dendrites not only are surrounded by different material, they also contain different material. Dendrites (like cell bodies of neurons) contain traces of endoplasmic reticulum, ribosomes, and ribonucleic acid (RNA), all of which are known collectively as *Nissl substance*. Nissl substance produces enzymes and other chemicals that play a crucial role in maintaining the structure and function of the neuron. None of this protoplasmic material is present in the axon. Lacking its own Nissl substance, the axon depends for its survival on the Nissl substance in the cell body and dendrites. Cylindrical structures, known as *microtubules*, connect the cell body and the axon, carrying life-sustaining chemicals from the Nissl substance in the cell body down the axon to the axonal endings by a process known as *axonal transport*. As these substances move from cell body to axonal endings, other substances—other nutrients and enzymes vital to the health of the neuron—are being transported in the opposite direction from axonal endings to cell body. Transport from axonal endings to cell body, commonly referred to as *retrograde transport*, completes the picture of the two-way traffic illustrated in Figure 2.3.

How Neurons Differ

Although all neurons share the same basic structural features (a cell body, dendrites, and an axon) and the same basic function (the capacity

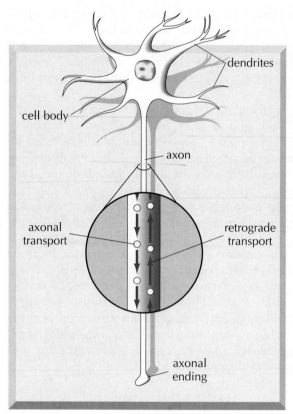

Figure 2.3 *Axonal and Retrograde Transport*
Enzymes manufactured in the cell body are carried by the microtubules to the axonal endings. Nutrients and enzymes are transported in both directions.

to transmit information), there are differences among them—specifically in their appearance and in the way they transmit information through the nervous system. There are three basic types of neurons: sensory neurons, motor neurons, and interneurons.

Sensory Neurons

Sensory neurons specialize in carrying information from receptors to the spinal cord and brain. This type of transmission is frequently described as *afferent* (from the Latin word for "bringing to"). Sensory neurons are of two types. If you look at Figures 2.4a and 2.4b, you will see that each sensory neuron has dendrites, a long axon, and a cell body. Notice, too, that sensory neurons differ in the way the axon is connected to the cell body. In one type, the *unipolar* neuron, the axon is connected indirectly, via a little "neck," to the cell body. In the other type, the *bipolar* neuron, the axon is connected directly to the cell body.

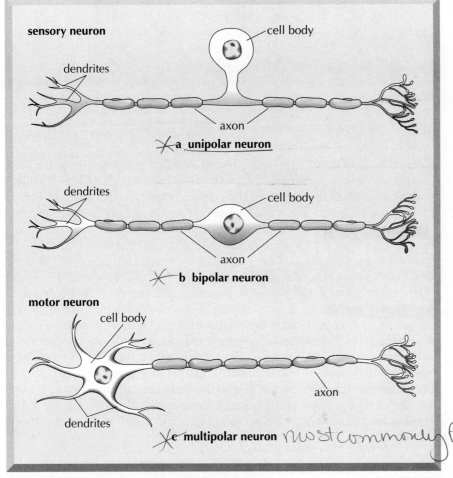

Figure 2.4 *Structural Variation among Neurons*
There are three classifications of neurons, determined by the number of extensions connected to the cell body. The cell body is connected to (a) one extension in a unipolar neuron, (b) two extensions in a bipolar neuron, and (c) many extensions (a single axon and many dendrites) in a multipolar neuron.

Motor Neurons

Motor neurons specialize in carrying information away from the spinal cord and brain to muscles and glands—a function frequently described as *efferent* (from the Latin word for "carrying outward"). A typical motor neuron consists of a single long axon and a number of dendrites, as shown in Figure 2.4*c*. Because of its multiple extensions, the motor neuron is commonly said to be *multipolar*.

Interneurons

Interneurons are located predominantly in the spinal cord and brain and are by far the most numerous neurons in the nervous system. As their

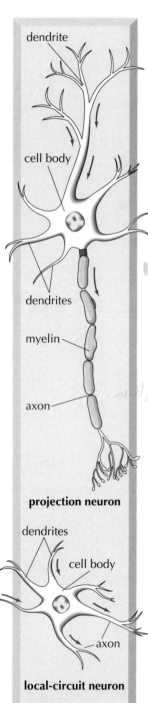

dendrite

cell body

dendrites

myelin

axon

projection neuron

dendrites

cell body

axon

local-circuit neuron

Figure 2.5 *Two Types of Interneurons, Projection and Local-Circuit*
Note that in local-circuit neurons, axons and dendrites are distinguished by the directions in which they conduct neural impulses. Dendrites conduct impulses toward the cell body, axons away from the cell body. The direction of impulse is denoted by arrows.

name indicates, interneurons are found *between* other neurons. Because these neurons are so numerous, anatomists have divided them into two types according to the length of their axons. One type, pictured in Figure 2.5, looks very much like a motor neuron and is generally referred to as a *projection neuron*. It has short, multibranching dendrites and a long axon, a structure that makes it ideally suited for transmitting information over long distances within the central nervous system, such as from the top of the brain to the spinal cord.

The other type of interneuron, pictured in Figure 2.5, is known as a *local-circuit neuron*. Its axons, unlike those of a projection neuron, are noticeably short, and both its axons and its dendrites show profuse branching. This feature underlies the local-circuit neuron's specialty: the ability to establish multiple relations with other neurons. Typically, a local-circuit neuron receives information from a large number of sensory neurons or other interneurons and delivers information to a large number of motor neurons or other interneurons. Thus we see the cellular basis for the ability of the nervous system to coordinate an enormous number of stimulus-response relationships.

Connecting the Neurons: The Synapse

Up to now, we have been talking about the relationships between neural structures primarily in terms of connections. We have spoken of the receptors that connect with sensory neurons, which in turn connect with interneurons, and of the interneurons that connect with motor neurons, which connect with muscles and glands.

The word "connection," however, does not really describe neural relationships accurately, for the term implies a *physical* relationship. If you were to examine two typical connecting neurons under an electron microscope, you would see that they are not connected at all; rather, there is a microscopic gap between them. If you did not know better, you might assume that this gap would *prevent* communication between neurons, but such is not the case. Although connecting neurons are not in physical contact, they nonetheless are linked by *functional* contact. The tiny gap that shows up under an electron microscope is known as the *synapse*. The term is derived from a Greek word that means "to clasp" and was originally coined in the early 1900s by Sir Charles Sherrington. Figure 2.6 shows a typical synapse enlarged millions of times. Such a synapse (i.e., the gap) usually measures 30 to 50 nanometers (nm), and it is found between the axon of one neuron and the dendrites or cell body or axon of another.

Neurotransmitters

Diffusing across the synapse are chemicals known as *neurotransmitters*. These chemicals can accurately be described as the "language of communication" from neuron to neuron. They represent, in effect, the functional contact between neurons.

Neurotransmitter activity, as you will see in Chapter 5, is one of the most important factors in the neural control of behavior. Virtually every behavior—from routine tasks like eating and walking to complex mental activities such as language and thought—can be affected by the slightest changes in the nature of the neurotransmitter activity going on from neuron to neuron. There is increasing evidence, for example, that the abnor-

Figure 2.6 *The Synapse*
The magnified view shows the neurotransmitters diffusing across the synaptic gap between two neurons. The neurotransmitters are released by the axonal endings of one neuron and act on the dendrite of the other neuron.

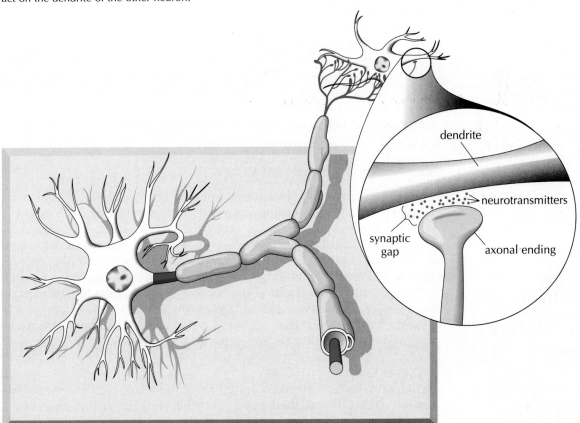

mal behavior of people who suffer from many forms of mental illness, chief among them depression and schizophrenia, is closely related to neurotransmitter activity that falls outside the norm. There is also increasing evidence that abnormal neurotransmitter activity may have important implications for the neurodegenerative disorders discussed later in this chapter, such as Parkinson's disease and Alzheimer's disease.

One final note: although most synapses are chemical in nature, some operate purely on the basis of an electric signal. They are found primarily in insects and, as you might expect, the adjoining neurons are not separated by a synaptic gap but rather are connected.

DEVELOPMENT OF THE NERVOUS SYSTEM

All behavior, from simple reflex actions to complex problem solving, is determined by communication among neurons—that is, communication among sensory neurons, interneurons, and motor neurons. The simplest hand movements—making a fist, for instance—could not occur unless specific neurons in the brain communicated with muscles in the hand. If we are to see, receptors in the eye must communicate with specific sensory areas in the brain. There is thus an intricate network of connections throughout the nervous system linking specific neural circuits to each other and to specific muscles and receptors.

All of which raises some fundamental questions: How, for example, does the network develop? How are the various connections that are the foundation of the network established? Finally, is the nervous system each of us has today the same basic system that was in place when we were born—or even before—or have life experiences produced significant changes? Let us now address these questions.

The Nervous System: Its Roots

The questions we have just raised are part of a much larger and more fundamental question having to do with behavior itself and the extent to which it is shaped by genetics or by the environment. The consensus today is that neither genetics nor the environment is the sole behavioral determinant and that different behaviors are rooted in a combination of genetic and environmental factors. This view, in turn, has led to a parallel view of the development of the nervous system—the idea that certain elements of the nervous system are genetically determined and are in place before birth but that other aspects of the development of the nervous system are subject to factors in the environment.

A Closer Look

Remarkable as it may seem—given the complexity of the nervous system—the groundwork (better still, the blueprint) for the nervous system can be found in the zygote, the fertilized egg. Through the process of mitosis (cell division) the fertilized egg proliferates into undifferentiated cells, the cells differentiate and those differentiated cells that assume the properties of neurons migrate to specific locations in the developing embryo. The type of neuron they become depends on the environment to which they migrate.

Most cells destined to become neurons originate, as far as we know, from a part of the embryo known as the *neural tube*, but there are two separate areas in the tube. One area, the interface between the neural tube and epidermal cells, houses those cells (known as *neural crest cells*) that eventually migrate from the neural tube and develop into the peripheral nervous system (that is, the sensory and motor neurons). The second area, in the core or ventricular zone of the tube, houses cells (known as *neuroblasts*) that eventually migrate from the neural tube and develop into the central nervous system (that is, the brain and spinal cord).

Once the neural precursor cells have migrated and have established their identity, their axons begin to grow and the connections they form will ultimately determine the role they play in behavior. Axonal growth occurs when a specialized structure on the tip of the axon—known as the *growth cone*—begins to grow. The growth process—that is, where the axons eventually connect—is determined by both genetic and environmental factors, but the degree to which each contributes appears to vary greatly not only among species, but among neurons in the same species (Jessell, 1991). Clearly, though, the overall development of the nervous system reflects the interaction of the two. Keeping this interaction in mind, we will now look at each aspect of development of the axonal connections: first genetic and then environmental.

The Genetic Factor

It is generally agreed that the connections made in the nervous system during embryological development are initiated and guided by genetic factors. Genes confer upon developing axons the capacity to seek out particular target sites (sensory receptors, muscles, glands, and other neurons). How the genes are able to do this is not yet completely understood, but evidence suggests a chemical affinity between developing axons and their target sites. The term "chemical affinity" is in need of elaboration. The pathways that developing axons take and the target sites with which they eventually connect are determined by two chemical factors: one, the actual chemical properties of the developing axons themselves; and two, the chemicals secreted by the target sites. Let's take a closer look at each.

Developing Axons
The process that governs the development of axonal connections begins when growth cones work their way through the surrounding tissue and form pathways that travel to target sites. Once this "journey" has been launched, the specific route the growth cones take is guided by a Velcro-like chemical interaction between genetically determined structures on the surface of the growth cones and genetically determined structures on the surface of the surrounding tissue along the pathway. The growth cones are endowed with *microspikes*—fingerlike projections that, in

effect, reach out and test the surface of the surrounding tissue. If the surface of the surrounding tissue is sufficiently "sticky" (that is, when the surfaces of the surrounding tissue and of the growth cone are chemically compatible) the microspikes take hold. If not, the microspikes continue to move and test the surface until the optimal degree of adhesion occurs. So it is that the growth process at this point is both "blind" and "guided." It is blind in the sense that the microspikes have no predetermined route. It is guided in the sense that the genetically determined adhesion properties of the surrounding tissue become the chemical guideposts.

Target Sites

Once the growth cone is in the neighborhood of the target sites, a new group of chemical agents enters the picture. The most prominent of these chemicals is known as *nerve growth factor*. Secreted by the target sites, nerve growth factor governs the final leg of the growth cone's journey in two ways: one, by creating chemical gradients that draw the growth cone to the target sites; two, by determining how many of the innervating neurons survive. As it happens, as many as 50 percent of the neurons that reach the target sites die because they are not stimulated by nerve growth factor. Those that *are* stimulated and that do survive, however, form synapses with the target sites but in a rather crude and undefined way. And it is at this point, after these synaptic connections have been made, that the role of genetics in neural development begins to diminish and the role of the environment becomes increasingly important.

The Environmental Factor

Neurons in general do not complete their development until after birth and it is believed that their postbirth development is greatly influenced by environmental factors. What is thought to happen, roughly speaking, is this: synaptic connections between developing axons and the target sites are formed, as we've just seen, and nerve growth factor produced by the target sites stimulates a portion of the developing axons to survive. The synaptic connections at this early stage, however, are tentative, and whether they "take" or "die" depends on the presence or absence of environmentally-induced neural activity—a classic example of the familiar "use it or lose it" principle. If the environment, because of its sensory qualities or motor demands, produces neural activity that stimulates the synaptic connections, the connections survive. Otherwise, the connections die.

Evidence that the environment plays an important role in shaping neural development comes from research on the mammalian visual system. In the visual system of both monkeys and humans, neural connections continue to develop after birth, and evidence indicates that this development can indeed be influenced by environmental factors.

In humans there is a visual condition known as *amblyopia* (lazy eye) in which children who have a tendency to squint fall into the habit of relying on only one eye for their visual stimulation, thus depriving the other eye of visual input. If this habit continues through childhood, the unused eye will usually become blind and impervious to corrective lenses—an indication that the problem is neural, not muscular. If, however, the squint is addressed early enough so that the child learns to use both eyes, vision in both eyes develops more or less normally (Alberts et al., 1994).

The assumption in this case is that, deprived of visual stimulation, the neural circuits connected to the nonstimulated eye die out. This assumption of course is difficult to confirm in humans, but it has been confirmed in monkeys. David Hubel and his colleagues reared infant monkeys for several months with one eye covered and found that when the patch was removed the monkeys behaved as if they were blind in the unstimulated eye. Hubel further determined, by mapping the neural connections from eye to brain, that the blindness was indeed the result of the death of neurons that normally were connected to the nonstimulated eye (Hubel, Wiesel, & LeVay, 1977).

Evidence for the effect of environmental stimulation on neural development is not restricted to the visual nervous system. In a classic study conducted in the 1960s, David Krech and his colleagues found that laboratory rats reared in an "enriched" environment (an environment in which the rats played with toys and with other rats) develop a more intricate, more dense network of neural connections than rats reared in a barren and isolated environment. Krech also found that rats that develop the denser network of neural connections demonstrate an ability to learn tasks more readily than their nonenriched counterparts (Krech et al., 1962).

Behavioral Implications

What these studies suggest, then, is that we may all be born with what might be termed "wild card" circuits that could conceivably come to control any number of behaviors, depending on environmental demands during a critical period early in our lives. These demands in turn determine which neural connections will become a permanent part of the nervous system, that is, which connections will be stimulated and which will not. On this basis, it could be argued that your ability to do certain things—speak a foreign language, play a musical instrument—depends to some degree on how early and to what extent you were exposed to each of these activities.

This is not to discount entirely the genetic factor—the fact that you have been born with a genetic inclination toward certain activities. It is to suggest, however, that even with a modest inclination you can still develop finely tuned skills if the environment encourages those skills. In many ways this process is analogous to the Darwinian view of natural selection: the environment shapes the structures of the nervous system to produce those behaviors that are appropriate to survival in that particular environment.

In summary, then, we are born with neurons that, as they grow and branch, confer upon the nervous system the potential to make new connections. Whether the nervous system makes those connections—that is, whether it realizes its potential—depends largely on the demands placed upon it by the environment. Presumably, without appropriate environmental stimulation the potential will be unrealized.

It is worth pointing out, before going on, that neural development continues throughout life, and that the capacity of the environment to shape the nervous system is not confined simply to the early stages of development. Each new experience we have in our lives—regardless of how old we are—has the potential to produce changes in the nervous system that in turn can change the way we think, feel, or act. Our ability to learn and remember—at any age—is rooted in the capacity of new experiences to produce changes in the nervous system and for those changes to endure. We will consider the neural changes that underlie learning and memory in detail in Chapter 16, but suffice it to say that it is the synapses and the connections they form with target sites that again hold the key.

True, our potential for neural change—and for the behavioral flexibility that it engenders—may diminish with age, as the aging process takes its toll on the number and complexity of neural connections. But evidence continues to mount, as we will soon see, that our capacity to retain our mental powers is not as vulnerable to aging as was once thought and that, barring physical illness, the key to how alert we remain as we grow older may have less to do with inevitable physiological decline and more to do with lifestyle and mental stimulation to which we are exposed.

HOW NEURONS DIE

As we have just seen, when certain neurons are *not* stimulated at a critical stage early in life, they die. But neurons, like all cells, die (the term commonly used is degenerate) from other causes as well. They die because of injury, because of disease, and because of the natural degeneration and chemical changes that accompany old age. We will now examine certain key aspects of how and why neurons die, with an eye toward the behavioral consequences of their death. We will look first of all at what happens to neurons that have been cut or injured, and, in particular, at the difference between the way neurons in the central nervous system respond to injury and the way neurons in the peripheral nervous system respond to injury. We will then look at what happens when neurons die or degenerate because of disease or old age, focusing in particular on two devastating diseases that have a neurodegenerative basis: Parkinson's disease and Alzheimer's disease.

When Neurons Are Injured

Any number of assaults to the nervous system—a cut, a sharp blow, a bullet wound and so forth—can produce neural injuries serious enough to kill neurons, but the way neurons respond to injuries depends on two factors: one, where in fact the injury to the neuron occurs, that is, the cell body or the axon; and two, where the neuron is located—that is, whether it is located in the central nervous system (the brain or spinal cord) or in the peripheral nervous system.

When an injury severely damages the cell body of a neuron, the neuron invariably dies, regardless of where the neuron is located (in the central or peripheral nervous system). That's because structural damage to the cell body destroys Nissl substance, which produces enzymes and other chemicals that maintain the structure and function of the neuron. Frequently, however, the injury occurs outside the cell body at some point along the axon, and in these situations, the fate of the neuron depends on where in the nervous system the neuron is located.

Figure 2.7 depicts a typical neuron whose axon has been experimentally cut, simulating an injury that would sever the axonal connection

Figure 2.7 *Degeneration and Regeneration of a Neuron*
A damaged neuron breaks down in stages. Wallerian degeneration occurs in the detached end, retrograde degeneration in the attached end, and chromatolysis in the cell body. Damaged neurons regenerate in the peripheral nervous system but not in the central nervous system.

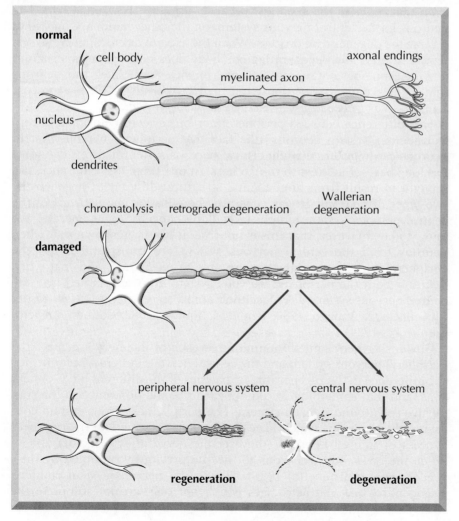

from the cell body of the neuron. As you can see from the figure, the detached section of the axon, because it has no means of sustaining itself (axons, remember, contain no Nissl substance of their own), dies—a stage of death referred to as *Wallerian degeneration*. In the meantime, the cell body—deprived now of life-sustaining chemical substances normally provided by the two-way exchange with the axon—begins to break down as well, with two interrelated physiological events happening more or less at the same time. The part of the axon still attached to the cell body breaks down—the process is known as *retrograde degeneration*—and the cell body itself, through a process known as *chromatolysis*, loses Nissl substance and, with the loss, the capacity to sustain itself.

All neurons, whether they are located in the central or peripheral nervous systems, are subject to these degenerative stages in the face of serious injury, but not all neurons respond in the same way. The neurons in the peripheral nervous system sometimes are able to reverse the effects of Wallerian degeneration, retrograde degeneration, and chromatolysis. That is, they regain their structural integrity and eventually sprout a new axon that replaces the axon lost because of injury (Fawcett, 1990). The neurons in the central nervous system, on the other hand, are unable to reverse the degenerative process. When the axon of a central nervous system is severed, the degenerating cell body does not regain its structure and the axon does not regrow. The neuron dies. Sometimes, too, neurons that form synapses with the dying neuron will die as well, a process referred to as *transneuronal* or *transynaptic degeneration*.

This difference between peripheral nervous system neurons and central nervous system neurons—the fact that peripheral nervous system neurons can regenerate while central nervous system neurons cannot—has long been of interest to researchers. At one time, this difference was thought to result from fundamental structural differences between the two types of neurons. It was generally thought that the neurons of the central nervous system simply lacked the capacity to regenerate. We know today, however, that this is not true. It has been shown that when neurons from the central nervous system are transplanted into the peripheral nervous system, they are able to regenerate, and that when neurons from the peripheral nervous system are transplanted into the central nervous system, they lose their ability to regenerate (Richardson, McGuiness, & Aquayo, 1980; Benfey & Aquayo, 1982; Cotman & Nieto-Sampedro, 1984).

Obviously, then, something unique to each of the environments—the peripheral nervous system and the central nervous system—accounts for the difference in the regenerating capacities of the different types of neurons, and that something would appear to be the difference in the supportive cells found in each system. The peripheral nervous system contains Schwann cells, which have the capacity to stimulate the regrowth process of injured neurons (they secrete nerve growth factor) and to guide the newly formed axons to the site previously occupied by their predecessors (Carbonetto, 1991). The central nervous system contains oligodendrocytes and astrocytes which not only do not stimulate the regrowth process but, in fact, inhibit regeneration by releasing inhibitory chemicals (from the oligodendrocytes) and by producing scar formation (in the astrocytes) (Louzzit & Lasek, 1987; Schwabb, 1990; Jessell, 1991).

Compensating Factors in the Central Nervous System

The fact that central nervous system neurons are unable to regenerate in the way that peripheral nervous system neurons can, explains—in part, at least—why the behavioral losses resulting from injuries or diseases that affect central nervous system function are often irreversible. Yet, as you undoubtedly know, many people who have suffered paralysis or other serious behavioral problems as a result of accidents or strokes have experienced all but complete recoveries, although it can sometimes take months and even years before normalcy is fully restored. All of which raises an obvious question: If, in fact, damaged central nervous system neurons are unable to regenerate, what happens inside the central nervous system to restore the behaviors that have been affected by the damage?

If neurons were like other cells, the answer to this question would be obvious. The damaged neurons, through the process known as *mitosis*, would simply be replaced by the division of other neurons. The problem with this explanation is that neurons, unlike other cells, do not reproduce themselves. When a neuron dies, it dies, and nothing replaces it. On the surface, the inability of a neuron to replace itself, coupled with the inability of central nervous system neurons to regenerate in response to disease or injury, would appear to pose monumental problems for recovery. What happens, you might wonder, to the function that is under the control of neurons that have died and not been replaced?

The not so obvious answer is that the brain appears to have a built-in capacity to compensate for the loss of dying neurons. For one thing, we are born with far more neurons than we need, and this excess means that when it comes to certain functions, the loss of neurons doesn't automatically translate into a loss of function. In other words, it's likely that, in certain situations, the function handled by the neurons that have been lost is only minimally affected (if at all) because there are enough surviving neurons handling the same function.

It also appears, as depicted in Figure 2.8, that once neurons in the central nervous system have been damaged, neighboring neurons can sometimes sprout new axonal endings to fill the sites that have been vacated by the degenerating neurons and, more important, to take over the function performed by the degenerating neurons (Reeves & Smith, 1987). In other words, the damaged neurons do not regrow, but neighboring neurons respond to the damage by undergoing new growth, a process known as *collateral sprouting* (Matthews, Cotman, & Lynch, 1976; Cotman & Nieto-Sampedro, 1984).

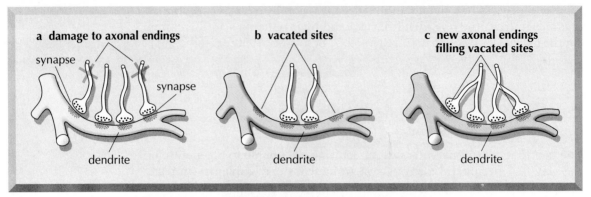

Figure 2.8 *Collateral Sprouting*
Once neurons in the central nervous system have been damaged, neighboring neurons compensate by sprouting new axonal endings.

The Aging Brain

The compensating factors we have just considered notwithstanding, there comes a time when the capacity of the brain to adjust to the death of neurons is outpaced by the number of neurons dying. And there is good reason to believe that many of the behavioral signs of old age—the deterioration of memory, for instance—can be traced to this change in the internal equation. With this pattern in mind, let us now take a closer look at the aging brain.

Age affects neurons in different ways: neurons degenerate or shrink (the term is *atrophy*) or their chemical makeup changes; that is, their cell bodies become laced with protein filaments known as *neurofibrillary tangles*. Areas outside neurons are also affected by age: an important chemical known as *beta-amyloid protein* accumulates in the fluid between neurons, in the blood vessels that fuel neurons, and in the membranes (known as the *meninges*) that surround the brain. Deposits of beta-amyloid protein scattered throughout the brain are known as *senile plaques* (Hayflick, 1980).

Having painted this gloomy picture of how aging affects the brain, let us now offer a few qualifications to the information we have just presented.

First, there is no firm rule for when the abnormalities in the brain begin to appear. In some people, abnormalities develop as early as their forties or fifties. For others, changes may not appear until they are in their seventies or eighties.

Second, the abnormalities do not appear uniformly throughout the brain. Rather, as you can see in Figure 2.9, they are much more prevalent in areas of the brain involved in the control of memory, language, thought, emotion, and motor behavior.

Finally, the abnormalities do not appear uniformly in all humans. The individual differences in fact are vast. Aging alone produces brain abnormalities (degeneration, neurofibrillary tangles, and senile plaques) in vir-

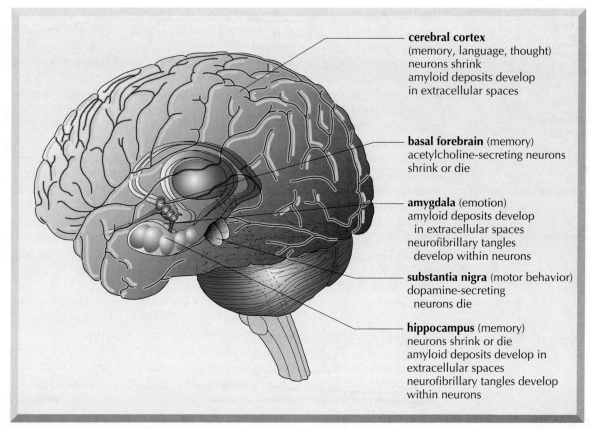

cerebral cortex
(memory, language, thought)
neurons shrink
amyloid deposits develop
in extracellular spaces

basal forebrain (memory)
acetylcholine-secreting neurons
shrink or die

amygdala (emotion)
amyloid deposits develop
  in extracellular spaces
neurofibrillary tangles
  develop within neurons

substantia nigra (motor behavior)
dopamine-secreting
  neurons die

hippocampus (memory)
neurons shrink or die
amyloid deposits develop in
extracellular spaces
neurofibrillary tangles develop
within neurons

Figure 2.9   *An Aging Brain*
Areas of the brain that develop abnormalities with age.

tually all of us (to different degrees), often with little or no effect on our behavior (Selkoe, 1992). Giuseppe Verdi, the Italian opera composer, wrote one of his most famous works—*Aida*—when he was in his eighties. Benjamin Spock, at the age of 90, is still writing books and lecturing.

There are, however, some important exceptions to this rule. Certain diseases—Parkinson's disease and Alzheimer's disease to name two of the most common—can significantly exacerbate the abnormalities that occur normally during the aging process. Let us take a closer look at the neural and behavioral effects of Parkinson's disease and Alzheimer's disease.

PARKINSON'S DISEASE AND ALZHEIMER'S DISEASE

Parkinson's disease and Alzheimer's disease are crippling neurological disorders that afflict mostly older people. Both diseases are classified as *neurodegenerative disorders* because they occur in stages, the brain deteriorating and the accompanying symptoms growing worse as the diseases progress. The neural abnormalities that characterize the two diseases affect different areas of the brain, as shown in Figure 2.9. Consequently, each disease produces different behavioral effects.

Parkinson's disease strikes mainly motor areas—the substantia nigra in particular degenerates and patients develop tremors in their hands, experience rigidity in their arms and legs, and have trouble keeping their balance. As the disease progresses, they find it increasingly difficult to walk and finally are confined to bed or to a wheelchair.

Alzheimer's disease affects primarily the memory, emotion, language, and thinking areas of the brain—among which are the hippocampus, basal forebrain, amygdala, and cerebral cortex; the brain abnormalities consist of neurodegeneration, neurofibrillary tangles, and beta-amyloid deposits, shown in Figure 2.10 (Selkoe, 1991). The symptoms of Alzheimer's disease begin quite innocently with seemingly harmless memory lapses (misplaced keys, a missed appointment). As time passes, however, the memory loss worsens to the point that memories of even a spouse or a child may fade. Other symptoms begin to appear as well. Alzheimer patients hallucinate and suffer from delusions. They lose the ability to speak and to understand language. They may lose the ability to recognize familiar objects or faces, or to walk or to swallow.

In summary, Parkinson's disease and Alzheimer's disease share certain features. Both are neurodegenerative diseases (i.e., they worsen with time), both are diseases of the elderly, and both are characterized by abnormalities that are normally present (but to a lesser degree) in elderly

Figure 2.10 *Beta-Amyloid Protein Deposit and Neurofibrillary Tangles Seen in Tissue from the Brain of an Alzheimer's Patient*
The beta-amyloid protein deposit is the large sphere at the center. The neurofibrillary tangles appear as small dark blobs.

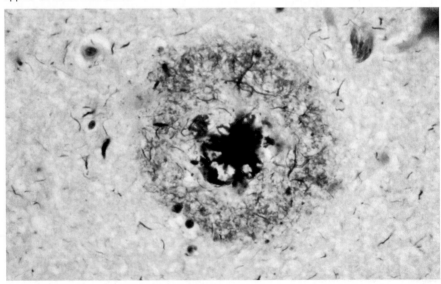

brains. And this brings us to the next question: What triggers the neural abnormalities—for example, the beta-amyloid protein deposits in the Alzheimer's patient and the neurodegeneration in the Parkinson's patient? We have no answer to this question, but we have some promising leads.

Parkinson's Disease: The Role of the Environment

There is a growing body of evidence that suggests a link between Parkinson's disease and the environment. The evidence comes from a rather unexpected discovery made in the early 1980s after several young adults injected themselves with heroin that had been accidentally contaminated with a chemical known as *MPTP* (Ballard, Tetrud, & Langstrom, 1985; Lewin, 1984). Within hours after taking the drug, they developed symptoms indistinguishable from Parkinson's disease. It was later found that MPTP selectively destroys neurons in the substantia nigra, thus providing the neurophysiological basis for the symptoms. The fact that MPTP can cause Parkinson's-like symptoms is significant for two reasons (Kopin & Markey, 1988).

First, MPTP is chemically similar to certain toxic agents found in the environment, raising the possibility that one or more of these agents may be the key factor in causing Parkinson's disease. Supporting, though not necessarily proving, this theory is the fact that areas of the country in which the herbicide paraquat (a chemical similar in structure to MPTP) is used, show an unusually high incidence of Parkinson's disease (Snyder & D'Amato, 1986).

Second, MPTP has been used in the laboratory to produce in lower animals (monkeys) the neurological conditions and behavioral symptoms that accompany Parkinson's disease (Langston et al., 1984; Langston, 1986). This lower-animal work has led to the discovery of a drug, known as *deprenyl*, whose principal function is to inhibit the destructive effects of MPTP. This drug is now being used to treat Parkinson's patients—with encouraging if limited success. Patients given deprenyl in the early stages of the disease still progress to the later stages but at a much slower rate than Parkinson's patients who do not receive the drug (Tetrud & Langston, 1989).

Alzheimer's Disease: Gene and Environment

The evidence surrounding Alzheimer's disease implicates both genetics and the environment as possible causes. In a small percentage of Alzheimer's cases there appears to be a family history of the disorder, implicating genetic factors, but in the majority of cases the families of Alzheimer's patients show no history of the disorder, suggesting environmental factors (Wurtman, 1985). Beyond this, the evidence becomes sketchy at best, perhaps more so for environmental factors than for genetic factors.

Environmental Factors

Two environmental agents commonly linked to the neural abnormalities that lead to Alzheimer's disease are slow-acting viruses and aluminum. Both are known to produce brain damage, but neither has been *directly* implicated in the type of brain damage seen with Alzheimer's disease (Wurtman, 1985).

One problem in linking these agents to Alzheimer's disease is that neither works selectively; that is, the damage they produce is not restricted to those areas of the brain (e.g., the cortex and hippocampus) that are typically damaged in Alzheimer's disease. Another problem is that aluminum, although it may be present in food and in drinking water, is filtered out of the circulatory system before it reaches the brain by a mechanism known as the blood-brain barrier (see Chapter 3 for details of the blood-brain barrier). These characteristics of slow-acting viruses and aluminum do not necessarily rule out a possible link to Alzheimer's disease, but a great deal of work needs to be done before the links are clearly established.

Genetic Factors

Evidence implicating a genetic factor in Alzheimer's disease is rooted in research seeking to understand the genetic basis of *Down's syndrome*, a form of mental retardation. Researchers have long been intrigued by the fact that people with Down's syndrome not only are born with limited cognitive ability, but as they grow older often lose whatever abilities they have more quickly than the population at large. This deterioration, moreover, is accompanied by abnormally high deposits of beta-amyloid protein and neurofibrillary tangles. Thus, it has been suggested that people with Down's syndrome, in addition to their retardation, may also suffer from a form of Alzheimer's disease. Because Down's syndrome has been traced to an abnormal gene on chromosome 21, it has been suggested that Alzheimer's disease may reflect a similar genetic abnormality (Goate et al., 1991).

This suspicion has recently been confirmed. There is evidence that families with a history of Alzheimer's disease have a genetic abnormality on chromosome 21, and this abnormality in turn has been linked to the production of beta-amyloid protein, the chemical substance that has been recently implicated as one of the possible causes of the disease (Levy et al., 1990; van Broeckhoven et al., 1990; Yankner et al., 1989).

Parkinson's Disease and Alzheimer's Disease: Treating the Disorders

Regardless of their underlying cause (gene or environment), Alzheimer's disease and Parkinson's disease are the result of unremitting, progressive degeneration of the brain. In Parkinson's disease, as we noted, the drug deprenyl has proven promising in slowing the degeneration and the progression of the disease. In Alzheimer's disease there are prospects (although still very much in the experimental stage) for the development of a similar treatment using nerve growth factor (Tuszynski et al., 1991).

But even if these drug therapies are perfected and the progressive neurodegeneration that causes Parkinson's disease and Alzheimer's disease can be impeded or prevented, the fact remains that literally millions of elderly patients are already afflicted with the diseases. What can be done for people in which the damage is already in place?

The approach again has been to use drugs, not necessarily to prevent or impede the brain damage but rather to compensate for it. The term "compensation" needs some elaboration. Not only do victims of Parkinson's disease and Alzheimer's disease undergo a loss of specific neurons, they also lose specific neurotransmitters produced by those neurons—dopamine in the case of Parkinson's disease, acetylcholine in the case of Alzheimer's disease. (See Chapter 5 for a detailed discussion of neurotransmitters.) Thus, it seems reasonable to assume that replenishing the brain with chemicals normally produced by neurons that no longer exist in the brains of Parkinson's and Alzheimer's victims might compensate for loss of the neurons themselves.

This therapeutic approach has begun to yield some important, if not conclusive, results. Drugs that compensate for reduced neurotransmitter activity have been administered to both groups of patients and with varied degrees of success. In the case of Parkinson's disease, drug treatment has proven successful in the early but less so in the later stages of the disease. In the case of Alzheimer's disease, drug treatment has not proven successful in either the early or the later stages of the disease (Growdon, 1992).

We will look at the action of these drug therapies in detail in Chapter 5, but for now it is enough to state that the therapeutic effectiveness of the drugs depends on the ability of brain areas, even when damaged, to produce at least *some* neurotransmitter. In the later stages of Parkinson's disease and in both the early and later stages of Alzheimer's disease, it is likely that because of the extensive degeneration, the damaged areas are unable to produce the neurotransmitter.

In summary, then, until recently the state of affairs surrounding these two diseases was as follows: two diseases in which major brain damage occurred and, because of the extensive and irreversible nature of the damage, very little if anything could be done. Today this picture may be about to change, clearly in the treatment of Parkinson's disease and perhaps in the near future in the treatment of Alzheimer's disease. The reason: neural damage produced by Parkinson's disease may not be as irreversible as originally thought.

REVERSING NEURAL DAMAGE: THE TRANSPLANT APPROACH

On the cutting edge of research into neurodegeneration is a series of extraordinary experiments whose purpose is to reverse the process of neurodegeneration that has long been considered irreversible. These experiments, all of which involve lower animals, have one feature in common: neural tissue from a healthy animal is transplanted into the brain of a brain-damaged animal. The rationale behind this procedure lies in the fact that the brain, unlike other parts of the body, is receptive to transplanted tissue. The reason for this is that the immune system's rejection responses that complicate transplant procedures in other parts of the body (e.g., the liver, heart, or kidney) do not occur in the brain.

In the original studies using the transplant approach, researchers damaged the area of the brain known as the substantia nigra, thus producing in laboratory animals the significant motor impairment normally seen in Parkinson's disease. Researchers then took tissue from a healthy brain and implanted it in the damaged area. The results were remarkable: neural tissue regrew and, most importantly, motor behavior improved significantly (Björklund et al., 1983).

The experiment has been repeated a number of times with a number of variations but with the same promising results (Kimble, 1990). For example, aged rats who had trouble balancing themselves on a wooden bridge suspended between two platforms were able to run along the bridge following a transplant, and rats whose ability to learn a maze was impaired by damage to the hippocampus were able to learn the maze much more readily after receiving a transplant (Gage et al., 1983).

There is one qualification, however, that cuts across all of the transplant work. Regardless of the location of the brain damage or the type of behavioral abnormality, the transplanted neural tissue must come from the brains of fetal (unborn) rats for the experiment to work, that is, for neural circuits to regrow and behavior to recover. Neural tissue taken from adult animals and implanted in the damaged areas of the brain simply does not work. Figure 2.11 summarizes the steps involved in the transfer procedure.

Parkinson's Disease and the Transplant Therapy

The transplant work in lower animals raises an obvious question with some not so obvious answers: Could similar transplants in humans conceivably help Parkinson's patients?

An implausible suggestion? Not in light of some very recent findings. In several recent studies, tissue taken from the brain (substantia nigra) of aborted human fetuses was transplanted into the damaged areas of Parkinson's patients—and with significant results. The implanted tissue survived, and the patients, who before the operation had suffered from severe rigidity in their limbs and from periods of immobility, showed moderate improvement. In no instance, however, did the operation restore their behavior to normal (Lindvall, 1990).

We must be careful, however, not to jump to conclusions. The transplant approach to treating Parkinson's disease is not only new and highly experimental but also raises a number of ethical and moral questions.

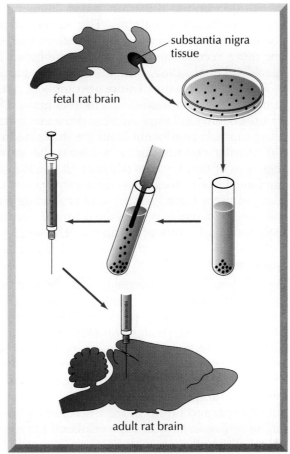

Figure 2.11 *The Transplant Procedure in Rats*
Substantia nigra tissue is taken from a fetal rat brain, transferred to a petri dish with saline, then to a test tube where
it is separated from other tissue, and finally to a syringe that
is used to inject the tissue into the adult rat brain.

The overriding issue—and the one that has caused scientists to rethink
the transplant approach—is the source of the transplanted tissue. Up to
now medical abortions have provided the tissue, but the idea of abortions providing the basis of a clinical treatment raises explosive ethical
issues. One alternative that has been suggested is that neural tissue be
taken from other animals (much as the heart valves of a pig have been
used to replace human heart valves), but studies to date indicate that
transplants from one species to another (e.g., mice to rats) do not work
nearly so well as transplants within species.

Another possibility now being explored is to use tissue from the
patient's own adrenal medulla gland and inject it into areas of the brain
known to be involved in Parkinson's disease. Adrenal medulla tissue,

when injected into the brain, works like neural tissue and releases the neurotransmitter dopamine. The results of this procedure, unfortunately, have been mixed. The procedure showed some promise at first, but more recent results have cast doubt on its ultimate effectiveness (Backlund et al., 1985).

Finally, there is the distinct possibility of not using implanted tissue—human or lower animal—at all to treat brain damage. Evidence indicates that the behavioral improvement produced by transplanted fetal tissue in lower animals results not from the implanted tissue substituting for the old missing circuits but rather from the implanted tissue stimulating regrowth of new circuits (Dunnett et al., 1987). Understanding how the implanted tissue does this—the assumption is that it releases a chemical that promotes the regrowth—and producing that chemical artificially in the form of drugs may hold the ultimate key to reversing brain damage. Only time and future research will tell.

A Final Look

By now you should understand that the nervous system is composed of an almost incalculable number of individual neurons that are structurally and functionally specialized to conduct and process information. This arrangement, though complex, is far from random. If we took a picture of the nervous system of every human being on earth, we would find, with very few exceptions, not only the same types of neurons—the same sensory and motor neurons and interneurons—but also the same general arrangement of neurons: the same peripheral nervous system, spinal cord, and brain. In the next chapter we shall examine this exquisite orderliness, first in the peripheral nervous system and then in the spinal cord and brain.

SUMMARY

1. *The neuron defined.* The basic unit in the nervous system is the nerve cell, or neuron. Its specialty is communication: transmitting information from one part of the body to another. The number of neurons in the human nervous system is now estimated to be in excess of 100 billion. Neurons, moreover, are far outnumbered by other cells, called neuroglial cells, found both in the central nervous system and in the peripheral nervous system. The function of these nonneural cells is supportive, providing nourishment and insulation for the neurons.

2. *How neurons are structured.* Neurons are structured and function much the same way as other cells, albeit for one striking difference: the presence of two types of extensions—axons and dendrites—that project from the cell body. Dendrites, in effect, "listen" to other cells. Axons, roughly speaking, are the communication lines from one neuron to another.

3. *Dendrites and axons.* Dendrites and axons differ in their basic structure. In a typical neuron, an axon is the long single extension at one end of the cell body, and dendrites are the cluster of smaller extensions at the other end. There are also branches at the end of the axon, known as axonal endings. These extensions promote communication of information. A key structural difference between dendrites and axons is the presence around axons of a whitish, fatty sheath known as the myelin sheath, whose main function is twofold: to speed the process of conduction and to prevent signals carried by adjacent neurons from interfering with one another. The disintegration of myelin is the primary cause of the degenerative disease known as multiple sclerosis. Another key difference between dendrites and axons is the presence in dendrites of Nissl substance, a group of cellular components involved in the production of vital chemicals. Deprived of Nissl substance, the axon depends on chemicals transported to it from the cell body and dendrites by a process known as axonal transport.

4. *How neurons are classified.* Neurons are commonly classified according to function: sensory neurons, motor neurons, and interneurons. Sensory neurons carry impulses from receptors toward the central nervous system, motor neurons carry impulses from the central nervous system to muscles, and both types of neurons are found in the peripheral nervous system. Interneurons, more numerous than either of the other two kinds of neurons, are found primarily in the central nervous system and are connected to sensory neurons, motor neurons, and other interneurons.

5. *Grouping neurons according to their appearance.* Neurons can also be grouped according to their appearance. Sensory neurons fall into two groups: those in which a single extension is connected to the cell body (unipolar neurons) and those in which two extensions are connected to the cell body (bipolar neurons). Motor neurons and interneurons are multipolar—that is, they have many extensions issuing from the cell body. Interneurons are classified as either projection neurons (having a long axon and little branching) or local-circuit neurons (having a short axon and profuse branching).

6. *Communication between neurons.* Neurons, except in rare instances, are not physically connected. Rather, they are linked by microscopic gaps known as synapses. The communication between neurons is governed by the activity of chemicals, known as neurotransmitters, whose activity constitutes, in fact, the basic language of the nervous system. It is now generally believed that many forms of mental illness can ultimately be traced to abnormalities in neurotransmitter activity.

7. *The development of the nervous system.* It is generally accepted today that the nervous system, at birth, is only partially formed, and that the manner in which the nervous system ultimately develops reflects an interplay between genetic and environmental factors. Genetics appears to confer upon developing axons the capacity to seek out certain target sites in the body, but whether the connections between those axons and the target site actually form and endure, depends on environmentally initiated stimulation at the target site. It has been shown in experiments on lower animals that young animals reared in "enriched" environments develop a denser and more complex system of neural connections than animals denied this enrichment. It has been shown, too, that certain aspects of visual behavior in monkeys and in humans can be influenced greatly by what happens, or doesn't happen, in the early stages of life.

8 . *When neurons are damaged.* The capacity of neurons to regenerate in the face of injury or disease is greater than was once originally thought, but there are nonetheless key differences between the regenerative capacities of neurons in the peripheral nervous system and neurons in the central nervous system. When the axons of neurons in the peripheral nervous system are severed, they are often able to regenerate primarily because of chemicals (nerve growth factor) secreted by the surrounding nonneural cells, known as Schwann cells. The regenerative capacity of injured neurons in the central nervous system, on the other hand, is blocked by the action of the surrounding nonneural cells, known as oligodendrocytes and astrocytes.

9. *Replacing neurons.* Unlike other cells in the body that replace themselves through a process known as mitosis, neurons that die are not replaced in the strict sense of the word. What happens instead in many instances is that surviving (and neighboring) neurons are able to assume functions that were formerly under the control of the dying neurons. How, in fact, neurons are able to assume this control is not yet understood, but it would appear as though we are born with far more neurons than we actually need and that this excess provides us with what is, in effect, a "backup" army of neurons ready to be pressed into service at any given time.

10. *The aging brain.* Notwithstanding the existence of surplus neurons, the aging process nonetheless takes its toll on the nervous system and, by doing so, on many aspects of behavior. As we age, neurons degenerate and undergo changes in their chemical makeup. Their cell bodies become laced with protein filaments, known as neurofibrillary tangles, and areas surrounding the neurons accumulate deposits of a chemical known as beta-amyloid protein. Certain diseases, however, can greatly exacerbate the behavioral consequences of the aging process. And two neurodegenerative diseases—Parkinson's and Alzheimer's—are particularly devastating in this regard. Parkinson's disease strikes areas of the brain that control motor behavior, producing symptoms such as motor tremors and, as the disease progresses, the inability to walk. Alzheimer's disease affects areas of the brain that control emotion, language, thinking, and memory.

11. *Parkinson's and Alzheimer's disease.* There is a growing body of evidence to suggest that the neurodegeneration at the root of Parkinson's disease is environmentally induced, but research into the cause of Alzheimer's disease has implicated both the environment and genetics as potential causes. Slow-acting viruses and aluminum have been suggested as potential environmental agents, but as yet there is no concrete evidence to support either claim. Evidence for a genetic link comes from studies on Down's syndrome and on families with a history of Alzheimer's disease, both of which implicate an abnormality on chromosome 21.

12. *Treating the diseases.* Drug therapies have proven successful in the early but less so in the later stages of Parkinson's disease. Drug therapies for Alzheimer's disease have not proven successful in the early or the later stages of the disease. A drug known as deprenyl has been shown to slow down the neurodegeneration brought on by Parkinson's disease, and there is optimism that a drug therapy involving nerve growth factor could yield similar results in Alzheimer's disease.

13. *Transplant therapy.* On the cutting edge of research into neurodegeneration are lower animal experiments in which neural tissue from healthy animals is transplanted into the brain of animals whose brains have been damaged to produce motor impairments normally seen in Parkinson's disease patients. These studies have shown that animals receiving these transplants do, in fact, regain motor function albeit with one condition: the transplanted tissue must come from the brains of fetal (unborn) rats for the experiment to work. The logical question here is whether similar transplants could work with Parkinson's patients, and recent findings of a highly experimental nature suggest a strong possibility that this could well be the case. On the other hand, transplant therapy, especially since the tissue originates in unborn fetuses, raises a number of moral and ethical issues—a fact that is leading researchers to explore alternative sources for the tissue to be transplanted.

KEY TERMS

afferent
Alzheimer's disease
astrocytes
axonal endings
axonal transport
axons
beta-amyloid protein
bipolar neuron
dendrites
deprenyl

Down's syndrome
efferent
local-circuit neuron
microglia
microspikes
microtubules
mitosis
MPTP
multiple sclerosis
multipolar neuron

KEY TERMS

myelin sheath
nerve growth factor
neurofibrillary tangles
neuroglial cells
neuron
neurotransmitters
Nissl substance
nodes of Ranvier
oligodendrocytes
Parkinson's disease

projection neuron
retrograde degeneration
satellite cells
Schwann cells
senile plaques
soma
synapse
unipolar neuron
Wallerian degeneration

SUGGESTED READINGS

Alberts, B., Bray, D., Lewis, J., Raff, M., Roberts, K., & Watson, J. D. (Eds.) *Molecular Biology of the Cell*, 3rd ed., New York: Garland, 1994.

Nicholls, J. G., Martin, A., Wallace, B. G., & Kuffler, S. W. *From Neuron to Brain*, 3rd ed., Sunderland, Mass: Sinauer Associates, 1992.

Selkoe, D. J. "Aging Brain, Aging Mind." *Scientific American*, 267, 1992, 61–67.

Shatz, C. J. "The Developing Brain." *Scientific American*, 267, 1992, 134–142.

3

THE NERVOUS SYSTEM

INTRODUCTION

By any measure, the study of the nervous system—how it is structured, how it works, and what it contributes to behavior—is one of the most challenging undertakings in science. Consider the numbers alone. The human nervous system consists of as many as 200 billion working parts, all of them interconnected in a way that makes the overall number of combinations almost impossible to calculate. Given this complexity, we will not attempt in this chapter to cover every known aspect of the nervous system. Rather, we will paint a general picture of the nervous system: how it is structured, how it functions, and how, in a broad sense, it controls behavior.

THE NERVOUS SYSTEM DEFINED

The nervous system can be best defined as a vast communication network of cells and their accompanying extensions. With the exception of unicellular and simple multicellular organisms, all species have such a system in one form or another. The network varies in complexity from species to species, but its function is the same throughout the animal kingdom. Nervous systems are transmitting devices: they transmit information back and forth throughout the body.

In humans and other higher animals, the nervous system is divided into two major parts, the *peripheral nervous system* and the *central nervous system*. Each system has a specific function. The peripheral nervous system is essentially an input-output system. It acts as an intermediary between the central nervous system and the environment. It transmits information (in the form of electrochemical signals) from the environment to the central nervous system and then transmits information (again in the form of electrochemical signals) from the central nervous system to the muscles and glands that ultimately carry out the behavior.

The central nervous system—that is, the brain and the spinal cord—can be best described as a decision maker. It processes the incoming signals and then dictates the appropriate motor response. Let us now look more closely at both systems.

THE PERIPHERAL NERVOUS SYSTEM

The peripheral nervous system comprises all neural material located outside the brain and spinal cord—all neurons, in other words, that are not part of the central nervous system. These neurons, as Figure 3.1 shows, do not exist in isolation. Instead, their axons are gathered into bundles known as *nerves*. Each nerve in the peripheral nervous system is made up of hundreds, sometimes thousands, of axons, but the axons of each neuron are able to operate independently. The cellular basis for this independence lies in the fact that each axon is insulated from the others by neuroglial cells, in this case *Schwann cells*. The same principle holds in the central nervous system as well. The difference is one of terminology: in the central nervous system bundles of axons are referred to as *tracts*, and the neuroglial cells that separate them as *oligodendrocytes*.

Figure 3.1   ***The Structure of a Nerve***
A nerve is made up of bundles of axons; each axon is insulated by a Schwann cell.

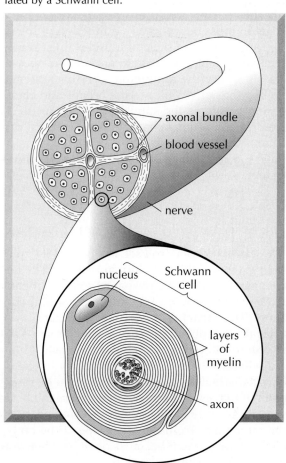

One other feature of the peripheral nervous system deserves mention here. By now you should know that a neuron consists of an axon, a cell body, and dendrites. But just as axons are gathered in groups, so are cell bodies. The name given to a group of cell bodies (as opposed to axons) in the peripheral nervous system is *ganglion*. The name given to a group of cell bodies in the central nervous system is *nucleus*, not to be confused with the nucleus found within each cell body.

Dividing the Peripheral Nervous System

The peripheral nervous system consists of two principal subdivisions: the skeletal nervous system and the autonomic nervous system. The *skeletal nervous system*, also known as the *somatic nervous system*, controls the activity of skeletal muscles—muscles attached to the skeleton and involved in the movement of limbs. The *autonomic nervous system* controls the activity of internal organs and glands.

Why do we need two separate systems to carry out the functions of the peripheral nervous system? The answer is that in order for behavior to take place, two conditions are essential. First, muscles that move the skeleton must be *activated*—a function of the skeletal nervous system. At the same time, the skeletal muscles must receive sufficient fuel and oxygen from the bloodstream to provide the necessary energy for movement. This is where the autonomic nervous system comes into play. By controlling the activity of internal organs and glands, the autonomic nervous system regulates the supply of energy to the skeletal muscles. We shall examine the unique characteristics of each of these systems—the skeletal and the autonomic—later in the chapter. First, however, let us consider some of the features they share as part of the peripheral nervous system.

The Structure of the Peripheral Nervous System

The schematic view you see in Figure 3.2 depicts the peripheral and central nervous systems of human beings. The column down the middle is the spinal cord. The egg-shaped mass at the top of the cord is the brain. Each extension from the brain and spinal cord represents a peripheral nerve. This structure underlies the function we mentioned earlier: it enables the peripheral nervous system to serve as an intermediary between the central nervous system and the environment.

As Figure 3.2 indicates, the nerves in the peripheral nervous system have a distinct distribution pattern. To be more precise, humans have 43 pairs of nerves. Each nerve that enters the brain or spinal cord from one side of the body has a counterpart that enters the brain or spinal cord in the same place from the other side of the body. The logic behind this bilateral arrangement becomes obvious when you consider that our bodies are bilaterally symmetrical: that is, we have two eyes, two ears, two arms, and so forth. Each member of a nerve pair represents one or the other side of the body.

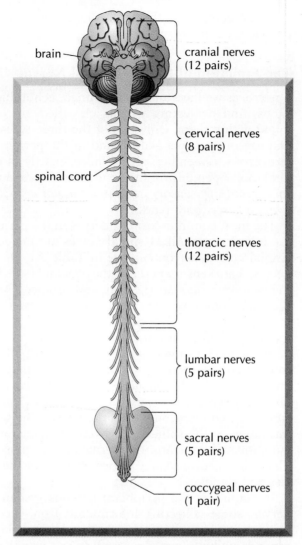

brain

cranial nerves
(12 pairs)

cervical nerves
(8 pairs)

spinal cord

thoracic nerves
(12 pairs)

lumbar nerves
(5 pairs)

sacral nerves
(5 pairs)

coccygeal nerves
(1 pair)

Figure 3.2   *Central and Peripheral Nervous Systems*
The simplest and commonest way of differentiating between the central and peripheral nervous systems is to
group all neural material within the brain and spinal cord
into the central nervous system and all other neurons into
the peripheral nervous system. Twelve nerves in the peripheral system are connected directly to the brain and are
called cranial nerves. The other peripheral nerves are connected with the spinal cord between vertebrae and are
called spinal nerves. The spinal nerves are divided into four
groups (plus the coccygeal nerves), depending on where
they connect with the spinal cord: in the cervical, thoracic,
lumbar, or sacral region.

Of the 43 pairs of nerves in the peripheral nervous system, 31 enter the
central nervous system below the neck, along the various levels of the
spinal cord. These 31 pairs are generally referred to as *spinal nerves*. The

other 12 pairs enter the brain directly and, appropriately enough, are known as *cranial nerves*.

The Function of the Peripheral Nervous System

A nerve, as we have already explained, is nothing more than a bundle of axons. And nerves are usually classified on the basis of the neurons found within them. Only two of the three types of neurons—the motor and sensory neurons—are found in the peripheral nervous system (interneurons, remember, are found primarily in the central nervous system). So, depending on the neurons within it, a nerve is known as a *sensory nerve* (only sensory neurons), a *motor nerve* (only motor neurons), or a *mixed nerve* (both types).

The most common form of nerves in the peripheral nervous system is the mixed nerve. All 31 spinal nerves are mixed nerves, as are 4 of the cranial nerves, as you can see in Table 3.1. Of the remaining 8 cranial nerves, 3 are sensory nerves—the *olfactory* (smell), the *optic* (vision), and the *auditory-vestibular* (hearing and balance). And 5 are motor nerves— the *oculomotor* (eye movement), *trochlear* (eye movement), *abducens* (eye movement), *spinal accessory* (movement of neck and viscera), and *hypoglossal* (tongue movement).

As Figure 3.3 shows, spinal nerves carry both motor and sensory neurons until they reach the spinal cord. There they divide into two branches known as *roots*. The *dorsal root* ("dorsal" means "toward the back") contains only sensory neurons; the *ventral root* ("ventral" means "toward the stomach") contains only motor neurons. The sensory neurons carry information to the spinal cord from the receptors in the skin (pressure, pain, touch, temperature), internal organs, muscles, tendons, and joints. The motor neurons carry information from the spinal cord to the muscles and glands.

In summary, the peripheral nervous system consists of 43 pairs of nerves, some collecting information from receptors (sensory nerves), some delivering information to muscles and glands (motor nerves), and some doing both (spinal nerves). In this way the peripheral nervous system plays an indispensable role in the control of behavior. But as we said earlier, for behavior to take place, two conditions are essential: skeletal muscles must move, and skeletal muscles must receive the necessary energy for movement. The peripheral nervous system, specifically the two divisions of the peripheral nervous system, are involved in the control of both; the skeletal nervous system controls movement, the autonomic nervous system controls the flow of energy.

THE SKELETAL NERVOUS SYSTEM

The skeletal nervous system consists of motor neurons that control external behavior. This behavior is of two types: voluntary and reflex. *Voluntary behavior* is any motion you make intentionally: lifting a glass,

TABLE 3.1

TYPE, FUNCTION, AND POINT OF ORIGIN OR TERMINATION OF CRANIAL NERVES

NUMBER AND NAME	TYPE	FUNCTION	POINT OF ORIGIN OR TERMINATION IN BRAIN
I Olfactory	Sensory	Smell	Cerebral hemispheres (ventral part)
II Optic	Sensory	Vision	Thalamus
III Oculomotor	Motor	Eye movement	Midbrain
IV Trochlear	Motor	Eye movement	Midbrain
V Trigeminal	Motor	Masticatory movements	Midbrain and pons
	Sensory	Sensitivity of face and tongue	Medulla
VI Abducens	Motor	Eye movement	Medulla
VII Facial	Sensory	Sensitivity of tongue	Medulla
	Motor	Facial movement	Medulla
VIII Auditory vestibular	Sensory	Hearing, balance	Medulla
IX Glossopharyngeal	Sensory, motor	Sensitivity and movement of tongue and pharynx	Medulla
X Vagus	Sensory, motor	Sensitivity and movement of heart, lungs, gastrointestinal tract	Medulla
XI Spinal accessory	Motor	Movement of neck muscles and viscera	Medulla
XII Hypoglossal	Motor	Tongue movement	Medulla

combing your hair, making a fist, and so on. *Involuntary*, or *reflexive, behavior* occurs without your conscious direction: you blink at a puff of air; your hand jerks back when it touches a hot stove. You might assume that because the skeletal nervous system controls two different types of behavior it contains two different types of motor neurons. But such is not the case. Both voluntary and involuntary behavior are controlled by the same motor neurons. Let us see how.

Structure and Function of the Skeletal Nervous System

Figure 3.3 depicts a typical motor neuron in the skeletal nervous system and in the process reveals the cellular basis for involuntary and voluntary behavior. As you can see, the motor neuron stretches in an uninterrupted fashion from the spinal cord to the skeletal muscle. If you trace this motor neuron to its origin in the spinal cord, however, you will find that, like a river fed by tributaries, it is fed by different neural inputs. Some of

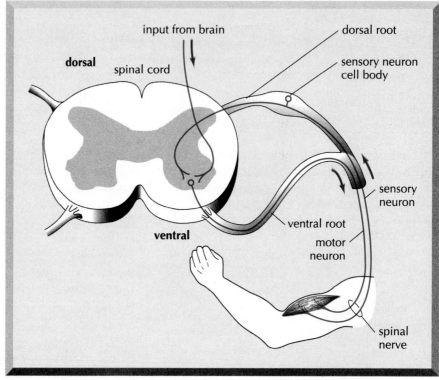

Figure 3.3 *A Spinal Nerve*
This magnified view of a section of the spinal cord shows how neurons contained in a single spinal nerve are connected to the cord. The sensory neuron enters the cord dorsally (at the back), and the motor neuron exits from the cord ventrally (at the front). The motor neuron receives input from sensory neurons and from the brain.

these inputs originate from sensory neurons. Others originate from higher centers in the brain. The site of origin is significant. Inputs that come directly from sensory neurons tend to produce reflexive behavior (the eye blink, the knee jerk). Those from higher centers tend to produce voluntary behavior. No matter where the input originates, however, it must travel down the same motor neurons and affect the same skeletal muscles to produce external behavior.

THE AUTONOMIC NERVOUS SYSTEM

The autonomic nervous system consists of motor neurons that connect the central nervous system to those internal organs and glands involved in life-sustaining internal processes, such as the heartbeat, digestion, and bladder function. With one exception—the heart—the muscles innervated by autonomic nervous system motor neurons have a smooth appearance and so are called *smooth muscles* or, occasionally, *viscera*. The heart, on the other hand, has the same striated appearance of skeletal muscles and for that reason is categorized separately as cardiac muscle.

The function of the autonomic nervous system, as we have already established, is to control the internal behavior necessary to respond to external behavioral demands. If you are relaxing in a comfortable chair, your respiration and heart rate remain low. In the final mile of a 10-mile race, your respiration and heartbeat need to work at maximum output. The autonomic nervous system makes the appropriate adjustment.

Two aspects of the autonomic nervous system function deserve special emphasis. First, the behavior controlled by the autonomic nervous system is, for all intents and purposes, *beyond* voluntary control. True, studies have shown that people can be trained, through meditation techniques and with the help of biofeedback, to exert a measure of voluntary control over certain internal responses—blood pressure, for example. Generally, however, the autonomic nervous system operates on automatic pilot. You do not have to consciously *make* your heart beat faster when you exercise: it does so automatically, responding to information channeled to it through the autonomic nervous system. Similarly, nearly all physiological processes that are vital for survival—digestion and respiration, for instance—take place without your direct intervention, and for an excellent reason. As Lewis Thomas wryly observes in his essay "Autonomy," our conscious involvement in these processes would not be in our best interests. Writes Mr. Thomas:

> If I were informed that I was in direct communication with my liver and could now take over, I would become deeply depressed. I'd sooner be told, forty thousand feet over Denver, that the 747 jet in which I had a coach seat was now mine to operate as I pleased; at least I would have the hope of bailing out, if I could find a parachute and discover quickly how to open a door. Nothing would save me and my liver if I were in charge. For I am, to face the facts squarely, considerably less intelligent than my liver. I am, moreover, constitutionally unable to make hepatic decisions, and I prefer not to be obliged to, ever. I would not be able to think of the first thing to do. (Thomas, 1974)

A second aspect of autonomic activity that deserves our attention at this point is that the system does not really "control" activity in the strict sense of the word. Even without the involvement of the autonomic nervous system, internal activity can still take place. The heart, for instance, will beat even if you detach it from the autonomic nervous system. Similarly, digestive processes, such as stomach contractions, can take place without autonomic involvement. What the autonomic nervous system does, though, is *modulate* internal activity. It makes sure that internal behavior keeps pace with the demands of external behavior and the external environment. Let us now consider how the autonomic nervous system accomplishes this task.

The Divisions of the Autonomic Nervous System

The ability of the autonomic nervous system to modulate behavior and to maintain an energy supply consistent with demand is rooted in its structure—the fact that it is, in effect, two systems. These systems, depicted in Figure 3.4, are generally referred to as the sympathetic and the parasympathetic nervous systems. Although both systems innervate most internal organs, they perform different energy-related functions. The *sympathetic nervous system* mobilizes and expends energy; the *parasympathetic nervous system* conserves and stores it. If you have just finished a heavy meal and you are relaxing, the parasympathetic nervous system does most of the work. It enhances the digestive process and si-

Figure 3.4 *The Autonomic Nervous System*
The autonomic nervous system is divided into two parts, the sympathetic and parasympathetic systems. Nerves making up the sympathetic system originate in the thoracic and lumbar regions of the spinal cord; nerves making up the parasympathetic system originate in the brain and the sacral region of the spinal cord. Most organs are innervated by nerves from both the sympathetic and parasympathetic systems.

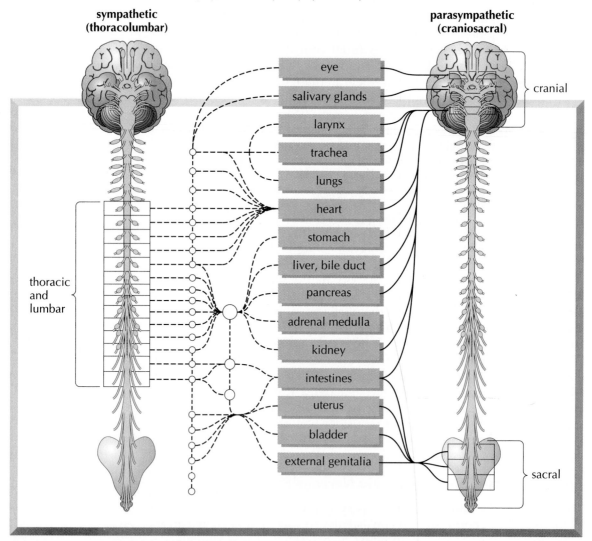

multaneously inhibits blood flow to the inactive skeletal muscles. Should something happen that requires quick action, the sympathetic nervous system takes control, inhibiting digestion and increasing blood pressure, thus helping the body meet the energy requirements of active skeletal muscles more effectively.

The Structure of the Autonomic Nervous System

In the same way that the function of the skeletal nervous system is linked to the structure of the neurons that compose it, so does the function of the autonomic nervous system relate to the structure of *its* neurons. The neurons in each system are similar in that they both originate inside the central nervous system. Otherwise there are significant differences, primarily in how they connect to the muscles. Unlike skeletal neurons, which run directly to the muscles, autonomic neurons do not run a direct route to the organs they innervate but form synapses with a second set of motor neurons. It is the second set that innervates the target organs.

The two sets of motor neurons and their relationships with the target organs are shown in Figure 3.5. The point at which synapses form between the two motor neurons is referred to as a *ganglion*. The neurons whose axons originate in the central nervous system are known as *pre-*

Figure 3.5 *The Autonomic and Skeletal Nervous System*
Note that the skeletal motor neuron runs an uninterrupted course from the spinal cord to the target muscles; the autonomic motor neurons do not.

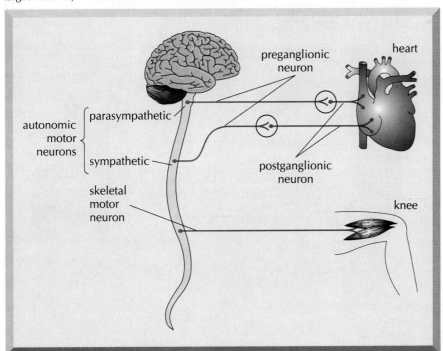

ganglionic; those that connect to target organs are known as *postganglionic*. The two sets of motor neurons communicate with one another through the neurotransmitter *acetylcholine*, which is released by the preganglionic neurons and excites the postganglionic neurons. We will discuss this aspect of nervous system function in Chapter 5.

The Structure and Chemistry of the Sympathetic and Parasympathetic Nervous Systems

Both parts of the autonomic nervous system, the sympathetic nervous system (the system that mobilizes and expends energy) and the parasympathetic nervous system (the system that conserves and stores energy), are made up of preganglionic and postganglionic neurons. As you can see in Figure 3.6, however, the structure and the function of the neurons in each system are different.

They differ, first of all, in their points of origin within the central nervous system. The preganglionic neurons of the parasympathetic nervous system originate in the lower part of the brain (the medulla) and in the

Figure 3.6 *Parasympathetic and Sympathetic Nervous Systems*
Shown are the differences between the two systems in their origins, in the lengths of their preganglionic and postganglionic neurons, and in the neurotransmitters they release at the target organ. ACh refers to the neurotransmitter acetylcholine, NE to norepinephrine.

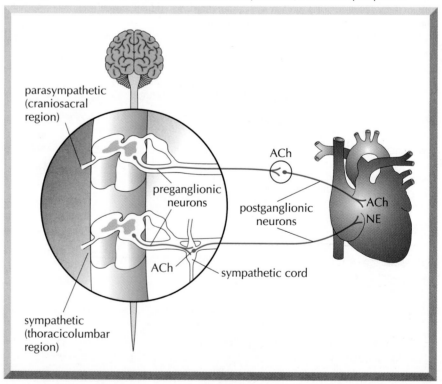

lower part of the spinal cord (the sacral region). Collectively, these two regions are known as the *craniosacral region*. Preganglionic neurons of the sympathetic nervous system originate in two regions of the spinal cord, the thoracic and the lumbar, known collectively as the *thoracico-lumbar region*.

A second difference between the preganglionic and postganglionic neurons in the two systems lies in the length of the neurons. Preganglionic neurons in the parasympathetic nervous system are long, traveling almost the entire distance from the central nervous system to the target organ and then, just outside the organ, forming synapses with the ganglia formed by the cell bodies of the postganglionic neurons. The postganglionic neurons, which continue to the target organ, are very short. In the sympathetic nervous system the reverse is true: the preganglionic neurons are short, and the postganglionic neurons long. The preganglionic neurons travel to ganglia that lie in chains running parallel to and located immediately outside the spinal cord. These chains of sympathetic ganglia make up the *sympathetic cords*, one on each side of the spinal cord. From them long postganglionic neurons extend to the target organs.

A final and crucial difference between the parasympathetic and sympathetic nervous systems lies in their chemistry—in the neurotransmitters that are released by postganglionic (as opposed to preganglionic) neurons to activate the smooth muscles and glands. This difference in neurotransmitters provides the basis for the difference between the way the two systems function—the fact that they have opposite effects on internal organs and glands. The postganglionic neurons in the parasympathetic nervous system release *acetylcholine* (ACh), which accounts for the ability of the parasympathetic nervous system during relaxation to enhance digestive processes while simultaneously inhibiting heart rate and blood pressure. The postganglionic neurons in the sympathetic nervous system release the neurotransmitter *norepinephrine* (NE), which accounts for the ability of the sympathetic nervous system to inhibit digestion and elevate heart rate and blood pressure during stress. As we indicated earlier, neurotransmitters are a subject unto themselves and will be dealt with in Chapter 5. For now it is enough to keep in mind that the difference in neurotransmitters accounts for the different effects that the two systems have on internal organs and glands.

A Final Look

Let us now take inventory of where we've been and where we are going. Figure 3.7 presents a schematic view of the subdivisions of the nervous system—the systems within the system.

1. There are two main divisions: the central nervous system, which consists of the brain and spinal cord, and the peripheral nervous system, which consists of the skeletal and autonomic nervous systems. The skeletal nervous system controls movement, and the autonomic nervous system controls the energy for movement.

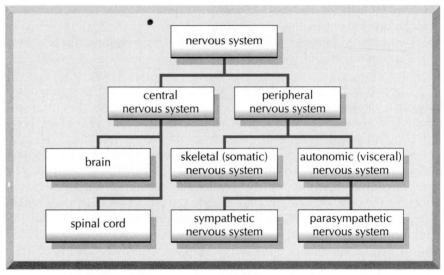

Figure 3.7   *The Major Divisions of the Nervous System*

2. The autonomic nervous system is divided into two parts: the parasympathetic nervous system and the sympathetic nervous system. The parasympathetic nervous system conserves and stores energy, and the sympathetic nervous system mobilizes and expends energy.

Up to now our concern has been with the peripheral nervous system, which is involved in collecting information from receptors and delivering information to muscles and glands. Now, to complete the picture, we turn to the central nervous system, the system involved in coordinating and processing the information in a manner that produces adaptive behavior.

THE CENTRAL NERVOUS SYSTEM

All but the lowest animals have some sort of central nervous system. The nature and complexity of the central nervous system, of course, varies considerably from species to species, and as you might expect, the complexity is greatest among human beings.

In humans, as well as in most other higher animals, the central nervous system is divided into two parts: the spinal cord and the brain. The spinal cord is a column of neurons that begins at the base of the skull and extends downward, following the route of the spinal column to a point along the column that is roughly two-thirds the distance between the base of the skull and the base of the spine. The brain itself, pictured in Figure 3.8, is an egg-shaped mass of cells that arises, mushroomlike, from the spinal cord and, in humans, weighs about 3 pounds. As Figure 3.8 also indicates, the neurons in the central nervous system consist of

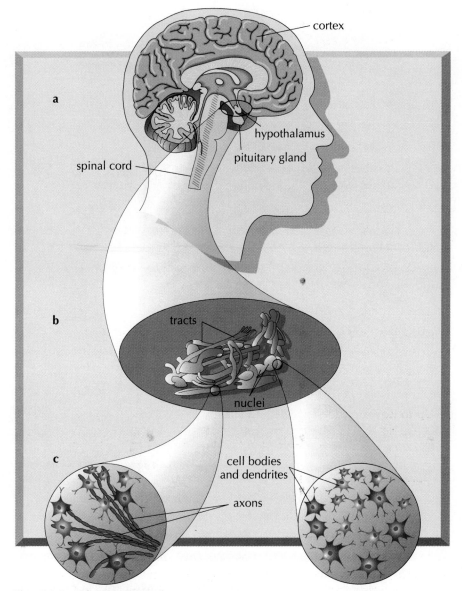

Figure 3.8 *The Human Brain*
(a) A midline view; (b) nuclei and tracts in the hypothalamus; (c) cell bodies, dendrites, and axons that make up the nuclei and tracts, respectively.

axons traveling in bundles known as tracts, and cell bodies and dendrites packed together in nuclei (also referred to as brain areas). Generally speaking, tracts are the communication lines in the central nervous system; nuclei are the decision makers.

These aspects of central nervous system function will be discussed later. First, however, let us briefly examine the structural features whose function is to protect and nourish the central nervous system.

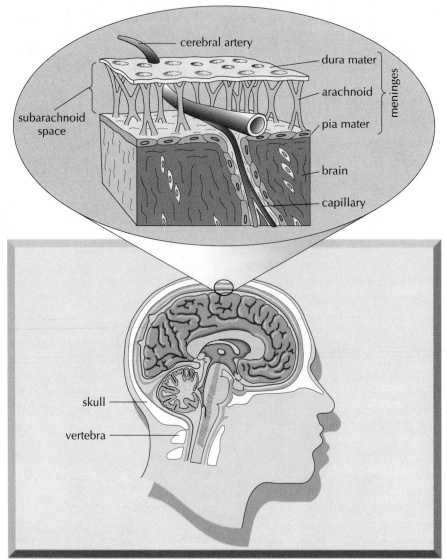

Figure 3.9 *The Meninges*
The magnified view shows the three layers of meninges, a cerebral artery in the subarachnoid space, and a capillary penetrating the surface of the brain.

Protecting and Nourishing the Brain and Spinal Cord

For the sake of protection, the brain lies within the skull, and the spinal cord is housed inside a canal formed by bony vertebrae. Additional protection comes in the form of nonneural material known as *meninges* (pictured in Figure 3.9). Inflammation of the meninges produces *meningitis*, a serious disease that can lead to paralysis and death.

As Figure 3.9 indicates, three layers of meninges envelop the brain and spinal cord. The outer layer is a tough, fibrous membrane called the *dura mater*. Next comes a thin membrane known as the *arachnoid*. Immediately surrounding the brain and the spinal cord, is a delicate membrane called the *pia mater*. Between the pia mater and arachnoid is the *subarachnoid space*, a spongy layer containing *cerebrospinal fluid* (discussed further on page 74) and blood vessels. All three layers serve a protective function and contain blood vessels that supply nourishment to the brain and spinal cord.

Blood Supply

The central nervous system, particularly the brain, is abundantly laced with blood vessels, and for good reason. Unlike most cells, neurons are unable to store nutrients (specifically glucose) in the form of protein and fat. Their survival is contingent on a steady supply of glucose and oxygen from the blood. Fortunately, keeping neurons supplied with sufficient glucose and oxygen is no problem—at least under normal circumstances. But if an injury deprives neurons of either glucose or oxygen for even a brief time, the result is usually irreversible damage.

You can appreciate just how dependent neurons are on glucose and oxygen when you consider that the typical aftermath of a cerebral stroke (i.e., an insufficiency of blood supply in the brain caused by closure of or bleeding from blood vessels) is usually some form of behavioral impairment. What happens in these situations is that neurons, deprived of blood and therefore of their energy supply, die in such great numbers that the behavior controlled by them is lost. This dependence also explains why the brain and the spinal cord, even though they account for less than 2 percent of total body weight, use roughly 15 percent of the body's blood supply.

Blood-Brain Barrier

Essential as the process is, the body's ability to supply the brain and spinal cord with blood is limited by one critical capacity of the body: its ability to protect the brain from foreign substances. More than any other area of the body, the brain and spinal cord are highly selective in the substances they allow to enter from the blood. The mechanism that underlies this selectivity is known as the *blood-brain barrier*, and its function is to control the inflow of substances and to make sure that only certain substances actually get into the brain and spinal cord. Common nutritive substances, such as glucose, pass freely into the brain and spinal cord. Substances capable of disrupting brain and spinal cord function are screened out.

One area left unprotected by the blood-brain barrier is known as the *area postrema*, and it is left unprotected for a good reason. Its job is to control vomiting. Thus it gives the body a means of ejecting toxic substances from the stomach before they can enter the bloodstream and reach the brain and spinal cord in massive amounts.

A Closer Look.   Scientists have known about the blood-brain barrier for some time, but only within recent years have they come to understand its workings. The "barrier" is created by the unique structure of blood vessels (specifically the capillaries) in the brain and spinal cord. Capillaries in other parts of the body have pores through which substances carried by the blood eventually pass to cells in the body. No such pores exist in the capillaries in the brain and spinal cord. Substances passing from the blood to the brain and spinal cord must penetrate the walls of the capillaries directly, and very few are able to do so. Even those substances that successfully penetrate the capillary wall must negotiate still another hurdle before they reach the neurons.

Between capillaries and neurons are nonneural astrocyte cells (a special type of neuroglial cell). To reach the neurons, substances leaving the capillaries must first penetrate the membranes of the astrocyte cells. These cells act, in effect, as "middlemen," carrying the substances from the capillaries to the neural cells. Not all substances leaving the capillaries are able to enter the astrocyte cells. Thus the blood-brain barrier actually consists of two membranes, one surrounding the capillaries, the other surrounding the astrocyte cells.

Cerebrospinal Fluid

Also present in the central nervous system is a colorless liquid known as *cerebrospinal fluid*. Its principal function is to cushion the brain and spinal cord, but it serves a number of other functions as well. Cerebrospinal fluid provides nourishment to and removes waste products from the brain and spinal cord. And because the fluid allows the brain to float, it helps reduce the weight of the brain. The reduction is significant: from roughly 1400 grams in the air to less than 40 grams in the skull.

Cerebrospinal fluid is found primarily in a group of cavities known as *ventricles* (see Figure 3.10), and it is constituted from the blood that filters into these ventricles through regions richly supplied with blood vessels known as *choroid plexuses*. The process by which cerebrospinal fluid is produced is continuous. Once the fluid reaches the ventricles, it circulates through them and around the spinal cord and outer surface of the brain before returning once again to the bloodstream.

You can get a general idea of the circulation path if you look at Figure 3.10. The fluid flows from the paired lateral ventricles located on either side of the brain to the third and fourth ventricles, both located along the midline of the brain, and finally into the subarachnoid space that surrounds the brain and spinal cord. There it reenters the blood through the arachnoid membrane. The steady flow of cerebrospinal fluid through the central nervous system is essential. When the flow is blocked, the fluid backs up and produces abnormal pressure that can cause brain damage and mental retardation. This condition is known as *hydrocephalus*— swelling of the brain.

The Structure of the Central Nervous System

We mentioned earlier that almost every animal has a central nervous system of sorts, but that humans and other vertebrates fall into a special category based on the structure of the nervous system. The central nervous

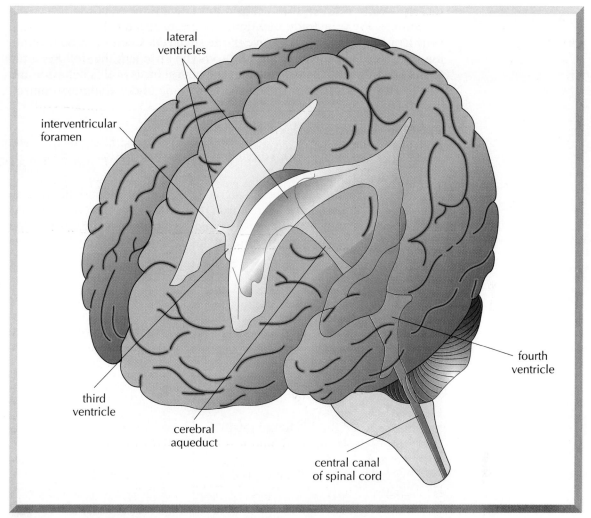

Figure 3.10 *The Ventricles*
The lateral ventricles, one on each side of the brain, connect with the third ventricle via the interventricular foramen; the third ventricle connects to the fourth ventricle via the cerebral aqueduct. There are no first and second ventricles.

system of vertebrates is divided into two parts: the spinal cord and the brain. Certain behaviors, as you will soon see, are controlled entirely by neural activity within the spinal cord. Most behaviors, however, involve both the brain and the spinal cord. In the rest of this chapter we shall consider the role that the spinal cord and the brain play in controlling human behavior.

The Spinal Cord and Behavior

To say that certain behaviors that are crucial to our survival are "controlled" by the spinal cord may be an overstatement, since these behaviors are really reflexes that occur automatically in response to certain conditions. We've already mentioned some of these behaviors—jerking your hand away from a hot stove is one such reflex behavior. So is blinking in response to a puff of air, and so is the knee jerk that follows a tap to the kneecap. Let us now consider the neural basis of this behavior and what needs to happen for the behavior to come under voluntary control.

The Monosynaptic Reflex

Reflexive behavior is rooted in neural circuits known as *reflex arcs*. The simplest of such arcs is a two-neuron chain, depicted in Figure 3.11. This arc represents the chain of events that produces the familiar knee-jerk reflex. When your knee is tapped, a signal travels along sensory neurons to the spinal cord, then back again through motor neurons to the muscles, producing the actual jerk. Because a single synapse links the sensory and motor neurons, circuits of this kind are known as *monosynaptic*. Most re-

Figure 3.11 *The Monosynaptic Reflex*
In the knee-jerk reflex, the impulse travels along the sensory neuron into the spinal cord and back to the skeletal muscle via the motor neuron.

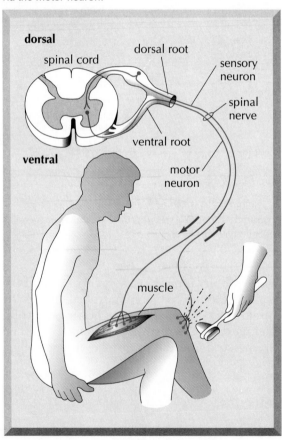

flex action is somewhat more complex than the knee jerk and depends on correspondingly more complex neural circuitry.

The Brain and Reflex Action

Although reflex action in the spinal cord takes place without involvement of the brain, the brain under certain conditions can control the reflex. If you tense your leg prior to the knee tap that normally produces a reflex response, you can generally prevent the knee from jerking. How do we explain this paradox? How can a reflex occur independently of the brain, on the one hand, and be controlled by the brain, on the other?

The answer lies in the linking patterns of the neural circuits directly involved in the reflex behavior. Even though spinal reflexes can operate independently of the brain, the circuits underlying them are linked to ascending and descending pathways that pass to and from the brain. These pathways all lie outside the H-shaped core of the spinal cord, illustrated

Figure 3.12 *The Connections Between Spinal Cord and Brain*
Sensory tracts carried in the spinal cord inform the brain of sensory activity below the neck, and motor tracts carried in the spinal cord allow the brain to exert control over muscles below the neck.

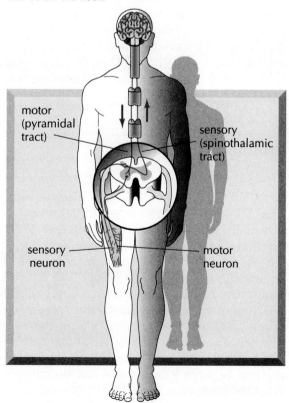

motor (pyramidal tract)

sensory (spinothalamic tract)

sensory neuron

motor neuron

in Figure 3.12. The myelin surrounding the neurons that make up these pathways give the region a whitish appearance.

The Spinothalamic and Pyramidal Tracts

Two of the most important pathways involved in the brain's ability to control reflex action are the *spinothalamic* tract and the *pyramidal* tract, both shown in Figure 3.12. The spinothalamic tract consists of pathways that form synapses with sensory neurons from receptors in the skin and with sensory neurons from receptors in muscles and joints and ascend the spinal cord to the brain. The pyramidal tract consists of descending pathways from the brain to spinal motor neurons. Both of these tracts link the sensory and the motor neurons in the spinal cord to the brain. They thus provide a communication network that, on the one hand, informs the brain that sensory activity is taking place below the neck and, on the other hand, allows the brain to control and modify movement below the neck.

The importance of these tracts cannot be overemphasized. We see their importance clearly in the tragic plight of *paraplegics*, in whom injuries have cut off the spinal cord from the control of the brain. The reflexes controlled by the isolated spinal cord remain operative, but paraplegics cannot exercise voluntary control over the reflex action. The knees of paraplegics will jerk when tapped, but paraplegics can do nothing to prevent the jerking, nor can they lift their legs voluntarily. Paraplegics, in fact, are not even aware of the sensations accompanying the tap on the knee. Thus, it is an oversimplification to think of the spinal cord as simply a relay station for producing reflex behavior. The spinal cord is also an extension of the brain, a means by which the brain becomes aware of and exerts control over parts of the body below the neck.

THE BRAIN

The structure and the function of the brain can be studied in any number of ways, but the most logical place to begin is in the way it develops. The human brain develops initially as a simple fluid-filled tube. Gradually, however, the tube gets larger and changes in shape, developing into separate fluid-filled chambers. These chambers are the ventricles, and they constitute the inner core of the brain. The tissue that surrounds these chambers, as Figure 3.13 indicates, develops into the three major divisions of the brain—the *hindbrain*, the *midbrain*, and the *forebrain*—and as the embryonic neural tissue undergoes further differentiation, it creates discrete areas within these divisions of the brain. Each of these areas has its own specific behavioral function, and if there is one basic rule that will guide and shape our discussion of the brain, it is the relation between location and function: *where* the brain area is dictates *what* the brain area does.

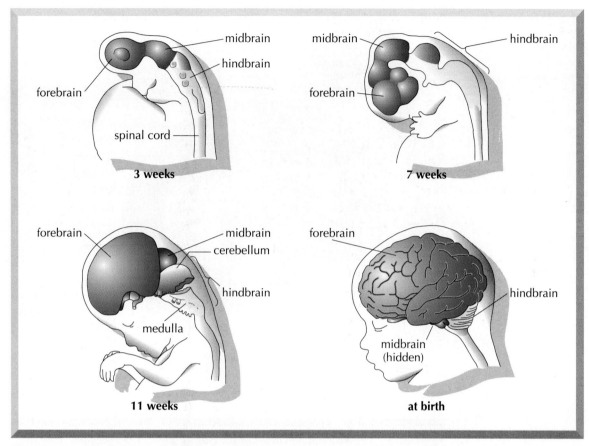

Figure 3.13 *Development of the Human Brain from the Third Week after Conception to Birth*

The Anatomy of the Brain

The three main divisions of the brain, as we have already established, are the hindbrain, the midbrain, and the forebrain. Let us now look at each division and at the behaviors it controls.

The Hindbrain

The hindbrain, as you can see in Figure 3.14, connects the spinal cord with the rest of the brain and is divided into two distinct sections: the *medulla*, which is connected directly to the spinal cord, and the *pons*, which lies above the medulla.

It is through the hindbrain that most sensory and motor pathways pass on their way to and from the upper portions of the brain. But more than simply being a conduit for sensory and motor information from the body to upper portions of the brain, the hindbrain contains areas that have their own motor functions. Areas in the medulla, for example, control such vital functions as breathing and heart rate. And mushrooming

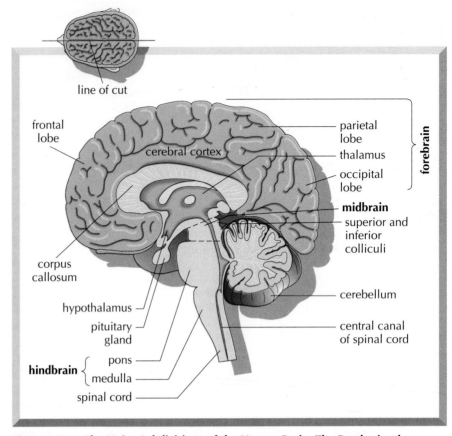

line of cut

frontal lobe

cerebral cortex

parietal lobe

thalamus

occipital lobe

forebrain

midbrain
superior and inferior colliculi

corpus callosum

cerebellum

hypothalamus

pituitary gland

central canal of spinal cord

pons

hindbrain

medulla

spinal cord

Figure 3.14 *The Major Subdivisions of the Human Brain: The Forebrain, the Midbrain, and the Hindbrain*

out of the pons is the *cerebellum,* a convoluted structure whose chief function is to maintain body balance and muscle coordination.

The hindbrain also contains several areas that give rise to neural tracts (axons) that project to a number of areas throughout the brain and spinal cord. Three of these hindbrain areas are especially important: the *reticular formation*, a network of neurons located in the core of the hindbrain and extending upward to the midbrain and forebrain; the *raphe* (meaning "seam") *nuclei*, a group of nuclei located along the midline of the reticular formation; and the *locus coeruleus*, an area located in the pons.

Each area has a different function. The reticular formation, in addition to maintaining wakefulness, is involved in controlling both attention and arousal: it screens sensory information as it travels to the upper portions of the brain while at the same time alerting the higher centers to the oncoming barrage of sensory information. The raphe nuclei play a prominent role in the control of pain suppression, sleep, aggression, and emotion. And the locus coeruleus functions to maintain emotion and regulate REM (rapid eye movement) sleep—a state of sleep in which the brain is aroused, dreaming occurs, and the skeletal muscles are temporarily paralyzed. We will be examining each of these hindbrain areas and their corresponding functions in later chapters.

The Midbrain

The midbrain, as the name implies and as you can see in Figure 3.14, lies between the hindbrain and the forebrain. Along with the hindbrain, it is commonly referred to as the *brain stem*.

Like the hindbrain, the midbrain contains sensory and motor pathways passing to and from the upper portions of the brain. And like the hindbrain, it contains several prominent areas that have their own sensory and motor function. These areas are known as the superior colliculus, inferior colliculus, substantia nigra, and red nucleus. The *superior colliculus* receives sensory information from the visual system and is involved in the control of eye movements. The *inferior colliculus* receives sensory information from the auditory system and plays a role in controlling the ability to orient one's head toward sound. The *substantia nigra* and the *red nucleus* receive motor information from the upper portions of the brain and the cerebellum, respectively, and are involved in motor control.

Figure 3.15 *The Forebrain*
A cross-section cut of the forebrain.

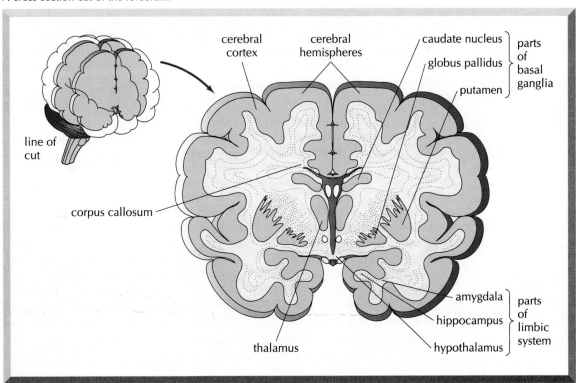

The Forebrain

The forebrain lies above the midbrain and is divided into two *cerebral hemispheres*. Though each hemisphere is a distinct structure, the two are connected (see Figure 3.15) by several large neural tracts, the most prominent of which is the *corpus callosum*. The corpus callosum is in fact a structural bridge between the two hemispheres; its chief function is to keep each hemisphere informed about what the other is doing. As you will see in Chapter 18, a breakdown in communication between hemispheres does not threaten survival, but it does produce some curious behavioral effects, such as the ability to hear a command without being able to obey.

Most areas that lie in one cerebral hemisphere have corresponding areas in the other, an arrangement that gives rise to duplicate areas in the forebrain. Among the most prominent of these areas, as shown in Figure 3.15, are the *hypothalamus*, the *cortex*, the *thalamus*, the *basal ganglia*, and the *limbic system*. Let us take a closer look at each.

The Hypothalamus

The hypothalamus is a tiny cluster of nuclei, but its size belies its importance. The hypothalamus is involved in one way or another in a broad range of behaviors, including eating, drinking, sex, fear, and aggression, all of which can be profoundly altered by either injury or artificial stimulation (electrical or chemical) of the hypothalamus. Often referred to as the "guardian" of the body, the hypothalamus is also involved in the regulation of cellular energy—the fuel for behavior. When internal nourishment or fluid drops below normal, the hypothalamus is informed of the change and initiates internal behavior—activating smooth muscles and glands—to regulate the internal environment. We will be looking at how the hypothalamus controls external behavior in later chapters. For now, however, let us look briefly at how the hypothalamus controls internal behavior.

Regulating Internal Behavior

The hypothalamus regulates internal behavior in two ways. To begin with, it controls the autonomic nervous system. It does so by giving rise to neural tracts that descend to both the medulla and to the spinal cord. Once in the medulla and the spinal cord, these tracts form synapses with the two divisions of the autonomic nervous system, the sympathetic and parasympathetic nervous systems, and it is through these neural connections that the hypothalamus controls heart rate and blood pressure.

Second, the hypothalamus exerts control over many of the glands found throughout the body. In this case, however, the hypothalamus controls glands not through neural connections but through chemicals and, more specifically, through the influence those chemicals have on the *anterior pituitary gland*. Chemicals known as *releasing hormones* are secreted by the hypothalamus and are transported, via a group of blood vessels known as the *portal system*, to the anterior pituitary, which in turn releases hormones that regulate the action of other glands: the *thyroid*, the *adrenal cortex*, and the *gonads* (the *testes* and *ovaries*). We will consider these glands in more detail in Chapter 10 and then again, particularly the gonads and the adrenal cortex and the role they play in the development and control of sexual behavior, in Chapter 13.

It isn't only the anterior pituitary gland that is under control of the hypothalamus. The posterior pituitary gland is under hypothalamic control as well, albeit in a different way. The hypothalamus produces two hormones—oxytocin and vasopressin—each of which is transported to the posterior pituitary gland but not through blood vessels, rather through neural connections. The hormones are produced in neural cell bodies in the hypothalamus and are transported along axons, via axonal transport, to the posterior pituitary. There they are stored in axonal endings and are released by neural impulses originating in the hypothalamus. Oxytocin promotes uterine contractions during childbirth and stimulates ejection of milk after birth; vasopressin regulates water content and blood pressure.

The Cortex

The cerebral cortex makes up the outer covering of the cerebral hemispheres and represents the most recent development in the evolution of the vertebrate nervous system. You will not find a cortex, for instance, in fish. And reptiles show signs of only a rudimentary one. Lower mammals, such as rats, have a cortex, but it is not a dominant feature of their brain structure. Only in higher mammals, such as porpoises, monkeys, and humans, do we begin to see a cortex that is disproportionately larger than other brain areas. And in no animal is the cortex as intricately structured and as densely packed as it is in humans.

There are an estimated 70 to 100 billion nerve cells in the human cortex, distributed among three types of neural tissue: the *neocortex*, located on the surface of the brain and distinguished from the other parts of the cortex by its multiple layers—six layers in all; the *juxtallocortex*, lying just beneath the neocortex; and the *paleocortex*, which lies beneath the juxtallocortex.

As you can see in Figure 3.16, the six layers of the neocortex envelop the outer portion of the brain in a series of miniature peaks and valleys that produce a large number of grooves. The smaller grooves are known as *sulci* (singular, *sulcus*), the larger ones as *fissures*. The bulges between grooves are called *gyri* (singular, *gyrus*). The convoluted structure of the cortex serves an important purpose: it gives the cortex a great deal more cellular mass than it would have if it were completely smooth.

The surface of the cortex, as shown in Figure 3.16, is divided into distinct lobes—the *frontal*, *parietal*, *temporal*, and *occipital* lobes, all of which are visible from the side. Each lobe has been associated with distinct behavioral functions.

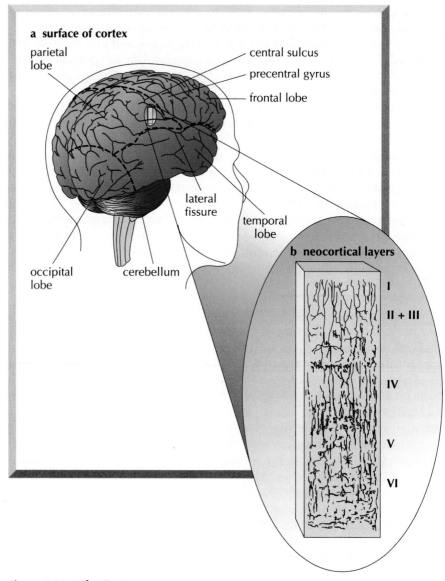

a surface of cortex

parietal lobe

central sulcus

precentral gyrus

frontal lobe

lateral fissure

temporal lobe

occipital lobe

cerebellum

b neocortical layers

I

II + III

IV

V

VI

Figure 3.16 *The Cortex*
(a) A view of the surface of the cortex, and (b) a view of the multiple layers of nerve cells.

Cortical Function

The frontal lobes are involved in motor control through a primary motor area along the precentral gyrus and a neighboring secondary area. The frontal lobes control different features of motor behavior. Circuits that originate in the frontal lobes and travel directly to the spinal cord are involved in the control of fine hand, finger, and facial movements. Circuits that originate in the frontal lobes and travel indirectly to the spinal cord (via synapses in the basal ganglia and red nucleus) are involved in the control of gross limb and body movement.

Adjacent to the motor area in the frontal lobe is the prefrontal cortex. It, too, is involved in the control of motor behavior, but from a different perspective. To do something as routine as walking across the room requires a sequence of behaviors occurring at the right time and in the right order. Evidence indicates that the prefrontal cortex is involved in organizing this behavior—remembering what you've just done and what you plan on doing—and timing the behavior (Goldman-Rakic, 1987). "Internal representation" and "temporal organization"—these are the terms that have been used to describe the "memory and timing" role of the prefrontal cortex in controlling motor behavior. This work will be discussed in greater detail in later chapters: the frontal and prefrontal cortices and motor behavior in Chapter 10, the frontal cortex and memory in Chapter 17.

In contrast to the frontal and prefrontal cortices the parietal, occipital, and temporal lobes are all involved in sensory processing: the parietal lobe with somatosensory information (pressure, pain, touch, temperature), the occipital lobe with visual information, and the temporal lobe with auditory information. This picture, however, is not as clear-cut as it seems, and for two reasons.

First, each sensory modality is represented by at least two and sometimes three areas in the cortex—a primary, a secondary, and sometimes a tertiary area. Hence there are, at least in humans, two somatosensory areas (S1 and S2) in the parietal lobe, two auditory areas (A1 and A2) in the temporal lobe, and three visual areas in the occipital lobe (areas 17, 18, and 19). The secondary and, in the case of the occipital lobe, tertiary areas neighbor on the primary area and tend to be less discriminating in their responsiveness, often reacting to information from other modalities. In cats, for example, the secondary somatosensory area (S2) responds not only to tactile pressure but to auditory stimulation as well.

Second, the parietal, occipital, and temporal lobes are involved in more than simply sensory processing. Areas in the parietal lobe, for instance, are involved in the control of attention and, along with areas in the frontal lobe in the control of speech. Areas in the occipital lobe have been implicated in learning and memory. And areas in the temporal lobe have been implicated in memory processing, control of emotions, and language.

Between the Hypothalamus and Cortex

As you can see in Figure 3.15, a number of areas lie between the hypothalamus and the cortex. These areas tend to fall into different functional groups, and to complete our discussion of the forebrain, we shall consider three of these groups: the *basal ganglia* (a misnomer because ganglia usually are groups of cell bodies in the peripheral nervous system), the *thalamus*, and the *limbic system*.

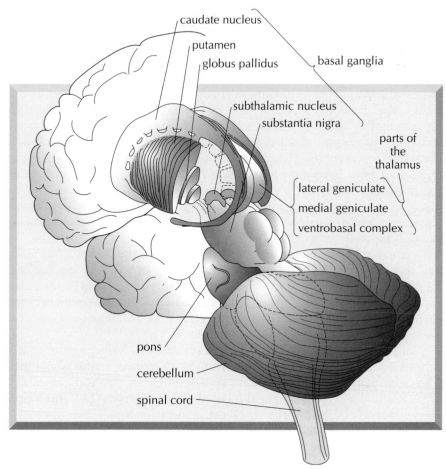

Figure 3.17 *The Basal Ganglia and the Thalamus*
The basal ganglia coordinate muscle movement with motor areas of the cortex, whereas the thalamus relays sensory information to the cortex.

The Basal Ganglia

The basal ganglia, pictured in Figure 3.17, consist of five areas: the *substantia nigra*, the *subthalamic nuclei*, the *putamen*, the *globus pallidus*, and the *caudate nucleus*. Collectively these areas coordinate muscle movement. The basal ganglia receive motor information from the cortex and in turn project it back to the cortex via connections to the thalamus. As we shall see in later chapters, damage in the basal ganglia results in motor abnormalities seen in Parkinson's disease as well as in cognitive abnormalities seen in obsessive-compulsive disorder (characterized by repetitive motor acts and thoughts) and in Huntington's disease (a neurodegenerative disorder marked by profound cognitive disturbances as well as motor tics).

Thalamus

The thalamus is also a collection of nuclei but its function, unlike that of the basal ganglia, is related more to sensory processes than it is to motor processes. The thalamus, in fact, can best be described as a sensory way station. It receives sensory information from the peripheral nervous system and relays it to the cortex. As Figure 3.17 shows, three thalamic nuclei are involved: the *lateral geniculate*, for relay of visual information to the occipital cortex; the *medial geniculate*, for relay of auditory information to the temporal cortex; and the *ventrobasal complex*, for relay of somatosensory information (touch, pressure, temperature, pain) to the parietal cortex.

Once again, however, we are looking at a picture that is more complex than one might think, for the term "sensory way station," while essentially correct, does not tell the whole story. To begin with, the thalamus relays not only sensory information but also motor and motivational information to the cortex. Second, through a complex system of interconnecting neurons, the thalamus funnels information back and forth among the various areas of the cortex—information concerned with motor control, motivation, and attention. Finally, the thalamus, apart from its role as a way station, imposes its own influence on incoming information, changing and transforming it as it passes to and from the cortex (Kelly, 1991).

Figure 3.18 *The Limbic System*

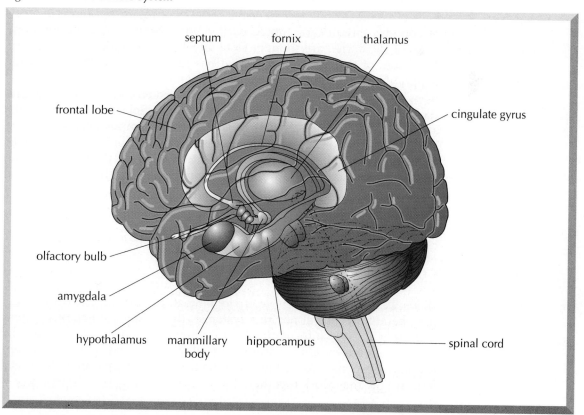

Limbic System

Not as circumscribed in structure as the basal ganglia or the thalamus, the limbic system contains interconnecting areas that run a circuitous route, pictured in Figure 3.18, between the cortex and the hypothalamus. The limbic system includes portions of the frontal cortex, temporal cortex, thalamus, hypothalamus, fornix, amygdala, hippocampus, septum, and mammillary bodies. Working as components in a complex chain, all these areas contribute, to one degree or another, to the control of emotional behavior. Aggression, fear, pleasure, pain—each of these behaviors can be profoundly altered through injury or through artificial stimulation (electrical or chemical) of the limbic system. Furthermore, the frontal and temporal cortices and the hippocampus and amygdala have been implicated in the control of learning and memory, functions we will consider in detail in Chapters 16 and 17.

A Cautionary Note

Before we leave the structure of the brain, a word of caution is necessary, particularly if we have left you with the impression that specific brain areas are directly related to specific behaviors. This picture is accurate, but only up to a point. Subdivisions of the brain notwithstanding, it is impossible to attribute a single behavioral function to a single anatomical site. Indeed, every area of the brain is related, directly or indirectly, to virtually every other area. So, in seeking an anatomical basis for behavior, we must think less in terms of simple centers and more in terms of complex circuits. We noted earlier, for example, that the temporal lobes of the cortex are thought to be involved in emotion and memory. The bases of this view are observations indicating that damage to the temporal lobes results in loss of emotion and memory. But the temporal lobes, as part of the limbic system, are connected to the amygdala, and the amygdala is connected to the hippocampus. Selective damage to the amygdala upsets emotion; damage to the hippocampus upsets memory. Therefore, emotional and memory disruptions accompanying damage to the temporal lobes may reflect the extent to which the amygdala and the hippocampus depend on the temporal lobes for their own normal activity.

INTEGRATING THE PERIPHERAL AND
CENTRAL NERVOUS SYSTEMS

When we look at behavior we are looking at the *combined* activity of the peripheral and central nervous systems—the peripheral nervous system collecting sensory information and issuing motor instructions, and the central nervous system coordinating information and selecting the appropriate response. We've looked at the two systems separately. Now let's look at how they work together.

Sensory Processing

We established earlier that sensory information travels, via the peripheral nervous system, along many different routes to the brain, with some information entering the central nervous system below the neck (the spinal nerves) and some above (the cranial nerves). But regardless of the route sensory information takes, this information (with the exception of olfactory cranial nerve input) does not go *directly* to the cortex. It must first be funneled through the lower areas of the brain. One such area is the already mentioned reticular formation (in the hindbrain); another is the thalamus (in the forebrain). The job of the reticular formation, as we stated earlier, is to alert the cortex—to prepare it for the oncoming barrage. The job of the thalamus is to sort out the sensory information and channel it to appropriate areas of the cortex. Only after both of these conditions have been met—the alerting of the cortex and the channeling of information to appropriate areas—is the cortex able to process sensory information with any degree of efficiency.

Figure 3.19 *Motor Processing*
A highly schematic view of cortical control of skeletal muscles and hypothalamic control of the autonomic and endocrine systems.

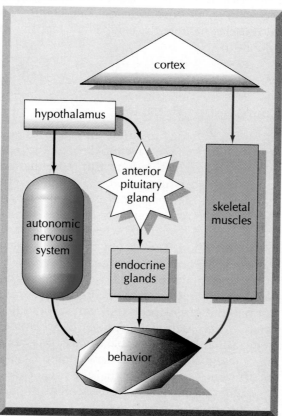

Motor Processing

The human brain is equipped to process a prodigious amount of sensory information, but no matter how much sensory information it processes, the information is useless unless it can be acted upon. Action involves motor neurons in the peripheral nervous system—the skeletal division which controls movement of the skeletal muscles, and the autonomic division which regulates energy for movement by controlling the smooth muscles and glands. Regardless of the route taken by motor information, skeletal or autonomic, it originates (with the exception of spinal reflexes) in the brain, as Figure 3.19 illustrates. Motor activity of the smooth muscles and glands is controlled primarily by the hypothalamus, via the autonomic nervous system and the anterior pituitary gland.

Motor activity in the skeletal muscles is primarily under the control of two circuits that originate in the frontal cortex. One circuit descends directly to the spinal cord and is involved in fine motor control, movement of the fingers, for example. The other circuit descends to the basal ganglia (which in turn provide feedback, via the thalamus, to the frontal cortex) and is involved in limb and body movement. A third circuit, originating in the prefrontal cortex, is also involved but not in producing actual movement. This circuit is involved instead in the organizing and planning of complex movements—making certain that the sequence of responses occurs at the right time and in the right order. Other areas of the brain outside the cortex that contribute to motor activity in the skeletal muscles include the cerebellum and the red nucleus (an area in the midbrain).

Coordinating Behavior

As we have already mentioned, the cortex is the ultimate destination of sensory information traveling through the nervous system and is also the origin of motor instructions. But more than simply receiving sensory information and issuing motor instructions, the cortex—on the basis of learning and memory—coordinates the two. This coordination ensures that when we read aloud, for instance, the seen word is translated into the spoken word, and that when we receive a verbal command, it is translated into action. This is why damage to the human cortex affects more than sensory and motor processes per se. Even if sensory and motor processes remain intact, the victim of cortical damage can still suffer severe behavioral loss. Some people with damaged cortices seem perfectly normal in every respect: they can see and hear, talk and move, they are bright, witty, and intelligent, yet they cannot read. Others are unable to write. Still others are unable to carry out motor commands. We shall discuss these disorders in greater detail in Chapter 18. For now, however, it is sufficient to remember that the role of the cortex in *coordinating* sensory and motor behavior is every bit as important as its role in *producing* sensory and motor behavior.

Now that you have a general picture of how the brain is structured and what behaviors are associated with specific areas of the brain, let us look briefly at how this picture has come to light. We will be looking specifically at the techniques used to study the anatomy of the brain and to study how the brain controls behavior.

Neuroanatomical Techniques for Tracing Pathways

When we talk about brain anatomy, we are talking about two features of the brain: specific areas, sometimes referred to as nuclei (groups of cell bodies), and tracts (groups of axons) that originate from and connect between brain areas. What an area does—what it contributes to behavior—is largely determined not only by where it is but where its tracts go: that is, the area's sphere of influence. The raphe nuclei (an area in the hindbrain), for example, give rise to tracts that go to both the cortex, where they initiate sleep, and the spinal cord, where they control pain. Thus we can say that the raphe nuclei, because of their connections to these areas, have an impact on both behaviors. The same pattern holds for all areas and their interconnecting tracts: to know how an area affects behavior, we need to know not only where that area is but also where its tracts go.

Determining where brain areas are located (i.e., the group of cell bodies from which tracts originate) and where tracts go (i.e., where axons terminate) is not a simple matter. But two recently developed techniques have enabled neuroanatomists to meet the challenge. Both techniques are built around the fact that life-sustaining chemicals are constantly flowing back and forth in the neuron between cell body and axonal endings, a process we referred to earlier as axonal transport.

In one technique, known as *amino acid autoradiography*, radioactively labeled amino acids are injected in the vicinity of the cell bodies. These labeled amino acids are taken up by the cell bodies and are combined to form radioactively labeled protein. The protein is then transported via the axon to the axonal endings, whose location can now be determined by exposing sections of neural tissue to chemically treated film, which reacts to the radioactivity and produces a photographic picture. In this way, the neuroanatomist is able to establish the connections between the site of injection (the cell bodies) and the axonal endings of the tracts that originate from that site.

A second technique involving axonal transport consists of injecting a special enzyme—*horseradish peroxidase* (an enzyme taken from the horseradish root)—in the vicinity of the axonal endings, where it is taken up by the endings and transported back to the cell body. The location of the horseradish peroxidase is then determined by exposing sections of neural tissue to special chemical stains that react with horseradish peroxidase, making it visible. In this way, the neuroanatomist is able to establish the connections between the site of injection (the axonal endings) and the cell bodies that send axons to that site.

Neurobehavioral Techniques to Establish Brain-Behavior Relations

Let us now turn from the techniques of neuroanatomy to the techniques of neurobehavior. Here, too, we need to confront some basic questions. How have we come to know how specific areas and tracts deep within the brain relate to specific behaviors? How have we come to connect the function of the hypothalamus, for instance, with eating, that of the hippocampus with memory, and that of the amygdala with aggression? Two approaches have been taken, one using lower animals and the other using humans.

Lower-Animal Research

Through the careful probing of the brain in lower animals, researchers have been able to construct with some precision a profile of the brain and its relationship to behavior. Three techniques have been used: lesion, stimulation, and recording. The lesion technique consists of removing specific brain tissue either by delivering electric current (direct current) or injecting neurotoxins (chemicals that kill neurons) and then noting the behavioral consequences. The stimulation technique consists of activating specific brain tissue either by delivering electric current (alternating current) or injecting chemicals that mimic the action of neurotransmitters and then noting the behavioral consequences. The recording technique consists of recording activity in various parts of the brain and noting the accompanying behavior. It is not unusual—indeed it is highly desirable—for all three procedures to be used in studying a particular brain area and its relation to behavior.

Stereotaxic Surgery

It is one thing to understand the rationale that underlies the three procedures, but it is another to actually implement the procedures. The surgical technique for all three is basically the same: it involves inserting a fine wire (known as an *electrode*) or, in the case of chemical injections, a fine hypodermic needle (known as a *cannula*), into specific areas of the brain. To achieve the required precision in placement, a special instrument, known as a *stereotaxic instrument*, is used to position the electrode or cannula in the brain.

A stereotaxic instrument, illustrated in Figure 3.20, serves two purposes. It holds the head of an anesthetized subject in a fixed position and its adjustable arm allows for precise placement of the electrode or cannula. A stereotaxic instrument is used in combination with a brain atlas, which contains maps of the brain. The maps locate specific brain areas with respect to their distance from ridges (equivalent to landmarks) on the skull known as *skull sutures*. The electrode or cannula is adjusted, relative to the skull sutures, in two directions, front-back (anterior-

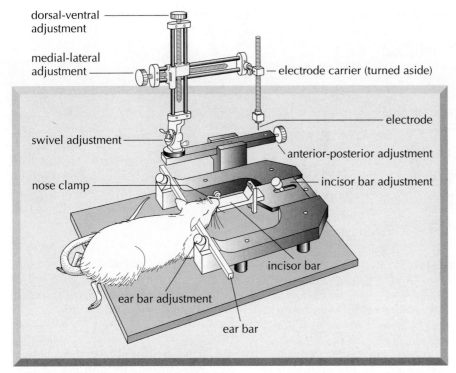

Figure 3.20 *Implanting with Precision*

The stereotaxic instrument, pictured here, allows for precise implantation of electrodes. The anesthetized animal's head is held fixed by the ear bars, incisor bar, and nose clamp. The electrode is attached to the electrode carrier and is positioned in the brain by moving the carrier in one of three directions: anterior-posterior, medial-lateral, and dorsal-ventral.

posterior) and left-right (lateral), and the electrode or cannula is then gradually lowered (relative to the surface of the skull) to a specific depth (dorsal-ventral) within the brain. Figure 3.21 presents a view of the surgical procedure.

The stereotaxic instrument solved one major problem in neurobehavioral research: the lack of precision in electrode or cannula placement. The electrode-cannula anchor, illustrated in Figure 3.22, solved the other problem: securing the electrode or cannula to the skull so that, after surgery, stimulation and recording studies could be conducted while the animal was moving about. Because there are no pain receptors in the brain, the implanted electrode or cannula put no apparent stress on the animal.

RESEARCH TECHNIQUES INVOLVING HUMANS

For obvious reasons, the experimental techniques we have been describing for lower animals do not readily lend themselves to humans, for there is an inherent physical risk to anyone who undergoes an experimental

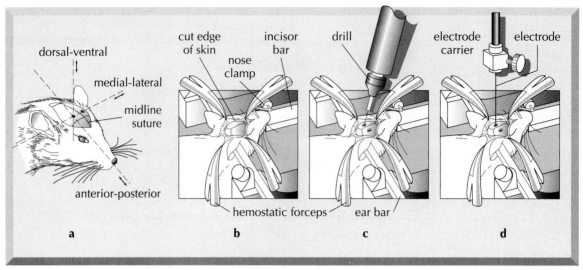

Figure 3.21 *Stereotaxic Surgery*
The three stereotaxic coordinates (a), exposing the skull for stereotaxic surgery (b), drilling holes corresponding to the stereotaxic coordinates (c), and inserting the electrode (d).

procedure involving brain tissue. Still, it is obvious that certain behaviors—those involving higher-order processes unique to humans—can be studied only in humans, and this fact raises a troublesome question. Where do human subjects come from?

The answer is that experimental work that has been done with humans in this field has rarely, if ever, involved "normal" people. Most of the work has focused on individuals who have suffered brain damage through disease or accident. Study of such individuals constitutes a kind

Figure 3.22 *The Electrode Anchor*
Electrodes are fixed in the brain and held in place by an electrode holder screwed to the skull.

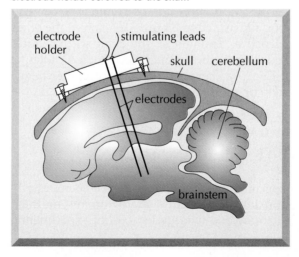

of "experiment in nature" in which conditions that prevail in laboratory experiments with lower animals are duplicated, albeit crudely. By noting the area and extent of the brain damage and by correlating these observations with the behavioral abnormalities manifested by a brain-damaged person, researchers have been able to construct a general profile, although not as precise as that for lower animals, of the human brain and its relationship to behavior. It has been noted, for instance, that people who suffer damage to specific cortical areas in the left cerebral hemisphere lose the ability to speak; on the basis of this observation, it has been concluded that areas controlling language are located in the left cerebral hemisphere. We shall consider these and related studies on language and the brain in detail in Chapter 18.

Visualizing a Living Human Brain

Establishing brain-behavior relationships in brain-damaged humans is difficult even under the best of circumstances. A stroke victim, for instance, may manifest the loss of a specific behavior, but the brain damage that produces the behavioral loss may be extremely difficult to locate. Because standard x-rays pass through all brain tissue with equal facility, they do not provide the contrast needed to distinguish healthy areas from damaged ones. Consequently, until recently physicians and scientists relied primarily on postmortem autopsies to determine the location of brain damage in humans.

Today, this is no longer the case. The problem of diagnosing the location and extent of brain damage in a living human still exists, but it has been greatly diminished by several technological advances. We will consider four: the *angiogram*, the *CAT scan*, the *PET scan*, and the *MRI*.

Angiogram

An angiogram is an x-ray that reveals the blood vessels in the brain. Before the x-ray is taken, a dye is injected into the blood vessels that enter the brain. The dye produces sufficient contrast to highlight the blood vessels, as shown in Figure 3.23, and the x-ray reveals any displacement of the blood vessels produced by changes in the surrounding brain tissue, such as abnormal growth produced by tumors.

CAT Scan

A computerized axial tomography (CAT) scan involves taking a series of x-rays from different positions around the subject's head. After passing through the head, the x-rays are monitored by a bank of detectors connected to a computer which generates a series of two-dimensional images of the brain from different vantage points and depths, two of which are pictured in Figure 3.24. The CAT scan is presently one of the most accurate methods of locating tumors and various intracranial lesions.

PET Scan

Positron emission tomography (PET) is a procedure that makes it possible to visualize energy metabolism in the neural cells of both normal and

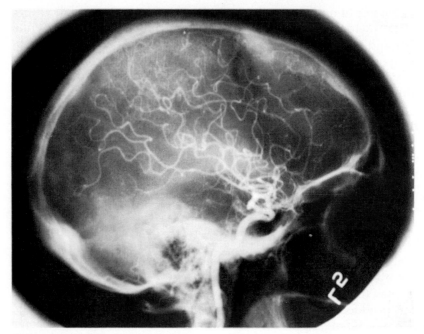

Figure 3.23   *Angiogram*
An angiogram consists of x-rays taken after a dye has been injected into blood vessels that enter the brain.

abnormal brains. The procedure is based on the principle that the more active a brain area is, the more glucose it takes up and uses for energy. The procedure consists of injecting a radioactive form of glucose into the bloodstream and then monitoring the radioactivity emitted by the brain while an individual is engaged in a particular type of behavior. The radioactive glucose is taken up by the brain areas active during the behavior. Because the radioactivity emitted by the areas increases with their activity, it is possible to gain a picture of the areas that are most active—and presumably most involved—in a particular behavior. Pictured in Figure 3.23 are PET scans comparing the activity in a subject's brain while the subject listened to language and then to music.

A variant of the PET scan procedure, known as *regional cerebral blood flow* (rCBF), uses cerebral blood flow rather than glucose metabolism to visualize activity in the brain. The procedure consists of injecting or inhaling a radioactive form of the substance xenon and then monitoring the radioactivity emitted by the brain. Xenon accumulates in regions of the brain in which blood flow increases and thus in regions that are most active—and presumably most involved—in a particular behavior.

Magnetic Resonance Imaging
In contrast to the PET scan and cerebral blood flow procedures, which monitor differential activity to visualize brain function, magnetic resonance imaging (MRI) monitors differences in chemical composition. MRI, also known as *nuclear magnetic resonance* (NMR), is a technique

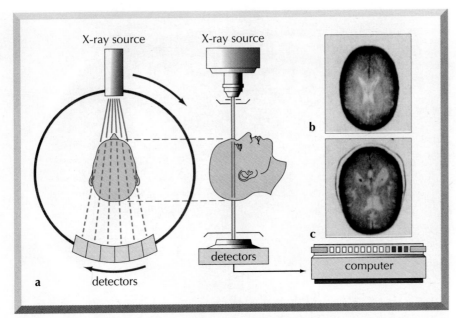

Figure 3.24 *CAT Scan*
In a CAT scan a series of x-rays is taken by moving an x-ray source around the head and measuring with detectors the amount of x-ray that passes through the head (a). The x-rays are then processed by a computer into a series of two-dimensional images corresponding to successive slices of the brain. The images shown are a normal brain (b) and the abnormal brain of a stroke victim (c).

that makes it possible to measure the chemical composition—for example, the concentration of hydrogen—in tissue. Because different tissue contains different concentrations of hydrogen, images can be generated that reflect these differences.

MRI does not measure the concentration of hydrogen directly. Instead it determines it indirectly in the following way: (1) the brain is exposed to a magnetic field which puts the hydrogen atoms in a state (spinning) capable of absorbing radio waves; (2) the brain is then exposed to radio waves, and the radio waves are then turned off; (3) the hydrogen atoms, which have absorbed the radio waves, release energy (i.e., the hydrogen atoms resonate) in the form of radio waves; (4) because different concentrations of hydrogen atoms (in different tissues) release different frequencies of radio waves, different images of the tissue are generated using computer techniques similar to those employed in CAT and PET scans. Pictured in Figure 3.25 is an MRI taken of a human brain.

Lingering Difficulties in Human Research

Despite the truly revolutionary developments in brain research technology, our ability to analyze the human brain in order to establish brain-behavior relationships is still in its embryonic stage. Even when we find a connection between an area of the brain and a specific behavior, ques-

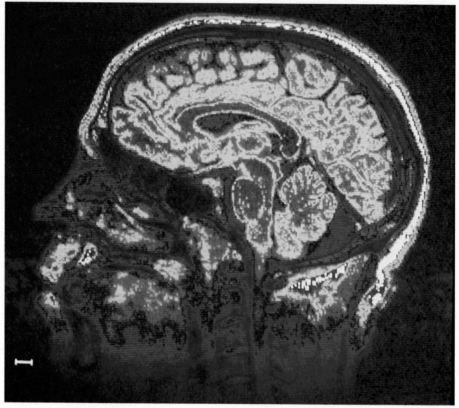

Figure 3.25 *Magnetic Resonance Imaging of a Living Human Brain*

tions frequently remain unanswered. Why is it, for example, that some brain injuries can affect certain behaviors so profoundly and leave related behaviors intact? Why is it that damage to the left hemisphere, which controls speech, can affect the ability to speak but not the ability to sing, read, or write?

But even with these built-in difficulties, the systematic study of brain-damaged individuals has contributed much to our knowledge of how the human brain controls behavior. Eventually, it seems safe to say, scientists will develop techniques that will allow us to study brain function in humans in a manner that poses no threat to their well-being yet provides the fine-grain analysis of brain-behavior relations that is now feasible only in experiments with lower animals.

SUMMARY

1. *The nervous system defined.* The nervous system can be best defined as a vast network of cells and their accompanying extensions. With the exception of unicellular and simple multicellular organisms, all species have such a system in one form or another. This network varies in complexity from species to species, but its function is the same throughout the animal kingdom. Nervous systems are transmitting devices: they transmit information back and forth throughout the body.

2. *Divisions of the nervous system.* In humans and other higher animals, the nervous system is divided into parts: the central nervous system, which consists of the brain and spinal cord, and the peripheral nervous system, which consists of all the neural material outside the brain and the spinal cord. The peripheral nervous system has two main divisions: the skeletal, or somatic, nervous system and the autonomic nervous system. Generally speaking, the skeletal nervous system is responsible for controlling skeletal muscles, whereas the autonomic nervous system controls the activity of internal organs and glands.

3. *Peripheral nerves.* Neurons in the peripheral nervous system do not travel in isolation. Rather, their axons are gathered into bundles called nerves. Peripheral nerves can be classified in two ways: by their points of entry (where they enter the central nervous system) and by their functions (sensory or motor). There are 43 pairs of nerves in the peripheral nervous system, 31 of which, known as spinal nerves, enter the central nervous system below the neck. The other 12, the cranial nerves, enter the central nervous system above the neck. The 43 nerves are classified on the basis of the function of neurons in the nerve. All 31 spinal nerves and 4 cranial nerves are mixed nerves, containing a combination of motor and sensory neurons. Of the 8 remaining cranial nerves, 3 are sensory and 5 are motor.

4. *Motor neurons and the skeletal system.* The skeletal nervous system consists of motor neurons that control external motor behavior, both voluntary and reflex. Both types of behavior are under the control of the same motor neurons, with the type of behavior ultimately determined by where the input to the motor neurons originates. Inputs that come directly from sensory neurons produce reflex behavior. Inputs from the higher centers in the brain produce voluntary behavior.

5. *Motor neurons and the autonomic nervous system.* The autonomic nervous system consists of motor neurons that connect the brain and the spinal cord to smooth muscles and glands. Its chief function is to regulate life-sustaining substances in the internal environment, and for all intents and purposes, this regulation takes place automatically. Like the neurons in the skeletal nervous system, the neurons in the autonomic nervous system originate inside the central nervous system, but they operate in different ways. Skeletal motor neurons run an uninterrupted course from the central nervous system to the muscles. Autonomic motor neurons leaving the central nervous system form synapses with a second group of motor neurons that innervates the target organs.

6. *Divisions of the autonomic nervous system.* The autonomic nervous system is itself divided into two parts: the sympathetic system and the parasympathetic system. The sympathetic system is activated during stress, when vigorous activity is called for. The parasympathetic system operates during periods of relaxation. The two systems differ in neural structure and chemistry. In the parasympathetic system, the preganglionic neurons are very long, traveling almost the entire distance from the central nervous system to the target organ and forming synapses with a postganglionic neuron very close to the target organ. In the sympathetic system, the pattern is reversed: the preganglionic neurons are short and the postganglionic neurons are long. Another key difference between the parasympathetic and sympathetic systems lies in the neurotransmitter released by the postganglionic neuron. In the parasympathetic system the neurotransmitter is acetylcholine; in the sympathetic system the neurotransmitter is norepinephrine.

7. *Protection for the central nervous system.* The brain is housed within the skull, and the spinal cord is housed within a canal formed by bony vertebrae. Both the skull and the spinal cord, moreover, are enveloped by three layers of nonneural material known as meninges. Because neural cells cannot store nutrients, neurons in the central nervous system rely on a steady supply of nutrients from the blood, which explains why the brain is abundantly laced with blood vessels. When this blood supply is cut off, even for brief periods, the results can be devastating. Yet another protective mechanism is the blood-brain barrier, a mechanism that serves to keep toxic substances in the bloodstream from infiltrating the brain. Also present in the central nervous system is the colorless cerebrospinal fluid, which cushions the brain and spinal cord against sudden blows to the skull and provides nourishment to the brain and spinal cord and removes their waste products.

8. *Reflex behavior and the spinal cord.* Some very simple behaviors, such as the knee-jerk reflex, involve only the spinal cord and, within the cord, only the sensory and motor neurons. Because a single synapse links the sensory and motor neurons, circuits of this kind are known as monosynaptic.

9. *The brain and voluntary behavior.* All behavior under voluntary control involves the brain. Even reflex behavior, in many cases, can come under voluntary control, demonstrated by the fact that with purposeful effort we can inhibit certain reflex actions, such as the knee-jerk reflex. Generally speaking, the brain's control over behavior at the spinal-cord level, reflex or otherwise, is based in two pathways—the spinothalamic and the pyramidal tracts—that connect the spinal cord with the brain. These tracts constitute a communication network that keeps the brain informed of sensory activity taking place below the neck and allows for movement below the neck to be modified and controlled by the brain.

10. *Dividing the brain.* It is customary to divide the brain into three general divisions: the hindbrain, the midbrain, and the forebrain, with each division having its own discrete areas involved in the control of specific behaviors.

11. *The hindbrain.* Three areas in the hindbrain are of particular importance: the reticular formation, which plays an important role in attention and arousal; the raphe nuclei, which play a key role in such behaviors as sleep, aggression, emotion, and pain suppression; and the locus coeruleus, whose function is closely tied to sleep behavior.

12. *The midbrain.* The midbrain consists of sensory and motor pathways that pass to and from the upper portions of the brain. Its key areas are the superior colliculus, involved in vision; the inferior colliculus, involved in audition; and the substantia nigra and red nucleus, both of which are involved in motor control.

13. *The forebrain.* The forebrain lies above the midbrain and is divided into two hemispheres connected by several tracts, the most important of which is the corpus callosum. Each hemisphere contains a number of areas including the hypothalamus, the cortex, the thalamus, the basal ganglia, and the limbic system. The hypothalamus is involved in the control of emotional and motivational behavior as well as internal responses via connections to the autonomic nervous system and the pituitary gland. The surface of the cortex is divided into four lobes: the frontal, parietal, occipital, and temporal. The frontal lobes are involved in motor control and memory processing and emotion. The other lobes are involved, to different degrees, in sensory processing, speech, motor control, memory processing, and the control of emotions.

14. *Between the hypothalamus and cortex.* A number of brain areas lie between the hypothalamus and the cortex. They tend to fall into three groups: the basal ganglia, involved in motor control; the thalamus, which relays sensory information to the cortex; and the limbic system, a complex network of areas involved in emotion, motivation, and memory.

15. *Coordinating behavior.* More than simply receiving sensory information and issuing motor instructions, the cortex coordinates the two. This coordination ensures that when we read aloud, for instance, the "seen" word is translated into the spoken word, and that when we receive a verbal command, it is translated into action. This is why damage to the human cortex affects more than sensory and motor processes per se. Even if these processes remain intact, victims of cortical damage can still suffer severe behavioral loss.

16. *Neuroanatomical techniques.* Two recently developed techniques have enabled neuroanatomists to gain a more precise picture of where brain areas are located and where tracts terminate. Both techniques rely on axonal transport. In one technique, known as amino acid autoradiography, radioactively labeled amino acids are injected in the vicinity of neural cell bodies where they are incorporated into radioactively labeled protein and are transported to the axonal endings. In the other technique, horseradish peroxidase is injected in the vicinity of the axonal endings where it is taken up and is transported back along the axon to the cell bodies. By then exposing the tissue to certain chemicals, the radioactively labeled protein or the horseradish peroxidase are made visible, making it possible for the neuroanatomist to establish the connections between the cell body and the axonal endings.

17. *Neurobehavioral techniques.* Three techniques have been used to study the relationship between specific brain areas and behavior: lesion, stimulation, and recording. The lesion technique consists of removing specific brain tissue either by delivering electric current or injecting neurotoxins and noting the behavioral consequences. The stimulation technique consists of activating specific brain tissue, either by delivering electric current or injecting chemicals that mimic the action of neurotransmitters and noting the behavioral consequences. The recording technique consists of recording from the brain and noting the accompanying behavior. It is not unusual—indeed it is highly desirable—for all three procedures to be used in studying a particular brain area and its relation to behavior.

18. *The stereotaxic instrument.* The surgical technique for all three procedures is basically the same. It involves an instrument known as a stereotaxic which holds the head of an anesthetized animal in a fixed position while its adjustable arm allows for precise placement of an electrode or cannula. Stereotaxic surgery is always done in conjunction with a brain atlas, which contains maps of the brain.

19. *Studying the human brain.* Most of the experimental brain-behavior work involving humans has focused on individuals who have suffered brain damage through disease or accident. Four recent technological advances have enhanced this research: the angiogram, the CAT scan, the PET scan, and the MRI. An angiogram is an x-ray taken after a dye has been injected into the blood vessels that enter the brain. A PET scan (positron emission tomography) is a procedure in which a radioactive form of glucose is injected into the bloodstream and the radioactivity emitted by the brain is monitored while an individual is engaged in a particular type of behavior. A CAT scan (computerized axial tomography) consists of a series of x-rays taken from different positions around the head. The x-rays are then processed by a computer into a series of two-dimensional images corresponding to successive slices of the brain. The MRI, also known as nuclear magnetic resonance (NMR), works on the principle that different tissue contains different concentrations of hydrogen; images can be generated that reflect these differences.

abducens nerve
acetylcholine
adrenal cortex
amino acid autoradiography
angiogram
anterior pituitary gland
arachnoid membrane
area postrema
autonomic nervous system
basal ganglia
blood-brain barrier
brain stem
cannula
caudate nucleus
central nervous system
cerebellum
cerebral hemispheres
cerebrospinal fluid
choroid plexuses
computerized axial tomography
  (CAT)
corpus callosum
cortex
cranial nerves
craniosacral region
dura mater
electrode
extrapyramidal tract
fissures
forebrain
frontal lobe
ganglion
globus pallidus
gonads
gyri
hindbrain
horseradish peroxidase
hypoglossal nerve
hypothalamus
inferior colliculus
juxtallocortex
lateral geniculate nucleus
limbic system
locus coeruleus
magnetic resonance imaging
  (MRI)

medial geniculate nucleus
medulla
meninges
midbrain
mixed nerve
monosynaptic reflex
motor nerve
neocortex
nerves
nervous system
norepinephrine
nucleus
occipital lobe
oculomotor nerve
olfactory nerve
oligodendrocytes
optic nerve
ovaries
paleocortex
paraplegic
parasympathetic nervous system
parietal lobe
Parkinson's disease
peripheral nervous system
pia mater
pons
positron emission tomography
  (PET)
postganglionic neuron
preganglionic neuron
putamen
pyramidal tract
raphe nuclei
red nucleus
reflex arcs
reflexive behavior
regional cerebral blood flow
releasing hormones
reticular formation
Schwann cells
sensory nerve
skeletal nervous system
skull sutures
smooth muscles
somatic nervous system
spinal accessory nerve

KEY TERMS

spinal cord
spinal nerves
spinothalamic tract
stereotaxic instrument
stereotaxic surgery
subarachnoid space
substantia nigra
sulci
superior colliculus
sympathetic cord

sympathetic nervous system
temporal lobe
testes
thalamus
thoracicolumbar region
thyroid
tracts
trochlear nerve
ventricles
ventrobasal complex

SUGGESTED READINGS

Angevine, J. B. & Cotman, C. W. *Principles of Neuroanatomy*. Oxford: Oxford University Press, 1981.

Nauta, W. J. H. & Feirtag, M. (Eds.) *Fundamentals of Neuroanatomy*, New York: W. H. Freeman, 1986.

Netter, F. H. *The CIBA Collection of Medical Illustrations. Vol. 1: Nervous System. Part 1: Anatomy and Physiology*. Summit, N.J.: CIBA Pharmaceutical Products Co., 1983.

THE ELECTRO-CHEMICAL BASIS OF BEHAVIOR

INTRODUCTION

The neural impulse can be best described as the language of the nervous system. It is the medium through which neurons communicate with one another and with the various parts of the body they activate. No behavior—no thought, no action, no feeling—can take place without this communication. Every image you see, every sound you hear, every tactile sensation you experience, every odor you smell—each of these experiences, at some stage in the behavioral chain, takes the form of an electrochemical signal coursing through the nervous system in and out of the brain. The stimuli that produce these experiences vary, as do the neural pathways that carry these signals throughout the body. But regardless of the behavior taking place, the basic nature of the impulse—its electrochemical dynamics—stays the same. The behavior may change; the language does not.

TRACKING THE NEURAL IMPULSE: THE EARLY DISCOVERIES

Most of what we know about the neural impulse today comes from discoveries that have come to light within the past 50 years, but the research that set the stage for this understanding dates back hundreds of years. One of the earliest discoveries was made in the late 1700s by the Italian physiologist Luigi Galvani and came about purely by accident. According to one account, Galvani and his wife were conducting a series of experiments designed to isolate the atmospheric force that produced nerve action and muscle movement. In one of their most significant experiments, the Galvanis took a dissected frog to an upstairs porch, attached a lightning rod to its head, and stretched a wire from the foot of the frog to a well filled with water. Later, a storm developed, and during the storm, lightning crackled, and the muscles of the frog, in Galvani's words, "fell into violent and multiple contractions."

On the basis of this observation, Galvani concluded that he had discovered an atmospheric force yet unknown to science. He labeled it "animal electricity." What he had witnessed, in fact, was the electrophysiological force known today as the neural impulse.

Beyond Galvani: Bernstein's Theory

The notion that neural communication was essentially an electrical affair held for roughly 150 years after Galvani's discovery. In the early nineteenth century, however, a number of physiologists, chief among them Emil Du Bois-Reymond and Julius Bernstein, made a puzzling discovery. They determined that the neural impulse travels much more slowly through the body [at 3 to 400 feet per second (ft/s)] than electricity travels along wires (up to hundreds of thousands of feet per second). Bernstein inferred from this discovery that the neural impulse, though electrical in nature, must also have a chemical component. Handicapped in his search for supporting data by a lack of sophisticated recording equipment (it had not been developed yet), he was never able to test his theory. The theory, however, has turned out to be substantially correct.

The Squid Axon

The limitations that kept Bernstein from verifying his theory persist to some degree to this day. For even with sophisticated recording equipment, such as the cathode-ray oscilloscope (pictured in Figure 4.4), studying neural transmission still presents monumental problems for researchers. The chief problem has to do with the size of the nerve fibers (i.e., axons) in the nervous system. They are so small that impulses within single neurons are extraordinarily difficult to measure.

A major breakthrough in neural research occurred in the early 1930s through the work of an Oxford University scientist named John Z. Young. Young discovered that the squid, a mollusk, possesses nerve fibers (i.e., axons) that are large enough (and we use "large" in the relative sense) to be isolated and studied individually during neural transmission. The largest of these "giant fibers" is about 1 millimeter (mm) in diameter. It is found in the body wall of the squid, and as Figure 4.1 shows, it innervates the muscles that give the squid its quick withdrawal responses. Since Young's discovery, scientists have been able to remove the nerve cell from the squid and keep it alive outside the body, thereby allowing its chemical and electrical properties to be studied.

Almost everything we know to date about the workings of the neuron is based on the pioneering experiments involving the giant axon of the squid, particularly those conducted by the British neurophysiologists Alan Hodgkin and Andrew Huxley. These two scientists developed a technique for microelectrode recording so precise that it allows recording electrodes to be inserted into single nerve cells. Such precision is crucial: it means electrodes can be inserted without damaging the nerve cells or disrupting the conducting properties of these cells.

The key result of Hodgkin and Huxley's work is the confirmation in principle of Bernstein's theory of neural action. This theory holds that

Figure 4.1
A top view of a squid showing the location of the giant axons.

giant axons

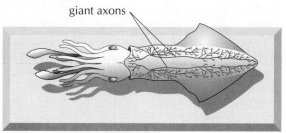

neural action is controlled in large part by chemical activity occurring around the neural membrane. Although a good deal of controversy still surrounds the issue, there is consensus regarding the electrochemical dynamics of the neural impulse. We shall consider these dynamics shortly, but first let us examine some of the features that underlie the electrochemical signal in general—what it looks like and the basic principles that govern it.

THE ELECTROCHEMICAL SIGNAL: AN OVERVIEW

As we saw in Chapter 2, a neuron is essentially an information-transmitting device consisting of a cell body, an axon, and dendrites. Generally speaking, the dendrites and cell body receive information from other neurons or from receptors, and axons deliver the information to other neurons or to muscles and glands. In either event, the information itself always takes the same form: an electrochemical signal produced by the movement of electrically charged particles called *ions*.

There is one qualification for this general point. The language of the neuron, in a manner of speaking, has two "dialects." One is the electrochemical signal in the dendrites and cell body, known as the *graded potential* or *synaptic potential*; the other is the electrochemical signal in the axon, known as the *action potential*. The difference is critical: for more than any other feature of the neuron, the difference in the electrochemical signal produced by dendrites and the cell body on the one hand and the axon on the other hand confers upon the nervous system a decision-making capacity of sorts. Figure 4.2 illustrates the two electrochemical signals. Let us take a closer look.

As the figure shows, up to the point of the *axon hillock* (the juncture point between cell body and axon) the form of the electrochemical signal in both the dendrites and cell body is *graded* and *decremental*. We say "graded" because its magnitude depends directly on the intensity of the stimulus. We say "decremental" because it dies out as it travels from the point of excitation.

In the axon, on the other hand, the electrochemical signal is neither graded nor decremental. Instead, the axon has a threshold, and once that threshold is reached, the electrochemical signal produced by the axon is complete and is unaffected by further increases in the intensity. The term used to describe this response is *all-or-none*. The action potential in the axon occurs completely or not at all. There is no in-between. Furthermore, unlike the electrochemical signal in the dendrites and cell body, which diminishes as it travels, the electrochemical signal in the axon does not diminish but rather maintains its full impact regardless of the distance it travels. The term used to describe this response is *nondecremental*.

The combined effect of the two signals, graded and all-or-none, is decision making at its most basic level: the axon makes the decision to re-

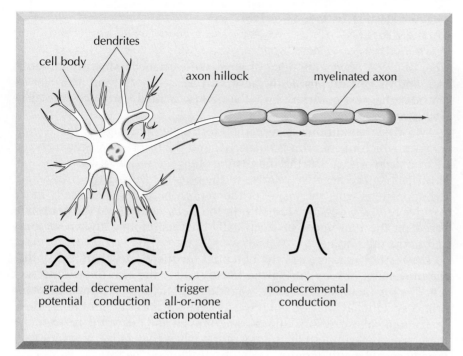

Figure 4.2 *The Relationship Between the Neural Impulse and Different Parts of the Neuron*
The cell body and the dendrites are characterized by a graded potential and decremental conduction, the axon by an all-or-none potential and nondecremental conduction. The axon hillock marks the point of transition from graded to all-or-none potential.

spond or not to respond, and the dendrites and cell body provide the information on which the decision is based—the graded signal reaching threshold or not reaching threshold. The decision-making process has been compared with the firing of a gun. Both result in all-or-none reactions, and both are "triggered" by a graded stimulus—in the gun by the gradual squeeze of the trigger, in the axon by the graded signal coming from the dendrites and cell body.

To summarize, the sequence of events is as follows:

1. An electrochemical signal (graded and decremental) is produced in the dendrites and cell body.
2. The signal travels to the axon, specifically the axon hillock.
3. Once it reaches threshold, a second electrochemical signal (all-or-none and nondecremental) is produced.
4. The two electrochemical signals differ in their relationship to stimulus intensity: the signal in the dendrites and cell body is graded, increasing or decreasing with changes in stimulus intensity; the signal in the axon is all-or-none, either occurring or not occurring depending on whether the stimulus intensity reaches threshold.

Now that you have some idea of what the electrochemical signal looks like, and its general profile in the dendrites, cell body, and axon, let us consider the next question: how the neuron actually produces the electrochemical signal.

Two basic conditions govern the electrochemical signal: the *resting state* (in which the neuron is *polarized*) and the *firing state* (in which the neuron *depolarizes*). During the resting state the inside of the neuron is electrically more negative relative to the outside. During the firing state the opposite is true: the inside of the neuron becomes electrically more positive than the outside. The shift in the electrical state of the neuron is based on the movement of electrically charged atoms, known as ions, across the membrane.

The resting state creates the potential for the electrochemical signal, the movement of ions during the firing state *is* the electrochemical signal. The key factor in both states—resting and firing—is the neural membrane, specifically the control it exerts over the movement of ions. More than simply allowing ions to pass randomly in and out of the neuron, the membrane determines which ions move, when they move, and in a very broad sense, how they move.

The Neural Membrane as a Gatekeeper

The ability of the neural membrane to control the movement of ions in and out of the neuron is rooted primarily in the microscopic pores, known as *channels*, that are depicted in Figure 4.3. As the figure indicates, these channels are of two types: passive (also known as nongated) and active (also known as gated). *Passive channels* are always open.

Figure 4.3 *The Two Types of Ion Channels, Passive (Nongated) and Active (Gated)*

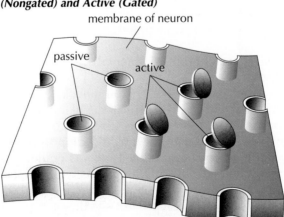

membrane of neuron

passive

active

Active channels, on the other hand, have "gates" that are open only when the neuron is stimulated. As you will see, these channels, each in its own way, control the movement of specific kinds of ions, and as you will also see, this selectivity, coupled with other aspects of neural function, is the reason the neural membrane is sometimes referred to as a "gatekeeper."

The ability of the neural membrane to control ionic movement is crucial. If ions were allowed to pass freely through the membrane (that is, if the neural membrane were completely permeable), two natural forces would eventually produce a state of equilibrium. The first is known as the *voltage gradient*—the tendency of ions to move until the regions they occupy are equal in electrical charge; the other is the *concentration gradient*—the tendency of ions to move until the regions they occupy are equal in concentration.

Obviously ions do not move freely in and around the neuron. If they did, there would be no separation of charge, no resting potential and no way for firing to occur. Controlling movement of ions during the resting and firing states are the unique properties of the neural membrane. Let us take a closer look, first at the resting state, then the firing state.

Figure 4.4 *Procedure for Recording a Membrane Potential*
(a) The oscilloscope. The main components of the oscilloscope are shown here. The electron gun emits negatively charged electrons. The path that the electrons travel is influenced by the electrical charges on two pairs of plates. One pair (y-plates) receives a charge from the neuron. The other pair (x-plates) receives a built-in charge. The electrons hit a fluorescent screen, which illuminates their path of travel. (b) Recording the resting potential across the neural membrane. Two electrodes—one on the outside of the neural membrane, the other inside the neural membrane—register a potential across the membrane indicating that the inside of the membrane is slightly more negative (−70 mV) with respect to the outside.

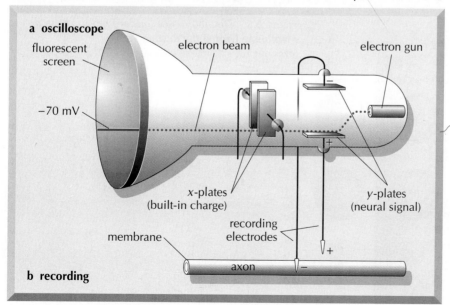

a oscilloscope
fluorescent screen
electron beam
electron gun
−70 mV
x-plates (built-in charge)
y-plates (neural signal)
membrane
recording electrodes
axon
b recording

The Resting State

If you were to record across the membrane of a neuron during the resting state (and resting states vary slightly among different neurons), you would find, as shown in Figure 4.4, that the neuron is more negative inside with respect to the outside—that is, there is a separation of charge across the membrane of −70 mV or roughly a tenth of a volt. A D-cell battery, by comparison, registers 1500 mV or equivalently 1.5 volts.

Understanding the source of the resting state—the reason the neuron is more negative inside relative to outside—begins with an appreciation of the chemical environment surrounding the neural membrane. One of the first discoveries made by Hodgkin and Huxley in their work on the squid axon was the presence of ions both inside and outside the neuron. The most common of these ions, as Hodgkin and Huxley have shown, are sodium (Na^+) and potassium (K^+), both of which are positively charged, and chloride (Cl^-) and organic ions (A^-), both of which are negatively charged.

If you look at Figure 4.5, you will see how these ions are distributed around the neural membrane during the resting state. The nature of this distribution is significant for it is what makes the inside of the neuron slightly more negative (−70 mV) than the outside. What is important to keep in mind, however, is the extent to which the membrane itself controls the distribution. Let's take a closer look.

Organic ions.   Negatively charged organic ions (A^-) are located exclusively inside the neuron simply because they are too large to escape through the pores in the membrane. Their constant presence inside the neuron is one of the factors that keeps the inside of the neuron negatively charged relative to the outside.

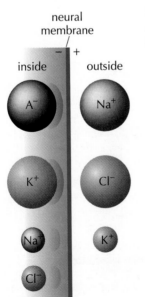

neural
membrane

inside   outside

Figure 4.5   *Distribution of Ions around the Neural Membrane During the Resting State*
Sizes of circles denote relative amounts.

Chloride ions.   Negatively charged chloride ions (Cl⁻) are located on *both* sides of the membrane with a greater concentration of ions outside the neuron than inside. Despite this disparity, however, these ions are in a state of equilibrium. Why? Because the voltage and concentration gradients governing the movement of these ions across the membrane are in equal and opposite directions. That is, the voltage gradient exerted by the −70 mV charge inside the neuron drives the negatively charged Cl ions out at the same rate that the concentration gradient exerted by the higher concentration of Cl ions outside the neuron drives the Cl ions in.

Sodium and potassium ions.   Figure 4.5 shows that during the resting state positive sodium (Na⁺) ions dominate the exterior of the neuron whereas positive potassium (K⁺) ions are found primarily inside the neuron. What is significant about this distribution is that these ions are not in a state of equilibrium. Rather they move from areas of greater concentration to areas of lesser concentration which produces a more or less constant flow of ions across the membrane, with K moving out and Na moving in.

There is a difference, however, between the way Na ions move and K ions move, and the reason for this difference is that the membrane is not equally permeable to both types of ions. The neural membrane is 50 to 75 times more permeable to K ions than to Na ions because—and this is crucial—it has 50 to 75 times more K than Na passive channels. This means that, although K ions can move out of the neuron with relative ease, Na ions can hardly penetrate the membrane at all. And it is this state of affairs, the movement of K out of the neuron and, to a lesser extent, the movement of Na into the neuron, that makes the inside of the neuron slightly more negative than the outside and produces the resting potential of −70 mV.

One question remains: If ions are in constant motion, how is the ionic balance that produces −70 mV maintained? Why do the Na and K ions not continue to move during the resting potential—Na inward, K outward—until they are in equilibrium and the resting potential is destroyed? To answer this question we are obliged to introduce yet another feature of the neuron, the so-called sodium-potassium pump.

Maintaining the Resting Potential

Once the −70-mV resting potential has been established, two things happen in and around the membrane to maintain the resting potential. Both are pictured in Figure 4.6. For one thing, any additional Na ions that leak into the neuron are ejected. For another, any additional K ions that move out of the neuron are drawn back in. So it is that Na ions never accumulate inside the neuron, and K ions never accumulate outside it. The result is a constant resting potential of −70 mV.

Scientists have proposed that the neuron maintains a constant resting potential by means of an energy-driven pump, often referred to as the *sodium-potassium (Na-K) pump*. This view is based on experiments indicating that when the neuron is prevented from producing energy through

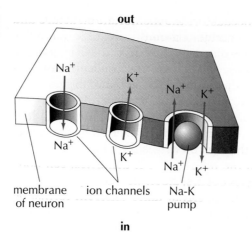

Figure 4.6 *The Sodium-Potassium (Na-K) Pump*
Energy is used by the neuron to prevent sodium ions from accumulating inside the neuron and potassium ions from accumulating outside the neuron.

the introduction of a poison (such as cyanide) or the deprivation of oxygen, the neuron promptly loses its power to extrude Na and to draw in K. This breakdown results immediately in an equilibrium of ion distribution on the two sides of the membrane. The resting potential is destroyed, and the neuron is rendered inoperative.

The actual means by which the pump works are not known, but its effect on ionic activity is clear: it controls the flow of ions in and out of the neuron in a way that keeps the inside of the neuron slightly more negative than the outside. In other words, the pump maintains an environment that keeps the potential for ion movement alive.

To summarize, the resting potential is the result of two factors. The first is the passive channels—the fact that there are more passive K channels than passive Na channels. This difference creates the resting potential, allowing movement of K out of the neuron and, to a lesser extent, movement of Na into the neuron. The second is the sodium-potassium pump, which maintains the resting potential by reversing the process, drawing K back in and Na back out. The result: the inside of the neuron is slightly more negative than the outside.

FIRING: INITIATING THE ELECTROCHEMICAL SIGNAL

Now that we have seen how the neuron establishes the first stage of the electrochemical signal, the resting potential, we are ready to look at the second stage, firing. Here the key factor is Na ions, although, as we will soon see, K ions are also involved.

During the resting state, Na ions "leak" into the neuron; but during the firing state, that leak turns into a "rush." It is, in fact, the sudden rush of positive Na ions through the membrane and into the neuron, be it of the dendrites, cell body, or axon, that initiates the electrochemical signal.

Na ions rush into the neuron because of the membrane structure and, in particular, the workings of the active channels. When the neuron is stimulated, active Na channels open, and the Na ions, now free to move across the membrane, are drawn into the neuron by the two natural forces: the voltage gradient (Na is positively charged, and the inside of the neuron is negatively charged) and the concentration gradient (Na is more concentrated on the outside than on the inside). The result of these two forces, combined with the opening of active Na channels, produces the electrochemical signal. Wherever and whenever the Na rushes through the membrane and into the neuron—be it dendrites, cell body, or axon—the electrochemical signal occurs, albeit with one qualification. As you will recall, the electrochemical signal takes different forms, depending on where it occurs in the neuron. In the dendrites and cell body, it is triggered by neurotransmitters (coming via synapses formed by receptors or other neurons), and it is graded. In the axon—specifically the axon hillock—it is triggered by the electrochemical signal coming from the dendrites and cell body, and it is all-or-none.

So, to understand the nature of the electrochemical signal (the firing state) is to understand not only what the signal is (the Na rush) but why the signal, depending on where it occurs, is different. Logic says that the signal is different because the Na rush is different. But the question is why? Why is it graded in the dendrites and cell body? Why is it all-or-none in the axon?

The answer, as you may have guessed, lies in the structure of the membrane, specifically in the ion channels. We classified the channels as passive and active. The passive channels (combined with the sodium-potassium pump) are responsible for the resting state, and the active channels are responsible for the firing state. And now we take the classification scheme one step further. There are two types of active channels, *chemical-sensitive* and *voltage-sensitive*. The two types of channels are located in different parts of the neuron, and the two types of channels account for the different types of electrochemical signals. Let's take a closer look.

Chemical-Sensitive Channels in the Dendrites and Cell Body

The graded signal in the dendrites and cell body is produced by chemical-sensitive channels found in the membrane surrounding the dendrites and cell bodies. The critical feature of these chemical-sensitive channels is their gates which open and shut as a result of neurotransmitter activity. During the resting state the gates are closed. But when the dendrites and cell body are stimulated by neurotransmitters (a process we will examine in detail later in this chapter), the gates open and Na and K ions move: Na ions move into the neuron (drawn by both concentration and voltage gradients), and K ions move out of the neuron (drawn by the concentration gradient). The result is two positively charged ions, Na and K, moving at the same time in different directions—Na in and K out.

This state of chemical affairs is similar to what happens during the resting potential, except for one critical difference. During the graded signal, chemical-sensitive channels are open and Na is able to move freely into the neuron. And because Na movement is driven by two factors (voltage and concentration gradients) and K movement by one (concentration gradient), more Na enters the neuron than K leaves. This difference leaves the neural membrane depolarized: the inside of the neuron becomes more positive than the outside. Thus is the electrochemical signal produced.

Graded Electrochemical Signal

Their ability to open chemical-sensitive channels explains why neurotransmitters are able to trigger the electrochemical signal in the dendrites and cell body. This ability does not explain, however, why the electrochemical signal in the dendrites and cell body is *graded*, that is, why the signal varies in strength with changes in stimulus intensity (i.e., with changes in the amount of neurotransmitter). To understand the graded phenomenon, we must take a closer look at the chemical-sensitive channels and their relation to the neurotransmitter.

Chemical-sensitive channels are keyed to the *amount* of neurotransmitter. As the amount of neurotransmitter increases, more and more channels open and more and more Na ions move across the membrane. The gradual accumulation of Na inside the neuron accounts for the graded nature of the signal. It does not account, however, for conduction.

Decremental Conduction

Up to now, our focus has been on the electrochemical signal in the dendrites and cell body as it is taking place in one area of the membrane—the area stimulated by the neurotransmitters. And the picture we have painted up to this point might suggest that when neurotransmitters act on one area of the membrane, the electrochemical signal caused by the rush of positively charged Na ions instantaneously spreads to the rest of the neuron.

Such is not the case. What happens instead is a much more gradual process. Neurotransmitters act on specific areas of the dendrites and cell body, and the electrochemical signals they produce in turn are conducted from the points of stimulation to the axon hillock. Furthermore, as it travels the signal tends to die out, a phenomenon known as *decremental conduction*.

To explain how conduction takes place in the dendrites and cell body and why it dies out, a key distinction needs to be made between two types of electrochemical signals: the one that occurs at the point of stimulation and the one that is conducted away from the point of stimulation. The signal that occurs at the point of stimulation—the *local signal*—is produced, as we've just seen, when neurotransmitters act on the membrane surrounding the dendrites and cell bodies: Na channels open, and Na ions move across the membrane. The signal *conducted* away from the point of stimulation is produced when the Na ions, after they have crossed the membrane and entered the neuron, move along the inner surface of the membrane away from the point of stimulation. The technical term for this movement along the inner surface is *electrotonic conduction*; and because the Na ions, as they move, encounter more and more resistance, the electrochemical signal they produce becomes weaker and weaker. The result: decremental conduction.

In summary, then, there are two distinctly different types of electrochemical signals in the dendrites and cell body. One is produced at the point of stimulation (the local signal) when Na channels open and Na ions move *across* the membrane into the neuron. The other (the electrotonic signal) is produced after the Na enters and Na moves *along* the inner surface of the membrane away from the point of stimulation. The same two-signal pattern holds for the axon, except there are important differences. In the dendrites and cell body, as we've just seen, the source of the local signal can be traced to channels that are *chemical*-sensitive. In the axon, as we are about to see, the sources of the local signal—the so-called action potential—are channels that are *voltage*-sensitive.

Voltage-Sensitive Channels in the Axon

The action potential, as depicted in Figure 4.7, has two distinct features: a firing stage and a recovery stage. Voltage-sensitive channels account for both.

As was the case with the chemical-sensitive channels in the dendrites and cell body, the critical feature of the voltage-sensitive channels in the axon is their gates, through which Na and K ions flow to generate the action potential. The gates of the channels in this instance, however, are controlled not by neurotransmitters but by the electric charge (i.e., the voltage) across the membrane. During the resting potential—that is, when the charge across the membrane is −70 mV—the gates are closed. But when the axon, specifically the axon hillock, is stimulated by electrochemical signals coming from the dendrites and cell body, the voltage across the membrane begins to drop, ultimately reaching a *threshold* (−60 mV) that, as Figure 4.7 indicates, opens the voltage-sensitive gates in an important sequence.

First, the gates of the Na channels open, accounting for the rush of Na (driven by both concentration and voltage gradients) into the neuron and the subsequent *firing state* (+30 mV). Then, roughly a millisecond later, the gates of the Na channels close and the gates of the K channels open, accounting for the rush of K out of the neuron (driven by the concentration gradient) and the subsequent *recovery state* (−90 mV).

If this sounds familiar to you, it should. For the movement of Na and K ions in the axon is similar to the movement of Na and K ions in the dendrites and cell body. The difference is that in the dendrites and cell body, the ions move *simultaneously*, whereas in the axon they move in sequence—Na in then K out. Moreover, while the ions are moving, the voltage-sensitive channels close, again in sequence. First, the Na channels

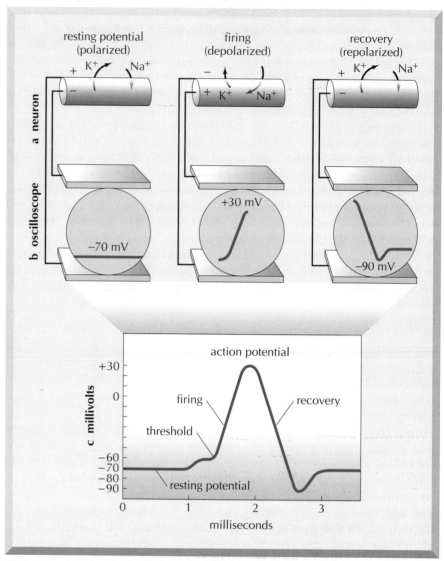

Figure 4.7 *Resting and Action Potentials: Electrical Properties*
The changes in polarization across the membrane (a) start with the resting potential and pass from the onset of depolarization (firing) through repolarization (the recovery period) back to the resting potential. Also shown are the changes in membrane permeability to sodium (Na^+) and potassium (K^+) ions during the course of the action potential. Note that an increase in arrow length denotes an increase in membrane permeability. The changes in the action potential are shown in (b) and (c).

close, followed by the closing of the K channels, bringing the ionic balance gradually back to its resting level (-70 mV) with Na ions concentrated on the outside leaking in and K ions on the inside moving out.

The All-or-None Action Potential

The voltage-sensitive channels account not only for the firing (Na in) and recovery (K out) states but also for the all-or-none feature of the action potential. The axon has a threshold (-60 mV), and once that threshold is reached, the action potential produced by the movement of Na into the axon is complete ($+30$ mV) and is unaffected by further increases in the intensity. The term used to describe this response is *all-or-none*.

The abrupt rise in the curve (from -60 mV to $+30$ mV), depicted in Figure 4.7, suggests that when the threshold is reached, all Na channels open and all Na ions rush in at the same time. Such is not the case. What happens instead is a more gradual process. Voltage-sensitive Na channels have different thresholds and open at different times. When an electrochemical signal from the dendrites and cell body arrives at the axon hillock and the threshold for the action potential is reached, the most sensitive channels open first, allowing some Na to enter. The resulting depolarization, albeit small, is enough to trigger the opening of the next set of channels, allowing more Na in. The resulting depolarization, now larger, is enough to trigger the opening of the next set of channels, which increases depolarization still further until finally the least sensitive channels open. So although Figure 4.7 gives the impression that Na ions are rushing in all at once, in fact the ions are rushing in incrementally in small, discrete steps. The process is referred to as *regenerative*: once begun, it is self-sustaining, regardless of the stimulus intensity. The cumulative effect on the movement of Na ions into the neuron at the axon hillock results in the all-or-none action potential.

Explaining Axonal Conduction

The cumulative action of Na ions accounts for how the action potential is initiated at the axon hillock. It also explains why the action potential is all-or-none: the voltage-sensitive channels open and do so in a regenerative fashion. What the cumulative action does not explain, however, is why the action potential is conducted along the length of the axon and why the conduction is nondecremental. Here again, curious though it may seem, the same elements—voltage-sensitive channels and a regenerative process—are at work.

Figure 4.8 illustrates how the action potential is conducted. As the figure indicates, the action potential travels along the axon in a nondecremental fashion. Once the action potential is produced, the movement of Na into the neuron and the change in the electric charge that it produces (from -60 mV to $+30$ mV) is the same regardless of the distance the action potential travels.

As is the case with dendritic and cell body conduction, axonal conduction begins when Na channels open at the point of stimulation. The Na ions move across the membrane, and after they enter the neuron they move along the inner surface of the axon, producing electrotonic flow.

There is, however, a critical difference between dendritic and cell body conduction and axonal conduction. Electrotonic flow in the dendrites

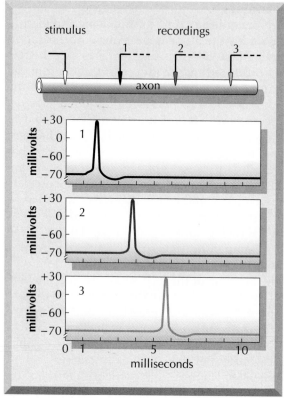

Figure 4.8 *Sequential Depolarization*
A stimulus initiates a succession of action potentials that propagate down the axon and produce the neural impulse.

and cell body gets progressively weaker as it travels and eventually dies out. In the axon the electrotonic flow does not die out, at least not to the same extent. The reason is the presence of voltage-sensitive channels that run the entire length of the axon's membrane, from axon hillock to axonal endings. (Voltage-sensitive channels tend not to occur in the dendrites and cell body.)

What happens in the axon is this. As the electrotonic flow travels from the axon hillock into neighboring areas, the charge drops across the membrane in the neighboring area, causing the following sequence: voltage-sensitive Na channels open, Na rushes in, and a new action potential followed by new electrotonic flow is produced. This process occurs over and over again along the entire length of the axon, with each part of the membrane passing through an immutable sequence of events alternating from electrotonic flow to action potential to electrotonic flow.

So, although Figure 4.8 may give the impression that conduction in the axon consists of a single action potential produced at the axon hillock and traveling to the axonal endings, conduction in the axon is actually the result of a *series* of action potentials. Each action potential occurs in a different segment of the membrane, and each produces the stimulus (i.e., the electrotonic flow) required to trigger the next. The result is non-decremental conduction. The magnitude of the action potential remains the same regardless of the distance it travels, and the process is regenerative: once it starts, it is self-sustaining. This is the nature of conduction in the axon, with one qualification, as we will now see.

Saltatory Conduction

In Chapter 2 we established that one important difference between dendrites and cell bodies, on the one hand, and axons, on the other hand, is the presence around many axons of a fatty sheath known as *myelin*, and that the basic function of myelin is to speed up conduction along the axon. The myelin sheath, if you recall, is not continuous; it has gaps, known as *nodes of Ranvier*, at which the axon membrane is left essentially uncovered.

The critical difference between the myelin sheath and the nodes of Ranvier and the reason conduction is so much faster in myelinated neurons is this: in myelinated neurons voltage-sensitive channels exist primarily in the nodes of Ranvier and are virtually absent in the myelinated sections of the axon. This absence of voltage-sensitive channels promotes electrotonic flow, a relatively fast electrochemical signal, from one node to the next and thus accounts for the speedy nature of the impulse in these neurons. In unmyelinated neurons, by contrast, voltage-sensitive channels run along the entire length of the axon, their presence producing a cumbersome succession of action potentials and in the process slowing down the impulse. As Figure 4.9 indicates, conduction along the myelinated axon is an express affair, the action potential skipping from node to node instead of moving along every part of the membrane as it does in unmyelinated axons. The term used to describe this response is *saltatory conduction*, from the Latin *saltare*, meaning "to dance."

Summing Up

Now let's take inventory. We began with the resting state (the separation of charge) and moved to the firing state (the movement of charge). We saw that membrane structure—specifically ion channels—accounts for both states. Passive channels (combined with the sodium-potassium pump) account for the resting state during which K tends to move out of the neuron while Na, to a lesser extent, leaks in. Active channels account for the firing state. And because there are two types of active channels, there are two types of firing states. In the dendrites and cell body, the opening of chemical-sensitive channels keyed to the amount of neurotransmitter produces an electrochemical signal that is graded and decremental. In axons, the opening of voltage-sensitive channels produces an electrochemical signal that is all-or-none and nondecremental.

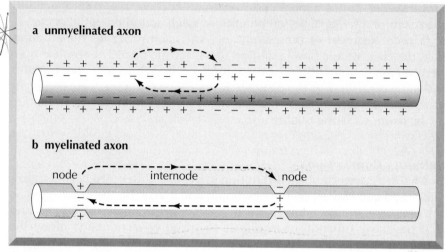

a unmyelinated axon

b myelinated axon

node   internode   node

Figure 4.9   *Neural Conduction*
An unmyelinated axon (a) conducts action potentials via a succession of ion movements be-tween neighboring areas along the entire membrane. In contrast, action potentials move along a myelinated axon (b) by skipping from one node of Ranvier to the next, speeding up impulse conduction.

Recovery after the All-or-None Action Potential

The picture we have just painted for you is reasonably complete. But it doesn't take into account one of the more intriguing—and certainly one of the most important—aspects of neural function: how a neuron reacts in the presence of constant, intense stimulation.

As you might expect there is a general relationship between the inten-sity of a stimulus and the firing rate of a neuron. What is important to keep in mind, however, is that the magnitude of an individual action po-tential (given that threshold is reached), has nothing to do with the rela-tive intensity of a stimulus. That is, an action potential produced by an intense stimulus is no different in magnitude from the action potential produced by a weaker stimulus. The action potential is all-or-none. What does change, however, with increases in stimulus intensity is the *number* of action potentials that are fired—the greater the intensity the more fre-quent the firing. But even the most intense stimulus, as it happens, is limited in the number of action potentials it can produce at any given time and this limitation is rooted in what happens during the state of the action potential generally referred to as recovery.

What happens, roughly speaking, is this: Immediately after an axon fires, it enters a stage known as the *absolute refractory period* during which it is incapable of being excited. This period is exceedingly brief—roughly 1 millisecond—and is followed by a stage known as the *relative refractory period* which, in turn, is followed by the resting state and the restoration of the resting potential. A neuron during the relative refrac-tory period is in a state of reduced sensitivity, which is to say that it is less sensitive than it is during the resting state (i.e., not as likely to fire) but sensitive enough to be excited, provided the stimulus—and this is the key point—is of sufficient intensity. Under constant and intense stimulation, in other words, a neuron doesn't have to return to the normal resting state in order to fire but can go through a more or less constant pattern of firing.

There is, however, one qualification to this repetitive firing pattern— the absolute refractory period. Given the fact that each action potential is followed by a brief period in which the neuron, in effect, is out of commission for roughly 1 thousandth of a second, the maximum rate of firing for a neuron—regardless of how intense the stimulus may be—is on the order of 1000 times per second. This limitation, it is important to emphasize, applies to individual neurons and doesn't necessarily limit, at least not entirely, the capacity of the nervous system to respond with a frequency of action potentials that exceed 1000 times per second. As you will see in subsequent chapters, the firing rate limitations of individual neurons are offset, at least in part, by the capacity of an intense stimulus to trigger simultaneous firing in a multitude of neurons.

NEURAL TRANSMISSION AND BEHAVIOR

Now that you have a general idea of how the electrochemical signal is produced and transmitted through the nervous system, let us consider how it influences behavior.

Up to now we have looked at the neuron as simply a transmitter of information: the axon receiving information from the dendrites and cell body in the form of a graded electrochemical signal and the dendrites and cell body receiving information from other neurons and receptors (via synapses) in the form of neurotransmitters. Because the electrochemical signal must travel long distances, it is easy to see why the signal is electrochemical: it is rapid and efficient. What's more, because behavior would be chaotic if we responded to every stimulus that impinged on our senses, it is easy to see why the stimulus, to produce a response, must reach threshold. The fact that axons have thresholds means that only the more intense stimuli will produce the action potential; weak stimuli will remain at subthreshold level at the axon hillock and will not trigger axonal firing.

But if we stop here, we are left with an incomplete neurobehavioral system. For if a neuron were capable only of bringing information in and sending information out, behavior would lack one indispensable ingredient: flexibility. Regardless of the circumstances, a particular stimulus, as long as it was sufficiently intense to exceed threshold, would always trigger the same response. Behavior in other words, would be "stimulus-bound."

Such of course, is not the case. With rare exceptions, human beings, and to a great extent most other animals as well, are able to respond to a stimulus not only on the basis of its intensity but on the basis of the context within which the stimulus occurs. If you smell smoke in a crowded theater, your first response is to look for the fire exit. If you smell smoke in a restaurant in which many people are smoking, you tend to ignore it. The flexibility principle holds for behavior because it holds for the nervous system. Before the neuron produces a response to a specific stimulus, that is, before the graded signal from the dendrites and cell body triggers the all-or-none action potential in the axon, the graded signal is "processed." The neuron assimilates (the technical term is *integrates*) information coming from many sources—the stimulus as well as the situational factors that accompany the stimulus. On the basis of this assimilation process, a neural "decision" is made, and a response, the all-or-none action potential, is either produced or not produced. At the root of this decision-making process are mechanisms found not only in the neuron (its ability to integrate information) but also in the synapse (its ability to collect information). Let's begin with the synapse.

THE SYNAPSE AND BEHAVIOR

Before information can pass from one neuron to another (or to a muscle or gland), a series of complex chemical events must take place across the microscopic gap separating the neurons. This gap, magnified millions of times in Figure 4.10, is called the *synaptic gap*, or *synapse*, and, as the figure shows, it is ideally suited for collection of information. It enables a single neuron, which is literally encrusted with *axonal endings*, to receive input in the form of neurotransmitters from many other neurons. It is worth emphasizing, as Figure 4.10 illustrates, that neurotransmitters (with few exceptions) are released by axons, that is, by axonal endings, and not by dendrites or cell bodies. Conduction across the synapse, in other words, moves in one direction: from the axon of one neuron to the dendrites, cell body, or (in some instances) the axon of the adjoining neuron. To avoid confusion, it has become common to refer to the neuron that releases the neurotransmitter as the *presynaptic* neuron and to the receiving neuron as the *postsynaptic* neuron. A neuron, of course, can go both ways: it can be postsynaptic to incoming neurons and presynaptic to outgoing neurons.

The Chemical Basis of Synaptic Activity

Much of what we know about synaptic activity originates in the work of Bernard Katz and his colleagues. Katz's research focused primarily on the chemical substances that govern the transmission of neural impulses from one neuron to the next, neurotransmitters. The importance of neurotransmitters and the postsynaptic membrane on which they act cannot be overstated. Once it crosses the synaptic gap, a neurotransmitter is capable not only of exciting but also of *inhibiting* neural activity. The post-

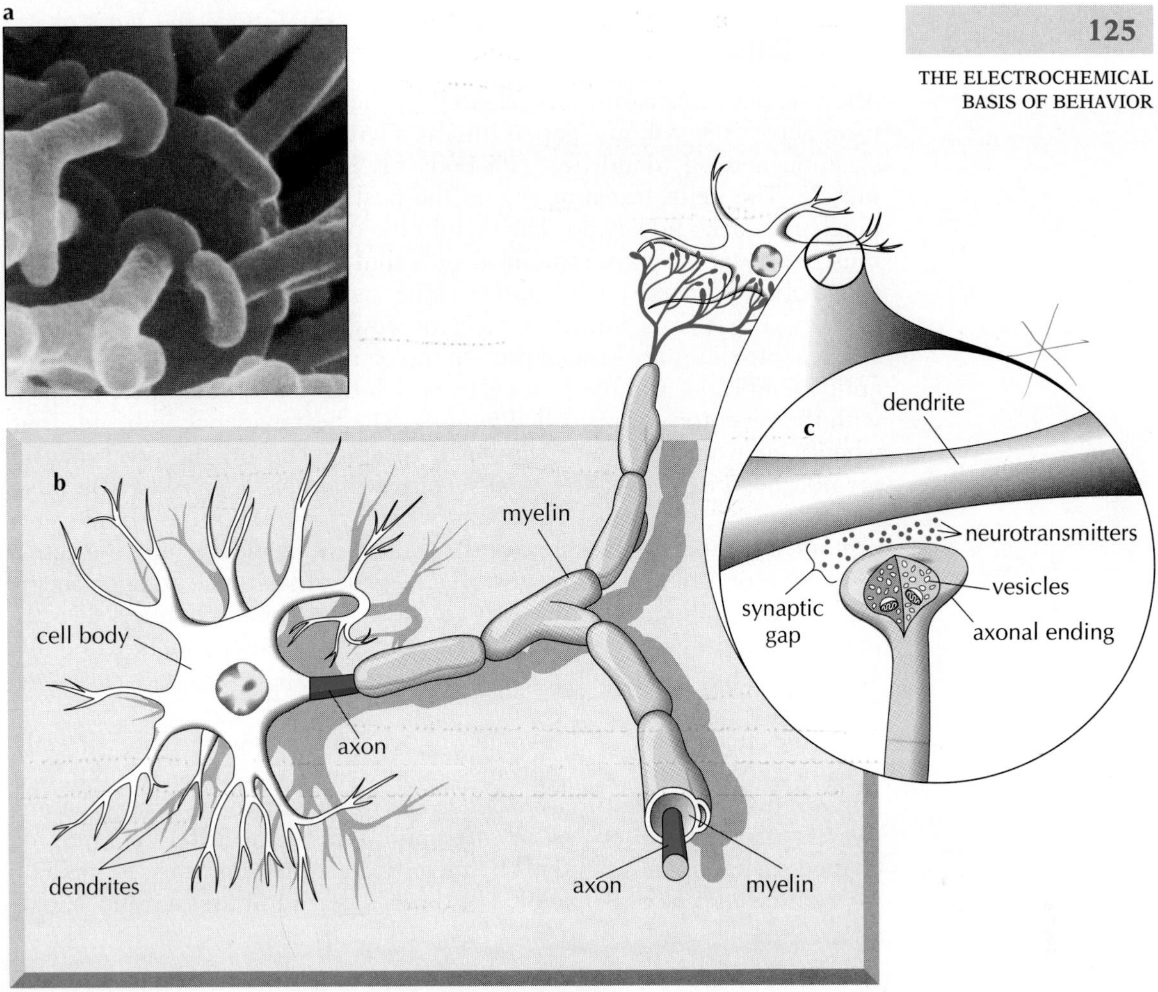

Figure 4.10 *The Synapse at Three Levels of Magnification*
(a) A photograph of axonal endings magnified millions of times. (b) Axonal endings forming synapses with a dendrite of another neuron. (c) A detailed view of the synapse.

synaptic membrane (the dendrites, cell body and, in some instances, the axon) on which a neurotransmitter acts is capable not only of transmitting but also of *summating* that neural activity.

The result is information processing at the most rudimentary level. Weak signals that ordinarily would not produce a response can be amplified (i.e., summated) and made to produce a response, and strong signals that ordinarily would produce a response can be attenuated (i.e., inhibited) and made not to produce a response. In other words, more than merely transmitting the neural signal, the neuron, in combination with the neurotransmitter, can *alter* the signal. No neural process is more critical to the flexibility of behavior than this capacity.

Let's take a closer look at the precise mechanisms: first the neurotransmitter and its ability to inhibit as well as to excite, and then the postsynaptic membrane and its ability to summate as well as to transmit.

Neurotransmitter Action: Excitation or Inhibition

After the neurotransmitter is released by the presynaptic neuron and diffuses across the synaptic gap, it interacts with the membrane of the postsynaptic neuron (dendrites, cell body or, in some instances, axon) or muscle. The neurotransmitter and the postsynaptic membrane interact much as a lock and key do. The membrane of the postsynaptic neuron or muscle appears to have structural slots that are related to the molecular shape of the transmitter substance, rather as a lock is related to the shape of a key. These slots, known as _receptor sites_, are pictured in Figure 4.11. The receptor sites are special protein molecules embedded in the postsynaptic membrane, and the process by which the neurotransmitter couples with the receptor sites is called _binding_. The best evidence indicates that when a neurotransmitter occupies a receptor site on the postsynaptic membrane, the gates of chemical-sensitive channels open. Why? Because the gates are protein molecules, and when neurotransmitters bind to receptors, they change the shape of the protein molecule opening the gates.

There is one complication, however. Neurotransmitters can open chemical-sensitive channels in one of two ways. They open channels directly in the manner just described, but they can also open channels, as Figure 4.12 illustrates, by inducing a second chemical—a _second messenger_—to open them.

On the surface, the ability of neurotransmitters to work either directly or indirectly through a second messenger seems to represent a duplication of effort. Why, you may wonder, do we need two systems? The answer is that the two types of interactions produce different kinds of changes in chemical-sensitive channels, each suited, it seems, to mediating a different type of behavior. The direct system initiates a rapid, short-

Figure 4.11 *The Lock-and-Key Relation between Neurotransmitter and Synaptic Receptors*

Two different types of neurotransmitters and their corresponding receptors—each with a unique shape—are shown in the figure.

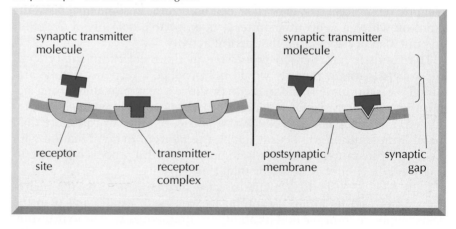

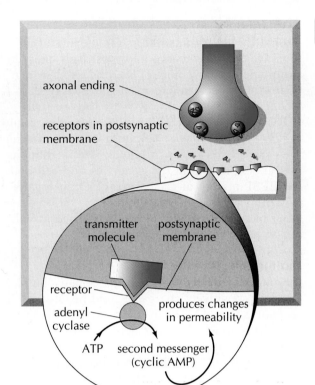

Figure 4.12 *The Second-Messenger System*
Located on the inner surface of the postsynaptic membrane
is an enzyme, *adenyl cyclase.* When a neurotransmitter (the
first messenger in this case) occupies a receptor on the postsynaptic membrane, this enzyme is activated to produce a
chemical reaction. The reaction consists of the conversion
of adenosine triphosphate (ATP) into the so-called second
messenger, cyclic adenosine monophosphate (*cyclic AMP,*
for short). Cyclic AMP, in turn, acts to change membrane
permeability by opening channels through a complex series
of chemical reactions that end with a change in the shape
of the protein molecule that constitutes the ion gate. After
cyclic AMP acts, it is destroyed by the enzyme *phosphodiesterase.*

lived change in the channels—a change ideally suited for rapid behavior
such as muscle contractions. The second-messenger system produces a
slow, relatively long-lasting change in the channels (from milliseconds to
minutes to even hours) that is better suited for long-term alterations in
behavior such as changes that occur during learning and memory. In either case, direct or indirect, after the neurotransmitter binds to a receptor it opens chemical-sensitive channels and, depending on which channels open, either excites or inhibits electrochemical signals. Let us look
at both possibilities.

Excitation

Excitatory neurotransmitters (as we already have seen) open chemical-sensitive channels to two ions, positively charged Na and K. The result is simultaneous movement of Na ions into the neuron and K ions out of the neuron. But because more Na is drawn in than K is drawn out, an electrochemical signal, known as the *excitatory postsynaptic potential* (EPSP), is produced. The EPSP is usually initiated by a transmitter acting on the dendrites or cell body of the postsynaptic neuron. The EPSP then spreads to the axon hillock, diminishing as it travels. (Remember, neural conduction in the dendrites and cell body is decremental.) Once the EPSP arrives at the axon hillock, it lowers the resting potential of -70 mV closer to the threshold of excitation of -60 mV. The axon is thus more likely to fire. If -60 mV is reached, it will fire and the all-or-none action potential will be produced.

Inhibition

Inhibitory neurotransmitters also open chemical-sensitive channels to two ions, positively charged K and negatively charged Cl ions. (Na ions are not affected.) The result is simultaneous movement of positively charged K ions out of the neuron (driven by a concentration gradient) and negatively charged Cl ions into the neuron (also driven by a concentration gradient). The inside of the neuron thus becomes more negative than normal in relation to the outside of the neuron, a state known as *hyperpolarization*, and the neuron becomes less likely to fire.

Why less likely? Remember that the normal resting potential is -70 mV and the threshold of excitation at the axon hillock is -60 mV. Hyperpolarization changes the resting potential at the axon hillock, raising it to, for example, -80 mV. This change means that the axon hillock must undergo additional stimulation (20 mV as opposed to the normal 10 mV) to produce the depolarization needed if the threshold is to be reached. The increase in membrane potential, from -70 mV to -80 mV, is known as the *inhibitory postsynaptic potential* (IPSP). Like the excitatory postsynaptic potential, it is usually initiated in the dendrites or cell body and spreads to the axon hillock. Figure 4.13 compares excitatory and inhibitory postsynaptic potentials.

The Postsynaptic Membrane: Summation and Transmission

It isn't only the type of neurotransmitter—excitatory or inhibitory—released that determines synaptic activity. It is also the *amount* of neurotransmitter released in the synapse. As you might expect, the amount of neurotransmitter released by a single action potential from a single axonal ending is hardly sufficient to determine whether ionic activity at the axon hillock will pass threshold level (i.e., become sufficient to change the resting potential from -70 mV to -60 mV). Rather, it is the accumulation of neurotransmitters released by many action potentials that creates the appropriate ionic effect. The cumulative process by which neurotransmitters affect ionic activity is

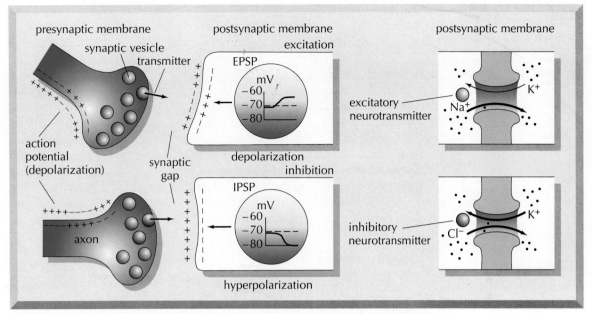

Figure 4.13 *Excitatory and Inhibitory Postsynaptic Potentials (EPSP and IPSP)*
A neural impulse travels along the axon and releases a neurotransmitter, which diffuses across the synaptic gap. On the postsynaptic neurons it produces either an EPSP, causing more sodium ions to move inward than potassium ions to move outward (top panel) or an IPSP, causing potassium ions to move out and chloride ions to move inward (bottom panel). (Bold arrows denote increased ion movement.)

called *summation*. There are two types of summation, *spatial* and *temporal*, and both are depicted in Figure 4.14.

Spatial Summation
Spatial summation is produced when action potentials occur *simultaneously* in a group of axonal endings that converge on and form synapses with one other neuron. Although each action potential may release only a small amount of neurotransmitter and cause only a small excitatory postsynaptic potential, the combined action of many action potentials produces the release of a large amount of neurotransmitter and a number of EPSPs which then spread to the axon hillock and cumulatively exceed threshold.

Temporal Summation
Temporal summation occurs when action potentials appear in rapid succession within *one* axonal ending, pumping out the neurotransmitter over an extended period of time. As we shall soon see, a neurotransmitter has a limited life span in the synaptic gap. If the release is frequent enough, however, the amount will overwhelm the normal means by which the neurotransmitter is removed, and the result will be a cumulative buildup of neurotransmitter. This buildup is called temporal summation because the buildup is critically dependent on the *time* between

129

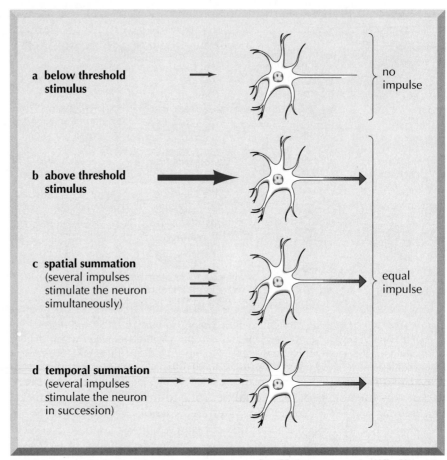

Figure 4.14   *Spatial and Temporal Summation*
(a) A weak stimulus will not produce a neural impulse because it does not exceed threshold. There are, however, two ways that stimuli can exceed threshold. A stimulus can be intense enough by itself (b) or several stimuli can summate either spatially (c) or temporally (d).

successive action potentials. A good way to visualize the difference be-tween spatial and temporal summation is to imagine a bucket being filled by the combined dripping of several faucets. The faucets represent axonal endings; the bucket represents the postsynaptic neuron. The image approximates spatial summation. Temporal summation is compa-rable to the dripping of only one faucet (or only one axonal ending) at a rate sufficient to raise the level of water in the bucket.

Summation of Inhibition
Like excitatory postsynaptic potentials (EPSPs), inhibitory postsynaptic potentials (IPSPs) summate spatially or temporally; that is, they produce cumulative effects. There is, however, a difference. The cumulative effect of IPSPs makes it harder for the impulse to fire; the cumulative effect of

EPSPs makes it easier. Furthermore, because a given neuron can receive input from different neurons at the same time, it is possible for the two potentials (EPSPs and IPSPs) to occur simultaneously. Let us now look at this simultaneous activity.

The Interaction of Synaptic Potentials

When we talk about synaptic potentials (excitatory or inhibitory) and summation (spatial or temporal), we are really talking about a decision-making process at the basic level of the neuron. Depending on the relative number of EPSPs and IPSPs, each axon has the capacity either to fire or not to fire an action potential.

What is more important, though, is how these relative numbers affect ionic activity at the axon hillock. Each time an EPSP or IPSP occurs, there is a change in the ionic balance at the axon hillock. EPSPs tilt the balance in one direction (from −70 mV toward −60 mV). IPSPs tilt it in the opposite direction (from −70 mV toward −80 mV). In order for the action potential actually to occur in the postsynaptic neuron, the balance must be tilted enough so that the threshold level at the axon hillock, −60 mV, is surpassed. When EPSPs dominate to the point of exceeding the threshold at the axon hillock, the axon will fire and the all-or-none action potential will occur. When IPSPs dominate, the likelihood of firing will decrease. Thus does the neuron act much like a computer, its output based on the total of all the incoming information it receives in the form of EPSPs or IPSPs. The adaptive value of this process cannot be overstated. It is the ability of individual neurons to make neuroelectrical decisions that enables the nervous system as a whole to make behavioral decisions. But it is also true that behavioral decisions are more complex and flexible than this. Not only do we respond or not respond to a given stimulus, but we are able to do so on the basis of the context in which that stimulus occurs. To repeat: we are not stimulus-bound. Behavior is flexible, and to understand this flexibility, we must take the analysis of neurotransmitters and the role they play in controlling behavior one step further.

SYNAPTIC MODULATION AND BEHAVIORAL FLEXIBILITY

Up to now we have focused primarily on the output side of the synapse—the ability of the neurotransmitter to inhibit and excite neural activity, and the ability of the neuron both to summate and transmit neural activity. Now let us shift our attention to the *input* side of the synapse—to the presynapse.

Neurotransmitters do not appear and disappear spontaneously. They are produced in the presynaptic neuron and released into the synaptic gap. Then, after they act on the postsynaptic membrane, they are cleared. Each of these factors—production, release, and clearance—is flexible or, to use the technical terminology, is subject to *modulation*.

The term "modulation" needs clarification. A good analogy is a simple radio. In the same way that a radio can be turned on, so can action potentials trigger the release of neurotransmitters. Once the radio is on, however, its sound can be adjusted. So, too, with neurotransmitters, once they have been released. They, too, can be adjusted or modulated. The modulation is controlled by any one or combination of three "switches": production, release, clearance.

Neurotransmitters: Production, Release, and Clearance

To date, nearly 40 different types of neurotransmitters have been discovered in the nervous system, and it is reasonable to assume that there are many more that have yet to be identified. We shall consider specific neurotransmitters in the next chapter. Now, however, let us examine some of the general features and functions neurotransmitters have in common, how these features are modulated, and the role they play in controlling behavior.

How Neurotransmitters Are Produced

Neurotransmitters are usually produced in the axonal endings of neurons where they are stored in tiny sacs known as *synaptic vesicles*. The chemical reactions that produce neurotransmitters are usually controlled by enzymes. The enzymes themselves are produced in the cell body of the neuron. They then move down the axon to the axonal endings through structures known as *microtubules*. This movement, shown in Figure 4.15, is known appropriately enough as *axonal transport*.

The critical factor in the production of the neurotransmitter is the enzyme. It is the "middleman" in the process, and it is subject to modulation. It determines production but is itself controlled by two factors: genes and hormones. The genetic and hormonal control of enzymes and the modulatory effect they have on transmitter production have been linked to behaviors ranging from Alzheimer's disease (a disease in the elderly marked by loss of memory) to sexual behavior in lower animals and humans.

How Neurotransmitters Are Released

Neurotransmitters are released as soon as the action potential (that is, the neural impulse), traveling down the axon of the presynaptic neuron, reaches the axonal endings where it triggers release of the neurotransmitter from the vesicles into the synaptic gap. This release takes place indirectly: the action potential causes calcium ions to enter the axonal endings, and the calcium triggers the release.

A Closer Look

Once the action potential arrives at the axonal endings, several events occur, all of which are important for release of the neurotransmitter.

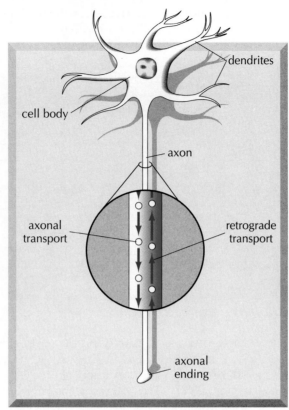

Figure 4.15 *Axonal and Retrograde Transport*
In axonal transport, enzymes manufactured in the cell body
are carried by the microtubules to the axonal endings. The
movement of nutrients and enzymes from axonal endings
to cell body is known as retrograde transport.

First of all, the action potential produces a change in voltage (i.e., depolarization) across the neural membrane. This change not only opens
the voltage-sensitive Na and K channels—something that happens whenever and wherever an action potential occurs—it also opens a set of voltage-sensitive channels we have yet to consider, the *calcium (Ca) channels*.
Second, the opening of the calcium channels causes positively charged
calcium ions, which normally lie in the fluid outside the neuron, to move
into the axonal endings drawn by both concentration and voltage gradients.
Third, the influx of calcium into the axonal endings triggers a process
known as *exocytosis*. During exocytosis, as pictured in Figure 4.16, the
vesicles move to and fuse with the inner surface of the membrane of the
axonal endings where they rupture, releasing the neurotransmitter into
the synaptic gap. The transmitter diffuses across the gap and binds to
postsynaptic receptor sites.

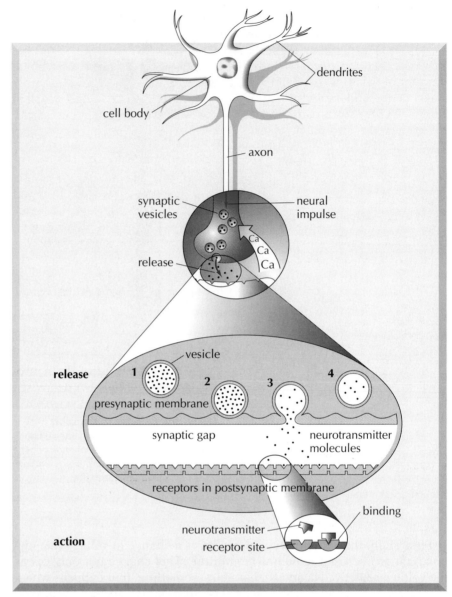

Figure 4.16 *Neurotransmitter Release and Action*
To release the neurotransmitter, calcium (Ca) enters, vesicles move to the inner surface of the presynaptic membrane (1), fuse with the membrane (2), rupture (3), and recycle for reuse (4). The neurotransmitter molecules diffuse across the synaptic gap and bind to the receptor site in a lock-and-key fashion.

Modulating the Release

The importance of the influx of calcium to synaptic transmission cannot be overstated. Without it, the synapse is rendered inoperative. With it, synaptic activity not only occurs but also varies in degree, depending on the amount of calcium that comes into the axonal endings. As more calcium enters the axonal endings, more vesicles fuse with the inner surface of the membrane and more neurotransmitter is released into the synaptic gap. It is no surprise, then, that one way of modulating the amount of neurotransmitter released into the synaptic gap is to modulate the amount of calcium that enters the axonal endings.

To better understand this type of modulation, it may help to look at Figure 4.17*a*. As you can see, the presynaptic neuron is, in effect, a middleman in the system. It forms a synapse with a so-called modulation neuron, and it releases neurotransmitters that act on a postsynaptic neuron. The key element in the circuit is the synapse formed between the modulation neuron and the presynaptic neuron. It is here that the modulation neuron releases a neurotransmitter that controls the amount of neurotransmitter released by the presynaptic neuron. The control, however, is indirect. The neurotransmitter released by the modulation neuron regulates the amount of calcium that enters the presynaptic neuron. The amount of calcium determines the amount of neurotransmitter released.

The function of the modulation neuron deserves elaboration. To say that a neuron modulates the amount of neurotransmitter released by the presynaptic neuron is not to say that it "triggers" release. That aspect of neurotransmission is reserved for the action potential in the presynaptic neuron. What it does say, however, is that once the action potential occurs in the presynaptic neuron, its impact on the release of the neurotransmitter can be either increased (*presynaptic facilitation*) or decreased

Figure 4.17 *Synaptic Modulation*
In (a) a modulation neuron forms a synapse with the presynaptic neuron. In (b) and (c) the modulation neuron increases or decreases synaptic transmission by increasing (presynaptic facilitation) or decreasing (presynaptic inhibition) the amount of calcium (Ca) in the presynaptic neuron.

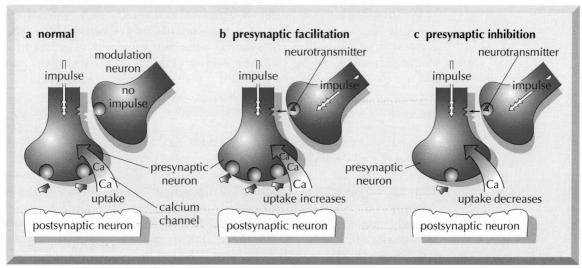

(*presynaptic inhibition*), depending on whether the modulation neuron increases or decreases the influx of calcium. Figures 4.17*b* and *c* compare the two types of presynaptic modulation.

Behavioral Implications

Modulation of neurotransmitter release is no trivial matter when it comes to behavior. In Chapter 9 we shall see that the inhibitory effect that modulatory neurons exert on synaptic transmission (i.e., presynaptic inhibition) may well constitute the physiological basis of pain suppression produced by opiates, acupuncture, and placebos. In Chapter 16 we shall see that the facilitatory effect of the modulation neurons (i.e., presynaptic facilitation) may account for some simple forms of learning and memory.

Clearing the Neurotransmitter

After the neurotransmitter is released and diffuses across the synaptic gap, it acts on the postsynaptic membrane and then it is cleared. As we've already seen, action on the postsynapse occurs when the neurotransmitter occupies receptor sites, opens chemical-sensitive channels to certain types of ions, and either triggers or inhibits the postsynaptic potential. The impact of the neurotransmitter on the postsynaptic neuron, however, is very brief. As soon as the interaction has occurred, the transmitter substance is cleared from the synaptic gap.

Clearance takes place in one of two ways. In some instances, the neurotransmitter is inactivated by an enzyme released from the membrane of the postsynaptic neuron. In other instances, the neurotransmitter, through a complex process known as *reuptake*, is drawn back into the vesicles of the presynaptic neuron. In either instance, the brevity of the interaction is critical, and for a highly adaptive reason: the limited life span of the neurotransmitter in the synaptic gap lends a critical measure of control to the overall communication process.

We can liken the clearing of neurotransmitter substances from the synaptic gap to the erasing of a blackboard. Before activity can start anew with each impulse, the synapse must be cleared of any neurotransmitter substance. As we shall see in later chapters, if neurotransmitters are not cleared quickly, the behavioral consequences can be devastating, ranging from memory loss to death.

PRESERVING NORMAL SYNAPTIC ACTIVITY: THE DEFENSE MECHANISMS

It should be obvious by now that normal synaptic transmission is vital to adaptive behavior. If synaptic activity is abnormal for any period of time, behavior breaks down. As we shall see in later chapters, *excessive* synaptic activity, for instance, has been linked to schizophrenia, whereas deficits in synaptic activity have been linked to mental depression. Given this importance, it should come as no surprise that the synapse has defense mechanisms of sorts designed to preserve normal activity. When postsynaptic activity is abnormal (either excessive or deficient) for any period of time, the synapse has the capacity to enlist responses to restore normality. These responses, known as *synaptic compensatory responses*, occur either in the presynapse or postsynapse, and they act in one of two ways to restore normal activity. When there is a deficit, synaptic activity is increased. When there is an excess, synaptic activity is reduced. Let's take a closer look at these compensatory responses, first in the presynapse and then in the postsynapse.

Autoreceptors on the Presynapse

One way that the synapse restores normal activity is to impose control, via a feedback system, over the amount of neurotransmitter released. Normally after a neurotransmitter is released, it not only diffuses across the synaptic gap and acts on postsynaptic receptors but also feeds back onto the presynaptic neuron and acts on a special set of receptors known as *autoreceptors*. The function of autoreceptors is to keep the presynaptic neuron "informed" about the amount of neurotransmitter in the synaptic gap. If there is either too little or too much, the production and release of neurotransmitter by the presynaptic neuron is adjusted accordingly and normality is restored.

Receptor Sensitivity on the Postsynapse

A second way that the synapse restores normal activity is to regulate the sensitivity of the postsynapse. Normally the sensitivity is determined by the number of receptors on the postsynapse, and the synapse has the capacity to regulate the number of receptors. When postsynaptic activity is abnormal (either excessive or deficient) for any period of time, the synapse has the capacity to either increase or decrease the number of receptors accordingly. The ability of the postsynaptic neuron to decrease the number of receptors (i.e., to decrease its sensitivity) when there is excess activity is known as *postsynaptic subsensitivity*. Its ability to increase the number of receptors (i.e., to increase its sensitivity) when there is a deficit in activity is known as *postsynaptic supersensitivity*. Postsynaptic subsensitivity and supersensitivity are illustrated in Figure 4.18.

Behavioral Implications
When we look at the ability of the synapse to regulate its own activity, we see built-in capacities that give the nervous system considerable flexibility in maintaining synaptic activity at optimal levels. As we shall see in later chapters, these built-in capacities underlie to a large degree an organism's ability to overcome disruptions in synaptic activity produced by neural damage, drugs, or even defective genes. There is a limit, however, to the amount of disruption the synapse can compensate for—to the amount of neurotransmitter it can produce and to its own capacity for

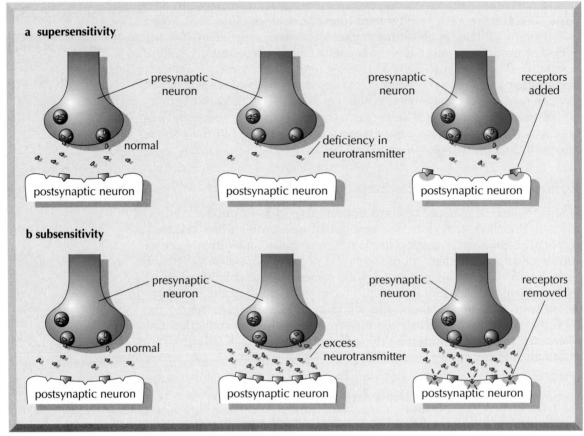

a supersensitivity

presynaptic neuron

normal

postsynaptic neuron

presynaptic neuron

deficiency in neurotransmitter

postsynaptic neuron

presynaptic neuron

receptors added

postsynaptic neuron

b subsensitivity

presynaptic neuron

normal

postsynaptic neuron

presynaptic neuron

excess neurotransmitter

postsynaptic neuron

presynaptic neuron

receptors removed

postsynaptic neuron

Figure 4.18   Synaptic Defenses
(a) Receptor sites increase in response to a deficiency in neurotransmitter, a process known as supersensitivity. (b) Receptor sites decrease in response to excess neurotransmitter, a process known as subsensitivity.

sensitivity and insensitivity. When the synapse is pushed beyond these limits, the behavioral results can be devastating, ranging from emotional to intellectual to sensory to motor breakdown. We shall look at these behavioral effects in subsequent chapters, but we should emphasize that there is one redeeming factor, and it is linked to neurotransmitter activity—the use of drugs to treat abnormal behavior.

With very few exceptions, behavior-altering drugs work by altering neurotransmitter activity, which they can do in many ways. A drug, for instance, can mimic the action of a neurotransmitter, interacting with the postsynaptic membrane just as the neurotransmitter does. A drug can also retard or accelerate the production of a neurotransmitter or the production of the enzymes that clear transmitters from the synaptic gap. Normally, drugs capable of doing these things serve only to disrupt behavior. But what if behavioral disruption already exists? Is it not logical to use drugs to restore normal activity? The answer of course, is yes, but as we shall see in the next chapter, the question of drugs and their impact on behavior goes well beyond these basic considerations.

SUMMARY

1. *The neural impulse defined.* The neural impulse is a chemically initiated electric signal that represents the basic language of the nervous system. No behavior can take place without this communication. And while the stimuli that initiate the signal may vary, the basic nature of the impulse is always the same.

2. *Early discoveries.* The first person to demonstrate the electrical nature of the neural impulse was an Italian physiologist named Luigi Galvani, who attributed the phenomenon to a force yet unknown and called it "animal electricity." The idea that the neural impulse is different from electricity per se did not develop until the early twentieth century, when researchers first attempted to measure the speed of the neural impulse. Julius Bernstein, in particular, speculated that the impulse, though electrical in nature, is chemically induced. This was an attempt to explain why the impulse travels more slowly along neurons than electricity travels along wires.

3. *Young's breakthrough.* A major breakthrough in research on the neural impulse came with John Z. Young's discovery that the giant nerve fibers in the squid can be isolated and studied individually during neural transmission. This discovery, together with the development of a microelectrode recording technique, enabled Alan Hodgkin and Andrew Huxley to confirm in principle Bernstein's chemical theory of nerve action.

4. *Two electrochemical signals.* Information flow in the neuron always takes the same form: an electrochemical signal produced by the movement of electrically charged chemicals called ions. This language has two "dialects." One is the electrochemical signal in the dendrites and cell body, known as the graded or synaptic potential; the other is the electrochemical signal in the axon, known as the action potential.

5. *The relationship between the two signals.* The sequence of events that constitutes the neural impulse begins with an electrochemical signal produced in the dendrites and cell body. The signal travels to the axon, and once it reaches threshold, a second electrochemical signal (all-or-none and nondecremental) is produced. The two electrochemical signals differ in their relationship to stimulus intensity: the signal in dendrites and cell body is graded, increasing or decreasing with changes in stimulus intensity; the signal in the axon is all-or-none, either occurring or not occurring depending on whether the stimulus intensity reaches threshold. The significance of this difference confers upon the nervous system a decision-making capacity of sorts.

6. *Resting state.* When a neuron is in the resting state, organic ions are trapped inside the neuron, chloride ions are in a state of equilibrium, and positively charged Na and K ions are in a constant state of motion, with K ions moving out of the neuron freely and Na ions "leaking" in. This ionic distribution produces a state in which the inside of the neuron is negative relative to the outside by -70 mV. Underlying the ionic distribution is the structure of the membrane and the sodium-potassium pump.

7. *The firing stage.* The second stage of the neural impulse—the firing stage—is triggered when the "leak" of Na ions through the membrane turns into a rush. This rush occurs because once a neuron is stimulated, its active Na channels open, drawing Na ions into the neuron. The Na rush is driven by two factors: the concentration and the voltage gradient.

8. *The source of the two signals.* Depending on whether it occurs in the dendrites or cell body, on the one hand, or in the axon, on the other hand, the electrochemical signal is either graded or all-or-none. Underlying the graded signal are chemical-sensitive channels found in the membrane surrounding dendrites and cell bodies. Because the opening of these channels is keyed to the amount of neurotransmitter (the more neurotransmitter, the greater the number of channels that open), the electrochemical signal is graded. Underlying the all-or-none action potential are voltage-sensitive channels found in the membrane surrounding axons. Because the opening of these channels is keyed to the change in voltage across the membrane and because voltage-sensitive channels have different thresholds and open at different times, the process is regenerative—once begun it is self-sustaining regardless of the stimulus intensity—and the result is the all-or-none action potential.

9. *Synaptic transmission.* Synaptic transmission begins when a neural impulse reaches the axonal endings and a neurotransmitter is released, diffuses across the synaptic gap, and acts on the postsynaptic membrane. Action of the neurotransmitter is determined by a "lock and key" relation between the molecular shape of the neurotransmitter and the structure of the receptor sites on the postsynaptic membrane. These receptor sites are protein molecules embedded in the membrane, and the process by which the neurotransmitter couples to them is called binding. After they bind to receptors, neurotransmitters change postsynaptic membrane permeability in one of two ways: directly, by opening chemical channels in the postsynaptic membrane, or indirectly, through a second messenger called cyclic AMP.

10. *Synaptic excitation and inhibition.* Excitation occurs when the neurotransmitter changes membrane permeability to Na ions, causing them to move inward and depolarize the neuron. This effect is known as the excitatory postsynaptic potential (EPSP). Inhibition occurs when the neurotransmitter changes membrane permeability to K and Cl ions, causing K ions to move outward and Cl ions to move inward. The result is that the outside of the neuron becomes more negative than it normally is, a state known as hyperpolarization, and the neuron becomes less likely to fire. The effect is known as an inhibitory postsynaptic potential (IPSP).

11. *Summation and transmission.* By itself the amount of neurotransmitter released by a single neural impulse is not sufficient to excite an impulse. It is the accumulation of neurotransmitter that produces excitation. This cumulative effect is known as summation. It occurs when impulses appear simultaneously in a number of axonal endings converging on one neuron (a process known as spatial summation) or when impulses travel in rapid succession along one axonal ending (a process known as temporal summation).

12. *Interaction between synaptic potentials.* Whether an axon fires or doesn't fire an action potential ultimately depends on the relative number of EPSPs and IPSPs. In this respect, the neuron acts as a computer, its output based on the total of all incoming information in the form of EPSPs and IPSPs. When EPSPs dominate, the neuron will fire. When IPSPs dominate, the likelihood of firing will decrease. This simple principle of synaptic activity—the fact that individual neurons are capable of making neuroelectrical decisions—enables the nervous system as a whole to make behavioral decisions and the organism to engage in flexible, adaptive behavior.

13. *Synaptic modulation.* Neurotransmitters are produced in the presynaptic neuron, released into the synaptic gap, and then, after they act on the postsynaptic membrane, they are cleared. Each of these factors—production, release, and clearance—is subject to modulation. Enzymes modulate production and clearance, calcium ions modulate release.

14. *Preserving normal synaptic activity.* Synapses are endowed with properties that enable them to regain a state of normalcy in the face of excess or deficient activity. These properties, known generally as synaptic compensatory responses, can occur in either the presynapse or the postsynapse. Underlying these responses are two factors: (1) the presence of autoreceptors on the presynaptic neuron that are able to monitor the amount of neurotransmitter in the synaptic gap and can adjust the amount of neurotransmitter released accordingly; (2) the ability of the postsynaptic neurons to either decrease or increase the number of receptors sensitive to the neurotransmitter.

KEY TERMS

action potential
active channels
autoreceptors
axon hillock
binding
calcium channels
cathode-ray oscilloscope
chemical-sensitive channels
concentration gradient
decremental conduction

depolarized
excitatory postsynaptic potential
  (EPSP)
exocytosis
firing state
graded potential
hyperpolarization
inhibitory postsynaptic potential
  (IPSP)
ions

KEY TERMS

neural membrane
passive channels
postsynaptic neuron
postsynaptic subsensitivity
postsynaptic supersensitivity
presynaptic facilitation
presynaptic inhibition
presynaptic neuron
receptor sites
recovery state
resting potential
resting state

saltatory conduction
second-messenger system
sodium-potassium pump
summation
synapse
synaptic compensatory response
synaptic gap
synaptic potential
synaptic vesicle
threshold
voltage gradient
voltage-sensitive channels

SUGGESTED READINGS

Kandel, E. R., Schwartz, J. H., & Jessell, T. M. *Principles of Neural Science*, 3rd ed. New York: Elsevier, 1991.

Mathews, G. G. *Cellular Physiology of Nerve and Muscle*, 2nd ed. Palo Alto, CA: Blackwell Scientific Publications, 1991.

Nicholls, J. G., Martin, A., Wallace, B. G., & Kuffler, S. W. *From Neuron to Brain*, 3rd ed. Sunderland, MA: Sinauer Associates, 1992.

Shepherd, G. M. *Neurobiology*, 2nd ed. New York: Oxford University Press, 1988.

THE NEURO-CHEMICAL BASIS OF BEHAVIOR

INTRODUCTION

As we saw in the last chapter, the capacity of the nervous system as a whole to make behavioral decisions is rooted in the neuroelectrical decisions made by individual neurons on the basis of neurotransmitter activity. In this chapter we will look at how neurotransmitter activity determines the *type* of behavioral decisions neurons make. We will begin by presenting a general picture of neurotransmitter activity. We will then look at how neurotransmitters operate in the nervous system and at the type of behavior their activity produces. At issue here is not only normal behavior but also abnormal behavior, and not only natural controls of neurotransmitters but also artificial controls—psychoactive drugs. Schizophrenia, depression, and obsessive-compulsive disorder—all have been linked to abnormalities in neurotransmitters, and all have been treated with drugs developed to correct those abnormalities.

NEUROTRANSMITTERS: AN OVERVIEW

At least 40 chemical substances have been identified so far as neurotransmitters, but it's likely that the nervous system contains many more that researchers have yet to isolate. Eight of the better known neurotransmitters are shown in Table 5.1. Of these we will look at four in detail, after which we will briefly survey what we know about the others.

Our concerns in this chapter will be guided and shaped by four questions. How and where do neurotransmitters act in the nervous system? What behaviors do they normally produce? What abnormal behaviors occur when they break down? And what drugs have been used to treat these abnormal behaviors?

As you read this chapter, it will help you to bear in mind that, as Figure 5.1 shows, all neurotransmitters work in basically the same way: they are produced in either the cell body or the axonal endings, they are

TABLE 5.1

LOCATIONS AND HYPOTHESIZED EXCITATORY OR INHIBITORY EFFECTS OF EIGHT KNOWN AND SUSPECTED NEUROTRANSMITTERS

NEUROTRANSMITTER	LOCATION	HYPOTHESIZED EFFECT
Acetylcholine (ACh)	Brain, spinal cord, autonomic ganglia, target organs of the parasympathetic nervous system	Primarily excitation in brain and autonomic ganglia, excitation or inhibition in target organs *muscle activity*
Monoamines		
Norepinephrine (NE)	Brain, target organs of sympathetic nervous system *counter part of*	Primarily inhibition in brain, excitation or inhibition in target organs
Serotonin (5-hydroxytryptamine, or 5-HT)	Brain, spinal cord *rate of heart*	Inhibition
Dopamine (DA)	Brain	Excitation or inhibition
Amino acids		
Glutamate	Brain, spinal sensory neurons	Excitation
Aspartate *excitatory*	Brain, spinal cord interneurons	Excitation
Gamma aminobutyric acid (GABA)	Brain (especially cortex and cerebellum)	Inhibition
Glycine	Spinal cord interneurons	Inhibition
Neuropeptides*		

*Because neuropeptides have different characteristics from the other neurotransmitters, they are presented separately in Table 5.2.

released by the axonal endings, they act by binding to receptors, and they are cleared. The key point we will be coming back to over and over is that neurotransmitters can affect behavior in two broad ways: one, *how* they operate (whether they excite or inhibit synaptic activity); and, two, *where* they act in the brain (the type of behavior they produce).

ACETYLCHOLINE

Acetylcholine is derived from choline and acetyl coenzyme A. It is produced in the axonal endings by a chemical reaction involving the enzyme *choline acetyltransferase*. It influences synaptic activity through its ability to bind to postsynaptic receptors, referred to as *cholinergic receptors*. When this binding occurs, chemical-sensitive ion channels are opened, and a postsynaptic potential is either excited or inhibited.

After acetylcholine acts on the postsynaptic receptors, it is cleared by an enzyme known as *acetylcholinesterase* (AChE). Acetylcholinesterase removes acetylcholine by breaking it down into choline and acetic acid. The enzyme works rapidly, thus limiting the amount of time acetylcholine has to act in the synapse. Once acetylcholine is cleared, choline then returns to the presynaptic neuron where it is recycled into new acetylcholine.

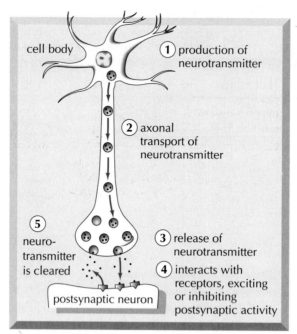

cell body   (1) production of neurotransmitter

(2) axonal transport of neurotransmitter

(5) neuro-transmitter is cleared

(3) release of neurotransmitter

(4) interacts with receptors, exciting or inhibiting postsynaptic activity

postsynaptic neuron

Figure 5.1   *A Summary of the Major Steps in Synaptic Transmission*

The importance of this breakdown process can be readily seen in light of what happens to behavior whenever the process is disrupted. If acetylcholinesterase works too slowly or not at all, the prolonged action of acetylcholine can cause consequences that range from memory loss to death. Indeed the lethal effects of certain poison gases and most insect sprays are the result of blocking the effects of acetylcholinesterase.

Acetylcholine in the Peripheral Nervous System

Acetylcholine operates in both the peripheral nervous system and the brain. But because the synapses in the peripheral nervous system are far more accessible to investigation than those in the brain, we know more about acetylcholine's action in the peripheral nervous system than we know about its action in the brain.

Acetylcholine is released in the peripheral nervous system by motor nerves and is involved primarily in the control of skeletal and smooth (including heart) muscle. It exercises this control through its ability to bind to cholinergic receptors located on the skeletal and smooth muscles.

There are two types of cholinergic receptors: muscarinic and nicotinic. Each type is named for the drug, muscarine or nicotine, that stimulates it. *Muscarinic* receptors are found almost exclusively on smooth muscles and glands—the target organs of the autonomic nervous system. *Nicotinic* receptors are found on skeletal muscles and in the ganglia of the autonomic nervous system. Whether acetylcholine excites or inhibits depends on the type of receptor with which it is interacting. When it interacts with nicotinic receptors, it has an excitatory effect, causing the skeletal muscles to contract and the limbs of the body to move. Its effect on the muscarinic receptors, on the other hand, is either excitatory or inhibitory. One of its principal effects, for example, is to slow down the heartbeat. Figure 5.2 illustrates some of the areas in the peripheral nervous system in which acetylcholine works.

Just as some drugs (muscarine and nicotine, for example) stimulate cholinergic receptors, others block their action. *Curare,* a poison used in hunting by some South American Indians, is one such drug. Its lethal effect is tied to its capacity to prevent acetylcholine from initiating activity in skeletal muscles. Curare occupies the cholinergic receptors on the muscles but does not itself produce activity. The result is total paralysis and eventual death.

Acetylcholine in the Brain

Identifying the brain areas that produce acetylcholine has proven to be exceedingly difficult, for there are no methods at present for studying acetylcholine directly in the brain. The information we have comes

[handwritten margin notes: blocks nicotinic ACh receptors / Atrophine blocks muscarinic ach receptors.]

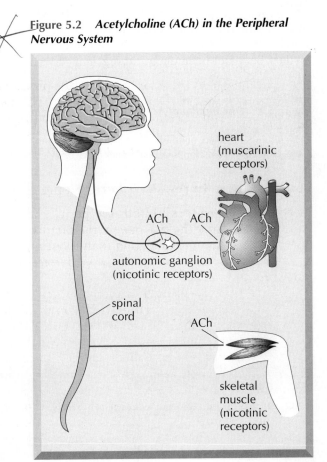

Figure 5.2 *Acetylcholine (ACh) in the Peripheral Nervous System*

heart (muscarinic receptors)

ACh   ACh

autonomic ganglion (nicotinic receptors)

spinal cord

ACh

skeletal muscle (nicotinic receptors)

largely from an indirect approach in which brain areas are stained in order to identify the presence of the enzyme (choline acetyltransferase) involved in the production of acetylcholine. The assumption behind the approach is that wherever this enzyme is present, acetylcholine must be present as well.

As you can see in Figure 5.3, neurons that produce acetylcholine in the brain originate primarily in two areas: the *septal area* and *nucleus basalis.* Axons originating in these areas project to the cortex and the limbic system, including the hippocampus and amygdala. In each area, the axons are involved in the control of a different behavior. In the human cortex, acetylcholine is thought to be involved in cognitive function—the ability to reason. In the hippocampus, acetylcholine has been linked to learning and memory. In the amygdala, it appears to control emotional behavior.

Acetylcholine and Alzheimer's Disease

Within the past few years acetylcholine has drawn a great deal of attention from researchers seeking to identify the physiological basis of Alzheimer's disease, a disorder that produces profound personality changes and intellectual impairment, the most notable of which is memory loss, in older people. Autopsies of Alzheimer's patients have revealed deficits of acetylcholine (specifically deficits of choline acetyltransferase) in the septal area and nucleus basalis (Coyle, Price, & DeLong, 1983), and therapeutic approaches to Alzheimer's disease have attempted to correct these deficits with drugs that increase acetylcholine. The results to date have not been encouraging. This doesn't rule out acetylcholine as

Figure 5.3   *Distribution of Acetylcholine in the Brain of a Rat*
Dots represent clusters of cell bodies; dark lines represent tracts projecting from groups of cell bodies.

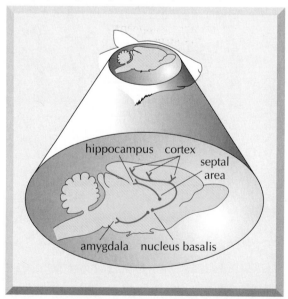

a factor in Alzheimer's disease, but it does indicate that other factors are at work as well (see Chapter 2 for details).

MONOAMINES

Monoamines is the generic term for three neurotransmitters: *norepinephrine*, *serotonin*, and *dopamine.* Frequently, a fourth neurotransmitter, *epinephrine* (also known as adrenaline), is grouped with these three, but epinephrine's function as a neurotransmitter is relatively minor (so far as we know) and therefore will not be considered in any detail.

Monoamines are so called because their chemical structure contains a single (mono) amine group. The production of norepinephrine and dopamine (and epinephrine as well) begins with the amino acid tyrosine and involves a complex series of chemical reactions, the final one of which determines which transmitter will be produced. Production of serotonin is a bit simpler, involving only two chemical steps. It begins with the amino acid tryptophan and ends with the production of serotonin (also known as 5-hydroxytryptamine). Figure 5.4 illustrates the chemical steps involved in the production of these neurotransmitters.

Figure 5.4   *Production of Monoamines*
The chemical steps involved in the production of the monoamines are mediated by enzymes, as is shown in the figure.

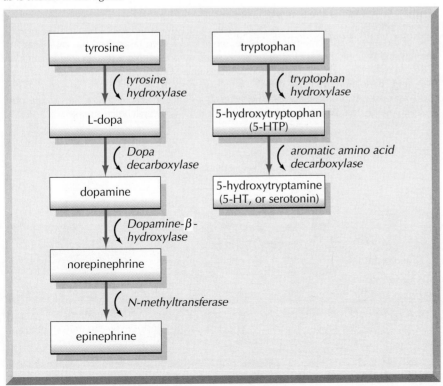

Action and Clearance of Monoamines

We have a reasonably good idea of how monoamines act in the synapse and how they are cleared. Monoamines act via one of several *second-messenger systems*. One common example of a second-messenger system is cyclic 3'-5-adenosine monophosphate (cyclic AMP): neurotransmitters bind to postsynaptic receptors, cyclic AMP is produced, a series of chemical reactions occurs, ion channels are opened or closed, and a neural impulse is either excited or inhibited. As we saw in Chapter 4, the behavioral significance of the second-messenger system is its long-lasting effect on the synapse. It is no surprise, then, that monoamines are involved in such long-term behaviors as motivation, emotion, and memory.

Like acetylcholine—and for that matter like all neurotransmitters—monoamines must be removed from the synapse immediately after they act. In contrast to acetylcholine, however, removal of the monoamines involves a *reuptake* process in which the bulk of the monoamines is drawn back into the axonal endings and is stored in the vesicles. In addition to the reuptake process a small amount of the monoamines is deactivated through the action of two enzymes: *catechol-O-methyltransferase* (COMT), which works *prior* to reuptake, and *monoamine oxidase* (MAO), which works *after* reuptake. If you look at Figure 5.5, you will see these steps as they apply to removal of norepinephrine and will be able to compare them with the steps involved in the removal of acetylcholine.

Figure 5.5 *Clearing the Synapse*

(a) A norepinephrine (NE) synapse. NE diffuses across the synapse and acts on the receptor sites of the postsynaptic membrane. Norepinephrine is then taken back up by the axonal endings and is stored in vesicles for reuse. A small amount of NE is deactivated through the action of two enzymes: catechol-O-methyltransferase (COMT), which works prior to reuptake, and monoamine oxidase (MAO), which works after reuptake. (b) An acetylcholine (ACh) synapse. ACh diffuses across the synapse and acts on the receptor sites of the postsynaptic membrane. ACh is then broken down by AChE (acetylcholinesterase).

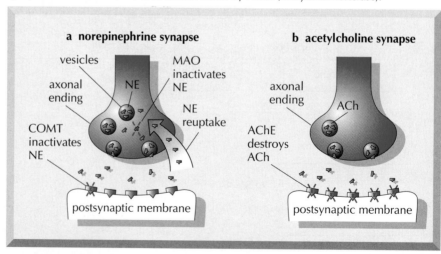

Location of Monoamines

Most of what is known about the location of monoamines in the nervous system has come through technological advances in a biochemical assay procedure called *fluorescent microscopy*. This procedure is based on the fact that when brain areas containing monoamines are viewed under a fluorescent microscope, they take on different colors, each color indicating the presence of a specific monoamine. Thus fluorescent microscopy has enabled researchers to link different monoamines to different areas of the nervous system and in turn to different behaviors. Let us now look more closely at the anatomical distribution of these neurotransmitters and their corresponding behavioral effects.

Norepinephrine in the Peripheral Nervous System

Norepinephrine is released in the peripheral nervous system during stress. It originates in the sympathetic motor nerves and is involved in control of smooth muscles, cardiac muscle, and glands, as depicted in Figure 5.6. Like acetylcholine, norepinephrine controls muscle activity

Figure 5.6 *Norepinephrine (NE) in the Peripheral Nervous System*

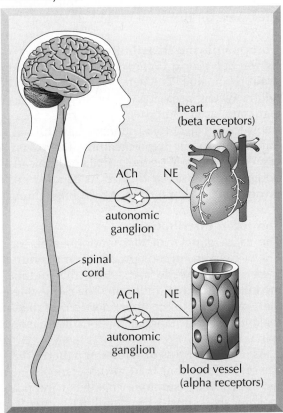

by interacting with specific receptor sites on the muscles, the *adrenergic* receptors. These receptors are of two types, alpha and beta, so called on the basis of their location. *Alpha* receptors are located in the blood vessels; *beta* receptors, of which there are two subtypes (beta-1 and beta-2), are located in the heart (beta-1) and in the intestines and lungs (beta-2).

How, specifically, norepinephrine operates—whether it excites or inhibits—differs depending on the type of receptors with which it interacts. On alpha receptors, norepinephrine has an excitatory effect, causing the blood vessels to constrict. On beta receptors norepinephrine has a mixed effect. Acting on the beta-1 receptors of the heart, norepinephrine has an excitatory effect, causing the heart muscle to contract. Acting on beta-2 receptors in the intestines and lungs it is inhibitory; it slows their action. The resulting behavioral effects—increased heart rate and decreased intestinal activity—are clearly adaptive responses when the body has to mobilize its resources for energy very quickly as in stressful situations.

[handwritten margin note: excitatory vs inhibitory]

Norepinephrine and Serotonin in the Brain

When we deal with the brain, it is best to treat norepinephrine and serotonin together, not because they affect the same areas of the brain (although there may be some overlap) but because of their unique and similar pattern of distribution. Much like spokes radiating from the hub of a wheel, neurons that produce norepinephrine and serotonin originate in a few areas of the brain yet travel to many.

Norepinephrine Distribution

As you can see in Figure 5.7, the distribution of norepinephrine in the brain is unusual. The neurons that produce norepinephrine originate in relatively few areas of the brain—the locus coeruleus and the lateral tegmental area. But after leaving these areas, these neurons give rise to tracts that project to a number of additional areas throughout the brain (among them the hypothalamus, thalamus, septal area, hippocampus, and cortex) as well as the spinal cord. Because the neurons that produce norepinephrine are so diffuse, its behavioral effects are widespread. They involve learning, memory, wakefulness, hunger, and emotion.

Serotonin Distribution

The same pattern of distribution holds for serotonin. As pictured in Figure 5.8, serotonin is produced in a group of neurons known as *raphe nuclei*, which are located along the midline of the brain stem in the medulla, pons, and midbrain. The raphe nuclei in turn give rise to tracts that travel both to the upper portions of the brain—to the hypothalamus, thalamus, basal ganglia, hippocampus, and cortex—as well as to the spinal cord.

As a result of this distribution pattern, the same broad and varied behavioral effects that hold for norepinephrine also hold for serotonin. In the spinal cord, serotonin has been implicated in pain suppression, a topic we shall consider in detail in Chapter 9. In the cortex, serotonin has

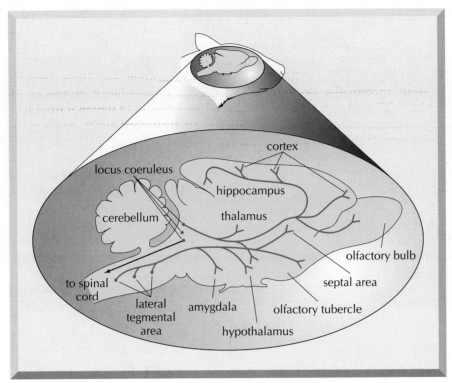

Figure 5.7 *Distribution of Norepinephrine in the Brain of a Rat*
Dots represent clusters of cell bodies; dark lines represent tracts projecting from the groups of cell bodies.

been linked to sleep and to heightened sensory awareness. Serotonin deficits in the basal ganglia have been implicated in obsessive-compulsive disorder, a behavioral disorder that we will cover in Chapter 15. This disorder is characterized by recurring thoughts or acts (washing one's hands repeatedly, for example) that are so intrusive and overbearing that they come to dominate the person's life and disrupt normal everyday behavior. Evidence that obsessive-compulsive disorder may be caused by a deficit in serotonin comes from the fact that drugs, known as *antiobsessional* drugs (*chlomipramine*, for instance), that relieve the extreme symptoms of the disorder increase serotonin in the nervous system (Zohar et al., 1988).

Norepinephrine, Serotonin, and Mental Depression

In addition to being similar in the way they are distributed in the brain, norepinephrine and serotonin have one other feature in common: deficits in both have been proposed as a possible cause of clinical depression. The evidence for this relationship comes from the fact that drugs known to increase norepinephrine and serotonin in the nervous system also produce noticeable behavioral improvement in people suf-

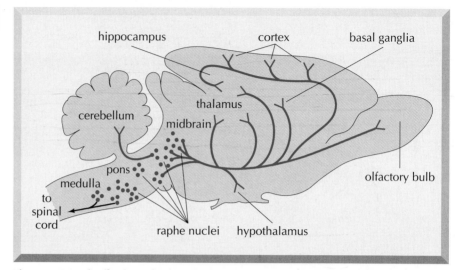

Figure 5.8 *Distribution of Serotonin in the Brain of a Rat*
Dots represent clusters of cell bodies; dark lines represent tracts projecting from the groups of cell bodies.

fering from clinical depression. Known as *antidepressant* drugs (*desipramine*, for instance), these drugs work by blocking the reuptake of norepinephrine and serotonin, making them more available for action at the postsynaptic receptor sites. We shall return to these drugs and their synaptic action later in this chapter and then again, in conjunction with depression, in Chapter 15.

Dopamine in the Brain

As depicted in Figure 5.9, the neurons that produce dopamine originate in three areas: the *substantia nigra* (which as part of the basal ganglia connects to the putamen and caudate nucleus), the *ventral tegmental area* (which connects with the limbic system and cortex), and the *hypothalamus* (which connects with the pituitary gland). The behavioral effects of dopamine include motor behavior (via the substantia nigra) and arousal and feelings of pleasure (via the ventral tegmental area).

Not surprisingly, abnormal levels of dopamine can produce profound behavioral effects. Its depletion in the substantia nigra, as you saw in Chapter 2, gives rise to the impaired motor conditions associated with *Parkinson's disease* and has led to a twofold pharmacological approach to the disorder. One drug used, *benzotropine*, inhibits the enzymes that normally break down dopamine. A second drug, *L-dopa*, a chemical precursor of dopamine (see Figure 5.4), increases dopamine production. Both drugs have proven effective in the early stages of Parkinson's disease, but each, at best, provides only a temporary solution. Once neu-

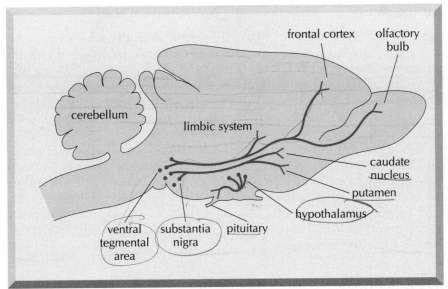

Figure 5.9 *Distribution of Dopamine in the Brain of a Rat*
Dots represent clusters of cell bodies; dark lines represent tracts projecting from the groups
of cell bodies.

rodegeneration has progressed to a point where little or no dopamine is
being produced, the drugs have little impact on the condition.

Within the past few years, dopamine also has figured prominently in
research whose goal is to identify the chemical basis of schizophrenia.
The reason is that drugs that block the action of dopamine—known as
antischizophrenic drugs (*chlorpromazine*, for instance)—often produce
noticeable improvement in the behavior of schizophrenics. This fact has
led some researchers to theorize that schizophrenia itself may be caused
by an abnormally high level of dopamine. As we shall see later in this
chapter and again in Chapter 15, however, schizophrenia is an extremely
complex disorder and an abnormally high level of dopamine is only one
of the many pieces in the puzzle.

OTHER NEUROTRANSMITTER SUBSTANCES

There are a number of neurotransmitters other than those we have just
described and, although less may be known about these neurotransmitters, there is no reason to believe that the general principles that govern
their production, release, action, and clearance differ from those that
govern the better known ones. Lesser known neurotransmitters fall
roughly into two chemical groups: *amino acids* and chains of amino
acids known as *neuropeptides*. We will look briefly at each group.

Amino Acids

Among the most common amino acid neurotransmitters are two excitatory transmitters, *glutamate* and *aspartate*, and two inhibitory transmitters, *gamma aminobutyric acid* (GABA) and *glycine*. Both glutamate and aspartate are thought to be the chief excitatory transmitters in the brain. And enough is known about GABA to suspect that more than a third of the brain may use it as an inhibitory neurotransmitter, most notably the motor areas in the cerebellum and basal ganglia.

Within the past few years glutamate has drawn a great deal of attention from researchers seeking to identify the chemical basis of learning and memory (see Chapter 16 for details). There is also evidence linking abnormal levels of glutamate and GABA to a rare and fatal genetic disease called *Huntington's disease*, whose symptoms include involuntary motor movements and severe mental deterioration culminating in death (see Chapter 10 for details).

Neuropeptides

Neuropeptides consist of short chains of amino acids, ranging from 2 to 39 amino acids in length. Table 5.2 lists a few of the more prominent neuropeptides. The table also presents a general view of the broad and varied behavioral effects of neuropeptides, many of which we will discuss in more detail in subsequent chapters.

When neuropeptides were originally discovered, many were identified only as hormones—chemicals that are produced by glands and travel in the blood to target organs. Later, when the same neuropeptides were discovered in the brain, it became reasonably clear that they are neurotransmitters as well. We shall now look briefly at some of the neuropeptides, although you should keep in mind that in virtually every case our knowledge of the neurotransmitter function—specifically the area of the brain and the behavior that we associate with it—is incomplete.

Cholecystokinin

As a hormone, cholecystokinin is produced and released by the gastrointestinal tract, where it promotes the digestion of fats. As a neurotransmitter, it is produced in several areas of the brain including the hypothalamus, and one of its functions appears to be regulation of food intake.

Adrenocorticotropic Hormone and Vasopressin

As hormones, adrenocorticotropic hormone (ACTH) and vasopressin are involved in energy production and water regulation, respectively. As neurotransmitters, however, they may play an entirely different role, working in the hippocampus and other areas of the brain to produce learning and memory.

TABLE 5.2	✗

HYPOTHESIZED BEHAVIORAL EFFECTS OF SEVEN NEUROPEPTIDES IN THE BRAIN

NEUROPEPTIDE	BEHAVIORAL EFFECT
Cholecystokinin	Food intake
Adrenocorticotropic hormone (ACTH)	Learning and memory
Vasopressin	Learning and memory
Substance P	Perception of pain
Endorphins	Suppression of pain, learning, memory, perception of pleasure
Enkephalins Leucine	Suppression of pain, learning, memory, perception of pleasure
Methionine	Suppression of pain, learning, memory, perception of pleasure
Angiotensin *blood/pressure*	Water regulation

Same

Angiotensin

As a hormone, angiotensin is produced and released by the kidneys and acts in both the brain and body to regulate water intake. As a neurotransmitter, it acts in areas in and around the hypothalamus to regulate water intake.

Substance P

Substance P is a neuropeptide that functions exclusively as a neurotransmitter. It is found in both the peripheral and central nervous systems and appears to play an important role in transmitting pain-related information to the brain.

Endorphins and Enkephalins

Endorphins and enkephalins are among the most recently discovered neuropeptides, and for a number of reasons they have created a great deal of interest. For one thing, opiates such as morphine and heroin mimic the action of endorphins and enkephalins. For another, they have been found in areas of the brain—the limbic system, for instance—that have been implicated in pain suppression and what we experience as pleasure. Studies we will describe in later chapters indicate, for example, that certain pain therapies, such as acupuncture, work by releasing endorphins in the limbic system and enkephalins in the spinal cord. Other studies have linked endorphins' action in the limbic system to feelings of reward and pleasure and to the formation of long-term memory.

Neuropeptides and Their Relation to Other Neurotransmitters

Evidence suggests that neuropeptides and such better known neurotransmitters as dopamine and acetylcholine may be produced in the *same* neurons and may be released together during synaptic transmission. If this is the case—and it appears that it is—we must reevaluate the long-standing belief, known as *Dale's law*, that a neuron is capable of producing and releasing only one type of neurotransmitter. We must also conclude that the potential for a single neuron to release two neurotransmitters at once may confer upon the nervous system a decision-making capacity far more versatile and complex than originally believed.

NEUROTRANSMITTERS AND BEHAVIOR: IN RETROSPECT

Even though our knowledge of individual neurotransmitters is still limited, the overall role of neurotransmitters in controlling behavior is reasonably well understood. Neurotransmitters appear to imbue the nervous system with a chemical code that permits one signal, the neural impulse, to control an enormous variety of behaviors. Were it not for this chemical code, the structure of the nervous system, with its indescribably complex interconnections, would produce behavioral chaos. The fact that neurons produce and release *specific types* of neurotransmitters, coupled with the fact that neurons, muscles, and glands have membrane characteristics (synaptic receptors) that are selectively sensitive to these neurotransmitters, establishes an orderly basis for behavior.

Figure 5.10   *The Lock-and-Key Relation between Neurotransmitter and Synaptic Receptors*
Two different types of neurotransmitters and their corresponding receptors—each with a unique shape—are shown in the figure.

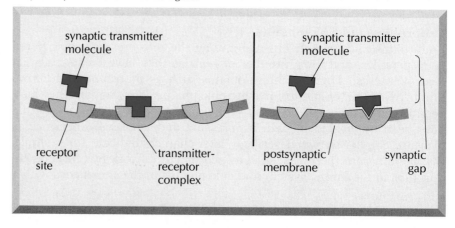

Figure 5.10 illustrates the point best. The critical feature is the "lock-and-key" relationship between neurotransmitters and receptors. This relationship ensures that neural impulses do not spread indiscriminately through the nervous system but are channeled into the precise areas for which they are intended.

NEUROTRANSMITTERS AND PSYCHOACTIVE DRUGS

If you bear in mind the relationship between synaptic activity and orderly behavior, it is easy to see why any disruption in this activity can produce profound behavioral consequences. We have mentioned some of these consequences and have noted briefly the means by which drugs have been used to treat abnormalities. But there is one key aspect of this overall picture that we have yet to address in any detail: the effects of drugs on synaptic activity and behavior. Up to now we have focused on only one side of the drug story: the therapeutic side. Even here our treatment has been rather superficial. We have seen that among the more significant advancements in the field has been the development of "anti" drugs: antiobsessional drugs, such as chlomipramine; antischizophrenic drugs, such as chlorpromazine; and antidepressant drugs, such as desipramine. There have been notable advances, too, in the development of drugs capable of relieving anxiety—*antianxiety* drugs. Two such drugs, Valium and Librium, have become two of the most widely used—and, many believe, widely abused—drugs in the world. Even with the progress of recent years, the overall question of how drugs affect brain chemistry and control behavior in many cases remains largely unanswered.

The general assumption, logical enough on the surface, is that drugs affect behavior by either enhancing or impeding the activity of certain neurotransmitters, thus altering the neurochemical environment of the brain. But the how and why of these consequences have yet to be determined in many instances. Breakthroughs are being made, but the struggle to understand the neurochemical dynamics of certain drugs is only just beginning. The scientific discipline that seeks to understand how drugs, through their action on the nervous system, affect behavior is known as *psychopharmacology*. In the remainder of this chapter we will give you an idea of where this scientific discipline is today—and where it needs to go.

THE FIVE GROUPS OF PSYCHOACTIVE DRUGS

Drugs that affect behavior are commonly known as *psychoactive* drugs. Ordinarily when we think of psychoactive drugs, we think of substances like heroin, cocaine, amphetamine, lysergic acid diethylamide (LSD), and marijuana—drugs that are usually taken for recreational not therapeutic reasons. But regardless of why a drug that affects behavior is taken, it affects neurotransmitter activity. As a group, psychoactive drugs are usually divided into five categories based on the manner in which they influence behavior. These five categories are summarized in Table 5.3. Also listed in this table are the neurotransmitters on which these drugs act to produce their behavioral effects.

The drugs listed in the table interact with neurotransmitters in various ways. Some affect the production of specific neurotransmitters in the neuron. Others affect the release of the neurotransmitter, its action, or its removal. Still others occupy the same receptor sites as the neurotransmitter and in the process either mimic or block its action. Figure 5.11 illustrates some of the sites of drug action in the synapse.

Regardless of how a psychoactive drug interacts with a neurotransmitter, it can have only one of two effects: it can either enhance neurotransmitter activity or impede it. Drugs that enhance activity by mimicking the action of neurotransmitters at the receptor level are known as *agonists*. Drugs that impede the action of neurotransmitters by blocking the effects of neurotransmitters at the receptor level are known as *antagonists*.

An example of an agonist is *morphine*, which has been used in the treatment of pain. Morphine enhances synaptic activity by occupying receptor sites normally occupied by endorphins. An example of an antagonist is *chlorpromazine*, a drug used to treat schizophrenia. It impedes the action of dopamine by occupying, but not acting at, dopamine receptor sites. We will now look at each of the five categories of psychoactive

TABLE 5.3

THE ACTIONS OF PSYCHOACTIVE DRUGS ON NEUROTRANSMITTERS

DRUGS	NEUROTRANSMITTER	ACTION OF DRUGS
Depressants		
Alcohol	GABA	Increases binding
Barbiturates	GABA	Increase binding
Benzodiazepines (Valium, Librium)	GABA	Increase binding
Stimulants		
Amphetamine	Dopamine, norepinephrine	Increases
Cocaine	Dopamine, norepinephrine	Increases
Opiates		
Morphine, heroin	Enkephalins, endorphins	Mimic
Psychedelics		
Marijuana	Anandamide	Mimics
LSD	Serotonin	Mimics
Antischizophrenics		
Chlorpromazine	Dopamine	Blocks
Antidepressants		
MAO inhibitors	Serotonin, norepinephrine	Increase
Tricyclic antidepressants	Serotonin, norepinephrine	Increase
Selective serotonin reuptake inhibitors	Serotonin	Increase

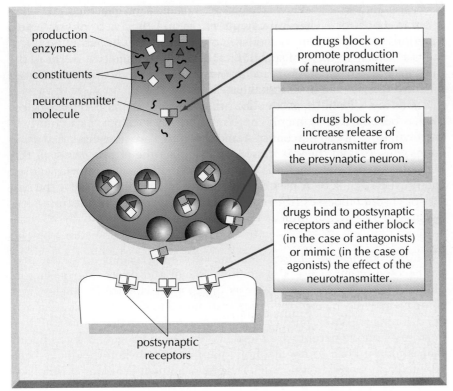

production
enzymes

constituents

neurotransmitter
molecule

drugs block or
promote production
of neurotransmitter.

drugs block or
increase release of
neurotransmitter from
the presynaptic neuron.

drugs bind to postsynaptic
receptors and either block
(in the case of antagonists)
or mimic (in the case of
agonists) the effect of the
neurotransmitter.

postsynaptic
receptors

Figure 5.11 *Some of the Ways Drugs Increase or Decrease Synaptic Activity*

drugs, examining their behavioral effects, their neurotransmitter activity, and how and where in the brain each produces this activity.

Depressants

Depressants, also known as sedatives or hypnotics, are a diverse group of drugs that include alcohol, barbiturates, and a group of drugs known as *benzodiazepines*. All these substances, in one way or another, tend to *decrease* behavioral activity, hence the term "depressant."

The behavioral effects of depressants vary with the drug and the dose. At their mildest, depressants help people sleep. Some depressants can also relieve anxiety, as do benzodiazepines, such as Valium and Librium. At their most dangerous, depressants can produce coma or even kill. More than a few famous people, among them the actress Marilyn Monroe, have died as the result of an overdose of barbiturates. Here is a brief description of the most common depressants: alcohol, barbiturates, and benzodiazepines.

Alcohol

By far the most widely known and widely used drug in the depressant category is alcohol, an organic substance customarily consumed in beverages like wine, beer, and whiskey. For most people, alcohol, when taken in moderation, has only a mild effect on behavior or physiological function. Indeed in many societies, American society in particular, alcohol is a basic ingredient of social interaction. More than two-thirds of the American adult population, according to recent studies, drink at least one or two alcoholic beverages a week.

That's one side of the story. The other side is that the overuse of alcohol has become a monumental problem in many societies, particularly in our own. Roughly 10 percent of American adults are now classified as alcohol abusers, and there is no way to calculate the ultimate cost of this abuse to society—whether it is the number of deaths and injuries caused each year by drunk drivers and by alcohol-related child abuse, or the battery of chronic illnesses (e.g., cirrhosis of the liver) that result from alcohol abuse.

The Causes of Alcohol Abuse.   No one knows for certain why some people become habitual users of alcohol. Social and psychological factors play a role, to be sure, but there is increasing evidence to suggest that some people may be more genetically disposed to alcohol abuse than others (Cloninger, 1987). Studies of adopted children indicate that children born to alcoholic parents are more likely to become alcoholics as adults than children born to nonalcoholic parents, even when they have been adopted and reared in a nonalcoholic environment (Valliant & Milofsky, 1982).

Genetic factors also appear to explain why many people (people of Asian descent, in particular) have an extremely low tolerance for alcohol, that is, cannot drink even small amounts of alcohol without becoming ill (Reed, 1985). The genetic factor underlying alcohol intolerance may well be related to the action of two enzymes involved in alcohol metabolism. One enzyme (acetaldehyde dehydrogenase) converts alcohol into a chemical (acetaldehyde) that produces sickness (e.g., nausea, vomiting, sweating). The other enzyme (aldehyde dehydrogenase) converts the chemical that produces sickness into a harmless chemical (acetic acid). Recent work has shown that people who get sick from small amounts of alcohol often have normal levels of the first enzyme but have a deficiency in the second enzyme (Harada et al., 1982).

Fetal Alcohol Syndrome.   New and important alcohol abuse research involves a condition known as *fetal alcohol syndrome*. The syndrome is caused by the ingestion of alcohol during pregnancy, and it has been implicated in a variety of birth abnormalities that include mental retardation, hyperactivity, distinctive facial features (see Figure 5.12), and heart defects (Mattson, Barron, & Riley, 1988). Exactly how much alcohol must be ingested to produce the syndrome is not known, but lower-animal work indicates that even small amounts of alcohol during pregnancy may have devastating effects on neural development (Goodlett, Marcussen, & West, 1990). Thus the best—and safest—strategy for a pregnant woman is to abstain.

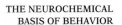
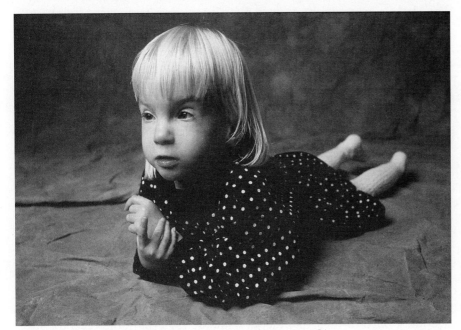

Figure 5.12 *A Child with Fetal Alcohol Syndrome*

Barbiturates

Next to alcohol, the most widely used drugs classified as depressants are barbiturates. In large doses, barbiturates, such as pentobarbital sodium, are used as anesthetics. In lower doses, they produce relaxation and mild euphoria. Like alcohol, barbiturates appear to be relatively harmless when taken in mild doses. In excessive amounts, however, they can produce a battery of destructive physiological effects—everything from insomnia to tremors to severe digestive problems—and can be fatal (Lickey & Gordon, 1991). Although less publicized than alcohol addiction, barbiturate addiction is rapidly mushrooming into one of the country's major health problems.

Benzodiazepines

Benzodiazepines, chiefly Valium, Xanex, and Librium, are depressants widely prescribed for the treatment of anxiety. As a rule they are not lethal, even in high doses, but their effects can last a relatively long time, anywhere from 8 to 50 hours, and have proved beneficial in the treatment of certain anxiety disorders such as panic attacks and generalized anxiety (see Chapter 15 for details). Compared to barbiturates and alcohol, benzodiazepines have a relatively low abuse potential, which is to say they are not as *physically* addictive. On the other hand, they have a tendency to produce psychological dependence.

How Depressants Work

Evidence to date indicates that the three depressants—alcohol, barbiturates, and benzodiazepines—work in essentially the same way: each enhances the action of GABA, one of the major inhibitory neurotransmitters in the brain. There are two types of GABA receptors—the $GABA_A$ and the $GABA_B$ receptors. To understand how the three drugs interact with GABA, we must take a closer look at the $GABA_A$ receptors. These receptors, along with several other receptor types, make up a group of receptors known as the *$GABA_A$ receptor complex* (Cooper, Bloom, & Roth, 1991). The $GABA_A$ receptors bind to GABA while the other receptors bind to benzodiazepines, barbiturates, or alcohol (Costa, 1991; Suzdak et al. 1986). When the binding of these receptors occurs simultaneously—GABA binding to its receptors and the drugs binding to their receptors—the binding properties of GABA are enhanced, increasing the inhibitory action of the neurotransmitter and producing the behavioral effects characteristic of each drug.

The discovery that benzodiazepines, barbiturates, and alcohol have their own binding sites on the $GABA_A$ receptor complex raises an important question regarding the intended function of these receptors. Human beings clearly did not evolve receptors solely as a means to respond to depressant drugs. Thus the assumption has been that there must be a naturally occurring neurotransmitter in the brain that resembles benzodiazepines, barbiturates, and alcohol, and acts on the same receptor sites. If this assumption is true (and it remains to be proven), then it means that just as there are neurotransmitters (endorphins) in the brain that act as opiates, so may there be other neurotransmitters in the brain that act as depressants. Identifying these neurotransmitters and understanding where and how they work in the brain is a topic of much current research (Barbaccia et al., 1989).

Stimulants

Stimulants are drugs that increase behavioral activity. They act on the nervous system in a variety of ways. Caffeine, for example, accelerates cellular metabolism, temporarily increasing energy. Nicotine, a milder stimulant, produces a similar effect by activating excitatory synapses. Still another stimulant, strychnine, *blocks* inhibitory effects of glycine on its receptors, but to such a degree that the unleashed excitatory activity in the brain can lead to convulsions and death.

Two stimulants that have aroused considerable attention of late are amphetamine and cocaine. Although they differ in chemical makeup, both drugs when taken in moderate doses serve as effective antidotes to fatigue. The problem with both, however, is that users can become dependent on them and can often experience schizophrenic-like symptoms, such as hallucinations and delusions. In some people cocaine produces an effect that can best be described as total indifference. Habitual users often reach a point at which nothing that once held meaning for them— job, home, family—is important anymore.

How Stimulants Work

Amphetamine and cocaine increase the level of two neurotransmitters, dopamine and norepinephrine, but each drug acts in a slightly different manner. Amphetamine increases both neurotransmitters by affecting the synapse in two ways: (1) by displacing the neurotransmitters from their storage sites, and (2) by blocking reuptake of the neurotransmitters once they have acted on the synapse. Cocaine apparently has only the second effect, blocking only the reuptake of neurotransmitters. The result, in each instance, is an increased level of dopamine and norepinephrine in the brain, a level that in moderate amounts triggers arousal, reward, and feelings of pleasure but in large amounts can trigger schizophrenic-like symptoms (see Chapter 15 for details).

Precisely how amphetamine and cocaine are able to exert their behavioral effects remains to be determined. Figure 5.13 summarizes the actions of amphetamine and cocaine that take place at the synapse.

Opiates

In the strict sense of the term, opiates are drugs derived from the opium poppy. Recently, however, it has become customary to include in this category any drug used chiefly for the relief of pain. Among the natural opiates in this category are opium itself, morphine, and codeine, all of which are derived from plants. Among the synthetic opiates made in the laboratory are meperidine (Demerol) and methadone. The infamous heroin falls somewhere in between. It is made in the laboratory, but the process involves a change in the chemical structure of morphine, a natural opiate.

Opiates do more than simply relieve pain. Most of them produce a temporary state of euphoria and at times can give a temporary feeling of boundless energy. Because of these effects, many people use opiates not to relieve pain but to relieve psychological pressures.

Figure 5.13 *Amphetamine and Cocaine in the Synapse*
Both drugs produce an increase in norepinephrine and dopamine in the synapse, amphetamine by promoting their release, and both cocaine and amphetamine by blocking their reuptake.

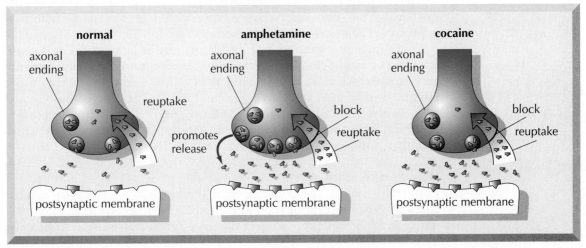

How Opiates Work

Opiates appear to have a widespread impact on the central nervous system, particularly on the spinal cord, the limbic system, and the cortex. It appears, too, that when opiates operate in the central nervous system, they bind to receptors and mimic the action of enkephalins and endorphins, two neurotransmitters that appear to be involved in the control of pleasure and the suppression of pain. Still to be understood are the specific processes by which opiates produce euphoria and create addiction. We shall look further into these topics later in this chapter.

Psychedelics

Psychedelics include all drugs that have the potential to alter consciousness: to produce hallucinations, to disturb thought processes—in short, to induce behavior similar to some forms of mental illness.

There are two types of psychedelics: natural and synthetic. Among the natural psychedelics, those derived from plants, are mescaline and marijuana. Synthetic psychedelics, manufactured in the laboratory, include LSD.

Much has been written about how closely the behavioral effects of some psychedelic drugs, LSD and mescaline, mirror the symptoms manifested by schizophrenics. On the surface these similarities are intriguing, but careful analysis suggests that the behaviors are not as similar as originally suspected. The principal behavioral effects of drugs like LSD or mescaline are *visual* hallucinations and disorientation in time and space. The hallucinatory symptoms of schizophrenia, in contrast, are mainly auditory (voices), not visual. Furthermore, disorientation in time and space, a common experience for LSD users, is *not* a prime symptom of schizophrenia. Finally, while schizophrenics routinely experience delusions of persecution or of grandeur, such delusions are rarely experienced by people under the influence of psychedelics.

Marijuana

Marijuana—the most commonly used psychedelic drug—comes from the dried leaves and flowers of a plant, *Cannabis sativa*. The plant's active ingredient is *delta-9-tetrahydrocannabinol* (THC), which in low doses produces feelings of euphoria and well-being but in large doses can cause paranoia and hallucinations. Synthetic forms of marijuana have recently been approved by the U.S. Federal Drug Administration for use in the treatment of nausea in cancer patients, weight loss in people afflicted with acquired immunodeficiency syndrome (AIDS), and glaucoma (a disorder in which there is an increase in fluid pressure within the eye, resulting in damage to the retina).

How Psychedelics Work

Even more varied and complex than the behavioral effects of psychedelics are their neural effects. The complexity arises from the fact that different psychedelic drugs affect different neurotransmitters. Mescaline, for instance, mimics the action of norepinephrine. LSD's ability to produce hallucinations is not well understood although there is evidence that LSD mimics the action of serotonin (Jacobs, 1987).

Recent evidence indicates that marijuana, more specifically its active ingredient THC, binds to its own receptors in the brain and mimics a newly discovered neurotransmitter (named *anandamide*) that has been isolated in the pig brain (Howlett, 1990; Fackelmann, 1993). Whether marijuana works the same way in the human brain is unknown, but the possibility that the human brain manufactures its own marijuana-like transmitter is certainly plausible in light of the ability of the human brain to manufacture endorphins, its own naturally occurring opiates.

Antipsychotics

Antipsychotics is the term used to describe a number of drugs that have proven somewhat effective in the treatment of psychotic illnesses—schizophrenia and affective disorders, especially depression. Thus, there are two major groups of antipsychotic drugs: antischizophrenic drugs and antidepressant drugs.

Antischizophrenic Drugs

Antischizophrenic drugs fall into two classes: *phenothiazines* (notably chlorpromazine) and *butyrophenones* (notably haloperidol). Antischizophrenic drugs, in general, help schizophrenics who are catatonic (exhibiting stuporlike motor behavior) or paranoid (subject to delusions). They also have a calming effect on schizophrenics who are highly agitated and hallucinatory much of the time.

The effectiveness of these drugs has spurred a good deal of research, particularly into their effects on neurotransmitters in the brain. We now know that antischizophrenic drugs block the action of neurotransmitters by occupying, but not activating, their receptor sites. What's more, because the newest and most potent antischizophrenic drugs—butyrophenones—selectively block dopamine, the evidence for a dopamine link with schizophrenia is now stronger than ever. But more of that in Chapter 15.

Side Effects. Antischizophrenic drugs are not without their limitations and side effects. To begin with, they do not work well in the treatment of *all* schizophrenic symptoms. Schizophrenia is a complex disorder manifested by a number of symptoms that fall roughly into two categories, positive symptoms (e.g., hallucinations) and negative symptoms (e.g., impoverished thinking). Antischizophrenic drugs are effective in the treatment of positive symptoms but not negative symptoms (see Chapter 15 for details).

Second, if taken repeatedly or in very large doses, the drugs can produce motor tremors and the kind of postural rigidity and shuffling gait frequently observed in victims of Parkinson's disease. This is because dopamine synapses are located in both the limbic and extrapyramidal systems, and thus antischizophrenic drugs affect both emotional and motor behavior—two behaviors normally controlled by these systems.

Finally, and perhaps most devastating, prolonged use of antischizophrenic drugs may produce a motor disorder known as *tardive dyskinesia* (which literally means "late developing movement disorder"). The disorder is characterized by tics of the face and involuntary movements of the legs and arms and may persist even after the drug is discontinued. The cause of tardive dyskinesia is not entirely clear, but one of the more widely held theories is that prolonged use of antischizophrenic drugs causes an abnormal increase of dopamine receptors in the extrapyramidal (motor) system. You will recall (see Chapter 4) that one of the ways the synapse responds to a neurotransmitter deficit is to offset that deficit by increasing the number of receptors on the postsynaptic neuron. Antischizophrenic drugs, by blocking the action of dopamine, cause such a deficit, and the resulting increase in dopamine receptors in turn, at least theoretically, causes tardive dyskinesia (Baldessarini & Tarsy, 1980).

There is one bright spot in the antischizophrenic drug picture. A new class of drugs, known as *atypical antischizophrenic drugs* (the most notable of which is *clozapine*), has changed the motor side effects story dramatically (Kane et al., 1988). The drugs are known as atypical for two reasons: one, they are effective in the treatment of schizophrenia, but they do not produce motor side effects; two, they block dopamine receptors in the limbic (emotion) system but not in the extrapyramidal (motor) system. We will consider the action of these drugs in detail in Chapter 15.

Antidepressant Drugs

Antidepressant drugs are used to treat clinical depression. They fall into two groups: *MAO inhibitors* and *tricyclic antidepressants*. Both produce increases in monoamines, primarily serotonin and norepinephrine. MAO inhibitors, as you can see in Figure 5.14, inhibit the enzyme responsible for deactivating monoamines. Tricyclic antidepressants, also depicted in Figure 5.14, block the reuptake of monoamines that normally occurs after their release in the synapse.

Aided by the discovery of a new class of antidepressant drugs known as *selective serotonin reuptake inhibitors* (SSRIs)—including *fluoxetine*, also known as *Prozac*, and *sertraline*, also known as *Zoloft*—researchers have been able to identify which of the monoamines (serotonin or norepinephrine) may be linked to depression (Lader, 1988). The antidepressant drugs used before the discovery of fluoxetine and sertraline increase both serotonin and norepinephrine, making it impossible to tell whether restoring one or both neurotransmitters is involved in alleviating the symptoms. No such ambiguity, however, exists with fluoxetine and sertraline. They relieve depression, and increase only serotonin by blocking its reuptake, thus implicating a deficit in serotonin as one of the primary causes of depression. We shall return to depression and the action of antidepressant drugs in more detail in Chapter 15.

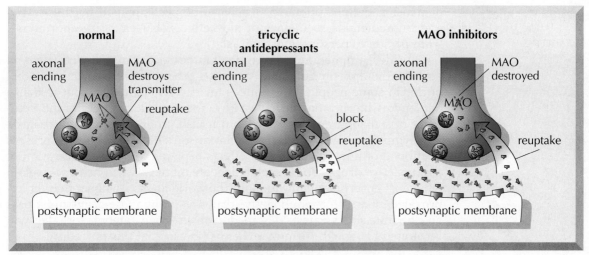

Figure 5.14 *Monoamine Oxidase (MAO) Inhibitors and Tricyclic Antidepressants in the Synapse*
MAO inhibitors increase monoamines by suppressing the action of MAO; tricyclic antidepressants increase monoamines by blocking their reuptake.

DRUGS AT WORK

Classifying drugs according to behavioral effects is convenient, but it should not lead you to think that a specific psychoactive drug has only a single behavioral effect. Far from it. Psychoactive drugs exercise very broad and often unpredictable effects on behavior. The reason: their impact on the nervous system is broad and often unpredictable.

This impression, of course, is not the one you gain from watching certain television advertisements for drugs. Some of these advertisements create the impression that psychoactive drugs work like guided missiles do, streaking through the brain and zeroing in on a specific area—the "sleep area," for instance—for which they are programmed. This is wishful thinking at best. Once a drug enters the brain, it is noticeably unselective in the path it travels, though there is a difference between a drug traveling unselectively and a drug acting indiscriminately in the brain.

The distinction is this: most psychoactive drugs affect the brain by acting on neurotransmitters, a given drug affecting a specific neurotransmitter in one way or another. But because a specific neurotransmitter, as we have seen, can act in a number of areas of the brain and be involved in the control of a variety of behaviors, it is logical that a drug that affects a neurotransmitter will also act in a number of areas of the brain and have multiple behavioral effects. This characteristic of psychoactive drugs—their multiple behavioral effects—presents a monumental problem for physicians prescribing the drugs for treatment of a behavioral disorder. The reason is simply that the therapeutic effects of a drug—its ability, for instance, to relieve anxiety or minimize the symptoms of depression or schizophrenia—can also be accompanied by unforeseen and unpredictable secondary or side effects that can vary enormously from person to person.

Consider amphetamines. Amphetamines are generally effective in curbing the appetite, but they can also produce schizophrenic-like behavior in some people. Morphine is an effective painkiller, but it is also addictive. Chlorpromazine, as we have mentioned, can help in the treatment of schizophrenic behavior, but it also produces tardive dyskinesia and symptoms similar to those of Parkinson's disease. This ever-present likelihood of unpredictable side effects explains why the prescription of psychoactive drugs can be such a delicate matter. It also helps to explain why most governments throughout the world are so stringent in their approval standards for psychoactive drugs and why these drugs must pass an elaborate series of tests designed to ensure their safety before they can be offered for sale to the public. Let us now look at this procedure.

Testing Drugs

The testing procedure for psychoactive drugs (and for most drugs in general) is known as screening. It is an elaborate process that begins with studies involving lower animals (mice, rats, rabbits, monkeys). Once the safety of the drug has been established in laboratory animals, testing is continued on humans, volunteer subjects at first (such testing usually takes place in prisons), and then, if the side effects prove to be mild, on patients in clinical situations.

The importance of screening should be obvious, yet it was not always recognized. Before governments instituted strict screening procedures, countless drugs reached the market before they had been carefully tested, sometimes with devastating consequences. Indeed, one of the more notorious of such cases involves none other than Sigmund Freud and the drug cocaine.

The Cocaine Affair

> "In my last severe depression," Sigmund Freud wrote to his then fiancee, Martha Bernays, in 1884, "I took cocaine again and a small dose lifted me to the heights in a wonderful fashion. I am just now busy collecting the literature for a song of praise to this magical substance." (Ray, 1974)

Freud first heard of cocaine during the 1880s, when reports from the German military indicated that the drug was useful in alleviating fatigue. Freud reasoned that if cocaine could alleviate fatigue, it might also be useful in treating depression. Because he himself was given to fits of depression, he served as his own guinea pig. He found that cocaine did in fact relieve his depression and at the same time renewed his energy. Convinced that he had made a medical breakthrough, he published a paper proclaiming the virtues of the drug.

Predictably enough, with Sigmund Freud's endorsement, cocaine became the rage of Europe. Physicians prescribed it routinely for depression, and people began to take it regularly to relieve everyday fatigue and tension. In time, however, it became increasingly clear that cocaine was not the panacea that Freud believed it to be. To the contrary, the drug proved to be habit-forming and, in many people, produced psychotic episodes.

It is logical to wonder why Freud himself was unaware of these effects. The reason apparently is that some people—a minority, to be sure—are able to take cocaine without experiencing negative symptoms, and Freud seems to have been one such person. Unfortunately, Freud's failure to recognize that what held true for him might not hold true for others, combined with his eagerness to deliver to the medical world a new wonder drug, resulted in a cocaine abuse problem during the 1880s that was every bit as severe as the one that afflicts American society today.

The lesson here is that screening is essential but doesn't necessarily eliminate side effects—it simply alerts us to them. Perhaps in the coming years we shall look back philosophically at the problem of side effects, for by then we may have developed drugs with *single* effects. But before this can happen, we will have to learn much more about drug action in general and about the particular mechanisms that underlie the two major side effects of psychoactive drugs that we will now consider: tolerance and addiction.

THE TOLERANCE FACTOR

Among the many side effects of psychoactive drugs, few are more basic and more significant than the manner in which the body responds to a drug taken over a long period of time. What happens, in short, is that the drug loses its effectiveness, an effect known as *tolerance*. Tolerance explains why people who use a given psychoactive drug over an extended period need increasingly higher doses of the drug to obtain the behavioral effect produced by the original dose.

Tolerance, of course, is not limited to psychoactive drugs. Its effect can also be seen in certain types of nonpsychoactive drugs, such as allergy medications and anti-inflammatories. As you probably know, our bodies become increasingly resistant to the therapeutic effects of certain medications when these medications are taken repeatedly, which explains why most physicians like to vary the medicines they prescribe to people with chronic illnesses.

Generally speaking, though, the tolerance that develops to nonpsychoactive drugs is governed by a different mechanism than the tolerance that develops to psychoactive drugs. The main reason tolerance occurs with many nonpsychoactive drugs is that the more frequently these drugs are taken the more actively the body acts either to eliminate them from the system before they reach the target sites or to make it more difficult for the drugs to cross the membranes of the target sites. This type of tolerance is known as *drug disposition* or *metabolic tolerance*. Extended use of psychoactive drugs, by contrast, doesn't appear in most cases to impede the ability of these drugs to reach their target sites. What happens instead is something known as *cellular tolerance*: the target sites become increasingly less responsive to the physiological action of the drugs.

How do we explain tolerance to psychoactive drugs—the fact that as the level of psychoactive drugs in the brain is on the rise, the neural and behavioral reactions begin to decline. Several theories have been proposed with one school of thought focusing on the synapse (Siegel, 1983; Poulos & Cappell, 1991) and another school focusing on nonsynaptic factors (Baker & Tiffany, 1985). The more commonly accepted of the two theories involves the synapse, but even here there are differences in emphasis and approach. Some researchers who have implicated the synapse as a key factor in tolerance propose a relatively simple cause-and-effect pattern, with increased levels of the drug promoting an antagonistic—that is, a compensatory—response in the synapse that reduces the drug's effect. Other researchers, though, maintain that the synaptic compensatory response, while an important factor in tolerance, is itself the product (to some extent at least) of behavioral factors in addition to the drug itself (Poulos & Cappell, 1991). In either case, the basic principle governing the synaptic compensatory response is essentially the same: as the drug levels increase, the synapse reacts to offset the effects of the increase. Let us now take a closer look at the synaptic defense.

The Synapse and Tolerance

As you will recall from Chapter 4, synapses have an optimal state of activity. They maintain this state by regulating either their sensitivity (i.e., their receptors) or the production of neurotransmitters. The optimal state is upset by drugs; synapses respond by defending it. It usually takes repeated administration of the drug to enlist this defense, at which point something of a tug-of-war ensues. The defense draws synaptic activity back to normal, meeting resistance from the activity produced by the drug. The defense is ultimately successful, which is to say that with repeated administration of the drug, the synaptic activity returns to normal, even though the drug is in the system.

This, in short, is what we mean by drug tolerance. The drug is present in the brain but, because of the synaptic defense, the effect on the brain and the behavior that the drug normally produces is not.

To be sure, there are valid elements in this explanation. We know today, though, that the picture is far more complex and, from a psychological point of view, even more interesting. Recent data indicate that tolerance is not simply the result of repeated administration of a drug. Equally important is the interval between administrations, commonly referred to as the *interdrug interval*. Important, too, curiously enough, is the environment in which the drug is taken.

Interdrug Interval and Environment: A Closer Look
Evidence from lower-animal research indicates that drugs such as morphine administered repeatedly at short intervals (once every few hours,

for instance) will invariably produce tolerance, regardless of where the drug is taken. As the interval lengthens, however, tolerance still occurs but a new factor assumes importance: the environment (Kesner & Baker, 1981). For example, animals made tolerant to morphine in a distinctive environment (i.e., in an environment that contains a distinctive sound or light or odor) will continue to show tolerance as long as the morphine is administered in that same distinctive environment. When the environment is changed, however, the animals do *not* show tolerance, or if they do it is significantly weaker (Siegel, 1976).

The environmental effect appears to hold for humans as well. Evidence indicates that heroin addicts who develop tolerance to the drug (and thus must take more and more of it to experience the original high) face the greatest risk of overdosing if they take the drug in a *new* environment—one in which they have never taken it before. An overdose occurs, it now seems, because addicts take a dose that is high enough to overcome tolerance in the familiar environment but is too high for the unfamiliar environment in which tolerance is weak or absent (Siegel et al., 1982; Siegel, 1983).

Interval, Environment, and Tolerance: An Explanation

Several theories have been proposed to explain the impact that the interdrug interval and the environment have on tolerance (Baker & Tiffany, 1985; Siegel, 1983). The details of the theories vary, but most agree on one point: to understand tolerance and its relationship to the interdrug interval and to the environment, we must understand the relationship between tolerance and the response produced by the synaptic defense (Siegel, 1983; Poulos & Cappell, 1991).

The response, known as the *compensatory response*, is always opposite the effect of the drug. The compensatory response to amphetamine (a stimulant), for instance, is a depression of both physical functions and mental processes. The compensatory response to barbiturates (a depressant) is just the opposite: a heightening of physical functions and mental processes. And it is the compensatory response—opposing and offsetting the drug effect—that, at least theoretically, lies at the root of drug tolerance and its relation to the interdrug interval and the environment (Poulos & Cappell, 1991).

The assumptions are as follows:

1. The key factor in tolerance is the compensatory response. When the response is present, tolerance is produced. When the response is absent, tolerance is lost.
2. The compensatory response has a limited life span. It persists if the interval between injections is brief. It wears off if the interval between injections is long.
3. Even if it has worn off, however, the compensatory response can be reinstated by environmental cues via a learning process.

Tolerance and the Learning Process: A Closer Look

The notion that the environment can produce tolerance via a learning process might seem odd at first, but the principle here is no different from the principle at the root of classical conditioning, the basic learning phenomenon you first encountered in introductory psychology. Just as Pavlov found that animals can learn to salivate in anticipation of food, so can animals being administered drugs "learn" a compensatory response in anticipation of a drug. Because the animals learn to anticipate receiving the drug in a specific environment, they learn to make the compensatory response in that same specific environment. And because the compensatory response is opposite the drug effect, tolerance is produced.

Such, then, is the general picture of drug tolerance. There are two types of drug tolerance, each related to a different interdrug interval and each, at least theoretically, related to a different compensatory response. The type of tolerance that occurs with short interdrug intervals, is produced by a compensatory response that lingers from one drug administration to the next, and does not depend on the environment is known as *nonassociative* or *physiological tolerance*. The type of tolerance that occurs with long interdrug intervals and is produced by a compensatory response that is conditioned to the environment is known as *environmental* or *associative tolerance*.

Curiously the same compensatory response that has been used to account for tolerance has been used to account for addiction. Let us take a closer look.

ADDICTION

> Remember when you had a case of the 24-hour virus. You're coming out of both ends—vomiting and diarrhea—and every joint in your body hurts. You wish that you could die but feel too badly to do anything about it. Take that, double and spread it over four to five days. That's cold turkey. (Ray, 1974)

This description of misery comes from a former heroin addict who went "cold turkey," that is, "kicked" his habit on his own. The agony he experienced is not unusual. It is in fact the agony that many drug addicts suffer when the drugs to which they are addicted are denied them for any length of time. These symptoms are real, not imagined. For once an addiction is established, the withdrawal procedure inflicts enormous punishment on the body, so much that addicts going through withdrawal have to be watched very carefully to prevent them from attempting suicide.

But what is addiction? How and why does it occur? And why has it become such an enormous problem throughout the world? The answers to these questions do not lie solely within the nervous system, for addiction has social and psychological dimensions as well. We know that environmental influences—stress, for instance—can often lead someone to addiction. And it appears that personality, too, is an important factor. We do not intend to delve into the social and personality aspects of addiction at any length, but we would like you to bear in mind that even if we fully understood the inordinately complex neurochemical processes that underlie addiction, we would still be a long way from solving the problem.

Addiction Defined

Addiction can best be defined as extreme dependence. We use the word routinely in everyday language to define an unusually strong desire or need for a particular food or activity. We speak of someone being addicted to music, to tennis, or to chocolate. When we talk about drugs, however, the word "addiction" becomes more than a figure of speech. Addiction is a physiological reaction; people who become addicted to a drug and are denied it for any length of time experience the same kind of violent changes they would experience if they were denied food or water for a prolonged period.

How Addiction Starts

Some people become drug addicts as the result of drugs they take when they are suffering from a severe injury or illness. More frequently, though, an addiction develops not because of illness but because of choice. Most addictive drugs produce some form of pleasure, providing a quick and easy escape from the tensions and stresses of everyday life. This pleasure becomes a powerful inducement to repeat the experience, but it also is often accompanied by another effect: physical dependence. Eventually, physical dependence as well as pleasure becomes the compelling motivation for staying on the drug.

Physical Dependence

Pleasure is one thing; physical dependence is another, and in some ways it is more difficult to understand. We usually measure dependence, as we have already established, by the severity of withdrawal behavior. The more severe the symptoms, presumably, the more severe the dependence. Withdrawal behavior, however, is highly complex. It involves not only physical symptoms—vomiting, sweating, diarrhea, changes in blood pressure—but psychological stress as well: severe depression or manic behavior, for instance. Furthermore, the severity of both categories of symptoms—physical and psychological—vary enormously from drug to drug and from individual to individual. And there is evidence to suggest, incredible though it may seem, that withdrawal, like tolerance, can also be strongly influenced by the environment. Animal studies have shown, for instance, that everything else being equal, when an animal undergoing withdrawal (i.e., is denied a drug to which it has become addicted) is placed in the environment in which the drug was originally administered, the withdrawal symptoms are more severe than they are when the animal goes through withdrawal in an unfamiliar environment (Hinson, Poulos, & Cappell, 1982). The same may hold for humans. Addicts who, after rehabilitation, return to the environment in which they are used to taking the drug are, at least in some cases, more likely to relapse than addicts who do not return to the environment (Siegel, 1983).

The complexity of withdrawal notwithstanding, we can make one important generalization about withdrawal symptoms: withdrawal produces physical and psychological effects that are the opposite of the effects produced by the addictive drug (Jaffe, 1985). When someone is withdrawing from a stimulant, for instance, the result is a depression in both physical functions and mental processes. But when a person is withdrawing from a depressant, the result is the opposite: a heightening of physical function and mental processes. Let us see if we can explain these opposing patterns in physiological terms.

The Compensatory Response Theory of Addiction

What is the physiological basis of a dependence so great that denial produces severe withdrawal symptoms? We cannot answer this question with certainty, but one theory seems to be particularly plausible (Siegel, 1983; Poulos & Cappell, 1991). The key feature of the theory is the compensatory response, the same compensatory response that accounts for tolerance but with one crucial difference: tolerance is produced when the compensatory response is present in combination with the drug; withdrawal is produced when the drug wears off and the compensatory response is present *alone*, in the absence of the drug.

The compensatory response explanation of withdrawal is compelling. It accounts for why withdrawal symptoms are always opposite the drug effect; the compensatory response is always opposite the drug effect. And it also accounts for why withdrawal, like tolerance, appears to be under the control of the environment; the compensatory response is under the control of (i.e., is conditioned) to the environment. For a better idea of how the compensatory response can produce withdrawal symptoms, let us look closely at how the body may react to one drug in particular—amphetamine.

Amphetamine

Amphetamine, a stimulant, increases both neural activity in the brain and cellular activity throughout the rest of the body, particularly the heart rate and blood pressure. In response to this increased activity, the brain and body initiate compensatory responses to *decrease* activity. Neural and cellular activity return to normal, even though the drug remains in the system and continues to have a stimulating effect.

The question then is, why, if normal activity is restored in the brain and the body, are there withdrawal symptoms? The answer provided by the compensatory response theory depicts the process as a tug-of-war in which one side (the drug) suddenly lets go of the rope. Presumably the wearing off of the stimulating effects of amphetamine, coupled with the continued depressing effect of the compensatory responses, result in what amphetamine users call "crashing" or "coming down." Eventually, of course, these withdrawal symptoms end, once the body's and brain's defenses, seeking to restore the internal environment to normal, reverse their action and increase neural and cellular activity until their levels return to normal.

Fine-Tuning the Theory

Withdrawal behavior, as we've just seen, is complex. It produces not only physical symptoms—vomiting, sweating—but psychological stress as well, including severe depression or manic behavior. In either event the presumption is that a compensatory response is at work—in the body it accounts for the physical symptoms, in the brain it accounts for the psychological symptoms.

Recent evidence indicates that the discomfort produced by the psychological symptoms may be a more important factor than the physical symptoms. Cocaine, for example, a highly addictive drug, produces powerful psychological withdrawal (intense craving for pleasure) but only minimal physical withdrawal (Gawin, 1991). And alcohol and opiates retain their addictive powers even after physical withdrawal has been alleviated.

What this means is that if we are to understand addiction—what causes it and how to treat it—we must understand not only the cellular changes in the body that underlie physical withdrawal but, perhaps more importantly, the neural changes in the brain that underlie psychological withdrawal. Much current research is focusing on this mechanism.

TREATING THE ADDICT

Should drug addiction be treated as an illness or as a crime? Few medical questions in the past 20 years have produced more controversy, one reason being that a large percentage of the crimes committed in urban areas are committed by addicts seeking money to support their habits. Historically, addicts in the United States have been sent to prison, but prison rehabilitation of drug addicts has not been notably successful. Approximately 90 percent of the addicts sent to prison return to their habits within 6 months after their release.

Given these statistics, the trend today is to view addiction less as a crime than as a medical and social problem. Two general medical approaches have developed over the past 20 years. One of them, typified by such organizations as Phoenix House, attempts to rehabilitate addicts by placing them in a homelike environment, surrounded by other addicts and supervised, in large part, by former addicts. Addicts take part in individual and group counseling sessions almost daily, and treatment can last anywhere from 6 months to 2 years. The goal of this therapeutic approach is to teach the addict how to cope with life without the help of drugs.

A second approach currently being used to treat heroin addicts relies on the drug *methadone*. Methadone is also addictive, but it appears to block the euphoric effects of opiates. It stops the desire for opiates and at the same time prevents the stress that normally accompanies heroin withdrawal.

No one can say at this time which treatment is more effective in dealing with the hard-core addict. Opponents of the methadone approach argue that the substitution of one addiction for another does not really solve the underlying problem. Opponents of the Phoenix House approach (and many offshoots of Phoenix House are now operating in the United States) argue that the programs do not adequately prepare addicts for life outside the therapeutic community.

Suffice it to say that there is logic on both sides of this issue and that neither approach represents a definitive answer to the addiction problem. Programs for addicts in the future will presumably combine a short-term chemical approach to treat the physiological addiction and a longer-term social therapeutic approach to keep addicts from returning to their former habits.

DIETARY CONTROL: AN ALTERNATIVE TO DRUG THERAPY

Is it possible that nutrients in many of the foods we eat could be substituted for drugs to alter neurotransmitters without producing the unwanted side effects of drugs? Indeed it is, and this possibility has led to some promising research, much of it being done by Richard Wurtman and his colleagues at MIT, who are examining the relationship between certain nutrients in our everyday diets and the activity of neurotransmitters in the brain (Wurtman, 1982).

Perhaps the best known and most widely studied example of this relationship concerns the neurotransmitter serotonin and the amino acid *tryptophan*. Serotonin, as you will recall, is produced from tryptophan, which is found in such protein-rich foods as meat, chicken, and fish. There is good evidence to show that in laboratory animals at least, changes in tryptophan in the diet can change serotonin levels in the brain and thus affect behaviors normally associated with serotonin, such as sleep and sensitivity to pain. Similar relationships have been reported in laboratory animals between choline (a nutrient found in egg yolks and liver) and acetylcholine, and between tyrosine (an amino acid) and norepinephrine.

The implications of these findings for human behavior have yet to be established, but the results of studies involving humans have been encouraging. Tryptophan, for instance, has been found to induce sleep in mildly insomniac patients and also to relieve pain in some chronic pain sufferers. Choline, in the meantime, has shown promise in the treatment of memory disorders associated with old age, and tyrosine has been used successfully to treat mental depression (Kolata, 1982).

These results must be viewed with caution, however. The data are heartening, but the findings are highly variable, and a number of problems need to be resolved before we can expect dietary therapies to become common practice in the treatment of behavioral disorders. One of the problems with most of the human studies to date—although it is more an experimental than a clinical problem—is that they lack biochemical validity. Although behavioral effects have been observed after certain nutritive substances have been administered, few if any of the human studies have been able to corroborate this relationship biochemically. If we are to establish definitive relationships between diet and neurotransmitters, we must have studies that not only observe the behavioral changes produced by the diet but also tie these changes to measurable changes in blood and brain chemistry. And even when we are able biochemically to confirm a behavioral relationship between nutrients and neurotransmitters, certain practical matters still need to be worked out before we can begin, for instance, to treat insomniacs with foods rich in tryptophan or older people who have memory disorders with foods rich in choline. To see how complex and delicate this whole matter is, let us consider the relationship between the amino acid tryptophan and serotonin.

Tryptophan, as we have said, is found in protein, but it is the consumption of carbohydrates (sweets, bread, and rice) and not protein that increases the level of tryptophan in the brain. The reason is that when protein is eaten alone, tryptophan competes with five other amino acids for attachment to a carrier molecule that transports the amino acids from the blood to the brain. And because there is less tryptophan in most proteins than other amino acids, less tryptophan is carried into the brain. If protein is eaten along with carbohydrates, however, the picture changes. Carbohydrates trigger the release of insulin, and, in doing so, cause all the amino acids in the blood to be taken up by body tissue—all, that is, except tryptophan. Now, with fewer amino acids to compete for attachment to the carrier molecule, more tryptophan reaches the brain, producing an increase in serotonin levels (Wurtman, 1982).

LOOKING AHEAD

In introducing you to the structure and function of the nervous system, we have examined how the neural impulse is produced and controlled by the movement of ions across the neural membrane and by the movement of chemical substances (neurotransmitters) across the synapse. We have examined how this function can be controlled by drugs and perhaps by nutrients. But if the neural impulse is the means by which information is communicated from one part of the body to another, what initiates the neural impulse and how does it act to produce behavior? In the following five chapters, we shall answer these questions by looking at the structure and function of the other cellular components of behavior—receptors and muscles.

SUMMARY

1. *Neurotransmitters in brief.* Neurotransmitters are chemicals in the nervous system that underlie the capacity of neurons to trigger neural impulses and to transmit information from one part of the body to another. All neurotransmitters work in basically the same way. They are produced in either the cell body or the axonal endings; they are released by the axonal endings; they act by binding to receptors and they are then cleared. All neurotransmitters, moreover, can affect behavior in two broad ways: how they operate (whether they excite or inhibit) and where in the brain they act. Of the roughly 40 chemical substances that have been identified as neurotransmitters, four—acetylcholine, norepinephrine, serotonin, and dopamine—have been studied extensively.

2. *Acetylcholine.* Acetylcholine, derived from acetyl coenzyme A and choline, operates in both the peripheral nervous system and the brain, where it influences synaptic activity through its ability to bind to post-synaptic receptors known as cholinergic receptors. In the peripheral nervous system acetylcholine is released by motor nerves and is involved in the control of skeletal and smooth (including heart) muscle. In the brain acetylcholine is produced primarily in two areas, the septal area and the nucleus basalis. From these areas axons project to the cortex and the limbic system, including the hippocampus and amygdala, where they are involved in the control of different behaviors—thinking in the cortex, memory in the hippocampus, and emotion in the amygdala.

3. *Monoamines.* The monoamines, so called because their chemical structure contains a single (mono) amino acid, include norepinephrine, serotonin, and dopamine. Monoamines act via a second-messenger system, which accounts for their long-lasting effect on the synapse and the role they play in long-term behaviors, such as emotion and memory. Most of what we know about their location in the nervous system comes from a biochemical assay procedure called fluorescent microscopy, based on the fact that brain areas containing monoamines take on different colors when they are treated chemically and viewed under a fluorescent microscope.

4. *Norepinephrine in the peripheral nervous system.* In the peripheral nervous system, norepinephrine is released by the sympathetic motor nerves—usually under stress—and is involved in the control of smooth muscles and glands, through its ability to interact with specific receptor sites on the muscles, so-called adrenergic receptors. Whether it excites or inhibits behavior depends upon the type of receptor—alpha or beta—with which it interacts. When norepinephrine binds to alpha receptors, located in blood vessels, it excites. When norepinephrine binds to beta receptors, found in the heart, intestines, and lungs it has a mixed effect; it excites beta 1 receptors in the heart and it inhibits beta 2 receptors in the intestines and lungs.

5. *Norepinephrine and serotonin in the brain.* The distribution pattern of norepinephrine and serotonin in the brain is similar. Each neurotransmitter is produced in relatively few areas, each neurotransmitter acts in a number of areas of the brain, and thus each neurotransmitter effects a multitude of behaviors including motivation, emotion, and sleep. Norepinephrine and serotonin share another feature; deficits of either neurotransmitter are thought to be a possible cause of clinical depression.

6. *Dopamine.* Dopamine production is confined primarily to three areas of the brain: the substantia nigra, the ventral tegmental area, and the hypothalamus. As with norepinephrine and serotonin, abnormal levels of dopamine in the brain can have profound behavioral effects, such as producing Parkinson's disease. Dopamine has also drawn a great deal of attention from researchers seeking to identify the chemical basis of schizophrenia. Certain drugs that block the action of dopamine produce noticeable improvement in the behavior of schizophrenics, leading some researchers to theorize that an abnormally high level of dopamine may be the key agent in schizophrenia.

7. *Other neurotransmitters.* Our awareness of the number of neurotransmitters thought to exist in the brain has grown dramatically in recent years. There are two general categories of these newly discovered neurotransmitters: amino acids and neuropeptides. Amino acids include two neurotransmitters—glutamate and aspartate—which may be the chief excitatory transmitters in the brain. This group also contains GABA (gamma aminobutyric acid) and glycine, two major inhibitory transmitters. Neuropeptides consist of short chains of amino acids. The group includes two transmitters, enkephalins and endorphins, whose action in the limbic system has led to studies that have linked them to behaviors as varied as pleasure, suppression of pain, drug addiction, and the formation of long-term memory.

8. *Neurotransmitters and behavior.* Even though our knowledge of individual neurotransmitters is still limited, the overall role of neurotransmitters in controlling behavior is reasonably well understood. Neurotransmitters permit one signal—the neural impulse—to control an enormous variety of behaviors. Were it not for this chemical code, the very nature of the nervous system, with its indescribably complex interconnections, would produce behavioral chaos.

9. *Psychoactive drugs.* Drugs that affect behavior are known as psychoactive drugs, and based on their behavioral effects they are usually divided into five categories: depressants, stimulants, opiates, psychedelics, and antipsychotics. Different though the behavioral effects of the drugs in each category may be, their effect on neurotransmitter activity is limited to two possibilities: they either enhance or impede synaptic activity.

10. *Depressants.* Depressants are substances that decrease behavioral activity. Alcohol, barbiturates, and benzodiazepines fall into this category. In moderate amounts, depressants can have beneficial effects: they relieve anxiety, help people relax, and help people sleep. On the other hand, the overuse of depressants—alcohol in particular—has become a monumental problem throughout the world. Although the issue is far from settled, there is evidence to suggest that genetic factors may predispose some people to alcohol abuse.

11. *How depressants work.* Current evidence suggests that the three depressants—alcohol, barbiturates, and benzodiazepines—work essentially the same way, enhancing the action of GABA, an inhibitory neurotransmitter. Recent evidence also suggests that the three depressants enhance the binding properties of GABA receptors by binding to their own receptors.

12. *Stimulants.* Stimulants, such as amphetamines and cocaine, increase behavioral activity. Both increase the amount of norepinephrine and dopamine in the synapse. Amphetamines do so by prodding the transmitters from their storage sites and then keeping them from returning. Cocaine does so simply by keeping the transmitters from returning.

13. *Opiates.* The opiate category of psychoactive drugs includes all drugs that have the capacity to relieve pain. Most opiates, however, also produce euphoria and are highly addictive. Morphine, codeine, and heroin are in this category. Opiates produce their behavioral effects by mimicking the action of endorphins and enkephalins, neurotransmitters found in the spinal cord, limbic system, and cortex.

14. *Psychedelics.* The psychedelic drugs include those that alter states of consciousness. Lysergic acid diethylamide (LSD), mescaline, and marijuana fall into this category. The behavioral effects of LSD and mescaline include visual hallucinations and disorientation in time and space. Marijuana in low doses produces feelings of euphoria and well-being but in large doses can cause paranoia and hallucinations.

15. *Antipsychotics.* Antipsychotics are drugs that have proved effective in the treatment of psychotic illnesses, such as schizophrenia and depression. Thus antipsychotic drugs fall into two broad categories: antischizophrenic drugs and antidepressant drugs. Antischizophrenic drugs are highly effective in treating schizophrenia, they work by blocking the action of dopamine, but they are not without their limitations and side effects. Antidepressant drugs, as the term implies, are used in the treatment of clinical depression. They, too, fall into two groups: monoamine inhibitors and tricyclic antidepressants. The newest class of antidepressant includes fluoxetine (better known as Prozac) and operates by blocking the reuptake of serotonin, thereby increasing serotonin levels.

16. *Drugs at work.* Because a specific neurotransmitter can act in a number of different areas in the brain and be involved in the control of a variety of behaviors, the study of psychoactive drugs has presented an ongoing challenge for researchers and clinicians. The problem, in brief, is that the therapeutic benefits of a drug can often be offset by unforeseen and unpredictable side effects. It is for this reason that psychoactive drugs, before they are approved, must undergo a thorough screening process.

17. *The tolerance factor.* Taken repeatedly, many drugs gradually lose their effectiveness. The body's response to repeated intake of these drugs is known as tolerance. The body builds up tolerance for the drug in two ways: first, in the case of nonpsychoactive drugs such as noninflammatories, the body acts either to eliminate the drugs before they reach the target sites or to make it more difficult for the drugs to cross the membranes of the target sites; this is known as dispositional or metabolic tolerance. Second, in the case of psychoactive drugs such as morphine, the drug reaches the target sites but the target sites themselves become increasingly less responsive to the drug. This is known as cellular tolerance.

18. *Cellular tolerance.* Cellular tolerance appears to be a function of how synapses respond to repeated exposure to a drug. When the optimal state of a synapse is upset by drugs, synapses respond in a compensatory fashion, altering their activity and restoring the optimal state. So it is that increasingly larger dosages of a drug are needed to supersede the synaptic compensatory responses, and the result is cellular tolerance.

19. *Interval and the environment as tolerance factors.* Tolerance can be affected by two factors: the interval between the administration of a drug and the environment in which the drug is taken. With short interdrug intervals tolerance occurs regardless of the environment. With long interdrug intervals tolerance is linked to the environment. The impact of the environment on tolerance has been demonstrated in studies in which animals made tolerant to morphine in a distinctive environment show tolerance as long as the morphine is administered in that environment, but do not show tolerance when the environment is changed. This finding would help to explain why heroin addicts who develop tolerance for the drug face the greatest risk of overdosing when they take the drug in a different environment. Several theories have been advanced to explain the impact that the environment has on tolerance, but the most commonly accepted focus on the synaptic compensatory response. It appears that animals being administered drugs learn to make a compensatory response to the environment (quite apart from the drug) and that when the environment is changed the compensatory response is abolished and so is tolerance.

20. *The nature of addiction.* Addiction is best defined as extreme dependence, and it is usually measured in terms of the symptoms that arise when the person is either denied or voluntarily chooses to reject the substance to which he or she is addicted. Withdrawal behavior among addicts has both physical and psychological ramifications, with symptoms varying greatly according to the individual and the drug. One of the more compelling theories advanced so far to explain the physiology of addiction has focused on the compensatory response. According to this theory, withdrawal symptoms are the result of the compensatory response occurring in the *absence* of the drug. Recent evidence indicates that it is the discomfort produced by the psychological symptoms and not the physical symptoms that may be the more important factor.

21. *Treating addicts.* The trend today is to treat drug addiction as an illness rather than as a crime. Treatment has taken two forms: behavioral therapy, directed at teaching addicts to cope with their environment, and drug therapy, to ease the trauma that accompanies withdrawal of the drug.

22. *Diet and drug therapy.* The possibility that nutrients in many of the foods we eat could alter transmitters without producing the unwanted side effects of drugs has led to some promising research, particularly on the relationship between the amino acid tryptophan and serotonin. Both animal and human studies have shown that tryptophan in the diet can change serotonin levels in the brain and thus affect behaviors normally associated with serotonin, such as sleep and sensitivity to pain.

KEY TERMS

acetylcholine
acetylcholinesterase
addiction
adrenergic receptors
adrenocorticotropic hormone
  (ACTH)
agonists
alcohol
alpha receptors
Alzheimer's disease
amphetamine
anandamide
angiotensin
antagonists
antianxiety drugs
antiobsessional drugs
antischizophrenic drugs
aspartate
associative tolerance
atypical antischizophrenic
drugs
barbiturates
basal ganglia
benzodiazepines
benzotropine
beta receptors
butyrophenones
caffeine
catechol-O-methyltransferase
  (COMT)
cellular tolerance
chlomipramine

chlorpromazine
cholecystokinin
choline acetyltransferase
cholinergic receptors
clozapine
cocaine
cold turkey
curare
Dale's law
delta-9-tetrahydrocannabinol
  (THC)
depressants
dopamine
endorphins
enkephalins
environmental tolerance
euphoria
fetal alcohol syndrome
fluorescent microscopy
fluoxetine
gamma aminobutyric acid
  (GABA)
glaucoma
glutamate
glycine
Huntington's disease
interdrug interval
L-dopa
lysergic acid diethylamide (LSD)
marijuana
mescaline
metabolic tolerance

methadone
monoamine oxidase (MAO)
monoamines
muscarinic receptors
neuropeptides
nicotine
nicotinic receptors
nonassociative tolerance
norepinephrine
nucleus basalis
obsessive-compulsive disorder
opiates
opponent responses
Parkinson's disease
phenothiazines
physiological tolerance
Prozac
psychedelics

psychoactive drugs
psychopharmacology
raphe nuclei
schizophrenia
screening
septal area
serotonin
stimulants
strychnine
substance P
substantia nigra
synaptic compensatory response
synaptic defense
tardive dyskinesia
tolerance
tryptophan
vasopressin
ventral tegmental area

SUGGESTED READINGS

Cooper, J. R., Bloom, F. E., & Roth, R. H. *The Biochemical Basis of Neuropharmacology*, 6th ed. New York: Oxford University Press, 1991.

Kandel, E. R., Schwartz, J. H., & Jessell, T. M. *Principles of Neural Science*, 3rd ed. New York: Elsevier, 1991.

Julien, R. M. *A Primer of Drug Action: A Concise, Nontechnical Guide to the Actions, Uses, and Side Effects of Psychoactive Drugs*, 6th ed. New York: W. H. Freeman, 1992.

Lickey, M. E. & Gordon, B. *Medicine and Mental Illness: The Use of Drugs in Psychiatry*. New York: W. H. Freeman, 1991.

SENSORY PROCESSING

INTRODUCTION

The world around us is a kaleidoscope of sensory stimuli—sights, sounds, smells, tastes, and things we can touch—and most of us are able to interact with this world on a variety of sensory levels. The fact that we are able to interact with the environment on so many different levels has obvious implications for our ability to survive, and you can begin to appreciate these implications by imagining what your day-to-day life would be like if for some reason you lost all or even some of your ability to see, to hear, to taste, to smell, or to feel objects around you.

Much less obvious than the importance of sensory processes is how the brain manages them all. What needs to happen, in other words, if you are to distinguish red from green, the trill of a flute from the thump of a tuba, the smell of fire from the smell of perfume, the taste of an apple from the taste of spinach, the smooth feel of silk from the scratchy feel of sandpaper?

We will be seeking answers to these basic questions in the three chapters that follow. Our goal in this chapter, however, is to give you an overview of sensory processing in general—of those structures and mechanisms that are at work whenever we are sensing and processing any form of sensory input—regardless of its source. We will be looking initially at a structure known as the receptor and at a process known as transduction. Later in the chapter, we'll look at a number of other sensory processes—attention and arousal, for instance—shared by all sensory systems.

TRANSDUCTION AND RECEPTORS: AN OVERVIEW

All sensory processes involve *transduction*—a term that can be roughly defined as any process that translates one form of energy into another. A simple example of transduction is an electric-eye door, which transduces (converts) your shadow across a light beam into movement of the door.

The specific type of transduction that concerns us in physiological psychology revolves around a cellular structure known as the receptor. A *receptor* transduces signals from the environment into a signal (the neural impulse) that is routed to the brain and produces the sensations we ultimately experience. A word of caution: while it is true that receptors play an indispensable role in converting environmental stimuli into neural impulses, that role is *indirect*. Receptors convert environmental stimuli into electrochemical signals, known as *generator potentials*, and it is the generator potentials that produce the neural impulse. Let us look at receptors, first at what they look like and then at how they work.

Receptors

Given the myriad stimuli to which humans are receptive, it should come as no surprise to you that we possess a variety of receptors, some of which are shown in Figure 6.1. As this figure indicates, some receptors (in the skin and muscles) are nothing more than dendritic endings of sensory nerves. Others (in the eyes and ears, for instance) are distinct cells separated from sensory nerves by synapses. No matter what their form, however, all receptors share certain features.

To begin with, every receptor has a membrane that is surrounded by ions. The presence of such a membrane and ions creates a *resting potential* in the receptor in much the same way that the presence of a membrane and ions creates a resting potential in the neuron. The resting potential enables the receptor to convert (i.e., transduce) a stimulus into an electrochemical signal, the generator potential. The receptor membrane is extremely sensitive, so sensitive that in some receptors (e.g., auditory receptors), it can convert movement as small as the diameter of a single hydrogen atom into a generator potential.

Figure 6.1   *Sensory Receptors*
Sensory receptors fall into two groups: those that are structural extensions of sensory neurons and those that are separated from and form synapses with sensory neurons. The arrows indicate where the neural impulse is initiated, either in the axon that extends from the receptor itself (in the case of smell, skin senses, and muscles) or in the sensory neuron with which the receptor forms a synapse (in the case of audition, vision, and taste). In vision, there are two sensory neurons, and the impulse is initiated in the second neuron.

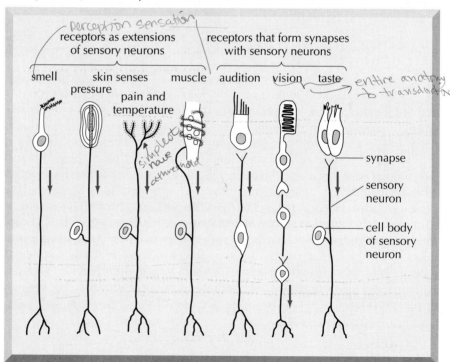

Transduction

All receptors carry out the transduction process in essentially the same way, regardless of the stimuli to which they are sensitive. What happens, in brief, is that environmental stimuli change the permeability of the cell membrane, which triggers the flow of sodium ions into the cell and causes the membrane to *depolarize*. The resulting electrochemical signal—the generator potential—travels from the receptor to the sensory neuron, where it produces the neural impulse. If this sounds familiar to you, it should. We saw a similar process in the synapse (see Chapter 4), except that in the synapse a neurotransmitter, not an environmental stimulus, triggers the electrochemical signal, and in the synapse, the electrochemical signal is called an excitatory postsynaptic potential, not a generator potential.

In any event, every receptor has the capacity to transduce a stimulus into a generator potential. The question then is, What exactly determines the selectivity of receptors? Why, for example, do receptors in the ear transduce sound, and why are receptors in our skin sensitive to touch? The answer to these questions lies chiefly in the membrane of each receptor cell, specifically in the differences between the membrane of one receptor and that of another. As you will soon see, auditory receptor cells have membranes uniquely sensitive to sound, and receptor cells in the skin have membranes uniquely sensitive to pressure.

With the exception of the eye, which we will cover in Chapter 7, the same principle holds true for all receptor cells in the body that interact with the environment: those in your nose, on your tongue, on the tips of your fingers. The membrane of each type of receptor is sensitive to a *specific type* of environmental stimulus. Different types of environmental stimuli (sound, touch, etc.) embody different forms of energy, and each form of energy, if it is to be detected, must have the capacity to change the receptor membrane's permeability and in the process to trigger the flow of sodium ions.

In summary, then, transduction is rooted in the relationship between the energy embodied in the environmental stimulus and the changes in the permeability of the receptor membrane—changes that trigger the flow of sodium ions across the membrane and in doing so convert the resting potential into the generator potential.

From Generator Potential to Action Potential

It is worth emphasizing that the generator potential we are discussing here is *not* the same thing as the action potential (the neural impulse) we described in Chapter 4. The generator potential does not "fire" in the sense that an action potential fires. It simply *produces* the action potential, and it does so in much the same way that the excitatory postsynaptic potential does (see Chapter 4).

To produce an action potential, the generator potential must satisfy two conditions: first, it must spread to the site of impulse initiation, the axon of the sensory neuron; second, it must produce enough depolarization to reach threshold—that is, it must depolarize the axon of the sensory neuron in order to fire the all-or-none action potential that travels to the brain.

The generator potential, like the excitatory postsynaptic potential, is a graded, decremental potential. Its magnitude depends directly on the intensity of the stimulus, and its strength diminishes as it travels to the axon of the sensory neuron. This is why a single generator potential is rarely sufficient to produce the action potential. Instead, it takes multiple generator potentials, all below threshold, to work collectively (i.e., to summate) in order to exceed threshold. Once the generator potential passes threshold, however, it elicits not only the action potential but also the "train" of action potentials depicted in Figure 6.2. The greater the magnitude of the generator potential, the greater the frequency of the action potentials.

One complication to this picture, as indicated in Figure 6.2, is a phenomenon known as *adaptation*. You have probably experienced this phenomenon yourself through your ability to adjust to sudden changes in your sensory environment. You jump into a swimming pool, are uncomfortably cold for a few seconds, but gradually grow accustomed to the temperature (assuming, of course, that the water isn't ice cold). What is happening in your nervous system during this experience is this: the initial stimulus is of sufficient intensity to produce the generator potentials needed to exceed threshold and produce neural impulses. But as that stimulus *continues* to act upon the receptors, the receptors lose their capacity to produce generator potentials. The decrease in generator potentials in turn reduces the number of action potentials produced and the intensity of the sensory experience. In short, you are not as cold because the action potentials are not as frequent.

Figure 6.2   *The Relationship between Stimulus Intensity, Generator Potential, and Action Potential*
(a) Stimuli of increasing intensity produce increasing generator potentials and increasingly frequent action potentials. (b) Stimuli of long duration produce decreasing generator potentials and progressively fewer action potentials. The relationship illustrated here is known as adaptation.

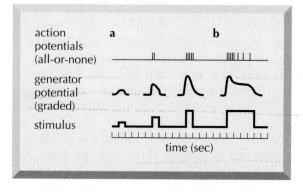

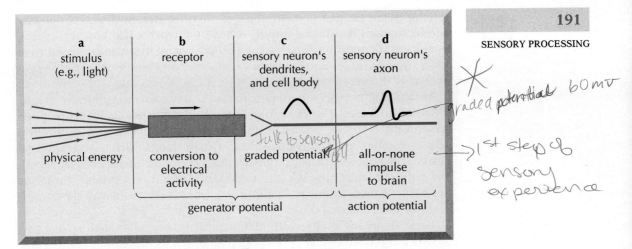

graded potential 60mv

→1st step of sensory experience

Figure 6.3 *From Stimulus to Neural Impulse*
A stimulus (a) arrives at a receptor and is transduced into a generator potential (b), is transmitted in the form of a graded potential to the axon (c), and finally is transmitted to the brain as a neural impulse in the sensory neuron (d).

Let us summarize the chain of events that occur from stimulus to neural impulse as shown in Figure 6.3.

1. When a stimulus is initially introduced, there is a one-to-one relationship between the intensity of that stimulus and the magnitude of the generator potential. In other words, the generator potential is graded: it increases or decreases directly with the increase or decrease in the intensity of the stimulus.
2. If the intensity of the stimulus is sufficient, the generator potential will meet the requirements necessary to produce the neural impulse. It will spread to the site of impulse initiation and produce depolarization sufficient to reach threshold.
3. If the stimulus is prolonged, the generator potential, regardless of the intensity, will diminish, which means increasingly weaker generator potentials spreading to the axon, less depolarization, fewer action potentials, and a decrease in the resultant sensory experience.

SENSORY CODING: AN OVERVIEW

The key to all sensory processing is the ability of the impulses transduced by receptors to produce actual sensations—to produce, for instance, sights, sounds, smells, tastes, and so forth. We use the phrase "produce actual sensations" advisedly since we do not know the exact relationship between what the brain is doing and what we are in fact experiencing. No one has ever observed anything in the brain that could be defined as a "sensation." The only thing we can observe in the brain is electrical activity. What we can say with reasonable certainty, however, is that certain features of the neural impulse—where it travels and how it travels—*correlate* with certain sensory experiences. We refer to these correlates as *codes*, and we refer to the brain's capacity to produce them as *coding*. Coding is the very essence of sensory experiences.

As you might expect, coding capacities vary enormously from species to species. Humans, in particular, have highly varied coding capacities. We can differentiate among a remarkable multitude of colors, sounds, tastes, smells, and tactile feelings. Green looks different from red. Limburger cheese smells and tastes different from Swiss cheese. Metals feel different from furs. We also make discriminations among stimuli on the basis of their intensity. A shout is louder than a whisper. The sun is brighter than the moon.

These differences in sensations introduce a crucial question, one that haunts the physiological psychologist as much as any other. If the transduction process converts different types of environmental stimuli into the same language (the neural impulse), how do these neural impulses (which are the same, regardless of the stimuli) produce such a vast array of sensations? Or, to pose the same question in another way, how does one language produce so wide a variety of experiences?

We are a long way from answering this question with precision, but at least two coding properties of the nervous system are known to be involved in the phenomenon. One, known as anatomical coding, has to do with the structure of the nervous system; the other, functional coding, has to do with the activity of the nervous system. We will now look at both.

Anatomical Coding

Visual, auditory, taste, smell, and tactile stimuli produce qualitatively different sensations, and it has been established that each category of stimuli produces neural activity in a different part of the brain. The term we use to describe the correlation between sensation and brain area is anatomical coding.

The idea that sensory coding is keyed to the anatomy of the brain has its roots in a theory proposed in 1826 by Johannes Müller, who called it the "doctrine of specific nerve energies." The main point of this doctrine is that sensations depend less on the environmental stimuli that activate them than on the nerves that are stimulated and ultimately on the part of the brain that the nerves stimulate. According to Müller's theory, sound and light produce different sensations because auditory nerves and optic nerves travel to different parts of the brain. Furthermore, according to the theory, if sound could stimulate nerves that travel to the visual part of the brain, sound would produce visual sensations. You would, in effect, "see" what you normally hear. This concept helps to explain why, for example, if you apply *pressure* to your eyes when they are closed, you experience visual sensations. The pressure apparently produces impulses that excite the visual area of the brain to produce visual sensations.

The specific nerve energies doctrine, interestingly enough, once played a role in a famous law case in which Müller himself gave expert testimony. The case involved a man who had been assaulted at night but who claimed nonetheless that he could identify his assailant. He claimed that the blow on the head had produced a flash of light that enabled him to get a glimpse of his attacker. Müller, testifying for the defense, agreed that a blow to the head could produce a sensation of light, particularly if the blow affected the part of the head that housed the visual areas of the brain. He pointed out, however, that this "light" is an entirely *internal* phenomenon that could in no way help the victim to identify his assailant (Shepherd, 1983).

Functional Coding

Functional coding, in contrast to anatomical coding, involves the differences in neural activity (i.e., the frequency of neural impulses) triggered by varying *amounts* of environmental stimuli. This type of coding is rooted in the observation that various sensations do not necessarily correspond to specific anatomical areas; they are also differentiated according to the degree of neural activity within an area. The sensation of brightness or loudness, for instance, varies according to the number of impulses arriving per unit of time (e.g., per second) at the visual or auditory cortex. The same can be said with respect to differences in the intensity of all stimuli.

A second crucial aspect of the functional code is the relationship between the stimulus and the actual firing of the neural impulse in the brain. Strictly speaking, a stimulus does not *initiate* this firing. That's because sensory areas in the brain and the neurons leading to these areas are firing spontaneously even if no stimulus is present. What the stimulus does is to *modulate* this spontaneous activity. An intense stimulus, for instance, will increase the level of firing and produce more impulses than a less intense stimulus. And in certain instances (in the coding that underlies color vision or brightness contrast, for instance) a stimulus will inhibit spontaneous activity and in so doing diminish the likelihood of impulses. As you will see throughout the next several chapters, this inhibitory aspect of coding is as potent a sensory code as excitation.

Arousal and Attention

Sensory processing calls for more than transduction and neural coding. If the signals produced by external stimuli are to be recognized, two things must happen in the nervous system. First, the signals must be received by an *aroused* brain; second, the stimuli must be *attended to*. Let's look at each.

Arousal

The principle of arousal in sensory processing is simply this: before a stimulus can have a psychological impact, the brain (specifically the

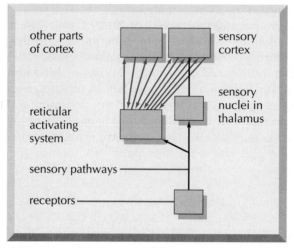

Figure 6.4 *The Two General Sensory Routes to the Cortex*
One route is diffuse, through the reticular formation; the other is specific, via the thalamic sensory nuclei.

cortex) must be in an aroused state, which is to say that the stimulus must produce generalized activity in the cortex. To express the same thought another way, the brain must be alerted to incoming sensory information.

If you look at Figure 6.4, you will see that sensory information takes two routes to the cortex: a direct route (the vertical line) through the thalamus, and an indirect route (the diagonal line) through the reticular formation. It is through the first route, through the thalamus, that we find the basis for anatomical coding—different stimuli affecting specific areas of the brain. It is through the second route, through the reticular formation, that we find the neural basis for arousal. You will notice how diffuse the projections are from the reticular formation to the sensory cortex. This diffusion means that regardless of the kind of signal traveling from the sensory pathway to the reticular formation, the result (assuming the signal is strong enough) will be a generalized arousal effect on the cortex. The stronger the signal (regardless of its nature), the more activity in the cortex.

That the reticular formation plays a pivotal role in alerting the cortex has been shown in studies conducted by Donald Lindsley and his colleagues (Lindsley et al., 1950). In one study, Lindsley showed that if two discrete flashes of light are delivered in succession to a monkey's eye, the flashes produce two discrete impulses (known as *evoked potentials*) in the visual cortex. When the interval between the flashes is very short, however, the two flashes produce only one evoked potential.

This finding indicates that the cortex itself has a threshold level below which two flashes are responded to as one. But something interesting happened when Lindsley applied electrical stimulation directly to the reticular formation. In this instance, the two flashes delivered in the time frame that had previously produced one evoked potential now produced two evoked potentials—an indication that the reticular formation has a decided effect on the ability of the cortex to detect stimuli.

One of Lindsley's colleagues, J. M. Fuster, went a step further to explore the phenomenon. Rather than limit his study to evoked potentials, Fuster examined the actual behavioral consequences of stimulation of the reticular formation (Fuster, 1958). After training monkeys to discriminate between two objects, Fuster decreased the time that an animal could attend to the objects by decreasing the amount of time the objects were exposed to light. Predictably enough, the reduction in light exposure produced an increase in errors. But Fuster also found that if he stimulated the reticular formation at the same time that he decreased the exposure time, the monkeys made fewer errors. His conclusion: stimulation of the reticular formation makes the animal more alert and in the process improves the animal's performance.

Attention

The impression we may have conveyed up to this point is that the sensory areas in the brain are passive receivers of sensory information—in other words, an audience, at the mercy of performers. Logically, it would seem that once a stimulus is transduced (assuming that its resulting generator potential is of sufficient magnitude to exceed axonal threshold), the impulses triggered in the sensory nerves should automatically travel to a specific area of the brain and produce a sensation.

Not quite. More than an audience at the mercy of performers, the brain is, in effect, an audience that can choose the type of performance it experiences. Experiments have shown, for example, that the brain plays an active role in actually selecting the stimuli that finally reach it. Among its remarkable properties is a *centrifugal influence* on sensory input—that is, an ability to allow some impulses access to the higher sensory areas of the brain while blocking others before they progress beyond the lower areas of the brain. The result: some stimuli can be sufficiently intense to excite an impulse and yet never be attended to. Why? Because their neural impact never reaches the sensory areas of the brain.

To see this process at work, you need only reflect on the fact that as you read these words, receptors other than those in your eyes are under constant stimulation. Your auditory receptors are picking up noise in the room. Tactile receptors are picking up the pressure of the chair against your back. Yet, you are not behaviorally torn between these competing claims on your attention. Behaviorally, as well as neurally, you automatically ignore some stimuli and attend to others.

The ability to block out all but relevant stimuli (i.e., to pay attention) is known as *selective inhibition of sensory input*, and it is easy to see how critical this capacity is to adaptive behavior. Without the ability to discriminate between relevant and irrelevant stimuli, the result would be total confusion.

The Brain as a Sensory Inhibitor

How does the brain selectively inhibit sensory input? There are two answers to this question.

To begin with, the brain is able to put up what is, in effect, a protective shield against stimulation that may be potentially harmful, thus preventing the stimulus from ever reaching the receptors. Reflex responses, such as closing the eyelids and constricting the pupils, help to prevent intense light from reaching the retina (the site of transduction). And reflexive contractions of muscles in the middle ear dampen the conduction of sound waves and in the process protect the inner ear (the site of transduction) from intense sound.

The brain also has the ability to block neural transmission in the sensory circuits, so that even if the stimulus initiates a neural impulse, the impulse does not necessarily reach higher centers in the brain. The block in this case is produced by inhibition of neural transmission early in the chain of sensory events, at the level of the receptors or the peripheral circuits just beyond.

Several areas of the brain have this blocking capacity. Each area is keyed to a different sensory system. If you apply electrical stimulation to two brain areas—the *olivary nucleus* (an auditory area) and the *periaqueductal gray* (a pain-suppression area)—the sensory input is inhibited. The reason: these areas give rise to circuits that exit from the brain and form synapses with their respective sensory systems. The circuits work differently. The circuits from the olivary nucleus form synapses directly with the auditory receptors, elevating their threshold (Dewson, 1967). Circuits from the periaqueductal gray form synapses with pain-related circuits in the spinal cord, blocking their transmission (Fields & Basbaum, 1978). Regardless of the mechanism, though, the result is the same—inhibition of sensory input.

It appears, too, that the reticular formation shares with the olivary nucleus and the periaqueductal gray the ability to control sensory input. The difference is that in the reticular formation, the inhibitory effect is not specific to one sensory modality but is more general. It includes sensory input from receptors located in muscles—sensory input involved in maintaining posture and balance, a phenomenon we shall look into in Chapter 10.

To conclude, then, it is clear that the reticular formation does more than simply alert the cortex to incoming sensory information. It also shares with certain brain areas—the olivary nucleus and the periaqueductal gray, to name two—the ability to *control* sensory input. Finally, to introduce yet another piece of the puzzle, experiments now suggest that even higher centers of the brain, areas in the thalamus such as the pulvinar nucleus and areas in the cortex—particularly in the temporal and parietal lobes of the cortex—are involved in attention (Wurtz, Goldberg, & Robinson, 1982; Wurtz & Goldberg, 1989). Evidence for pulvinar involvement comes from PET scan work on humans indicating that neurons in the pulvinar nucleus increase metabolic activity during selective attention (LaBerge & Buchsbaum, 1990). Evidence for cortical involvement comes from recording work on single neural cells in monkeys indicating that some cells in the posterior parietal cortex and inferior temporal cortex become extremely active when the monkeys are visually tracking significant objects—in other words, when they are paying attention (Mountcastle, Andersen, & Molter, 1980; Desimone et al., 1990). Furthermore, humans who suffer damage to the parietal lobes show a peculiar loss of attention to stimuli on one side of their body, a phenomenon we shall look into further in Chapter 18.

How these data fit into the overall picture is still not clear. The best guess is that the pulvinar nucleus in the thalamus and areas in the parietal and temporal cortex may play an "executive role" in the sensory system, selecting the channels that are being blocked and opened during selective attention.

SENSORY PROCESSING: THE PSYCHOLOGICAL IMPACT

It would be misleading to suggest that the picture we have painted so far of sensory processing is complete. Indeed, a critical question remains. Given that a stimulus is transduced and attended to (i.e., given that it produces neural impulses that reach the higher sensory areas of the brain), what then is its psychological impact? What do we experience?

It is tempting to answer—and indeed we have conveyed the impression—that we experience a "sensation." This is true, except that in some situations—such as those involving the kinesthetic senses (the sensory information from your muscles and joints)—we don't experience a sensation at all, even though our brain is being bombarded with impulses. At this very moment, as you are reading, stimuli are impinging on receptors in your muscles and joints, stimuli that must be processed for you to maintain balance and movement, yet no sensory experience is produced. Why? Because these stimuli are being processed at the *unconscious level* outside your awareness.

What is clear here is that not all information is of equal value; nor does all information require the same type of processing to be responded to effectively. Some information can be processed automatically outside our consciousness, for example, the sensory signals from your muscles and joints. Some information requires thought and deliberation, for example, the words on this page. What our ability to process information both consciously and unconsciously enables us to do is to respond to the two types of information at the same time, to, in effect, do two things at once: to sit and read, to walk and talk, to drive a car and listen to the radio.

Unconscious Processing: A Closer Look

Unconscious processing of sensory information does not apply solely to sensory signals from muscles and joints. In fact, some of the most compelling evidence for unconscious processing comes from experiments on the auditory system and selective attention and from a procedure known as *dichotic listening* (Cherry, 1953).

The dichotic listening procedure is designed to simulate in the laboratory a selective-attention phenomenon known as the *cocktail party effect*. Faced with listening to several conversations at once at a noisy party, you are able to attend to one while shutting out the others. In the dichotic listening procedure, subjects are given two different auditory messages (e.g., different words) at the same time through earphones, one for each ear, and are asked to attend to the words in one ear but not the other.

In most cases, subjects are able to do this task very easily. That is, they are able to report the words delivered to the attended ear but are unable to report the words delivered to the unattended ear. It is as if the words were not, in fact, delivered to the unattended ear at all. Something different occurs, however, when the words delivered to the unattended ear have special significance to the subject—when they are the person's name, for instance. In these situations, even though the subject is not forewarned that significant information may be delivered to the unattended ear, he or she takes notice and the words delivered to the unattended ear are now reported (Moray, 1959).

How is this possible? How, on the one hand, can the subject be oblivious to information in the unattended ear yet, on the other hand, attend to it if it becomes significant? Subjects must somehow judge the information to be significant. But how, if they are not paying attention to it?

The answer is that they *are* paying attention to it, but in a subtle way. What is thought to happen is this: while the subjects are processing and reporting the information that enters the attended ear, they are also processing the information entering the unattended ear, but, and this is the critical point, the processing is done outside their awareness, at the unconscious level. If the message is judged to be significant (e.g., one's name), it enters consciousness and subjects can report it. If the message is judged to be insignificant, it does not enter consciousness and subjects cannot report it.

There is experimental evidence to support the view that the message in the unattended ear is being processed at the unconscious level (McKay, 1973). In one of the most interesting of these experiments, subjects were given two types of messages: a message consisting of a sentence was delivered to the attended ear, and a message consisting of a single word was delivered to the unattended ear.

As expected, the subjects were able to report the sentence that had been delivered to the attended ear but were unable to report the word that had been delivered to the unattended ear. Variations on this procedure, however, indicated that, though unreported, the words delivered to the unattended ear were nonetheless processed, albeit at the unconscious level. When, for example, the sentence delivered to the attended ear contained a word with two different meanings, the interpretation of that word was affected by the word that was delivered to the unattended ear. In the sentence, "They threw stones at the bank yesterday," "bank" could mean one of two things, a financial institution or a sloping terrain.

Subjects who were given the word "money" in the unattended ear interpreted "bank" in this sentence to mean a financial institution. Subjects who were given the word "river" in the unattended ear interpreted "bank" to mean a hill along the slope of a river.

It is clear from these and other studies that sensory processing does indeed occur at the unconscious level and that information processed unconsciously can have a profound effect on behavior (Marcel, 1983). The question is, Where in the brain do unconscious and conscious processing occur? We have no answer to this question, but we do have some clues, at least with respect to visual information. The evidence comes from people who suffer damage to the visual cortex (Zeki, 1992).

Blindsight

Depending on precisely where the visual cortex is damaged, some people behave in a rather bizarre way. If you show them a flashing light, they cannot verbally report its presence. They behave as if they are blind. Show them the same flashing light and ask them to guess where the light is, and they can point to it. They behave as if they are not blind (Campion, Latto, & Smith, 1983; Weiskrantz, 1986).

This intriguing behavior is commonly referred to as *blindsight* and has been taken as evidence that visual information is processed at two levels, conscious and unconscious, and that each process is mediated by a different area in the brain. The assumption is that blindsight patients, because they are unaware of the object yet are able to point to it, have damage in the conscious but not in the unconscious area. Similar observations have been made in the auditory system. Two patients with damage in the auditory cortex reported that they could not hear, yet they showed startle reactions to loud sounds (Tanaka et al., 1991). Like people suffering from blindsight, the deaf patients were unaware of the stimulus yet they were able to react to it.

Sensory Processing: The Interpretive Stage

Let us take inventory. Sensory processing consists of a series of steps beginning with transduction and culminating in attention, coding, and consciousness. But this picture, as tidy as it is, is still incomplete. For there is more to processing a stimulus then just sensing its physical features. Just as important is our ability to interpret these features, to collect the raw sensory information, and then to process it on the basis of our past knowledge into a meaningful sensory experience. We "sense" lines and colors and clicks and tones, but what we actually see and hear are scenes and paintings, voices and music. So, in addition to sensing the physical features of a stimulus, we interpret and then classify these features in terms of our past knowledge. The term used to refer to the sensing stage—the stage determined by the physical properties of the stimulus—is *bottom-up processing*. The term used to describe the interpretive stage governed by past experience, knowledge, and expectation is *top-down processing*.

Agnosia: Sensing without Knowing

To appreciate just how important the interpretive process is in shaping our sensory world, let us consider what happens if past knowledge is missing. It is hard to imagine sensing an object without knowing what that object is, but there are brain-damaged people who suffer from this very problem. The disorder is known as *agnosia*, from the Latin meaning "without knowledge." Depending on the extent and location of the brain damage, the agnosia can be very broad (applying to any one or a combination of all the senses) or very narrow (applying to a very specific sensory experience within a given modality). Of all the agnosias, perhaps the most bizarre is a disorder known as prosopagnosia (Damasio, Tranel, & Damasio, 1990).

Prosopagnosia

Brain-damaged patients suffering from *prosopagnosia* can be normal in every respect except one: they cannot recognize *familiar* faces. It is not that such patients are blind; they can reproduce on paper a rough facsimile of any face they look at. What's more, they can frequently identify people by their clothes or by their voice. What they cannot do is recognize people by simply looking at their faces. When they look in a mirror, in fact, they cannot even recognize their own faces. The disorder may seem bizarre to you, but it becomes easier to understand when you realize that recognizing a familiar face involves two separate faculties: the ability to "see" the face and the ability to "know" the face you see. Assuming that each process—seeing a face and knowing a face—is mediated by a different area of the brain, it is reasonable to assume that a prosopagnosic has damage in the "knowing" area, not the "seeing" area.

We must be careful not to oversimplify the prosopagnosic picture. Recent evidence indicates that not all prosopagnosics suffer from a knowing deficit. Some are simply unable to see a face as a face; they are able to see the features of the face but cannot integrate the separate features into a meaningful whole (Sergent & Poncet, 1990).

A Closer Look

We saw earlier that sensing a stimulus involves unconscious as well as conscious processing and that each process is mediated by a different area of the brain. This conclusion is based on studies of brain-damaged patients suffering from blindsight. Recent work indicates that the same pattern—unconscious and conscious processing mediated by different areas of the brain—may hold for knowing a stimulus as well. And we base this conclusion on studies conducted on brain-damaged patients suffering from prosopagnosia.

In one study, two prosopagnosic patients were given the opportunity to view photographs of familiar and unfamiliar faces. They were then asked to report verbally whether the faces were familiar, and while they were responding, researchers monitored their autonomic response (specifically, changes in skin resistance, which is a measure of autonomic arousal). The results are surprising: the patients' verbal reports showed no signs of recognition; the patients' autonomic activity, however, did (Tranel & Damasio, 1985).

Clearly, then, the two patients in this experiment (and, remember, it is risky to generalize from two subjects to all prosopagnosics) were able to recognize familiar faces at the autonomic or unconscious level. What they were unable to do is to bring the information to verbal or conscious awareness. The conclusion: there are two knowing areas for faces, conscious and unconscious, and in this case the damage is in the conscious (verbal) area and not the unconscious (autonomic) area.

Localization of Function

The implications of prosopagnosia are intriguing, especially when it comes to the issue of localization of function (i.e., the extent to which a specific area of the brain controls a specific behavior). Because the prosopagnosic's symptoms are specific (applying to faces and only to faces), the implication is that localization of function must also be very specific—specific brain areas controlling the knowing of faces and only the knowing of faces.

The question, though, is, How general a rule is this? Does it apply to all sensory experiences? Are there specific areas in the brain that code for, say, the knowing of a familiar dog or the knowing of a familiar car? Or is it unique to knowing familiar faces? The answer to this question requires a fuller understanding of the complexities of sensory processing. We will return to the issue of localization of function in subsequent chapters.

LOOKING AHEAD: COMMON MECHANISMS AND SENSORY PROCESSING

By now it should be obvious that adaptive behavior depends on the ability to interact successfully with the environment. The more information humans can extract from the environment and the more elaborate and sophisticated their means of acting upon such information, the more efficient, generally speaking, their behavioral patterns will be. In the next four chapters we will focus on the precise mechanics of this interaction. Chapters 7 through 9 deal primarily with mechanisms that detect and absorb information from the environment. These mechanisms, referred to collectively as sensory processes, include vision, audition, smell, taste, touch, pain, and the internal (kinesthetic and proprioceptive) senses that control body movement and balance. Chapter 10 deals with the action systems—specifically the means by which information is channeled from the brain to the muscles and glands.

As you might expect, sensory processes (the ability to detect, absorb, and convey information to the brain) vary in accordance with the particular sensory system involved. Yet all sensory systems are rooted in the same basic process—converting environmental stimuli into the sensations that humans commonly experience when they see, hear, touch, smell, and taste. And all sensory systems are governed by basically the same mechanisms—transduction (converting the stimulus into the neural impulse) and coding (representing the stimulus in the brain in terms of place or frequency of the neural impulses).

Sensory coding, as you will soon see, is one of the most fascinating areas of physiological psychology but also one of the most mystifying. We know far more today about sensory coding then we knew 10 years ago, but even so no one has been able as yet to say with certainty why red looks different from green, why salt tastes different from sugar, and why certain tactile experiences produce pain whereas others produce pleasure. There is, however, one thing we can say with certainty: whatever

Figure 6.5 *Phantom Limbs*
A composite picture of phantom limbs (depicted as transparent) that are perceived as real by many amputees.

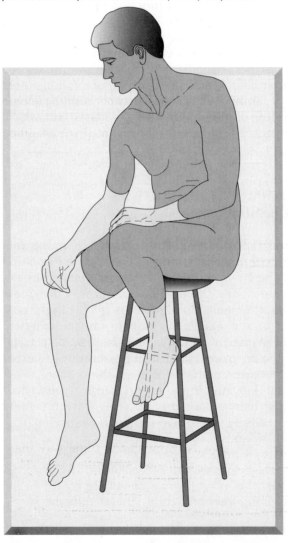

the sensory codes may be, it is the brain that ultimately determines the nature and quality of sensory experiences. No phenomenon illustrates this point better than a clinical problem known as phantom limb.

Phantom Limb

Many amputees report that they still experience sensations in the leg or arm that they no longer have (see Figure 6.5). This phenomenon is known as *phantom limb*, and the amputees who experience it not only *feel* the missing limb, they sometimes attempt to *use* it. On occasion, an amputee experiencing this phenomenon will perceive that the missing limb is in an awkward position. One amputee who has been studied reported that he felt as if his "phantom arm" was always extended so much that he would turn sideways to walk through a doorway. A second patient perceived that his phantom arm was bent behind his back, and he slept on his stomach or side to avoid sleeping on it. Amputees often report sensations of pressure, cold, warmth, pain, and even itching in the phantom limb. Particularly distressing is pain. Reported by roughly 70 percent of patients, phantom limb pain in some cases is continuous and excruciating—their toes, they report, "are being seared by a red-hot poker" (Melzack, 1992).

Why should an image of the limb persist even though the actual limb is missing? Logic says that the image of the limb exists because the activity in the brain that normally is produced by the limb exists. But why? The answer, according to Ronald Melzack, a pioneer in phantom limb research, is that after a limb is removed neural activity is released in areas of the brain that are normally connected to the limb and that this activity, because it persists even though the limb does not, gives rise to an image of the limb (see Chapter 8 for details). The critical point, and one that will be made throughout this book, is that when it comes to sensory experiences—or for that matter all psychological experiences—the brain is the key. If the brain *reports* the experience, the experience *is* present with or without the external physical stimulus needed to produce it.

SUMMARY

1. *Transduction.* Our ability to interact with our environment on a variety of levels (sight, sound, touch, etc.) is rooted in a process known as transduction—the conversion of one form of energy into another. The specific type of transduction that underlies sensory behavior revolves around a cellular structure known as the receptor, whose function is to transduce signals from the environment into the neural impulse.

2. *Receptors.* Receptors generate signals in much the same way that neurons generate the neural impulse—with one key difference. The action of receptors is triggered by environmental stimuli, rather than neurotransmitters. The membrane of each type of receptor is sensitive to a *specific type* of environmental stimulus, and each receptor is able to transduce a stimulus into a generator potential.

3. *The generator potential.* The generator potential produced by a receptor that has been stimulated is not the same as the neural impulse. The receptor, in other words, doesn't fire in the sense that a neuron fires. When a stimulus is initially introduced, the resulting generator potential increases or decreases directly with the increase or decrease in the intensity of the stimulus. If the stimulus is prolonged, however, the generator potential, regardless of the stimulus intensity, will diminish, which means smaller generator potentials spreading to the axon, less depolarization, fewer impulses, and a decrease in the resultant sensory experience.

4. *Sensory coding.* Certain features of the neural impulse—where it travels and how it travels—*correlate* with certain sensory experiences. These correlates are known as codes, and the brain's capacity to produce them is known as coding. Coding is the very essence of the sensory experience. Two properties of the nervous system are known to be involved in coding: anatomical coding, which is linked to the structure of the nervous system (different areas of the brain correlated with different sensations), and functional coding, which is linked to the nature of neural activity in the nervous system (different frequency of neural impulses correlated with different sensations).

5. *Anatomical and functional coding.* The idea that coding is keyed to the anatomy of the brain has its roots in a theory, the doctrine of specific nerve energy, proposed in 1826 by Johannes Müller. Its main point is that sensations depend less on the environmental stimuli that activate them than on the nerves that are stimulated and ultimately on the part of the brain that the nerves stimulate. Functional coding is rooted in the fact that various sensations do not necessarily correspond to specific anatomical areas; instead, they are differentiated according to the degree of neural activity within an area.

6. *Arousal and attention.* Before a stimulus can have a psychological impact, the brain must be in an aroused state and the stimulus must be attended. The neural basis of arousal is found in a section of the brain stem known as the reticular formation. Attention is linked to one of the brain's more remarkable properties—a *centrifugal influence* on sensory input. The brain, in other words, is able to allow some impulses access to the higher sensory areas while blocking others before they progress beyond the lower areas. Several areas of the brain have the capacity to block sensory input, chief among them the olivary nucleus (an auditory area) and the periaqueductal gray (a pain-suppression area). Other areas that are highly active during the attention process are located in the thalamus (the pulvinar nucleus) and the cortex (temporal and parietal).

7. *Unconscious sensory processing.* Sensory information can be processed at the unconscious level outside of your awareness and still have an impact on your behavior. One procedure used to study unconscious processing is known as *dichotic listening.* The procedure consists of presenting the subject two stimuli at the same time, one to each ear, and instructing the subject to attend the stimulus in one ear but not the other. Evidence for unconscious processing comes from observations indicating that information in the unattended ear influences behavior even though the subject is unaware of it.

8. *Blindsight.* Exactly where in the brain unconscious processing occurs and how the mechanisms differ from conscious processing is not known. But studies involving brain-damaged patients who are suffering from blindsight—that is, who claim that they cannot see and yet are able to point accurately to a stimulus such as a flashing light—have been taken as evidence that visual information is processed at two levels, conscious and unconscious, and that each process is mediated by a different area in the brain. Blindsight patients presumably have damage in the conscious, not the unconscious, area.

9. *Bottom-up and top-down processing.* In addition to sensing the physical features of a stimulus, we interpret and classify these stimuli in terms of our past knowledge. The term used to refer to the sensing stage—the stage determined by the physical properties of the stimulus—is bottom-up processing. The term used to describe the interpretive stage governed by past experience, knowledge, and expectation is known as top-down processing. And just as there are areas of the brain involved in *sensing* a stimulus, so are there areas involved in *knowing* a stimulus. Damage a "knowing" area and the person loses the ability not to sense but to know or recognize the stimulus, and the loss can be highly selective such as the loss of the ability to recognize familiar faces.

10. *Prosopagnosia.* Brain-damaged people suffering from a condition known as prosopagnosia are unable to recognize familiar faces. The disorder strongly suggests that seeing a face and knowing a face are mediated by different areas of the brain, and that prosopagnosics have damage in the "knowing" area not the "seeing" area. Complicating the picture, however, is the fact that some prosopagnosics are simply unable to see a face as a face; they are able to see the features of the face but cannot integrate the separate features into a meaningful whole.

11. *The brain and sensory processing.* The phenomenon known as phantom limb illustrates a critical principle about sensory coding: whatever the sensory codes may be, it is the brain that ultimately determines the nature and quality of sensory experiences. Phantom limb is a condition in which people who have had an arm or leg amputated continue to feel as though the arm or leg were still there. Some amputees, in fact, feel continuous and excruciating pain in a limb they no longer have. This phenomenon graphically illustrates that if the brain reports an experience, the experience is present—with or without the external physical stimulus.

KEY TERMS

agnosia
anatomical coding
arousal
attention
blindsight
centrifugal influence
cocktail party effect
dichotic listening
evoked potentials
functional coding
generator potentials
olivary nucleus

parietal cortex
periaqueductal gray
phantom limb
prosopagnosia
pulvinar nucleus
receptor
resting potential
reticular formation
sensory codes
temporal cortex
transduction

SUGGESTED READINGS

Barlow, H. B. & Mollon, J. D. *The Senses*. New York: Cambridge University Press, 1982.

Kolb, B. & Whishaw, I. Q. *Fundamentals of Human Neuropsychology*. New York: Freeman, 1990.

Sekuler, R. & Blake, R. *Perception*, 3rd ed. New York: McGraw-Hill, 1994.

Spillman, L. & Werner, J. S. (Eds.). *Visual Perception: The Neurophysiological Foundations*. San Diego: Academic Press, 1990.

THE VISUAL
SYSTEM

COLOR BLINDNESS
Explaining Color Blindness

INTRODUCTION

The sense of sight—our ability to see what is happening around us—has obvious implications for survival, and so it is no surprise that virtually all animals are endowed with this capacity. As you might expect, however, the extent and versatility of an animal's visual capacity differ widely among species, and so does the degree to which specific species rely on vision as a prime survival mechanism. Very simple animals (e.g., certain insects) can make only *phototropic responses*; that is, they merely approach or avoid light. Humans, on the other hand, have a highly sophisticated visual system.

True, we do not see as well in certain situations as some other animals (cats, for example, have better night vision than humans), but no other species has as versatile a visual capacity as humans and no species can absorb and process as many different kinds of visual stimuli. We can detect shapes, follow movement, differentiate colors, and judge distances. We can view the glimmer of a star at one moment and focus on the pages of a book the next.

The physiological basis for the visual versatility enjoyed by humans is not yet fully understood and, as you might imagine, is exceedingly complex. Little by little, though, we are beginning to uncover the intriguing mysteries of sight—specifically how our visual system produces the broad spectrum of visual sensations that most of us take for granted. Before we examine the physiological processes that underlie vision, let us first look at some of the features of light and how they relate to what we see in the world around us.

Understanding Light

Light is a form of electromagnetic radiation generated by the oscillation of electrically charged particles. The oscillating charges travel in a wave-like form that varies in three respects: length, amplitude, and purity. All visual sensations are produced by the relative differences in these three properties of light. The *length* of the wave determines *hue*—the sensation we identify as color. The *amplitude* of the wave determines the *intensity* of the light—how bright it is. And the *purity* of the wave determines how *saturated* or how deep the color is.

Wavelengths are measured in nanometers (nm)—units of measure equal to one-millionth of a meter. Wavelengths vary enormously, but only a small fraction—those between 380 and 760 nm—are visible to the human eye. Wavelengths shorter than 380 nm (including ultraviolet rays, x-rays, and gamma rays) require special equipment for detection, as do wavelengths longer than 760 nm, which include infrared waves. The shortest wavelength visible to humans, 380 nm, produces the color we recognize as violet. The longest wavelength, 760 nm, produces red. (The color spectrum is shown in Figure 7.15.)

The purity or saturation of colors depends on the homogeneity of the light waves. If, for instance, only one kind of wavelength, such as 650 nm, is sensed, the resulting sensation, in this case red, will be exceptionally pure or saturated. But if other wavelengths are present along with those of 650 nm, the purity of the red will be diminished even though the 650-nm wavelengths predominate.

HOW HUMANS SEE

Vision is a twofold process—*optical* and *neural*. Certain devices in the eye serve an optical function; that is, they gather light from objects and *refract* (i.e., bend) this light so that it is brought into focus. The optical stage of the process ends at the *retina*, a membrane of cells whose specialty is transducing light. Once the light interacts with the retina and is transduced into neural impulses, vision becomes a neural process. To understand vision, you need to understand both processes.

Figure 7.1 *The Human Eye*

Light enters the cornea, passes through the pupil and lens, and is focused on the retina. The layers of tissue in the eye consist of the sclera, choroid layer, and retina.

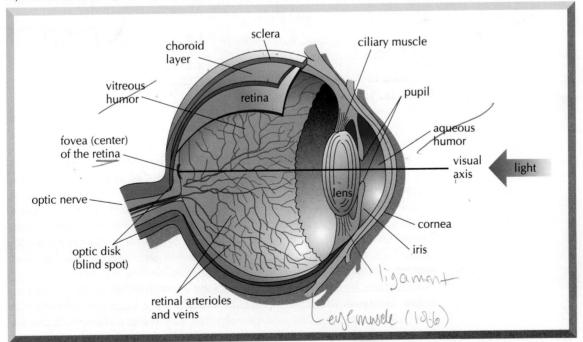

The Anatomy of the Eye

Figure 7.1 depicts the human eye. As you can see, the eyeball is basically round but bulges slightly in front. The entire eyeball is sheathed by a fibrous layer that consists of two parts. About five-sixths of the surface—everything but the bulge—is covered by an opaque white coating called the *sclera*, or white of the eye. The bulge is covered by a transparent shield known as the *cornea*. Light enters the eye through the cornea, whose principal function is to initiate the focusing process.

One intriguing characteristic of the cornea is that is has no blood vessels. It draws its fuel from a fluidlike substance known as the *aqueous humor*, which occupies the chamber between the cornea and the lens. There is a reason. Blood vessels in the cornea would impede the entry of light waves into the eye. Because blood is the source of immune defenses against foreign substances, the absence of blood vessels in the cornea makes it one of the few tissues in the body that can be transplanted from one person to another with little chance of rejection.

The Choroid Layer

Adjacent to the sclera, as pictured in Figure 7.1, is a structure called the *choroid layer* or *coat*. It is a darkly pigmented layer of tissue with two basic functions: it supports the blood vessels that supply fuel to the retina, and it absorbs light waves that have scattered after they enter the eyes. If the choroid layer did not prevent these scattered rays from striking the retina, our vision would be blurred.

Not all animals have this choroid layer. The layer adjacent to the sclera in the eye of a cat cannot absorb scattered light. It operates instead as a mirror, reflecting light back into the eye. This luminescent layer, known as the *tapetum*, gives cats and other nocturnal animals unusually keen eyesight at night. It is also what endows the eyes of the feline family with that familiar nocturnal glow.

The Iris

As light passes through the cornea and the aqueous humor, it encounters the *iris*, a contractile membrane whose color determines the color of the eye. A small opening in the center of the iris, the *pupil*, controls the amount of light that reaches the back of the eye. The pupil can open (the word frequently used is *dilate*) to a diameter of $\frac{5}{16}$ inch at its widest; at its narrowest, it has a diameter of about $\frac{1}{16}$ inch.

The widening and narrowing of the pupil are governed by two sets of smooth muscles under the control of the autonomic nervous system. These muscles work to regulate how much light enters the eye's interior. In periods of stress or intense concentration, the sympathetic nervous system stimulates the pupil to dilate, thus *increasing* the amount of light entering the back of the eye. In periods of relaxation or in bright sunshine, the parasympathetic nervous system stimulates the pupil to contract, *decreasing* the amount of light that can enter the back of the eye.

The Lens

The *lens* is a flattened, spherical structure located behind the pupil, and its principal role is to bring visual images into focus. The relatively common eye condition known as *cataracts* results from a clouding of the lens. If left untreated, it can often lead to blindness.

Working in tandem with the cornea, the lens narrows the scattered light entering the eye into a single ray that is focused as a single point on the retina. This bending process is known as *refraction*. The cornea, which has roughly twice the refractory power of the lens, does most of the work; but what the lens lacks in refractory power it makes up for in flexibility. Unlike the cornea, whose refractory powers are fixed, the lens can vary in shape, contracting or relaxing under the control of the ciliary muscles. The lens, in other words, can change refraction according to the demands of the moment. Under normal conditions, it is flat; but when greater refractory powers are called for, the lens becomes more spherical, that is, it bulges.

Focusing Disorders

Most common eye problems are related to refraction. In *nearsightedness*, also known as *myopia*, light rays entering the eye are bent too much, causing the rays to come into focus in front of the retina and to begin to scatter again before they reach the retina. This problem comes about in one of two ways. In some instances, the lens bulges too much, over-bending the light. In other instances, the distance between the lens and the retina may be abnormally long, as Figure 7.2b shows. In any event, myopia produces a blurred image, and corrective lenses (glasses) are needed to compensate for the overbending light rays. Glasses for a myopic person have a concave shape, which causes light rays to scatter or diverge more than they normally would before they enter the eye.

With *farsighted* (also known as *hyperopic*) people, the problem is the opposite and so is the correction, as shown in Figure 7.2c. Light rays entering the eye of a farsighted person are not bent enough, so that they hit the retina while they are still partially scattered. Here, too, there are two possible causes. First, the lens may not bend the light rays sufficiently, that is, the lens may not bulge enough. Second, the distance between the lens and the retina may be abnormally short, as Figure 7.2c shows. Corrective lenses for farsighted people have a convex shape, which increases the bending of light rays before they enter the eye.

THE VISUAL NERVOUS SYSTEM: ANATOMY

The neural processing of visual information begins in the retina, a membrane consisting of three layers of cells. As shown in Figure 7.3, one layer is made up of two types of receptor cells: *rods* and *cones*. The other two layers are made up of neural cells that take two forms: *bipolar* and *ganglion* cells. Also present in the retina are two types of neurons that inter-

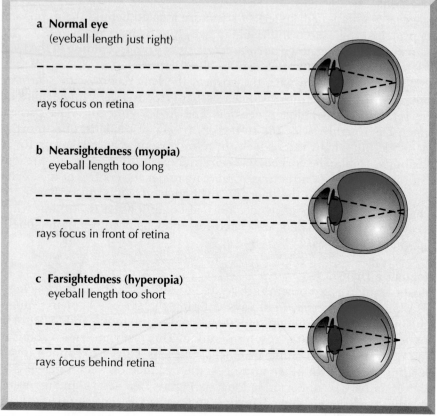

a Normal eye
(eyeball length just right)

rays focus on retina

b Nearsightedness (myopia)
eyeball length too long

rays focus in front of retina

c Farsightedness (hyperopia)
eyeball length too short

rays focus behind retina

Figure 7.2   *Nearsightedness and Farsightedness*
In a normal eye (a) the focal point of the lens (that is, the point at which light rays converge to form a sharp image) is located on the retina. In a nearsighted eye (b) the focal point of the lens is located in front of the retina and the light rays begin to scatter again as they hit the retina, resulting in a blurred image. In a farsighted eye (c) the focal point of the lens is located behind the retina and the light rays are still scattered when they hit the retina, resulting in a blurred image.

connect the cells within each layer. Those interconnecting the receptors are known as *horizontal* cells. Those interconnecting the ganglion cells are known as *amacrine* cells.

The arrangement of the three layers warrants special mention. Logically, you would expect receptor cells to occupy the layer closest to the front of the eye. As you can see in Figure 7.3, however, this is not the case. The receptor cells (rods and cones) are located *behind* the two neural layers. This means that when light hits the retina, it must first filter through the neural layers (first the ganglion cell layer, then the bipolar cell layer) before it reaches and activates the receptor cells (the rods and cones). It also means that the neural impulse, once it is triggered by the receptors in the rear portion of the retina, travels toward the front of the eye through the bipolar and ganglion cells. Ultimately, however, it is routed to the back of the retina through the axons of the ganglion cells

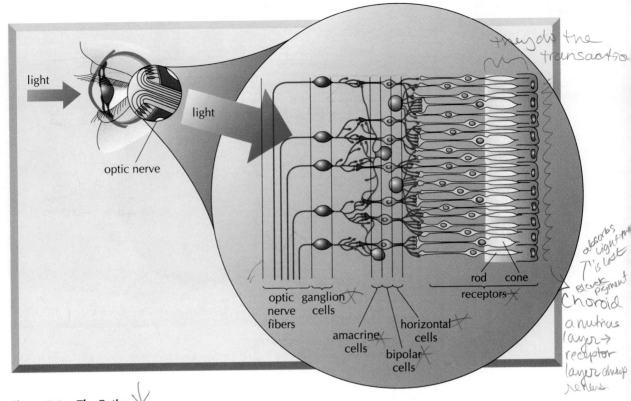

they do the transaction

absorbs light so I's lost

Black pigment

Choroid a nutrius layer → receptor layer always returs.

Figure 7.3 *The Retina*
When light hits the retina (at the back of the eye), it must filter through the neural layers before reaching the receptor cells.

that make up the *optic nerve* and from there to the brain. Notice that where the optic nerve leaves the retina of each eye, there are neither rods nor cones. This particular area is known as the *blind spot* or *optic disk.*

You can detect the blind spot in your own eye by holding a tiny object at arm's length, closing one eye, and moving your other eye in the direction of the closed eye. You should discover that at one point (when the object is projected on the blind spot) the object disappears, only to reappear as you continue turning your gaze. The reason you are not normally aware of this blind spot and that it does not interfere with your vision is that you usually fixate on an image with both eyes. Because each eye detects a slightly different aspect of the image, the image never falls on both blind spots at once.

From Retina to Cortex

Each eye, of course, has its own optic nerve, but the two nerves converge at the base of the brain at a place called the *optic chiasma.* The nerves do not form synapses at this point of convergence; instead, they go through a re-sorting process—one that differs widely among species. In lower ani-

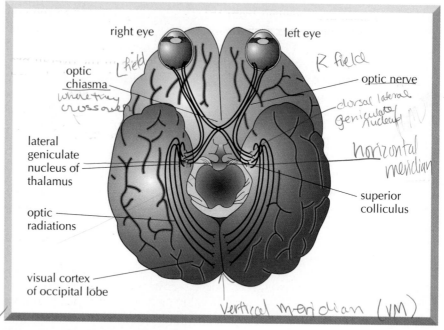

handwritten annotations on figure: "L field", "where they cross over", "R field", "dorsal lateral Geniculate Nucleus IV", "horizontal meridian", "Vertical meridian (VM)"

Figure 7.4 *The Visual Nervous System*
The optic nerves originate in the retina and go through a re-sorting process at the optic chiasma. Neurons from the nasal portion of each eye cross to the opposite side of the brain whereas neurons from the temporal portion of each eye do not cross. In both cases the neurons form synapses with neurons in the lateral geniculate nucleus that project (via the optic radiations) to the visual cortex of the occipital lobe. (View of the brain is from the bottom looking up.)

mals, such as the frog, the optic nerves from the two eyes simply cross to the opposite sides of the brain. In humans and other mammals, as pictured in Figure 7.4, only half of the neurons contained in the two optic nerves cross. The neurons that cross originate in the nasal half of each retina (i.e., the half of the retina closest to the nose). The neurons that do not cross originate in the temporal half of each retina (i.e., the half of the retina closest to the temple); these neurons simply continue back on the same side of the brain. So it is that visual information from each eye travels to both sides of the brain.

Once the re-sorting process in the optic chiasma is complete, the optic nerve branches and its axons travel in one of two directions. Some axons branch off to the *superior colliculus*, where they form synapses with motor nerves that control eye movement. Most, however, go to the *lateral geniculate nucleus* in the thalamus. There they form synapses with neurons which in turn give rise to axons that project (via *optic radiations*) to areas located in the visual cortex of the occipital lobe.

In summary, the three major areas that mark the path traveled by neural impulses in the visual system are the retina (where transduction takes place and impulses are initiated), the lateral geniculate nucleus (where impulses are received from the retina and projected to the cortex), and the visual cortex (where impulses are processed and coding takes place). Bearing this in mind, we will now move from structure to function and examine the role that each area plays in the overall processing of visual information. We begin at the beginning, with the rods and cones and transduction.

THE VISUAL NERVOUS SYSTEM: FUNCTION

Transduction in the retina is carried out by the rods and cones, the *photoreceptors*. Rods and cones are unique to the eye and are named for their shape. Rods are slender and cylindrical; cones are broad and bulbous. Some animals—rats, for instance—have only rods. Others—turtles, for instance—have only cones. Most animals, however, have both, although the ratio of rods to cones in different species varies considerably. Humans are thought to have about 125 million rods and 7 million cones.

The distribution pattern of rods and cones in the human retina is significant. Rods are located primarily in peripheral areas; cones are more numerous in the interior. One section in the center of the retina, an area smaller than a square millimeter, contains nothing *but* cones—more than 50,000. This area is known as the *fovea*. Areas along the periphery of the retina, on the other hand, contain only rods. Between the two extremes (fovea and periphery), there is a mixture of rods and cones, with the number of cones declining steadily as you move toward the periphery.

The Sensitivity of Rods and Cones

Rods and cones are both sensitive to light, but the nature of their sensitivity differs, and it is this difference that establishes the physiological bases for several different visual experiences. Rods have a characteristically low threshold of excitation, which means that relatively small amounts of light can trigger impulses from them. For this reason, they operate primarily under conditions of low illumination—at night, for instance. Rods are highly sensitive to the presence of light but do not abstract color from it. Rods function in ways that are *achromatic* (colorless) and *scotopic* (related to darkness). If there were only rods in your retinas, your visual world would be an assortment of grays, blacks, and whites. The more rods that are stimulated by a particular wavelength, the brighter an object will appear.

Cones are different. They demonstrate a marked *chromatic* (colorful) and *photopic* (related to light) capacity. With a much higher threshold than rods, they function mainly under high-illumination conditions—in sunlight, for instance. The more cones that are stimulated by a particular wavelength, the brighter and more colorful an object appears.

Cones and rods differ in other ways as well. You have probably noticed that you can see the details of an object better when it is directly in front of you than when it is off to one side. The reason for this is that the center of the retina (the fovea) contains only cones and the periphery of the retina contains only rods. Although rods are better than cones at detecting very weak visual stimuli, they are less adept at resolving the details of these stimuli—a capacity known as *visual acuity*.

In summary, rods are better than cones at detecting the mere presence of a stimulus, and cones are better than rods at discerning the details of a stimulus. The differences between rods and cones are rooted in two factors: one is chemical and the other is anatomical. Before we consider these differences, however, let us consider the one feature that both rods and cones share: transduction.

Rods and Cones as Transducers

As photoreceptors, both rods and cones convert light waves into neural impulses, and both carry out transduction on the basis of photochemicals in their membranes. Light hits the rods and cones, photochemicals break down, membrane permeability to the surrounding ions changes, and a generator potential (i.e., the electrochemical signal in receptors that initiates neural impulses in sensory neurons) is produced. Let's take a closer look.

Transduction

The way photoreceptors (both rods and cones) react to light is different from what you might expect. Rather than producing excitation (depolarization) of photoreceptors, light produces inhibition (hyperpolarization) of photoreceptors. Darkness, in contrast, excites photoreceptors. The fact that photoreceptors whose function is to detect light are inhibited by light and excited by darkness may seem like a paradox. And indeed it is— albeit a paradox with an explanation.

The explanation is found in the activity that characterizes sensory neurons (the bipolar and ganglion cells) connected to the photoreceptors. Like most sensory neurons, these neurons show spontaneous activity, and this activity is affected differently by light than by darkness. Light increases the spontaneous activity of sensory neurons even though it inhibits the activity of photoreceptors. Darkness, in contrast, decreases the spontaneous activity of sensory neurons even though it excites photoreceptors.

The reason for this phenomenon is that the spontaneous activity of sensory neurons is controlled by a neurotransmitter (released by photoreceptors when they are excited) that is inhibitory, not excitatory. So when this neurotransmitter is released—under conditions of darkness— spontaneous activity in the sensory neurons diminishes, activity in the brain diminishes, and the result is the visual sensation of darkness. Under conditions of light, with less inhibitory neurotransmitter present, the spontaneous activity in sensory neurons is increased, neural activity in the brain increases, and the result is the visual sensation of light.

Thus, our ability to detect light depends on the relative presence or absence of the inhibitory neurotransmitter. As the level of the neurotransmitter increases (as it does in the dark), <u>our ability to detect light diminishes. As the level of the neurotransmitter decreases</u> (as it does in the light), our ability to detect light increases.

Figure 7.5 presents a detailed view of the unique relationship between light and its effect on neural activity. The critical point here is the fact that inhibition of receptors (i.e., hyperpolarization) is just as capable of converting stimuli into neural impulses (i.e., of acting as a generator potential) as excitation of receptors (i.e., depolarization). The question though is, Why should light cause photoreceptors to hyperpolarize rather than depolarize? The answer, according to most researchers today, lies in the photochemical makeup of the receptors, although exactly how these photochemicals interact with the receptor membrane to produce hyperpolarization remains to be determined. Less speculative is the manner in which the photochemicals interact with light.

Figure 7.5 *Transduction in the Photoreceptors*

Light produces inhibition in the photoreceptors, which in turn produces an excitatory graded potential in the bipolar cells and increasingly frequent action potentials in the optic nerve. Darkness, in contrast, produces excitation in the photoreceptors, which in turn produces an inhibitory graded potential in the bipolar cells and decreasing action potentials in the optic nerve.

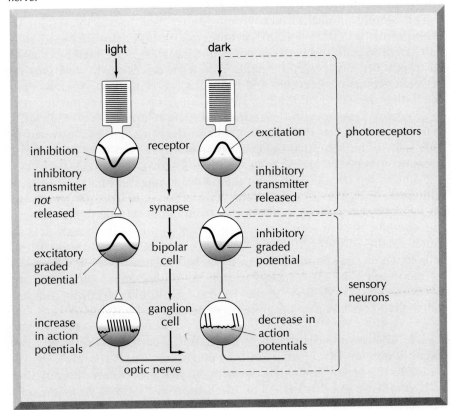

Photochemicals: A Closer Look

Transduction, as we've just seen, begins with the breakdown of photochemicals in both cones and rods. But the photochemicals differ in each instance. Rods contain a photochemical called *rhodopsin*, which is composed of *opsin* (a protein found only in photoreceptors) and *retinene* (a yellowish substance related to carotene, which is found in carrots). Cones do not contain rhodopsin. They contain three types of *iodopsin*, a substance made up of retinene and a protein known as *photopsin*.

The behavioral significance of these chemical differences lies mainly in the difference in sensitivity to light between the rhodopsin found only in rods and the iodopsin found only in cones. Rhodopsin is about 10 times more sensitive to light than iodopsin. This difference explains, in part, why rods are more sensitive to light than cones. There is another difference, however, between rods and cones that accounts for their differences in sensitivity as well as their differences in acuity: the nature of their connections with the brain.

Anatomical Differences

The approximately 130 million rods and cones in the eye funnel information into about 1 million ganglion cells that make up the optic nerve and travel to the brain. But because there are far more rods than cones in the retina, the typical ganglion cell in the optic nerve receives far more information from rods than it does from cones.

This simple numerical fact has enormous significance for vision. To begin with, the difference in the numerical relationship between rods and ganglion cells and between cones and ganglion cells introduces us to an important term: *receptive field*. This term refers to the relationship between groups of receptors and individual neurons to which they connect either directly or indirectly. When we use the term in vision, it refers to groups of receptors in the retina and their relationship to individual neurons, in this case the ganglion cells in the optic nerve, illustrated in Figure 7.6. The receptive field, in other words, is the total area of the retina from which a ganglion cell receives input.

You can see the differences in the neural connection patterns of rods and cones in Figure 7.7. Notice that the receptive field of ganglion cells in the optic nerve receiving impulses from cones is much smaller than the receptive field of ganglion cells receiving impulses from rods. It is so much smaller, in fact, that the relationship of cones and the ganglion cells to which they connect can be described (figuratively if not literally) as one-to-one. The differences in receptive fields explain why cones are better than rods at discerning the details of a stimulus, and why rods are better than cones at detecting the mere presence of a stimulus.

Acuity. Discerning the details of a stimulus is commonly referred to as visual acuity, and it depends on how accurately that stimulus is represented to the brain. The chief operatives in this process are the ganglion cells, and for a good reason. The small receptive field of ganglion cells connected to cones lends itself to analysis of details. When different parts of an image are projected on different cones, the cones, because of their

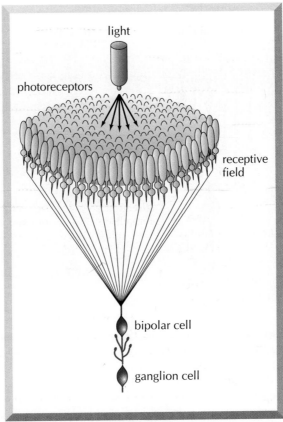

Figure 7.6 *The Receptive Field*
A single ganglion cell receives (via the bipolar cell) input
from many photoreceptors.

one-to-one "private line" relationship with ganglion cells, have a high
likelihood of stimulating different ganglion cells and eventually different
areas of the brain. This pattern of stimulation results in a detailed representation of the image.

In contrast, when different parts of an image are projected on different rods, the rods, because of their converging "party line" relationship
with ganglion cells, tend to stimulate the same ganglion cell and eventually the same area in the brain. This convergence of the stimuli results in
a less accurate representation of the image.

Sensitivity. The difference in the receptive fields of ganglion cells connected to rods and cones also accounts, in part, for the difference in sensitivity between rods and cones. Rods, as it happens, are 1000 times more
sensitive than cones, but only a small part of this difference in sensitivity can be accounted for chemically—the fact that rhodopsin in the rods
is 10 times more sensitive than iodopsin in the cones. The remainder is
explained by the difference in receptive fields.

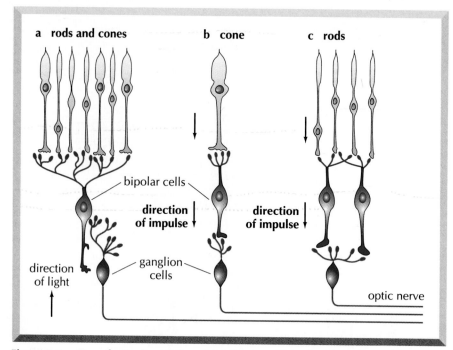

Figure 7.7 *How the Rods and Cones Are Connected to the Nervous System*
(a) Both rods and cones may form synapses with the same bipolar cell. (b) Cones tend to have "private lines" to the brain; individual cones connect to individual bipolar cells. (c) Rods tend to have "party lines" to the brain: groups of rods connect to a few bipolar cells.

The convergence of rods on ganglion cells increases the sensitivity of these cells by promoting their capacity to work in concert when they produce a neural impulse. Thus, even though each rod may be receiving only weak stimulation (i.e., below threshold), a neural impulse in the ganglion cell may still result. Why? Because information from a large number of rods converges on a single ganglion cell and promotes *spatial summation*, a process by which neural activity coinciding in time and space may accumulate to exceed threshold. Conversely, the same weak stimulation projected on a number of cones is unlikely to produce an impulse since cones tend to work alone and do not benefit from spatial summation. Therefore, in order for cones to produce an impulse in their corresponding ganglion cells, the stimulus must be notably more intense than for rods.

NEURAL CODING

Vision involves more than simply detecting objects and discerning their details. It also involves differentiating objects on the basis of certain properties, such as color, shape, and brightness. Our ability to make these distinctions—to distinguish red from green, to tell a triangle from a square, and so forth—is rooted in the ability of our visual system to take raw electromagnetic light waves and convert (the technical term is *code*) them into the spectrum of visual sensations that humans experience.

The Retina and Neural Coding

Neural coding is primarily a function of the brain (specifically of the lateral geniculate nucleus and the visual cortex, as shown in Figure 7.4). Research has shown, however, that the retina (specifically the neurons in the retina) also plays an important part in the process. Far from being a simple relay station for transducing light waves into neural impulses, the retina abstracts and processes certain types of visual stimuli, thus playing a preliminary but indispensable role in the coding process ultimately completed by the brain. And there is no better example of this than the role played by the retina in coding for an object's contour or shape.

The Contour Code

We all take for granted our ability to distinguish among the various objects that make up our environment. We recognize the object in the corner of the room as a chair, and the object beside it as a lamp. To make these distinctions, however, our eyes must be able to perform a critical function: they must be able to view an object as *distinct* from its background. If the object and the background were indistinguishable (i.e., if the object had no contour or no edges), it would be impossible to identify the object.

Our ability to distinguish an object from its background is rooted in differences in reflected light. What we actually see when we look at an object is not the object itself but the light reflected from that object. And because the amount of light reflected by an object differs from the amount of light reflected by the background, that object has contour or edges. If the amount of light reflected in each case were the same, there would be no contour or edges.

An important feature of object and background is the fact that the edges separating the object from its background often appear sharper than they really are. If you look at Figure 7.8, you will see what we mean. The figure depicts different gray stripes, each of uniform intensity. Yet, if you focus on one of the stripes toward the middle, its left- and right-hand edges will seem to vary in brightness: the left-hand edge (the one next to the darker stripe) appears ultrabright, and the right-hand edge (the one next to the lighter stripe) appears ultradark.

In reality, each edge is of uniform intensity. What you are seeing is, in fact, an illusion—an illusion referred to as *Mach bands*, named after Ernst Mach who discovered them. Such illusions, moreover, occur not only with Mach bands but whenever and wherever there are differences in light reflected from adjacent surfaces, that is, wherever there are contours or edges. This phenomenon is known as *brightness contrast*, and it is highly adaptive. It accentuates the edges of objects and in the process sharpens our vision.

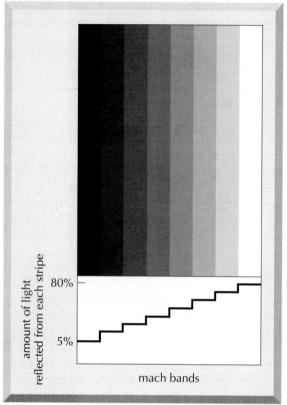

Figure 7.8
The edge of each stripe (upper portion of the figure) varies in brightness even though the intensity of each stripe is uniform (lower portion of figure).

The questions concerning us here are the following: What in the nervous system enables us to code for edges (i.e., for *differences* in the amount of light reflected by the object and its surroundings)? And why are these edges accentuated (i.e., why is there brightness contrast)? The answer to these questions comes from two lines of work, one on invertebrates (*Limulus*) and the other on mammals (cats and monkeys). Let's begin with the invertebrate work.

Retinal Inhibition and *Limulus*

As has been the case with the neural impulse, research into neural activity at the retinal level poses monumental methodological problems. The main problems are the minute size of receptor cells in the mammalian retina and the complexity of their interactions. In Chapter 4 we talked about John Z. Young's discovery that one of the neurons in the squid, because of its giant size, is ideally suited for study of the electrochemical nature of the neural impulse. Similarly, Floyd Ratliff and H. Keefer Hartline have significantly aided research on the neural mechanisms underlying vision through their discovery that the eye of the horseshoe crab (*Limulus*), shown in Figure 7.9*b*, is ideally suited for visual analysis (Ratliff & Hartline, 1959).

What makes the eye of the *Limulus* unique is that it contains only about 800 photosensitive cells, all of which, by biological standards, are fairly large—large enough, at any rate, to allow for detailed examination of an individual cell. Each of these cells is known as an *ommatidium*. Each is, in effect, a miniature eye.

Sharpening the Image

The most significant finding to emerge from the early work of Ratliff and Hartline is that neural mechanisms at the level of the retina play a larger role in sharpening an image than had originally been suspected. Placing electrodes on a single neuron (ganglion cell) leading from a single ommatidium, Ratliff and Hartline noted that the single neuron had a spontaneous firing rate. That is, even though the ommatidium was not stimulated, the neuron fired. A fine beam of light was then projected onto the ommatidium connected to that ganglion cell, and the firing increased.

The increase itself was not surprising. What *was* surprising, however, was the activity in the neighboring ganglion cell. For, although the neigh-

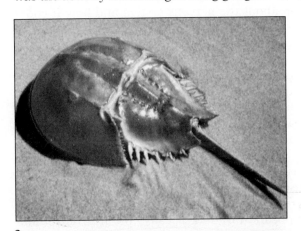

a

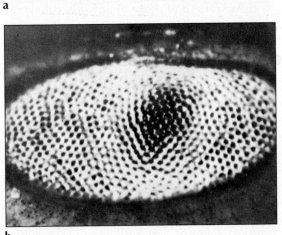

b

Figure 7.9 *The Limulus Used in Visual Analysis*
(a) The *Limulus* (Photograph courtesy of Gordon S. Smith/National Audubon Society/Photo Researchers). (b) The *Limulus* eye, with hundreds of ommatidia (Photograph courtesy of Dr. Floyd Ratliff, Rockefeller University). (c) The rate of firing of the ganglion cells, depending on the position of their ommatidia in relation to the light-dark border. The greatest difference in rate of firing occurs at the border.

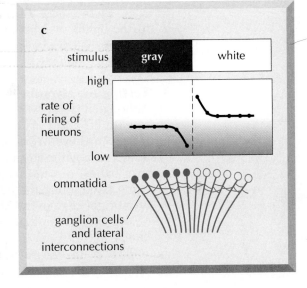

boring ommatidium was *not* stimulated by the light beam, the activity of its ganglion cell changed—and did so in a rather peculiar way. Its spontaneous activity *decreased*.

These findings led Ratliff and Hartline to draw an important conclusion: stimulating an ommatidium does two things. It excites activity in the ganglion cell with which it is connected and it *inhibits* activity—through cross-connections—in neighboring ganglion cells. The name they gave to this phenomenon is *lateral inhibition*. They confirmed their conclusion through experiments in which two adjacent ommatidia were stimulated simultaneously. The firing rate of each was found to be less than if the two ommatidia were stimulated at different times. With simultaneous stimulation, each ommatidium inhibited the firing of the other, a phenomenon they termed *mutual inhibition*.

You may be wondering what all this has to do with visual coding and, in particular, with the basic visual capacity of being able to distinguish objects. The answer lies in Ratliff and Hartline's contention that lateral inhibition is the key to understanding how the nervous system codes for contour and edges and for the special feature of contour known as Mach bands (the ultradark and ultrabright edges in Figure 7.8). But before considering how lateral inhibition accounts for contour and Mach bands, we must clarify an assumption about the nervous system and how it codes for brightness in general.

Sensory neurons (i.e., ganglion cells) are known to have a spontaneous firing level. On this basis, we can assume that increasing the frequency of firing above the spontaneous level will code for increases in brightness, while decreasing the frequency of firing below the spontaneous level will code for increases in darkness. Bearing in mind this relationship among brightness, darkness, and frequency of firing, we can now return to contour and Mach bands, offering the following hypothesis. The left-hand edge of the stripe (the one next to the darker neighbor) appears ultrabright because the neurons stimulated by the edge have a *higher* firing rate than those of any other neurons stimulated outside the edge. By the same token, the right-hand edge of the stripe (the one next to the lighter neighbor) appears ultradark because the neurons stimulated by the edge have a *lower* firing rate than those of any other neurons stimulated outside the edge.

Testing the Hypothesis
Although it is not yet possible to test this hypothesis with the mammalian eye, Ratliff and Hartline have been able to test and confirm it by using the *Limulus* eye. Working with a stimulus consisting of a gray stripe bordering on a white stripe, they found evidence, as shown in Figure 7.9c, of two "bands" of neurons along the two edges between the stripes: a high-firing band along the edge of the white stripe that corresponds to the ultrabright edge in the Mach band, and a low-firing band along the edge of the gray stripe that corresponds to the ultradark edge in the Mach band.

To explain this pattern of firing, Ratliff and Hartline have cited the phenomenon of lateral inhibition. Neurons stimulated by the white stripe, they hypothesize, are excited by direct stimulation of their receptor cells and, because of lateral inhibition, are inhibited by the stimulation of neighboring receptor cells. This is true of all neurons stimulated by the white stripe except those that lie on the edge of the stripe. These neurons are also excited by direct stimulation of their receptors and, because of lateral inhibition, are inhibited by stimulation of their neighbors. But, and this is the critical point, because only half of their neighbors are stimulated (the other half lie on the border of the gray stripe), the inhibitory effect is diminished by half. Thus the firing rate of the neurons at the edge of the white stripe is higher than that of any other neurons stimulated by the white stripe, and the edge of the stripe appears the brightest.

Lateral inhibition has also been cited to explain the ultradark edge seen along the gray stripe. In this case the neurons stimulated by the gray stripe fire at or near spontaneous level because their receptor cells are *not* excited. This is true of all neurons stimulated by the gray stripe except those that lie on the border of the stripe. These neurons are not themselves stimulated by their receptors either; they are, however, stimulated by neighboring receptors (the receptors that lie on the edge of the white stripe), thus producing lateral inhibition and a decrease below spontaneous level in the firing rate of the neurons. Thus the firing rate of the neurons at the edge of the gray stripe is lower than that of any other neurons stimulated by the gray stripe, and the edge appears the darkest.

What all this means is this: whenever light borders dark, maximum firing occurs at the perimeter of the light area, and maximum inhibition occurs at the perimeter of the dark area. Consequently, when dark and light areas are side by side, the contrast appears stronger at the border between them than at any other points of comparison. The result is brightness contrast and an enhanced ability to see objects as distinct from their background.

Implicit in and critical to this explanation is the fact that inhibition, which in this case modulates spontaneous activity downward, carries as much information and is about as potent a code as excitation, which modulates spontaneous activity upward. Both increased and decreased firing serve to abstract features of the visual world into the neural code.

Edge and Contour: A Closer Look

In the early 1950s a group of researchers at Massachusetts Institute of Technology, led by Jerome Lettvin, were able to distinguish in the optic nerve of the frog's eye several types of neurons, each sensitive to a specific type of visual stimulus. Some neurons responded to the presence of sharp edges, but only if the edges remained stationary. Other neurons responded to sharp edges, but only if the edges were moving (Lettvin et al., 1959).

Of all the neurons they found, however, the most curious were those that were sensitive to small, dark, moving objects and unresponsive to large, stationary objects. Lettvin dubbed these neurons "bug detectors" and surmised that they confer upon the optic nerve (and presumably the frog) the uncanny ability to detect moving insects. The presence of these so-called bug detectors indicates that neurons in the frog's optic nerve can perform a function normally associated with the brain. Given the primitive nature of the frog's brain, it is not surprising that higher-order abstracting and coding (as in the detection of bugs) should occur in the optic nerve. Relating these coding properties of the visual system to the frog's behavior, W. R. Muntz, one of Lettvin's colleagues, has noted that "the eye is not a physical instrument like a camera, but a biological instrument adapted to meet the animal's needs" (Muntz, 1964).

CODING IN THE MAMMALIAN VISUAL SYSTEM

In simple animals, such as the frog, complex features of a visual stimulus—size, mobility, stationary or moving edges—are coded in peripheral areas such as the optic nerve. In animals with more complex nervous systems (cats and monkeys, for instance) there is a shift in function. What we see, in effect, is a neural division of labor. The simple features of a visual stimulus are coded in peripheral areas, and more complex features are coded in central areas, particularly the cortex. In the following section we shall examine this division of labor, but before we begin, let us review briefly the anatomy of the mammalian visual nervous system.

Figure 7.10 *The Visual Nervous System*
A schematic view of the neural circuits from the retina to the cortex.

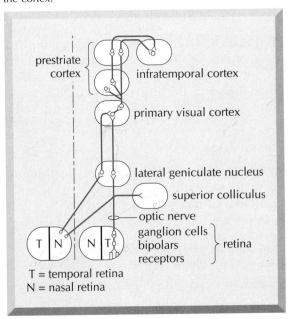

prestriate cortex

infratemporal cortex

primary visual cortex

lateral geniculate nucleus

superior colliculus

optic nerve

ganglion cells
bipolars   } retina
receptors

T   N   N   T

T = temporal retina
N = nasal retina

An Anatomical Overview

In Figure 7.10, you will notice that neurons (ganglion cells) from the retina travel in two directions. Some branch off to the superior colliculus, but most go to the lateral geniculate nucleus in the thalamus. From the lateral geniculate nucleus, information is projected to the visual cortex. You will notice that three areas in the visual cortex are involved: the *primary visual cortex*, which receives input directly from the lateral geniculate nucleus; the *prestriate cortex*, which receives input from the primary visual cortex; and the *infratemporal cortex*, which receives input from the prestriate cortex.

Generally speaking, each of the three major areas of the visual system—the retina, the lateral geniculate nucleus, and the cortex—is involved in coding different features of the visual stimulus. The retina codes for brightness contrast. The lateral geniculate nucleus codes for brightness contrast and color. The cortex codes for lines and angles, and motion and color. Let us now examine the coding process of each of these areas in more detail.

The Work of Kuffler

Much of what we know about coding in the retina we owe to Stephen Kuffler, one of the first researchers to study the mammalian retina at the single-cell level (Kuffler, 1953). Using cats as subjects, Kuffler placed microelectrodes in single ganglion cells and observed, not surprisingly, that the cells had a spontaneous firing rate. Even in the dark, the single ganglion cells of cats showed a firing rate of roughly five impulses per second.

Kuffler then discovered that he could change the spontaneous firing rate of a single ganglion cell by projecting small spots of light on certain areas of the retina. This type of selectivity—a single ganglion cell's response depending on the precise location of a spot of light on the retina—is not surprising when you remember that ganglion cells have their own receptive fields, each cell receiving input from a specific area of the retina. Surprisingly, though, Kuffler found that when he directed a spot of light on different parts of the receptive field of a specific ganglion cell, the activity of that cell changed in a peculiar way. Light focused on the center of the receptive field *excited* the ganglion cell's spontaneous firing; light shining on the perimeter of the receptive field *inhibited* the cell's spontaneous firing. Kuffler called these ganglion cells *on-center* cells because they turn on (i.e., they fire) when the center of their receptive field is illuminated. Kuffler also found other ganglion cells in which the opposite is true: their center is inhibitory and their perimeter excitatory. Kuffler called these ganglion cells *off-center* cells. The important point to remember is this: illumination in the center of the receptive field produces one type of response in the ganglion cell, while the same illumination in the perimeter of the receptive field produces exactly the opposite response.

Brightness Contrast in the Mammalian Eye

To relate Kuffler's findings to visual coding, we need to take his experiment one step further and consider what happens when the center and perimeter of a receptive field are stimulated at the same time.

If diffuse light is projected over the entire receptive field, stimulating both the center and the perimeter with the same intensity of illumination, the ganglion cell does not respond, that is, its spontaneous activity does not change. If, however, the diffuse light varies—that is, if the light is brighter in one area of the receptive field than in another—the ganglion cell responds in proportion to the difference in illumination. Why? Because illumination of the same intensity in the center and perimeter of a receptive field produces equal and opposing effects on the ganglion cell, thus canceling each other out. Illumination that varies between the center and perimeter still produces opposing effects, but the effects are not equal (input from the brighter area is greater than input from the dimmer area) and the difference is reflected in ganglion cell activity. Figure 7.11 illustrates the response of on-center cells to different types of illumination.

Figure 7.11 *Kuffler's Experiment*
(a) A microelectrode is implanted in a ganglion cell of a cat and various parts of its retina are stimulated by small spots of light. (b) The four panels show the firing rates of the ganglion cell. When no light is shone (1), the ganglion cell fires at a spontaneous rate. When light is projected on the center of the receptive field (2), the firing rate increases above the spontaneous level. When light is projected on the perimeter of the receptive field (3), the firing rate decreases below the spontaneous level. When two spots of light (or diffuse light) are projected on the center and the perimeter of the receptive field (4), the firing rate remains at the spontaneous level.

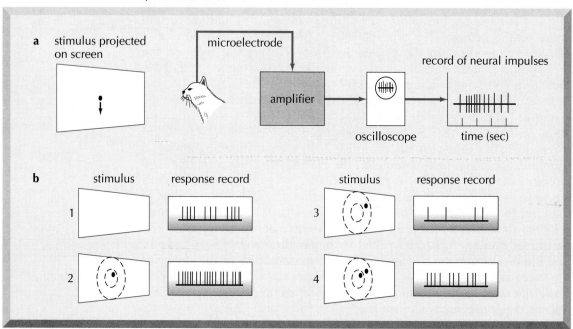

The conclusion: opposing inputs from the center and the perimeter of a receptive field confer upon the ganglion cell (and presumably the organism) the ability to detect brightness contrast, that is, to detect differences in illlumination between neighboring areas on the retina.

If this effect sounds familiar to you, it should. This capacity represents the mammalian counterpart to the brightness contrast produced by lateral inhibition in the *Limulus* eye that we considered earlier. Both systems enable an organism to discard diffuse background illumination and to highlight the relation of figure to ground. A patch of light projected on a cat's retina by its very nature produces differences in illumination at its edges, and it is these differences that the on-center and off-center cells respond to and report to the brain. The reporting, however, comes not from one but from thousands of ganglion cells, and it is the function of the brain to process this prodigious amount of information and to make some sense of it. Exactly how the brain does this is not yet known, but we have some very good leads. Let us now consider the role of the brain in visual coding.

THE WORK OF HUBEL AND WIESEL

In the early 1960s, two Harvard Medical School researchers, David Hubel and Torsten Wiesel, undertook a series of experiments seeking to discover how the brain codes visual information (Hubel & Wiesel, 1959). Their work would eventually earn them the Nobel Prize in 1981.

Hubel and Wiesel's approach was basically the same as Kuffler's and is illustrated in Figure 7.12a. They exposed cats to various patterns and forms of white light on a screen and recorded the resultant activity of single neurons in the brain. It was slow, painstaking work, involving hours of tedious probing to isolate a particular neuron sensitive to a particular visual stimulus, but the experiments yielded valuable data.

To understand the implications of Hubel and Wiesel's findings, it may help to look back at Figure 7.10, which presents a schematic view of the visual nervous system. We shall begin our examination of Hubel and Wiesel's work by considering experiments in which they recorded from single neurons in the lateral geniculate nucleus, the major relay station between the retina and the cortex. We will then consider studies in which they placed their electrodes in single neurons in the visual cortex.

The Lateral Geniculate Nucleus

The lateral geniculate nucleus consists of layers of neural cells: three layers in cats, six layers in monkeys and humans. The layers in monkeys and humans are divided into two sections based on their size: the two large layers are known as the *magnocellularis layers*, and the four smaller layers are called the *parvocellularis layers*. The significance of this division will become apparent when we consider how the lateral geniculate nucleus codes for color and motion.

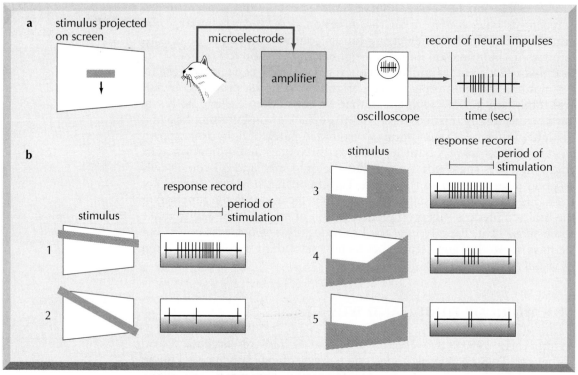

Figure 7.12 *Hubel and Wiesel's Experiment*
A cat with a microelectrode implanted in the visual cortex (a) is stimulated with lines of different orientations (b). Some single neurons are selectively responsive—that is, firing occurs only when the line is horizontal (1). If the line is tilted (2), the horizontal detector stops firing. Other single neurons are sensitive only to right angles (3). As the visual form deviates from a right angle (4 and 5), the firing rate of the cell diminishes.

The neurons in each layer form synapses with axons from the ganglion cells in the retina. Hubel and Wiesel found that the receptive fields of the neurons in the lateral geniculate nucleus were essentially the same as those in the ganglion cells. These receptive fields share three important characteristics: (1) they have opposing centers and perimeters, (2) they are on-center or off-center cells, and (3) they are responsive to spots of light. In short, the neurons in the lateral geniculate nucleus, like those in the retina, code for brightness contrast.

Given these data, why do we need the lateral geniculate nucleus? If the lateral geniculate nucleus merely duplicates the function of the ganglion cells, why not project visual information directly from the ganglion cells to the cortex? We have no answer to this question as yet, but there is at least one plausible explanation. We know that the lateral geniculate nucleus is more than simply a relay station for visual information. It also has a role in attention and in sharpening of images, thus contributing to the precision of the visual information ultimately projected to the cortex.

The Visual Cortex

The primary visual cortex consists of six layers of neural cells. Counting down from the surface of the cortex, it is layer IV that receives input from the lateral geniculate nucleus. Higher-order analysis of visual information begins at layer IV and the layers (II and III) immediately above.

Recording from single neurons in the primary visual cortex, Hubel and Wiesel found a major transformation in the visual code, reflected in the stimulus required to initiate a response. The stimulus most likely to initiate a response in single neurons in the retina and the lateral geniculate nucleus—a spot of light—was less effective for neurons in the cortex. The spot of light was still able to stimulate neurons in the cortex. To be maximally effective, however, it had to be combined with other spots of light, and the array had to be arranged in a straight line, as illustrated in Figure 7.12b. In other words, the stimulus on the retina required a linear feature—an edge—for cortical neurons to respond maximally.

What Hubel and Wiesel apparently found, then, were single neural cells in the cortex that coded for the basic ingredient for seeing objects, the code for contour or edges. They called these neurons "feature" cells and classified them into three groups: simple, complex, and hypercomplex. All are maximally responsive to linear stimuli—to edges—but there are differences, which we will now examine (Hubel & Wiesel, 1959).

Simple Cells

Simple cells respond best when a line is in a very specific orientation—vertical, horizontal, oblique—and in a very precise position on the retina. One cell, for example, may fire in response to a vertical line projected to one part of the retina but not to that same vertical line projected to a different part of the retina. The reason, Hubel and Wiesel theorize, has to do with the manner in which simple cells receive information from the lateral geniculate nucleus.

You can gain a better picture of the theory by looking at Figure 7.13. Notice that the lateral geniculate nucleus acts as an intermediary in the system. It receives information from an array of receptor cells that are stimulated by a straight line (an edge) on the retina. It then relays this information in a converging manner to a *single* simple cell in the cortex.

The convergence is critical. It explains why a straight line can stimulate many receptors on the retina but only a single—simple—cell in the cortex. It also explains why a straight line is more effective in stimulating a simple cell than a spot of light: the straight line benefits from spatial summation (input from many cells converging on one); the spot of light does not. Hubel and Wiesel suggest that this same basic convergence principle occurs over and over again in the visual nervous system, thus creating the complex and hypercomplex cells we are about to consider.

Complex Cells

Complex cells also respond maximally when a line is in a very specific orientation, but the precise place on the retina where a line is projected

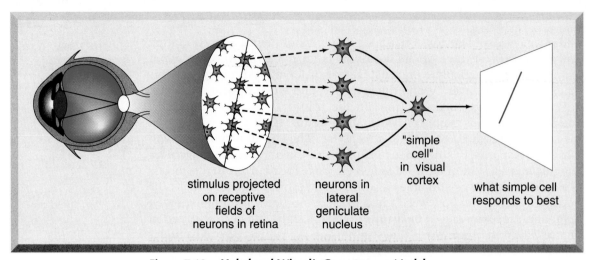

Figure 7.13 *Hubel and Wiesel's Convergence Model*
A diagram of Hubel and Wiesel's model of the neural circuits that determine simple cells.

does not seem to be as critical as it is in simple cells. The line can be placed virtually anywhere on the retina and still affect the complex cells. According to Hubel and Wiesel, the response pattern of complex cells is the result of convergent input from simple cells, each simple cell being sensitive to the same orientation of a line and to a different part of the retina.

Hypercomplex Cells
Hypercomplex cells also respond best when a line is in a very specific orientation, but what differentiates them from complex cells is that the line must also be of a specific length. If the line deviates from this length, the firing rate of the cell declines. Hypercomplex cells are also coded for particular angles (Hubel & Wiesel, 1965). A hypercomplex cell, for example, may fire maximally in response to right angles but to a lesser degree as the angle deviates from a right angle, as shown in Figure 7.12*b*. The response pattern of hypercomplex cells, according to Hubel and Wiesel, is the result of convergent input from complex cells.

The Arrangement of Cells
Apart from discovering that there are three types of cells in the visual cortex, Hubel and Wiesel found that the cells, specifically the simple and complex cells, are arranged in a very orderly way (Hubel, Wiesel, & Stryker, 1978). They are organized in narrow columns that cut across the six layers of the cortex, each column containing cells with the same line orientation. A specific column, for instance, may contain simple and complex cells sensitive to the same vertical line. Another column may contain cells sensitive to a horizontal line. Hubel and Wiesel also found that as they moved their electrodes from one column to the next, the line orientation of the cells changed in a highly systematic way, the angle of

orientation shifting roughly 10 degrees from column to column. Figure 7.14 presents a diagram of this pattern.

We need to ask ourselves what purpose other than that of bringing cells together in a tidy arrangement is served by these columns. Some researchers have proposed that columns work as building devices, sorting simple cells on the basis of their line orientation and then putting cells with similar orientation near one another so that they can interact to produce complex cells. This idea is certainly appealing, but no one has actually observed that columns promote the construction of more complex cells from simple cells. On the contrary, there is some evidence to suggest that the columns play no such role, or that if they do, they are not the exclusive building devices in the process.

Evidence casting doubt on the idea that columns are the exclusive building devices (and, for that matter, on Hubel and Wiesel's convergence model) comes from a study comparing the speeds with which simple and complex cells respond to a visual stimulus (Stone, 1972). If Hubel and Wiesel's convergence explanation and the building model are correct, we would expect complex cells, because they presumably depend on input from simple cells, to respond *after* simple cells. The results of this study, however, indicate that in some cases at least, complex cells respond *before* simple cells. This sequence indicates that some complex cells may not depend on input from simple cells but instead may receive input directly from the lateral geniculate nucleus. Exactly how complex

Figure 7.14 *A Diagram of the Orientation Columns in the Visual Cortex*

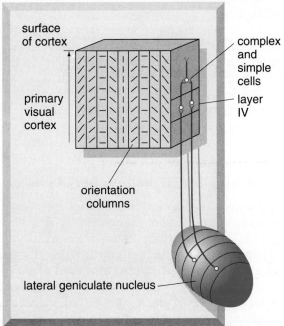

cells are formed from these connections is still a matter to be worked out, but it seems clear that while some complex cells may depend on input from simple cells, others may not.

Summing Up

Let us take inventory. The data to date indicate that as we progress level by level through the visual nervous system, at each level the cells abstract more information than at an earlier level. At the level of the retina and thalamus—the ganglion cells and the lateral geniculate nucleus—brightness contrast and the position of the stimulus are critical. In simple cells, both the position and the linear quality of the stimulus are essential. In complex cells the linear quality is still important, but the position is less so. And in hypercomplex cells, lengths of lines and angles become significant (Kandel, 1991).

To account for these findings, Hubel and Wiesel proposed a model based on the principle of convergence. Lateral geniculate neurons, according to the model, converge on simple cells; simple cells converge on complex cells; and complex cells converge on hypercomplex cells. At each level, a cell receives more information and processes more information about the stimulus than at an earlier level. Thus, according to Hubel and Wiesel, a hierarchy of cells is formed, beginning in the retina and ending in the cortex.

NEW DIRECTIONS IN CODING RESEARCH

Today, roughly 30 years after Hubel and Wiesel's original experiments, certain questions remain unanswered, and two questions are particularly intriguing.

The first question concerns what lies beyond hypercomplex cells in the nervous system. Could there be cells we have yet to identify that are even more complex than hypercomplex cells? In other words, what is the limit of the amount of information about a stimulus a single cell can code?

The second question is whether Hubel and Wiesel's hierarchical view is correct or, as the data suggest, whether there is another process, in addition to a hierarchical process, involved in organizing and abstracting visual information. Let us briefly consider both issues.

Searching for "Grandmother" Cells

To answer the question of what lies beyond hypercomplex cells to abstract information, some researchers have suggested the following possibility: that sitting on top of the pyramid are single cells that receive information from line cells and angle cells and as a result code for triangles and squares. A related and even more intriguing possibility is that there are perhaps super-higher-order cells: cells that put together a composite picture of the entire visual scene and enable us to recognize landscapes or faces—"grandmother" cells (as some researchers have facetiously put it) that enable us to recognize, say, the face of our grandmother.

Oddly enough, higher-order grandmother cells do seem to exist, albeit in limited situations. Some single cells in the visual cortex of monkeys, for instance, respond best (i.e., fire maximally) to the image of a monkey hand; other single cells respond best to a monkey face (Perett, 1991; Desimone, 1991). In the auditory cortex of monkeys are single cells that respond best to a pattern of sound that resembles a mating call (Wollberg & Newman, 1971).

Evidence indicates that there are also areas in the human brain that code for images of faces, although in these cases we have no way of knowing if the perceptual analysis is accomplished at the single-cell level. PET scan studies indicate that when subjects look at pictures of faces, neural activity increases in the parietal and temporal areas of the brain (Lu, 1991). Brain damage studies indicate that patients with selective damage in the parietal cortex can be perfectly normal in every respect except that they cannot recognize familiar faces, a disorder known as prosopagnosia (see Chapter 6 for details) (Damasio, 1985; Sergent & Poncet, 1990).

The fact is that, other than those we have mentioned, very few examples of higher-order cells have been found. Common sense tells us that a set of higher-order cells for every complex stimulus that we perceive or might conceivably perceive would require a network of neural connections whose scope and complexity would be far beyond the capacity of the human cerebral cortex.

So we are brought to the final question regarding higher-order perception. If the nervous system is not equipped to account for all perceptions in terms of a hierarchical arrangement, how does it account for perception?

Mechanisms of Underlying Perception

Researchers are beginning to believe that while hierarchical processing has an important place in visual analysis, another type of relationship among neurons may be just as important: *parallel processing*.

Looked at in its most elementary form, hierarchical processing suggests that the ability to perceive, say, a human face requires that a number of cells, each coding for a different feature of the face (shape, color, etc.), converge on a single higher-order cell, a "face" cell. Parallel processing, on the other hand, does not require convergence on higher-order cells. It merely requires the *simultaneous* activation of a number of different subordinate cells—feature cells—each of which may be formed by a hierarchical process. Presumably, the subordinate cells are located in parallel areas of the brain, and it is their simultaneous activation that produces the overall perception. Eric Kandel has drawn an apt analogy between parallel processing and a photograph. "The individual silver halide grains of a photograph," he notes, "do not represent the photograph of a face, but the ensemble of grains does" (Kandel, 1981).

Evidence for Parallel Processing

Critical to the notion of parallel processing is the assumption that different areas of the brain code different features of a visual stimulus at the same time. Anatomical evidence supports this view.

Careful analysis of the retina and its connections to the brain has uncovered parallel circuits mediated by different types of ganglion cells emerging from the retina. These cells are known simply as *M cells* and *P cells*. Each gives rise to circuits that project to the lateral geniculate nucleus, the M cells to the magnocellular layers, the P cells to the parvocellular layers. And each circuit in the lateral geniculate nucleus in turn projects to different areas in the visual cortex, M cells to the V4 area, P cells to the V5 area.

Studies on both lower animals and humans indicate that each circuit is involved in coding a different feature of the visual stimulus. In one study lesions were placed in the M or P circuits in monkeys, and the animals' ability to see color and motion was disrupted: M-circuit lesions disrupted motion, and P-circuit lesions disrupted color (Schiller and Logothetis, 1990). In a second study PET scans were taken while people viewed visual displays, in one case a Mondrian (an abstract painting containing different colors) and in the other case black-and-white moving images, and the results indicated that the two areas of the visual cortex (V4 and V5) to which the M cells and P cells project are activated by different features—color and motion—of the visual stimulus, respectively (Zeki et al., 1991). By the same token, patients with damage to one or the other of these areas show selective loss of ability to recognize motion (V4 area) or color (V5 area) (Rizzo et al., 1992; Zihl et al., 1991).

What is significant about these findings from a parallel processing point of view is that coding of color and movement involves not only different areas in the visual cortex but also areas that engage in coding in an independent and presumably parallel fashion. So the anatomical potential for parallel processing clearly exists, although the extent to which it is actually involved in perception remains to be determined.

Summing Up: Bottom-Up and Top-Down Processing

Although researchers have barely scratched the surface of higher-order perceptual coding, recent findings have profoundly changed the way psychologists think about the visual coding process. Today, we can safely say that a substantial amount of abstracting and processing of information is related to the activity of single neurons, and we can begin to see a general pattern emerging when we move from lower animals, such as frogs, to higher animals, such as cats and monkeys. In frogs, for instance, codes for complex information are formed in the optic nerve, but in cats and monkeys (and possibly in humans), the coding for complex information appears to be tied to the cortex.

But this picture, tidy as it is, is still incomplete. As we emphasized in the last chapter, there is more to sensing a stimulus than just determining its physical properties. We sense lines and edges, but we see scenes and paintings. In addition to sensing the physical properties of a stimulus, we interpret and then classify these properties in terms of our past experience.

The term used to refer to the sensing stage—the stage determined by the physical properties of the stimulus—is *bottom-up processing*. The term used to describe the interpretive stage—the stage governed by past experience, knowledge, and expectations—is *top-down processing*. We've just looked at bottom-up processing, transducing and coding the physical features of visual stimuli. Now let us take a brief look at top-down processing, the physiological basis of the ability to interpret these stimuli on the basis of past knowledge.

Agnosia Revisited

As we saw in the last chapter, some brain-damaged humans suffer from agnosia: they can see objects but are unable to identify them, even when objects are familiar. When some people suffering from agnosia look into a mirror, for instance, they can't even identify the person they see. Agnosia is a rare condition, but the fact that some people are afflicted by it indicates that the ability to recognize and identify the things we see involves two different processes—"seeing" and "knowing"—each mediated by a different area of the brain. People with agnosia presumably have damage in the "knowing" area of the brain but not the "seeing" area—a presumption that raises an interesting possibility—that knowing an object may be physiologically rooted in principles of coding similar to those we encountered in seeing an object. Conceivably, like the circuits for coding different physical features of a visual stimulus, there may be circuits or areas in the brain that code for different memories of that visual stimulus, and indeed, evidence from lower-animal work has strengthened the likelihood of this possibility.

The evidence for this view comes from studies in which monkeys subjected to damage in brain areas connected to the visual cortex were divided into two groups: one group receiving damage in the anterior part of the infratemporal cortex, the other receiving damage to the posterior parietal cortex. The monkeys in both groups retained the ability to "see" but lost some aspect of "knowing" behavior. Significantly, though, the nature of the loss differed, depending on the site of the damage. Monkeys receiving damage to the anterior infratemporal cortex lost the ability to identify visually familiar objects; monkeys receiving damage to the posterior parietal cortex lost the ability to remember the visual location of the objects (Mishkin, Ungerleider, & Macko, 1983).

The conclusion: there appear to be two distinct visual *memory* systems, at least in monkeys, one for recognizing a familiar object and the other for remembering where the object is located. We'll return to the physiological basis of memory in detail in Chapter 17.

NEURAL CODING:
INHERENT OR ACQUIRED?

Is neural coding an inherent or an acquired capacity? The early work of Hubel and Wiesel produced evidence for both views. The work showed, on the one hand, that newborn kittens have single neural cells that code for line and angles. On the other hand, their work showed that this unique coding capacity is lost if kittens are deprived of visual stimulation during the first 20 days of life (Hubel & Wiesel, 1963). Adult cats subjected to comparable sensory deprivation, on the other hand, show no such deficit in visual coding. These findings suggest strongly that there is a critical period, early in an animal's life, for sustaining the inherent circuits and that deprivation of sensory experience during this period leads to loss of coding.

Experiments by Helmut Hirsch and D. N. Spinelli have shown that, although the cells may be present at birth and may be abolished by early sensory deprivation, they may also be *altered* by early sensory stimulation (Hirsch & Spinelli, 1970). In one study, Hirsch and Spinelli subjected kittens to different visual stimulation (via goggles). The visual stimulation presented to one eye was a series of black lines arranged vertically on a white background. The visual stimulation presented to the other eye was a similar group of black lines arranged horizontally on a white background. The kittens spent the first 10 to 12 weeks of their lives in this environment. Neural activity was then recorded from single cells in the visual cortex.

The results of this study would appear to confirm the notion that inborn coding capacities can indeed be altered by visual experiences early in life. Cells connected to the eye exposed to only horizontal lines fired in response to only horizontal stimuli, while cells connected to the eye exposed only to vertical lines fired to only vertical stimuli. But there was another—and rather surprising—finding. The kittens in both groups lost the ability to respond to oblique (that is, angular) lines, and this absence could not be attributed to atrophied or inactive cells because no silent cells were found. The likely explanation: the sensory stimulation *altered*, but did not abolish, the inherent coding of oblique lines.

Hirsch and Spinelli's data indicate that early visual experiences affect the activity of neurons but the data do not indicate that such activity can ultimately alter visual *behavior*. It remained for another study, conducted by Colin Blakemore and G. F. Cooper, to establish a relation between early visual experience and visual behavior (Blakemore & Cooper, 1970).

Blakemore and Cooper followed Hirsch and Spinelli's procedure, raising newborn kittens in controlled visual environments. One group of kittens saw only horizontal lines for the first 5 months of their lives, another group saw only vertical lines. The question Blakemore and Cooper sought to answer was this: Would the kittens whose visual experiences were devoid of vertical lines be able to see vertical lines, and would the kittens whose visual experiences were devoid of horizontal lines be able to see horizontal lines?

The behavior of the kittens suggested strongly that they *could not* see any lines that they had not been exposed to during the first 5 months of their lives. Placed in a maze, the kittens reared in a "vertical" environment could negotiate the maze when confronted by vertical obstacles but not when confronted by horizontal obstacles. Kittens reared in a "horizontal" environment showed just the opposite behavior: they could handle the horizontal obstacles but not the vertical ones.

Evidence that the environment plays an important role in the development of the human visual system comes from observations on children who suffer from a visual condition known as *amblyopia*. Children suffering from this condition have a tendency to squint and fall into the habit of relying on only one eye for their visual stimulation, thus depriving the other eye of visual input. If this habit continues through childhood, the unused eye will usually become blind and impervious to corrective lenses—an indication that the problem is neural not muscular. If, however, the squint is addressed early enough so that the child learns to use both eyes, vision in both eyes develops more or less normally (Alberts et al., 1994).

In conclusion, then, studies on lower animals and humans point to a definite relationship between early visual experience and visual behavior. But what are the implications of this relationship? Does it mean that neural circuits and, ultimately, visual behavior early in life can be engineered by the environment? Perhaps. But it is worth pointing out (as discussed in Chapter 2) that neural changes continue throughout life, and that the capacity of the environment to shape the nervous system is not confined simply to the early stages of development—although in some cases it may be—nor to the visual nervous system. Our ability to learn and remember—at any age—is rooted in the capacity of new experiences to produce changes in the nervous system and for those changes to endure. We will consider the neural changes that underlie learning and memory in detail in Chapter 16.

COLOR VISION

Apart from being able to differentiate objects on the basis of their shape and form, humans and a few other animals (e.g., birds and monkeys) are able to sense and differentiate colors. As we have already seen, coding color involves a circuit that begins in the retina and, via the lateral geniculate nucleus, ends in the cortex. Now we will consider the coding process itself—what actually happens in the retina and in the lateral geniculate nucleus that gives rise to the code for color in the cortex.

The range of colors or hues experienced by humans, as pictured in Figure 7.15, is called the *color spectrum*. For all practical purposes, this spectrum begins at 400 nm with blue. It changes to blue-green at around 500 nm, then to green, yellow-green, yellow, orange, red, and reddish purple as wavelengths increase, until they are no longer visible.

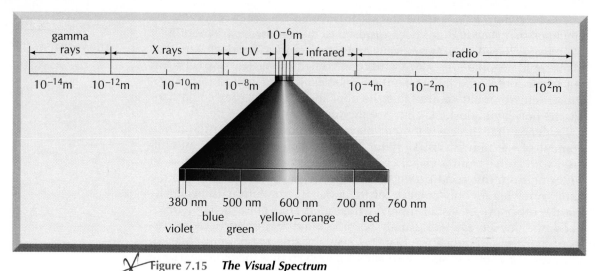

Figure 7.15 **The Visual Spectrum**
Light waves visible to humans fall in a very small range of the electromagnetic spectrum. Within the visible band, different wavelengths produce different color sensations (wavelengths are represented in terms of nanometers [nm]).

The determining factor in the ability to respond to wavelengths ranging from 380 to 760 nm is the fact that only these particular wavelengths are capable of being transduced—that is, of producing neural impulses. And the reason, as we will see shortly, is that receptors in the eye contain special chemicals that are sensitive to and transduce certain wavelengths but not others.

How Colors Are Produced

Although Figure 7.15 depicts colors as a result of single wavelengths, the fact is that colors are usually produced by a mixture of wavelengths. In fact, when mixed in varying proportions, wavelengths in three different areas of the visual spectrum—red, green, and blue—can produce every color in the spectrum. If you mix red and green light, for instance, the resulting wavelengths will produce the color yellow. If you mix blue and yellow light, the resulting wavelengths will be seen as gray.

This fact may be surprising to you. You probably know, for example, that if you take blue paint and mix it with yellow paint, the resulting color will be green. Why the difference between mixing lights and mixing paints? The reason is that color produced by mixing (whether lights or paints) depends on the wavelengths that reach the eye. Paints absorb some wavelengths and reflect others, and it is the reflected wavelengths that reach the eye. The combination of blue and yellow paint, for example, absorbs the light of all wavelengths except those in the green range. Only these wavelengths reach the eye. Mixing lights, on the other hand, does not work by absorbing wavelengths. The combination of blue and yellow light is the combination that actually reaches the eye. The result is gray.

To demonstrate how a mixture of wavelengths of light can produce a single color, let us consider a hypothetical color-mixing experiment. If we select a long wavelength in the red range—671 nm, let us say—and mix it with wavelengths from the green range one at a time, the resulting colors will vary from orange to orange-yellow until we mix it with a green wavelength of 536 nm. At that point the result will be yellow (a yellow that is indistinguishable from "pure" yellow produced by a single wavelength of 589 nm). We call colors that result from the mixing of different wavelengths (orange, orange-yellow, and yellow, in this case) *intermediate colors*.

If, however, we continue to mix the red wavelength with progressively shorter and shorter green wavelengths (again, one at a time), at a certain point—specifically at 493 nm—the mixture will result in no color: we will see gray. As it happens, every color (i.e., wavelength) in the spectrum, when mixed with one other color in appropriate proportions, will produce gray, and the sets of colors that together produce gray (e.g., red of a particular wavelength and green of a particular wavelength) are known as *complementary colors*.

You will begin to appreciate the importance of these distinctions when we consider some of the theories of color coding. For now it is enough to bear in mind two facts:

1. There are two ways of producing colors, either by a single wavelength (which is rare) or by mixing wavelengths (which is more common).
2. Mixing wavelengths can produce one of two results—new colors (intermediates) or no color (complementaries).

Thus, the physiological mechanism that underlies color coding, whatever it may be, must also account for both of these features—intermediates and complementaries.

TRACKING THE COLOR CODE

Researchers who have studied the physiological basis of color coding have differing views of how, in fact, coding takes place, but everyone agrees on one point: the sensation of color depends primarily on the receptors in the retina that are stimulated, specifically, on the cones and their relationship to the brain. Earlier in this chapter we spoke of the different visual sensations (acuity and sensitivity) mediated by rods and cones and discussed how these differences may be explained by dissimilarities in chemical makeup and in neural connections with the brain. The chief difference that concerns us here is that color sensations depend on stimulation of the cones. Rod stimulation produces only varying sensations of grayness.

The most obvious way of explaining color coding is to assume that there is a specific set of cones sensitive to each color-producing wavelength. But the problem with this explanation is that many colors—the intermediate colors, as we have seen—are products of mixed wavelengths. This means, obviously, that a specific type of cone is not needed for every color. It is more likely that a few types of cones, sensitive to a few primary colors, may suffice, and that stimulating these cones in various combinations (mixing them as you would primary colors) may be sufficient to account for all the color sensations we experience. In any case, two theories proposed in the nineteenth century share this premise. Each suggests the existence of a few groups of primary cones, each group being capable of producing one color sensation by itself but capable of producing the entire color spectrum when stimulated simultaneously to various degrees. Although both theories are more than 100 years old, technological advances have made it possible to confirm some portions of each.

The Trichromatic Theory

The trichromatic theory of color vision was originally proposed in 1802 by Thomas Young and was revised about 50 years later by Hermann von Helmholtz (Young, 1807; Helmholtz, 1852). Briefly stated (in its updated version), it is as follows.

The retina consists of three groups of cones, each of which is *maximally sensitive* to a different wavelength (long, intermediate, or short), with each wavelength corresponding to one of the three primary colors (red, green, or blue). "Maximally sensitive" is a key concept. It means that each group of cones is attuned to a broad range of wavelengths, but that each responds "best" to certain wavelengths and less well to others.

If a long wavelength (say, 671 nm) produces a red sensation, for instance, we can assume that even though the three groups of cones have been activated, the group of cones maximally sensitive to long wavelengths (the red receptors) has been activated the most. If an intermediate wavelength (say, 536 nm) produces a green sensation, we can assume that the group of cones maximally sensitive to intermediate wavelengths (the green receptors) has been activated the most. A single wavelength (589 nm) between these levels or a mixture of two wavelengths (671 and 536 nm) will then produce a yellow sensation, not because yellow receptors have been stimulated but because *both* red and green receptors have been activated the most. Presumably, the effect of this combined activation in the brain is different (yellow) from the effect of the activation of either red or green receptors alone. A basis for a code, a neural distinction for each color, is thus formed.

Support for the Trichromatic Theory

Evidence to support the trichromatic theory of color vision comes from the work of Nobel Prize winner George Wald. Wald found that the cones can be differentiated on the basis of their chemical makeup, specifically, in the nature of their iodopsin. Iodopsin, Wald discovered, can take one of three different forms, known as cyanolabe, chlorolabe, and erythrolabe (Wald, Brown, & Smith, 1954; Wald, 1964). Wald also discovered that each type of iodopsin is maximally sensitive to a specific wavelength that, in turn, corresponds to one of the three primary colors (red, green, or blue). Figure 7.16 illustrates the sensitivity curves for the three groups of cones.

The Three Groups of Cones: Summing Up

Color vision is apparently governed by three groups of cones, each group sensitive to a broad range of wavelengths in the visible spectrum and each group more responsive to certain wavelengths than to others. Thus what is reported to the brain is not the activity produced in one group of cones per se but the *relative activity* produced in all three groups of cones. The brain's job is to process this information and to code it into the neural activity that represents color. Exactly how the brain does this is not yet known, but we have some good leads. They come from experiments concerned with the opponent-process theory of color vision.

The Opponent-Process Theory

The *opponent-process theory* of color vision was originally advanced by the German physiologist Ewald Hering in 1870 and was revised in the late 1950s by Leon Hurvich and Dorothy Jameson (Hurvich & Jameson,

Figure 7.16 *Sensitivity Curves for Three Groups of Cones*
Each group of cones contains its own iodopsin maximally sensitive to certain wavelengths and less sensitive to others: one group is maximally sensitive to (that is, absorbs) the shorter wavelengths (445 nm), a second group is maximally sensitive to the intermediate wavelengths (535 nm), a third group is maximally sensitive to the longer wavelengths (570 nm).

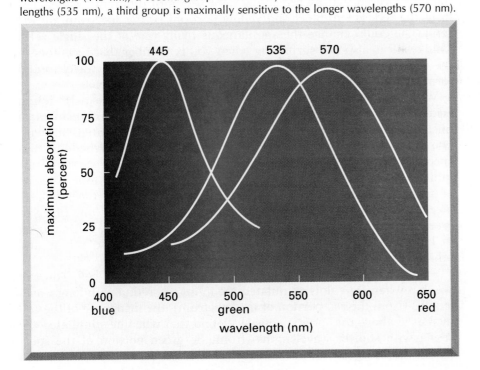

1957). Like Young and Helmholtz, Hering believed that there were only a few primary colors and that the rest of the spectrum was derived from the mixing of these primaries. Unlike Young and Helmholtz, however, Hering postulated that yellow was not derived from a mixture of red and green (as the trichromatic theory proposed) but, along with red, green, and blue, was itself a primary color. More significant, perhaps, Hering suggested a much different coding mechanism.

Unlike Young and Helmholtz, who theorized that each primary color was coded by a different group of cones, Hering proposed that a single chemical process (he never identified it) could code two primary colors, with the buildup of a certain chemical coding for one primary color and the breakdown of the same chemical coding for a second primary color. This meant that two chemicals could account for all four primaries. From Hering's conceptualization—the same chemical working in opposite directions to produce different colors—came the name "opponent process."

Support for the Opponent-Process Theory

Much as advances in biochemical assay technology helped George Wald to marshal support for the trichromatic theory, so have advances in microelectrode technology led to data supporting the opponent-process theory. In one important set of experiments involving monkeys, Russell De Valois placed microelectrodes in single neural cells in the lateral geniculate nucleus and noted, not surprisingly, that the single cells (like Kuffler's single ganglion cells) had a spontaneous firing rate. De Valois then discovered that by projecting light waves of different frequencies, from the red, green, blue, and yellow portions of the spectrum, on the retina, he could change the spontaneous firing rate of the single cells. This result is also not surprising when you remember that receptors in the retina are connected to ganglion cells, which in turn travel to and form synapses with neurons in the lateral geniculate nucleus.

What was surprising was what De Valois discovered next. He found evidence that the four primary colors are coded in the lateral geniculate nucleus in terms of opponent processes, as Hering postulated, but with one difference. Coding is rooted not in the buildup and breakdown of a specific chemical, as Hering theorized, but rather in the excitation or inhibition of activity in single neurons. De Valois found four types of opponent neurons in the lateral geniculate nucleus: two types of red-green cells (one firing to red and inhibiting to green, and one firing to green and inhibiting to red) and two types of blue-yellow cells (one firing to blue and inhibiting to yellow, and the other firing to yellow and inhibiting to blue) (De Valois, 1960; De Valois & De Valois, 1975).

Figure 7.17 shows the firing rate of a typical red-green cell. You can see that when De Valois stimulated the monkey's retina with long wavelengths (from the red portion of the spectrum), the firing rate of the cell increased above the spontaneous level, and that when he stimulated the retina with shorter wavelengths (from the green portion of the spectrum), the firing rate of the *same* cell decreased below the spontaneous

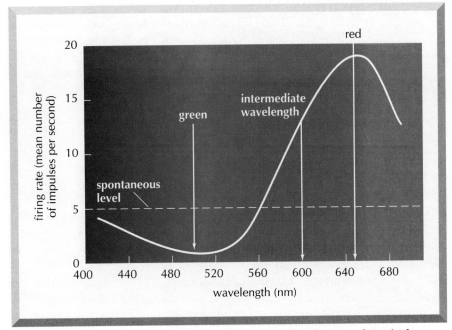

Figure 7.17   *Recordings from a Single Red-Green Cell in the Lateral Geniculate Nucleus*

The average firing rate increases above spontaneous level to long wavelengths (in the red range) and decreases below spontaneous level to shorter wavelengths (in the green range). The average firing rate approaches spontaneous level with intermediate wavelengths.

level. De Valois found a similar pattern of firing in blue-yellow cells—the cell firing to some wavelengths and the *same* cell inhibiting to other wavelengths, except in this case the wavelengths were from the blue and yellow (rather than the red and green) portions of the spectrum.

Combining the Trichromatic and Opponent-Process Theories

How do we reconcile De Valois's findings with Wald's? In other words, how can there be three groups of cones (i.e., three types of iodopsin) maximally sensitive to wavelengths from three different portions of the visible spectrum (red, green, and blue), as Wald found, and four sets of opposing cells in the lateral geniculate nucleus (two for red-green and two for blue-yellow), as De Valois found?

If you look at Figure 7.18, you will see a theoretical model of how "conversion" from the chemical reactions of cones to the neural response of the lateral geniculate nucleus might occur. As the figure indicates (and we are simplifying an extremely complex process), the explanation lies, at least theoretically, in the circuits (the ganglion cells) connecting the receptors in the retina with the opponent neural cells in the lateral genic-

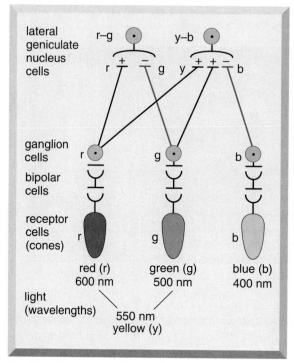

Figure 7.18   *Color Vision*
A theoretical model of how neural interactions in the retina can convert the chemical responses of three types of cones into neural responses in four types of color-coded opponent cells. Plus sign denotes excitation; minus sign denotes inhibition; r-g denotes red-green opponent cells; y-b denotes yellow-blue opponent cells.

ulate nucleus. Let's look at the opponent cells and the connections more closely, first the red-green opponent cells, then the blue-yellow opponent cells.

Red-Green Opponent Cells

How can an opponent cell—the red-green cell in this case—fire to long wavelengths (from the red portion of the spectrum) and inhibit to shorter wavelengths (from the green portion of the spectrum)? The answer, according to the theory, is that the red-green opponent cells receive neural input from two sources: from red receptors and green receptors. The input from the red receptors is excitatory, the input from the green receptors is inhibitory, and when the two inputs occur simultaneously, the neural activity they produce in the opponent cell depends on which is dominant. If excitation outweighs inhibition, firing in the opponent cell *increases* above the spontaneous level and the red portion of the spectrum is signaled. If inhibition outweighs excitation, firing in the opponent cell *decreases* below the spontaneous level and the green portion of the spectrum is signaled. If excitation and inhibition are equal and opposite, firing in the opponent cell does not change, no signal in the red or green portion of the spectrum is produced, and we see gray.

The absence of a signal, in this case, is particularly significant, for it accounts for complementary colors. Remember, two wavelengths (e.g., a specific wavelength from the red portion of the spectrum and a specific wavelength from the green portion of the spectrum) when mixed are known to produce gray and the opponent cell's response, or in this case absence of a response, explains why.

Blue-Yellow Opponent Cells

How can an opponent cell—the blue-yellow cell in this case—fire to intermediate wavelengths (from the yellow portion of the spectrum) and inhibit to shorter wavelengths (from the blue portion of the spectrum)? The answer, according to the theory, is that the blue-yellow opponent cells receive neural input from *three* sources: from the blue, green, and red receptors. The input from the blue receptors is inhibitory and would account for why wavelengths from the blue portion of the spectrum produce inhibition. The input from the red and green receptors is excitatory and would account for why wavelengths from the yellow portion of the spectrum produce excitation. Let us look at the coding for yellow more closely.

Coding Yellow

Look at Figure 7.18. Notice that when the eye is stimulated by wavelengths from the yellow portion of the spectrum, red and green receptors are stimulated simultaneously—remember there are no yellow receptors. The simultaneous stimulation in turn is projected to the blue-yellow *and*, as we saw earlier, to the red-green opponent cells. But the impact that the simultaneous stimulation has on the two types of cells is much different: it has no effect on the red-green opponent cells, but it does increase firing in the blue-yellow opponent cells. Why? Because the simultaneous stimulation projected to the red-green opponent cells produces equal and opposing effects (remember input from red receptors is excitatory and input from green receptors is inhibitory) that cancel each other out. Simultaneous stimulation projected to the blue-yellow opponent cells does not produce equal and opposing effects; rather, stimulation from *both* the red and green receptors is excitatory, the effects summate, and the firing of the blue-yellow opponent cells increases above the spontaneous level.

Something should bother you about this explanation. If, as Figure 7.18 indicates, the simultaneous stimulation of red and green receptors is projected to the blue-yellow opponent cells, why, then, when red receptors are stimulated *alone* or when green receptors are stimulated *alone*, do they not (in addition to exciting or inhibiting the red-green opponent cells) stimulate the blue-yellow opponent cells? The answer, at least theoretically, is that the blue-yellow opponent cells have a high threshold of excitation that can be exceeded only when red and green receptors are stimulated *simultaneously* and the excitatory effects of each summate.

In any event, whether we are dealing with blue-yellow opponent cells or red-green opponent cells, the coding process is the same. If excitation outweighs inhibition, firing in the opponent cell *increases* above the spontaneous level and the yellow portion of the spectrum is signaled. If inhibition outweighs excitation, firing in the opponent cell *decreases* below the spontaneous level and the blue portion of the spectrum is signaled. If excitation and inhibition are equal and opposite, firing in the opponent cell does not change, no signal in the blue or yellow portion of the spectrum is produced, and we see gray.

Summary

On the surface, the model just described appears logical enough. It accounts for intermediate colors (colors that result from the mixing of different wavelengths) and it accounts for complementary colors (the sets of colors that together produce gray). The mechanism in both cases is the same. When opponent neural cells fire, either *above* or *below* the spontaneous level, the intermediates are produced; when they fire *at* the spontaneous level, the complementaries are produced.

You must keep in mind, however, that no one has observed the circuitry (the connections between receptors and opponent cells) that underlies this model of color vision. Moreover, we do not want to leave you with the impression that the opponent cells in the lateral geniculate nucleus are the only cells in the brain involved in coding color. Cells in the cortex, as we saw earlier, are also involved, their activity presumably reflecting the activity in the cells in the lateral geniculate nucleus, but their role is still being worked out (Zeki, 1980; Zeki et al., 1991).

COLOR BLINDNESS

As you know by now, and as you will come to appreciate more when we look into higher-order behaviors, physiological psychologists routinely study abnormalities to gain insights into normal functioning. Color vision is no exception, and one of the abnormalities that has been studied with this objective in mind is color blindness.

There are several types of color blindness, and all seem to be genetically determined. In rare cases color blindness is total, causing the victim to sense wavelengths of light only as varying shades of gray. Most cases of color blindness, however, are partial. The two most common types of partial color blindness, summarized in Table 7.1, are *protanopia* and *deuteranopia*. Both involve red-green blindness. Protanopes see long wavelengths that normally produce red as black, and intermediate wavelengths that normally produce green as yellow. Deuteranopes have essentially the same problem except that their color blindness is reversed: they see intermediate wavelengths that normally produce green as black, and long wavelengths that normally produce red as yellow. There is a third type of partial color blindness known as *tritanopia*, but it is almost as

TABLE 7.1

COLOR BLINDNESS: THE COLOR SENSATIONS PRODUCED BY LONG, INTERMEDIATE, AND SHORT WAVELENGTHS IN NORMALS, PROTANOPES, AND DEUTERANOPES

	LONG WAVELENGTHS 600 nm	INTERMEDIATE WAVELENGTHS 500 nm	SHORT WAVELENGTHS 400 nm
Normals	Red	Green	Blue
Protanopes	Black	Yellow	Blue
Deuteranopes	Yellow	Black	Blue

rare as total color blindness and very little is known about it other than the principal symptom: tritanopes can see neither yellow nor blue.

Explaining Color Blindness

To consider color blindness in light of the two theories of color vision is to run into a number of problems. The opponent-process theory, for instance, suggests that because they are red-green-blind, protanopes and deuteranopes lack the neurons in the lateral geniculate nucleus essential for the red-green opponent process. But if this is so, why does a protanope see yellow from wavelengths that normally produce green, and why does a deuteranope see yellow from wavelengths that normally produce red?

The quandary is not eased when we attempt to explain color blindness within the framework of the trichromatic theory. Wald's discovery of the three different iodopsins may explain why protanopes are red-blind (they lack the iodopsin sensitive to the wavelengths that normally produce red) and why deuteranopes are green-blind (they lack the iodopsin sensitive to wavelengths that normally produce green). But Wald's findings do not explain why protanopes see yellow from wavelengths that normally produce green and why deuteranopes see yellow from wavelengths that normally produce red. According to the trichromatic theory, remember, yellow is not a primary color but a mixture of red and green. Thus we must ask ourselves how a person unable to see red or green could see the color that presumably results from the mixture of red and green.

There is a possible resolution of these inconsistencies. It is conceivable that protanopes and deuteranopes are normal in every respect but one: the nature of their iodopsin. Protanopes, for instance, might have cones that would normally contain iodopsin maximally sensitive to long wavelengths (the red portion of the spectrum) that instead contain iodopsin maximally sensitive to shorter wavelengths (the green portion of the spectrum). This would explain why protanopes are red-blind: when stimulated by wavelengths from the red portion of the spectrum, because there is no iodopsin sensitive to these wavelengths, no cones are excited, and they see no color at all. It also explains why protanopes see wavelengths from the green portion of the spectrum as yellow. When the retina of a protanope is stimulated by wavelengths from the green portion of the spectrum, the error in iodopsin results in excitation of both groups of cones: the green cones that are normally sensitive to wavelengths from the green portion of the spectrum and the red cones which, because of the error in iodopsin, are also sensitive to wavelengths from the green portion of the spectrum. The result: the simultaneous action of the green cones and red cones excites the blue-yellow cells in the lateral geniculate nucleus, producing the code for yellow.

A similar explanation—an error in iodopsin—can be applied in the case of deuteranopes, the only difference being that deuteranopes lack the iodopsin sensitive to wavelengths from the green portion of the spectrum and have in its place iodopsin sensitive to wavelengths from the red portion of the spectrum.

SUMMARY

1. *Light and vision.* Light is a form of electromagnetic energy that travels in waves, whose variations correspond to specific visual experiences: length corresponds to hue, amplitude corresponds to brightness, and purity corresponds to saturation.

2. *The basics of vision.* Vision is a twofold process: an optical process and a neural process. In the optical process, scattered light rays are gathered as they enter the eye and are focused on the retina, which acts as a transducer. In the neural process, the light rays are transduced into neural impulses and the impulses are coded into particular visual experiences. Structures in the eye can be categorized according to the roles they play in the two processes. Nonneural structures are involved in optics and nourishment, and neural structures are involved in transduction and coding.

3. *Nonneural structures in the eye.* The first structures encountered by light when it enters the eye—the cornea and lens, in particular—are nonneural, and their principal function is to focus light on the retina. Light enters the eye in scattered form; the cornea and lens combine to project the scattered light as a single point (that is, focus the light) on the retina. The focusing capacity of the two structures comes from their ability to bend (refract) light. The cornea, which does most of the work, has fixed refractory powers. The lens, because it can change in shape, has varied refractory powers.

4. *The lens and refraction.* The varied refractory powers of the lens are important because of variations in the extent to which light must be bent. The greater the distance light travels before it reaches the eye, the less the scatter and hence the less refraction needed. The most common visual disorders, myopia (nearsightedness) and hyperopia (farsightedness), are related to problems in refraction. Myopia is the result of over-refraction (that is, light waves are bent too much and are focused in front of the retina). Hyperopia results from underrefraction (that is, light waves are not bent enough and hit the retina while still scattered).

5. *The retina.* Neural processing of visual information begins in the retina, a structure consisting of three layers of cells. One layer is made up of photoreceptor cells, the rods and the cones. The other two layers are made up of nerve cells, a layer of bipolar and a layer of ganglion cells. The ganglion cells give rise to axons, which leave the retina in a bundle of fibers known as the optic nerve.

6. *Rods and cones.* Rods and cones are unique to the eye. Both are named for their shapes. Both are sensitive to light, but the nature of their sensitivity differs, and these differences are related to both their structure and their chemical makeup. Rods function in ways that are achromatic (colorless) and scotopic (related to darkness). Cones require more light to be excited and they demonstrate a chromatic (color) and photopic (related to light) capacity. Rods are better than cones at detecting very weak visual stimuli, but cones are more attuned to visual details—a capacity known as visual acuity.

7. *The breakdown of photochemicals.* Their differences notwithstanding, rods and cones operate in similar ways. They both convert light waves into neural impulses, and they do so on the basis of photochemicals in their membranes. Rods contain rhodopsin, which is composed of opsin and retinene. Cones have no rhodopsin but contain three types of iodopsin. The behavioral significance of these chemical differences lies in the difference in light sensitivity between the rhodopsin found only in rods and the iodopsin found only in cones. Rhodopsin is about ten times more sensitive to light than iodopsin. This explains, in part, why rods are more sensitive to light than cones.

8. *Acuity and sensitivity: their relation to receptive fields.* The receptive field is the total area of the retina from which a ganglion cell receives impulses. The receptive field of ganglion cells connected to cones is much smaller than the receptive field of ganglion cells receiving impulses from rods. The difference in receptive fields explains why cones are better than rods at discerning the details of a stimulus, and why rods are better than cones at detecting the mere presence of a stimulus.

9. *Coding for contour.* The ability to distinguish an object as distinct from its background calls for the ability to see its contour—that is, to code the differences in reflected light between an object and its background. The neural recording work of Hartline and Ratliff on ommatidia in the *Limulus* (horseshoe crab) eye indicates that the code for contour, specifically the code for brightness contrast that highlights figure from ground, is rooted in a neurophysiological process known as lateral inhibition. Lateral inhibition occurs when receptors that are stimulated not only activate their own circuits but inhibit activity in neighboring circuits. The result is an increase in activity in the stimulated areas, a decrease in activity in the neighboring areas and a code for brightness contrast, that is, a code for the contrast that occurs at the edges between object and background.

10. *Kuffler's discovery.* Recording from single ganglion cells in the monkey retina, Kuffler found evidence for ganglion cells receiving opposing inputs from the center and the perimeter of their receptive field. He called the cells on-center and off-center cells and concluded that they represent the mammalian counterpart to the brightness contrast produced by lateral inhibition in the *Limulus* eye.

11. *Coding for lines.* Extending the analysis of contour coding to the cortex of cats, Hubel and Wiesel found single neural cells that code for lines and edges. Hubel and Wiesel called these cells feature cells and classified them into three groups. Simple cells respond best when a line is in a very specific orientation—vertical, horizontal, oblique—and in a very precise position on the retina. Complex cells also respond maximally when a line is in a very specific orientation but the position of the line on the retina is less important. Hypercomplex cells fire only to lines of a particular length or particular angle. To account for their findings, Hubel and Wiesel have proposed a model of visual coding based on the principle of convergence. Lateral geniculate neurons, in their view, converge on simple cells, simple cells converge on complex cells, and complex cells converge on hypercomplex cells.

12. *Parallel processing.* The convergence, or hierarchical, model explains many aspects of visual coding, but another process, known as parallel processing, may be just as important. In parallel processing, it is the simultaneous (rather than the convergent) activation of subordinate cells that produces the image. Critical to the notion of parallel processing is the assumption that different features of a visual stimulus affect different areas of the brain at the same time, and it is their simultaneous activation that produces the final image. There is anatomical evidence to support this assumption.

13. *M cells and P cells.* Analysis of the retina and its connections to the brain has uncovered parallel circuits mediated by two different types of ganglion cells—M cells and P cells—emerging from the retina. M cells connect to the magnocellular layers of the lateral geniculate nucleus where they form synapses with circuits that project to the cortex. P cells connect to the parvocellular layers of the lateral geniculate nucleus which in turn give rise to circuits that project to the cortex. Studies in monkeys indicate that each circuit is involved in coding a different feature of the visual stimulus, the M circuit coding for motion, the P circuit coding for color.

14. *Environmental impact on coding.* The question of whether neural coding for vision is an acquired or inherent capacity has been studied extensively and the results suggest a relation among early visual experience, development of neural circuitry, and development of visual behavior.

15. *Color coding: the basics.* Color is the result of a mixture of wavelengths, and the wavelengths of three colors in particular—red, green, and blue—can produce every color in the spectrum. This has led to the notion that color vision is governed by a few groups of cones attuned to a broad range of wavelengths in the visible spectrum but responding best to certain wavelengths and less well to others. Two theories have been proposed to explain how stimulation of these cones in different combinations account for all the color sensations.

16. *The trichromatic theory.* The trichromatic theory of color coding, originally proposed by Thomas Young in 1802 and revised by Hermann von Helmholtz in the 1850s, holds that the retina consists of three groups of cones, and that each group, stimulated alone, will produce one primary color sensation (red, green, or blue). Stimulated in various combinations, the groups will produce all the remaining colors in the spectrum. Evidence supporting this theory comes from the work of George Wald, who has isolated three photochemicals, each maximally sensitive to a wavelength that corresponds to one of the three primary colors.

17. *The opponent-process theory.* The opponent-process theory, originally advanced by the German physiologist Ewald Hering in 1870, shares with the trichromatic theory the idea that a few primary colors combine to produce the rest of the spectrum. The difference, though, is that it designates yellow in addition to red, green, and blue as a primary color. This theory holds that two chemical processes are needed to account for these four primary colors and that two primary colors are coded by the same chemical working in opposite directions. Supporting this theory is the work of Russell De Valois, who found that the lateral geniculate nucleus of monkeys does not contain different chemicals, as Hering proposed, but different cells coding in terms of opponent processes: two types of red-green cells (one firing to red and inhibiting to green and one firing to green and inhibiting to red) and two types of blue-yellow cells.

18. *Reconciling the theories.* In an effort to reconcile the two theories of color vision, researchers have proposed that both theories may be correct and that complex neural interactions between the retina and lateral geniculate nucleus convert the chemical response of the three types of cones into the neural response of the four types of color-coded neurons. This explanation accounts for intermediate colors—colors that result from the mixture of different wavelengths—and it accounts for complementary colors, the sets of colors that together produce gray. The theory is logical, but no one to date has observed the circuitry that might underlie it.

19. *Color blindness.* There are several types of color blindness, all of which appear to be genetically determined. The two most common types are protanopia, whose victims see red as black and green as yellow, and deuteranopia, whose victims see green as black and red as yellow. These symptoms, on the surface, cast doubt on the two principal theories of color coding. The opponent-process theory, for instance, would suggest that because they are red-green blind, protanopes and deuteranopes lack the neurons in the lateral geniculate nucleus essential for the red-green opponent process. But if this is so, why would a protanope see yellow from wavelengths that normally produce green, and why would deuteranopes see yellow from wavelengths that normally produce red? By the same token, the trichromatic theory fails to explain why people unable to see red or green could see the color that presumably results from the mixture of red and green. One possible explanation for these inconsistencies is that protanopes and deuteranopes are normal in every respect but one: the nature of their iodopsin.

KEY TERMS

achromatic
agnosia
amacrine cells
amplitude
aqueous humor
blind spot
blue-yellow opponent cells
bottom-up processing
brightness contrast
"bug detectors"
chlorolabe
choroid layer
chromatic
complementary colors
complex cells
cones
contour code
cornea
cyanolabe
deuteranopia
erythrolabe
fovea
"grandmother" cells
horizontal cells
hue
hypercomplex cells
infratemporal cortex
intermediate colors
iodopsin
iris

lateral geniculate nucleus
lateral inhibition
lens
Limulus
M cells
Mach bands
mutual inhibition
myopia
off-center cells
ommatidium
on-center cells
opponent-process theory
opsin
optic chiasma
optic disk
optic nerve
optic radiations
P cells
parallel processing
photochemicals
photopic
photopsin
photoreceptors
phototropic responses
prestriate cortex
primary colors
primary visual cortex
protanopia
pupil
purity

receptive field
red-green opponent cells
refraction
retinal inhibition
retinene
rhodopsin
rods
sclera
scotopic

simple cells
spatial summation
superior colliculus
tapetum
top-down processing
trichromatic theory
tritanopia
visual acuity
visual memory system

SUGGESTED READINGS

Hubel, D. H. *Eye, Brain, and Vision*. New York: Scientific American Library, 1988.

Livingstone, M. S. "Art, Illusion and the Visual System." *Scientific American*, 258, 1988, 78–85.

Miyashita, Y. "Inferior Temporal Cortex: When Visual Perception Meets Memory." *Annual Review of Neuroscience*, 16, 1993, 245–264.

Spillman, L. & Werner, J. S. *Visual Perception: The Neurophysiological Foundations*. San Diego: Academic Press 1990.

Zeki, S. "The Visual Image in Mind and Brain." *Scientific American*, 267, 1992, 69–76.

CHAPTER

8

AUDITION, TASTE, AND SMELL

INTRODUCTION

The physiological dynamics that underlie our ability to see are paralleled in many ways by the dynamics that underlie our ability to hear, to taste, and to smell. Just as we are endowed with a complex array of cellular mechanisms that enable us to transduce and code light waves into visual sensations, so are we equipped with cellular mechanisms that enable us to transduce and code sounds, odors, and tastes into a remarkable variety of sensory experiences: the music we like to listen to, the flowers we love to smell, and the food we love to eat, to mention a few.

As in the previous chapter, we will be examining each of these sensory processes with an eye toward understanding the dynamics within the nervous system that underlie what we experience as sensations. We will begin by looking into audition and then, for reasons you will quickly discover, treat smell and taste as a single topic.

AUDITION: AN OVERVIEW

Our ability to hear is rooted in our capacity to convert sound into neural impulses. Sound itself is produced by vibrations (such as those of a tuning fork or a violin string) that cause molecules to move back and forth. What we actually "hear" at any given time are molecules being disturbed. The molecules first move together, that is, they become *compressed*. When this happens, air pressure increases, creating a momentary vacuum (decreased pressure) that draws compressed molecules back into it. The term for this oscillation from compression to decompression is *rarefaction*.

Seen another way, sound is a wave of varied states of pressure radiating in all directions from a vibrating object. This wave moves relatively slowly, much more slowly than light: 330 meters per second (m/s) as compared to 300 million m/s for light. It has been measured in three respects: frequency, amplitude, and timbre. A glance at Figure 8.1 will show you the physical features of sound.

Frequency and Pitch

Frequency refers to the *rate of vibration*. Differences in frequencies of sound are to audition what differences in wavelengths of light are to vision. Just as the human eye can respond only to those light waves within a specific range, the human ear can detect only those sound waves that fall within a limited range of frequencies.

Sound-wave frequencies are commonly measured in cycles per second or hertz (Hz). The lowest frequency detectable by the human ear is about 16 Hz, a long wavelength; the highest frequency that most human beings can respond to is 20,000 Hz, a very short wavelength. Frequencies within this range produce the sound sensation known as *pitch*. The higher the frequency, the higher the pitch; the lower the frequency, the lower the

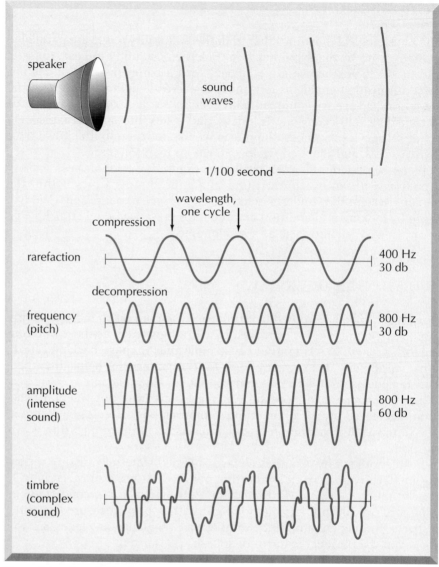

Figure 8.1 *Sound Waves*
Frequency (measured in hertz), amplitude (measured in decibels), and timbre.

pitch. Frequencies above or below these limits usually go undetected by human ears.

The auditory limitations, however, are not universal. Infants, for instance, can pick up frequencies as high as 40,000 Hz, and dogs can generally detect frequencies up to 30,000 Hz (thus explaining why high-frequency whistles can be heard by dogs but not by humans). Some animals (bats, moths, and porpoises) can pick up frequencies as high as 100,000 Hz. In Table 8.1 you will find a comparison of the frequencies of common sounds.

TABLE 8.1	
THE FREQUENCIES OF SOME COMMON SOUNDS (From Lindsay & Norman, 1972)	
SOUND	FREQUENCY (Hz)
Lowest note on piano	27.5
Lowest note of bass singer	100.0
Lowest note on clarinet	104.8
Middle C on piano	261.6
Standard tuning pitch (A above middle C)	440.0
Upper range of soprano	1000.0
Highest note on piano	4180.0
Harmonics of musical instruments	10,000.0
Limit of hearing for older persons	12,000.0
Limit of hearing	16,000–20,000.0

Amplitude and Loudness

Amplitude denotes how much pressure there is in a given sound wave, that is, the number of molecules compressed into a given area. You can also think of it as the force exerted on the molecules by the vibrating object. Variations in amplitude reflect the differences between how loud or soft a sound is. The more molecules moved or compressed into a given space, the greater the pressure, or amplitude, and the louder the sensation. Table 8.2 compares the amplitude of various sounds. Loudness is measured in decibels (dB), which are the basic units of intensity of sound.

Timbre

Timbre is to sound what saturation is to light. It refers to the purity or quality of a tone. *Pure* tones, in the strict sense of the term, are rare. That's because tones are not normally represented by sound waves of a

TABLE 8.2	
THE AMPLITUDES OF SOME COMMON SOUNDS (From Lindsay & Norman, 1972)	
SOUND	AMPLITUDE (dB)
Manned spacecraft launch (from 150 feet)	180
Pain threshold	150
Loud thunder, rock band	130
Shouting	100
Conversation	80
Soft whisper	30

single frequency. Without a mixture of frequencies, all musical instruments would sound the same; middle C on a piano would be no different from middle C on a violin. To understand how a mixture of frequencies determines the quality of a sound, we need to take a closer look at what we mean by "a mixture of frequencies."

A simple vibrating object, such as a tuning fork, produces a simple sound wave, or *sine wave*, whose pressure variations produce a *simple sound*. Most of the sounds we hear, however, come from *complex* vibrating objects—objects that consist of a number of vibrating parts, each with its own amplitude and frequency.

Consider a violin. If you pluck a violin string, it will vibrate up and down, producing pressure changes. If you could observe the vibrating string in slow motion, you would see that the movements of the string vary in amplitude. You would notice some very large vibrations, known as *fundamental tones*, and a variety of vibrations of smaller amplitude, known as *overtones*. You would also notice that the vibrations are characterized by a mixture of frequencies: the fundamental tone by low frequencies and the overtones by higher frequencies. A violin, having its own variety of vibrating parts, produces its own mixture of frequencies. That mixture is what enables you to distinguish the sound of a violin from the sound of a flute.

Harmonics: Musical Sounds

Harmonics is usually defined as the science of musical sounds, and *harmonic analysis* is the term used to describe the method by which sounds are measured and analyzed. A basic principle of harmonics is that fundamental tones and overtones (i.e., the waves in a complex sound) interact with one another. When sound waves coincide, as they do when a choir sings, they are known as *periodic*, and the effect is usually pleasant. When sound waves are produced at random, they are said to be *aperiodic*. The result, not always pleasant, is commonly referred to as *noise*.

How Sound Travels

Sound is produced initially by an object that disturbs molecules when it vibrates, causing each molecule to be pushed by a neighboring molecule. This sequential pushing causes successive molecules to vibrate. Once disturbed, the vibrating molecules spread in all directions, like billiard balls scattering across a table. The degree to which sound waves are sustained depends basically on two factors: the distance they must travel and the environment in which they make their journey. Distance reduces amplitude (loudness) but does not affect frequency (pitch). Environment, on the other hand, can affect both, as evidenced by the fact that restaurants with thick carpeting and drapes are not nearly as noisy as restaurants with bare windows and wood floors. Accounting for this difference is the distinct way certain materials either absorb or reflect sound waves, a principle that applies of course to light as well.

As you can see from Figure 8.2, the human ear has three basic parts: the outer ear, the middle ear, and the inner ear. The outer ear collects sound, the middle ear amplifies it, and the inner ear transduces it.

The Outer Ear

The first thing sound hits when it encounters the auditory system is the *pinna*, or *auricle*, pictured at the far left of Figure 8.2a. The pinna is what you normally think of as your "ear"—that flap projecting from the side of your head. Prominent though it may be, however, the pinna plays only a minor role in hearing. Even if the pinna is removed, hearing remains largely unaffected.

Figure 8.2   *The Ear*
(a) The outer, middle, and inner ear; (b) a magnified view of the bones in the middle ear and their articulation with the cochlea of the inner ear, shown unwound.

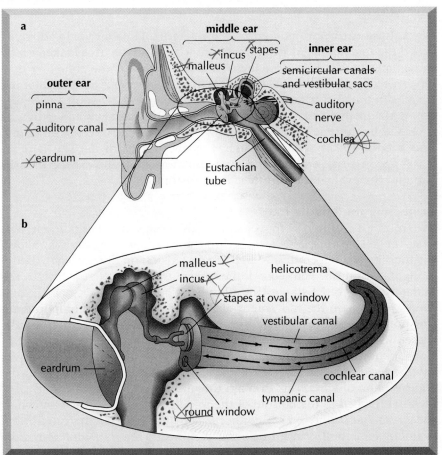

The role of the pinna is to orient us to the direction of sound, especially sounds originating in front or in back of us. Sound waves originating behind us must wind around the pinna and thus take a slightly different form from those originating in front. Some animals—dogs and bats in particular—can control the position of the pinna, thus giving them the ability to orient themselves to the direction of the sound.

A small hole in the pinna opens into an inch-long tunnel commonly known as the *auditory canal*. Its function is to conduct airborne sound inward (see Figure 8.2*a*). At the end of this passage is the membrane (the *tympanic membrane*) commonly known as the *eardrum*. The cone-shaped eardrum is pulled over the opening of the auditory canal and acts rather like the diaphragm of a microphone. Its chief quality is its elasticity—the capacity to move back and forth. This capacity allows it to match the incoming sound in frequency and amplitude. So sensitive is the eardrum that it can move, literally, at the drop of a molecule. The displacement of the eardrum created by the movement of a single molecule is in fact calculated to be *one-billionth of a centimeter*. Hence little is lost when airborne sound is converted into the mechanical movement of the eardrum.

The Middle Ear

Beyond the eardrum (as Figure 8.2*b* illustrates) sits an air-filled cavity called the *middle ear*. Most of the space within this cavity is taken up by three bones: the *malleus*, the *incus*, and the *stapes*. These bones are usually referred to by the shapes they roughly resemble: the *hammer* (malleus), the *anvil* (incus), and the *stirrup* (stapes). As you can see, the bones are arranged like a chain, beginning at the eardrum and ending at a second membrane (the *oval window*), which opens into the inner ear. The three bones are set in motion by the vibrating eardrum. The hammer starts the process, prodding the anvil into movement and driving the stirrup into the oval window, rather like a piston.

Protecting the Middle Ear

Two muscles control the movements of the bones in the middle ear. The first, the *tensor muscle*, is attached to the hammer in a way that allows the muscle, when it contracts, to increase tension on the eardrum, dampening its vibration. The second, the *stapedius muscle*, is attached, as the name implies, to the stapes (the stirrup). When this muscle contracts, it serves to dampen the movement of the stirrup so that the amplitude of the pressure exerted against the oval window is reduced. Both the stapedius muscle and the tensor muscle protect the inner ear (the site of transduction) from intense sound. When high-amplitude sound waves hit the ear, the muscles in the middle ear tighten reflexively, reducing the transmission of vibrations through the middle ear to the inner ear.

Also attached to the bottom of the middle ear is a thin tube known as the *Eustachian tube*, which connects with the back of the mouth and maintains an equilibrium in air pressure inside and outside the middle ear. When you open your mouth to chew or to yawn, the air pressure in the middle ear changes to permit equalization. Maintaining pressure equilibrium becomes necessary whenever there is an abrupt change in environmental pressure, as when you are in a plane that is taking off or landing.

Amplifying Sound

The bones in the middle ear, known collectively as *ossicles*, are among the smallest in the body, but their function in sound conduction is crucial. They serve to amplify sound pressure exerted against the oval window of the inner ear, and they do so by conducting sound through progressively smaller areas.

The surface of the eardrum measures approximately 1 square centimeter, an area much larger than that of the stirrup which measures approximately 3 square millimeters. Thus the sound initially spread over a large surface area is eventually funneled by the bones and concentrated on the small surface area of the oval window. Since the same force is maintained while the surface area is decreased, the power of the sound wave is amplified about 22 times before it reaches the oval window.

You can appreciate this principle better if you think of a shoe with a spiked heel. The heel funnels pressure spread across its tapered end, amplifying the pressure to such a degree that the heel can make an indentation in a wooden floor. The same pressure exerted by a flat heel does not benefit from amplification and hence cannot damage the floor.

The Inner Ear

The *inner ear* (as Figure 8.2 illustrates) begins on the other side of the oval window and is the most intricately structured of all the ear components. It consists of three main structures: the *semicircular canals* and *vestibular sacs*, both of which are found in its upper portions, and the *cochlea*, which is found in the lower portion.

Semicircular Canals and Vestibular Sacs

Despite their presence in the ear, neither the semicircular canals nor the vestibular sacs are involved in hearing per se. Their main role is to help maintain body balance and posture, the dynamics of which will be discussed in Chapter 9. The vestibular sacs are sensitive to head position and movement and in this way help to control the muscles that maintain posture. The semicircular canals respond mainly to head movements. Damage to them impairs the ability to maintain balance.

The Cochlea

The cochlea is the organ of hearing—the "retina of the ear." It consists, as you can see in Figure 8.2, of three fluid-filled canals within a single coiled tube: the *vestibular canal* (not to be confused with the vestibular sacs or the semicircular canals), which begins at the oval window and tapers to a small opening called the *helicotrema*; the *tympanic canal*, which interconnects with the vestibular canal at the helicotrema and ends at the *round window*; and the *cochlear canal*, which lies between the other two canals.

The Organ of Corti

One of the key features of the cochlea is a structure called the *organ of Corti*, which is shown in Figure 8.3. Named after its discoverer, Alfonso

Figure 8.3   *The Inner Ear*

The cochlea and organ of Corti in the inner ear (a) are shown in cross section (b) and in a magnified view (c) that shows the relationship between the basilar membrane, the hair cells, and the auditory nerve.

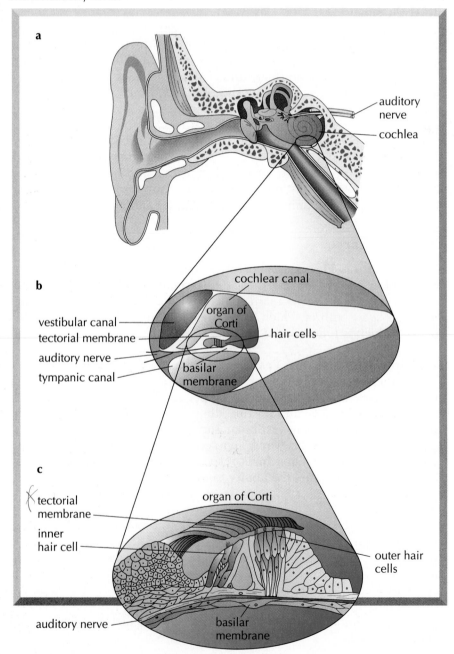

Corti, it rests on the floor of the cochlear canal, supported by the *basilar membrane*. Inside it are receptor cells that connect with neurons making up the auditory nerve. These receptor cells are called *hair cells* because hair, literally, is what they look like. Hair cells are located on the basilar membrane beneath the surface of an overhanging gelatinous structure known as the *tectorial membrane*. The number of these cells in the human ear has been placed at approximately 28,500, and they are arranged in two layers (25,000 in the outer layer and 3500 in the inner layer).

Hair Cells and Sound Production

Hair cells are activated as soon as sound is transmitted through the ossicles of the middle ear and the fluid of the inner ear is pushed from the vestibular canal to the tympanic canal. The compressed fluid creates an upward push of the basilar membrane, which heaves the hair cells up and down against the relatively immobile tectorial membrane. It is this mechanical deformation of the hair cells that defines the moment of transduction. Surrounded by cell membranes, hair cells, like neurons, are polarized with ions, and their bending triggers the movement of sodium ions that causes depolarization. Once the hair cells have been bent, the resultant generator potential sums with other generator potentials to produce a neural impulse that then travels to the brain via the auditory nerve.

THE AUDITORY NERVOUS SYSTEM

The circuit that transmits neural impulses from the ear to the brain is depicted in Figure 8.4, and, as you can see, one of the main structures in this network is the *auditory nerve*. The auditory nerve is a bundle of bipolar neurons whose dendrites form synapses with the hair cells and whose cell bodies collect in the spiral ganglion located just outside the walls of the cochlea. The axons of these neurons, one bundle from each cochlea, course inward, entering the brain stem at the level of the medulla. There they form synapses in an area called the *cochlear nucleus*. Just as there are two auditory nerves (one from each ear), there are two cochlear nuclei (one on each side of the brain stem).

From the cochlear nuclei, the neurons travel in two directions, represented by the arrows in Figure 8.4. They either ascend the brain stem directly or they cross to the other side of the brain stem and then ascend it. In either case, the ascending tract is known as the *lateral lemniscus*.

The complexity of this circuit comes primarily from the crossing pathways, which are sometimes referred to as *trapezoid bodies*. A nucleus, known as the *superior olive* (in the lower part of Figure 8.4), is located on each side of the brain stem. The superior olives receive crossing neurons from the cochlear nuclei, and they give rise to pathways that join neurons ascending directly from the cochlear nucleus to form the lateral lemniscus.

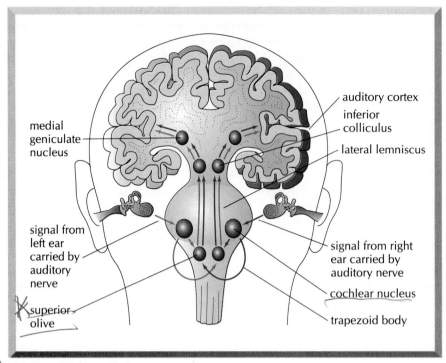

medial geniculate nucleus

auditory cortex

inferior colliculus

lateral lemniscus

signal from left ear carried by auditory nerve

signal from right ear carried by auditory nerve

cochlear nucleus

superior olive

trapezoid body

Figure 8.4 *The Auditory Nervous System*
A schematic representation of the neural connections between the cochlea and the auditory cortex.

One important thing to remember about this circuit is that neural information from each ear, like neural information from each eye, ultimately travels to *both* cerebral hemispheres. What's more, some of the neurons in the lateral lemniscus travel to a nucleus called the *inferior colliculus*, which is located in the midbrain. This nucleus plays a role in orienting body reflexes to sound. Other auditory neurons in the lateral lemniscus branch off into the reticular formation and the cerebellum, but most of the auditory neurons traveling in the lateral lemniscus either indirectly or directly project to the thalamus (specifically to the *medial geniculate nucleus*) and then to the auditory cortex in the temporal lobe.

From Ear to Cortex: A Summary

Now that you are somewhat familiar with the anatomy of the auditory system, we can better trace the sequence of events that take place from the moment sound hits the outer ear until impulses arrive at the auditory cortex.

Sound begins, remember, with vibrations (changes in pressure) in the environment. These vibrations are triggered in either air or water and travel to the external ear. Once inside the ear, they slip through the auditory canal, strike the eardrum, and cause vibrations to occur at the same frequency and amplitude as the sound wave. The vibrations then set in motion the bones in the middle ear, which function in a pistonlike fashion, pushing the membrane at the oval window of the inner ear in and out in tempo with the pressure changes.

As sound moves past the large surface area of the eardrum to the small surface area of the oval window, the force of the vibrations is amplified. Such amplification, of course, is crucial. Without it, the fluid in the canals of the cochlea could not be moved. Thus with each inward push of the oval window, fluid moves from the vestibular canal to the tympanic canal, causing an outward bulge of the round window and an upward push of the basilar membrane. Conversely, when pressure is released at the oval window, the bulge disappears and the process is ready to begin again. The bulging of the basilar membrane, meanwhile, produces a mechanical deformation of the hair cells of the cochlea. This deformation triggers the movement of sodium ions that produces the generator potential and then the neural impulses that travel along the auditory nerve into the central nervous system. The impulses pass through a series of four relay stations—the cochlear nucleus (the first relay station) and the superior olive, inferior colliculus, and medial geniculate nucleus (three additional relay stations)—before arriving at the auditory cortex of both cerebral hemispheres.

Deafness

Deafness occurs when the neural impulse is prevented from reaching the auditory cortex. And because two general processes are involved (middle-ear conduction and neural transmission) in producing neural impulses, there are also two types of deafness. One type is known as *conduction deafness* and is normally caused by disease in the middle ear. If either the eardrum or the ossicles are rendered inoperative, no sound can be heard, even though the transducer in the inner ear is normal. This particular type of deafness can frequently be corrected by surgery designed to free the movement of the ossicles. It can also be corrected by a hearing aid, which is based on the principle that sound, even in normal hearing, can reach the inner ear through the skull as well as through the middle ear.

The second type of deafness is *nerve deafness*. As the term implies, the problem here is usually the result of disease or degeneration of the auditory nerve or the hair cells connected to the nerve. Nerve deafness can be caused by a variety of factors including genetics, loud sounds, and old age. Often the deafness is restricted to a particular frequency of sound, such as selective loss of high-frequency sounds. In other words, only the part of the auditory nerve involved in the transmission of particular frequencies is damaged. Unlike conduction deafness, nerve deafness cannot be corrected because the auditory nerve cannot regenerate once it has been damaged.

CODING AUDITORY INFORMATION

The principles we discussed in Chapter 7 on visual coding apply to audition as well. Just as every feature of light detected produces a distinctive neural response (i.e., a neural code), so too does every detectable feature of sound produce a neural response—a neural code. We will now explore the nature of this code: the properties of the receptors and the nervous system that produce the neural response that indicates whether sound is indeed present, what pitch it is, and how loud it is.

Coding for the Presence of Sound

If sound is to influence your behavior, you must be able to transduce it. As we pointed out at the beginning of this chapter, sound waves generally must fall within a frequency range of 16 to 20,000 Hz to be heard by the average adult. Humans are most sensitive, however, to frequencies within the rather limited range of 1000 to 4000 Hz. At frequencies outside that range, sounds must be intensified before we can hear them.

Middle-Ear Sensitivity

The physiological basis for this peak in sensitivity is the eardrum—and for a logical reason. The mechanical conversion to movement of the ossicles by the eardrum seems to be more efficient in the range of 1000 to 4000 Hz. In this frequency range, conversion calls for the least amount of sound energy. To express this idea in another way: the ability to detect a sound may depend not only on whether that sound can be transduced by the inner ear but also on whether sound can be conducted by the bones in the middle ear.

Inner-Ear Sensitivity

The inner ear is *ultrasensitive* to sound. Indeed, if it were any more sensitive, any random collision of air molecules would be detected as sound and would produce a constant roaring sensation in the ears. For this reason, the receptor cells in the inner ear are nourished not by blood but by a fluid known as *perilymph* in the vestibular canal and the tympanic canal and a fluid known as *endolymph* in the cochlear canal. If the inner ear were nourished by blood, the sound of the heartbeat echoing through the blood vessels would interfere with the detection of incoming sounds. If you recall, we examined a similar situation in the case of the eyes and light waves. The cornea and the lens, remember, are nourished not by blood but by transparent humors (aqueous and vitreous, respectively); thus incoming light waves are not distorted by blood vessels coursing through the optical system.

Coding for Pitch

In Chapter 7 you read about two theories that have been advanced to explain the neural coding process in color vision. The two theories were initially at variance, but their differences have been partially resolved by technological advances. A similar situation exists in audition. Two seemingly conflicting theoretical positions regarding the code for pitch have been partially reconciled through the help of technological advances.

One theory is known as the place, or resonance, theory; the other is known as the frequency, or telephone, theory. Both attempt to answer the basic question, How are variations in the frequency of sound waves coded into different sensations of pitch?

The Place Theory

The *place theory* was originally proposed by Hermann von Helmholtz, who, as you may remember from the last chapter, was one of the scientists responsible for the trichromatic theory of color coding. Helmholtz's contention was that coding for pitch is primarily a matter of *place*, with different frequencies of sound stimulating different areas on the basilar membrane.

To understand this theory fully, you must first understand the phenomenon of *resonance*. All objects in the environment have resonating or vibrating properties, some more than others. This is why an opera singer with a finely trained voice can break a glass by singing a certain note, but you cannot. The soprano's voice simply resonates much more than yours. Helmholtz believed that the basilar membrane also has a vibrating or resonance property. He compared the membrane to a piano and the membrane's fibers to piano strings, each tuned to vibrate to sound of a very specific frequency.

The Frequency Theory

In 1886, shortly after the telephone was invented, physicist William Rutherford proposed the *frequency theory* of pitch. Rutherford's theory, like Helmholtz's, involves the basilar membrane, but whereas Helmholtz believed that the membrane works like a musical instrument, Rutherford saw the entire cochlea as a kind of telephone, and he compared the basilar membrane to the diaphragm in a telephone. The vibrations of the membrane, he believed, mimic the incoming sounds, and different frequencies of sound are coded into pitch simply by producing different frequencies of neural impulses in the auditory nerve.

The Volley Principle

The early evidence seemed to favor Rutherford's view over Helmholtz's, but not entirely. Recording from the auditory nerve in cats, Ernest Wever discovered that the number of neural impulses does in fact follow sound frequency but only up to 4000 impulses per second (Wever, 1949). This finding posed a problem. The rate of neural firing is limited by the refractory period that follows each impulse. Because of this refractory period, the fastest a single neuron can fire is 1000 impulses per second. How can the number of impulses recorded from the auditory nerve (a bundle of neurons) be as high as 4000 impulses per second if the fastest a single neuron can fire is 1000 impulses per second?

To resolve this problem, Wever advanced the following explanation: neurons, in his view, respond to sound frequencies on the basis of what he called the *volley principle*. The principle is based on the supposition that the auditory nerve contains several sets of neurons, each set capable of responding maximally at 1000 impulses per second. The unique aspect of this arrangement is that these neurons do not all fire at the same time; rather, they fire alternately, so that while one set is responding, the others are in various stages of the refractory period. To understand how this arrangement works, consider a group of soldiers with single-shot rifles. They can maintain a constant volley of fire if, while one is shooting, the others are reloading.

Hence the frequency code for pitch is confirmed for sounds up to 4000 Hz. What about the code for sounds from 4000 Hz to 20,000 Hz? To answer this question, we will consider the work of one of the foremost figures in audition research, George von Bekesy.

Reconciling the Place and the Frequency Theories

Bekesy began his research on auditory coding in the early 1950s. Perhaps his most important discovery is that the coding for pitch is consistent with both Helmholtz's place theory and Rutherford's frequency theory.

Figure 8.5   *The Traveling Wave*
(a) The basilar membrane shown uncoiled in the cochlea. (b) A schematic view of a wave-like bulge moving along the basilar membrane. The location of the peak of the wave relative to the oval window varies with the frequency of sound. The lower the frequency, the farther from the oval window the peak occurs (1kHz = 1000 Hz).

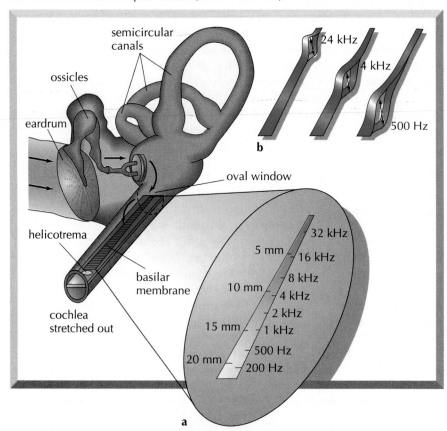

Using cochleas from recently deceased humans, Bekesy stimulated the oval window with an electrically powered piston and then observed through a microscope the movement of the basilar membrane (Bekesy, 1960). He discovered, for one thing, that a stimulus of a given frequency causes the basilar membrane to bulge in a wavelike manner, as pictured in Figure 8.5b. First the bulge appears at the base of the cochlea near the oval window and then gradually moves (Bekesy called it a traveling wave) along the basilar membrane toward the apex, at the helicotrema. The frequency of the sound determines where along the membrane the wave peaks. A high-frequency sound produces the highest bulge at the base of the cochlea near the oval window. With progressively lower frequencies, the highest peak moves closer and closer to the apex (the tip) of the cochlea. Finally, very low frequencies (below 400 Hz) produce a broad bulge that covers the entire membrane and causes it to vibrate uniformly at the frequency of the incoming sound.

There is a structural reason for the differential displacement of the basilar membrane. As you can see in Figure 8.5a, the width of this membrane varies from its base (at the oval window), which is very narrow and stiff, to its apex (at the helicotrema), which is wide and flexible. The difference in width means that there is more fluid in the wide part of the canal than in the narrow part. It has been shown that low-frequency sound waves are able to move more fluid than high-frequency sound waves. Thus it is not surprising that low-frequency sound waves cause the bulge to travel farther and farther along the membrane and that the increased flexibility of the membrane causes the size of the bulge to increase as the wave moves toward the tip. And with very low frequencies, the stimulus is powerful enough to cause the entire membrane to bulge and vibrate uniformly.

We can draw several conclusions from Bekesy's findings. The most important is that there are two codes for pitch. Pitch produced by sounds of low frequencies (i.e., by frequencies that cause the entire membrane to vibrate uniformly) is coded in terms of *rate* of firing of the auditory nerve (consistent with Rutherford's frequency theory). In this case, a low-frequency sound causes the entire membrane to vibrate; this vibration in turn causes the hair cells to bend and the auditory nerve to fire at a certain frequency. Pitch produced by sounds of high frequencies is coded in terms of the place stimulated on the basilar membrane (as Helmholtz proposed). In this case, different high-frequency sounds cause the maximum bulge in the basilar membrane to occur in different *places*, thus stimulating different hair cells and ultimately different neural pathways to the cortex. In fact, there seems to be a one-to-one relationship between regions on the basilar membrane undergoing displacement and auditory regions in the cortex undergoing firing. The spatial relationship between regions on the basilar membrane and regions in the cortex is referred to as a *tonotopic representation*.

In summary, then, pitch depends on two codes: frequency of firing codes for low pitch, place of firing codes for high pitch. Exactly where the transition from one code to the other occurs is not known. It seems safe to say, however, that the frequency code works below 400 Hz, that the place code works above 4000 Hz, and that both codes (along with the volley principle) work together to represent the frequencies in between.

Sharpening the Code

Bekesy, who won the Nobel Prize in 1961, has shown that the cochlea, like the retina, is more than simply a transducer. It also has inhibitory and excitatory mechanisms that sharpen the relationship between incoming sound frequencies and the area of maximum displacement on the basilar membrane. Impulses created by dominant frequencies are maximized; impulses created by stray frequencies are suppressed. Here again we can draw a direct analogy to retinal function and the role that excitatory and inhibitory mechanisms play in sharpening the contour of an image. Bekesy noted that without inhibitory effects a tone would not sound like a pure tone but like a noise of a certain pitch.

But sharpening or maximizing the spatial relationship between activity in the cochlea and activity in the auditory cortex does not stop with the inhibitory processing of stray frequencies in the cochlea. Microelectrode recording, for instance, reveals that sharpening occurs at each relay station along the way. As a result, when the impulse finally reaches the auditory cortex, it is in its most precise form.

On the surface, this sharpening pattern suggests that the closer to the auditory cortex we probe, the more we will find single neurons coded for only a small range of frequencies. This is not quite true, however. There are many such single neurons in the auditory cortex, but there are also neurons that are less selective and respond to a wide range of frequencies. The difference between the two types is this: the neurons that respond selectively do so to only high-frequency sounds; the less selective neurons make their broad-band responses to low-frequency sounds. The presence of these two types of cortical neurons lends further support to Bekesy's observations that in the cochlea, high-frequency sounds are distinguishable in terms of their effects on different parts of the basilar membrane (i.e., are coded by place), whereas low-frequency sounds tend to affect the entire basilar membrane indiscriminately (i.e., are coded by frequency).

Coding for Loudness

Loudness, as we explained earlier, is related to changes in the amplitude of a sound wave. Bekesy investigated the code for loudness and found that increases in the amplitude of sound waves cause the basilar membrane to be displaced in general over increasingly large areas and with increasing vigor. This displacement in turn produces an increase in the *number* of impulses per second arriving at the auditory cortex.

There are two reasons why displacement of the basilar membrane produces an increase in the number of impulses: first, the more expansive displacement of the basilar membrane stimulates more hair cells and thereby more neurons; second, the more vigorous (higher-amplitude) displacement bends the hair cells sufficiently to excite neurons with high thresholds of firing as well as those with low thresholds. In summary, the frequency of sound waves determines the distance the bulge travels—the code for pitch. The amplitude of the sound wave determines the height and expanse of the bulge—the code for loudness.

CODING FOR SOUND LOCALIZATION

Humans have an uncanny ability to localize the source of sound. If you close your eyes and listen closely to a sound, you can nearly always tell whether it is coming from right or left, front or back, above or below. On the other hand, front-back and up-down localization is more difficult to discriminate than right-left localization. Then, too, if you cover one of your ears, you lose the general ability to localize sound.

The key to our capacity to localize sound lies in the fact that we have two ears. Depending on its direction, sound stimulates the two ears differently. These differences in stimulation are referred to as *binaural* (two-ear) *cues*. Sounds hit the ear that is closer to them first, and they have greater intensity at the near ear than at the far ear. Why? Simply because the head creates a sound barrier that weakens sounds before they reach the far ear. What this means is that there are two binaural cues: a difference in the time of arrival and a difference in the intensity of sound between the two ears, as Figure 8.6 illustrates.

Figure 8.6 *Sound Localization*
Binaural cues enable us to localize sound that originates at the side of the head. High-frequency sounds are blocked by the head, so that the intensity of sound differs in the two ears. In addition, both low- and high-frequency sounds arrive slightly later at the more distant ear than at the closer ear.

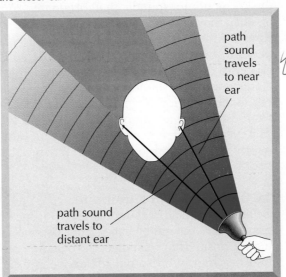

path
sound
travels
to near
ear

path sound
travels to
distant ear

It is logical to wonder which of the two cues is more important. The answer, in brief, is that it depends on the pitch—the frequency of the sound wave. Low-frequency sounds tend to wrap around the head and thus reach the far ear with virtually the same intensity as the closer ear. High-frequency sounds, on the other hand, tend to be reflected by the head and thus arrive at the far ear with less intensity than at the closer ear. In low-frequency situations, therefore, the primary cue is a difference in time of arrival. In high-frequency situations, the primary cue is the difference in intensity.

Binaural Coding and the Auditory Nervous System

The coding process for binaural cues appears to take place at several points in the auditory system, most notably the superior olive, the inferior colliculus, and the auditory cortex, all pictured in Figure 8.4.

The first of these structures to receive input from both ears (i.e., the first relay station) is the superior olive, which codes sound localization on the basis of time and intensity differences (Dobak & Johnson, 1992). This capacity comes from two separate areas in the superior olive: the *medial superior olive*, which is sensitive to time differences, and the *lateral superior olive*, which is sensitive to intensity differences (Heffner & Masterson, 1990).

Individual neurons in these areas respond best when the two ears receive sound at slightly different times or at slightly different intensities. Some neurons respond when the left ear receives sound first; other neurons respond when the right ear receives sound first. The same holds for intensity differences—some neurons responding when the left ear receives sound that is slightly more intense than that in the right ear, other neurons responding when the right ear receives sound that is slightly more intense than that in the left ear. In this way different neurons respond to sounds that originate from different locations, and together the neurons are able to provide a map of the auditory space (King & Moore, 1991; Sekuler & Blake, 1994). A similar coding process occurs in the inferior colliculus and the auditory cortex, but only with respect to time differences (Masterson, 1974; Neff et al., 1956).

To summarize, sound localization is based on the response pattern of cells in the superior olive, the inferior colliculus, and the auditory cortex. It is the selective action of these cells—the fact that their firing patterns are keyed to differences in arrival time and intensity of sound—that enables an organism to transform binaural cues into the code for sound localization.

The Owl and Sound Localization

The ability to localize sound varies from species to species, and these differences, as you might expect, correspond to differences in brain circuitry. Consider, for instance, the owl. A nocturnal animal, the owl relies almost primarily on sound to survive and, not surprisingly, has neural circuitry exquisitely attuned to sound localization (King & Moore, 1991).

The neurons in the owl's equivalent of the inferior colliculus, for instance, can track the source of sound as it moves through space. Indeed, a given neuron can respond to a sound coming from a very specific area in the environment, while a neighboring neuron can respond to the same sound coming from a neighboring area (Knudsen & Konishi, 1979; Knudsen, 1981).

The owl's brain, in other words, has an elaborate representation of auditory space, and for a good reason. Its survival depends on it. We examined a similar situation in Chapter 7 in the case of frogs and "bug detectors." What we concluded there, in principle, holds here. The ear is not simply a physical instrument like a tape recorder, but a biological instrument adapted to meet the animal's needs.

Coding for Vocalization

Removing the auditory cortex from a cat or a monkey has little or no effect on the animal's ability to discriminate frequency or loudness of sound, but it has devastating effects on more complex auditory analyses, such as the ability to localize sound and the ability to discriminate sound patterns—the difference between a high-low-high tone pattern and a low-high-low tone pattern (Neff et al., 1977).

Microelectrode work, patterned after Hubel and Wiesel's work on the visual system, reveals that the auditory cortex codes complex auditory stimuli at the single-cell level. Zvi Wollberg and John D. Newman have found that more than 80 percent of the neurons in the auditory cortex of squirrel monkeys respond to *species-specific* vocalizations (Wollberg & Newman, 1971). Just as in higher-order visual coding, some cells respond more selectively than others. Some, for example, fire to many different types of sounds, including clicks, noise, and tone bursts, whereas others fire to very specific vocalizations, often to only one. Again, sensory coding corresponds to adaptive behavioral niches. Not only do frogs have bug detectors in the visual system and owls have auditory space detectors, but it also appears that monkeys are endowed with single cells that attune them to sounds vital for social communication.

Where do humans fit into this higher-order coding picture? Evidence from brain-damaged humans indicates that the auditory cortex and neighboring areas are involved in coding complex sounds important for speech perception (Philips & Farmer, 1990) and voice recognition (Lancker, Krieman, & Cummings, 1989). Hearing in these brain-damaged patients remains intact; what is lost is the ability to recognize the *patterns* of sounds that characterize speech (e.g., words sound like a buzz or noise) or to recognize the *intonations* of sounds that characterize a familiar voice.

TASTE AND SMELL

Like the ability to see and hear, our ability to detect stimuli on the basis of their taste and smell has important implications for survival. A foul taste in food alerts us to the possibility of food poisoning, and the smell of smoke or gas fumes alerts us to impending danger. These two senses—smell and taste—are known as the *chemical senses*. They are not as highly evolved in humans as the two senses we've already covered, sight and hearing, but they are governed to a large extent by similar principles of transduction and coding, albeit with a number of critical differences.

The main reason we are considering taste and smell at the same time is that they depend on similar transduction processes. Each sense is tied to receptors, known as *chemoreceptors*, whose specialty is the ability to transduce chemicals into neural impulses. Chemoreceptors fall into two categories. The first type, located in the nose, connects with the part of the brain associated with the sensation of smell, also known as *olfaction*. The second group, located in the mouth, connects with the part of the brain associated with the sensation of taste, also known as *gustation*.

Although the chemoreceptors for taste and smell are both sensitive to stimulation by chemicals, the actual chemicals that stimulate them differ. Chemicals that stimulate the chemoreceptors in the mouth are either solid or liquid; chemicals that stimulate the chemoreceptors in the nose take the form of gases.

Differences apart, the chemoreceptors in the mouth and the nose frequently work together. One of the reasons hot foods are tastier than cold foods, for instance, is that hot foods vaporize more and stimulate both smell receptors and taste receptors. You have probably noticed, too, that when you have a bad cold, nothing you eat seems to have any taste. Why? Because excess mucus in your nasal cavity has rendered smell receptors inoperative. The vapors given off by the food exert no effect on the receptors. But it works the other way, too. Because vapors from odors often filter through the nasal passage and stimulate taste receptors, noxious odors can frequently leave a bitter taste in your mouth.

As we did with vision and again with audition, we will now look at both the structure and function of the gustatory (taste) and olfactory (smell) systems. We will begin with receptors and how they connect to the brain, and then we will move on to transduction and coding.

THE ANATOMY OF TASTE

The receptors involved in taste, as pictured in Figure 8.7, are commonly referred to as *taste buds* and are located in microscopic recesses or pits at the top and sides of the tongue and throughout the oral cavity (in the pharynx and larynx). These receptors, which number approximately 3000, transduce chemicals into the neural impulses that eventually code for the sensation of taste.

Each taste bud consists of two kinds of cells: supporting cells and receptor cells. Supporting cells, curiously enough, seem to have no neural function at all, and this lack of neural function has led researchers to believe that they are actually degenerated receptor cells. Receptor cells, in the meantime, have a very limited life span, functioning for only

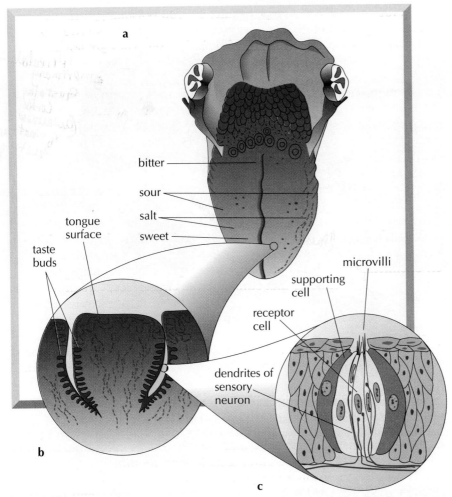

a

bitter

sour

salt

tongue
surface

sweet

taste
buds

microvilli

supporting
cell

receptor
cell

dendrites of
sensory
neuron

b

c

Figure 8.7 *Taste Receptors*
(a) The distribution of taste receptors on the tongue. (b) A close-up of a taste bud. (c) A close-up of the structures contained within a taste bud.

a few days. This short life span means that the cellular environment in the mouth is in a constant state of turnover, with some receptor cells forming while others are dying.

Microvilli

Like the receptor cells in the ear, taste receptors are equipped with hair-like projections. These projections are called *microvilli*, and they project onto the surface of the tongue. It is here, within the microvilli, that the actual transduction process takes place. Once the microvilli are stimulated, they trigger generator potentials in the receptor cells, which ultimately summate to produce a neural impulse in the connecting neural circuits.

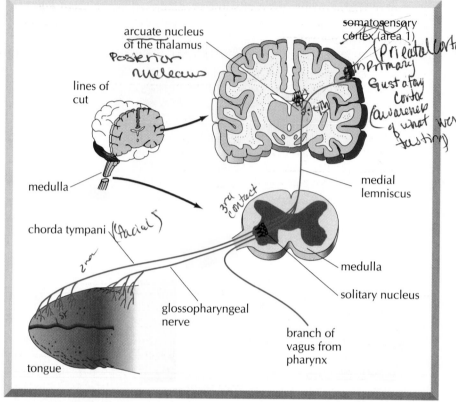

Figure 8.8 *The Gustatory (Taste) Nervous System*
The neural pathways from the tongue to the cortex.

Neural Pathways

The transmission process that carries impulses from taste receptors to the brain involves three cranial nerves, each of which is pictured in Figure 8.8. The first, as the figure illustrates, is the *chorda tympani* branch of the *facial nerve*, which innervates the anterior two-thirds of the tongue; the second is the *glossopharyngeal nerve*, which innervates the remaining one-third; and the third is the *vagus nerve*, which innervates the taste buds located in the pharynx.

These three cranial nerves are multipurpose: only a portion of the neurons in each is concerned exclusively with taste. The remaining neurons are involved in tactile and temperature sensations in the head and in control of the muscles in the face and tongue.

From Tongue to Cortex

As you can see in Figure 8.8, the cranial nerves conducting the impulses that eventually code for the taste sensation enter the brain at the same place: the medulla. There they form synapses in the *solitary nucleus*.

From there the neurons diverge, some crossing the brain stem and others remaining on the same side. In either case, they ascend to the thalamus in the same neural tracts that carry sensory information from below the neck: the *medial lemniscus*. At the thalamus, the neurons carrying the taste signal form synapses again, this time in an area called the *arcuate nucleus*, before continuing to the somatosensory cortex (area 1).

What all this means is this: the neural pathways that define the route of taste signals from tongue to cortex follow the same general pattern as those that conduct signals from visual and auditory receptors. They do not go directly from the receptors to the cortex; rather, they go through relay stations on the way to the cortex. Two such stations concern us here: the solitary nucleus, which is in the medulla, and the arcuate nucleus, which is in the thalamus.

CODING FOR TASTE

Taste sensations are generally divided into four categories: sweet, sour, salty, and bitter. Each sensation, as you might expect, is produced by a different group of chemicals, and each sensation begins the same way. Chemicals taken into the mouth stimulate the taste buds and change the permeability of the membranes in the receptor cells. This action initiates the generator potential. Exactly what properties of the chemicals initiate the change and why the membranes undergo any change at all have not yet been determined. It is clear, however, that for some people the coding process is flawed. For just as there are people who are unable to detect colors or recognize sounds at a certain pitch, so, too, are there people for whom every taste is the same. They are, for lack of a better description, "taste-blind."

Tracking the Code

Much of the research on taste coding has involved insects—and for the same reason that the giant axon in the squid has been the chief object of research on the neural impulse and the ommatidium in *Limulus* (the horseshoe crab) has been the focal point of research into visual coding. Certain insects by virtue of biological structures unique to the species make ideal subjects for researchers studying the neurophysiology of taste. The black blowfly is a classic example. Extending from the feet of the blowfly are hair cells that serve as chemoreceptors as the blowfly plods through food. These hair cells can be stimulated experimentally with different taste-related substances (sugar or salt, for instance), enabling researchers to study the relationship between chemical stimuli and their abstractions into the neural code for taste. Some of the most important work to emerge from this approach was conducted by Edward Hodgson and Kenneth Roeder who on the basis of their findings proposed the stereochemical theory of taste.

The Stereochemical Theory of Taste

Recording from the taste-sensitive neurons of the blowfly, Hodgson and Roeder found that the critical feature determining how taste receptors will react to stimuli is the shape of the chemical molecule, not its chemical constituents. Their procedure was to stimulate hair cells with four types of alcohol and found that inositol, an alcohol that differs from the others most clearly in its molecular shape, produces a distinct neural response (Hodgson & Roeder, 1956). On this basis, Hodgson and Roeder advanced the *stereochemical*, or *lock-and-key, theory* of chemical-receptor relationships.

Put simply, the stereochemical theory proposes that the membrane surrounding the taste receptor has distinct structural slots that can be filled only by chemicals of a particular shape. Once these slots are filled, according to the theory, a chemical reaction occurs, triggering the generator potential. This idea, of course, is not unique. As we noted in Chapter 4, it also applies to the action of neurotransmitters in the synapse, and we shall encounter it again later in this chapter when we consider the chemical-receptor interactions that relate to smell.

Coding at the Receptor and Neural Levels

Assuming that the stereochemical theory (that specific chemicals excite specific taste receptors on the basis of shape) is essentially correct, we must still determine what *type* of coding may occur for taste, first at the receptor level and then at the neural level. The basic question is, How does the nervous system abstract the four primary tastes and all of the intermediate ones?

To answer this question, we begin at the receptor level. Receptors for each of the four basic taste sensations tend to be concentrated on different parts of the tongue, as pictured in Figure 8.7. Sweet and salt receptors (i.e., receptors that transduce particular chemicals that produce sweet and salt sensations) are located toward the front part of the tongue. Sour receptors tend to be located on the sides. Bitter receptors are found at the back of the tongue.

Current thinking holds that these receptors code for taste in much the same way that receptors in the eye code for color. In color coding, as you will recall, the mixing of neural activity from three groups of cones accounts for the intermediate colors. Similarly, taste appears to involve the mixing of activity from the four primary taste receptors to produce all of the intermediate tastes.

Reinforcing this view are studies by Carl Pfaffman and his colleagues, who recorded from single neurons in the chorda tympani (one of the sensory nerves for taste) of cats and monkeys and found evidence for four groups of taste-related neurons, each firing to a broad range of tastes but some firing best to certain tastes and less well to others (Pfaffman et al., 1976; Pfaffman et al., 1979). These findings suggest that the code for taste (like the code for color) may result not from the activity produced in one group of taste-related neurons but from the *pattern* of activity produced to various degrees in all taste-related neurons (Bartoshuk, 1978; DiLorenzo, 1989).

Parallels between taste and vision can also be seen at the anatomical level. Microscopic analysis of the taste receptors, for example, reveals that a single taste receptor (like a single photoreceptor) may be connected with a number of neurons and that a number of receptors may be connected with a single neuron.

There is, however, a special technical problem in this area of research. It relates to the nature of the stimuli that produce taste—the fact that chemicals diffuse across the surface of the tongue. Such random diffusion makes it highly difficult, if not impossible, to control the receptors stimulated and to make the sort of direct electrochemical analysis in higher animals that can be made with the blowfly. Technical difficulties notwithstanding, the current view is that taste coding is related more to the collective action of multiple neurons than to the responses of single neurons or receptors programmed to respond to specific tastes.

SMELL

For most animals—humans being one of the notable exceptions—the sense of smell has a much greater bearing on survival than other senses. More than simply guiding animals to food, the sense of smell enables many animals to avoid predators and, in many instances, controls mating behavior. A male dog or a male moth can detect the odor of a female in heat miles away.

It is logical to question why the sense of smell is so much less important to humans than the other senses. One frequently voiced explanation is that as humans evolved from simpler forms and moved from sea to land and then up into trees and down again, vision and audition became more important to survival than smell. Supporting this view is the fact that odor-laden vapors tend to concentrate near the ground. Thus it might be said that humans, by virtue of their evolving from four-legged animals to two-legged animals rose, in a real sense, *above* these stimuli. What's more, it appears that in humans the neural mechanisms initially involved in smell became involved in the control of other behavior functions, particularly those related to emotional-visceral reactions.

Even so, humans are far from being the lowest mammal on the olfactory detection scale. As relatively weak as our sense of smell may be in comparison with that of dogs or cats, humans have a much keener sense of smell than porpoises and whales. And *what* we smell can often motivate our behavior in a number of ways. It is not by accident, for instance, that bakeries deliberately vent their ovens in the direction of the sidewalk, creating, in effect, an olfactory magnet to passers-by. Neither should it surprise you that many car dealers make it a practice to spray the interior of the second-hand cars they sell with a substance known in the trade as "new car" scent (Sekuler & Blake, 1994).

It also appears, based on several studies, that each of us emits a smell as unique as any aspect of our appearance. It is well known, for instance, that bloodhounds can distinguish the scent of a fugitive from the scent of all the people who are in pursuit of the fugitive, but humans, too, can make similar distinctions—to some degree at least. Evidence indicates that humans can identify their own clothing on the basis of odor and that they can even distinguish between clothing worn by males and by females (Russel, 1976).

The Physical Essence of Smell

In order for an object to have an odor, it must release molecules into the air. This capacity is known as volatility, and while it does not take much volatility to generate an odor (two-millionths of a milligram of vanilla per cubic millimeter, for instance, is detectable), not all objects have this property. But even with objects that do have this property, a second condition must be satisfied before they can generate an odor. The airborne molecules they release must stimulate the olfactory receptors and, because the receptors are covered by mucus, these molecules must be water-soluble to penetrate the mucus.

Olfactory Receptors

Tucked away in two clefts in the upper part of the nasal passage is a square inch of tissue known as *epithelium*. On it are located the receptors for smell. Because the epithelium is tucked away and not located in the air passage, it is often necessary to sniff (i.e., draw air over the olfactory receptors) in order to experience the sensation of smell.

Unlike taste buds, which are distinct from neural cells, olfactory receptors *are* neural cells. Their cell bodies lie embedded in the epithelium, and their dendrites branch out and project to the surface of the epithelium where they act as transducers. Their axons issue from the cell bodies and make up the olfactory nerve that travels to the brain.

Olfactory receptors are distinct in yet another way. They are neurons, but more so than other neurons they are in a constant state of turnover. They live for about 5 to 8 weeks, die, and are then replaced. No other neurons are capable of reproducing themselves in this way (Moulton, 1974).

Smell and the Nervous System

The olfactory nerve is unique. Alone among cranial nerves, it does not form synapses in the lower areas of the brain, such as the medulla (as do the neural circuits related to audition and taste). Nor does it have direct connections to relay stations in the thalamus (as do the neural circuits related to vision). Instead, as Figure 8.9 shows, it travels to the base of each cerebral hemisphere, an area called the *olfactory bulb*. There, at each bulb, axons numbering in the millions collect in separate clumps known as *glomeruli*.

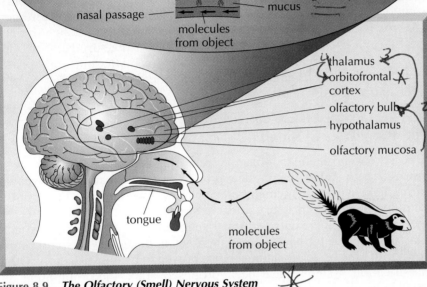

Figure 8.9   *The Olfactory (Smell) Nervous System*
The neural pathways from the olfactory receptors to the cortex.

The density of these clumps varies among animals, but in all animals the axons in the glomeruli converge on and form synapses with only a handful of dendrites of a second group of neurons found inside the olfactory bulb. After these neurons leave the olfactory bulb, they travel to the *prepyriform cortex* and the *amygdala* where they divide into two pathways, as pictured in Figure 8.9. Both pathways project to the *orbitofrontal cortex*, but by different routes: one via the hypothalamus (to the lateral posterior area), the other via the mediodorsal nucleus of the thalamus (to the centroposterior area) (Takagi, 1979).

It is logical to wonder what function is served by having a circuit for olfaction that forms synapses in the hypothalamus, an area in the brain that is involved in motivation and emotion. We have no answer to this question at present, but we can speculate. We know that some reptiles and mammals (not monkeys or humans) have a second set of olfactory receptors, known as *vomeronasal organs*, that connect to the hypothalamus. We also know that the vomeronasal organs are sensitive to specific kinds of chemical substances: scents of prey, in the case of snakes; of mates, in the case of rodents (Lehman & Winans, 1982). Given these findings, it is conceivable that even though monkeys and humans do not possess vomeronasal organs, the hypothalamic circuit has remained as a remnant of evolution and still serves as a link between olfaction and motivated behavior such as sex and aggression (Keverne, 1978).

CODING FOR SMELL

Before a stimulus can produce a sensation of smell, it must of course excite a neural impulse in the olfactory system. What this requirement calls for is clear: a stimulus in gaseous form that can change the permeability in the dendrite-type receptor cells on the surface of the epithelium. But the manner in which receptors in the olfactory system transduce airborne chemicals into neural impulses is not clear. Neither is the entire process of olfactory coding.

The Properties of Smell

A persistent problem in olfactory research has been the inability of researchers to isolate the physical properties and sensations that accompany smell. With taste, remember, researchers were able to break sensations down into four primary categories: sweet, sour, salty, and bitter. No such tidy grouping exists for smell sensations. A classification system was suggested as far back as the late nineteenth century, breaking smell down into nine basic sensations, but it proved to be unsatisfactory. Other classification systems have been proposed since then, but none has gained universal acceptance.

The basic question regarding the physical properties of smell is why certain airborne molecules stimulate one sensation and others stimulate another sensation. There is no lack of theories, and for a time two theories were in particular favor. One, the *infrared theory*, maintained that the heat of airborne molecules stimulated certain olfactory receptors to produce smell. The other, the *Raman shift theory*, held that ultraviolet rays were the stimulating factor.

Both theories have been disproved. The problem with each is that when you shield receptors from odorous molecules with a thin membrane but still allow heat and ultraviolet light to penetrate, olfactory sensations do *not* occur. This indicates that the role played by heat or by ultraviolet rays in the olfactory process is minor, at best.

The Stereochemical Theory of Olfaction

In 1949 the Scottish scientist Robert W. Moncrieff proposed the basis of what is today the most widely accepted theory of olfaction. Moncrieff theorized that the relationship between airborne molecules and olfactory receptors is essentially chemical. Different smells, he suggested, result from the different ways in which certain chemicals affect certain receptors. Moncrieff's notion is known today as the *stereochemical theory of olfaction* (Moncrieff, 1954; Moncrieff, 1955).

Moncrieff's theory was not without precedent. Even before he advanced his suggestion, the prevailing view among physiologists had been that olfactory coding is a chemical process. Prior to the late 1940s, however, there was no means of reconciling the fact that chemically similar substances often have different smells and that chemically different substances often have the same smell.

Moncrieff's method of dealing with this contradiction was to suggest that the size and shape of the chemical molecule (and not necessarily its chemical constituents) are the keys to its capacity to stimulate different receptors. Thus chemically *dissimilar* molecules could be similar in shape and size, and for this reason produce similar smell sensations. It seemed plausible to Moncrieff that receptor sites could vary in shape, so that only chemicals of a particular size or shape could fit the membrane and cause a generator potential—a kind of lock-and-key concept much like that proposed by Hodgson and Roeder in regard to taste.

Categorizing Odor

A few years after Moncrieff introduced his theory, an American scientist, John Amoore, elaborated on it extensively (Amoore, 1963; Amoore, 1967). What Amoore did was to synthesize chemically different molecules of the same size and shape and to demonstrate that different chemicals do in fact smell the same if they are identical in size and shape. He went even further. He examined more than 600 chemical compounds and then classified them, on the basis of their size and shape, in seven categories of primary odors, providing detailed descriptions of the size and shape of the molecule of each primary odor.

These primary odors are the following: *camphoraceous, musky, floral, pepperminty, ethereal, pungent,* and *putrid*. Each of these odors, according to Amoore, is produced by a molecule that has a specific shape and size. Simply by noting the shape and size of a specific molecule (e.g., a roughly spherical molecule with a diameter of 6 angstroms), he was able to predict the smell sensation it would produce (in this case, musky).

Ambiguities in Amoore's Findings

Subsequent studies have introduced some worrisome ambiguities regarding Amoore's findings. Susan Schiffman, for example, has conducted several experiments, none of which has found a relationship between the shape of a chemical molecule and its ability to produce specific odors (Schiffman, 1974). So, whether Amoore's theory is correct remains an open question. Assuming, however, that chemical molecules, even at the most general level, interact with olfactory receptors, we must still ask ourselves what happens next: that is, what type of coding occurs for smell, first at the receptor level and then at the cortical level?

Coding at the Receptor and Neural Levels

Evidence to date suggests strongly that the code for smell, like the code for color and taste, begins at the receptor level—with different groups of receptors coding for different odors. The evidence comes from studies on people who have lost the ability to smell, a condition known as *anosmia* (Wysocki & Beauchamp, 1984). The loss of smell in these cases is often selective, involving only one odor, and the condition is rarely permanent. The temporary nature of the loss suggests that it is the result of damage to olfactory receptors since the receptors can regenerate. And the selectivity of the loss suggests that there are indeed distinct receptors keyed to specific odors.

Coding Beyond Receptors

If odor is, in fact, coded by distinct receptors, it should also be coded by distinct areas of the brain to which these receptors project. Curiously, though, evidence from lower-animal work indicates that this is not the case. Recording from single neurons in the olfactory cortex of monkeys, researchers have found that the vast majority of neurons respond to a large number of odors, responding best to certain odors and less well to others. So it is not that separate neurons or areas of the brain are coding for different qualities of smell; it is that the same neurons, firing at different *patterns* across the entire olfactory cortex, are coding for different qualities of smell (Slotnick et al., 1987; Kauer, 1991; Freeman, 1991).

Reinforcing the "pattern" view of coding are lower-animal experiments in which the removal of specific areas of the olfactory cortex have little or no effect on the animal's olfactory behavior in general—a finding that tends to rule out that "place" is a factor in the coding of smell.

How do we reconcile the receptor findings with the neural recording data? In other words, how can there be distinct groups of receptors responding to specific odors while at the same time a large group of neurons in the cortex respond to all odors but with different patterns of firing? The answer, it is safe to say, lies in the circuits that connect receptors and cortex, but the precise nature of these interconnections remains to be determined. One possibility is that a given group of receptors (keyed to a specific odor) projects diffusely to the olfactory cortex. When these receptors are damaged, the effect extends presumably to the entire olfactory cortex and to the code for that specific odor. Damage to a specific area of the cortex, on the other hand, affects activity in that area only, leaving unaffected the code for the specific odor.

SUMMARY

1. *The basics of sound.* The reason we are able to hear is that our ears are able to transduce sound waves into neural impulses. Sound itself is the result of vibrating objects that cause molecules to move back and forth. The varied states of pressure created by this movement radiate out as waves in all directions from the vibrating object. Sound waves can be measured in three respects: (1) by frequency, or rate of vibration, which corresponds to pitch; (2) by amplitude, or the degree of pressure in a sound wave, which corresponds to loudness; and (3) by timbre, or the number of different frequencies, which corresponds to the purity or quality of sound. Differences in timbre—i.e., the mixture of frequencies—account for the different sounds produced by musical instruments.

2. *The anatomy of the ear.* The ear has three main parts: the outer ear, the middle ear, and the inner ear. The outer and middle ears, much like the nonneural parts of the eye, are involved in gathering and preparing sound for transduction. The inner ear, like the retina of the eye, is involved in the actual transduction of sound into neural impulses.

3. *Structures in the outer ear and middle ear.* Among the structures found in the outer ear are the pinna (the flap of the ear), the auditory canal (an inch-long tunnel from the outer to the middle ear), and the tympanic membrane, better known as the eardrum. The middle ear, an air-filled cavity just beyond the eardrum, contains three bones—commonly known as the hammer, the anvil, and the stirrup—and two muscles, the tensor and the stapedius. Besides conducting sound to the inner ear, the middle ear amplifies weak sounds and protects the inner ear from damage by intense sounds. The bones in the middle ear amplify sound by funneling it from the large surface of the eardrum to the small surface of the stirrup. The muscles protect the inner ear from damage by reflexively tightening in response to intense sound and preventing the middle ear bones from vibrating.

4. *The inner ear.* The inner ear consists of three structures, two of which (the semicircular canals and the vestibular sacs) are not involved with hearing per se but play a role in the maintenance of body balance and posture. The third structure in the inner ear, the cochlea, is the "retina" of the ear. It consists of three fluid-filled canals: the vestibular canal, the tympanic canal, and the cochlear canal.

5. *The organ of Corti and transduction.* One of the key structures in the cochlea is the organ of Corti, which rests on the floor of the cochlear canal, supported by the basilar membrane, and contains receptors, known as hair cells, that form synapses with the auditory nerve. Like all receptors, the hair cells have cell membranes that are polarized with ions. The actual moment of transduction in the ear comes when sound, transmitted through the ossicles of the middle ear and the fluid in the inner ear, causes the hair cells to bend and depolarize. The resulting generator potential—provided it is of sufficient magnitude—produces a neural impulse.

6. *From hair cells to brain.* Impulses initiated by the bending of the hair cells are conveyed to the brain through the auditory nerve, a bundle of bipolar neurons whose dendrites form synapses with the hair cells and whose cell bodies are found in the spiral ganglion, located just outside the walls of the cochlea. The neural network conveying information from hair cells to the auditory cortex includes several relay stations: the cochlear nucleus, the superior olive, the inferior colliculus, the medial geniculate nucleus, and the auditory cortex of the temporal lobe.

7. *Deafness.* Deafness normally occurs when the neural impulse is prevented from reaching the auditory cortex. Because two general processes are involved, there are two types of deafness: conduction deafness, usually caused by disease in the middle ear, and nerve deafness, the result of disease or degeneration of the auditory nerve or the hair cells connected to the nerve.

8. *Coding for pitch.* Two theories have been advanced to account for the relationship between the frequency of sound and pitch. The place theory, advanced by Helmholtz, proposes that different frequencies of sound stimulate different areas of the basilar membrane that have vibrating or resonance properties. The frequency theory, proposed by William Rutherford, argues that the basilar membrane, like the diaphragm in a telephone, mimics incoming sounds, and that different frequencies of sound are coded into pitch by producing different frequencies of neural impulses in the auditory nerve.

9. *Reconciling the theories.* The work of George Bekesy has helped to reconcile some of the differences between Helmholtz's place theory and Rutherford's frequency theory. Bekesy's theory, in brief, is that there are two codes for pitch. Low frequencies of sound are coded in terms of the frequency of impulses, and high frequencies of sound are coded in terms of "place." He based this view on the observations that low frequencies of sound cause the entire basilar membrane to bulge uniformly whereas high frequencies cause the basilar membrane to bulge maximally in different places. Bekesy's work has also shown that the cochlea, like the retina, does more than simply transduce sound but has inhibitory and excitatory mechanisms that can sharpen the relationship between incoming sound frequencies and the area of maximum displacement on the basilar membrane.

10. *Coding for sound localization.* The coding for sound localization—the ability to determine where a sound is originating—is determined by two binaural cues, a difference in the time of arrival and a difference in the intensity of sound between the two ears. Which cue is used depends on the frequency of sound. With low-frequency sound the primary cue is time of arrival, with high-frequency sound the primary cue is intensity. Binaural coding takes place at several points in the auditory system, most notably the superior olive, the inferior colliculus, and the auditory cortex. Individual neurons in these areas appear to respond best when the two ears receive sound at slightly different times or intensities.

11. *Coding for vocalization.* In monkeys more than 80 percent of the neurons in the auditory cortex respond to sounds vital to social communication. Evidence from studies on brain-damaged humans indicates that in humans, too, the auditory cortex is involved in coding for specific patterns of sounds and intonations important for speech perception.

12. *The similarities of taste and smell.* The senses of taste and smell depend on similar transduction processes. Each sense is tied to receptors, known as chemoreceptors, whose specialty is the ability to transduce chemicals into neural impulses.

13. *Chemoreceptors.* Chemoreceptors fall into two categories. One type, located in the nose, is sensitive to chemicals in a gaseous form and connects with the part of the brain associated with the sensation of smell, also known as olfaction. The second type, located in the mouth, is sensitive to chemicals in either solid or liquid form and connects with the part of the brain that is associated with the sensation of taste, also known as gustation.

14. *Taste buds.* The receptors involved in taste, commonly referred to as taste buds are located in microscopic recesses or pits at the top and sides of the tongue and throughout the oral cavity (in the pharynx and larynx). Like the receptor cells in the ear, taste receptors have hairlike projections, known as microvilli. The transduction process begins in the microvilli.

15. *Transmitting taste signals.* Three cranial nerves are involved in transmitting impulses from the taste receptors to the brain: the facial, the glossopharyngeal, and the vagus. The three nerves enter the brain at the level of the medulla, where they form synapses with the solitary nucleus. There they give rise to circuits that ascend in the medial lemniscus to the arcuate nucleus of the thalamus and then to the somatosensory cortex.

16. *Categorizing taste.* Taste sensations are generally divided into four categories: sweet, sour, salty, and bitter. Each sensation is produced by a different group of chemicals, and each sensation begins the same way, with chemicals stimulating the taste buds and changing the permeability of the membranes in the receptor cells. It is generally agreed that the stimulus works on a stereochemical (also known as a lock-and-key) principle and that it is the size and shape of the chemical molecule (and not necessarily its chemical constituents) that determine its capacity to stimulate different receptors.

17. *Coding for taste.* Coding for taste begins on the tongue where the receptors for the four basic tastes are neatly distributed: sour receptors at the sides, bitter receptors at the back, sweet and salt receptors in front. Current thinking holds that these receptors code for specific tastes in much the same way that photoreceptors in the eye code for color: by mixing of activity from the four primary taste receptors to produce all of the intermediate tastes. Recording from single neurons in the chorda tympani of cats and monkeys, researchers have found evidence for four groups of taste-related neurons, each firing to a broad range of tastes but some firing best to certain tastes and less well to others.

18. *The essence of smell.* In order for an object to have an odor, it must release molecules into the air, and the airborne molecules must stimulate the olfactory receptors. Olfactory receptors are located in two clefts in the upper part of the nasal passage, embedded in tissue known as epithelium. Because they are covered by mucus, the airborne molecules must be water-soluble. Like taste, it is generally agreed that it is the size and shape of the chemical molecule (and not necessarily its chemical constituents) that determine its capacity to stimulate different receptors. Olfactory receptors are unique among neurons in one key respect: they are the only neurons capable of reproducing themselves.

19. *The olfactory nerve.* The olfactory nerve, unlike other cranial nerves, does not form synapses in the lower areas of the brain, such as the medulla, and does not have direct connections to relay stations in the thalamus. It travels to the base of each cerebral hemisphere, an area called the olfactory bulb. There, at each bulb, axons numbering in the millions collect in separate clumps, known as glomeruli, where they form synapses with neurons that project either to the cortex or the amygdala.

20. *Coding for smell.* How smell is coded in the nervous system is still in the process of being worked out. At the receptor level, the evidence favors a "place" code with different groups of receptors responding to different odors. In the brain, however, the evidence points to a "pattern" code. Recording from single neurons in the olfactory cortex of monkeys, researchers have found that the vast majority of neurons respond not on the basis of place but in terms of pattern of firing, a given neuron responding best to certain odors and less well to others. Why it is that different receptors respond to different odors while at the same time neurons in the olfactory cortex respond to all odors but with different patterns of firing is as yet an unanswered question.

KEY TERMS

anosmia
anvil
arcuate nucleus
auditory canal
auditory nerve
basilar membrane
binaural cues
chemical senses
chemoreceptor
chorda tympani
cochlea
cochlear canal
cochlear microphonics
cochlear nucleus
conduction deafness
eardrum
endolymph
epithelium

Eustachian tube
facial nerve
frequency theory
glomeruli
glossopharyngeal nerve
gustation
hair cells
hammer
harmonics
helicotrema
incus
inferior colliculus
infrared theory
inner ear
lateral lemniscus
malleus
medial geniculate nucleus
medial lemniscus

medial superior olive
microvilli
middle ear
nerve deafness
olfaction
olfactory bulb
olfactory nerve
orbitofrontal cortex
organ of Corti
ossicles
oval window
perilymph
pinna
pitch
place theory
prepyriform cortex
Raman-shift theory
resonance
round window
semicircular canals
solitary nucleus

stapedius muscle
stapes
stereochemical theory of
    olfaction and taste
stirrup
superior olive
taste blind
taste buds
tectorial membrane
telephone theory
tensor muscle
timbre
tonotopic representation
trapezoid bodies
tympanic canal
tympanic membrane
vagus nerve
vestibular canal
vestibular sacs
volley principle
vomeronasal organs

SUGGESTED READINGS

Edelman, G. M., Gall, G. W., &
Cowan, W. M. (Eds.). *Auditory
Function: Neurobiological Bases
of Hearing*. New York: Wiley,
1988.

Finger, T. E., & Silver, W. L.
(Eds.). *Neurobiology of Taste and
Smell*. New York: Wiley, 1987.

Pfaff, D. W. (Ed.). *Taste,
Olfaction, and the Central
Nervous System*. New York:
Rockefeller University Press,
1985.

Zwislocki, J. J. "Sound Analysis
in the Ear: A History of
Discoveries." *American Scientist*,
69, 1981, 184–192.

CUTANEOUS SENSES INCLUDING PAIN AND PROPRIO-CEPTION

INTRODUCTION

The sensory processes that have occupied our attention so far—vision, audition, smell, and taste—are triggered by stimuli that for the most part originate outside ourselves, in the external environment. Some stimuli, however, originate either on the surface of or within the body itself, and the sensory system that receives and processes surface or internal stimuli is known as the *somatic sensory system*. This system derives its name from the Greek word for body—*soma*—and its receptors fall into two categories. Receptors sensitive to stimuli on the body surface are generally referred to as *skin* or *cutaneous* receptors. They underlie our capacity to experience pressure and pain and to differentiate heat from cold. Receptors operating within the body are known as *proprioceptive* receptors. The stimuli they sense underlie our capacity to adjust to the changes that occur in the body whenever we move.

As you will see in this chapter, most of the basic principles that govern cutaneous and proprioceptive senses are similar to the principles that underlie the sensory processes we have already considered, but there are significant differences, particularly when it comes to one cutaneous sensation we're all familiar with: pain. In this chapter we will be looking first at the cutaneous senses, with special attention to pain, after which we will look at the proprioceptive senses.

CUTANEOUS SENSES

"Cutaneous senses" is a general term that describes a number of different sensations that occur when substances in the environment come into contact with receptors on the skin. Cutaneous senses have traditionally been grouped into four broad categories: pressure, pain, warmth, and cold. This system of categorization, however, leaves a good deal to be desired. How do you categorize, for instance, such a common skin sensation as an itch or a tickle?

Difficulties with categorization notwithstanding, cutaneous senses, like the other senses we have studied, have their own receptors, their own peripheral circuits, their own tracts to the brain, and their own centers in the brain. Let us now look at the elements of this sequence, beginning with receptors.

The Anatomy of the Cutaneous Senses

The notion that a specific cutaneous sensation—the feeling of pressure, for instance—is keyed to special receptors first came to light nearly 100 years ago through an experimental procedure known as skin mapping. *Skin mapping* consists of applying discrete stimuli to various areas on the skin in an effort to isolate specific areas sensitive to stimuli for pressure, pain, warmth, and cold. Studies using this technique have revealed the presence of microscopic structures in the skin known as *end organs*.

These end organs, illustrated in Figure 9.1, and the stimuli to which they are sensitive are as follows:

Meissner's corpuscles: sensitive to touch and vibration
Merkel's disks: sensitive to light touch and pressure
Pacinian corpuscles: sensitive to deep pressure
Krause's end bulbs: unknown
Ruffini endings: sensitive to touch and pressure
Free nerve endings: sensitive to pain and temperature

Figure 9.1   *The Skin Game*
Skin end organs are found in three layers of the skin—epidermis, dermis, and subcutaneous fat. The close-ups show some of the end organs and their corresponding sensations.

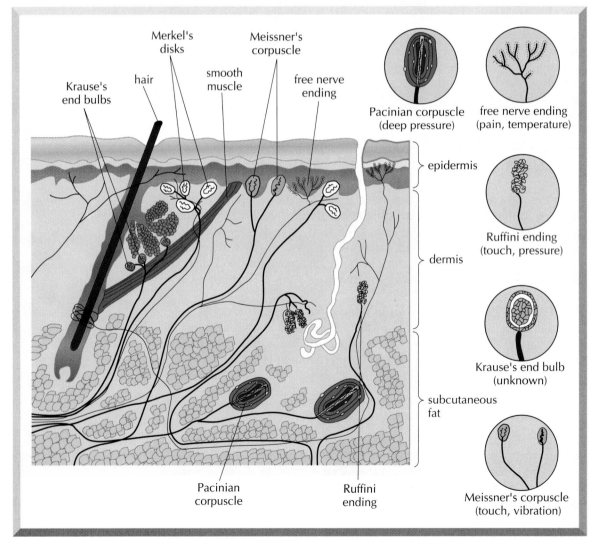

Defining the Relationships

The relationship between end organs and specific stimuli was originally thought to be clear-cut, with each end organ acting as a receptor for a specific stimulus. Subsequent findings, however, brought to light a somewhat more complex picture. Free nerve endings in the cornea, for instance, have been found to be responsive not only to pain but also to warmth and cold (Lele & Weddell, 1956).

The current view, in light of these findings, is that the end organs are not themselves receptors (i.e., the sites of transduction). The receptors, rather, are nerve endings contained within the end organs. Much like the lens in the eye, the end organs appear to serve nonneural functions: they transmit the stimulus to the receptor but do not transduce the stimulus into the neural impulse. This view explains why researchers in search of the sensory code for cutaneous senses have been concentrating their efforts not so much on the end organs themselves but on the receptors and the neural circuitry that lie between the end organs and the brain.

Peripheral Circuits for the Cutaneous Senses

Cutaneous receptors are no different from receptors in general. They are transducers. They convert stimuli into neural impulses and, like other receptors, initiate impulses in neurons that go to the central nervous system. Cutaneous receptors located below the neck produce impulses that travel to the spinal cord via the spinal nerves (see Chapter 3 for details). Cutaneous receptors located above the neck, in the head and face, produce impulses in the spinal nerves from the scalp and in the trigeminal nerve from the face. Critical to the function of the cutaneous receptors are beltlike regions of the skin wrapped around the trunk, limbs, neck, and scalp. These regions, illustrated in Figure 9.2, are called *dermatomes*.

A dermatome represents the region of skin innervated by a single spinal nerve. Each dermatome is innervated by its own spinal nerve. Just as there are 31 spinal nerves, so there are 31 dermatomes. Significantly, however, a section of each dermatome is also innervated by a neighboring spinal nerve. This means that in addition to innervating its own dermatome, a given spinal nerve also innervates the top or bottom half of the neighboring dermatome. The behavioral significance of this overlap is protection. If a spinal nerve is severed, neighboring spinal nerves assume the functions previously handled by that nerve, thus minimizing sensory loss.

Spinal Nerves

Spinal nerves contain three types of sensory neurons, classified according to how fast they conduct the signal: fast-conducting A-beta fibers (which conduct at a speed of about 35 to 75 meters per second), moderate-conducting A-delta fibers (5 to 30 m/s), and slow-conducting C fibers (0.5 to 2 m/s). The speed of conduction in each instance is determined by the diameter of the neuron: the larger the diameter, the faster the conduction.

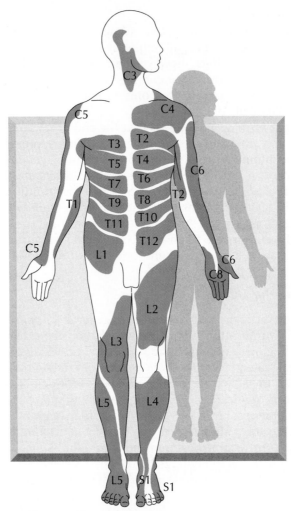

Figure 9.2 *The Dermatomes*

Each spinal nerve innervates a region of skin wrapped around a limb or the trunk of the body. The skin regions are known as dermatomes. They are labeled according to the regions of the spinal cord in which their corresponding spinal nerves enter—that is, cervical (C), thoracic (T), lumbar (L), sacral (S). Although this figure depicts the dermatomes as alternating from one side of the body to the other (T3 on one side of the body and T4 on the opposite), in reality each dermatome is represented on both sides of the body and overlaps with the dermatomes above and below it.

It is generally believed that cutaneous coding actually begins in these fibers. Large-diameter A-beta fibers appear to code pressure and touch; smaller-diameter A-delta and C fibers appear to code pain and temperature. We shall return to this notion shortly. The important point to bear in mind at this stage of our discussion is that the three groups of neurons travel to the spinal cord *collectively* in a given spinal nerve. Once the cutaneous information enters the spinal cord, it has two destinations: the motor neurons in the spinal cord through which it initiates spinal reflexes, and the ascending tracts to the brain where it initiates sensations.

Figure 9.3 *The Neural Pathways for the Cutaneous Senses*
Cutaneous information is projected to the cortex by two ascending systems. Each system takes a different route to the brain. The dorsal column–medial lemniscus system crosses at the medulla, the anterolateral system crosses at the spinal cord, but both travel to the same areas in the thalamus (the ventral posterior lateral nucleus) and the same areas in the cortex (somatosensory primary and secondary areas).

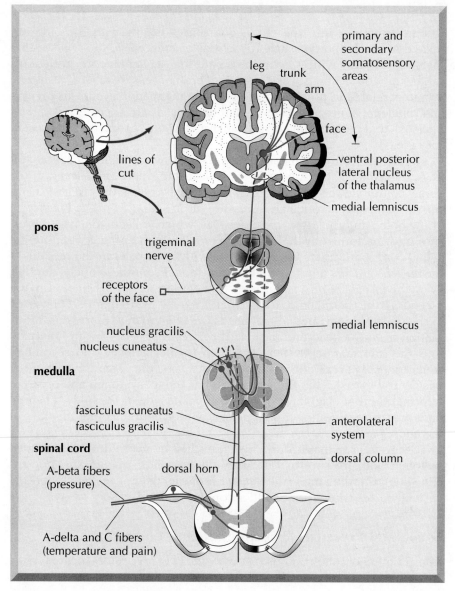

As Figure 9.3 illustrates, cutaneous information is carried from the spinal cord to the brain by two ascending systems (they are referred to as "systems" because each contains several tracts). One system, the *dorsal column–medial lemniscus* system, carries information related to touch and pressure. The other, the *anterolateral* system, carries information related to pain and temperature.

We shall now consider each system—its structure and function in detail—discussing first pressure and touch and then pain and temperature. Because much more is known about pain than about temperature, we shall focus primarily on the physiology of pain.

Touch and Pressure: The Neural Pathways

Our investigation into the cutaneous senses begins with the circuitry related to touch and pressure. If you look at Figure 9.3, you will see that the circuit begins with A-beta fibers entering the spinal cord in the dorsal horn. You will also see that the brain areas reached by neural impulses related to touch and pressure are the medulla (nucleus gracilis and nucleus cuneatus), the thalamus (the ventral posterior lateral nucleus), and the parietal cortex (the primary and secondary somatosensory areas).

The circuit from spinal cord to brain, as shown in Figure 9.3, is as follows: the axons of the A-beta fibers collect into tracts and ascend in the dorsal column to the medulla. Two tracts are involved: the *fasciculus gracilis*, which collects touch and pressure information from the lower part of the body; and the *fasciculus cuneatus*, which collects touch and pressure information from the upper part of the body. After ascending the spinal cord, both tracts form synapses with two nuclei in the medulla— the *nucleus gracilis* and the *nucleus cuneatus*. From these nuclei another tract, the *medial lemniscus*, crosses to the opposite side of the brain and ascends to the *ventral posterior lateral nucleus* of the thalamus. On its way to the thalamus, the medial lemniscus collects touch and pressure information from the head and face via the *trigeminal nerve*. From the thalamus the information is then projected to the primary and secondary somatosensory areas of the parietal cortex (i.e., the posterior part of the postcentral gyrus). The primary area tends to receive touch and pressure information that originates from the opposite side of the body. The secondary area receives touch and pressure information from both sides of the body, particularly the face.

To sum up, the major brain areas reached by neural impulses related to touch and pressure are the medulla (nucleus gracilis and nucleus cuneatus), the thalamus (the ventral posterior lateral nucleus), and the parietal cortex (the primary and secondary somatosensory areas).

Touch and Pressure: Transduction and Coding

Transduction of touch and pressure begins in the receptors located in the cutaneous end organs—the *Pacinian corpuscles*. Pacinian corpuscles operate rather like the hair cells in the cochlea of the inner ear: when stimulated, they undergo mechanical deformation. The difference between the Pacinian corpuscles and the hair cells of the cochlea is that deformation of the Pacinian corpuscle does not, in and of itself, transduce pressure and touch into generator potentials and ultimately the neural impulses. The actual transduction is done by the dendritic endings of the sensory neurons (the A-beta fibers) that lie within the corpuscle.

There is a direct relationship between the amount of pressure ultimately exerted on the Pacinian corpuscle and the magnitude of the generator potential. With continued pressure, however, the generator potential diminishes, and so does the resultant tactile experience. The result, in other words, is adaptation, which we talked about in Chapter 6. What is happening physiologically is that with continued pressure the Pacinian corpuscle changes shape, producing a decrease in the generator potential and, consequently, a decrease in neural firing (Lowenstein & Mendelson, 1965).

Coding in the Somatosensory Cortex

The coding of pressure and touch takes place in the area of the brain known as the somatosensory cortex and appears to be governed by a place arrangement. Impulses related to each sensation are conveyed to the brain by a separate set of neurons, with each set terminating at a different place in the cortex. The intensity of the tactile sensation—how much pressure we actually feel—corresponds to the number of impulses firing per unit of time in the different cortical areas.

You will recall that in audition, neighboring areas of the cochlea project to neighboring areas in the auditory cortex. Somatosensory coding, as pictured in Figure 9.4, shows a similar topographical arrangement. Impulses from pressure and touch receptors on the skin surface are projected to the cortex such that stimulation of neighboring areas of the body produces neural activity in neighboring areas of the cortex. The more sensitive to touch a particular part of the body is, the more densely packed is the cortical area devoted to coding stimuli originating from the receptor area. In monkeys, for instance, a disproportionate amount of cortical area consists of neurons that receive sensory input from the hands and feet; in humans, a disproportionate amount of the cortex is devoted to sensory input from lips, tongue, and fingers.

There is, however, a complication to this topographical relationship between pressure and touch receptors on the body and corresponding sensory neurons in the cortex: the cells that code the two sensations are more than surface-deep (Straile, 1969). The pressure we feel in our hands, for instance, is coded not only at the *surface* of the cortex but also in a column of cells extending downward through the cortex. This means that while one column of cells may code for pressure, an adjacent column may code for light touch from the same segment of skin (a dermatome). We saw a similar arrangement for vision in Chapter 7, except that one column of cells in the visual cortex coded for a line of a specific

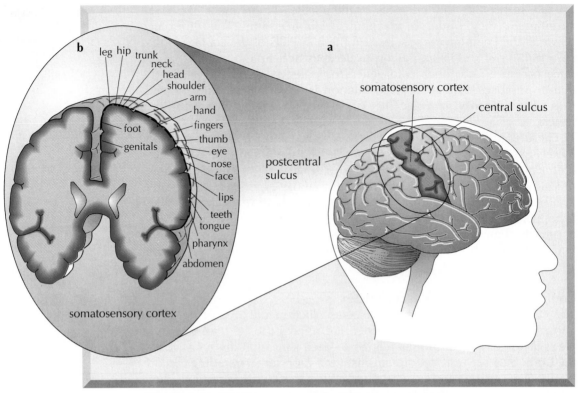

Figure 9.4 *Cortical Representation of the Cutaneous Senses*
(a) The location of the primary somatosensory cortex and (b) the arrangement and relative size of the cortical areas corresponding to the cutaneous senses of the various parts of the body.

orientation while an adjacent column coded for the same line at a slightly different orientation. No such orderly arrangement exists for coding pain, which we will consider shortly.

The Somatosensory Cortex: The Effect of Environmental Experience

In the late 1980s a group of researchers headed by Michael Merzenich conducted a series of studies that not only yielded additional information about the workings of the somatosensory system but also brought to light new insights into the larger question of how environmental experiences can shape the nervous system. Working with adult monkeys, Merzenich and his colleagues have produced findings indicating that the topographical arrangement of the somatosensory cortex (i.e., neighboring areas of the cortex representing touch or pressure information from neighboring areas of the body) is not as "fixed" as once had been thought and that new experiences can produce changes in the cortical map.

Their procedure consisted of exposing monkeys to somatosensory stimulation the monkeys never experienced before and then observing the effect of these experiences on the somatosensory cortex. In one study, the monkeys underwent a surgical procedure in which the skin of two adjacent fingers was connected so that both fingers received the same somatosensory stimulation, as if they were a single finger (Clark et al., 1988). Comparisons were then made between the arrangement of the somatosensory cortex prior to the surgery (when the two fingers received the sensory stimulation independently) and the arrangement of the somatosensory cortex after surgery (when the two fingers received the sensory stimulation as a unit for several weeks). The difference was dramatic. Prior to surgery, the somatosensory information from the two fingers was represented in separate but neighboring areas of the somatosensory cortex. After surgery, however, the information was represented in the *same* area of the cortex—a clear indication that the rearrangement of the sensory input resulted in the reorganization of the cortical circuits.

The practical implications of Merzenich's findings became evident in light of yet another monkey experiment conducted by Gregg Recanzone, one of Merzernich's colleagues (Recanzone et al., 1992). Recanzone delivered a series of vibrating stimuli to a spot on the skin of one of the fingertips of the monkeys with one stimulus vibrating at a frequency slightly different from all the others. The task of the monkeys was to learn to identify the stimulus with the unique frequency. Not surprisingly, the animals in this study, with increased training, were able to make the necessary discrimination with increasing accuracy. More significantly, the improved performance correlated with changes in the somatosensory area of the cortex. The somatosensory area responding to touch from the stimulated fingertip grew larger and more sensitive as a result of the sensory experience.

A therapy based on the principles underlying the monkey studies has been used—with some success—to treat brain-damaged patients suffering from a loss in touch sensitivity. The therapy consists of requiring patients to make fine discriminations on the basis of touch. Studies have found that with time and practice, the patients' ability to distinguish among objects on the basis of touch improves significantly (Dannenbaum & Dykes, 1988).

Implications of the Somatosensory Work

The results of these experiments are significant not only because of what they tell us about the physiological basis of touch, but also because of what they indicate about neural connections in general and about the degree to which those connections are shaped by environmental factors.

Researchers have long accepted, as a given, that all behavior—from rudimentary reflexes to higher-order behavior such as language and thought—is determined by neural connections. And it has become increasingly apparent over the past several years that where and how these connections are formed depend, in part, on genetics and, in part, on the environment. Genes determine the initial mapping, roughing in the circuitry (see Chapter 2 for details). The environment does the fine tuning, although where and how this fine tuning takes place remains very much a mystery.

All of which underscores the significance of the new somatosensory findings. We know from work on the visual system (see Chapter 7) that in kittens, at least, there is a critical period, early in life, in which environmental influences can produce structural changes in the nervous system. The work of Merzenich and Recanzone in the somatosensory system indicates that the potential for structural changes in the nervous system initiated by the environment isn't limited to early development. Merzenich's and Recanzone's monkeys, remember, were adults not infants.

Clearly then the nervous system is turning out to be a good deal more malleable than early studies would have led us to believe. And, as we will soon discover, the neural changes observed in the visual and somatosensory systems are only part of the story. To look ahead for a moment, it now appears that each new experience we have—that is, our ability to learn and remember—has the potential to change the nervous system in ways that can change the way we think, feel, or act. We will consider the changes in the nervous system that underlie learning and memory in detail in Chapters 16 and 17.

THE PHYSIOLOGICAL BASIS OF PAIN

Pain is a sensation that most of us recognize all too well. Its adaptive function is obvious: pain is usually a signal that something is going wrong in our bodies. Research over the last decade has given us a general idea of what happens in the nervous system to produce pain, but important questions remain unanswered. Why, for instance, do some people experience excruciating pain even though there is no apparent physical problem? And what are the mechanisms that enable certain chemical and nonchemical agents alike—morphine, on the one hand, and hypnosis, placebos, and acupuncture, on the other hand—to block or minimize pain? These are some of the questions we will be looking into as we explore this obviously important and often mystifying aspect of sensory processing.

Defining Pain

As you undoubtedly know, pain comes in a variety of "flavors." The quick, sharp pain you experience when you bump your elbow against your desk is different from the dull, throbbing pain of a toothache. Pain, moreover, is not a simple sensation; it is not rooted in a simple mechanism. But complicated though the mechanism may be, the basic elements of pain—receptors, neural circuitry, and neural coding—are the same in principle as those that relate to other sensory systems. Let us look at each element.

Pain Receptors

The receptors related to pain are reasonably well understood. They are free nerve endings, and they fall into two categories: the endings of small-diameter A-delta fibers (not to be confused with the large-diameter A-beta fibers for pressure) and the endings of C fibers. Both types are found throughout the body: in the skin, in the internal organs, in the muscles, and in the tissue surrounding the bones. Studies have established, too, that the two different types of fibers are associated with different sensations of pain: the A-delta fibers play a role in short-duration, pricking pain; the C fibers play a role in longer-lasting, burning pain.

It is important to stress that not all A-delta and C fibers are involved exclusively with pain. Some of these fibers are sensitive to temperature as well. What differentiates pain fibers from temperature fibers is their high thresholds—that is, their sensitivity to intense stimulation (electrical, mechanical, chemical, and thermal). Intense stimulation, however, does not act directly on pain fibers. The generally held view today is that intense stimulation produces tissue damage, which in turn releases a chemical that acts on the fibers. Although the precise nature of this chemical is unknown, there are a number of candidates, among them potassium ions, histamine, and a neurotransmitter known as *substance P* (Fields, 1987; Campbell et al., 1989).

From Receptors to Spinal Cord

As you can see in Figure 9.5, A-delta and C fibers enter the spinal cord in the dorsal horn, an area of the spinal cord consisting of layers of neural cells known as *laminae*. These fibers terminate primarily in two laminae: lamina I (the outermost layer) and lamina V. There they form synapses with neurons whose axons cross the cord and ascend to the brain in several tracts collectively known as the *anterolateral system*. The A-delta and C fibers in these synapses release the neurotransmitter substance P, and when substance P decreases, pain in both lower animals and humans decreases (Pearson, Brandeis, & Claudio, 1982; Yaksh et al., 1979).

What we have presented so far is at best a sketchy picture of the spinal cord and its role in relaying pain-related information to the brain. What is important to bear in mind at this point is that the spinal cord is more than simply a relay station for input from the peripheral nerves (Ruda, Bennett, & Dubner, 1986). It also contains interneurons that play a vital role in the *control* of pain. On the basis of input received from the brain, these interneurons, located in an area known as the *substantia gelatinosa* (laminae II and III), either block or transmit pain-related information. We shall discuss this regulatory action later. For now, keep in mind that the spinal cord is not just a passive receiver of signals but an active *filter*

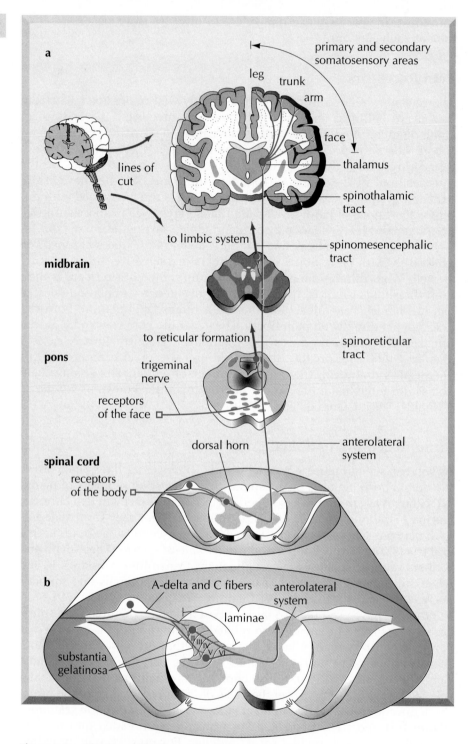

Figure 9.5 *The Neural Pathways for Pain*
(a) The anterolateral system collects pain-related information from receptors of the body and face and projects it to the reticular formation, the limbic system, and the thalamus. (b) A-delta and C fibers form synapses with neurons in the lamina I and lamina V, which cross the cord and ascend to the brain in the anterolateral system.

as well: it constantly modulates and regulates the pain-related information before transmitting it to the brain.

From Spinal Cord to Brain

Figure 9.5 illustrates the circuitry that underlies pain. The main structure in this circuit—the tracts that make up the anterolateral system—collects pain-related information from three sources: from A-delta and C fibers at the level of the spinal cord and from the trigeminal nerve from the face and head.

The axons of the tracts, as you can see, course upward into the brain. There they convey pain-related information to three general areas: the reticular formation (via the spinoreticular tract), the limbic system (via the spinomesencephalic tract), and the thalamus (via the spinothalamic tract). Why three different areas? Presumably, because each area is involved in coding a different aspect of pain. The reticular formation accounts for arousal. The limbic system (including its connections to the prefrontal lobes) accounts for emotion. The thalamus, in addition to being involved in the actual sensations of pain, integrates information from the other two areas (Wall, 1980).

The Thalamus

Projections from the spinal cord to the thalamus are far from random. Anatomical work has shown that neurons from lamina I and lamina V in the spinal cord project, via tracts in the anterolateral system, to different areas in the thalamus. Lamina I neurons tend to project to an area in the thalamus known as the *posterior nuclear group*, and lamina V neurons project to an area in the thalamus known as the *intralaminar nuclei*. There is also a group of pain-related fibers in laminae VI, VII, and VIII, but their central projections have not yet been worked out (Fields & Basbaum, 1978; Kelly, 1991).

That the thalamus is involved in the perception of pain has become evident through the observations of cancer patients who have undergone brain surgery to relieve pain. Two areas of the thalamus, the *ventrobasal complex* (part of the posterior nuclear group) and the *intralaminar nuclei*, have been implicated, but each area appears to code a different type of pain. Vernon Mark and his colleagues have found that lesions in the ventrobasal complex will alleviate sharp, pricking pain but will have little effect on dull, burning pain (Mark, Ervin, & Yakovlev, 1962). Lesions in the intralaminar nuclei, on the other hand, have the opposite effect: they relieve dull, burning pain but not sharp, pricking pain. Apparently, then, the sharp and dull pain sensations that follow many injuries are rooted in neural activity taking place in two distinct areas.

The Cortex

One other feature of the neural circuit involving pain warrants our attention. The thalamic nuclei give rise to circuits that project to the primary and secondary somatosensory areas in the cortex, as shown in Figure 9.5. Surgical removal of these areas has no effect on the perception of pain, and so we don't know exactly what function this routing serves (Kelly,

1991). There is, however, evidence linking pain to two other cortical areas—areas that do not receive direct projections from pain-related nuclei in the thalamus; and there is evidence to suggest that each of these areas plays a distinctive role. Removing one area, the *prefrontal lobes*, eliminates pain, but the loss appears to be more emotional than sensory. Prefrontal lobotomy patients report feeling the sensation of pain but claim that it is no longer bothersome (Mark, Ervin, & Yakovlev, 1962). The second area is the *cingulate gyrus*. Patients who undergo the removal of the anterior portion of the cingulate gyrus (the operation is called a *cingulotomy*) report that they no longer feel pain at all (Teuber, Corkin, & Twitchell, 1977).

The Code for Pain: Pattern versus Place

We do not wish to leave you with the impression that specific brain areas are related *directly* to specific features of pain: the ventrobasal complex and its circuit from lamina I related to sharp pain, the intralaminar nuclei and its circuit from lamina V related to dull pain. These relationships are far from clear-cut. Pain does not always operate as if it were coded by single circuits traveling to their own centers in the brain. In their thalamic studies, for instance, Vernon Mark and his colleagues have found that patients receiving electrical stimulation (as opposed to lesions) of the thalamus do not report pain (Mark, Ervin, & Yakovlev, 1962). This finding has raised the nettlesome question of how electrical stimulation of an area in the brain that presumably codes for pain can fail to produce pain.

A possible explanation for this apparent paradox is that coding is probably more than simply a matter of *where* the pain circuits from spinal cord to brain go (the place) but of *how* the circuits actually fire: the pattern of neural activity. Conceivably, then, the electrical stimulation used by Mark was simply too crude a procedure to mimic the pattern of firing that normally produces pain.

These issues aside, the coding for pain appears to be basically no different in principle from coding for touch and pressure or, for that matter, from coding for vision and audition. Pain has receptors (high-threshold free nerve endings), peripheral nerves (A-delta and C fibers), tracts to the brain (the anterolateral system), and centers in the brain (the posterior nuclear group and intralaminar nuclei). Pain, though, may have a unique pattern of firing in the brain—a pattern that is apparently not easily mimicked by electrical stimulation.

Once we get beyond these basic elements, the similarity between pain and other sensations quickly begins to vanish. If pain worked like other sensations, we might expect it to stop when the stimulus that produces it is removed. But as most of us know from personal experience, pain does not always disappear when the stimulus that produces it stops. Herein lie two of the most troubling questions about pain—why it persists and what underlies it. Logic tells us that pain persists because neural activity in the pain areas of the brain persists even after the noxious stimulus has been removed. But logic, unfortunately, does not tell us why.

Most of us know what it is like to have a headache, a toothache, or an occasional dull pain in one part of the body or another. Imagine, though, what it would be like to go through life experiencing pain every moment of every day. This, tragically, is the plight of hundreds of thousands of people throughout the world—people who suffer from a condition commonly known as *chronic pain*.

Chronic pain has been an object of fascination to human beings throughout recorded history, and science has done an admirable job of developing treatments and drugs to alleviate it. Still, nobody seems to know for certain how or why chronic pain occurs.

What makes chronic pain so difficult to understand is that it does not fit into the normal pain pattern. Pain is usually produced by an injurious stimulus—a cut, a sprain, an infection, for instance—and logic dictates that healing should produce relief from pain. But there are at least three instances, known as *chronic pain syndromes*, in which removing the injurious stimulus does not produce a corresponding relief of pain and, worse, often leaves the patient with pain more intense than that produced by the injury itself.

The first of these instances is *phantom limb pain* experienced by some amputees long after a limb has been removed and healing has occurred (Melzack, 1992) (see Chapter 6 for details). The second is *causalgia*, pain that is caused by a bullet wound and that often continues after the wound has healed. The third is *neuralgia*, pain produced by infection or disease in the peripheral nerves; it, too, persists after the original infection has cleared up (Melzack & Wall, 1965).

Explaining Chronic Pain:
The Melzack-Wall Theory

How can the sensation of pain be present without a corresponding stimulus to produce it? According to two prominent pain researchers, Ronald Melzack and Patrick Wall, the answer lies in the fact that the nervous system, under certain conditions, is capable of producing its *own* pain, even after a noxious stimulus has been removed (Melzack & Wall, 1965). The capacity of the nervous system to do so, according to Melzack and Wall, is rooted in a curious relationship between pain fibers and other fibers, namely, A-beta fibers for pressure. Melzack and Wall's contention, in brief, is this: pain depends not only on the state of pain fibers (A-delta and C fibers) but on the state of the A-beta fibers as well.

Melzack and Wall base their theory on their contention that even before a noxious stimulus is ever delivered, pain and pressure fibers are constantly active, firing at a spontaneous rate. According to Melzack and Wall, this spontaneous activity—and this is the critical feature of their theory—reflects the unique way that pressure and pain fibers interact. The spontaneous activity of the pressure fibers *inhibits* the spontaneous activity of the pain fibers, and it is this inhibitory effect exerted by the A-beta (pressure) fibers that, in the view of Melzack and Wall, represents the critical factor in chronic pain. If for any reason the A-beta activity slows down or if the fibers are selectively destroyed by damage or injury (which, according to Melzack and Wall, is what happens in chronic pain syndromes), the inhibitory effect of the A-beta fibers is diminished. The result: spontaneous activity of the pain fibers is released, the neurons in the anterolateral system are stimulated, and pain is produced.

To boil the Melzack and Wall theory down to its essentials, chronic pain is produced by selective damage to the inhibitory A-beta fibers. This damage either eliminates or weakens the normal inhibitory effect of these fibers, allowing A-delta and C fibers to transmit neural activity unchecked to the anterolateral system.

The Melzack-Wall theory is illustrated in Figure 9.6, which provides a detailed view of the relationship between pressure and pain fibers. Notice, in particular, that Melzack and Wall have theorized that the inhibitory effect the pressure fibers (A-beta) exert on the pain fibers (A-delta and C) is not direct but rather is mediated by a group of interneurons in the *substantia gelatinosa*. This neural arrangement has important therapeutic implications which we will consider shortly.

Evidence for the Theory

Researchers have been seeking evidence to support the Melzack and Wall theory ever since the theory was introduced, but the results have been mixed. Some researchers have found evidence that does indeed link a decrease in A-beta fiber activity to an increase in the activity of A-delta and C fibers—a finding that lends credibility to the Melzack-Wall theory

Figure 9.6   Melzack and Wall's Theory of Pain

Two sets of peripheral neurons, A-beta fibers (pressure) and A-delta and C fibers (pain), enter the spinal cord. In the cord they form synapses with interneurons in the substantia gelatinosa and with ascending pathways to the brain (the anterolateral system). The firing of the neurons in the anterolateral system determines pain. The interneurons in the substantia gelatinosa inhibit firing of these neurons and thereby decrease pain. The A-beta fibers excite (+) the interneurons, whereas the A-delta and C fibers inhibit (−) them.

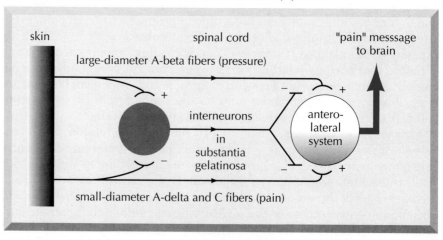

(Hentall & Fields, 1979). But other researchers have found no such relationship (Whitehorn & Burgess, 1973).

Why the discrepancy? The reason might be purely technical. A-delta and C fibers are extremely small, even by normal neurophysiological standards. Thus even with advanced microelectrode technology it is difficult to obtain clear and reliable recordings.

Melzack himself, in the meantime, presented evidence that called into question some elements of his theory (Melzack & Loeser, 1978). His evidence came from clinical reports on paraplegic patients who, in an effort to alleviate phantom limb pain, had undergone surgical removal of sections of their spinal cords. Melzack has reported that despite the spinal cord cut, pain persists, indicating that pain does *not* depend solely on input from the peripheral circuits that enter the spinal cord below the cut.

Does this evidence refute the Melzack-Wall theory? Not necessarily, although it does oblige us to rethink it. The original Melzack-Wall theory held that chronic pain is produced by *abnormal*, or uninhibited, activity in the A-delta and C fibers—the peripheral circuits that enter the spinal cord. Observations on paraplegic patients notwithstanding, Melzack contends that this assumption is still valid, but with one qualification: once the abnormal activity produced by these peripheral circuits reaches the brain, the peripheral factors are no longer important. In other words, input from the peripheral sensory nerves is needed to *initiate* abnormal activity in the brain, but once this activity begins it is able to continue on its own, even if the spinal cord is cut.

In conclusion, even if the specific details of the original Melzack-Wall theory are incorrect, certain elements of the theory may nonetheless be valid, in particular the capability of the nervous system not only to excite but also to *inhibit* the sensation of pain. Given that this is the case, let us now look at the therapeutic implications of the Melzack-Wall theory—the possibility that external agents can indeed be used to trigger the natural ability of the nervous system to inhibit pain.

Therapeutic Implications of the Melzack-Wall Theory

Certain chemical agents—morphine, for instance—can block pain, and certain nonchemical agents—acupuncture, for instance—can relieve pain as well. How do we explain these phenomena within the framework of the Melzack-Wall theory?

Melzack and Wall's explanation is that morphine and acupuncture work like A-beta pressure fibers: they activate interneurons in the substantia gelatinosa and these interneurons, in turn, inhibit activity in the anterolateral system. According to Melzack and Wall's view, therapeutic agents like morphine and acupuncture stimulate an area of the brain—the reticular formation—triggering impulses that travel down the spinal cord to the substantia gelatinosa where they close a spinal "gate," shutting off the neural activity that normally produces pain.

This theory, sometimes known as the *gate-control theory* of pain, was originally proposed by Melzack and Wall in the 1960s, at a time when next to nothing was known about pain suppression (Melzack & Wall, 1965). Today we know that the theory is essentially correct, if not in detail, then certainly in principle. Studies we are about to consider have shown that there is indeed a descending circuit from the brain and that the circuit does indeed impose an inhibitory influence on the firing of neurons in the anterolateral system. Evidence also indicates that it is through this circuit that such painkilling agents as morphine and acupuncture may work. Let us examine the evidence that indicates the presence of this circuit—first for the circuit itself, then for the effects of painkilling agents.

THE PAIN-SUPPRESSION CIRCUIT

If specific areas of the brain are to qualify as part of the pain-suppression circuit, they must meet certain criteria. Above all, these areas, when stimulated, must *suppress* pain—that is, produce a phenomenon known as *analgesia*. At least two areas of the brain fit this description: one is the *periaqueductal gray*, an area in the midbrain (Mayer et al., 1971); the other is the *nucleus raphe magnus*, a nucleus in the raphe's system that is located in the medulla (Oliveras et al., 1975). Both of these areas, when stimulated, suppress pain. One study, by David Reynolds, has shown that by electrically stimulating the periaqueductal gray (and neighboring areas) it is possible to produce analgesia to such a degree that abdominal surgery can be performed on unanesthetized rats without causing them any apparent distress (Reynolds, 1968).

A similar brain stimulation technique has been used with humans, and the results are promising. Yoshio Hosobuchi and his colleagues implanted electrodes in the periaqueductal gray of six patients suffering from pain so intractable that no other therapy had produced relief (Hosobuchi, Adams, & Linchitz, 1977). The results were striking. Five of the six patients reported complete relief as the result of the brain stimulation, and the sixth patient reported partial relief. Unfortunately, however, this therapy, like drugs, loses its effectiveness when administered repeatedly over a 4- to 5-week period, although the effectiveness returns when the stimulation is stopped for a few weeks and then resumed. More recently similar results have been reported with larger groups of patients (Hosobuchi, 1986; Barbaro, 1988).

The Bridge between Brain and Spinal Cord

If it is true that stimulating the periaqueductal gray and the nucleus raphe magnus suppresses pain, the obvious question is, Why? The likely answer is that stimulating these two brain areas inhibits the transmission of impulses in other parts of the nervous system, specifically in neurons conducting pain-related information in the spinal cord and the trigeminal nerve (the sensory nerve from the face).

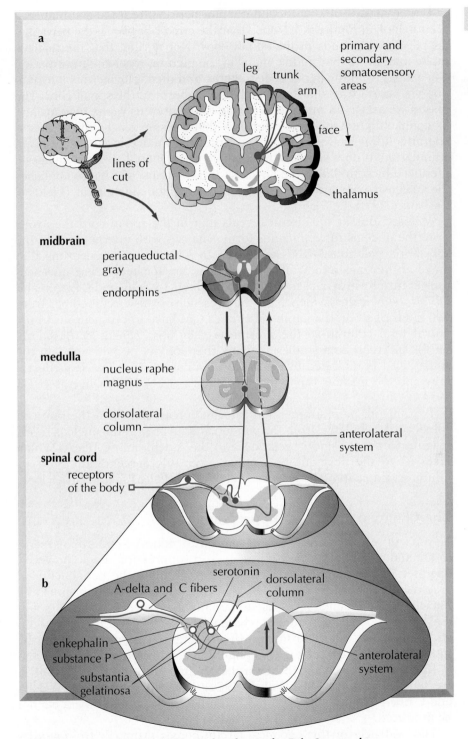

a

primary and
secondary
somatosensory
areas

leg trunk
arm

face

lines of
cut

thalamus

midbrain

periaqueductal
gray

endorphins

medulla

nucleus raphe
magnus

dorsolateral
column

anterolateral
system

spinal cord

receptors
of the body

b

serotonin dorsolateral
column

A-delta and C fibers

enkephalin
substance P

substantia
gelatinosa

anterolateral
system

Figure 9.7 *The Neural and Chemical Pathways for Pain Suppression*
(a) The periaqueductal gray is stimulated by endorphins and sends information to the nucleus
raphe magnus, which conveys the information via the dorsolateral column to the spinal cord.
(b) The dorsolateral column releases serotonin, the interneurons in the spinal cord release
enkephalin, which then prevents the A-delta and C fibers from releasing substance P.

To get an idea of how this interaction between brain and spinal cord occurs, look at Figure 9.7. Notice that the circuit begins in the periaqueductal gray and ends in the spinal cord. Notice, too, that the nucleus raphe magnus is the "middle man" in the picture, receiving information (via axons) from the periaqueductal gray and then relaying this information via neural tracts in the dorsolateral column to the spinal cord. The reason we assign an intermediary role to the nucleus raphe magnus and its connecting dorsolateral column is that a lesion placed in the dorsolateral column has been shown to upset the analgesic effects of brain stimulation. It does so, moreover, in two ways: it abolishes the analgesia produced by stimulating the nucleus raphe magnus, and it also abolishes the analgesia produced by stimulating the periaqueductal gray (Fields & Basbaum, 1978; 1979).

A closer look at the circuit reveals that in the spinal cord the axons from the nucleus raphe magnus form synapses with interneurons in the substantia gelatinosa—the same area in which the interneurons that make up Melzack and Wall's spinal "gate" are located. These interneurons in turn form synapses with the pain fibers (A-delta and C fibers) and *inhibit* their firing. Evidence for the presence of this circuit comes from two kinds of studies: anatomical studies that have traced neurons in the dorsolateral column to the substantia gelatinosa (Fields & Basbaum, 1979), and recording studies showing that activity in pain fibers in the spinal cord is inhibited by electrical stimulation of the periaqueductal gray and the nucleus raphe magnus (Fields et al., 1977; Oliveras et al., 1974).

To sum up, pain suppression information passes from the brain to spinal cord as follows: from the periaqueductal gray to the nucleus raphe magnus to the substantia gelatinosa to the A-delta and C fibers. Which takes us to the next question: What gives this descending circuit its inhibitory capacity? The answer is chemistry. Let us take a closer look.

The Chemistry of Pain Suppression

As you can see in Figure 9.7, three neurotransmitters—endorphins, serotonin, and enkephalin—play a role in pain suppression. Each, however, operates in a different way. Endorphins stimulate the periaqueductal gray, which in turn increases activity in the nucleus raphe magnus; the nucleus raphe magnus gives rise to circuits that travel (via the dorsolateral column) to the spinal cord where they release serotonin. Serotonin stimulates the interneurons in the substantia gelatinosa, and the interneurons in turn release enkephalin, which prevents the A-delta and C fibers from releasing the neurotransmitter substance P (Jessell & Iversen, 1979; Ruda, 1982; Yaksh, 1979). Without substance P, A-delta and C fibers cannot stimulate the anterolateral system and pain cannot be produced.

The evidence for this chemical circuit comes primarily from studies showing that drugs capable of decreasing the production or blocking the action of the neurotransmitters also block the analgesia produced by stimulating the periaqueductal gray or nucleus raphe magnus. The analgesic effects of brain stimulation, for instance, have been significantly reduced by injections of two drugs in particular: *parachlorophenylalanine* (PCPA), which decreases the production of serotonin, and *naloxone*, which blocks the action of endorphins and enkephalin (Akil, Mayer, & Liebeskind, 1976; Oliveras et al., 1977).

Treating Pain

The discovery of the pain-suppression circuit, along with a clearer understanding of its anatomy and its chemistry, has enabled scientists studying pain to make some sense out of what was once a bewildering set of clinical observations. Prior to these discoveries, no one doubted that pain could be alleviated by drugs, acupuncture, hypnosis, and even placebos, but no one really knew how these treatments achieved their results. Now we are beginning to understand.

What we now know about the manner in which pain therapies work can be stated very generally as follows: the analgesic effects of the treatments just mentioned, except hypnosis, are mediated to a large extent by the periaqueductal gray and its descending circuit to the spinal cord. In each case, the interaction between treatment and the nervous system appears to be mediated by endorphins and enkephalin. Let us briefly consider these interactions.

Opiates

It is well established that pain can be alleviated by various drugs, the most potent of which are opiates, particularly morphine. How opiates achieve this powerful effect was once a mystery, but it now appears that they owe their painkilling properties to the fact that their structure enables them to act in the same sites of the brain and the spinal cord as endorphins and enkephalin. One of these sites is the periaqueductal gray, which presumably responds to opiates in the same way that it responds to endorphins: it becomes stimulated, and thus suppresses pain. The sites in the spinal cord are the A-delta and C fibers, which presumably respond to opiates in the same way that they respond to enkephalin: their capacity to activate the ascending pain tracts in the anterolateral system is inhibited (Yaksh et al., 1980).

Findings in lower animals support these hypotheses. Receptors sensitive to opiates have been found in the periaqueductal gray and the spinal cord (Fields & Basbaum, 1978; Pert, Kuhar, & Snyder, 1976). And injecting opiates directly into the periaqueductal gray or spinal cord suppresses pain (Fields & Basbaum, 1979; Yaksh & Rudy, 1976). The conclusion: opiates relieve pain because they mimic the action of endorphins and enkephalin in the periaqueductal gray and spinal cord.

Acupuncture, Placebos, and Hypnosis

Let us begin with some definitions. *Acupuncture* is an ancient Chinese treatment in which needles are inserted into specific areas of the body.

Placebos are inert substances (sugar pills) that have no known therapeutic powers but, in some cases, can relieve symptoms. *Hypnosis*, of course, is a trancelike state in which a person is highly suggestible. All are effective treatments in the relief of pain. The question is, Why?

One of the ways researchers have been trying to answer this question is by administering a drug known as *naloxone* to people whose pain relief has been induced by acupuncture, placebos, or hypnosis. Naloxone is known to *block* the action of endorphins. Therefore, if endorphins in fact mediate the treatments' analgesic effect, naloxone should block it.

David Mayer and his colleagues have found that naloxone does indeed block the analgesia produced by acupuncture, and Jon Levine and his colleagues have reported a similar effect for placebos (Mayer et al., 1976; Levine, Gordon, & Fields, 1979). Patients who are given placebos and think they are painkillers report a decrease in pain. But patients given naloxone in addition to placebos report no such effect. These findings lead to the conclusion that endorphins mediate the analgesic effects of acupuncture and placebos.

Hypnosis, however, is a different and more mystifying story. Unlike the cases of acupuncture and placebos, the analgesic effect of hypnosis is *not* reversed by naloxone, a fact that has led to the suspicion that hypnosis exerts its effects through circuits that lie outside the influence of endorphins (Goldstein & Hilgard, 1975). Locating these circuits, however, is not going to be easy because hypnosis for the most part is a uniquely human phenomenon, and there are obvious limitations to the types of experiments that scientists can conduct on human beings.

Finding the mechanism by which hypnosis reduces pain represents only one of the many problems that need to be resolved before pain suppression can be fully understood. Another and in some ways even more puzzling problem has to do with the natural function of the pain-suppression circuit.

The Puzzle of Pain Suppression

As we have just seen, considerable evidence now supports the notion of a neural pathway whose function is to suppress or block pain. The puzzle here is why such pathways should exist. Pain, after all, tells us there is something wrong with our bodies; it conveys information that should not be ignored. Why would we ever want to ignore it? Are we to assume that nature has endowed us with these circuits as a vehicle for analgesic drugs, placebos, acupuncture, or hypnosis? Are we to believe, in other words, that we carry with us circuits that we could not use without first going to a drugstore or to a physician? Hardly. Clearly, there are adaptive reasons for these circuits apart from their relationship with analgesic agents. And while we do not have definitive answers to these questions, we do have some clues.

One reasonable explanation for the existence of pain-suppression circuits is that in some situations an organism's survival might depend on the ability to ignore pain temporarily. You have undoubtedly heard about or read about people who, after being seriously injured in a plane or car crash, have walked for miles to get help, or, for that matter, of athletes who have finished a game despite a serious injury. Such anecdotal accounts are not scientifically valid, but a growing body of experimental literature on lower animals lends increasing weight to the hypothesis that pain-suppression circuits serve an important adaptive function.

Animal Research

Several studies have shown that if you subject laboratory rats to a stressor, such as inescapable shock, and then test their reaction to a painful stimulus—the frequency with which they flick their tails in response to radiant heat—they show more tolerance to pain (fewer tail flicks) than rats that receive the same painful stimulus but are not subjected to the stressful situation (Lewis, Cannon, & Liebeskind, 1980; Watkins & Mayer, 1982). The studies suggest that stress makes animals much more tolerant to pain than they ordinarily are. Even more significant, perhaps, the analgesic effect that stress produces (much like the analgesic effect produced by opiates or acupuncture) can be reversed by naloxone. The logical conclusion: the analgesic effect is mediated by endorphins.

Unfortunately, other findings complicate an otherwise clear picture (Grau et al., 1981). Naloxone, for instance, reverses the analgesia produced only by intense stress (80 shocks), not mild stress (40 shocks) (Terman & Liebeskind, 1986; Meagher, Grau, & King, 1990). Apparently, then, as in the case of hypnosis, a factor other than endorphins mediates the analgesia produced by mild stress. Even so, the findings are significant and have led researchers to wonder whether the same effect may apply to humans.

Human Research

It would be naive to conclude on the basis of the rat data alone that humans release endorphins and as a result experience pain relief under stress. Yet there is reason to believe that in some instances, at least, humans can do so.

We know that athletes who have been injured often turn in remarkable performances without realizing until after they have competed that they have done so with a serious sprain or broken bone. We know, too, that wounded soldiers often report that in the midst of battle they were not aware of pain. Are these episodes flukes of nature? Are the verbal reports a result of failing memory or matters of pride? Or does the human brain, like the rat brain, release endorphins to suppress pain under stress? We have no definitive answer to these questions, but controlled experiments on humans have yielded some data—sketchy, to be sure—that are consistent with the animal studies.

In these experiments, naloxone is administered to human patients who are already experiencing some level of pain from having had wisdom teeth extracted (Levine et al., 1978). The assumption here is that if ongoing pain (and the stress that accompanies it) releases endorphins, then naloxone, which blocks the effects of endorphins, should increase the pain experienced by the patients. This is precisely what has been observed: naloxone does in fact increase pain in patients already suffering from pain. On the basis of these findings, we can conclude that in certain situations—situations that produce intense pain and stress—the human brain is prepared to block pain even though the block is obviously not complete.

Some Conclusions

It seems safe to say that the brain is organized not only to perceive pain but also to inhibit it. Paradoxically (despite its importance to survival), pain can be suppressed almost at the point of its origin in the nervous system. Our growing understanding of this pain-suppression circuit has had a profound effect in recent years on both the scientific and clinical views of pain. It has helped to clarify the effects of a number of treatments used to relieve pain. It has clarified the role that the brain plays as a painkiller—its ability to manufacture and use its own natural brand of opiates (endorphins). Finally, it has changed attitudes concerning the study of pain. Scientists no longer look upon the effects of placebos and hypnosis as mysterious phenomena outside the realm of experimentation. Instead, many researchers are now approaching these therapies within a new scientific framework and are trying to gain a better understanding of how each of these treatments interacts with the brain. A better understanding of this relationship could well hold the key to the development of new and better therapies for the control of pain.

NEURAL CODING FOR TEMPERATURE

Our ability to experience the common sensations of being cold or warm is rooted in distinct areas of the skin (roughly 1 mm in diameter) that are sensitive to thermal stimulation. These areas contain both cold receptors and warmth receptors. The cold receptors are nerve endings belonging to A-delta fibers, and the warmth receptors are nerve endings belonging to C fibers (Iggo, 1959; LaMotte & Campbell, 1978). Beyond the receptors and their connections to the spinal cord, however, we know very little about the neural circuit for temperature other than that it ascends the spinal cord in the anterolateral system (shown in Figure 9.3), a system that it shares with circuits for pain.

One curious feature of the sensation of temperature is something you have probably noticed for yourself: the fact that the same thermal stimulus can be perceived as either hot or cold, depending on the conditions under which you sense it. Cold water on very cold hands, for instance, feels warm; but once your hands warm up, the same water feels cold.

Clearly, then, it is the combination of the thermal properties of the stimulus and the temperature of the skin that determines the sensation. Skin temperature is usually referred to as *physiological zero*. Whether the touch of an object is experienced as hot or cold depends on whether its temperature is above or below physiological zero. If it is higher than physiological zero, it will be experienced as warmth; if it is below physiological zero, it will be experienced as cold.

The simplest way to explain this phenomenon is in terms of a place code. Temperature differences between an object and physiological zero are sensed by different receptors: A-delta fibers respond to temperatures below physiological zero, and C fibers to temperatures above physiological zero. These fibers in turn are connected to cold- and warm-coded areas in the brain. This theory also accounts for the outcomes of experiments in which warm stimuli applied to cold receptors (i.e., A-delta fibers) produce cold sensations; presumably the cold sensation reflects the connections between A-delta fibers and cold-coded areas in the brain. The phenomenon is known as *paradoxical cold*.

The cutaneous receptors respond to external stimuli. We now turn to the proprioceptive receptors that respond to internal cues.

PROPRIOCEPTION

Behavior, as we have seen throughout this book, is keyed to cues in the environment: visual cues, auditory cues, chemical cues, cutaneous cues. These environmental or external cues are known collectively as *exteroceptive* cues.

But just as there are two environments that govern behavior (external and internal), there are also two sets of cues. We refer to the internal cues as *interoceptive*, and their function, in brief, is to provide the brain with two types of information crucial to adaptive behavior. First, they provide cues that tell us about internal need states: whether we are thirsty or hungry. Second, they provide cues that keep the brain informed about the position of the limbs and body. We shall look into the first category, the so-called *visceral* cues, in later chapters. In the remainder of this chapter, our concern is with the second category of cues, known as *proprioceptive* cues.

Proprioception Defined

Behavior demands that you move your body in response to events taking place in the external environment. Related to this crucial ability is a sensory capacity that functions to keep the brain constantly informed of any *changes* in movement. This capacity serves primarily to help balance the body, but it also generates signals about the position of the limbs. When you close your eyes, you are still aware of where your hands are, an indication that your brain is getting its information about hand position from a source other than your eyes.

Two questions, above all, need to be asked with respect to this ability. First, where does this information originate, and, second, how is it neurally coded? At least part of the answer to these questions lies in a special category of receptors that gather information triggered by the body itself. These receptors are sometimes referred to as *self-receptors*. The technical term is *proprioceptors*, and the sensation they produce is called *proprioception*.

The Sources of Proprioceptive Cues

Proprioceptive stimulation has two sources. The first is balance, which is nothing more than awareness of body position with respect to gravity. Balance is sensed by receptors located in the nonauditory part of the inner ear—the *vestibular sacs* and the *semicircular canals*. The term used to describe the sense that helps you keep your balance is the *labyrinthine sense*. The second source, known as the *kinesthetic sense*, is awareness of limb position, which is monitored by receptors located in the joints and ligaments.

The primary job of all proprioceptors is to provide a background of bodily awareness within which discrete responses can be made to external cues. Consider what happens when you run. Your legs move back and forth, but you must remain in an upright, balanced position. Labyrinthine receptors enable you to do so. Balance also involves an awareness of your limbs at any given moment, and here is where the kinesthetic receptors assume importance. Damage to either the labyrinthine or kinesthetic receptors will interfere with your balance and your ability to move. People whose labyrinthine receptors have been damaged, for instance, cannot keep their balance when their eyes are closed. (This inability, often used as a clinical sign for labyrinthine damage, is known as the *Romberg sign*.) Closing your eyes puts the brunt of balance control on the labyrinthine receptors, and when these receptors are damaged, they are unable to feed enough equilibrium information to the muscles. Similarly, selective damage to sensory nerves from kinesthetic receptors produces a condition known as *tabes dorsalis*. This affliction reduces kinesthetic feedback concerning the position of the limbs and makes the gait of the afflicted person disjointed and robotlike.

We shall now consider each of these systems in detail: first kinesthetics and then the labyrinthine sense.

KINESTHETICS: A SENSE OF MOVEMENT

A good typist can work without looking at the keys. Many brilliant pianists have been blind. The ability that makes these things possible—that is, the ability to control the movement of your limbs without visual cues—is rooted in the kinesthetic sense, which in turn has its physiological basis in receptors located in the joints. Whenever you move an arm or leg, the angle between adjacent bones changes. This angle change occurs in the joints (the junctures between bones), and with each angle change, different receptors respond.

Transducing Angles to Impulses

Receptors in the joints are no different from receptors in general. They transduce stimuli (in this case, angular relationships between hinged bones) into generator potentials and eventually into neural impulses that relay information about limb position to the brain. If there is anything distinctive about these particular receptors, it is that they generate impulses by virtue of spray-type nerve endings that act as receptors. These receptors are located in capsules, known as *Ruffini endings* and *Pacinian corpuscles*, that surround the joints and ligaments. As the position of the limb changes, the receptors undergo varying degrees of deformation. As in the case of the touch receptors in the skin and the hair cells in the ear, this mechanical deformation is transduced into generator potentials, which then summate to produce a neural impulse.

Coding Limb Position

It is clear that each movement you sense is represented in a distinctive way to the nervous system, so the question we must ask ourselves is, How is limb movement coded? In other words, in what distinctive way is each movement you sense represented in the nervous system?

The answer seems to lie in the fact that within a given joint there are sets of neurons sensitive to the various bone relationships created when the limb is bent. If you extend your right arm in front of you and close your eyes (shutting out visual cues) and then gradually bend your forearm upward, you will be aware of each new position. What is happening neurally is that a new set of neurons in the joint fires with each movement. One set of neurons, for instance, is maximally sensitive (and fires most) when the joint angle is 90 degrees. Another set, meanwhile, is maximally sensitive (and fires most) at a 45-degree angle. And each firing rate tails off as you move away from that angle in either direction. In brief, changes in limb position are expressed as changes in the angle between adjacent bones in the joint. These changes are then coded by sets of neurons firing in response to different angles.

Coding for Speed of Limb Movement

Now that we have established that the *angle* in the moving joint determines which set of neurons fire, we can ask whether the *speed* of limb movement has an effect on the firing rate of neurons. Indeed it does. The longer a limb remains in a given position, the lower the firing rate of the neurons attuned to that angle—a manifestation of the adaptation phenomenon common to all receptors. As a limb moves rapidly from angle to angle through an arc, however, each neuron (which is tuned to a new angle) is deprived of an opportunity to adapt and therefore fires maximally. The same limb moving slowly through an arc allows each neuron the opportunity to adapt. This means that each neuron fires maximally when the joint is entering a new angle but that the firing then decreases. So the code for speed of movement can best be thought of in terms of adaptation to firing. As movement of a limb slows, the firing rate declines; as movement quickens, the firing rate increases.

Coding Kinesthetics in the Brain

Kinesthetic receptors give rise to sensory impulses that take essentially the same route to the brain as pressure and touch information from the skin. Kinesthetic information is carried from the spinal cord to the medulla in two tracts: the *fasciculus cuneatus* and the *fasciculus gracilis*, both of which are pictured in Figure 9.3. The tracts form synapses in the medulla with the medical lemniscus, which ascends to the thalamus (ventral posterior lateral nucleus). From there the information is projected to the *anterior* part of the postcentral gyrus of the cortex (the primary somatosensory area). You will recall that the pathways from the touch and pressure receptors on the skin take a similar route but project to the *posterior* part of the gyrus. Also, like the cortical cells that code pressure and touch and, for that matter, visual-line orientation, the cells that code limb position are arranged in roughly columnar patterns within the cortex. One column of cells running from the surface downward, for example, may be sensitive to a 90-degree angle in a particular joint; another column may be sensitive to a 50-degree angle in the same joint. Thus sensitivity to each particular angle expresses itself spatially in a particular column of cortical cells.

LABYRINTHINE SENSE

Consider a gymnast performing somersaults. With each moment-to-moment change in body position—each acceleration and rotation, each upside-down and right-side-up position—different responses are needed to maintain balance. The gymnast's muscles must tense in both legs simultaneously to cushion the landing. Both arms must fly out during the middle of the stunt in order to keep the body from falling to one side. As the gymnast approaches the mat, his or her eyes must fix on it. Eye movement must compensate for head movement. All of these responses occur rapidly, without much thought; all call for different sensory signals produced by changes in position as the body moves through the environment. And all these responses are described by a single term: *postural reflexes*. Underlying these reflexes is the *labyrinthine sense*.

You do not have to be a gymnast, of course, to benefit from postural reflexes and labyrinthine sense. Adjustments in postural reflexes take place in the simplest of movements—walking, sitting down, and even standing. Usually we are unaware that these reflexes, initiated by balance receptors, are taking place, for balance receptors are unique. Unlike other receptors, they produce conscious sensations not directly but *indirectly*, and usually only when they are overstimulated. The dizzy feeling you experience after spinning around for a few seconds, for example, is an indirect effect produced by overstimulated balance receptors. What happens is this: the spinning action stimulates the balance receptors to elicit reflexes, such as eye movements and stomach contractions. These reflexes in turn initiate stimuli of their own, which are sensed as specific sensations and collectively labeled as a feeling of dizziness. For the most part, though, balance receptors work at an unconscious reflex level.

The Semicircular Canals and the Vestibular Sacs

Our sensitivity to changes in body position with respect to gravity comes from several sources. Eyes are one such source. Kinesthetics is another. Our concern here is with the sources found in the head, in the same skull cavity that houses the inner ear. This cavity, called the *labyrinth*, is aptly named, for it contains a complex series of bony tunnels and canals arranged much like a maze. The sense organs it houses are known as the *labyrinthine organs*. There are two such organs in the labyrinth (see Figure 9.8). One organ consists of three fluid-filled canals called the *semicircular canals*. These canals specialize in sensing *rotating* movements such as those that occur whenever you twist or turn your head. The other sense organ, consisting of two fluid-filled canals known as the *vestibular sacs*, is sensitive to *linear* (as opposed to rotating) motion. It enables you to tell, for instance, whether you are accelerating or decelerating in a car. The vestibular sacs are also sensitive to the position of your head when your body is stationary. In other words, it allows you to tell up from down with respect to gravity.

Hydrodynamics and the Labyrinthine Organs

The semicircular canals and vestibular sacs operate on hydrodynamic principles. To understand these principles, imagine a glass of water balanced on the dashboard of a car. When the car accelerates forward, the water lags behind. Why? Because of the inertia created by a greater degree of pressure on the back of the glass than on the front. As the car's speed becomes constant, the water in the glass levels off, returning eventually to a resting position, at which time all sides of the glass are stimulated equally. Then, with deceleration, the fluid presses more to the front than to the back of the glass.

So it is with the fluid in the vestibular sacs and semicircular canals. When your head moves in a linear direction or rotates, the fluid lags in each of the sacs and canals, exerting an increase in pressure on the receptors lying opposite the direction of movement. The receptors in the vestibular sacs and semicircular canals are sensitive only to *changes* in movement (acceleration and deceleration), each change stimulating a different set of receptors. When movement reaches a constant speed, the fluid in the sacs and canals returns to a resting position, and receptors are no longer differentially stimulated. Thus movement at a constant speed cannot be distinguished from motionlessness because the fluid is in the same level state in both conditions. This is why we say the vestibular sacs and semicircular canals are sensitive to *changes* in movement (acceleration and deceleration) rather than to movement per se.

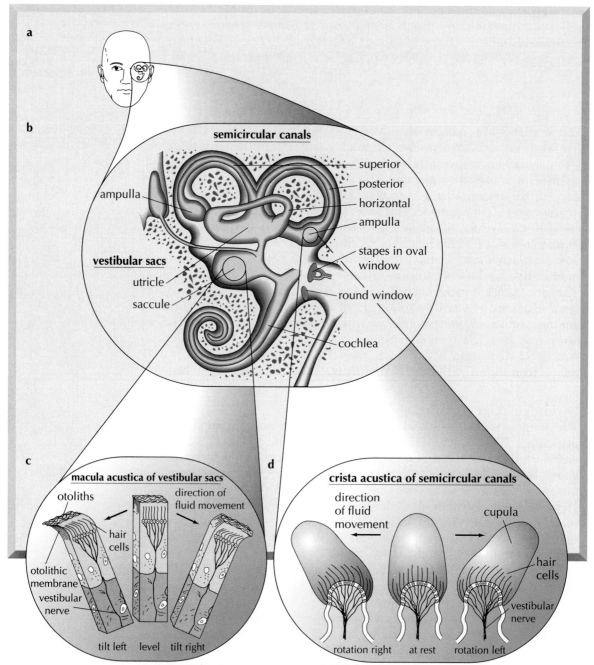

Figure 9.8 *The Labyrinthine Apparatus*

The semicircular canals and vestibular sacs are shown (a) in position in the head, (b) in position in the inner ear, and (c and d) in detail with a diagram of their membranes (otolithic and cupula) and hair cells. In the left-hand panel (c) a tilt of the head moves the otolithic membrane in the vestibular sacs causing the attached hair cells to bend and the vestibular nerve to fire. In the right-hand panel (d), changes in speed of rotation cause the cupula to move, the hair cells to bend, and the vestibular nerve to fire.

Semicircular Coding: Rotating Movement

Any time you swing your head from side to side or spin around, two things help to maintain your balance. One is compensatory eye movement known as the *nystagmus reflex*. The other is a chain of events that takes place in the semicircular canals.

To understand the chain of events, it helps to understand something about the structure of the semicircular canals, pictured in Figure 9.8*b*. These canals are filled with fluid known as *endolymph*. Whenever the semicircular canals move, endolymph moves. At the base of each canal, at the point where each joins with a vestibular sac, is an enlarged cavity called the *ampulla*. Within each of the three ampullae is another structure, called the *crista acustica*, in which the semicircular canal receptors are located. The receptors take the form of hair cells, one end projecting into the gelatinous mass known as the *cupula*, the other end connecting with the vestibular nerve as shown in Figure 9.8*d*. Neurons from the vestibular nerve join with those from the auditory nerve to form cranial nerve VIII.

When the body rotates and the head moves, the endolymph exerts a kind of hydraulic pressure that moves the gelatinous cupula into which the hair cells are projected. As the cupula moves, the hair cells bend, as shown in Figure 9.8*d*. The bending triggers generator potentials and eventually a neural impulse in the vestibular nerve. One aspect of this movement should be stressed: the fluid tends to move *only* when the body is accelerating or decelerating in a rotating motion, hence the physiological connection between the semicircular canals and the rotating motion of the body.

Coding for Direction and Speed of Rotation

As we have explained, limb movement is coded on the basis of its relationship to neural firing. The slower the movement, the slower the firing. A similar principle applies to the coding for direction and speed of rotation by the semicircular canals.

When your head is still, the neurons in the vestibular nerve are *not* inactive. Instead, they are firing spontaneously at a rate of approximately 100 to 300 impulses per second. When your head moves, the fluid in each semicircular canal pushes against the cupula, causing the hair cells to bend. Because the three semicircular canals (superior, posterior, and horizontal) are arranged at right angles to one another (rather like the two walls and the floor in the corner of a room), each canal is maximally sensitive to movement in one of three directions: forward-backward, up-down, left-right. So, depending on the direction and speed of rotation, the movement of the fluid in one canal lags behind that of the fluid in another. These varying movements bend some hair cells and unbend others to produce a unique mixture of excitation with each variation in direction of speed. This movement of hair cells in turn causes an increase in the firing of some neurons and a decrease in the firing of others. In this way the neural code for direction and speed is established.

Vestibular Coding: Up-Down and Linear Movement

The key to the body's ability to differentiate between up and down and among variations in speed of straight-line movement lies in two fluid-filled sacs contained within the vestibule, an area that lies between the semicircular canals and the cochlea, as shown in Figure 9.8*b*. These vestibular sacs, known as the *utricle* and the *saccule*, work on roughly the same principle as the semicircular canals. They are arranged at right angles to each other. The fluid in the utricle, which sits in a horizontal plane, moves when the body accelerates either forward or backward. The fluid in the saccule, which is in a vertical plane, moves when the body is accelerated in a vertical direction—as when, for example, you jump up and down.

Like the semicircular canals, the utricle and saccule contain hair cells that project into a gelatinous mass. In the case of the utricle and saccule, however, the gelatinous mass is embedded with calcium carbonate crystals known as *otoliths* and consequently is referred to as the *otolithic membrane*. Collectively, the otolithic membrane and the hair cells are called the *macula acustica* and are pictured in Figure 9.8*c*.

The actual neural coding that originates in the macula acustica works roughly as follows: when your head is in an upright position, the hair cells projecting into the overlying otolithic membrane are in an unbent vertical position. But when your head is tilted or when there is a change in the speed of movement along a straight line (as during the accelerating or decelerating of a car), fluid shifts. This shift causes the otolithic membrane to move. The result of such movement, as shown in Figure 9.8*c*, is the bending of the hair cells, which excites the neural impulses. In this way, different head positions cause the stimulation of different hair cells, which ultimately stimulate different neurons to establish the code for up-down and linear movement.

From the Vestibular Sacs to the Brain

The neural pathways from the vestibular sacs to the brain are similar to those that run from the semicircular canals. The hair cells in the vestibular sacs form synapses with neurons that join neurons from the semicircular canals to make up the nonauditory (vestibular) part of cranial nerve VIII.

The impulses from both the vestibular sacs and the semicircular canals travel to the medulla. There the vestibular nerve forms synapses in the vestibular nuclei. As it happens, the vestibular portion of the auditory nerve contains neurons that are relatively large in diameter. Their size enables them to conduct impulses more rapidly than average-sized neurons. This added speed is needed for the rapid reflex adjustments in posture or eye movement which rapid changes in body position dictate.

From the vestibular nuclei, neurons travel to several areas in the brain. Some go to the oculomotor nerve, where eye movements can be regulated to compensate for head movement. Others go to visceral nuclei in the medulla, where, for instance, the stomach can now become involved, producing the nausea that accompanies the condition known as motion sickness. Still others go to the cerebellum, the reticular formation, and the cortex, in each case affecting motor coordination. Finally, some go to the spinal cord, where muscle tone is controlled. We shall consider these pathways more closely in Chapter 10.

SUMMARY

1. *The somatic system defined.* The sensory system that receives and processes stimuli that originate on the surface of or within the body itself is known as the somatic sensory system, and the receptors in this system fall into two categories. Receptors sensitive to stimuli on the body surface are referred to as skin or cutaneous receptors. They underlie our capacity to experience pressure and pain and to differentiate heat from cold. Receptors operating within the body are known as proprioceptive receptors. The stimuli they sense underlie our capacity to adjust to the changes that occur in the body whenever we move.

2. *The end organs.* The skin contains end organs—nonneural structures that transmit stimuli to receptors—grouped according to the specific stimuli to which they are sensitive: Meissner's corpuscles (touch and vibration), Merkel's disks (light touch and pressure), Pacinian corpuscles (deep pressure), Krause's end bulbs (unknown), Ruffini endings (touch and pressure), and free nerve endings (pain and temperature). The end organs are not themselves the receptors (that is, the sites of transduction) but rather are nonneural structures that transmit stimuli to receptors.

3. *Cutaneous receptors.* Cutaneous receptors below the neck are connected with the central nervous system by spinal nerves. Those above the neck are connected with the central nervous system by the trigeminal nerve (from the face) and spinal nerves (from the scalp). Critical to the function of the cutaneous receptors are beltlike regions of the skin known as dermatomes. Just as there are 31 spinal nerves, so there are 31 dermatomes, each of which is innervated by not only its own spinal nerve but the neighboring spinal nerve as well.

4. *From receptor to spinal cord to brain.* Cutaneous information is carried to the spinal cord by three types of sensory neurons: A-beta fibers for pressure, A-delta and C fibers for temperature and pain. The three groups of neurons travel collectively in each spinal nerve to the spinal cord and then from the spinal cord to the brain via two ascending systems. One system (the dorsal-column lemniscal system) carries information related to touch and pressure; the other system (the anterolateral system) carries information related to pain and temperature.

5. *Coding pressure and touch.* A-beta fibers are the receptors for pressure and touch. They are located in the Pacinian corpuscles and they transduce the deformation of the corpuscle produced by pressure into neural impulses. Once transduced, pressure and touch are coded on the basis of a place principle. Pressure and touch information from adjacent areas on the body are represented in different but adjacent areas in the cortex. The more sensitive to pressure or touch a given area of the body is, the more neurons there are in the corresponding projection area in the cortex. The cortical map that underlies the ability to discriminate tactile sensations can be modified by environmental stimulation, and these findings have led to new therapies for brain-damaged people who have lost their sensitivity to touch.

6. *Coding temperature.* The sensations of cold and warmth are rooted in distinct areas of the skin that contain receptors (low threshold A-delta and C fibers) sensitive to both cold and warmth, and a coding pattern that is governed primarily by place. Differences between the temperature of an object and skin temperature (physiological zero) are sensed by different receptors that are connected to cold- and warm-coded areas in the brain.

7. *Pain receptors.* Pain receptors are free nerve endings, high threshold A-delta and C fibers. These receptors are sensitive to intense stimulation, albeit indirectly, via a chemical that is released by the injured areas and that acts on the fibers. A-delta and C fibers enter the spinal cord in the dorsal horn, forming synapses with neurons that ascend the cord to the brain in several tracts known collectively as the anterolateral system.

8. *Pain circuitry in the brain.* The tracts of the anterolateral system collect pain-related information from three sources: from A-delta and C fibers at the level of the spinal cord and from the trigeminal nerve from the face and head. These tracts convey pain-related information to three areas: the reticular formation, the limbic system, and the thalamus. Each area is thought to control a different aspect of pain—arousal, emotion, and sensation, respectively.

9. *Chronic pain.* Up to a point, the coding for pain seems to follow a pattern similar to the coding of other sensory experiences. It involves receptors, peripheral nerves, tracts to the brain, and centers in the brain. One striking difference, however, is that the experience of pain doesn't automatically disappear when the stimulus is removed. There are, in fact, three instances—known as chronic pain syndromes—in which removing a pain-inducing stimulus does not produce corresponding relief. One is phantom limb pain (experienced by amputees). Another is causalgia—pain caused by a bullet wound that has long since healed. The third is neuralgia, pain that lingers after the infection or disease in the peripheral nerves has cleared up.

10. *The Melzack-Wall theory.* According to two prominent pain researchers, Ronald Melzack and Patrick Wall, chronic pain is produced by selective damage to the A-beta fibers. Their theory is based on the assumption that A-delta and C fibers, even before a noxious stimulus is introduced, are constantly firing but are normally inhibited by the A-beta fibers. Damage to the A-beta fibers, in the view of Melzack and Wall, either eliminates or dims the normal inhibitory effect of these fibers, allowing A-delta and C fibers to transmit neural activity unchecked to the anterolateral system. Some researchers have found evidence that does indeed link a decrease in A-beta fiber activity to an increase in the activity of A-delta and C fibers, but other researchers have found no such relationship.

11. *The pain-suppression circuit.* Although the specific details of the original Melzack-Wall theory may not be correct, the basic premise of the theory—that the nervous system has the capability not only to excite but also to inhibit the sensation of pain—appears to be true. Two areas of the brain when stimulated produce relief from pain. One is the periaqueductal gray, an area in the midbrain; the other is the nucleus raphe magnus, located in the medulla. Stimulating these areas inhibits the transmission of impulses in the anterolateral system. Three neurotransmitters—endorphins, serotonin, and enkephalin—are involved, each of which works in a different area of the pain-suppression circuit. There is good reason to believe, too, that the pain-suppression circuit is the mechanism that accounts for the pain-killing properties of morphine, acupuncture, and placebos.

12. *How pain therapies work.* Most therapies known to relieve pain—the key exception is hypnosis—do so by actions mediated to a large extent by the periaqueductal gray and its descending circuit to the spinal cord. In each case, the interaction between treatment and the nervous system appears to be mediated by endorphins and enkephalin. Opiates owe their pain-killing properties to the fact that they mimic the action of endorphins and enkephalin in the periaqueductal gray and spinal cord. Acupuncture and placebos both appear to bring pain relief by stimulating the release of endorphins.

13. *The adaptive function of pain suppression.* Why there is a circuit in the nervous system whose function is to suppress pain is still something of a mystery, but one theory holds that in certain situations, adaptive behavior calls for the ability to ignore pain. A growing body of experimental literature on lower animals, coupled with a handful of studies on humans, has led to the conclusion that under extreme stress, the body releases endorphins that block pain, enabling the organism to respond adaptively to emergency situations.

14. *Proprioception defined.* Behavior is keyed to cues from inside the body (interoceptive stimuli) and outside the body (exteroceptive stimuli). Internal cues provide two types of information: proprioceptive cues, which are related to the position and balance of the body, and visceral cues, which are related to internal states, such as hunger and thirst.

15. *Sources of proprioceptive cues.* Proprioceptive cues convey two kinds of information: awareness of body position and balance with respect to gravity and awareness of limb position. Body balance is sensed by receptors in the nonauditory parts of the inner ear, which are known as the labyrinthine sense organs. Limb position is sensed by receptors located in the joints and ligaments, which provide what are known as the kinesthetic senses. Receptors collecting balance and kinesthetic information mainly furnish a background of body awareness within which discrete responses can be made. Damage to either set of receptors can have a crippling effect on the ability to move.

16. *Kinesthetics in brief.* Kinesthetic receptors gather information by sensing the angular relationship between the hinged bones of a limb and transducing it into neural impulses. Each change in the relationship causes a different set of neurons to fire. The code is represented in the cortex in much the same way as the code for pressure and touch: different columns of cells are responsive to different angles.

17. *Balance and labyrinthine sense.* The chief sources of balance information are two receptor organs located in the nonauditory part of the inner ear. One organ consists of the semicircular canals, which are three fluid-filled canals sensitive to rotating movement. The other consists of the vestibular sacs, which are two fluid-filled sacs sensitive to linear movement. The transduction process in both organs is based on the same hydraulic principle. Each canal and sac contains hair cells, and when the body moves, the fluid in the canals and sacs moves. Depending on the direction of movement, the hair cells bend and neural impulses are produced.

18. *The neural basis of balance.* The neural circuits that connect the semicircular canals and the vestibular sacs to the brain take similar paths. The hair cells in both organs form synapses with neurons that make up the vestibular nerve, the nonauditory part of cranial nerve VIII. The nerve enters the brain at the level of the medulla and forms synapses in the vestibular nuclei. From the vestibular nuclei the neural fibers travel to several areas, each involved in a different reflex. The oculomotor nerve produces reflexive eye movements; the visceral nuclei produce reflexive stomach contractions; the cerebellum, the reticular formation, and the spinal cord produce reflexive muscle tone.

KEY TERMS

A-beta fibers
A-delta fibers
acupuncture
ampulla
anterolateral system
C fibers
causalgia
chronic pain
chronic pain syndromes
cingulate gyrus

cingulotomy
crista acustica
cupula
cutaneous senses
dermatomes
dorsal column–medial
  lemniscus system
end organs
endolymph
endorphins

enkephalin
exteroceptive cues
fasciculus cuneatus
fasciculus gracilis
free nerve endings
gate-control theory
hypnosis
interoceptive cues
intralaminar nuclei
kinesthetic sense
Krause's end bulbs
labyrinth
labyrinthine sense
laminae
macula acustica
medial lemniscus
Meissner's corpuscles
Melzack-Wall theory
Merkel's disks
naloxone
neuralgia
nucleus cuneatus
nucleus gracilis
nucleus raphe magnus
nystagmus reflex
opiates
otolithic membrane
otoliths
Pacinian corpuscles
pain-suppression circuit
paradoxical cold
PCPA (parachlorophenylalanine)

periaqueductal gray
phantom-limb pain
physiological zero
placebo
posterior nuclear group
postural reflexes
proprioception
proprioceptive cues
proprioceptive receptors
proprioceptors
Romberg sign
Ruffini endings
saccule
semicircular canals
serotonin
skin mapping
skin receptors
somatic sensory system
somatosensory coding
spinal nerves
spinomesencephalic tract
spinoreticular tract
substance P
substantia gelatinosa
tabes dorsalis
thalamus
trigeminal nerve
utricle
ventral posterior lateral nucleus
ventrobasal complex
vestibular sacs
visceral cues

SUGGESTED READINGS

Lund, J. S. (Ed.). *Sensory Processing in the Mammalian Brain: Neural Substrates and Experimental Strategies*. New York: Oxford University Press, 1989.

Melzack, R., & Wall, P. D. *The Challenge of Pain*. New York: Basic Books, 1993.

Sathian, K. "Tactile Sensing of Surface Features." *Trends in Neuroscience*, 12, 1989, 513–519.

Wall, P. D., & Melzack, R. (Eds.). *Textbook of Pain*, 2nd ed. Edinburgh: Churchill Livingston, 1989.

Wilson V. J., & Melvill Jones, G. *Mammalian Vestibular Physiology*. New York: Plenum Press, 1979.

MUSCLES AND GLANDS

INTRODUCTION

The human brain, as you should well appreciate by now, can process a prodigious amount of sensory information. No matter how much information is processed, however, it is of no use unless it can be acted upon.

Action involves muscles—skeletal, smooth, and cardiac—and glands. All are controlled, either directly or indirectly, by specific areas in the brain. The cortex, by giving rise to tracts that descend the spinal cord, plays a critical role in the control of skeletal muscles. The hypothalamus, by exerting control over the autonomic nervous system and pituitary gland, plays a critical role in controlling the smooth muscles, heart, and glands. In this chapter we shall be concerned with both types of action systems. Let us begin with the control of skeletal muscles.

THE MECHANICS OF MOVEMENT

Every animal moves, and every animal consists of parts that move. Even single-cell animals have appendages that move—and with good reason. Without some means of movement, an animal would not be able to react to challenges in the environment and survival would be impossible.

Movement in humans is under the control of specialized cells that make up the skeletal muscles. Skeletal muscles are so called because they are connected to the skeleton by tendons. Movement occurs through the combined action of bones and muscles. The specific form a movement takes is determined by the structure and placement of the bones. How the movement is made is under the control of the muscles. Bones without muscles would be the equivalent of a puppet without strings.

Bones are connected at fluid-filled spaces known as joints. When you bend your arm, you are not really bending the arm bones; you are making use of the elbow joint. The number and the shapes of joints determine how a particular limb moves. The more joints in a particular appendage, the more versatile its movement.

The versatility of movement made possible by joints is not always obvious. The movement of limbs can be likened to the movement of a door on a hinge, except that a limb can do much more than open and close. It can also rotate. You can do more with your arm, for instance, than straighten it and fold it inward; you can also rotate it a few degrees to the right or left. Your ability to do so gives you far more movement versatility than you would have if your arm could move only on a single axis.

How Muscles Move

Bones are versatile, but muscles are not. A muscle can do only two things: it can contract (i.e., tighten) or it can relax. When a muscle contracts, it becomes shorter and it pulls. The fact that a muscle can only pull raises an interesting question: since much of our routine behavior calls for what seems to be pushing, how do we manage with a set of muscles that can only pull?

The answer to this question has to do with the ways in which muscles are tied to the skeleton. Two sets of muscles are attached to the skeleton, and, as Figure 10.1 shows, they are attached in such a way that the limb can be pulled in either of two directions. When one set of muscles contracts, the limb is pulled in one direction; when the other set contracts, the limb is pulled in the other direction.

Let us be more specific. Muscles that straighten or extend a limb—the muscles in your arms, fingers, and legs that enable you to stretch these appendages—are known as *extensors*. Every time you stretch or extend your arm or leg, you are contracting an extensor muscle. But limbs can be flexed as well as extended. That is because of a different type of muscle which, when it contracts, works antagonistically to the extensors. These muscles are known as *flexors*.

Coordinating Antagonistic Muscles

Because a single limb is under the control of antagonistic muscles, it is not surprising that a special relationship exists between the two muscles. Neither set of muscles works in isolation. When extensors contract, flexors relax. When flexors contract, extensors relax. In other words, all

Figure 10.1 *To Bend or Not to Bend*
The reciprocal relationship between flexors (biceps) and extensors (triceps) and its effect on the bending and straightening of a jointed limb. When the limb is partially flexed (a), both extensor and flexor are partially contracted. When the limb is extended (b), the extensor is contracted and the flexor is relaxed. When the limb is flexed (c), the extensor is relaxed and the flexor is contracted.

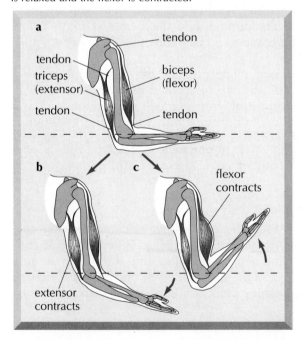

movements, simple and complicated alike, call for the reciprocal action of two sets of muscles, as Figure 10.1 shows. Movement, in fact, can occur *only* when the two sets of muscles act reciprocally. If flexors and extensors were to contract at the same time, the result would be a muscular tug of war—and no movement. Thus the two sets of muscles are innervated in a specific manner, assuring that when one set contracts, the other relaxes. The term for this relationship is *reciprocal innervation*.

THE NEURAL ASPECTS OF MUSCLE MOVEMENT

Muscles may be the means by which we move, but they are not the *reason* we move. If movement is to be adaptive, it cannot be random. It must have direction, and it must be coordinated with incoming stimuli and other movements. To meet these requirements, movements must be under neural control.

The Final Common Pathway

The neural control of muscle movement is related mainly to the capacity of muscles to contract on the basis of neural information received from the spinal cord and the brain. This information is delivered by a special type of neuron: the *alpha motor neuron*. The cell bodies of the alpha motor neurons are located in the ventral horn of the spinal cord. As you can see in Figure 10.2, no matter where the impulse comes from (sensory neurons in the spinal cord or tracts from the brain), it always takes the same route on the last part of the trip to the muscles: the alpha motor neuron. Hence the alpha motor neuron has been labeled the *final common pathway*.

The key structural feature of a typical alpha motor neuron is its multi-branching axonal endings. These endings enable a single motor axon to innervate a large surface of the muscle, which is itself composed of many individual muscle fibers. The actual number of muscle fibers innervated by a single axon varies and is measured by the *innervation ratio*. The ratio can go as high as 150 muscle fibers to 1 neuron or as low as 3 to 1. The larger the ratio, obviously, the larger the area of muscle that contracts in response to the excitation of one neuron. Hence, in large muscles used for crude or gross movements such as bending your back, the ratio of muscle fibers to neurons is high; in situations calling for fine movement such as digital dexterity, the ratio is low. In any case, a single axon and the muscle fibers it innervates are known collectively as a *motor unit*.

Neuromuscular Junctions

Although muscles consist of muscle cells, they are similar in certain respects to nerves. A nerve, as you already know, is a bundle of many neurons; a muscle is a bundle of many muscle fibers. In addition, each

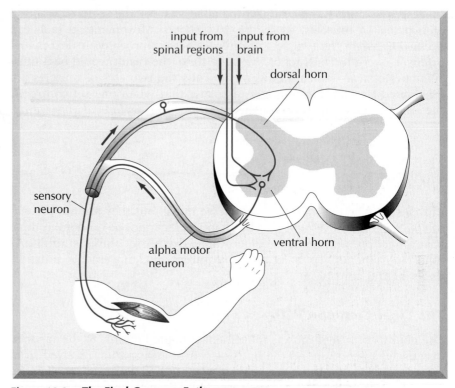

Figure 10.2 *The Final Common Pathway*
Activation of the alpha motor neuron in the spinal cord may originate in the sensory neurons, in other regions of the spinal cord, or in motor areas in the brain.

muscle fiber, like each neuron, is surrounded by a thin membrane, although in muscle fibers, the membrane is known as the *sarcolemma*. Ions are distributed across this membrane to create a resting potential, as can be seen in Figure 10.3.

We have already described how information is transmitted across the synaptic gap between neurons by neurotransmitters. The same principle holds for transmission between neurons and muscles. As you can see in Figure 10.3, a microscopic gap, known as the *neuromuscular junction*, separates the motor neuron from the muscle it innervates. The muscle surface at this junction is characterized by a slight elevation known as the *end plate*. When a neural impulse arrives at the end of the motor neuron, it stimulates the release of *acetylcholine* from the vesicles in the axonal endings. And just as it does in synapses that separate neurons, the acetylcholine does three things: it diffuses across the gap, binds to receptor sites, and changes the permeability of the membrane to trigger the flow of sodium ions. This change in permeability causes the muscle fibers to depolarize.

The depolarization recorded from the end plate region on the muscle fibers is called an *end plate potential* (EPP). The depolarization caused by the acetylcholine takes the same general form as the excitatory post-

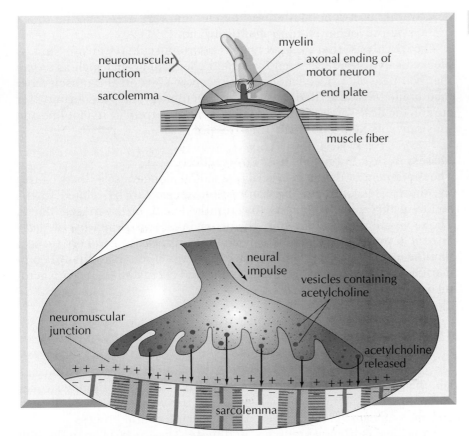

Figure 10.3 *Neuromuscular Junction*
A neuromuscular junction and the events that occur there to produce a muscle action potential.

synaptic potential in synapses between neurons. It is graded, which is to say that depolarization at the end plate increases as the release of acetylcholine increases. It is "all or none" in the sense that when the threshold is reached, sodium ions rush in, and the impulse, known as the *muscle action potential*, propagates itself down the muscle fiber.

Acetylcholine in Muscle Action

Acetylcholine, as we noted in Chapter 5, is rapidly broken down by the enzyme acetylcholinesterase. This means that the muscle action potential passes through a refractory period and quickly recovers. The role of acetylcholinesterase in this process is seen most vividly in the treatment of a disease called *myasthenia gravis*, which is characterized by severe muscle weakness especially in the muscles of the eyes, the eyelids, the mouth, and the throat, as well as the limbs. The cause of myasthenia gravis appears to be a deficiency of acetylcholine receptors in the neuromuscular junctions. The deficiency prevents muscle fibers from depolarizing and treatment includes drugs that compensate for the deficiency by deactivating acetylcholinesterase, thereby allowing acetylcholine to act in the synapse longer than normal (Rowland, 1991).

The paralysis that results when neuromuscular transmission is blocked can also be triggered by certain chemical agents such as *curare* that compete with acetylcholine for receptor sites on the muscle-fiber membrane. Because the muscle-fiber membrane has an affinity for curare, the drug serves to insulate the membrane from acetylcholine and thus prevents neuromuscular transmission.

Muscle Action Potentials and Contraction

The movement of the muscle action potential along muscle fibers causes the muscle to contract. The contraction appears to be related to the action of threadlike *myofibrils* that run the length of the muscle fibers. These myofibrils contain fine filaments made up primarily of *acto-myosin*, a protein that has the capacity to contract. Researchers suspect that the muscle action potential releases energy through a series of complex chemical reactions, and that the released energy interacts with acto-myosin to produce contraction.

THE FORM OF MOVEMENT

Movement obviously takes many forms. The bulletlike thrust of a boxer's jab, the graceful arc of a ballet dancer's arms, the short, choppy strokes of a carpenter hammering nails—each of these movements is distinct and each, presumably, is triggered by a specific neural process.

To behave is to move muscles, and more. The "more" has to do with the conditions that must be present before movement can take place. Chief among these conditions is a state of existing tension or support in muscles known as *muscle tone*. Muscle tone is the behavioral background, the condition that must exist before discrete motor responses (i.e., movement) can take place. To understand movement you need to understand both background tone and discrete movement. We shall explore first how muscle tone is initiated at the level of the spinal cord. Then we will look at how the brain fits into the process. Finally, we will consider the source of the fine movement and discrete responses that are superimposed on the background state.

Background Tone and the Stretch Reflex

A basic condition of movement is the body's capacity to adjust muscle tone very quickly to abrupt shifts in weight. This capacity is clearly illustrated by your ability to jump up and down and, at the same time, to keep your body level and upright. The reason you can do so is that adjustments are taking place automatically at the level of the spinal cord. The process that controls these adjustments is known as the *stretch reflex*.

The stretch reflex is constantly at work whenever you move. Similar to the load levelers in a car, it constantly adjusts muscle tension to shifts in weight. It does this in routine behavior—such as when you are taking a leisurely stroll. And it does it during highly specialized behavior—such as when a pole vaulter is arching upward. It is obvious that these adjustments must take place rapidly, which explains why the muscle support provided by the stretch reflex is controlled automatically at the level of the spinal cord. If the muscle reactions that adjust to sudden shifts in weight had to depend on signals from the brain, there would be no time to make the adjustments.

Adjustments to shifts in body weight take place because the muscles have a unique capacity: they can regulate their own tension. When you stand up, for instance, your muscles automatically tense to support your body. When you lie down, the muscles relax, again automatically. The reason behind this automatic tensing and relaxing can be traced to the following sequence of events: when you stand up, the added weight causes the muscles to stretch, the stretch causes neurons to fire, and the neural firing causes the muscles to tense. The resulting tension supports the added weight. This sequence of events involves anatomical structures that are unique to skeletal muscles. Let us take a closer look.

Regulating Muscle Tension

In every skeletal muscle, there are two types of muscle fibers, *extrafusal* and *intrafusal.* These fibers lie side by side, and they work in synchrony, shadowing each other's movement. As Figure 10.4 shows, the middle region of the intrafusal fiber, an area commonly referred to as the *nuclear bag*, is wrapped in a group of nerve endings known as *stretch receptors* or *spindle organs.* The nerve endings are unique: they produce neural firing whenever any tension is exerted on the intrafusal fibers.

The inner workings of these structures are depicted in Figure 10.4. As you can see, putting added weight on a muscle stretches both the extrafusal and intrafusal fibers, causing the receptors in the nuclear bag to stretch and to produce neural impulses. The impulses travel to the spinal cord and then back to the extrafusal fibers, whose contractions produce muscle tension.

But the cycle does not end there. Muscle tension, by eliminating the stretching in both the extrafusal and intrafusal fibers, brings about a temporary end to the firing of the stretch receptors. As firing decreases, the extrafusal fibers begin to relax. If the load remains on the muscle, the fibers stretch again, starting the process anew. This cycle from stretch to tension to stretch explains why the stretch reflex is often referred to as a self-regulating process.

Types of Stretch Receptors

The nerve endings, or stretch receptors, wrapped around the nuclear bag are actually of two types, as Figure 10.5 indicates. One type, known as an *annulospiral ending,* is wrapped around the center of the nuclear bag and ultimately forms synapses in the spinal cord with the alpha motor neurons that return to the extrafusal fibers in the stimulated muscle. The other type, known as a *flower-spray ending,* is wrapped around the outer

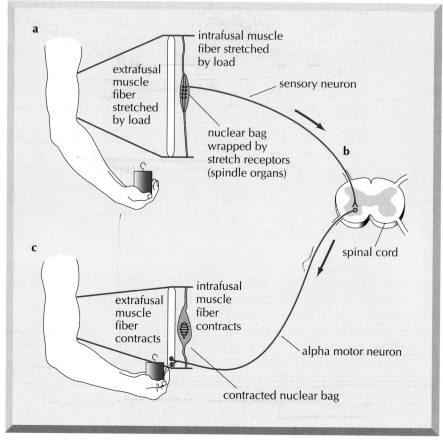

Figure 10.4 *Extrafusal and Intrafusal Muscle Fibers in Action*
(a) The load on the muscle causes the extrafusal and intrafusal fibers to stretch and the stretch receptors to fire. (b) The neural impulses initiated by the stretch receptors travel to the spinal cord and return to the muscle via the alpha motor neurons, causing extrafusal fibers to contract. (c) This contraction reduces both the tension (stretch) on the intrafusal fibers and the firing in the stretch receptor. The arrows indicate the direction of neural impulses toward and away from the spinal cord.

part of the nuclear bag and takes a different path to the spinal cord. It eventually forms synapses with alpha motor neurons that travel to the extrafusal fibers of the muscle that is functioning antagonistically to the stimulated muscle.

As you might expect, these two types of nerves work reciprocally. The annulospiral endings work to trigger the contraction of extrafusal fibers in the stretched muscle, while the flower-spray endings work via interneurons to inhibit contractions in the antagonistic muscle. This reciprocal action ensures that tension occurs only in the stretched muscle.

Spinal Reflexes
The stretch reflex is not the only reflex mediated by the spinal cord. To appreciate the other reflexes involved, consider what happens when the

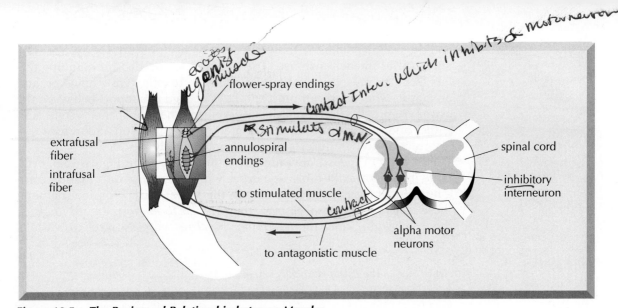

Figure 10.5 *The Reciprocal Relationship between Muscles*
The stretch reflex consists of two circuits, one involved in contracting the stimulated (stretched) muscle, the other involved in inhibiting (relaxing) the antagonistic muscle.

spinal cord is severed and detached from the brain. The reflexes controlled by the isolated spinal cord (known as a spinal preparation) remain operative, but the voluntary control of behavior is lost. Included among the spinal reflexes is the scratch reflex in cats, elicited by touching the skin, and, of course, the knee-jerk reflex in humans.

The spinal preparation demonstrates something significant about the brain and motor behavior. With the involvement of the brain, motor behavior no longer is limited to robotlike reflexes. Balance, fluidity, spontaneity—each of these added dimensions of movement reflects brain involvement. Each feature involves a different part of the brain, and all must fit together to form an integrated response. Let us now look at these features.

THE BRAIN AND MOVEMENT

The brain has a dual role in the control of muscle movement. First, it provides information that allows muscles to assume the background condition necessary to perform movement. Second, it controls the discrete movements themselves. The first of these functions falls within the domain of the extrapyramidal system; the second is under the control of both the extrapyramidal and pyramidal systems. We shall now look at these systems in detail.

The Extrapyramidal System and Muscle Tone

You have been sitting in a chair for about 15 minutes; suddenly you rise and walk across the room. For each movement—the sitting, the rising, and the walking—muscle tone is necessary to support the body. Yet your needs differ in each instance. The muscle tone needed for standing differs from the muscle tone needed for sitting. In either case, however, and no matter what degree of muscle tone is needed to support behavior, the extrapyramidal system underlies its control. The role of this system is to gather and process information related to body position and to feed this information to the muscles that support the body.

Pathways in the extrapyramidal system, pictured in Figure 10.6, originate in the cortex but form synapses with and gather information from a number of areas before they reach the spinal cord. Prominent among these areas are the *basal ganglia*, the *reticular formation*, the *red nucleus*, the *cerebellum*, and the *vestibular nucleus*—all involved to various

Figure 10.6 *The Extrapyramidal System*
A schematic rendering of the extrapyramidal system.

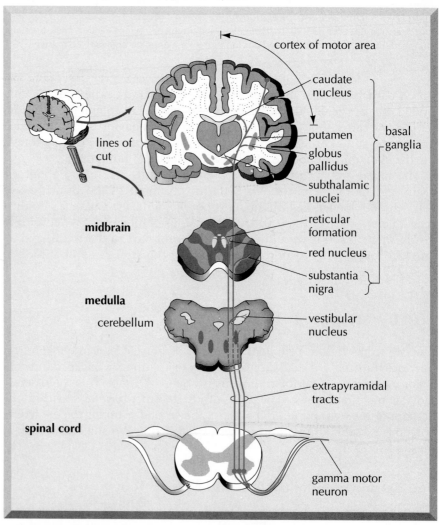

degrees in sensing the position and balance of the body. This information is carried by the extrapyramidal system to the spinal cord, where the extrapyramidal tracts form synapses with a special set of motor neurons, the *gamma motor neurons*. It is through the gamma motor neurons that the extrapyramidal system regulates muscle tone. Let us examine this regulatory process.

The Gamma Motor System

As we noted earlier in our discussion about the stretch reflex, the key to regulating long-lasting tension states in the muscles lies in the action of intrafusal fibers of the muscle. These fibers are controlled by the extrapyramidal system, which exerts control over muscle tone by causing the intrafusal fibers to contract and relax. It does so via gamma motor neurons, as shown in Figure 10.7. Excitation in the gamma motor neurons causes the intrafusal fibers to contract, a crucial part of the

Figure 10.7 *The Gamma Motor System in Action*
After gathering information about the position of the body from the cortex, the extrapyramidal system sends impulses to the intrafusal fibers (1), causing them to contract and the stretch receptors to fire (2). The neural impulses initiated by the stretch receptors travel to the spinal cord (3) and return to the muscle via the alpha motor neurons (4), causing extrafusal fibers to contract. This contraction reduces both the tension (stretch) on the intrafusal fibers and the firing in the stretch receptors.

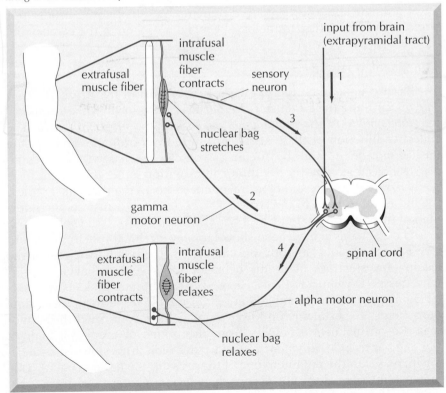

process because selective contraction of this sort (in which extrafusal fibers remain uncontracted and intrafusal fibers contract) brings about stretching in the elastic nuclear bag, which in turn causes the stretch receptors to fire. The result is a contraction of the extrafusal fibers, producing tension in the muscle as a whole. As the degree of extrafusal fiber contraction approaches that of the intrafusal fibers, the tension on the nuclear bag gradually diminishes. As soon as the extrafusal and intrafusal fibers have contracted equally, the strain is taken off the nuclear bag and the firing rate decreases in the stretch receptors. The intrafusal fibers, in other words, provide a model of contraction for the extrafusal fibers to follow; the model is determined by information from the brain conveyed by gamma motor neurons.

The Extrapyramidal System and Discrete Muscle Movement

Although the precise function of the extrapyramidal system is enigmatic, its role clearly goes beyond regulating muscle tone to maintain posture. Considered as a whole, the extrapyramidal system seems to play a role in controlling discrete motor behavior and making it fluid and continuous. This, at any rate, is the picture that emerges after the functions of some of its component parts—specifically the basal ganglia and the cerebellum—are pieced together. Investigations to determine the function of the extrapyramidal system in controlling discrete behavior have involved lower animals and brain-damaged humans. We shall now consider this work, with respect first to the basal ganglia and then to the cerebellum.

The Basal Ganglia

The basal ganglia, pictured in Figure 10.8, consist of five areas: the *caudate nucleus* and the *putamen* (together they are known as the *striatum*), the *globus pallidus*, the *subthalamic nuclei*, and the *substantia nigra*. The collective function of these areas is to initiate, coordinate, and execute muscle movement, and the circuit, as you can see, is anything but simple. The basal ganglia receive motor information either directly or indirectly from the cortex and then, via connections to the thalamus, project the information back to the cortex. The cortex then transmits the information through tracts that travel (via the brain stem) to the spinal cord.

The basal ganglia have been shown to play a critical role in the voluntary control of slow, smooth movements. H. H. Kornhuber, one of the leading investigators of motor behavior, calls such behavior "ramp" movements (Kornhuber, 1974). He reports that human patients who suffer damage in the basal ganglia are often unable to perform these slow movements. Experiments on lower animals have confirmed these findings. Recording neural activity from the brains of monkeys, Mahlon DeLong has found that when monkeys move their arms slowly neural firing increases in the putamen (one of the areas in the basal ganglia). This increase in firing does not occur when the monkeys move their arms quickly (DeLong, 1974).

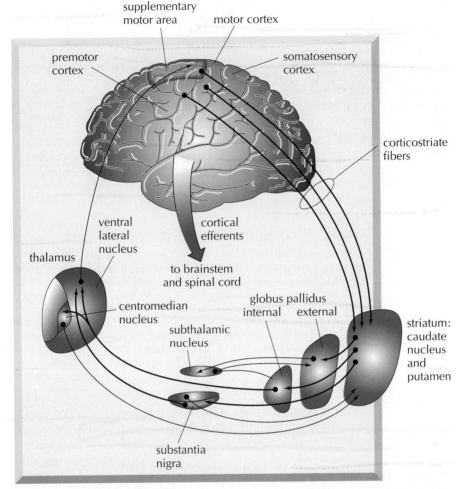

Figure 10.8 *The Basal Ganglia*
The basal ganglia (caudate nucleus, putamen, globus pallidus, subthalamic nucleus, and substantia nigra) receive motor information either directly or indirectly from the cortex (premotor, supplementary, and motor cortex) and in turn project it back to the motor cortex via connections to the thalamus. The motor cortex then gives rise to tracts (cortical efferents) that project via the brain stem to the spinal cord.

Animal experiments have also shed light on the function of two other areas in the basal ganglia—the caudate nucleus and the globus pallidus. Stimulation and lesion work indicate that both are involved in the control of spontaneous activity (Laursen, 1963). Studies have shown that damage to the globus pallidus (part of the basal ganglia) diminishes spontaneous motor activity in rats and that stimulation of the same area induces spontaneous motor activity. The conclusion: the globus pallidus plays an excitatory role in spontaneous motor activity.

Damage to the caudate nucleus (also part of the basal ganglia) produces a condition called *obstinate progression* (Waller, 1940). The lesioned animal may walk into a wall and continue moving its feet, even though it is not going anywhere. Conversely, stimulation of the caudate nucleus tends to arrest ongoing behavior. Thus it may be concluded that the caudate nucleus works antagonistically to the globus pallidus, playing an inhibitory role in spontaneous motor activity.

Diseases of the Basal Ganglia

Abnormalities in the basal ganglia and related circuits have been linked to several motor disorders in humans. These disorders fall into two groups: those characterized by a deficit in motor activity and those characterized by excessive motor activity (DeLong, 1990). The most prominent example of the first category is Parkinson's disease. An example of the second category is a disorder known as Huntington's disease. Let us take a closer look at each disease.

Parkinson's Disease.   Parkinson's disease strikes roughly 1 percent of the population and almost always begins after the age of 50. People suffering from Parkinson's disease, like the former heavyweight champion Muhammad Ali, exhibit a variety of symptoms, the most prominent of which are motor tremors, muscular rigidity, difficulty in initiating movement and, once initiated, a general slowness of movement. Moreover, the tremors occur only in limbs that are at rest or motionless; they disappear when the limbs begin to move. In its latter stages, Parkinson's disease brings with it a decline in intellectual and cognitive skills.

   The primary cause of the disorder has been traced to degeneration of circuits originating in the substantia nigra and terminating in the striatum (the caudate nucleus and putamen). The degeneration produces a deficit in the neurotransmitter dopamine. Thus drugs (L-dopa, for example) that increase the production of dopamine have been used with some success to treat the disorder. The cause of the degeneration in the substantia nigra, on the other hand, is unknown. Recent evidence points to the environment, although the specific factors in the environment have yet to be determined (see Chapter 2 for details of the treatment and cause of Parkinson's disease).

Huntington's Disease.   Huntington's disease is a rare illness that strikes roughly 5 persons in 100,000 and almost always between the ages of 30 and 50 years old. The symptoms begin quite innocently—absentmindedness and irritability accompanied by seemingly harmless fidgeting (Cote, 1991). As time passes, however, the fidgeting turns into random involuntary movements, the body writhes and jerks incessantly, and the patient is unable to walk or stand. Other debilitating symptoms appear as well. Patients are unable to maintain muscle tone for any period of time. They cannot grasp an object, for example, and hold on to it without dropping it. Speech becomes slurred and eventually stops; thinking, reasoning, and the ability to learn and remember deteriorate (Kolb & Whishaw, 1990). People afflicted with Huntington's disease ultimately become bedridden or confined to a wheelchair. Death comes on average 10 to 20 years after onset.

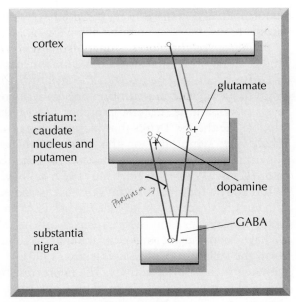

Figure 10.9 *Huntington's Disease*
A theoretical model of the neural circuits and neurotransmitters involved in Huntington's disease.

Figure 10.9 presents a theoretical model of the neural circuits thought to be involved in Huntington's disease (Kolb & Whishaw, 1990). As the figure indicates, the model consists of three circuits. One circuit originates in the cortex and travels to the striatum (caudate nucleus and putamen), where it releases the neurotransmitter *glutamate*. Another circuit originates in the striatum and travels to the substantia nigra, where it releases the neurotransmitter *GABA*. And the third circuit originates in the substantia nigra and travels back to the striatum, where it releases the neurotransmitter *dopamine*.

The symptoms that characterize Huntington's disease have been traced to the degeneration occurring in the second of these circuits—the one originating in the striatum—and, more specifically, to the chain of neurotransmitter events that results from this degeneration. As you can see from Figure 10.9, the relationship between the striatum and substantia nigra normally is a more or less reciprocal affair, the striatum imposing inhibitory control over the substantia nigra via the release of GABA and the substantia nigra in turn exerting excitatory control over the striatum via the release of dopamine. Keeping this pattern in mind, you can now appreciate what happens if the inhibitory influence on the substantia nigra is removed.

What appears to happen in Huntington's disease is that the circuit originating in the striatum degenerates, the inhibitory effect that it exerts over the substantia nigra decreases, and the activity in the substantia nigra and the dopamine that it releases in the striatum (now unchecked) increases. The result: activity in the striatum increases and the motor abnormalities that are among the chief symptoms of the disease are produced.

Evidence for the theory comes from several sources. Brain imaging studies done on Huntington's patients, for instance, reveal selective loss of GABA-producing neurons in the striatum, and postmortem assays of brain tissue taken from Huntington's patients reveal higher than normal levels of dopamine (Cote & Crutcher, 1991). Drug action, too, seems to support the theory. Drugs that increase dopamine, such as L-dopa, exacerbate the symptoms of the disease whereas drugs that decrease dopamine activity (phenothiazines, for instance) ameliorate the symptoms (Chase, Wexler, & Barbeau, 1979; Kolb & Whishaw, 1990).

If it is true that Huntington's disease is rooted in a degenerating striatum circuit, the question we need to ask is, What causes the degeneration in the first place? One theory focuses on the third in the trio of circuits we have been considering—the one that originates in the cortex and travels to the striatum (Kolb & Whishaw, 1990). Here, too, we're concerned with neurotransmitter activity. The neurotransmitter released by this circuit is glutamate, which, in moderate amounts, produces normal synaptic activity (Choi, 1988), but in excessive amounts produces neural degeneration. It is now suspected that the striatum degeneration that triggers the syndrome underlying Huntington's disease is produced when excessive amounts of glutamate are released in the striatum causing neural damage and death (DeFiglia, 1990).

It remains to be seen if excess glutamate is indeed the triggering mechanism for Huntington's disease, but one thing appears clear. The disease has a strong genetic component. A child born to a parent suffering from Huntington's disease has a 50 percent likelihood of contracting the disease—an all but unequivocal indication that a single dominant gene is the culprit. The presumption today is that this single gene, once it is transmitted, results in an abnormally high level of glutamate release in the striatum, thus setting into motion the deadly sequence of degeneration and abnormal neurotransmitter activity that ultimately disrupts the neural activity essential to motor control.

Logical though it may seem, the model that we have described to you is at this stage highly speculative. What's more, even if the model turns out to be an accurate picture of how Huntington's disease originates and manifests itself, it accounts for only one set of the symptoms that characterize the disease—the abnormalities in motor control. Huntington's patients, as a rule, suffer from not only the motor symptoms that we have been stressing but also from a variety of cognitive abnormalities as well, including thinking, reasoning, memory, and learning.

To sum up, Parkinson's disease and Huntington's disease share certain features. Both are motor disorders, and both are rooted in abnormalities in the basal ganglia and related circuits. But that is where the similarities end. In Parkinson's disease the source of the degeneration appears to be environmental, while in Huntington's disease it is genetic. In Parkinson's disease there is a deficit in dopamine activity in the striatum; in Huntington's disease there is an excess. Finally, in Parkinson's disease the result is a deficit in motor behavior (difficulty in initiating movement) accompanied by tremors, while in Huntington's disease the result is excessive motor behavior (random involuntary movements) accompanied by loss of motor tone.

The Cerebellum

As you can see in Figure 10.6, the cerebellum, like the basal ganglia, feeds into the extrapyramidal system. It is involved in two functions: regulating the fluidity of movement and controlling rapid muscle movement.

Fluidity

In regulating fluidity of movement, the cerebellum serves, in effect, as a go-between for the cortex and the muscles that control discrete movement. If a movement is to be fluid, remember, the motor command issued by the cortex must be coordinated with the existing tension and position of the muscles. The cerebellum is equipped to handle both pieces of information: the motor instructions from the cortex, and the existing tension and position of the muscles. If the position of the muscle or the existing tone prevents the muscle from responding, the cerebellum can change either the motor command or the position and tone of the muscle. It changes the motor command through ascending connections to the cortex. It changes the position and tone of the muscle through the descending extrapyramidal tract.

People suffering from cerebellar damage cannot perform movements smoothly. Their responses are mechanical and robotlike. To lift one of their legs, for example, they move each of its parts in sequence—first the thigh, then the knee, then the ankle. They are unable to combine the individual responses into a continuous, fluid movement. Moreover, each response is made with a jerkiness that may become a tremor. The tremor stops, however, as soon as the movement stops. Thus the tremor, known as an *intentional tremor*, is just the opposite of the resting tremor resulting from damage to the basal ganglia and seen in Parkinson's disease.

Rapid Movement

The ease with which normal people perform rapid automatic movements—catching a ball, swinging a golf club, braking a car—belies the complexity of the process involved. Consider the amount of information that must be processed in a split second: the position of the limb before the movement, the position of the limb during and after the movement, the time and force necessary to make the movement. It is a job for a high-powered computer and, in the view of Kornhuber, the cerebellum serves just such a function (Kornhuber, 1974).

In support of this contention, Kornhuber points to the types of motor loss shown by people with cerebellar damage. Such people lose the ability to make rapid preprogrammed movements. They are also unable to make involuntary rapid eye movements, known as *saccades*, and they cannot perform rapid movements with their hands, either such aimed movements as catching a ball or such spontaneous movements as rotating the wrist rapidly. In each instance the movement is slow and irregular.

Summary

In summary, then, the cerebellum and basal ganglia play complementary roles in the control of movement. The basal ganglia are involved in slow, calculated movement, the cerebellum in rapid, automatic movement. It should be emphasized that neither the basal ganglia nor the cerebellum is involved in the control of specific movements—flexing a finger, wiggling a toe. Rather, the two areas control features of general movement that apply to all skeletal motor behavior—speed, fluidity, and smoothness. This is not to say, however, that the extrapyramidal system is completely without control over specific movements. It does exert some control, but, as we are about to discover, the finer and more delicate the movement, the more likely it is to come under the control of the pyramidal system.

The Pyramidal System

The pyramidal system differs from the extrapyramidal system in two primary ways: first, in the degree to which synapses are formed and, second, in the number of sources from which it draws information. Whereas the extrapyramidal system forms synapses with several subcortical areas, including the cerebellum and the basal ganglia, the pyramidal system is mainly under the control of areas in the cortex. And whereas the extrapyramidal system draws upon the basal ganglia and cerebellum for information, the pyramidal system relies primarily on the somatosensory cortex—cutaneous senses—for information.

As you can see in Figure 10.10, the pyramidal system originates in the cortex, along the precentral gyrus, where it gives rise to tracts that stretch uninterrupted to the spinal cord. Most of the neurons in this system cross to innervate muscles on the opposite side of the body from the side of the brain in which they originate. Neurons originating, for example, in the left hemisphere descend in the *internal capsule* to the lower part of the medulla. There they cross to the right side of the brain and continue their descent along the right side of the spinal cord. Consequently, damage in the left cerebral hemisphere may result in paralysis of limbs on the right side of the body, and damage in the right cerebral hemisphere may result in paralysis of limbs on the left side of the body.

The pyramidal system derives its name from the area it crosses in the medulla. The tracts pass through an area of the medulla that contains large, pyramid-shaped neural bundles, but not all the pyramidal tracts cross this way. In humans, about 20 percent of the tracts remain on the same side of the body as the hemisphere where they originate. The crossed neurons descend the cord in the *lateral corticospinal tract*. The uncrossed neurons descend in the *ventral corticospinal tract*. Both tracts form synapses, either directly with alpha motor neurons or with

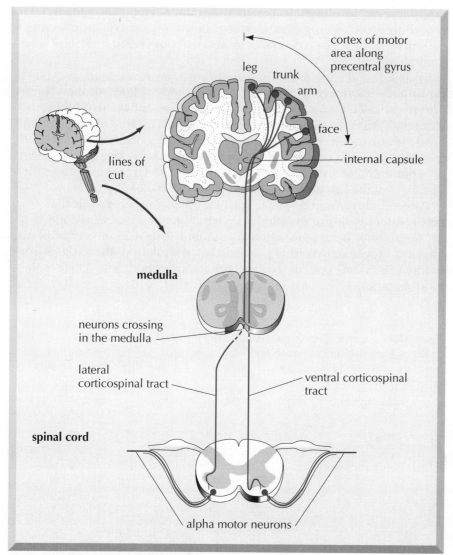

Figure 10.10   *The Pyramidal System*
A schematic rendering of the pyramidal system showing how neurons cross in the medulla.

interneurons that form synapses with alpha motor neurons. It is through the alpha motor neurons that the pyramidal system exerts control over skeletal muscles and discrete movement.

Pyramidal Control of Discrete Motor Function

Much of what we know about the pyramidal control of discrete motor function comes from electrical stimulation experiments originally conducted by Wilder Penfield. Using a procedure known as brain mapping, Penfield stimulated the cortical areas of conscious patients. (This is possible because there are no pain receptors in the brain and a local anesthetic is used to eliminate the pain accompanying the incision.) This procedure enables surgeons, before removing diseased brain tissue, to determine which tissue can be removed without creating serious behavioral abnormalities.

The picture Penfield assembled through brain mapping is roughly this: motor control of various parts of the body is laid out more or less topographically along the precentral gyrus, as shown in Figure 10.11 (Penfield, 1954). At one end of the precentral gyrus are areas that control head movement; at the other end are areas that control movement of the feet. The finer the movement under cortical control, the larger the area of representation in the cortex. In humans, the largest areas are those that control the lips and fingers.

Penfield also found evidence for two other motor areas in the cortex that connect with the pyramidal system. One area is located along the *Sylvian fissure*. What makes this area unique is that it exerts control over bilateral movement. Penfield found that stimulation along the Sylvian fissure caused one patient to raise both hands or both legs. This response to stimulation is in obvious contrast to that of the precentral gyrus,

Figure 10.11   *Cortical Representation of the Pyramidal System*
(a) The location of the primary motor cortex (precentral gyrus) and supplementary motor area and (b) the arrangement and relative size of the cortical areas as they correspond to the areas they control in various parts of the body.

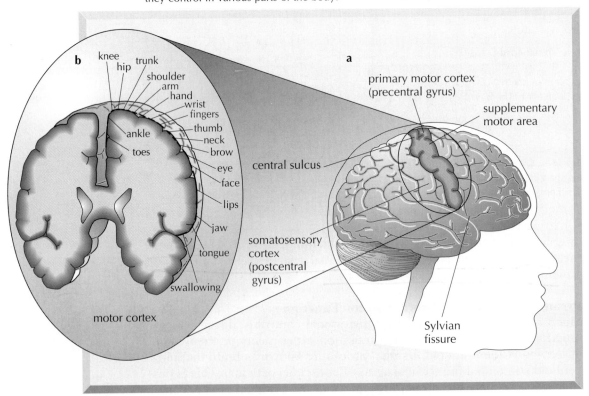

which typically produces responses on the side of the body opposite the hemisphere stimulated.

The second area found by Penfield borders on the precentral gyrus. Penfield named it the *supplementary motor area* (see Figure 10.11). Stimulation of this area produces responses that usually involve several muscles. People stimulated in this area characteristically lift their arm and turn their head to gaze at it.

One fascinating aspect of the brain-mapping procedure is that when movements are electrically stimulated, as in Penfield's work, the person is unaware that they are happening and has no memory of them afterward. The movements are robotlike, out of conscious control.

Fine versus Coarse Control

Earlier we established that the extrapyramidal system controls discrete movement. Now we discover that the pyramidal system, too, is involved in control of discrete movement. Why, you might wonder, is there this duplication of effort?

The answer, in short, is that the apparent duplication of effort is not quite what it appears to be. Each system seems to control a *different* aspect of discrete movement. The pyramidal system is involved in the control of fine movement—manual dexterity—and receives its major input from the cutaneous senses (touch, pressure, temperature, and pain). Significantly, in most people manual dexterity, regardless of the hand, is under the control of the left hemisphere. People who suffer damage to the motor area in the left hemisphere retain the general ability to *move* their hands, but lose the delicate and precise *control* of their hands, left or right.

The extrapyramidal system is involved in control of coarse movement—movement of large muscles in the arms and legs—and receives its major input from balance and position circuits in the cerebellum and basal ganglia. Studies on monkeys tend to bear out this distinction. Discrete responses produced by electrical stimulation in the pyramidal system are not totally lost in monkeys after the system is damaged. There is of course a noticeable decrease in the efficiency of movement; that is, fine control of movement is definitely affected. But coarse responses such as the flexing and extending of limbs still go on. This finding suggests that coarser responses are under the control of extrapyramidal areas in the subcortex (such as the basal ganglia) and that the reason they are activated by electrical stimulation after the pyramidal system is damaged is that the stimulation spreads to these subcortical areas.

A good deal of information concerning brain-motor relationships comes from lesion work of this sort in lower animals. But we must again be cautious about applying conclusions drawn from lower animals to humans because cortical control of movement varies markedly among species. The lower a species is on the evolutionary scale, the less will be the motor disability produced by damage in the motor cortex. A lesion in the motor cortex of a rat, for instance, may cause only a temporary loss in muscle tone; a lesion in the motor cortex of a monkey, however, will have a noticeable effect on the fine movements of fingers and hands. It is also important to remember that selective lesions in the motor cortex of higher animals do not necessarily produce complete paralysis in the muscle; rather, they seem to affect one type of movement within that muscle. People suffering from a particular form of motor cortex damage may not be able to move their fingers individually but may still be able to move them simultaneously.

Organizing Motor Behavior

Apart from the two motor systems (pryamidal and extrapyramidal) we have just described, there is a third aspect to motor control—an organizational aspect that enables the two motor systems to operate in a coordinated and organized fashion. This aspect of motor behavior is controlled by the prefrontal cortex which is located in the frontal lobe adjacent to the motor cortex.

It is important to keep in mind that even the most routine of behaviors—walking across the room to turn down your stereo, for instance—calls for a staggeringly complex series of responses occurring not only at the appropriate time but in the proper sequence. Evidence indicates that the prefrontal cortex, in a sense, oversees the organizational and timing aspects of this behavior (Goldman-Rakic, 1987). A person with damage to the prefrontal cortex would have the motor capability of walking across the room and turning down the stereo but may have difficulty organizing the behavior. Midway across the room for instance the person might suddenly "forget" what he or she intended to do and why. "Internal representation" and "temporal organization"—these are the terms that have been used to describe the "memory and timing" role of the prefrontal cortex in controlling motor behavior.

Protective Devices

Because motor control is indispensable for the survival of all species, virtually all animals are equipped with built-in devices to protect their motor systems. Without such devices, muscles could conceivably be stimulated by neural impulses to contract with a force strong enough to rip tendons or even break bones.

Muscle contraction is directly related to the frequency of impulses in the alpha motor neuron. As firing increases, contraction increases. There are two protective mechanisms that place a ceiling on the frequency with which the alpha motor neuron can conduct impulses, thus preventing overcontraction that might produce tendon or bone damage. One such device is known as the *recurrent circuit*; the other is related to a receptor known as the *Golgi tendon organ*.

Recurrent Circuits

To illustrate how the recurrent circuit works, let us take another brief look at the neural circuitry of muscle control in general. Every skeletal muscle, as we have been saying, is innervated by motor neurons commonly referred to as alpha motor neurons. As Figure 10.12 shows, the

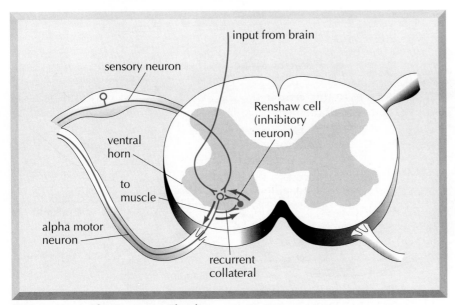

Figure 10.12 *The Recurrent Circuit*
The Renshaw cell is excited by a branch (the recurrent collateral) of the alpha motor neuron and in turn inhibits neural activity in the cell body of the same alpha motor neuron.

cell bodies of these neurons are located in the ventral part of the spinal cord, and their axons branch immediately before they leave the cord. One branch goes directly to the muscle where it forms synapses with the extrafusal fibers. The other branch, the *recurrent collateral*, forms synapses with an interneuron known as a *Renshaw cell*. The axon of the Renshaw cell returns to and forms synapses with the alpha motor neurons, including the one that stimulates it. Moreover, it acts in an inhibitory manner on these alpha motor neurons.

You should now be able to see what happens. When an alpha motor neuron is stimulated, it excites not only a muscle but also an interneuron (the Renshaw cell) that then inhibits the alpha motor neuron's own subsequent firing. This inhibitory effect is very brief, lasting up to 200 milliseconds, but it is sufficient to keep the muscle from being contracted too forcefully by prolonged stimulation of the alpha motor neuron. The Renshaw cell, in other words, acts to dampen the action of the alpha motor neuron and in the process dampens the contraction of the muscle.

Golgi Tendon Organs
As if the recurrent circuits were not enough, there is a second protective device. Skeletal muscles are connected with the skeleton by tendons, and the strength of these muscles is such that if they were allowed to contract unbridled, they might tear the tendons from the bones. Preventing this from happening is the Golgi tendon organ (shown in Figure 10.13), a sensory receptor that senses the strain at the tendon and inhibits firing in the motor neuron if the strain becomes excessive.

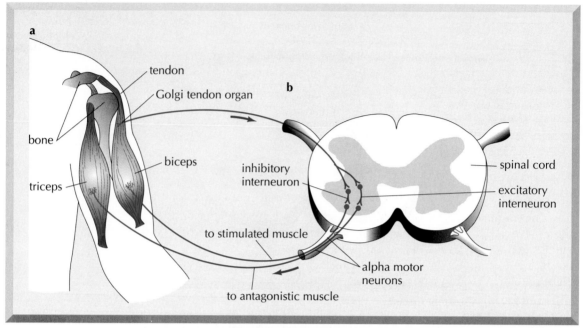

Figure 10.13 *The Golgi Tendon Organ in Action*
(a) Contraction of the muscle (the biceps in this case) causes the Golgi tendon organs to stretch and fire. (b) The neural impulses initiated by the stretch travel to two circuits in the spinal cord, one involved in inhibiting the stimulated (stretched) muscle, the other involved in contracting the antagonistic muscle.

Basically, the process works as follows: as the muscle contracts, the tendon pulls, stretching the Golgi tendon organ. A critical feature of the organ is its high threshold for exciting a neural impulse. It does not fire every time the tendon pulls, but only when the pull on the tendon exerted by the contracting muscle approaches a dangerous level, threatening damage. When the tension reaches that level, the threshold of firing is exceeded, and neural impulses are triggered along axons that enter the spinal cord. There the impulses travel to two groups of interneurons, as shown in Figure 10.13. One group forms synapses with and *inhibits* the firing of the alpha motor neuron causing the excessive contraction. The contraction diminishes and so does the tension on the tendon. A second group of interneurons excites the alpha motor neuron connected with the antagonistic muscle, causing it to contract. Here, too, the contraction of the antagonist acts to counter and relieve the tension created by the overstimulated muscle.

CONTROL OF INTERNAL BEHAVIOR

No discussion of the action system would be complete if it were limited to external behavior; the action system is involved in the control of internal behavior as well. Like external behavior, internal behavior is controlled to a large extent by the brain. But in this case it is the hypothalamus, not the cortex, that is the center of activity.

The hypothalamus exerts control over internal behavior in two ways. Through its connections with the autonomic nervous system it controls smooth and cardiac muscles, and through its connections with the pituitary gland it controls most of the glands in the body. We covered the autonomic nervous system in Chapter 3. Here we shall consider the glands.

The Glands

Glands consist of specialized secretory cells; their specialty is to produce and release chemical substances known as hormones. There are two types of glands: *exocrine* and *endocrine*. Exocrine glands secrete hormones that are transported throughout the body via special ducts. One example is the salivary glands, whose secretions are carried through the digestive tract into the stomach. Endocrine glands secrete hormones that require no special pathways or ducts for transport. Hormones secreted by endocrine glands are transported by the bloodstream and therefore reach most of the cells in the body. But not all cells in the body are programmed to respond to these hormones. Cells whose structures are keyed to interacting with hormones are known as *target-organ cells*. They are equipped with receptor sites and react to hormones in the same way as postsynaptic receptors react to neurotransmitters. Like neurotransmitters, hormones bind to receptors, and like neurotransmitters, hormones act on target cells via a second-messenger system (see Chapter 4 for details).

By acting on target organs, hormones produce a variety of behavioral effects. Figure 10.14 presents the major endocrine glands and their behavioral effects, many of which will be treated more fully in subsequent chapters.

Hormone Control

It is obvious from Figure 10.14 that hormones have profound effects on behavior. But what controls the hormones? As we mentioned earlier, the hypothalamus and pituitary gland play the major roles. The pituitary gland is divided into two parts: the anterior and the posterior.

The posterior pituitary, as described in Chapter 3, releases two hormones: oxytocin, which promotes uterine contractions during childbirth and ejection of milk after birth, and vasopressin, which regulates water content and blood pressure. Both hormones are produced in the hypothalamus and are transported to the posterior pituitary via axonal transport (see Chapter 3 for details of the hypothalamus–posterior pituitary interaction).

The anterior pituitary gives the gland its "master" status by releasing hormones that regulate the activity of other glands, as pictured in Figure 10.15. But the hypothalamus in turn controls the anterior pituitary.

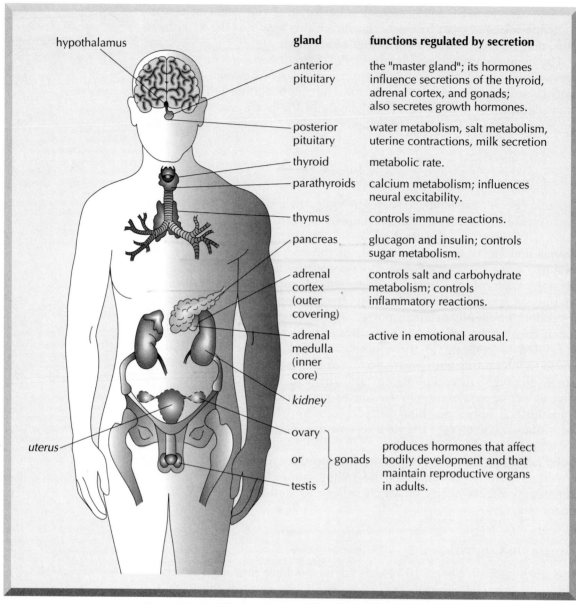

gland	functions regulated by secretion
anterior pituitary	the "master gland"; its hormones influence secretions of the thyroid, adrenal cortex, and gonads; also secretes growth hormones.
posterior pituitary	water metabolism, salt metabolism, uterine contractions, milk secretion
thyroid	metabolic rate.
parathyroids	calcium metabolism; influences neural excitability.
thymus	controls immune reactions.
pancreas	glucagon and insulin; controls sugar metabolism.
adrenal cortex (outer covering)	controls salt and carbohydrate metabolism; controls inflammatory reactions.
adrenal medulla (inner core)	active in emotional arousal.
kidney	
ovary or gonads testis	produces hormones that affect bodily development and that maintain reproductive organs in adults.

Figure 10.14 *The Location and Function of the Endocrine Glands*

In other words, it is the interplay between the hypothalamus and the anterior pituitary that regulates many hormonal levels in the body. The process starts with the hypothalamus, which "reads" the hormonal levels in the blood. When the hormone level drops below optimum, the hypothalamus releases a chemical, known as a *releasing hormone*, that acts on the anterior pituitary. The anterior pituitary in turn releases a hormone that travels to the "delinquent" gland and stimulates it to release more of

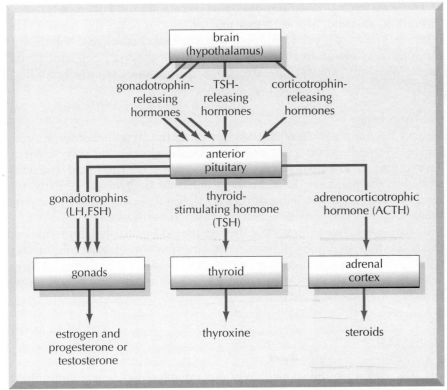

Figure 10.15 *The Hypothalamus and Its Relations to the Anterior Pituitary and the Target Glands*

its hormone. The stimulation continues until the optimum level is restored.

The Target Glands

The glands under the control of the anterior pituitary are the *thyroid*, the *adrenal cortex*, and the *gonads*. The thyroid releases the hormone *thyroxine*, which has two primary effects on behavior. First, it regulates adenosine 5-triphosphate (ATP) production and hence potential energy for behavior (ATP amplifies energy and carries it through the cell). A deficiency in thyroxine, known as *hypothyroidism*, results in general fatigue. Second, the thyroid plays a critical role in the formation of the nervous system of the developing fetus; a deficiency of thyroxine in the fetus results in *cretinism*, a birth defect characterized by a dwarflike body, protruding tongue, and mental retardation.

The adrenal cortex produces at least 40 hormones, each chemically unique. Most hormones produced by other glands are proteins. The hormones of the adrenal cortex are different. They are known chemically as *steroids* and can be classified on the basis of four functions: regulating metabolism, maintaining blood pressure, determining sexual appearance, and controlling sexual behavior.

The gonads (ovaries and testes) also secrete steroid hormones: testosterone in the male, and estrogen and progesterone in the female. The hormones control the development of sexual appearance and behavior in the fetus and maintain reproductive organs and sexual behavior in the adult. We shall examine the effect of sex hormones in detail in Chapter 13.

Self-regulation

Not all hormones are under the control of the hypothalamic-pituitary system. Some hormones are regulated by the glands that secrete them. Two examples are insulin and glucagon. Both are produced and controlled by the pancreas. Like the hypothalamus, the pancreas "reads" the level of insulin and glucagon in the blood. If a deficiency exists, the pancreas responds by increasing secretion of the hormones.

In any event, hormones—whether regulated by the glands themselves or by the hypothalamus-pituitary system—play an integral role in controlling behavior, particularly motivated behavior. Eating, drinking, sex—each is controlled to one degree or another by hormones, as we shall see in upcoming chapters.

SUMMARY

1. *The function of movement.* Without some means of movement, there would be no way to react to the environment, and survival would be impossible. In most animals, overt behavior is controlled by the action of skeletal muscles, which are connected to bones by tendons. The actual movement of these bones is produced by rotating action in the joints, which are fluid-filled spaces between the bones. The number and shape of joints determine the form and type of movement of a particular limb.

2. *How muscles move.* Versatility of movement notwithstanding, a muscle can do only two things: contract (pull) or relax. Two sets of muscles are attached to the skeleton. One set, known as flexors, pulls limbs toward the body; the other set, known as extensors, pulls limbs away from the body. The two sets work reciprocally; that is, when extensors contract, flexors relax, and vice versa.

3. *Coordinating movement.* The nervous system coordinates movement with incoming stimuli and with other movements. Neural information from the brain and the spinal cord is conducted to muscles by the alpha motor neurons (also known as the final common pathway). The neurons are called so because regardless of where the impulse comes from (sensory neurons in the spinal cord or tracts from the brain), it always takes the same route on the last part of the trip to the muscles: the alpha motor neurons. The actual number of muscle fibers innervated by a single axon varies from as high as 150 to 1 to as low as 3 to 1 and is measured by the innervation ratio. In any case, a single axon and the muscle fibers it innervates are known collectively as a motor unit.

4. *Neuromuscular connections.* The synaptic connection between alpha motor neurons and muscles is no different than the synaptic connection between neurons. When neural impulses arrive at the ends of motor neurons, they stimulate the release of acetylcholine from the vesicles in the axonal endings. The acetylcholine then diffuses across the synaptic gap between neuron and muscle (also known as the neuromuscular junction), binds to receptors, and produces muscle contraction. A deficiency of acetylcholine receptors appears to be the cause of myasthenia gravis, a disease characterized by severe weakness in the muscles of the eyes, the eyelids, the mouth, and the throat, as well as the limbs.

5. *Background muscle tone and the stretch reflex.* Movement can take place only after background muscle tone, or tension, has been established. Muscle tension is constantly monitored and changed in accordance with changes in body position and posture. The stretch reflex controls these adjustments. This reflex involves the interaction between two groups of muscle fibers (extrafusal and intrafusal fibers) and a specific set of receptors (the stretch receptors). Stretch receptors are actually nerve endings wrapped around a segment of the intrafusal fiber known as the nuclear bag. When the nuclear bag stretches, the receptors fire, setting into motion a sequence of events (impulses traveling into the spinal cord and back to the extrafusal fibers) that ends in muscle tension. For instance, stretch receptors regulate muscle tension when we stand up or lose our balance.

6. *The brain and muscle control.* The brain plays a dual role in the control of muscles. It controls both muscle tone and limb movement. Muscle tone is regulated by the extrapyramidal system. Limb movement, however, is regulated by both the extrapyramidal and pyramidal systems.

7. *Muscle tone, limb movement, and the extrapyramidal system.* The pathways in the extrapyramidal system originate in the cortex and receive input from several brain areas (most notably the cerebellum and basal ganglia) on their way to the spinal cord. In the spinal cord the extrapyramidal pathways form synapses with the gamma motor neurons, and it is through these motor neurons that the extrapyramidal system controls muscle tone. The extrapyramidal system also plays a role in controlling limb movement, making it fluid and continuous. The basal ganglia and cerebellum are involved in this control. The basal ganglia appear to play an important role in the regulation of slow, voluntary behavior, sometimes referred to as "ramp" movements. The cerebellum regulates fluid and rapid movements.

8. *Diseases of the basal ganglia.* Malfunctioning of the basal ganglia has been linked to several different motor disorders, chief among them Parkinson's disease and Huntington's disease. The primary cause of Parkinson's disease, whose chief symptoms are motor tremors, muscular rigidity, and general slowness of movement, is the degeneration of circuits originating in the substantia nigra and ending in the striatum (the caudate nucleus and putamen). The primary cause of Huntington's disease, whose symptoms begin with seemingly harmless fidgeting but whose victims ultimately become physically and mentally debilitated, is degeneration of an inhibitory circuit originating in the striatum, which theoretically results in excess activity in the substantia nigra and an increase in release of dopamine in the striatum.

9. *Limb movement and the pyramidal system.* Limb movement is also controlled by the pyramidal system. This system differs from the extrapyramidal system mainly in the number of sources from which it draws its information. Whereas the extrapyramidal system forms synapses in several subcortical areas on its way to the spinal cord, the pyramidal system does not form synapses until it reaches the alpha motor neurons in the spinal cord. The pyramidal and extrapyramidal systems exert complementary control over limb movement. The pyramidal system controls fine movement (flexing the fingers, for instance); the extrapyramidal system controls coarse movement (such as lifting an arm or leg).

10. *A closer look at the pyramidal system.* Much of what is known about the pyramidal system's control of discrete movement in humans comes from brain-mapping studies. The general picture that has emerged shows motor control of various parts of the body to be laid out along a cortical strip, known as the precentral gyrus, with head movement controlled at one end of the strip and foot movement at the other. Moreover, the finer the movement, the larger the cortical area controlling it.

11. *Protecting the motor system.* Virtually all animals are equipped with built-in devices to protect their motor systems. Two protective mechanisms that place a ceiling on the frequency with which the alpha motor neuron can conduct impulses are the recurrent circuit, and a receptor known as the Golgi tendon organ. When an alpha motor neuron is stimulated, it excites not only a muscle but also an interneuron, known as the Renshaw cell, which acts to dampen the action of the alpha motor neuron and in the process dampens the contraction of the muscle. The Golgi tendon organ senses the strain at the tendon and inhibits firing in the alpha motor neuron if the strain becomes excessive.

12. *Internal behavior.* Internal behavior is also controlled by the brain, but the hypothalamus, rather than the cortex, is the center of activity. The hypothalamus exerts its control through two routes, the autonomic nervous system and the pituitary gland. The pituitary gland, particularly the anterior part, acts as a "master" gland, exerting control over the thyroid gland, the adrenal cortex, and the gonads. The thyroid releases the hormone thyroxine, which regulates energy production and plays a critical role in the development of the nervous system. The adrenal cortex produces at least forty hormones, known as steroids, involved in controlling metabolism and blood pressure, determining sexual appearance and controlling sexual behavior. The gonads (ovaries and testes) produce hormones (estrogen, progesterone, and testosterone) that control the development of sexual appearance and behavior in the fetus, and maintain reproductive organs and sexual behavior in the adult.

acetylcholinesterase
actomyosin
adrenal cortex gland
alpha motor neuron
annulospiral ending
anterior pituitary gland
basal ganglia
caudate nucleus
cerebellum
cretinism
curare
end plate
end plate potential (EPP)
endocrine glands
exocrine glands
extensor muscle
extrafusal fibers
extrapyramidal system
final common pathway
flexor muscle
flower-spray ending
GABA
gamma motor neurons
globus pallidus
glutamate
Golgi tendon organ
gonads
Huntington's disease
hypothalamus
hypothyroidism
innervation ratio
intentional tremor
internal capsule
intrafusal fibers
L-dopa

lateral corticospinal tract
motor unit
muscle action potential
muscle tone
myasthenia gravis
myofibrils
neuromuscular junction
nuclear bag
obstinate progression
Parkinson's disease
posterior pituitary gland
putamen
pyramidal system
ramp movements
reciprocal innervation
recurrent circuit
recurrent collateral
releasing hormone
Renshaw cell
reticular formation
saccades
sarcolemma
skeletal muscles
spindle organs
steroids
stretch reflex
striatum
substantia nigra
supplementary motor area
Sylvian fissure
thyroid
thyroxine
ventral corticospinal tract
vestibular nucleus

SUGGESTED READINGS

Becker, J. B., Breedlove, S. M., & Crews, D. *Behavioral Endocrinology*. Cambridge, MA: MIT Press, 1992.

Brooks, V. B. *The Neural Basis of Motor Control*. New York: Oxford University Press, 1986.

Kandel, E. R., Schwartz, J. H., & Jessell, T. M. (Eds.). *Principles of Neural Science*, 3rd ed., New York: Elsevier, 1991.

Rosenbaum, D. A. *Human Motor Control*. San Diego: Academic Press, 1991.

EATING AND DRINKING

INTRODUCTION

Virtually every behavioral action taken by humans and other animals has some purpose, or motive, behind it. Certain motivations of course are purely biological—present at birth and operating largely beyond our conscious control. The feelings we recognize as "hunger" or "thirst" occur automatically, a physiological response to events taking place in our bodies. Other motivations, though, are based on what we have learned. Hungry though we may be, we may choose *not* to eat for any number of reasons: vanity (we want to slim down), religion (we want to fast in observance of a holy day), or health (we want to fast to cleanse our system). Still other motivations, such as ambition and competitiveness, are known as cognitive motivations, and are based partly on learning and partly on our genetic makeup. They are unique to each of us.

It goes without saying that if we are to understand the totality of human behavior, we must understand the dynamics of motivation on each of its levels. In this chapter, however, we will be concerned primarily with only one aspect of motivation: the mechanisms that underlie its *biological* dynamics. The behaviors we shall be examining in this chapter—eating and drinking—are keyed in one way or another to biological survival.

The questions that we will be examining in this chapter are similar to those we asked ourselves in the sensory chapters. Here, too, we are interested in stimuli, in receptors, and in the mechanisms by which stimuli are transduced. The difference, though, is that in this chapter our focus will be confined almost entirely to the internal behavioral pattern regulated by a process known as *homeostasis*—the state of inner equilibrium that underlies optimum body functioning.

The reason homeostasis figures so prominently in our study of motivation is that, with the exception of sex, behaviors keyed to our biological survival occur largely as the result of disruptions in the internal environment. When the internal environment is disrupted, certain behaviors are provoked. When the internal balance is restored, the behavior is terminated.

As you will see, homeostasis controls two types of behavior. The first type involves internal nonvoluntary reflexive actions such as the breakdown of stored fats into usable nutrients when the body has been denied nourishment for a certain period. The second type of behavior is overt and voluntary and is directed toward the satisfaction of various needs: eating in the case of hunger, drinking in the case of thirst. We will be concerned with both the internal and the overt.

BIOLOGICAL BASIS OF HUNGER

Most of us take for granted our ability to regulate what we eat. We experience hunger, and we eat. When we have had our fill, we stop.

Not everyone's eating behavior, however, runs this smoothly. Some people eat compulsively, whether they are hungry or not. Others—anorexics, for instance—are so repulsed by food that they sometimes starve themselves to death. Some people can consume enormous amounts of food without gaining any weight. Others eat very little and remain seriously overweight.

How do we explain this diversity of eating patterns? To answer this question, we must approach eating much as we would approach any other behavior—with an eye to uncovering the neural mechanisms that control it.

Historical Perspective

Research into eating behavior has focused primarily on two key questions: the first question has to do with the signals that trigger and terminate eating behavior, and the second has to do with the areas of the brain to which these signals project. The search for the answers to these questions has been going on for nearly 100 years, but it has been only within the past few years that we have been able to draw a reasonably consistent set of conclusions. At that, there is much we have yet to learn.

As so often happens in brain-behavior research, the first clues to how the nervous system controls eating behavior originated in clinical observations of humans. In the early 1900s, a Viennese physician named Alfred Fröhlich discovered that patients with tumors in the pituitary gland often became obese and suffered atrophy of the genitals. These conditions came to be known as *Fröhlich's syndrome*, and they led to the early assumption that eating was under the control of the pituitary gland. That assumption, however, turned out to be incorrect, for subsequent studies showed that the real source of the syndrome discovered by Fröhlich is not the pituitary gland itself but rather the neural structure immediately above it: the hypothalamus (Hetherington & Ransom, 1940).

Early Studies on the Hypothalamus

The first significant animal experiments designed to pinpoint the precise role of the hypothalamus in eating behavior were conducted by John Brobeck, whose work centered on two areas in the hypothalamus—the ventromedial area and the lateral area (Brobeck, 1946). By making lesions in the ventromedial area (as pictured in Figure 11.1), Brobeck was able to produce in laboratory rats the same kind of obesity that Fröhlich saw in human patients. Brobeck thus concluded that the role of the ventromedial hypothalamus, when intact, is to *curb* appetite. Brobeck also found that lesions in the lateral hypothalamus disrupted eating behavior, but in the opposite direction; the lesioned animals refused to eat and lost weight—prompting the view that the role of the lateral hypothalamus, when intact, is to produce hunger.

The implications of these findings are not as clear-cut as they must have seemed at the time. Subsequent work has shown, for instance, that if an animal whose lateral hypothalamus has been lesioned is carefully nursed and given injections of nutrients, it will recover its appetite, albeit very gradually (Teitelbaum & Epstein, 1962). Recovery may take as long as 60 to 70 days and occurs in stages: as time passes, the animal moves from complete abstinence from eating and drinking to eating only wet food and then to eating normal dry food.

In any event, Brobeck's basic conclusions—that the ventromedial hypothalamus when intact curbs appetite and the lateral hypothalamus when intact excites appetite—drew later support from the work of Neal Miller and others, who found that *stimulating* the ventromedial hypo-

Figure 11.1 *The Lateral and Ventromedial Hypothalamus*
(a) A schematic view of the lateral and ventromedial hypothalamus. (b) The rat that has been lesioned in the ventromedial hypothalamus (right) weighs almost three times as much as the normal rat (left). (From Philip Teitelbaum. "Appetite." *Proceedings of the American Philosophical Society* 108 (1964): 464–72; Figure 1, p. 467).

a

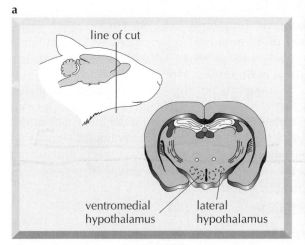

line of cut

ventromedial
hypothalamus

lateral
hypothalamus

b

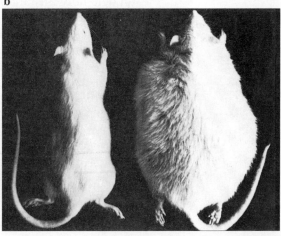

thalamus in rats, as opposed to making lesions in the area, inhibits eating, and that stimulating the *lateral* hypothalamus induces eating behavior even after an animal is satiated (Delgado & Anand, 1953; Miller, 1960).

From Data to Theory: The Interaction of Centers

The early data led to what at the time seemed to be unequivocal conclusions: the lateral hypothalamus was thought to be the "hunger center," the area in the brain that triggered eating behavior; and the ventromedial hypothalamus was thought to be the "satiation center," the area in the brain that curbed eating behavior. The two areas, moreover, were thought to work in tandem. When the level of nutrients in the body is high, so the early theory went, the ventromedial hypothalamus is excited and the lateral hypothalamus is inhibited. The result is a decrease in hunger. If nutrients are low, the opposite occurs: the ventromedial hypothalamus is not excited, and the lateral hypothalamus is not inhibited. The result is an increase in hunger.

Reasonable as this view may have seemed at the time, we know today that the relationship between the hypothalamus and eating behavior is a good deal more complex. Elements of the original theory have remained, but the views of precisely what the signals are and what role the ventromedial and lateral hypothalami play have changed. Let's begin with the signals.

THE SEARCH FOR EATING SIGNALS

It is logical to assume that the signals that control eating behavior—the signals that turn on eating and the signals that turn it off—are related to the nutrients (i.e., the energy levels) in the body. According to a strict homeostatic principle, the *on signal* ought to be triggered when nutrients in the body fall beneath an optimal level. The *off signal* should be triggered when nutrients are restored.

Logic notwithstanding, there are problems with this model. The main problem is that eating behavior frequently does not conform to homeostatic rules. Lower animals and humans are often motivated to eat when energy deficits are not present, and lower animals and humans frequently stop eating before the metabolic (energy) deficiencies are corrected—that is, before the food can be digested and circulated to the cells. This inconsistency helps explain why, early on in the search for eating signals, researchers began to suspect that eating behavior was under the control of not one but of *two* signals: one, a speedy neural signal that can turn eating on or off before a second, and slower, metabolic signal takes effect. Subsequent studies have verified this initial suspicion.

The Speedy On-Off Signal

Asking ourselves what specific form an eating signal takes is asking, in effect, three questions: what makes people feel hungry, what makes people feel full, and by what means is information routed to the brain to initiate or to terminate eating?

Walter Cannon addressed these questions as early as 1910 when he advanced a theory known today as the *local theory of motivation*. Cannon believed that the conditions for translating deprivation-related stimuli into neural impulses are similar to conditions surrounding the sensory coding of stimuli from outside the body. Receptors, he theorized, are present in those areas of the body through which food and water must pass—the mouth and stomach, for instance. He theorized further that these receptors are sensitive to stimuli produced by deprivation of food and water (Cannon, 1934). These local stimuli, he proposed, are transduced into neural impulses by their respective receptors. The impulses are then conveyed to specific areas of the brain, producing the corresponding sensations—hunger and thirst.

Today we know that local factors do not account for all aspects of eating behavior, but they may account for at least part of the on and off signal. Consider what happens during eating. Food enters the mouth, passes down the esophagus to the stomach, then to the intestine and then finally to the blood where it is transported to the cells throughout the body. Each of these areas—the mouth, the stomach, the intestine, the blood—is thus a candidate for producing an on or off signal.

Oral Factors

We all know how hard it is to resist desserts we love, even though we are not necessarily hungry when the dessert tray is presented to us. Clearly, then, factors other than energy deficits play at least some role in controlling food intake.

Experimental evidence indicates that one of these factors involves the mouth. In experiments using a procedure known as *sham feeding*, animals were surgically prepared so that food taken in their mouths never reached their stomachs. The results showed that even when food doesn't reach their stomachs, animals are still able to regulate food intake. True, regulation isn't normal—the animals take in more food than normal—but the key point is that the animals do stop eating (Young et al., 1974).

Oral factors can not only turn eating off but they can also turn eating on. When the diet of rats in one study was varied among four tastes, the rats overate by as much as 30 percent. Indeed, with each new taste, their eating behavior began anew, as if they had not eaten before (Le Magnen, 1969).

The same pattern appears to hold for humans. In one study, a group of subjects was asked to rate the pleasantness of taste, smell, and texture of food before and after they ate. As expected, the ratings dropped after the meal was eaten. Significantly, though, they dropped in a selective way: only for the taste of the food that was consumed. "New" tastes were still rated high, even after the meal (Rolls, Van Duijvenvoorde, & Rolls, 1984).

Clearly, then, how *much* we eat is determined to some extent by how the food tastes to us, although it is also true that even when it comes to foods we love to eat, there can be too much of a good thing. No matter what the food, with repeated intake the attractiveness of the taste diminishes. But it works in the other direction as well. Generally speaking, food usually tastes better to us when we are hungry, specific hungers developing for the taste of specific foods (specific hungers will be considered later in the chapter). In extreme states of hunger, virtually anything remotely edible becomes appetizing (Mook, 1991).

Adaptive Implications

That taste is one of the ways we regulate food intake makes sense from an adaptive point of view. It is important to our health that we maintain a balanced diet, that is, that we eat a variety of foods: carbohydrates, proteins, fats, vitamins, and minerals. The foods that contain these nutrients differ in taste, thus helping to ensure that we will eat a variety of foods. As satiation for one taste develops, hunger for the other tastes (and the nutrients they represent) remains. Each change in taste, in effect, renews our interest in eating, albeit not completely.

Taste Factors and Bulimia

The importance of taste as a factor in regulating eating behavior has led some researchers to focus on taste as one of the factors in *bulimia*, the highly publicized eating disorder in which people first gorge themselves with food and then induce vomiting (Drenoski et al., 1987). For most of us, there is a correlation between how hungry we are and how "tasty" the food seems. Once we reach a certain level of satiation, even foods we love lose their appeal. Judith Rodin and her colleagues (1990) have found a different pattern among bulimic subjects they have studied. In one of her studies, bulimics were asked to rate the taste of a sweet substance both before and after they had ingested a glucose solution. In contrast to what you might expect, the substance was rated as sweet and pleasurable after the glucose as it had been rated before. Rodin's conclusion is that the taste for foods does not diminish as bulimics eat but rather is maintained throughout the meal. The result, according to Rodin, is binging.

Bypassing the Mouth

Numerous studies have shown that factors other than taste have an impact on eating behavior. Alan Epstein and Philip Teitelbaum, for instance, have shown that animals can regulate food intake without the benefit of neural feedback related to taste and smell cues (Epstein & Teitelbaum, 1962). The procedure they used in their studies is known as *intragastric feeding*. It consists of training animals to press a lever in order to receive injections of a liquid diet administered through a tube connected directly to the stomach. Their results showed convincingly that even when animals can neither taste nor smell food, they are still capable of regulating their diet and weight. Similar results, interestingly, have been obtained as well in intragastric feeding studies with humans (Jordan, 1969).

The Stomach versus the Small Intestine

The work of Epstein and Teitelbaum makes a strong case for the involvement of the stomach in the control of eating behavior. But the anatomy of the digestive tract introduces yet another possibility: the small intestine. Because the stomach, as shown in Figure 11.2, is connected to the small intestine, food must pass through both before it reaches the circulatory system. Thus it is possible that what is happening in the intragastric studies is that the regulation is being controlled not by receptors in the stomach but by receptors in the small intestine.

J. Anthony Deutsch studied the question of the small intestine versus the stomach by devising a surgical preparation that eliminates small intestine involvement (Deutsch, 1983). By closing off the *pylorus*—the

Figure 11.2 *The Human Digestive System*
Notice the relationship between the stomach and small intestine and the interconnecting pylorus.

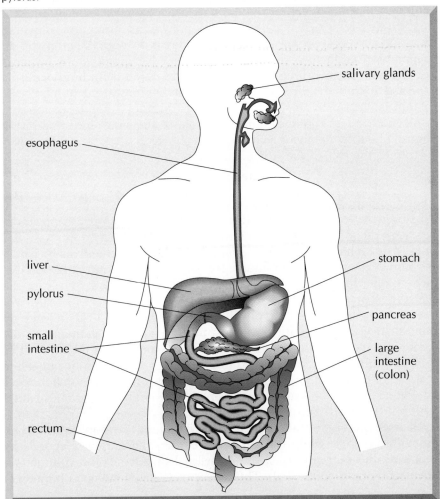

opening that connects the stomach with the small intestine—with an inflatable cuff, Deutsch was able to study the eating behavior of animals in which food never reached the small intestine (Deutsch, Puerto, & Wang, 1977). Significantly, Deutsch found that the animals were still able to regulate their food intake normally.

Deutsch's findings seem to confirm the notion that the stomach, and not the small intestine, is the site of food regulation. But other studies have called this notion into question. Some researchers have shown that when food is introduced directly into the small intestine, animals will curtail their eating (Snowdon, 1975). Other studies have shown that eating behavior can be curtailed by giving animals cholecystokinin, a hormone that is normally released when food is present in the small intestine (Gibbs, Young, & Smith, 1973). These results suggest that the small intestine, in addition to the stomach, is involved in food regulation.

Deutsch and others do not agree with this view (Deutsch & Hardy, 1977). Their explanation for why animals stop eating when their small intestines have been injected with food or when they have been given cholecystokinin is not that the animals are no longer hungry but that they are simply sick. Deutsch has found that when animals are trained to associate cholecystokinin with a specific flavor of food, they develop an aversion to that flavor—so much so that after the cholecystokinin wears off, the animals continue to avoid the taste. Such a finding would be expected if the curtailment of eating behavior produced by cholecystokinin is caused by an aversive stimulus (sickness) and not satiation.

All in all, then, the question of the role of the small intestine in the control of eating behavior remains open. No such uncertainty, however, surrounds the role of the stomach itself.

The Stomach: A Closer Look

Whatever the role of the small intestine may be, the stomach appears to be one of the principal sites of food regulation. Working on this assumption, Deutsch has attempted to isolate the specific mechanisms by which the stomach regulates food intake. He has focused, in particular, on two factors: one, the *volume* of food that enters the stomach; and, two, the *caloric content* of the food.

Deutsch studied the effect of volume on eating behavior by injecting a nonnutritive saline solution directly into an animal's stomach at the same time the animal was drinking milk. He found that the amount of milk the animal drank decreased in proportion to the amount of saline injected into the stomach. This finding indicates that the stomach regulates food intake, at least in part, on the basis of the *volume* of food within it (Deutsch, Young, & Kalogeris, 1978).

Deutsch has also found, however, that if you remove nutrients from an animal's stomach while the animal is eating, the animal responds by replacing the nutrients (i.e., the calories) lost but not the volume lost (Deutsch & Gonzalez, 1980). Thus it seems that the stomach may regulate eating on the basis not only of food volume (distension) but on the basis of food content (calories) as well.

The Stomach and the Brain

The presence of receptors in the stomach sensitive to distension and calories represents only one aspect of the stomach's control of eating behavior. The question is, How do the signals generated by the receptors in the stomach reach the brain?

The answer appears to be twofold: stomach distension is signaled via neural connections, calories are signaled by nonneural factors, perhaps hormones. This conclusion was drawn after Deutsch and his colleagues found that severing the vagus nerve (specifically the branch of the vagus that connects the stomach to the ventromedial hypothalamus) affects the two signals differently (Gonzalez & Deutsch, 1981). With the vagus nerve severed, animals tend to ignore stomach distension (that is, they continue to eat when saline is injected directly into the stomach), but they do not ignore nutrients in the stomach (that is, when nutrients are removed from the stomach they eat to restore the caloric value of the nutrients).

Confirming the role of the nonneural factors in the control of eating is an experiment in which the stomach and parts of the intestine were transplanted from one rat into another, giving the recipient rat two stomachs—one with neural connections and one without (Koopmans, 1981). After the animals recovered from surgery, food was injected directly into the transplanted stomach and was confined there.

The findings were striking. Even though the stomach had no neural connections to the brain and even though the food never reached the intestine or the circulatory system, the animals were nonetheless able to regulate their food intake according to the amount of food injected into the transplanted stomach. The conclusion: a hormone, not a neural signal, is apparently involved in signaling the contents of the stomach to the brain. What that hormone is, however, remains to be determined.

There is yet another aspect of how the brain and stomach interact to produce eating behavior that warrants attention: the fact that the signals travel both ways—not only from the stomach to the brain but from the brain to the stomach as well. How do we know this? Simply because lesions in the ventromedial hypothalamus can affect how quickly food is emptied from the stomach: in lesioned animals food is emptied more quickly than in nonlesioned animals (Dugan & Booth, 1986).

All told, then, it seems safe to conclude that an off signal for eating travels from the stomach to the brain and safe to conclude that there are two different signals: a neural signal and a chemical (i.e., hormonal) signal. It is important, however, to put these conclusions into perspective. The stomach may indeed be the source of an off signal, but this is not to say that it is the source of *the* off signal. As stated earlier, we need a speedy signal that can prevent eating long enough for a slower metabolic off signal to take effect. The stomach may be the source of the speedy off signal. Now let us turn to the slower, more enduring metabolic signal.

The Metabolic Factors

It is one thing to stop eating and another thing to stop eating for an extended period of time. If, in fact, the stomach signal were the only off signal, you would expect a normal (nonlesioned) animal to resume eating once the stomach signal ceased. This, however, does not happen. The fact that it does not happen raises the possibility of a second off signal— one that is more prolonged than the stomach signal and that keeps eating behavior turned off from one meal to the next. What is that second signal? Evidence points to the blood as the vehicle and to metabolic change as the signal.

Blood as the Vehicle

A convincing experiment implicating blood as the vehicle for the prolonged off signal has been carried out by John Davis and his colleagues (Davis et al., 1969). Davis transferred blood from a group of sated rats to a group of hungry rats and found that the transfused animals no longer behaved as if they were hungry. Presented with food they would have ordinarily devoured, they ate very little. Davis took this finding to mean that the blood does carry an off, or satiation, signal.

Davis also discovered something significant regarding the length of time it takes for this off signal to become operative. He found that blood taken from donors who had eaten *immediately* before the transfusion had no effect on the eating behavior of the recipients, but that blood taken from donors who had eaten 45 minutes before the transfusion had a noticeable inhibitory effect. His findings indicate strongly that in rats, at least, the blood off signal takes time to develop—perhaps as long as 45 minutes.

THE SEARCH FOR METABOLIC SIGNALS

Assuming that blood is the vehicle for the metabolic signal, a question still remains, What is the signal itself?

At least two properties of blood qualify as potential metabolic signals: glucose and fat. Each has been the focal point of a different theory, the glucostatic and lipostatic theories, respectively. Each theory falls within the dynamics of the homeostatic model, and each postulates the same general principles: that an optimum state—be it glucose or fat—prevails in the blood, that deviation below the optimum state produces the on signal, and that a return to the optimum state produces the off signal. Let us examine the theories more closely.

The Glucostatic Theory *Read*

In its original and simplest form, the *glucostatic theory* of feeding maintains that eating behavior is controlled primarily by the level of blood glucose in the body.

The first person to propose this theory was Jean Mayer, whose original suggestion, advanced in the early 1950s, was that the hypothalamus contains receptors that are sensitive to glucose levels in the blood and that fluctuations in these levels determine whether eating is triggered or suppressed. Mayer theorized that when glucose levels drop below optimum, eating is triggered. When glucose levels rise above optimum, eating ceases (Mayer, 1952).

At first glance, Mayer's theory is compelling. After all, the slightest glucose deficiency in the brain can impede neural activity, producing dizziness and nausea. Moreover, a prolonged deficiency of glucose can produce coma and eventually death. Even so, the theory runs into problems when you take into account the eating behavior of diabetics. Diabetes (technically, *diabetes mellitus*) in its most common form is characterized by a deficiency in insulin, a hormone produced by the pancreas. Lacking insulin, diabetics have abnormally high levels of glucose in their blood. Thus, according to Mayer's theory, diabetics should never feel hungry. As it happens, though, the opposite is true. Diabetics are generally in a constant state of hunger—a condition known as *hyperphagia*.

Mayer has since revised his original theory, basing his revision on the fact that before it is metabolized, glucose must pass into cells. He has maintained his original premise—that eating is regulated by glucose levels—but has shifted the focal point of the theory from glucose levels in the blood to glucose levels in the *cells* (Mayer, 1953).

Mayer's revised theory would explain why diabetics, despite the high glucose levels in their blood, are constantly hungry. The main effect of insulin is to change the permeability of the cell membrane, making it receptive to the flow of glucose. A shortage of insulin in the body results in a high level of glucose in the blood but little in the cells. According to Mayer's revised theory, diabetics are in a constant state of hunger because a low level of glucose in the cells is the signal for hunger.

Logical as it may seem, Mayer's revised theory has nonetheless come under attack. Pointing out that brain cells, unlike other cells in the body, do not use insulin to take up glucose, some scientists have argued that diabetes has no bearing on the amount of glucose in the brain, while other scientists have countered that brain cells—in particular, those in the hypothalamus—do need insulin (Debons, Krimsky, & From, 1970). The issue may be irrelevant. Experiments suggest that it is not the glucose levels in the brain that affect eating behavior, it is the glucose levels in the liver. Let us look at these experiments in more detail.

Experimental Support for the Glucostatic Theory

Since Mayer introduced his glucostatic theory, many researchers have sought to determine whether glucose is indeed the signal for hunger. Among the procedures used in these studies is one in which glucose is injected into a hungry animal just before the animal is set to begin a meal. The rationale behind this procedure is that if low cell glucose is indeed the signal for hunger, glucose injections should inhibit eating behavior.

Maurio Russek and his colleagues have used this procedure and have found that hungry (food-deprived) animals do indeed refuse to eat following glucose injections (Russek, 1971). Russek has also reported, however, that the satiation effect of glucose varies according to where in the body the injection is administered. When glucose is injected into the jugular vein (allowing glucose to circulate throughout the body before it reaches the liver), eating behavior is unchanged. When glucose is injected into the hepatic portal vein (the blood vessel connected to the liver), eating behavior is prevented. More recent studies have confirmed Russek's results (Novin et al., 1983; Tordoff & Friedman, 1988). Figure 11.3 summarizes the findings.

Russek has concluded from these observations that although most cells in the body need glucose for energy production, the cells in the liver have an additional capacity: they can act as receptors. That is, they can monitor glucose levels and regulate eating behavior accordingly. More recently it has been proposed that it is not glucose per se that is monitored by the liver, but rather the *energy* that is produced by glucose in the

Figure 11.3   *Russek's Findings*
Glucose injected into the liver (hepatic portal vein) blocks eating; glucose injected into the jugular vein has no effect on eating.

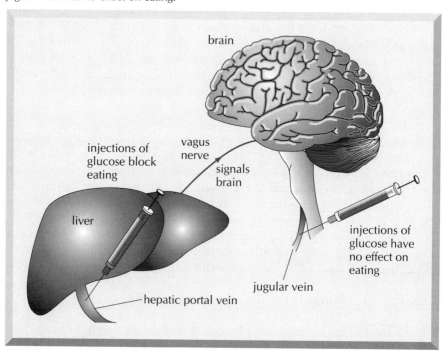

liver cells: when energy levels are up (i.e., when glucose levels are high), eating is suppressed; when energy levels are down (i.e., when glucose levels are low), eating is excited (Friedman & Stricker, 1976). We'll return to this theory in detail later.

A Caveat. There is little doubt that the liver plays a regulatory role in hunger and eating behavior. But recent studies have clouded what once appeared to be a fairly straightforward picture. A key assumption behind most studies involving the liver and the hunger signal is that messages concerning hunger are transmitted to the brain from the liver via the vagus nerve. Recent liver transplant studies have called that assumption into question. When an animal is subjected to a liver transplant the neural connections between the liver and brain are severed, which, according to the glucostatic theory, should severely disrupt the animal's eating pattern. Yet experiments have shown that the feeding patterns of liver-transplanted rats are quite normal (Louis-Sylvestre et al., 1990). And humans who have undergone liver transplants continue to eat normally as well.

One way to interpret the eating behavior of liver-transplanted animals (and humans) is that the liver is not necessary for normal eating but is important under conditions of severe metabolic challenge. A second possibility is that there are redundant mechanisms for the control of hunger, perhaps shared by both the brain and the liver, and that these mechanisms compensate for the loss of the liver. These and related issues are topics of ongoing research.

The Lipostatic Theory

Compelling as the evidence for the glucostatic theory may be, it cannot be said that glucose is the *only* metabolic factor controlling eating behavior. As more and more studies are reported, it appears that body weight—specifically, fat—may also be involved.

The chief reason body weight is a candidate for the eating signal is that animals have been shown to regulate eating according to their weight. When subjected to forced feeding and fattened, they stop eating. Deprived of food and made thin, they start eating.

The theory linking body weight to the control of eating is known as the *lipostatic theory*. According to this theory, the brain (specifically the hypothalamus) acts as a "scale," constantly weighing the body by monitoring a correlate of weight traveling in the blood. When weight or some correlate rises above optimum, eating stops. When weight drops below optimum, eating starts.

The lipostatic theory was originally advanced by George Kennedy in 1953, but its best known proponent has been Philip Teitelbaum, whose work has focused on animals suffering from an eating disorder known as hyperphagia—a condition of overeating and obesity that results from lesions in the ventromedial hypothalamus (Kennedy, 1953; Teitelbaum, 1955).

Hyperphagia: A Closer Look

Hyperphagia is marked by two distinct behavioral phases. During the first phase, immediately after the lesion is made, animals behave as if they are determined to eat themselves to death. After weeks of incessant overeating, however, food intake returns to slightly above normal. During the first, or *dynamic*, phase, hyperphagic animals often triple their normal weight. During the second, or *static*, phase, they eat only enough to maintain their new heavy weight. Figure 11.4*a* illustrates the two phases.

Because a lesioned animal's eating behavior seems to be directed at achieving a new body weight, Teitelbaum postulated that the signal by which the ventromedial hypothalamus normally controls eating is body weight or some correlate. Lesions in the ventromedial hypothalamus, in his view, make the receptors in the ventromedial hypothalamus less sensitive to a weight-related signal, thus calling for a compensatory increase in stimulation to turn off eating. This hypothesis has inspired numerous studies, one of the most important of which we will now examine (Hoebel & Teitelbaum, 1961).

Experimental Support for the Lipostatic Theory

To test the theory that weight or some correlate of it is the signal by which the ventromedial hypothalamus inhibits eating, Teitelbaum studied rats made obese by lesions in the ventromedial hypothalamus. The rats in his studies weighed anywhere from 400 to 1500 g (normal weight is from 200 to 300 g). According to the lipostatic theory, this excessive

Figure 11.4 *Ventromedial Hypothalamic Syndrome*
(a) The dynamic and static stages after lesioning of the ventromedial hypothalamus.
(b) Superobesity after forced feeding followed by return to "normal" obesity after normal feeding.

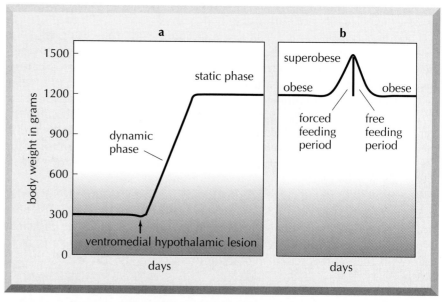

weight was a consequence of the dulled ventromedial hypothalamus's failure to inhibit eating. In other words, it takes more weight to stimulate the relatively insensitive ventromedial hypothalamus to turn eating off.

If this reasoning is correct, it should follow that when obese rats are forced to gain even more weight, the weight-related signal should be present in excess, the dulled ventromedial hypothalamus should be *overstimulated* and, paradoxically, the superobese animals should stop eating. In fact, they should stop eating until their weight returns to the original level of obesity (400 to 1500 g).

Teitelbaum confirmed this prediction. In one study he made animals obese by lesioning the ventromedial hypothalamus. He then forced the animals to eat and gain weight beyond their obese level by training them to eat in order to avoid shock. As illustrated in Figure 11.4*b*, when animals made superobese in this way were allowed to eat freely again, they refrained from eating until their weight had dropped to its normal obese level (400 to 1500 g). These results indicated that a weight-related signal is critical for control of eating. What they did not indicate is what, specifically, that weight-related signal is.

Fat as the Signal

Ever since the lipostatic theory was first introduced, it has been assumed that the weight-related signal is fat, but it remained for Robert Liebelt and his colleagues to provide concrete evidence to support the notion (Liebelt, Bordelon, & Liebelt, 1973). Liebelt's procedure consisted of removing fat tissue surgically from rats that had been made obese by lesions in the ventromedial hypothalamus. If the presence of fat is the signal for satiation, reasoned Liebelt, then a shortage of fat should be a signal for hunger.

Consistent with this hypothesis, Liebelt found that the surgically slenderized rats ate incessantly and stopped only after their weight reached the original obese level. Earlier suspicions therefore have proven correct: fat content in the body plays a major role in the regulation of eating behavior.

Revising the Lipostatic Theory

At first glance, the lipostatic theory seems highly plausible. There is little doubt, in light of Liebelt's study, that fat plays an important role in controlling eating behavior. And there is little doubt, in light of Teitelbaum's lesion experiments, that the ventromedial hypothalamus is involved in regulating eating behavior.

Its plausibility notwithstanding, however, the lipostatic theory has run into a number of problems, particularly with respect to Teitelbaum's work on the ventromedial hypothalamus. These problems do not refute the theory, but they do oblige us to reassess the role that the ventromedial hypothalamus plays in the process and they oblige us to take a closer look at how fat itself is metabolized and how metabolic (i.e., energy) factors figure into hunger, eating behavior, and weight gain.

The Lipostatic Theory: An Anatomical Reassessment

It wasn't long after Teitelbaum reported the results of his hypothalamic lesion studies that researchers following up on Teitelbaum's work made an important anatomical discovery. They found that the behavioral effects Teitelbaum reported had less to do with damage to the ventromedial hypothalamus itself than with damage that the ventromedial hypothalamic lesions had inadvertently produced in two adjacent sites: a tract known as the *ventral noradrenergic bundle* and an area in the hypothalamus known as the *paraventricular nucleus*. When Richard Gold, for instance, confined lesions to the ventromedial hypothalamus itself, the eating behavior of the lesioned animals was unaffected. Confining damage to either of the adjacent areas, on the other hand, produced the disruption that Teitelbaum had originally reported (Gold, 1973; Gold et al., 1977; Leibowitz, Hammer, & Chang, 1981). (Note: Despite these findings, and primarily because the adjacent areas are so closely associated with the ventromedial hypothalamus, many researchers continue to refer to the behavioral effects as a result of ventromedial hypothalamic lesions and we will do the same.)

The Lipostatic Theory: A Behavioral Reassessment

A more serious problem with the lipostatic theory, however, had come to light several years earlier when P. J. Han uncovered an aspect of eating behavior in ventromedial hypothalamic-lesioned animals that could not be explained by the lipostatic theory. Ventromedial hypothalamic-lesioned animals in Han's study *gained weight whether they overate or not* (Han, 1967). In other words, Han found that even under normal feeding conditions, ventromedial hypothalamic-lesioned animals show an abnormal tendency to gain weight. The significance of this behavioral pattern is that it should not have occurred if, in fact, the lipostatic theory were correct.

Central to the lipostatic theory, let us remember, is the idea that overeating and gaining weight are related—that one (the need to gain weight and restore the optimum) motivates the other (overeating). Han's findings, however, indicate that the two behaviors—overeating and gaining weight—are not necessarily related. But if they are not related, how then do we account for them? Why do ventromedial hypothalamic-lesioned animals overeat, if not to gain weight? And why do ventromedial hypothalamic-lesioned animals gain weight even when they do not overeat? There is a logical answer to these questions, but to understand the answer, you have to understand the role that fat plays not only in eating behavior but in weight gain as well.

Fat in the Body

Fat is formed from excess food—food that the body does not need for immediate energy production. Fat is important in body functioning because it provides a supply of backup energy. Once the food we eat is metabolized, cells need to receive energy from elsewhere, and the chief source of this alternate energy is stored fat. When it is needed, fat is broken down and used as a source of energy. It is this breakdown of fat—producing *free fatty acids*—that keeps us going from one meal to the next. With this overview in mind, let us now try to get a clearer picture of why, on the one hand, ventromedial hypothalamic-lesioned animals overeat, and why, on the other hand, these animals gain weight even when they do not overeat? The answer to both questions, as you will soon see, obliges us to incorporate into the lipostatic theory a new factor: the release of insulin by the pancreas, and, more specifically, how insulin release is affected by ventromedial hypothalamic lesions.

Abnormal Overeating

Evidence indicates that the ventromedial hypothalamus exerts *inhibitory* control over the pancreas and its release of insulin. Thus, when lesions occur in the ventromedial hypothalamus, the pancreas releases more insulin than normal, and the excess insulin in turn prevents fat from breaking down (Frohman & Bernardis, 1968; King, Smith, & Frohman, 1984). The result? The body is deprived of a major source of energy—the breakdown products of fat (free fatty acids). To correct this deficit, the lesioned animals overeat.

In short, then, the ventromedial hypothalamic-lesioned animals are deceptive. Even though they overeat and seemingly have an abundance of food in their systems, the food seems to be "stuck" in a state (fat) which cannot be used for energy production. Their bodies are thus starved of energy-producing fuel (free fatty acids), and the animals behave as any food-deprived animals normally would—they overeat (Friedman & Stricker, 1976).

Abnormal Weight Gain

The link between the ventromedial hypothalamus, insulin, and levels of fat in the body also helps to explain why ventromedial hypothalamic-lesioned animals show an abnormal tendency to gain weight even under normal feeding conditions. Here again, the culprit is excess insulin (Powley, 1977). More than simply preventing the breakdown of fat, excess insulin actually promotes the *buildup* of fat. Thus, when nutrients normally metabolized for energy are exposed to excess insulin, they are stored as fat. The result: normal amounts of food in ventromedial hypothalamic-lesioned animals produce abnormal weight gain.

Summing Up

What can we conclude, finally, about the validity of the lipostatic theory, and in particular, about the role of the ventromedial hypothalamus in controlling eating behavior? The answer, in brief, is this: the essential components of the lipostatic theory have been confirmed. Fat, as Liebelt's early studies indicated, is indeed a key hunger signal. And the ventromedial hypothalamus (more accurately, two adjacent areas of the ventromedial hypothalamus) is clearly involved in regulating the behavior, as Teitelbaum originally proposed. What we now know, however, is that the ventromedial hypothalamus does not monitor the fat signal in the normal sense of the term "monitor." Its role is a good deal more indirect. Through the control it exerts over the pancreas and the release of insulin, it regulates the buildup and the breakdown of fat.

If this sounds familiar to you, it should. We saw the same pattern with the glucostatic theory. Yes, glucose is a signal for hunger. No, the ventromedial hypothalamus does not monitor the signal. That function apparently is handled by the liver and perhaps brain areas other than the ventromedial hypothalamus.

All of which brings us to our final question regarding the lipostatic theory. If fat is a signal for hunger, where, if not in the ventromedial hypothalamus, is the fat signal monitored? To answer this question we must reconsider the glucostatic and lipostatic theories in a more general light.

Combining the Glucostatic and Lipostatic Theories

The glucostatic theory and the lipostatic theory agree on one point: eating occurs when a metabolic signal (i.e., energy production) falls below an optimum level. Where the theories differ is on the source of the signal. The glucostatic theory argues that eating occurs because energy produced by *glucose* is not at the optimum level. The lipostatic theory argues that eating occurs because energy produced by *fat* is not at the optimum level.

It is too early to predict which of the two theories will ultimately be proved correct. Supporting the glucostatic theory are Russek's data indicating that hungry animals stop eating after injections of glucose into the hepatic portal vein. Supporting the lipostatic theory are Liebelt's data, which indicate that surgically slenderized rats eat incessantly and stop only after their weight reaches the original obese level. More recent findings, however, indicate that both theories may be correct: animals may be using the liver to monitor energy produced by both glucose and fat to regulate eating accordingly.

To understand how this is possible, we must take a closer look at glucose, fat, and their relation to the liver.

The Liver, Glucose, and Fat

As we mentioned earlier, fat is formed from excess food; when needed, it is broken down into free fatty acids and used as a source of energy. The organ chiefly involved in both the buildup and breakdown of fat is the liver, which itself requires fuel for energy.

In other words, the liver needs fuel to make fuel. When producing fat, immediately after a meal, the liver relies on glucose for energy. When breaking down fat and converting it into usable nutrients, the liver depends on free fatty acids (derived from fat) for energy. But there is a difference between glucose and free fatty acids as sources of energy; glucose provides more energy to the liver during the buildup of fat than free fatty acids provide during the breakdown of fat. According to Mark

Friedman and Edward Stricker, it is this *shift* in energy—detected and responded to by the liver—that is the signal for hunger (Friedman & Stricker, 1976). It is not that the energy provided by free fatty acids cannot satisfy hunger, it is that the energy required calls for far more free fatty acids than glucose. On the basis of this key assumption, Friedman and Stricker explain the eating patterns of normal and ventromedial hypothalamic-lesioned animals as follows.

When normal (nonlesioned) animals are deprived of food, fat breaks down, free fatty acids are produced, and the resulting energy deficit in the liver signals hunger. When normal animals are fed or (in the case of Russek's experiment) injected with glucose, energy levels are restored in the liver and the liver signals satiation.

When animals with lesions in the ventromedial hypothalamus (or for that matter any animal suffering from excess insulin) are fed, they are able to use the food for energy. Once the food has been metabolized, however, excess insulin impedes the use of fat for energy. As a result, there is an abnormal energy deficit in the liver (i.e., a deficit in free fatty acids), and the liver signals intense hunger.

Originally introduced in the 1970s, the theory remains highly speculative. The theory, however, has generated a great deal of interest and has opened several lines of research that continue today.

NEURAL MECHANISMS FOR EATING

Up to now we have been concentrating primarily on the signals for eating. Evidence suggests that the stomach signal serves as a speedy off signal, preventing eating long enough for a slower metabolic (energy) signal to take effect. Energy produced by glucose and fat, on the other hand, functions over longer periods of time, holding off eating from one meal to the next. Only after the signals stop—that is, only after the stomach signals cease and energy levels drop following the shift from glucose to free fatty acids—is *hunger* signaled.

But what does it mean to say that *hunger* is "signaled"? As we emphasized earlier, the same principles that apply to sensory processing hold for motivation as well. Hunger, like vision or audition, depends less on the stimuli that activate the sensation than on the nerves that are stimulated and ultimately on the part of the brain that the nerves stimulate.

So, to complete the picture of the physiological basis of eating we move from the signal to the brain. The question we seek to answer is where in the brain neural activity must occur for hunger to be produced? Not long ago the answer would have been the lateral hypothalamus. It still may be, but not without qualifications. Let us take a closer look.

The Lateral Hypothalamus: A Closer Look

Electrical stimulation and lesion studies have clearly established that the lateral hypothalamus is involved in the control of eating. Stimulate the lateral hypothalamus and eating is produced; make lesions in the lateral hypothalamus and eating is abolished.

But what is the nature of the involvement? Does an animal receiving stimulation of the lateral hypothalamus eat because it is hungry (i.e., because it is motivated), or does stimulation elicit eating for some other reason? The same question can be posed for animals that receive lesions: Do the lesions abolish eating because they abolish hunger, or do they affect some other process that is necessary for eating to take place?

These questions do not lend themselves to simple answers. In fact, we still don't have a full account of the role that the lateral hypothalamus plays in the control of eating. What we do know, however, is that if the lateral hypothalamus and hunger are indeed related, it is not a simple relationship. The evidence comes from stimulation and lesion studies.

Stimulation Studies

Elliot Valenstein and his colleagues were among the first to challenge the notion that the lateral hypothalamus controls eating through its control of hunger (Valenstein, Cox, & Kakolewski, 1968; 1970). They based their argument on some compelling data. Electrical stimulation of the *same* area in the lateral hypothalamus, they discovered, can elicit a variety of behaviors. If food is present, the stimulation can produce eating. If food is removed and water is substituted, the animal begins to drink. Furthermore, the eating and drinking do not appear necessarily to be related to hunger or thirst. Electrical stimulation of the lateral hypothalamus elicits eating of food pellets but not of food powder. It also elicits drinking from one type of container but not another type. Valenstein thus contends that the animals could not be hungry or thirsty; if they were, they would consume both the powder and the pellets and would drink water from one container as well as from the other.

These findings, in Valenstein's view, suggest that the lateral hypothalamus may not trigger a specific motivational state such as hunger but rather a general state of arousal that has the potential to release several different well-established response patterns, such as chewing or licking. The significance of this explanation is that it calls into question the view of other researchers—Neal Miller, in particular—who have long argued that the eating and drinking behavior elicited by lateral hypothalamic stimulation reflects motivations such as hunger and thirst. Miller's view was based on studies in which animals stimulated in the lateral hypothalamus were able to perform behaviors—lever pressing, for instance—that were previously learned in response to deprivation of food or water while the animals were presumably hungry or thirsty (Miller, 1960; 1961). Because the behavior produced by the stimulation is not limited to a specific motor response related to eating or drinking but is more versatile and can be learned, Miller argued that the behavior reflected motivational states—hunger and thirst—and not the arousal of built-in response patterns. How do we resolve the contradiction between Miller and Valenstein?

In the face of these contradictions, the only reasonable solution is a compromise. Miller and Valenstein could both be correct, for it is possible that the behaviors each scientist has observed result from the activation of two different circuits in the lateral hypothalamus: a circuit for the execution of built-in response patterns, and a circuit for motivation. Such a possibility seems likely, given the work of Peter Morgane (Morgane, 1961).

Morgane's Experiment

Morgane's work has established that stimulation of two different areas within the lateral hypothalamus can produce different behaviors. Electrical stimulation of the far lateral region of the lateral hypothalamus produces intensely motivated behavior, such as crossing an electrified grid for the opportunity to press a lever to receive food. Stimulation to the midlateral region of the lateral hypothalamus elicits eating, the consummatory component of the behavior, but does not motivate the animal to cross the grid.

These findings suggest that different circuits in the lateral hypothalamus may control at least two components of eating behavior. The far lateral region appears to control motivation; the midlateral region appears to control the consummatory component—the actual eating. These findings may also help to resolve the contradictions between Miller's findings, which indicate that stimulation of the lateral hypothalamus produces motivation (hunger and thirst), and Valenstein's, which indicate that stimulation of the lateral hypothalamus produces built-in response patterns. Keep in mind, however, that these conjectures are based on a key assumption—that Miller and Valenstein placed their electrodes in slightly different areas of the lateral hypothalamus. That is yet to be determined.

Lesion Studies

The lesion work gives us a different perspective. Animals with damage in the lateral hypothalamus not only refuse to eat, but they also refuse to drink, lose interest in sexual behavior, exhibit motor impairment, and are unresponsive to sensory input—visual, auditory, and touch. The behavioral deficit is referred to as *sensory neglect* (Marshall, Turner, & Teitelbaum, 1971).

How should we interpret these results? What does sensory neglect have to do with eating and drinking? As you may recall, sensory processing calls for arousal—a general alerting response to stimuli—and the behavior, or lack of it in this case, indicates that lesions in the lateral hypothalamus may interfere with the arousal process. It may seem like a minor point, but it is not. The original motivation explanation was that lateral hypothalamic-lesioned animals fail to eat and drink because they are not hungry or thirsty. The sensory neglect view is that lateral hypothalamic-lesioned animals fail to eat and drink because sensory input no longer can arouse a reaction to food or to water or, for that matter, to any object in the environment (Wolgin, Cytawa, & Teitelbaum, 1976; Stricker, 1983).

Which is it—motivation or sensory arousal? The answer may be both. When lesions are placed in the lateral hypothalamus, two anatomical structures are often damaged, the lateral hypothalamus and, inadvertently, the *nigrostriatal tract* (a neural tract which passes very close to the lateral hypothalamus), and evidence indicates that each structure may be involved in the control of a different component—motivation or sensory arousal—of eating behavior. Before we consider the evidence, however, let us take a closer look at the anatomy (see Figure 11.5) and chemistry of the lateral hypothalamus and nigrostriatal tract.

Nigrostriatal Tract versus the Lateral Hypothalamus

Because the nigrostriatal tract and lateral hypothalamus are located so closely together, it is virtually impossible—with existing research technology—to lesion or stimulate one without lesioning or stimulating the other. How then does a researcher go about manipulating one independently of the other? The answer lies in the structure and chemistry of the lateral hypothalamus and the nigrostriatal tract. The lateral hypothala-

Figure 11.5 *The Nigrostriatal Tract*
The nigrostriatal tract originates in the substantia nigra and travels to the putamen and caudate nucleus.

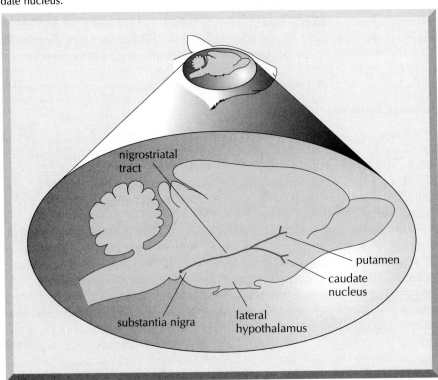

mus is made up largely of neural cell bodies. The nigrostriatal tract consists of axons that release the neurotransmitter dopamine.

This difference has led to experiments involving two kinds of chemicals known as *neurotoxins*. One type kills cell bodies; the other kills dopamine-releasing axons. Inject *kainic acid* into the lateral hypothalamus, and it kills the cell bodies in the lateral hypothalamus but not the dopamine-releasing axons in the nigrostriatal tract. Inject *6-hydroxydopamine* into the nigrostriatal tract, and it kills dopamine-releasing axons in the nigrostriatal tract but not the cell bodies in the lateral hypothalamus.

In both cases the two types of damage—damage in the nigrostriatal tract or damage in the lateral hypothalamus—produce similar behavioral effects: animals refuse to eat and drink. But this is not to say that they do so for the same reason. Brain damage can produce loss of eating and drinking for a variety of reasons, among them the disruption of sensory, motor, or motivational processes. Thus we must ask exactly where damage to the nigrostriatal tract (independent of the lateral hypothalamus) and damage to the lateral hypothalamus (independent of the nigrostriatal tract) fit into the overall behavioral picture.

The answer is this: damage in the nigrostriatal tract (produced by 6-hydroxydopamine) appears to disrupt arousal but not hunger. The lesioned animals show little or no responsiveness to external stimuli, including food and water. Yet, when food is placed directly in their mouths they behave as if they are hungry and they eat (Berridge, Venier, & Robinson, 1989). Curiously, too, they also resume eating and drinking when their tails are gently pinched (O'Brien, Cheshire, & Teitelbaum, 1985). Apparently, then, damage to the nigrostriatal tract disrupts the arousal component of eating and drinking, and tail-pinching restores it.

Damage in the lateral hypothalamus (produced by kainic acid) has a different effect (Grossman et al., 1978). It appears to disrupt hunger but not arousal. The animals refuse to eat, regardless of whether food is placed in their mouths, yet they remain responsive to objects in their environment.

Fine Tuning the Lateral Hypothalamus. If the lateral hypothalamus is indeed a hunger area (as the neurotoxin work suggests) we would expect that stimulation of the lateral hypothalamus should elicit eating.

But as we noted earlier, stimulating the lateral hypothalamus poses methodological problems, chief among them the likelihood that stimulation to one area will also stimulate a neighboring area. To resolve this problem (that is, to limit the effects of stimulation to discrete areas), recent studies have injected minuscule amounts of a neurotransmitter (10 nanoliters) into different areas in the hypothalamus (Stanley et al., 1993). The neurotransmitter injected in this case is neuropeptide Y and the areas injected (there were 47) included the lateral hypothalamus. Of the 47 areas stimulated, eating has been elicited by injections into at least seven. The lateral hypothalamus, not surprisingly, is one of the seven, but it turns out that another area—the *perifornical area*—has a greater impact on eating behavior than any other area, including the lateral hypothalamus.

What can we conclude from these results? How do we reconcile, in other words, the neurotoxin-lesion work, which suggests that the lateral hypothalamus is involved in the control of hunger, and the neuropeptide Y work, which implicates the perifornical area? The answer should be fairly obvious to you by now. For as we have seen over and over throughout this book, no behavior or in this case component of behavior is under the control of a single area of the brain—and hunger is clearly no exception.

The Lateral Hypothalamus: Its Role in Controlling Hunger

We now come to the final question regarding the lateral hypothalamus. How, in fact, does the lateral hypothalamus control hunger? Does it produce hunger directly or does it control conditions which in turn produce hunger?

The answer, as far as we know today, is this: the lateral hypothalamus is *not* a "hunger" center per se. Rather it receives metabolic input and controls hormonal output which, together with activity in other areas of the brain, may result in hunger.

On the input side, this view has been confirmed by recording studies showing that the lateral hypothalamus, via the vagus nerve, receives metabolic information from the liver. These studies have shown that when glucose levels (i.e., energy) in the body are *low*, activity is high in the liver, the vagus nerve, and the lateral hypothalamus, apparently signaling hunger. When glucose levels in the body are *high*, activity in all three of these areas drops, apparently signaling satiation (Niijima, 1969; Schmitt, 1973).

When it comes to output, the picture for the lateral hypothalamus is much the same as for the ventromedial hypothalamus with one major difference. Like the ventromedial hypothalamus, the lateral hypothalamus exerts control over the release of insulin by the pancreas, but rather than inhibiting release it excites release (Morley et al., 1985). You will recall that the ventromedial hypothalamus, among other things, inhibits release of insulin and that lesions in the ventromedial hypothalamus, by removing the inhibitory effect, release insulin and trigger overeating.

The same holds for the lateral hypothalamus, except in the opposite direction. The lateral hypothalamus excites the release of insulin, and lesions in the lateral hypothalamus result in animals that refuse to eat and that lose weight because the lesions remove the excitatory effect and produce a decrease in insulin. Why should a decrease in insulin result in animals that refuse to eat and that lose weight? The decrease in insulin promotes fat breakdown, the animals lose weight, and an excess of fat-related nutrients (free fatty acids) is dumped into the blood (Shimazu, Fukuda, & Ban, 1966). The lateral hypothalamic-lesioned animal is, in effect, drowning in its own food (breakdown products of fat), energy levels (produced by the excess free fatty acids) rise in the liver, and thus eating stops (Friedman & Stricker, 1976).

Historical Reflections: The Satiety and Hunger Centers Revisited

Before going any further, let us emphasize an important point that the hypothalamic stimulation and lesion studies have taught us about the brain and its relation to behavior. To say that there is a single brain center that controls a single behavior is rather like saying that there is a single component in a television set that controls the picture. Eating is a complex behavior involving a number of component parts. So, even though the traditional approach has been to talk about the ventromedial hypothalamus as though it were a "satiety center," and of the lateral hypothalamus as a "hunger center," we know today that they are not centers at all; rather, they are integral parts of satiety and hunger circuits. In and of themselves they do not control eating behavior. It is only when their activity is combined with activity in other areas of the body and brain that eating occurs adaptively.

This idea of combined activity is one that we have been making throughout this book and one we shall make again and again. It reinforces the point that no single area of the brain controls a single behavior.

Reconstructing the Circuit

What has all this research taught us about the eating circuit and its component parts? To answer this question it helps to consider the circuit in sections—the signals, the receptors, and the brain areas, as illustrated in Figure 11.6.

We shall begin with the signals. We know of three: stomach, glucose, and fat. Stomach signals (distension and calories) are "read" by receptors in the stomach, and the information is relayed to the ventromedial hypothalamus. The energy produced by the use of either glucose or available free fatty acids is "read" by the liver and signaled to the lateral hypothalamus. Finally, the ventromedial and lateral hypothalami, in addition to receiving signals from the stomach and liver, control the buildup and breakdown of fat via the release of insulin by the pancreas.

How do the three signals regulate eating? Evidence suggests that the stomach signal serves as a speedy off signal, preventing eating long enough for a slower metabolic signal to take effect. The glucose and fat signals, on the other hand, function over longer periods of time, holding off eating from one meal to the next.

Such, then, is the general picture of the internal circuitry that controls eating behavior in experimental animals. To what extent, though, does this picture reflect the internal circuitry in human feeding patterns? Like other forms of behavior, eating is far more complex in humans than in lower animals. The eating habits of humans are influenced by a variety of factors, ranging from religious beliefs to health consciousness and

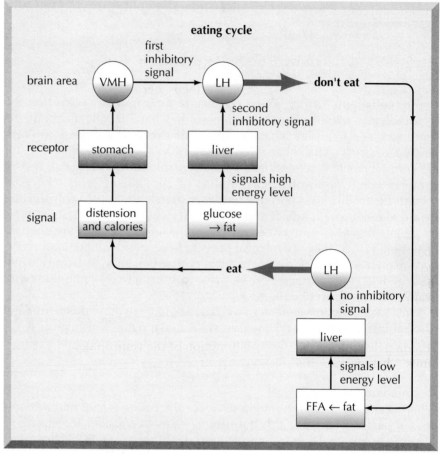

Figure 11.6   *The Systems Hypothesized to Regulate Eating*
The ventromedial hypothalamus (VMH) and lateral hypothalamus (LH) receive neural input from the stomach and liver, respectively. When stomach distension, calorie level, or energy level produced by glucose is high, the lateral hypothalamus is inhibited and satiation is signaled. When stomach distension, calories, *and* energy level produced by free fatty acids (FFA) are low, the lateral hypothalamus is released from inhibition and hunger is signaled.

social pressures. Still, regardless of external influences, the ultimate control of eating behavior in humans is *internal*. And, just as disruption in the internal circuitry of lower animals can disrupt eating behavior, so any disruption in the internal circuits of humans can have similar consequences. We shall now examine some of these consequences.

EATING BEHAVIOR: THE HUMAN FACTOR

Roughly one out of four Americans is overweight, and it is generally agreed that obesity is a key factor in any number of life-threatening diseases ranging from diabetes to heart disease. We also know, given the enormous popularity of diet books and diet programs, that most obese people would like to lose weight, but for a variety of reasons are unable to do so.

Obesity itself, however, is still very much a mystery, primarily because obesity is not produced by a single factor. Nor does it manifest itself in a single set of behaviors. So, while we focus here on the physiological aspects of obesity, we do not mean to underplay the role of cognitive, personality, environmental, and social factors. Even if we were to uncover the physiological basis of obesity, we would still be a long way from solving the problem.

Human and Animal Obesity: Finding Parallels

At least one type of obesity in humans shows a striking similarity to the animal studies we have been considering throughout this chapter. Some obese people, like ventromedial hypothalamic-lesioned animals, gain weight even though they do not overeat. Furthermore, they have great difficulty in losing weight, even on very strict diets, and once they lose weight they have difficulty keeping it off.

It would be naive to conclude, on the basis of the similarity between obese people and ventromedial hypothalamic-lesioned animals, that human obesity is caused by a malfunction of the ventromedial hypothalamus. There is, however, reason to believe that at least in some instances there may be a connection between lesioned rats and obese people.

The Pancreas and Eating Behavior

There is a strong possibility that obesity in humans is caused, in some cases, by malfunctioning of the pancreas and its release of insulin. The process through which the body controls the storage of fat is regulated by insulin: when insulin is high, fat storage is high, and when insulin is low, fat storage is low.

Earlier we noted that in ventromedial hypothalamic-lesioned rats, fat storage is high because insulin levels are high. The suspicion is that the same may hold for some obese people—fat storage is high because insulin levels are high. Exactly why this occurs in the human is not clear, and although we cannot rule out damage in the ventromedial hypothalamus, the more likely candidate is malfunction of the pancreas itself.

To say that obesity in the human is caused by physiological abnormalities, be it hormonal (pancreas) or neural (ventromedial hypothalamus) or both, is to raise a second and more fundamental question: What causes the abnormalities in the first place? There is a possibility that some forms of obesity can be traced to either inborn traits or traits formed very early in a child's life.

This contention has been reinforced by findings of both lower animal studies and human studies. The lower animal studies, initially reported in the 1970s, found that different strains of rats show different genetic potentials for accumulating fat (Schemmel, Mickelsen, & Gill, 1970). The human work, of more recent vintage, has found that the body weights of adults who were adopted as young children correlates more closely with the body weights of their biological (genetic) parents than with their adopted parents (Strunkard et al., 1986).

The Metabolic Factor

If it is true, as it appears to be, that there is a genetic component to weight control, we must ask ourselves, What mechanism in the body is under the control of that component? Among the more likely candidates, according to recent studies, is metabolism—the capacity to burn calories.

The notion that genetically produced differences in metabolism can account, in part, for the weight-gain patterns of individuals is hardly new. It has long been suspected, for instance, that certain ethnic groups are able to eat more "fattening" foods than other ethnic groups without, however, showing a corresponding weight gain. Recently, though, scientific evidence has emerged that makes a strong case for a genetically induced metabolic component to weight gain.

One study involved 12 pairs of identical male twins, all of whom were given a daily diet that had roughly the same number of calories—1000 more than they needed to maintain their normal body weight—and all of whom were put on a similar but minimal exercise schedule (Bouchard et al., 1990). The experiment ran for 100 days and, as expected, everyone who took part in the study gained weight. Significantly, however, there was considerably more variation in weight gain among the *pairs* of twins than among the individual twins in each pair. This variability among the pairs of twins (keeping in mind, again, that everyone in the study ate and exercised virtually the same amount) is presumably the result of individual differences in metabolic efficiency. And the fact that the twins in each pair tended to gain roughly the same amount of weight strongly suggests that the metabolic efficiency (or lack thereof) was genetically induced. What's more, the manner in which the subjects gained weight (i.e., whether the fat was deposited in the abdomen, the thighs, the hips) was strikingly similar on a twin to twin basis and much less so when the sets of twins were compared.

Fat Cells

There is evidence that yet another factor in weight gain is the number of adipocyte (fat) cells in the body. Adipocyte cells specialize in storing fat, and studies have shown that these cells are far more numerous in obese people than in people of normal weight (Hirsch & Knittle, 1970). Adipocyte cells, moreover, may contribute to obesity in more than one way. First of all, it is next to impossible to get rid of adipocyte cells through dieting. Dieting simply shrinks the cells; it does not reduce their numbers. Second—and this notion is more theoretical—the urge to eat may be controlled by the state of fat in the adipocyte cells; when the cells are depleted of fat, the urge to eat is triggered until fat is restored. This would account for why an overweight person who goes on diets may lose weight—their fat cells shrink—but do not lose their craving for food.

Environmental Factors

The fact that some people, because of a genetic predisposition, may be more prone to gaining weight than others—because of either inefficient metabolism or an abnormally high number of fat cells—does not rule out environmental factors in weight control (Knittle & Hirsch, 1968). Animal studies have shown, for instance, that if young rats are overfed before they are weaned, they are far more likely to gain weight—that is, to add new fat cells—than rats that are overfed after weaning. This finding has led to the contention that people who are overfed as infants are more likely to have trouble controlling their weight when they become adults than people who are fed normally as infants. The view linking early eating patterns to adult obesity is more theoretical than factual, and, as you know, it is always risky to draw human implications from rat studies. Even so, however, the traditional notion that the chubbier the baby is the healthier he or she is, is no longer as predominant as it once was. And while evidence for a genetic link to weight control continues to mount, most weight control specialists continue to believe that except in rare instances the impact of these genetic predispositions can be greatly affected by lifestyle factors, such as diet and exercise.

Anorexia Nervosa: A Cautionary Note

What we have learned about obesity from animal work, useful and fascinating as it is, represents a tiny part of what we need to learn before we can eliminate the problem of obesity in humans. People eat and become obese for a variety of reasons, some directly rooted in physiology, but others only indirectly rooted in physiology.

The same is true for people who refuse to eat. Consider yet another highly publicized eating disorder—*anorexia nervosa*. This condition, as you probably know, chiefly affects women in their teens and early twenties. What happens with anorexics is that they suddenly manifest an intense and irrational fear of becoming fat and develop so distorted an image of themselves that they see themselves as overweight even though, as you can see in Figure 11.7, they are emaciated.

There is a strong temptation to draw parallels between people suffering from anorexia nervosa and rats made thin by lesions in the lateral hypothalamus. Both, after all, are skinny and may die of starvation. But beyond these superficial similarities, there is very little to suggest that anorexia nervosa—except in rare cases—is caused by lesions in the lateral hypothalamus.

No one knows at this point what causes anorexia. The fact that anorexics often stop menstruating prior to their abnormal weight loss suggests that the condition has a hormonal component. But psychological factors appear to be involved as well (Logue, 1986). A large percentage of anorexics are perfectionists; many of them are products of a conflict-ridden upbringing. All told, it is far too early to make a case for a hormonal, personality, or environmental cause of the condition. And because eating, as we have seen, involves such a complex behavioral system, it is likely that all three are involved.

Figure 11.7 *Anorexia Nervosa*
The singer Karen Carpenter before (left) and after (right) anorexia nervosa.

LEARNING TO EAT: SPECIFIC HUNGERS

We have been treating hunger as if it depended only on the *amount* of food taken into the body. But there is considerable experimental evidence to suggest that hunger is controlled by not only the amount of food intake but also by the *nature* of that food intake.

In a series of fascinating experiments based on a procedure known as *cafeteria feeding*, infants were allowed to select their own diets. Most ended up choosing diets similar to the normal and balanced diet that would have been selected for them. Moreover, when a particular nutrient was deliberately withheld for a short period, infants then selected foods containing that ingredient when they were given the opportunity.

This ability to select foods according to their nutrients reflects a phenomenon known as *specific hungers* and appears to involve a number of essential nutrients, including protein, carbohydrates, fat, calcium, salt, thiamine, and other B-complex vitamins (Rodgers, 1967; Zahorik, Maier, & Pies, 1974). The idea is that when we are deprived of these nutrients, we develop hungers or "cravings" for foods that contain them. Rats, for example, when given the opportunity to choose their diets in cafeteria style, also make choices consistent with dietary needs. If deprived of protein, they increase protein intake, and if deprived of carbohydrates, they increase carbohydrate intake (Rozin, 1968).

The implication of these experiments is that we have neural circuits whose function is to determine not only when we eat and don't eat but also which foods we eat. Experiments on lower animals (studying the chemistry of the hypothalamus and its relation to specific hungers) substantiate this view. Sarah Leibowitz and her colleagues have found that injections of different chemicals into the paraventricular nucleus (the same area which has been linked to the obesity produced by lesions in the ventromedial hypothalamus) activate specific hungers: norepinephrine enhances consumption of carbohydrates, galanin (a neuropeptide) increases fat consumption, and endorphins increase protein intake (Shor-Posner et al., 1985; Kyrkouli, Stanley, & Leibowitz, 1986). Injections of serotonin into the lateral hypothalamus and surrounding areas, on the other hand, suppress carbohydrate intake (Weiss et al., 1986).

Thus, just as the brain codes for different qualities of a sensory experience—color, pitch, taste, smell—so does the brain appear to code for different qualities of the hunger experience. Here again, we can see the adaptive implications of this capacity. Our survival depends on maintaining a balanced diet of nutrients, vitamins, and salts in the body. Multiple hungers (along with the multiple tastes that identify the foods satisfying these hungers) ensure that the balance is achieved.

Exploring the Bases of Specific Hungers

Are we born with circuits that regulate the kinds of food we eat, or do we develop eating patterns on the basis of experience? Once again we are faced with the classic nature-nurture question, and once again the answer appears to lie on both sides of the fence. Data suggest that animals may use both built-in circuits and learning to regulate what they eat (Rozin & Kalat, 1971). Regulation of sodium, for example, appears to be built-in, inasmuch as animals deprived of sodium from birth show a preference for it even though they have never experienced it before (Rowland, 1990). Regulation of intake of such vitamins as vitamin B, on the other hand, may be learned. Edward Scott and Ethel Verney found, for example, that when animals deprived of vitamin B were given that vitamin in food with a particular flavor, they quickly learned to prefer that flavor to the extent of choosing it even after the vitamin had been omitted (Scott & Verney, 1947). More recent evidence indicates that this type of learning holds for a variety of nutrients (Arbour & Wilkie, 1988; Lucas & Sclafani, 1989).

Learned Taste Aversion
Finally, our ability to survive goes beyond selecting foods that contain essential nutrients. It also requires selection of foods—especially plants—that do not contain poisons. Rats have evolved a highly adaptive food selection process to avoid poisons in their natural environment.

Rats have a built-in aversion (called *neophobia*) to anything new including tastes. Thus, when encountering a new taste they will eat only a little and then stop. If the food contains poison and they become sick (and this is where learning enters the picture), they associate the sickness with the taste and later will avoid the taste. If the food does not contain poison and they do not become sick, they will return to the food and include it in their diet (Rozin, 1976).

DRINKING BEHAVIOR: AN OVERVIEW

Much of what we have said about eating behavior applies as well to drinking behavior—albeit with one exception. You can go without eating for long periods—even months—and still live. Without water, you can live for only a few days. The reason is that our bodies can store nutrients, specifically in the form of fats, but have no capacity to store water. When we are deprived of water, we literally shrivel up.

Research into drinking behavior is directed toward the same goal as research into eating behavior: to uncover the nature of the neural mechanisms involved in its regulation. As it is with eating, the process that regulates drinking behavior, at least in part, is homeostasis: on signals are triggered when water levels in the body drop below normal; off signals are triggered when the normal level is reached. Here again, to understand water intake at a physiological level, we must understand not only the responses that regulate the behavior but also the signals that turn it on and the receptors that monitor these signals.

Responding to Water Deprivation

Depriving an animal of water triggers two responses aimed at restoring normality. You are familiar with one response: drinking. But there is another, less widely recognized response that is just as important. It is an internal response directed at reducing the amount of water lost in urine.

The internal response to water deprivation involves a set of neurosecretory cells located in an area of the hypothalamus known as the *supraoptic nuclei*, pictured in Figure 11.8. These cells synthesize a hormone known as *vasopressin*, whose principal function is to act as an *antidiuretic*—that is, to decrease the volume of urine produced. Although it is manufactured in the hypothalamus, vasopressin is transported to and stored in the *posterior pituitary* gland and is released whenever there is a water shortage in the body. Its target organ is the kidney. There it works to promote reabsorption of water by the blood. As a result, the amount of water excreted in the urine is reduced.

People deficient in vasopressin suffer from a condition known as *diabetes insipidus*, the chief symptom of which is excessive loss of water through urination. This water loss, known as *polyuria*, is accompanied by a corresponding increase in thirst and drinking behavior, known as *polydipsia*.

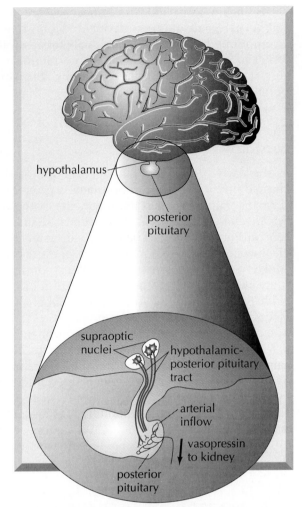

Figure 11.8 *Relation of the Hypothalamus to the Posterior Pituitary and Kidneys*
Vasopressin is manufactured in the supraoptic nuclei of the hypothalamus, transported to the posterior pituitary via the hypothalamic-posterior pituitary tract, and released by the pituitary into the bloodstream.

THE SEARCH FOR THE SIGNALS

The search for the signals that regulate water intake has been as intensive as the search for those that regulate food intake and has followed a similar pattern. We know that the primary signal to stimulate drinking and the release of the antidiuretic hormone vasopressin is a deficit of water in the body. But it is one thing to speak of a water deficit as the signal for water intake and something else to understand what we mean by a water deficit at the cellular and neural levels.

Here again, as we did with hunger, we are looking for two signals: one that turns on drinking behavior and one that turns it off. The basic assumptions regarding these signals are as follows: the on signal is a deficit in water, the off signal is a correction in the deficit, and signaling takes place in the hypothalamus. Studies have confirmed these assumptions.

The Hypothalamus and Thirst: The Early Studies

In the early 1950s Bergt Andersson found that a mild salt solution injected into a goat's brain produced a pronounced increase in drinking behavior, but only when the target site of the injection was the *anterior hypothalamus* (Andersson, 1953). Because salt mimics the effect of water deprivation (a topic we shall deal with later), Andersson concluded that the anterior hypothalamus is one of the sites related to control of water intake. Andersson and his colleagues confirmed this conclusion in a study showing that electrical stimulation of the anterior hypothalamus induces drinking and that lesions abolish drinking (Andersson & McCann, 1955). Neal Miller later extended the analysis to show that the water intake produced by stimulation of the anterior hypothalamus is indeed related to thirst. He found that animals trained to perform a response when deprived of water (and therefore presumably thirsty) will perform the same response when sated and stimulated in the anterior hypothalamus (Miller, 1961).

Research over the past three decades has added immeasurably to this original picture of water intake. We no longer speak of one set of receptors or one signal for drinking; indeed, we no longer speak of one type of thirst. We shall now consider some of these discoveries.

THE TWO THIRSTS: OSMOTIC AND VOLEMIC

All of us know what it is like to feel thirsty. But what is thirst? And what causes it? Answering these questions obliges us to introduce a fact about thirst that you may not have been aware of—the existence of two different types of thirst: osmotic and volemic thirst. Both types produce the same sensation, but their causes and dynamics differ.

Why are there two different types of thirst? Because there are two different types of water deficits in the body—that is, two different on signals that can trigger drinking behavior. We shall now look at the nature of these two signals.

Maintaining Fluid Balance

To understand what thirst is, you first have to understand one of the chief functions of water in the body. As soon as water is taken into the body, it passes through the stomach and into the small intestine, where it is absorbed into the bloodstream. The blood then transports it to cells throughout the body.

Once water reaches the cells, one of its main jobs is to help maintain the chemical balance between the environment inside the cells and the environment surrounding them. We have already seen how essential this balance is for proper cell function. Only when this balance exists can neural cells, for example, produce neural impulses. The key to the balance is the relative concentration of water and certain minerals, chiefly salt, in and around the cells.

Water and salt are present in both the inner environment of the cell, the *intracellular fluid*, and the outer environment, the *extracellular fluid*. When the concentration of salt increases either inside or outside the cell, fluid moves across the cell membrane to restore the balance. But because the cell membrane tends to resist the movement of salt more than it resists the movement of water, the water, as illustrated in Figure 11.9, does most of the moving. When the concentration of salt outside the cell becomes excessive, water from inside the cell crosses the membrane to dilute it. When the concentration of salt outside the cell drops *below* normal and becomes diluted, then water moves from outside in, thus diluting the salt levels inside the cell. The consequence of the movement either in or out is water depletion. Once depleted, water has to be replenished. The need for replenishment produces thirst.

Differentiating Osmotic from Volemic Thirst

Thirst is differentiated on the basis of *where* the fluid deficit exists: inside or outside the cell. As you can see in Figure 11.9, when the deficit exists *inside* the cell—in the intracellular fluid—the thirst is *osmotic*, and when the deficit exists *outside* the cell—in the extracellular fluid—the thirst is *volemic*.

Osmotic Thirst
Osmotic thirst is the thirst you experience after eating something very salty, such as salted peanuts. The salt content creates a high concentration of salt outside the cells, which in turn produces a compensatory movement of water from inside the cells in order to dilute the excessive salt. The result of the movement is a deficit *inside* the cells: osmotic thirst.

Volemic Thirst
Volemic thirst is the thirst that arises when you perspire and *lose* salt. The loss of salt results in a low concentration of salt outside the cells. To compensate for this imbalance, water from outside the cells moves inside. The result is a deficit *outside* the cells: volemic thirst.

Water Deprivation
The thirst we all experience when we are deprived of water for several hours is a combination of volemic and osmotic thirst. When water is not

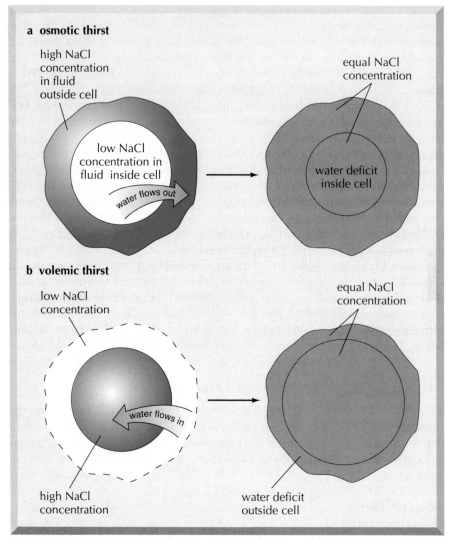

a osmotic thirst

high NaCl concentration in fluid outside cell

low NaCl concentration in fluid inside cell

water flows out

equal NaCl concentration

water deficit inside cell

b volemic thirst

low NaCl concentration

water flows in

equal NaCl concentration

high NaCl concentration

water deficit outside cell

Figure 11.9 *Two Types of Thirst*
(a) An increase in salt (NaCl) outside the cell causes water to move out of the cell; the result is osmotic thirst. (b) A decrease in salt outside the cell causes water to move into the cell; the result is volemic thirst.

constantly replenished by drinking, it is lost outside the cells through urination, producing volemic thirst. And because excess salt is left behind after urination, water moves from the inside to the outside of the cell, leaving a water deficit within and producing osmotic thirst.

Water Deficits and Blood Pressure
Whether thirst is osmotic or volemic in origin, the fluid deficits that produce it affect other functions in the body. One of the chief effects is on blood pressure. Have you ever wondered why people who suffer from high blood pressure are instructed to limit their salt intake? The reason

is that the more salt you take in, the more fluid must move from inside to outside the cell (osmotic thirst), and movement of fluid into the extracellular environment increases blood pressure.

Thirst Receptors

Although all cells in the body are subject to intracellular and extracellular water deficits, not all cells are capable of converting these deficits into thirst signals. Only a small percentage of the cells in the body have this capability. These highly specialized receptor cells, known as *thirst receptors*, are of two kinds: osmotic receptors and volemic receptors.

Osmotic Receptors

Experimental findings indicate the presence of osmotic receptors (cells selectively sensitive to intracellular deficits) in an area of the hypothalamus known as the *preoptic nucleus*. The research that has yielded these findings is of two types. In the first type, salt is injected directly into the preoptic nucleus. The fact that these injections provoke drinking behavior, whereas similar injections in other areas of the brain produce no such behavior, is strong evidence for the presence of osmotic receptors in this area of the hypothalamus (Blass & Epstein, 1971). In the second type of experiment, animals that have undergone lesions in the preoptic nucleus show no osmotic thirst; that is, they do not respond to intracellular fluid deficits, but they *do* respond to extracellular deficits. It is thus a reasonable conclusion that the preoptic nucleus contains only osmotic thirst receptors and that receptors for extracellular deficits—volemic receptors—are located elsewhere (Blass & Hanson, 1970).

Volemic Receptors

Just as the search for glucose receptors involved in food intake took us from the brain to the liver, so the search for volemic receptors takes us away from the brain as well. In an important series of experiments conducted by James Fitzsimons, receptors sensitive to volemic thirst were found in two places: the *vena cava*, a major vein connected to the heart, and the *kidneys* (Fitzsimons, 1971). These locations were determined after Fitzsimons, by decreasing blood flow to both areas (conditions normally produced when there is a deficit in extracellular fluid), was able to induce animals to drink excessively.

Again, why the overlap? Why *two* sets of volemic receptors? Nobody knows for certain, but the redundancy may well represent a defense mechanism. It has been found, for example, that when one set of receptors is out of commission—as in animals whose kidneys have been surgically removed—the other set continues to respond to extracellular deficits (Stricker, 1973).

Signaling the Brain

The presence of receptors sensitive to osmotic and volemic thirst represents only one aspect of the neural control of drinking behavior. The signals generated by these receptors must reach the brain. For osmotic receptors, this requirement does not pose much of a problem. These receptors, after all, are located *in* the brain (the preoptic nucleus), and thus communication poses no special logistical problems. But what of the volemic receptors in the vena cava and the kidneys? How do they communicate with the brain? This problem is much more complex and is not yet fully understood.

A likely messenger is the hormone known as *angiotensin II* (Epstein, Fitzsimons, & Rolls, 1970). Experiments indicate that extracellular fluid deficits stimulate the receptors in the kidneys to release this hormone, which is carried to the brain by the bloodstream and stimulates drinking. At least three areas of the brain, as shown in Figure 11.10, appear to be involved: the preoptic area and two areas that border on the ventricles, the subfornical organ and the organum vasculasum of the lamina terminalis (OVLT, for short). All these areas elicit drinking when injected with angiotensin II (Epstein, Fitzsimons, & Rolls, 1970; Simpson, Epstein, & Camardo, 1978; Simpson & Routtenberg, 1973).

But as simple and straightforward as this explanation appears, it is not without complications. The brain, you will recall, is protected from certain chemical substances by the so-called blood-brain barrier (see Chapter 3 for details), and angiotensin II happens to be one of these chemicals. The inability of angiotensin II to penetrate the brain poses no problem for the subfornical organ or the OVLT, which are two areas of the brain left relatively unprotected by the blood-brain barrier. But what of the preoptic area, which *is* protected by the blood-brain barrier? How does angiotensin II reach it?

Several theories have been advanced to answer this question. One view is that angiotensin II is taken up by the subfornical organ and then

Figure 11.10 *Brain Areas Involved in the Control of Drinking*
Two of the areas are located on the border of the ventricles, the subfornical organ above the third ventricle, the organum vasculasum of the lamina terminalis (OVLT) below the third ventricle.

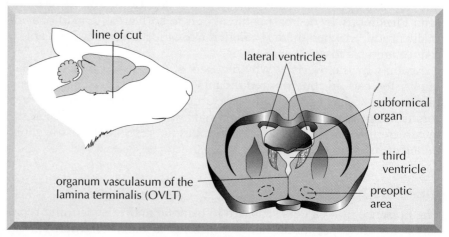

transported, via axonal transport, to the preoptic area. A second theory is that angiotensin II is manufactured in the preoptic area itself (in other words, angiotensin II is not only a hormone but a neurotransmitter as well) and thus does not have to cross the blood-brain barrier to stimulate the brain (Epstein, 1987). These, as well as other possible explanations, are currently under investigation.

As far as receptors in the vena cava are concerned, they communicate with the brain via neural impulses. The precise brain areas involved, however, remain to be determined.

REGULATING DRINKING BEHAVIOR

Despite the fact that osmotic and volemic thirsts are controlled by different signals and different receptors, both appear to be regulated by the same homeostatic principle. Deprivation of water produces a deficit of fluid in and around the cells, which triggers drinking behavior. When the normal balance of fluid is restored, an off signal stops the drinking behavior.

There is a problem, however, in attributing the off signal *exclusively* to restored balance of fluid in and around the cells. The problem is that drinking stops *before* the circulatory system has had an opportunity to absorb an appreciable amount of water and to convey the water to the osmotic and volemic receptors. There must therefore be a *speedy* off signal that can act quickly to shut off drinking long enough for the fluid off signals to take effect.

The Search for the Speedy Off Signal

Originally, scientists believed that the source of the speedy off signal was neural input from the mouth—a logical suspicion because one of the principal symptoms of thirst is a dry mouth. Studies by Alan Epstein and Philip Teitelbaum, however, show that water-deprived rats trained to press a lever in order to receive water injections directly into the stomach appear to regulate their water intake as effectively as normal rats do—a finding that indicates that the mouth does not play the *primary* role in the regulation of water intake (Epstein & Teitelbaum, 1962).

Here again we must be careful about drawing conclusions when eliminating a variable produces no visible effect on behavior. For the possibility always exists that compensating factors may mask the significance of the mouth. As it happens, the mouth may indeed play an important role in water regulation, particularly in stopping water intake. Evidence supporting this position has come from experiments in which animals are surgically prepared so that water taken into their mouths cannot reach their stomachs. The esophagus (the tube that connects the mouth with the stomach) is severed in the middle, and both cut ends are brought outside the body. When an animal surgically altered in this way drinks, water passes through the mouth and down the esophagus but never reaches the stomach.

Experiments of this nature have shown that, although water never reaches the stomach and never enters the bloodstream, animals are still able to regulate their water intake (Adolph, 1950). Do not misunderstand: regulation is not normal. The animals—known as *esophageal* animals—take in about four times more water than normal animals. But even though the water never passes beyond the esophagus, the animals *do* stop drinking. And stopping is not the result of simple fatigue. How do we know? If fatigue were the reason, we would expect the animals to drink the same amount of water no matter how thirsty they were. But experiments have shown that the greater their thirst—that is, the longer they are deprived—the more they drink (Blass & Hall, 1976). Apparently water passing through the mouth and esophagus satisfies thirst, though not completely, for the animals do drink four times as much as normal animals.

Stomach Factors

When we drink normally, water passes through the mouth, esophagus, and stomach, enters the small intestine, and is then absorbed by the bloodstream. We have just seen that water passing through the mouth and esophagus contributes to the off signal. But what happens when we move down the line and add the stomach to the chain? Does the off signal become more nearly normal?

In studies designed to examine this question, animals are surgically prepared so that water taken into their mouths passes through the esophagus and stomach but no farther (Blass & Hall, 1976; Hall, 1973). To accomplish this end a noose is placed around the pylorus, the tube that connects the stomach with the small intestine. When the noose is closed, it blocks the passage of water from the stomach to the intestine and prevents water from being absorbed by the bloodstream. When the animals are allowed to drink, they do *not* regulate their water intake normally. They improve—that is, they drink *less* than the esophageal animals—but they still drink more than normal animals do. Water entering the stomach improves the off signal, presumably a neural signal to the brain, but something is still missing.

A process of elimination leaves us with three potential sources of the off signal: the small intestine, the bloodstream, and the fluid balance in and around cells. The consensus is that the missing link is the fluid balance in and around cells.

Anticipatory Off Signal

The inability of esophageal and pyloric animals to regulate water intake normally is presumably caused by the fact that water never reaches their cells and thus never reaches the osmotic and volemic receptors. Work by Donald Novin, however, indicates that this assumption may be wrong—that water may, in fact, reach the cells of esophageal and pyloric animals (Novin, 1962).

By monitoring fluid movement in the hypothalamus following drinking, Novin has found that fluid returns to the inside of the cells almost as soon as water reaches the stomach of normal animals. It returns there, oddly enough, *before* water is absorbed by the blood and conveyed to the cells directly. What appears to happen is that the cells in the hypothalamus anticipate receiving water from the stomach and react as if they had already received it as soon as the water reaches the stomach. Thus water may enter cells in esophageal and pyloric animals even though it has not actually passed beyond the esophagus or stomach. The fact remains, though, that esophageal and pyloric animals drink abnormal amounts of water. Therefore, even if water enters their cells, the anticipatory effect apparently does not have the same impact as when water is actually carried to the cells by the bloodstream in normal animals.

Reconstructing the Circuit

In summary, as illustrated in Figure 11.11, there appear to be two speedy off signals, one from the mouth and one from the stomach. Each signal reaches the brain via neural impulses, and each holds off drinking long enough for fluid to enter the bloodstream, travel to the cells, and offset fluid deficits in the osmotic and volemic receptors.

You may have already noticed that there are some striking similarities between regulation of drinking behavior and regulation of eating behavior. Both behaviors involve cellular on and off signals. Both involve speedy neural off signals. Both involve receptors that lie outside the brain—the stomach and liver for eating, the kidneys and vena cava for drinking.

All told, the research into eating and drinking has added two important new dimensions to the picture of motivation we have presented in this chapter. First, the studies have reinforced the view that motivated behavior is the result of complex interactions among a variety of behavioral elements, each of which is mediated by different circuits in the brain and all of which are vital if behavior is to occur. Second, these studies indicate that the elements involved in the control of eating and drinking are so integrated that a disruption of any one of them is usually sufficient to disrupt the entire system. This characteristic of the eating and drinking circuits reflects a recurring theme throughout our exploration: every behavior is a manifestation of a number of behavioral elements. To seek a physiological basis for behavior, we are obliged to think not of single processes but of complex interactions.

SUMMARY

1. *The hypothalamus and eating behavior.* Research into eating behavior has focused primarily on two key questions: what are the signals that trigger and terminate eating behavior? And to what areas of the brain do these signals project? Early studies identified the lateral hypothalamus

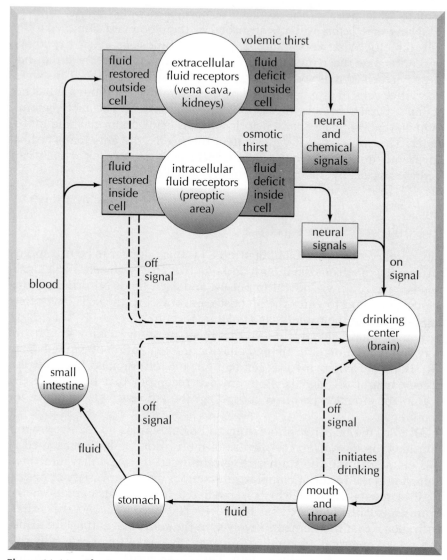

Figure 11.11 *The Sequence of Events Regulating Drinking*
Drinking is initiated when fluid levels are low either within the cells (osmotic thirst) or in the space surrounding the cells (volemic thirst). Drinking stops when fluid passes through the gastrointestinal tract and restores intracellular and extracellular levels to normal.

as the "hunger center"—the area in the brain that triggers eating behavior—and the ventromedial hypothalamus as the "satiation center"—the area in the brain that curbs eating behavior. The two areas, moreover, were thought to act in tandem. We know today that the relationship between the hypothalamus and eating behavior is a good deal more complex than was originally thought, but elements of the original theory have remained. Research into eating behavior has been guided by the premise that there are two signals: a speedy neural signal that can turn eating on or off, before a slower, metabolic signal takes effect.

2. *Cannon's theory and taste factors.* One of the earliest theories of eating behavior was proposed by Walter Cannon in 1910. Known as the local theory of motivation, Cannon's theory linked on and off eating behavior with local signals, that is with signals originating in areas of the body—the mouth and stomach, for instance—through which food passes before reaching the blood. Lending credence to this theory are studies showing that the eating behavior of laboratory animals is determined to some extent by taste and to some extent by stomach factors. Two stomach signals are involved—the volume of food entering the stomach and the caloric content of food. Each is signaled to the brain by a different vehicle—stomach distension via neural connections, calories via nonneural factors such as hormones.

3. *Blood as the vehicle.* John Davis and others have shown that when the blood of sated rats is transferred to the blood of hungry rats, the hungry rats behave as if they are no longer hungry—a discovery that makes a strong case for the presence in the blood of a signal that controls eating. Two properties of blood—glucose and fat—qualify as the signal, and each has been the focal point of its own theory.

4. *The glucostatic theory.* According to the glucostatic theory of feeding, originally proposed by Jean Mayer in the early 1950s, eating behavior is controlled primarily by the level of blood glucose in the body. When glucose levels drop below optimum, eating is triggered. When glucose levels rise above optimum, eating ceases. The theory in its original form doesn't account for the eating behavior of diabetics, who are in a constant state of hunger, even though their glucose levels in the blood are abnormally high. Mayer has since revised his original theory, suggesting that the glucose signal originates in the cells and not the blood. Current thinking implicates the liver as the organ in which eating-related glucose signals are detected and suggests further that it isn't glucose itself, but rather, the energy produced by glucose in the liver cells that is the actual signal.

5. *The lipostatic theory.* The fact that animals have been shown to regulate eating according to their weight has led to a theory, known as the lipostatic theory, that implicates body weight as a key eating signal. This theory draws much of its support from the work of Philip Teitelbaum, who has studied hyperphagia—a condition of overeating and obesity that results from lesions to the ventromedial hypothalamus. The eating patterns of hyperphagic animals suggest that body weight is the signal by which the ventromedial hypothalamus normally controls eating—a relationship that Teitelbaum has confirmed in several studies.

6. *Fat as the signal.* The suspicion that fat is the signal at the root of the lipostatic theory has been confirmed by Robert Liebelt, who removed fat tissue surgically from rats that had been made obese by lesions in the ventromedial hypothalamus and found that the obese animals continued to eat incessantly until their weight reached the original obese levels. Studies, however, have shown that even when ventromedial hypothalamic-lesioned rats are prevented from overeating, they still gain weight, suggesting the possibility that the two behaviors—overeating and gaining weight—are not necessarily related.

7. *Explaining the paradox.* The reason hypothalamic-lesioned animals gain weight even when they don't overeat would appear to be related to how the hypothalamus, when normal, controls the release of insulin by the pancreas. Because lesions produce excess insulin, the breakdown of fat is impeded, depriving the body of a major source of energy, explaining why lesioned animals overeat. And because nutrients not used for energy are stored as fat, an excess of insulin results in an increase in fat storage, explaining why lesioned rats accumulate weight even when they are given normal rations of food.

8. *The liver and eating behavior.* Both the glucostatic and lipostatic views of eating behavior may be correct, which is to say glucose and fat both act as signals and that they are monitored in the liver. Mark Friedman and Edward Stricker have proposed that the hunger signal is related to the difference between the energy produced by glucose and free fatty acids in the liver. In their view, when normal (nonlesioned) animals are deprived of food, fat breaks down, free fatty acids are produced, and the resulting energy deficit in the liver signals hunger. When normal animals are fed or injected with glucose, energy levels are restored in the liver and the liver signals satiation.

9. *Eating behavior and the lateral hypothalamus.* Electrical stimulation and lesion studies have established that the lateral hypothalamus and tracts that pass very close to it are central factors in controlling eating behavior, but determining how the lateral hypothalamus actually controls the behavior has proven to be a difficult challenge. The work of Eliot Valenstein suggests that the lateral hypothalamus, rather than triggering a specific motivational state, produces a general state of arousal that releases several well-established response patterns. Peter Morgane, exploring this possibility, has found that stimulating two different areas in the hypothalamus can produce different behaviors, suggesting that different circuits in the lateral hypothalamus may control two components of eating behavior: a motivational component and a response component. Neurotoxin-lesion studies lend credence to this view by implicating a neighboring tract—the nigrostriatal tract—as the circuit controlling arousal, and the lateral hypothalamus itself in controlling hunger.

10. *Human implications.* The eating habits of humans are influenced by a variety of factors, ranging from religious beliefs to health consciousness and social pressures, but regardless of external influences, the ultimate control of eating behavior in humans is *internal*. The one aspect of eating behavior that has generated the most interest is obesity, and one of the basic questions surrounding the research on obesity concerns the degree to which it is genetically determined.

11. *Obesity, genetics, and metabolism.* Evidence indicates that obesity in the human, at least in some cases, is genetically determined. The evidence also indicates that metabolism may be the key factor. In one study different pairs of twins gained different amounts of weight on a similar diet and exercise schedule, implicating differences in metabolism as the controlling factor. Within each pair, however, the twins tended to gain the same amount of weight suggesting that the metabolic efficiency (or lack thereof) is genetically determined.

12. *Specific hungers.* A series of studies involving a procedure known as cafeteria feeding has suggested the existence of neural circuits whose function is to determine not only *when* we eat and don't eat but *which* foods we eat. Rats given the opportunity to choose their diets cafeteria style make choices consistent with their dietary needs. The ability to select foods according to their nutrients is known as specific hungers, and several researchers have shown that the food choices animals make can be controlled by chemical injections in the brain. Whether this aspect of eating behavior is the result of built-in circuits or learning has not yet been determined, but recent data suggest that our food choices are shaped by both factors.

13. *How the body responds to a water deficit.* The neurobehavioral processes regulating water intake follow the same general sequence as those regulating food intake. A deficit in water is signaled to the brain, and responses are evoked to correct it. Two responses restore normality. One is, of course, drinking. The other is an internal response directed at reducing the amount of water lost in the urine. The internal response is governed by the hormone vasopressin, which is manufactured in the supraoptic nucleus of the hypothalamus and is stored in the posterior pituitary gland. A deficit in water triggers the release of vasopressin, which travels to the kidney. There it acts to decrease water loss in urine by increasing water reabsorption into the blood. A deficiency in vasopressin results in diabetes insipidus, a disorder characterized by excessive urination and thirst.

14. *Categorizing thirst.* Like eating, drinking has an on signal and an off signal. In the case of drinking, there appear to be two distinctly different on signals. Each signal is associated with a different type of thirst, osmotic or volemic. Osmotic thirst occurs when something we eat or drink creates a high concentration of salt outside the cells, causing water to move from inside to outside and creating a water deficit inside the cell. Volemic thirst arises when, through perspiration, we lose salt, creating a higher concentration of salt inside the cells, causing water to move from outside to inside, creating a water deficit outside the cell.

15. *The receptors underlying thirst.* Each type of thirst is under the control of different receptors. The preoptic area of the hypothalamus contains receptors for osmotic thirst; lesions in the preoptic area eliminate osmotic thirst. The vena cava and kidneys contain receptors for volemic thirst. Decreasing blood flow to the vena cava or kidneys, which simulates loss of extracellular fluid, induces drinking. The vena cava signals the brain via neural impulses, whereas the kidney releases a hormone known as angiotensin II that is thought to stimulate the subfornical organ, OVLT, and the preoptic area.

16. *Searching for the off signal.* It was originally suspected that the source of the speedy off signal for drinking behavior was neural input from the mouth, but studies indicate that the mouth plays only a secondary role in water intake and the three most likely sources of the off signal are the small intestine, the bloodstream, and fluid balance in and around cells. It now appears, in fact, that there may be two speedy off signals, one from the mouth and one from the stomach. Each signal reaches the brain via neural impulses, and each holds off drinking long enough for fluid to enter the bloodstream, travel to the cells, and offset fluid deficits in the osmotic and volemic receptors.

17. *Implications.* Viewed as a whole, research into eating and drinking has added two important new dimensions to our understanding of motivation. The first is that motivated behavior is the result of complex interactions among a variety of behavioral elements, each of which is mediated by different circuits in the brain and all of which are vital if behavior is to occur. The second is that the elements involved in the control of eating and drinking are so integrated that disruption of any one of them is sufficient to disrupt the entire system.

KEY TERMS

6-hydroxydopamine
angiotensin II
anorexia nervosa
anterior hypothalamus
antidiuretic
cafeteria feeding
cholecystokinin
diabetes insipidus
dynamic phase
extracellular fluid
free fatty acids
Fröhlich's syndrome
glucostatic theory
homeostasis
hyperphagia
intracellular fluid
intragastric feeding
kainic acid

lateral hypothalamus
lipostatic theory
local theory of motivation
neuropeptide Y
neurotoxins
nigrostriatal tract
off signal
on signal
osmotic thirst
paraventricular nucleus
perifornical area
polydipsia
posterior pituitary
preoptic nucleus
pylorus
sham feeding
specific hungers
static phase

stomach distension
supraoptic nuclei
thirst receptors
vasopressin
vena cava

ventral noradrenergic bundle
ventromedial hypothalamus
volemic receptors
volemic thirst

SUGGESTED READINGS

De Caro, G., Epstein, A. N. & Massi, M. *The Physiology of Thirst and Sodium Appetite*. New York: Plenum, 1986.

Le Magnen, J. *Neurobiology of Feeding and Nutrition*. San Diego: Academic Press, 1992.

Logue, A. W. *The Psychology of Eating and Drinking*. New York: W. H. Freeman, 1991.

Walsh, B. T. *Eating Disorders*. Washington, DC: American Psychiatric Press, 1988.

12

SLEEP

The motivation to sleep is a powerful one. We humans in fact spend more time sleeping—roughly 25 years of an average life—than we do engaging in any other single activity. Deprived of sleep for any period of time, most of us will be as driven to seek sleep as we are to seek food when we are hungry or water when we are thirsty. Yet despite the fact that we have an unrelenting need to sleep, nobody has been able to establish the specific physiological function it serves.

There are two general theories. One theory, known as the *restorative theory of sleep*, depicts sleep as a restorative mechanism—the means by which our bodies restore vital chemicals and substances that are depleted in daily activities. The second theory, known as the *evolutionary theory of sleep*, views sleep as mainly a vestige of our prehistoric past—important for our survival during the course of evolution but not important for our survival today.

There is evidence to support both theories, but in the case of the restorative theory the evidence is not as clear-cut. On the one hand, it has been reported that marathon runners sleep on average 1.5 hours longer than normal on the first two nights following a race, lending weight to the restorative theory (Shapiro et al., 1981). On the other hand, if sleep does indeed serve a restorative function, there should be a relationship between sleep deprivation and physiological deficits. Such is not the case. True, people who are deprived of sleep for any length of time become irritable and, according to several studies, lose their ability to concentrate on boring, repetitive tasks (Meddis, 1977). But the evidence to date shows that sleep deprivation has a surprisingly minor effect on most physiological functions such as blood pressure, heart rate, body temperature, and so forth (Horne, 1982). What's more, sleep deprivation appears to have little effect on our overall ability to reason and comprehend (Percival et al., 1983).

So, sleep may serve a restorative function—perhaps related to energy—but if it does, it may not be as vital to our survival as the restorative theory contends. Which brings us back to our original question: Why do we sleep? Why are we motivated to engage in a behavior—occupying roughly a third of our lives—which, on the surface, we could survive without?

According to the evolutionary theory of sleep, originally introduced by Wilse Webb (1975), our need to sleep is linked not to vital physiological functions but in fact is the result of evolution. In Webb's view sleep has evolved mainly as a protective device, a carryover from prehistoric times when an animal's chances for survival were enhanced by the ability to remain inactive during the hours of darkness, when the environment is most threatening. Lending credibility to this theory is the fact that hibernation patterns of certain animals coincide with those periods in their lives in which environmental conditions pose the gravest threat to survival. Humans of course have developed the means to survive even in widely divergent environments, but Webb contends that our nervous systems still bear the vestiges of behavioral patterns that were necessary long before such adaptability evolved.

Regardless of its purpose, sleep is a clearly important behavior for physiological psychologists to study, particularly in light of the millions of people whose lives are disrupted by their *inability* to sleep. Our exploration of the physiological basis of sleep will focus on several aspects of the subject. We will look first at some of the general physiological characteristics of sleep. Then we will examine the nature and the source of the physiological signals thought to control sleep, and, as the chapter draws to a close, we will look into the nature and causes of certain sleep disorders.

SLEEP DEFINED

Most people think of sleep as a unitary process: a single behavior that is the opposite of being awake. The picture is not quite that simple. Thanks to the invention of the electroencephalograph (EEG)—a machine that enables researchers to measure brain activity—it is possible to observe, measure, and analyze what happens in the brain while people sleep. Studies using the EEG show that brain-wave patterns of sleeping people undergo changes during various periods or stages of the sleeping experience (Carskadon & Dement, 1989; Kelly, 1991).

To understand these changes, you first have to know something about brain-wave patterns during waking periods. Most of the time when we are awake, our brains show a rapid pattern known as *beta waves* (see

Figure 12.1 *Sleep Patterns*
(a) EEG recordings from a human subject during wakefulness and four stages of sleep. (b) Time spent in slow-wave and paradoxical sleep (indicated by dark bars) during the course of a night. Note that as sleep progresses, time in slow-wave sleep decreases and time in paradoxical sleep increases.

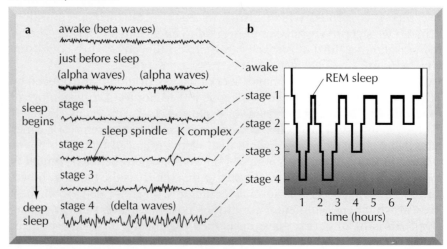

Figure 12.1*a*). The beta wave is a low-amplitude desynchronized wave varying between 13 and 30 cycles per second (Hz). The reason for this pattern is that during wakefulness (i.e., the state of being awake), cortical neurons are active in a random fashion, producing fluctuations in voltage so out of phase that they tend to cancel one another out.

There are also times during wakeful periods when brain waves slow down, producing a larger, slower, and more synchronized pattern known as *alpha waves*. Alpha waves are usually present when we are awake but relaxed.

Beyond Alpha Waves: Sleeping in Stages

The onset of what we normally think of as sleep produces a brain-wave pattern that is similar to—but slightly slower than—the low-amplitude, high-frequency wave that normally occurs when we're awake. As sleep grows deeper, the waves go from 9 to 12 Hz (alpha waves) to 1 to 4 Hz. The latter pattern consists of *delta waves*.

The transition from the alphalike patterns of relaxed wakefulness to the delta pattern of deep sleep is gradual and normally takes about 45 minutes. As you can see in Figure 12.1*a*, the transition consists of four stages, beginning with the onset of sleep (stage 1) and progressing to deep sleep (stage 4), with delta waves appearing periodically during stage 3 and dominating in stage 4. After deep sleep is reached, the brain-wave pattern reverses, gradually moving from stage 4 back to stage 2 over a similar time span.

Sleep taking place during stages 2, 3, and 4 is commonly referred to as *slow-wave sleep*, or *S sleep*. It is distinguished by the presence of not only slow waves but also, in stage 2, by two distinct wave forms: occasional bursts of 14- to 18-Hz waves known as *sleep spindles*, and a sharp high-amplitude spikelike wave known as the *K complex*. During slow-wave sleep skeletal muscles are relaxed and parasympathetic activity is dominant, heart rate and blood pressure decrease, while gastrointestinal activity increases.

Stage 4 Sleep: A Closer Look

The role stage 4 sleep plays in sleep in general varies on a number of levels (Kelly, 1991). Stage 4 sleep, for instance, is more prevalent in young children than in adults and, not surprisingly, is also the time in which growth-promoting hormone is secreted (Takahashi, 1979). As we grow older, stage 4 sleep not only declines but virtually disappears in many people by the age of 70. Stage 4 sleep is also the stage in which we are most likely to see the sleep abnormalities common among young children, such as bed wetting (enuresis) and sleepwalking (somnambulism—walking around with the eyes open and a blank stare, but with no later recollection). Finally, stage 4 is the stage that is most affected by physical fatigue; recall that marathon runners sleep on average 1.5 hours longer than normal on the first two nights following a race. Most of that extra time is spent in stage 4 sleep (Shapiro et al., 1981).

REM Sleep

If you were to observe an EEG machine recording neural activity during sleep, you would notice a dramatic change taking place in the brain-wave pattern approximately 90 minutes after the subject first goes to sleep. Suddenly the cortical activity enters an aroused, desynchronized state, the EEG pattern becoming far more rapid with a lesser amplitude. If you didn't know better, you would assume that the subject was awake, for this pattern is similar to the desynchronized beta-wave pattern that occurs during wake. Accompanying this desynchronized cortical arousal is movement of the eyeballs under the closed lids, as if the person were tracking a moving object.

This active stage of sleep has been referred to by different terms: *paradoxical* (because of its similarity to wake), *D* (for desynchrony of the brain waves) and, the most common term, *REM* (for *rapid eye movement*).

For most people REM sleep continues for about 10 minutes, then the slow-wave cycle resumes. A little less than an hour later, the REM pattern returns, lasting slightly longer than the first time. The slow-wave cycle then repeats itself. Thus, as Figure 12.1*b* shows, the pattern of slow-wave and REM sleep experienced by an average person during a typical night consists of several periods of each type of sleep. As the night progresses, the periods of slow-wave sleep gradually diminish (stage 4 and eventually stage 3 drop out) and the periods of REM sleep gradually increase. In general, slow-wave sleep in normal adults accounts for roughly 80 percent of the time we spend sleeping; REM sleep makes up the remaining 20 percent.

Differences between Slow-Wave and REM Sleep

No one knows as yet why sleeping behavior is characterized by the cycles we have just described. What we do know, however, is that most mammals go through similar cycles. We know, too, that there are significant differences in physiological and behavioral activity during each of the two main types of sleep: slow-wave and REM. Let us now look at some of these differences.

Dreaming

Although some dreaming occurs during slow-wave sleep (Dement, 1957), it is far more likely to occur during REM sleep. In studies conducted by Nathaniel Kleitman and his colleagues (Kleitman, 1963), most people awakened during REM sleep reported that they had been dreaming.

The fact that dreaming has been found to occur primarily during REM sleep has led to a change in thinking regarding dreaming itself. Long before the advent of the EEG, Sigmund Freud wrote extensively about dreaming, maintaining that dreams are the masked and censored representations of unconscious desires that are suppressed during wakefulness. But like many of the theories Freud proposed about the unconscious and the role it plays in controlling behavior, his view of dreaming has fallen out of favor among mainstream behavioral scientists.

Among the more influential theories that have been advanced in recent years to explain dreaming is the *activation-synthesis theory* proposed by Alan Hobson (1989). In Hobson's view, dreaming is triggered by the neural arousal that accompanies REM sleep. The actual dream itself—what the dream is about—is determined by two other factors: memories that are activated by the neural arousal, and the brain's attempt to make sense of those memories. Because the memories are not linked to any specific environmental stimuli, the resulting dream is often chaotic and disjointed. The only reason that dreams have some semblance of reality, in Hobson's view, is that the brain tries its best—with its limited resources—to make sense of the memories.

Autonomic Behavior

The two types of sleep are marked by different types of autonomic behavior (Dement and Mitler, 1974). During slow-wave sleep, heart rate and respiration tend to be much more regular than during REM sleep, and some studies suggest that the irregularities during REM sleep correspond to the contents of dreams: the more emotional the dreams, the more intense the autonomic signs. Changes also occur in the sex organs. Penile erections and increased vaginal blood flow occur more frequently during REM sleep than during slow-wave sleep, even though neither seems to be correlated with erotic dreams.

Muscle Tone

In contrast to the upper parts of the brain, particularly the cortex, which become more active during REM sleep than during slow-wave sleep, the skeletal muscles (with the exception of the muscles controlling the eyes, respiration, and the ossicles in the middle ear) go into a deep state of inhibition during REM sleep, producing a loss of muscle tone. In light of all the other active signs during REM sleep, muscle inhibition seems out of place, but animal research suggests that it may serve as an important safety device. The fact that the body turns limp during REM sleep may protect dreamers from physically acting out their dreams. Lesion work in cats lends support to this hypothesis, as we shall see later in the chapter.

SEARCHING FOR SLEEP SIGNALS

Although we are not sure why we sleep or why we sleep in cycles, it is generally agreed that the control of sleep, much like the control of eating and drinking, involves an on signal and an off signal. One reason we can make this assumption is that humans and most other animals appear to have built-in biological clocks that control sleeping and waking patterns on a remarkably rhythmic cycle (Richter, 1967). This cycle, which averages about 25 hours in humans, is called the *circadian rhythm*, from the

Latin words for "about" and "day." In humans the sleep-wake cycle is biphasic—that is the cycle dips twice: once in the late afternoon (which is when most of us become drowsy), and once again in the wee hours of the morning (around 4 A.M.) when sleepiness for most people reaches its peak.

In addition to the sleep-wake cycle, humans have over 100 different rhythms in their body. One of these rhythms is body temperature, which is highest during the day, usually in the late afternoon, and lowest at night around 4 A.M. Circadian rhythms in the human apply to a number of other bodily functions as well, including flow of urine, secretion of hormones, cell division, blood pressure, heart rate, and even time of childbirth, which is most likely to occur between 12 and 6 A.M. (Coleman, 1986; Moore-Ede, Czeisler, & Richardson, 1983).

Another aspect of the circadian rhythm is a change in mental alertness which may (or may not) account for the fact that a number of major industrial catastrophes traced to human error—the nuclear power plant accidents at Chernobyl, Russia, and Three Mile Island, Pennsylvania, and the poison gas accident at Union Carbide in Bhopal, India—occurred late at night around 4:00 A.M. (Coleman, 1986).

As you might expect, the cycle varies among species. Certain animals, mainly predators, tend to sleep during the day and search for food at night. Humans, on the other hand, tend to sleep at night and carry out the active parts of their lives in the daylight. But even among humans there are individual differences in sleep-wake cycles especially related to age: newborn infants take frequent naps, young children nap usually once a day, adults tend to go without naps, and elderly adults often return to taking naps (Kelly, 1991).

Circadian Rhythms: A Closer Look

Evidence for circadian rhythms comes from studies in which eliminating external time cues—referred to as *free-running conditions*—have little effect on the sleep-wake cycle of lower animals or humans. Animals kept in a laboratory environment in which lighting conditions are held constant (always light or darkness) show sleeping patterns consistent with circadian rhythms. The same pattern appears to hold true for humans. Studies in which people have volunteered to live for several weeks in underground caves indicate that constant-light conditions have little effect on circadian rhythms (Kleitman, 1963).

There is, however, one curious aspect about the behavior of people taking part in these studies. Without temporal cues (i.e., without cues that indicate changes in time) the biological clock in humans tends to run a little slower than normal, producing a day that lasts about 25 hours. At the end of each day subjects in constant-light conditions go to sleep approximately an hour later than they did the day before. Once time-related cues such as light and dark (referred to as *zeitgebers*— German for "time-giver") are introduced, the biological clock is reset and the subjects return to their normal 24-hour cycle.

The same principle holds true not only for sleep and wake but also for all bodily functions that exhibit a circadian rhythm. When temporal cues are absent, the cycles that govern temperature, blood pressure, and hormone secretions tend to fall into longer rhythms than normal; when the temporal cues are reinstated, each function returns to the 24-hour rhythm.

There are significant differences among the rhythms. Although the rhythms for bodily functions become longer when cues are removed, they do *not* become longer in the same way. The sleep-wake and temperature cycles, for instance, are closely synchronized when external cues are present, the onset of sleep occurring at the same time that body temperature drops (Johnson & Hastings, 1986). When the cues are removed, the two cycles uncouple—the term is *desynchronize*—prompting speculation that the cycles for the two functions are controlled by different mechanisms.

Biological versus Environmental "Clocks"

By now you're aware of what happens to your body in two situations relating to circadian rhythms: one, when temporal cues—that is, environmental cues that signal different times of the day—are present; and, two, when temporal cues are absent. In the first situation, your biological clock is *entrained*—that is, comes into phase with the environment. In the second situation, your biological clock simply "free runs."

Let us now look at what happens when temporal cues are present but out of phase with your biological clock—that is, when the environmental clock is operating according to one schedule but your biological clock is operating under a different schedule. This inconsistency arises, of course, whenever you go on a trip that takes you into different time zones. You fly from New York to San Francisco, for instance, and on the day you arrive begin to feel tired right about the time you normally go to bed, which might be, say, 11 P.M. New York time. The problem, though, is that at 11 P.M. New York time, it is still only 8 P.M. in San Francisco. You can force yourself to stay up, of course, and eventually your biological clock adjusts to the new schedule; but it usually takes a few days to adjust and, in the meantime, you don't feel as energetic or as sharp as you normally feel. The term used to describe the symptoms you experience until your biological clock readjusts is *jet lag*.

To a certain extent, too, nearly all of us experience a conflict of this nature every Monday morning, when the alarm clock goes off and we find it a little harder than normal to wake up. The reason: we usually change our sleep-wake patterns on the weekends, going to bed a little later than usual and waking up later than usual. Thus, our biological clocks get slightly out of sync with the environmental clock, producing the feeling sometimes referred to as the "Monday morning blues."

Night Work

As it happens, there is one large and varied group of people for whom sleep-related, jet-lag type symptoms are an almost constant problem—

people who, in effect, have to fight the Monday morning blues almost every day of the week. This group consists of the millions of people throughout the world—more than 7 million in the United States alone—who work at night and thus have to sleep during the day. Included in this group are factory workers, nurses, doctors, all-night radio personalities, and law enforcement officers, to name just a few.

Considering the fact that our bodies, given a sufficient amount of time, can readjust to travel patterns that involve shifts in the time zone, you might assume that people whose work and sleep schedules put them in direct conflict with their biological clocks would eventually adjust to the change as well. The facts, however, speak otherwise. True, most people who work at night and sleep by day are frequently able to function at what would appear to be normal or near normal levels, but sleep researchers have known since the beginning of the century that even after years of working the same hours, the bodies of people who work these schedules never make a complete physiological adjustment to the inverted schedule. Studies since then, moreover, have shown that people who adhere to work-at-night-sleep-by-day schedules for any length of time are more susceptible to a number of physical and psychological problems (cardiovascular disease, ulcers, hypertension, insomnia, and so forth) than people who work and sleep according to normal schedules (Moore-Ede, Czeisler, & Richardson, 1983). And as we noted earlier, numerous studies have shown that people who work at night are more prone to fatigue-related accidents than people who work by day.

It is obvious, of course, that if a complex, technologically oriented society like ours is going to function effectively, a certain percentage of the population needs to be working at night, and so it is no surprise that research has sought to find ways to minimize (if not totally eliminate) the behavioral consequences of these schedules. In the forefront of this work is the research of Charles Czeisler (Czeisler et al., 1990).

Czeisler's work is based on evidence indicating that the "human circadian pacemaker"—the mechanism, in his words, that controls our circadian rhythms—can come under the control of light-dark cycles (Czeisler et al., 1989). That being the case, he surmises that the circadian rhythm of people who work at night and sleep by day is in a state of constant conflict with the work schedule they are obliged to follow, thus contributing to the battery of problems that are common among people who work under inverted schedules. Czeisler thus proposes that if the light-dark cycle could somehow be rearranged to coincide with the work-inverted schedule, the conflict would be resolved and night workers would have an easier time of adjusting to the demands of their jobs.

Czeisler's results appear to bear out this hypothesis (Czeisler et al., 1990). In one experiment, for instance, he and his colleagues compared the behavior and the physiological responses of two groups of young men who volunteered to spend a week at a simulated "job" that obliged them to work all night and sleep during the day. The subjects in one group—the treatment group—were subjected to 8 hours of bright light during the evening (when, of course, they needed to stay awake) and to nearly complete darkness during the day (when, of course, they were trying to sleep). The subjects in the other group—the control group—were exposed to ordinary room light during the evening and were not shielded from light during the day.

Consistent with his hypothesis, Czeisler found that the group exposed to bright light adjusted more quickly and more successfully to the night-time work schedule than subjects in the other group. Within four days the subjects that were exposed to the bright light were finding it easier to sleep during the day than the subjects in the control group, and there were substantive differences, too, in their sleep-related physiological responses (body temperature, for instance) and in their on-the-job alertness.

Viewed as a whole, Czeisler's work reaffirms the suspicion that work performance differences (i.e., less productivity, more accidents, etc.) between night shift and day shift workers are rooted, in large part, in the light-related misalignment of the circadian rhythm and the sleep problems that result from this misalignment. His work also indicates that, to some extent at least, these problems can be minimized. Czeisler has been careful to point out, however, that his work is still in its early stages and that there are a number of important questions for which he has yet to find reasonable answers. He has yet to determine, for instance, which is more significant to circadian adaptation: bright light during night work or darkness during daylight sleep. And apart from differences in individual physiology, it appears that several variables—the intensity of the light, the duration of the light, and the precise timing of the light—can affect the adjustment process.

Czeisler's findings might also have practical implications for anyone whose travel schedules create an abrupt change in the time zone and in the sleep-wake cycle. The key to making the adjustment easier, it would appear, is to try your best to bring into synchrony as soon as possible the environmental cues—whether it is light or dark out—and your sleeping schedule, even if it means losing a few hours of sleep at first. Indeed a frequently reported finding is that people who travel west tend to experience fewer effects of jet lag than people traveling east (Nicholson et al., 1986). The reason, in the context of Czeisler's findings, is that you usually gain daylight when you travel west and that it is a little easier to stay awake (regardless of the time) when it is light out than when it is dark.

Circadian Rhythms: The Underlying Mechanism

If the sleep-wake cycle is indeed controlled by circadian rhythms—as appears to be the case—it is logical to ask ourselves, What controls the circadian rhythms? Presumably these rhythms are under the control of a built-in signal that originates in the brain or elsewhere in the body. But how and where is this signal produced, and what are the neural mechanisms that monitor it and regulate the sleep-wake cycle accordingly? We shall look into these questions next.

If an area of the brain is to qualify as an area that controls the circadian rhythm for the sleep-wake cycle, it must have three properties:

1. An intrinsic rhythm of its own to account for the rhythm produced without external temporal cues.
2. Input from the visual system to account for the fact that the circadian rhythm can be influenced by changes in illumination, the zeitgebers.
3. Output to the sleep-wake areas of the brain to account for the control that the rhythms exert over the sleep-wake cycle.

At least one area of the brain fits this description well. It is known as the *suprachiasmatic nucleus* and is located in the hypothalamus in an area immediately above the optic chiasm (see Figure 12.2). Implicating it as the source of the circadian rhythm for the sleep-wake cycle are the following observations:

1. *Intrinsic rhythm.* The suprachiasmatic nucleus has a rhythm of its own: the activity of its neurons exhibits a circadian rhythm even after the neurons have been detached surgically from the rest of the brain (Green & Gillette, 1982).

    The autoradiographs presented in Figure 12.3 illustrate the degree to which the rhythm is linked—the technical term is *entrained*—to light and dark cues but can continue on its own in the absence of external cues. The autoradiographs (obtained by monitoring the utilization of a radioactive form of glucose by neural cells) indicate which cells in the brain are the most active and presumably most

Figure 12.2 *Suprachiasmatic Nucleus*
The suprachiasmatic nucleus receives input from the visual system via the retinohypothalamic tract.

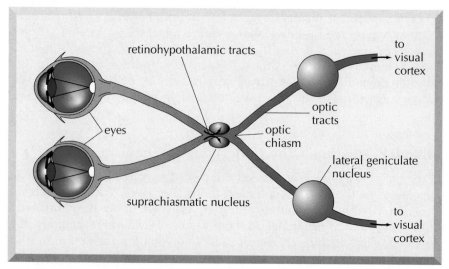

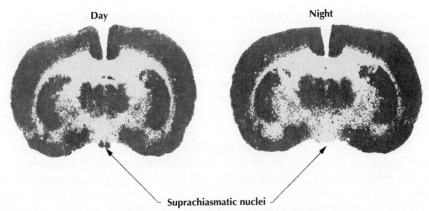

Day   Night

Suprachiasmatic nuclei

Figure 12.3 *Autoradiographs of the Suprachiasmatic Nucleus*
Autoradiographs of tissue taken from rats injected with radioactive labeled 2-deoxyglucose during the day or during the night. The increased metabolic activity in the suprachiasmatic nuclei during the day is indicated by the darker area at the base of the brain (see arrows).

involved in controlling a particular behavior (see Chapter 3 for details). When both light and dark cues are present, the neural cells in the suprachiasmatic nucleus increase activity in light and decrease activity in dark. In short, the rhythm is entrained. When light and dark cues are absent (not shown in Figure 12.3), the cells in the suprachiasmatic nucleus still increase and decrease activity, but now the rhythm is endogenous—that is, it occurs in the absence of the external cues—coinciding with what would ordinarily be the normal light and the normal dark periods (Schwartz & Gainer, 1977).

2. *Input from visual system.* The suprachiasmatic nucleus receives input (known as the *retinohypothalamic tract*) from the visual system. When these circuits are severed, the light and dark cues that normally reset the clock and restore the 24-hour interval, become in effect inoperative, although the animals retain the ability to see (Rusak, 1977). The reason: Vision itself is controlled by other circuits (the optic tracts) from the eye (see Figure 12.2), and when these circuits are severed, animals lose the ability to see, but they retain circadian rhythms to light-dark cues (Moore & Eichler, 1972).

3. *Output to sleep and wake areas.* Lesions in the suprachiasmatic nucleus abolish the periodicity of sleep and wake, but do not affect the animals' overall ability to sleep and wake (Turek, 1985; Moore, 1972). Sleep and wake behavior in the broad sense are apparently controlled by other areas in the brain—areas outside of, yet influenced by, signals from the suprachiasmatic nucleus. Determining where these areas are and the role they play in controlling sleep defines the aim of much of the current research on the neurobiology of sleep and wake today.

THE NEURAL MECHANISMS OF WAKEFULNESS

As we have just seen, most evidence today points to the suprachiasmatic nucleus as the source of the signal in the brain that controls sleep and wakefulness. But this has not always been the case, and it will help your understanding of sleep to see how our current views of sleep have evolved.

The original theory of what signals underlie sleep and wakefulness was based on the assumption that during sleep the nervous system is in a "fatigued" state and is thus less responsive to external sensory stimulation than when we are awake. The theory, in other words, linked sleep and wakefulness to the impact of sensory stimulation.

One of the first researchers to test this idea was Fredric Bremer, who in 1937 surgically interrupted sensory input to the brain of a cat and observed the resulting EEGs recorded from the cortex during sleeping and waking hours (Bremer, 1937). Bremer surgically prepared cats in one of two ways. In one preparation, he made a cut between the base of the brain stem and the spinal cord and thus eliminated all sensory input from below the neck. He called this preparation, illustrated in Figure 12.4*a*, the *encéphale isolé*. He found that even though all sensory input

Figure 12.4 *Bremer's Two Preparations*
In the *encéphale isolé* (a), a cut between the base of the brain stem and the spinal cord does not disturb sleep-wake patterns. In the *cerveau isolé* (b), a cut at the midbrain level abolishes waking activity. Although a comatose animal's eyes may remain open, the animal is unresponsive to its environment.

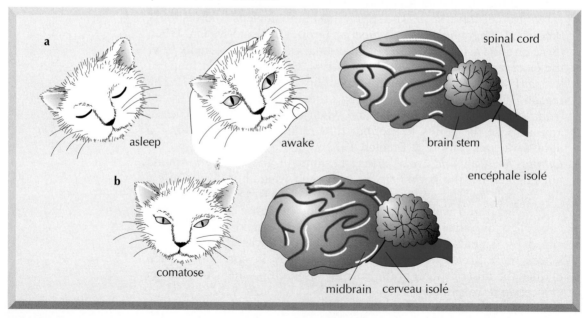

from below the neck was eliminated, EEG activity still exhibited normal sleep-wake patterns.

To confirm that the sensory input from the cranial nerves entering the brain stem above the cut was sufficient to sustain wakefulness, Bremer used a second surgical preparation. This time he made a cut between the upper part of the brain stem at the midbrain level and the rest of the brain. This procedure eliminated all sensory input to the cortex except that from the optic and olfactory nerves, both of which enter the brain above the midbrain cut. He called this preparation, illustrated in Figure 12.4b, the *cerveau isolé*.

Bremer discovered that the midbrain cut did indeed abolish waking activity. And because moving the cut from the base of the brain stem to the midbrain level prevented most sensory stimulation from reaching the cortex and put animals in a comatose state, Bremer concluded that the signal for wakefulness depends on sensory stimulation.

What Bremer didn't take into account, however, was the fact that a cut at the midbrain level has two effects: first, it reduces the amount of sensory stimulation that reaches the cortex; second, it severs connections between the other parts of the brain stem and the cortex. This second effect raises the possibility that detaching the brain stem from the upper part of the brain produces sleep for reasons other than the reduction of sensory input. It is possible, for instance, that the brain stem does something to the cortex to maintain wakefulness quite apart from acting as a conduit for sensory information from head and body to cortex.

These suspicions were confirmed by a number of experiments. Donald Lindsley and his colleagues, for instance, found that the brain stem per se (rather than its sensory connections) was the critical factor in the control of wakefulness (Lindsley, Bowden, & Magoun, 1949). Taking great care to leave the sensory pathways to the cortex intact, they lesioned an area within the brain stem, the *midbrain reticular formation*, and found that this lesion abolished wakefulness; the animals, in fact, went into permanent coma.

It thus appeared that Lindsley's procedure damaged a center for waking. Confirming this notion were the findings of Giuseppe Moruzzi and Horace Magoun, who reported that electrical stimulation delivered to the midbrain reticular formation was sufficient to wake a sleeping cat, whereas the same stimulation applied to other areas had no such arousing effect (Morruzi & Magoun, 1949). This finding ruled out the possibility that the stimulation acts simply as a general arouser.

To further validate the findings that sensory input is *not* critical to the sleep-wake cycle, Lindsley and his colleagues carefully eliminated sensory input to the cortex but left the reticular formation intact. Their findings: Despite the absence of sensory input, the animals went through the normal sleep-wake cycle.

The implications of these findings are twofold. First, sensory input does not appear to be necessary to maintain the sleep-wake cycle, although the precise nature of the signal remains something of a mystery. Thus it may be helpful for now to think of signals that are inherent in the activity of a particular area in the brain. All signs, as we've seen, point to the suprachiasmatic nucleus as one of those areas.

Second, it appears that wakefulness is controlled by the midbrain reticular formation and its circuits to the upper parts of the brain. When active, these circuits turn wakefulness on; when damaged, they turn wakefulness off.

THE NEURAL MECHANISMS OF SLEEP

If wakefulness is controlled by a waking center or circuits, what controls sleep?

Two theories have been proposed. One theory argues that sleep is a passive phenomenon resulting from the *absence* of stimuli, rather like the slowing of a car when you take your foot off of the accelerator. The other theory submits that sleep is an active phenomenon, like the slowing of a car when the brakes are applied. According to the passive view, sleep occurs when fatigue reduces activity in the waking center. According to the active theory, sleep is not merely a result of the absence of neural activity. Instead, like wakefulness, it is produced by the presence of activity in specific areas of the brain: when active these areas turn sleep on, when inactive they turn sleep off. Evidence favors the active theory.

The Early Studies

In 1959 Giuseppe Morruzi and his colleagues conducted a series of experiments that revolutionized the modern-day view of sleep (Magni et al., 1959). Working with cats, they found that injections of an anesthetic directly into areas in the upper sections of the brain stem (upper pons and midbrain reticular formation) put waking animals to sleep—a predictable finding. They also found, and this was the unexpected result, that injections of an anesthetic directly into areas in the lower sections of the brain stem (the lower pons and medulla) *awakened* sleeping animals. Their results suggested that sleep, like wake, depends on activity in specific areas of the brain. When that activity is turned off (in this case by an anesthetic), the animals awaken. Identifying those sleep areas—where they are located and how they work—has been the goal of much of the research on the neural basis of sleep conducted over the past 30 years.

Indeed, the most recent studies indicate not only that sleep is controlled by specific areas of the brain but also that the two types of sleep—slow-wave and REM—are controlled by different areas of the brain. But let us not overstate the case. Frustrating though it may be for researchers to admit, the fact of the matter is that we are less certain today about the specific areas of the brain that control slow-wave sleep and REM than we were 30 years ago.

In 1969 Michel Jouvet proposed a theory linking slow-wave and REM sleep to two areas in the brain stem, the raphe nuclei and locus coeruleus, and to two neurotransmitters, serotonin and norepinephrine, produced in those areas (Jouvet, 1969). Jouvet based his theory on what at the time appeared to be very compelling data—drug-induced deficits in serotonin disrupted slow-wave sleep, and drug-induced deficits in norepinephrine disrupted REM sleep.

Logical as this view may have seemed at the time, we now know that the picture is a good deal more complex. The elements of the original theory have remained—slow-wave and REM sleep are controlled by different areas of the brain stem—but the view of precisely what those areas are and how they control the two types of sleep has changed.

SEARCHING FOR SLEEP AREAS

One basic rule guides research seeking to identify sleep areas. For an area of the brain to qualify as a sleep area, it must meet at least one of the following requirements:

1. Stimulating the area should produce sleep.
2. Lesioning it should produce wake.
3. Recording from it should indicate that its activity increases with sleep and decreases with wake.

Several areas, presented in Figure 12.5, meet these criteria in one way or another. None, however, meets all three criteria without some qualification. We will now look more closely at each of the areas, beginning with the area involved in slow-wave sleep and then considering those areas involved in the control of REM sleep.

Slow-Wave Sleep: The Preoptic Area

Evidence for preoptic area involvement in slow-wave sleep comes from both lesion and stimulation studies. Lesions made in the preoptic area, a nucleus in the basal forebrain located near the hypothalamus, produce insomnia in laboratory animals. Stimulating the same area, either electrically or with drugs that increase the neurotransmitter serotonin, induces slow-wave sleep. Both results are consistent with the view that the preoptic area is a slow-wave sleep area (McGinty & Sterman, 1968; Sterman & Clemente, 1962).

The picture becomes murkier, however, when viewed in the context of recording work. If the preoptic area is a sleep area, it should behave like a sleep area. That is, it should increase activity during sleep, and it should decrease activity during wake. Recording studies do not reflect this pattern, and there is no clear explanation. One possibility—and it is

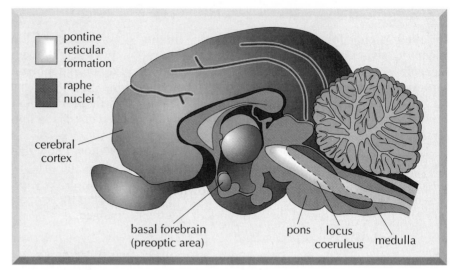

Figure 12.5   Sleep Areas
Areas in the cat brain that play a role in producing sleep.

a possibility that always exists when one fails to observe an effect—is that the preoptic area is indeed active during slow-wave sleep, but the recording technique is simply not sensitive enough to detect the activity.

REM Sleep

REM sleep, as we've seen, consists of two distinct features: cortical arousal (also known as cortical desynchrony), and motor paralysis in which muscle tone is lost in most skeletal muscles throughout the body. Each feature of REM sleep appears to be under the control of different areas of the brain.

Cortical Arousal

Three areas of the brain, shown in Figure 12.5, have been implicated in the control of cortical arousal during REM sleep: the raphe nuclei, the locus coeruleus, and the pontine reticular formation. Alan Hobson and his colleagues have proposed a theory to account for how these areas interact to produce cortical arousal (Hobson, 1989).

The key assumption in Hobson's theory is that the pontine reticular formation, via its diffuse connections to the cortex, produces cortical arousal, and that the raphe nuclei and locus coeruleus in turn "control" the pontine reticular formation. "Control" in this case is in need of elaboration. During wake and during slow-wave sleep, the control imposed by the raphe nuclei and locus coeruleus over the pontine reticular formation is *inhibitory*. During REM sleep, inhibition stops, activity in the pontine reticular formation is released, neurons connecting the pontine reticular formation to the cortex transmit neural activity unchecked, and cortical arousal is produced.

Hobson bases this view on recording studies in cats during slow-wave and REM sleep (Hobson, 1989). He and his colleagues have found the kind of "seesaw" effect in neural activity that you would expect to find if the locus coeruleus and raphe nuclei imposed inhibitory control over the pontine reticular formation. During slow-wave sleep, neurons in the raphe nuclei and locus coeruleus are active, while neurons in the pontine reticular formation are inactive—evidence for inhibition. Conversely, during REM sleep neurons in the raphe nuclei and locus coeruleus are inactive, while neurons in the pontine reticular formation become active—evidence for release of inhibition (Hobson, McCarley, & Wyzinski, 1975; Hobson, 1977).

All of this leads of course to the following question: What gives the raphe nuclei and locus coeruleus their inhibitory capacity and what gives the pontine reticular formation its excitatory capacity? The answer is their chemistry. The raphe nuclei and locus coeruleus (when active) release serotonin and norepinephrine, respectively, and the effect of the neurotransmitters is inhibitory. The pontine reticular formation (when active) releases acetylcholine, and its effect is excitatory.

Evidence for the chemistry comes from drug work. Drugs that increase serotonin (Wyatt, 1972) or norepinephrine (Dunleavy et al., 1972), the presumed inhibitors, decrease REM sleep. Drugs that decrease the two neurotransmitters increase REM sleep (Vaughan, Wyatt, & Green, 1972). The same pattern holds for acetylcholine, the excitator, but in the opposite direction. Drugs that increase acetylcholine increase REM sleep; drugs that decrease acetylcholine decrease REM sleep (Qualtrochi et al., 1989).

Motor Paralysis

REM sleep is marked not only by cortical arousal but also by motor paralysis. The locus coeruleus is involved in the control of both.

Recording and drug work, as we've just seen, show that the locus coeruleus (along with the raphe nuclei and pontine reticular formation) is involved in cortical arousal. Lesion work on cats, on the other hand, indicates that the locus coeruleus is also involved in producing motor paralysis, and the lesion effects are rather dramatic. The motor paralysis normally seen during REM sleep is abolished, and cats subjected to the lesions exhibit a variety of behaviors, such as attacking, hissing, grooming, and flight, that are normally held in check during REM sleep (Jouvet & Delorme, 1965).

To understand how the locus coeruleus can control both cortical arousal and motor paralysis during REM sleep, we need to take a closer look at the anatomy and physiology of the locus coeruleus. As you can see in Figure 12.6, it consists of two sections, rostral (upper) and caudal (lower).

The rostral section gives rise to tracts that ascend to and inhibit the pontine reticular formation. These are the tracts that become inactive during REM sleep, release activity in the pontine reticular formation, and produce cortical arousal. The caudal section of the locus coeruleus

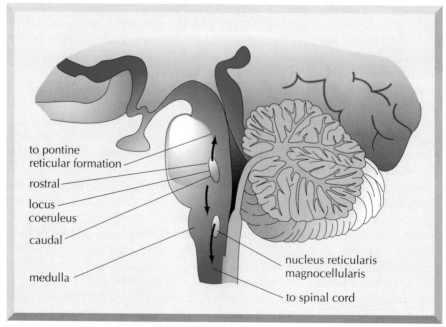

to pontine reticular formation

rostral

locus coeruleus

caudal

medulla

nucleus reticularis magnocellularis

to spinal cord

Figure 12.6 *Arousal and Inhibition*
The neural circuits originating in the locus coeruleus involved in producing cortical arousal (rostral) and motor inhibition (caudal).

gives rise to tracts that descend to the medulla (specifically, the nucleus reticularis magnocellularis). There they form synapses with neurons that travel to and inhibit activity in the spinal cord, thus producing motor paralysis (Kanamori, Sakai, & Jouvet, 1980).

Both tracts, it is worth emphasizing, are inhibitory. The rostral tract directly inhibits the pontine reticular formation, and the caudal tract indirectly inhibits the spinal cord via circuits originating in the medulla. There is, however, a crucial difference between the two. During REM sleep the ascending rostral tract becomes *inactive*, releasing the pontine reticular formation to produce arousal, and at the same time, the descending caudal tract becomes *active*, inhibiting the spinal cord and producing motor paralysis (Sakai, 1980).

This difference between the rostral and caudal sections of the locus coeruleus—the simultaneous decrease and increase in activity—explains how the locus coeruleus can govern two seemingly opposing responses: how it can arouse the cortex (via the pontine reticular formation) at the same time that it inhibits the spinal cord (via the nucleus reticularis magnocellularis).

Reflections on the Circuit

Sleep is an active process, and the stages of sleep, slow-wave and REM, are controlled by different areas of the brain and different neurochemical systems. It would be misleading to suggest, however, that this picture of slow-wave and REM sleep is complete. At every level of the analysis—from the signals that turn sleep on and off to the brain areas and the brain chemistry that underlie slow-wave and REM sleep—we are faced with nettlesome questions and we are introduced to other factors that play at least some role in the behavior. Let us now consider these other factors.

Factor S as a Sleep Signal

In experiments involving sleep-deprived goats, John Pappenheimer and his colleagues found that sleep can be affected by a chemical found in cerebrospinal fluid. The chemical is known as Factor S, and Pappenheimer has shown that when Factor S is extracted from sleep-deprived goats and injected into normal animals, it increases the duration of slow-wave sleep but not that of REM sleep (Pappenheimer et al., 1975).

The Nucleus of the Solitary Tract as a Slow-Wave Area

Although the preoptic area, from all indications, is one of the most likely sources of slow-wave sleep, other areas—in particular, the nucleus of the solitary tract, for one—may also fit into the picture. Like the preoptic area, the nucleus of the solitary tract when stimulated will produce sleep. Lesions in this nucleus, however, do not produce wakefulness (Magnes, Moruzzi, & Pompeiano, 1961).

The Pontine Reticular Formation: A Reappraisal

The case for the pontine reticular formation as the chief source of REM sleep may be overstated. The work of Jerome Siegel and Dennis McGinty (1977) shows that activity in the pontine reticular formation not only increases during REM sleep but also increases during wake and appears to correlate closely with motor behavior. This observation raises the possibility that the increase in activity in the pontine reticular formation seen during REM sleep is not related to cortical arousal, as Hobson contends, but to the motor activity (such as the rapid eye movements and rapid breathing) that occurs during REM sleep.

The Interaction of Sleep Circuitry: A Question

If it is true that the preoptic area controls slow-wave sleep and that the raphe nuclei, locus coeruleus, and pontine reticular formation are involved in producing REM sleep, we still need to ask ourselves how everything fits together. What is the coordinating mechanism? And what ensures that the components of REM sleep (e.g., dreaming and motor paralysis) do not spill into wake?

We raise these questions not to confuse the issue but simply to caution you against jumping to specific conclusions about sleep and its relationship to the brain. As much as we have learned in recent years about the physiological basis of sleep, numerous problems need to be worked out before the sleep-wake cycle is fully understood. We will now look at what may be the most enigmatic of these problems: the function served by REM sleep.

THE NEED FOR REM SLEEP

Our need for sleep itself seems to be paralleled by our need for REM sleep. When human subjects in sleeping experiments are awakened night after night as soon as EEG readings show them slipping into REM sleep, they become irritable and confused (Dement, 1960). When finally left alone and allowed to sleep normally, the subjects behave as you might expect they would if they had a need for REM sleep: they make up for the deficit and show an abnormal amount of REM sleep, as much as 60 percent more than usual. They then finally return to normal. This phenomenon of compensating for lost REM sleep is known as *REM rebound*.

Why is REM rebound necessary? What purpose does REM sleep serve? At this point, we can only speculate. Among the theories that have been advanced, one of the more influential ones centers on neural development.

REM Sleep and Neural Development

Among the more intriguing aspects of sleep behavior is the fact that infants spend much more of their sleeping hours in REM sleep than adults do. Particularly intriguing are the sleep patterns of premature infants. Evidence indicates that the younger the infant, the greater the need for REM. In infants born 10 weeks premature REM sleep consumes as much as 80 percent of sleep time, whereas the percentage of REM sleep in infants born 2 to 4 weeks premature drops to 60 to 65 percent of sleep time. A normal 2-year-old exhibits REM sleep roughly 30 to 35 percent of sleep time, and a young adult exhibits REM 20 to 25 percent of sleep time (Kelly, 1991).

Because increased REM sleep in infants coincides with developmental changes in the nervous system, Howard Roffwarg and his colleagues have speculated that it may be related to neural growth and development (Roffwarg, Muzio, & Dement, 1963). There is evidence that sensory stimulation from the external environment influences neural growth during maturation. David Krech and his colleagues (Rosenzweig et al., 1962) have shown that rats reared in an enriched sensory environment have larger brains than those reared in an impoverished sensory environment. Possibly, then, REM sleep in Roffwarg's view, is a form of stimulation that serves to promote growth of the brain during its early development. The function of REM sleep in adults remains unknown, although there is some evidence that it may play a role in memory processing (Karni et al., 1994) (see Chapter 17 for details).

Just about everybody has trouble sleeping on occasion. Worry, excitement, overeating, pain, unfamiliar surroundings—any number of factors can interfere with sleep. For some people, however, sleep problems are more than merely an occasional inconvenience. They are chronic. And, given the behavioral consequences that sleeplessness can produce, people who suffer from such problems are susceptible to a variety of behavioral disorders. Our interest here is in the two principal sleep disorders: insomnia and narcolepsy.

Insomnia

An estimated one out of five people suffer from insomnia—the inability to sleep—at some time in their lives. The insomnia we refer to here goes well beyond having trouble falling asleep for one or two nights. It refers instead to a general pattern of sleeplessness. The widespread nature of the condition is apparent from the public demand for prescription and over-the-counter sleeping pills.

Logic leads us to assume that insomnia is rooted in damaged sleep circuits, but we have no real basis for this assumption. Indeed, we know very little about the condition, and what little we know indicates that underactive sleep circuits are *not* the cause. It is possible in fact that in some cases the brain may not even be involved in insomnia.

Among the many problems facing researchers who study insomnia is the fact that the condition takes a number of forms. Some insomniacs fall asleep easily enough but dream that they are awake, and when they awaken, they feel the same grogginess they would have felt had they in fact spent a sleepless night (Hartmann, 1974). Still other insomniacs suffer from a problem known as *sleep apnea* (Dement & Villablanca, 1974). Shortly after they fall asleep, they suddenly stop breathing and are forced to gasp for air. Most attacks are mild, and the person usually does not wake up. In rare cases, however, people suffering from this frightening condition wake about every 60 seconds (roughly 500 times a night) to take a breath. In some instances, they have no memory of the attacks. Because the time they spend asleep is extended by the frequent awakenings, they actually complain of too much sleep. Others, roughly one-third, are aware of the episodes and complain of insomnia (Sewitch, 1984; Sewitch, 1987).

Sleep Apnea: A Closer Look
Two factors have been implicated in sleep apnea. One relates to the respiratory center, which, during normal sleep, monitors and adjusts oxygen levels in the blood. The respiratory center in the brains of some insomniacs who suffer from sleep apnea does not function properly, which explains why they keep waking up (Mendelson, 1987).

In other insomniacs who suffer from sleep apnea, the problem is related to the overrelaxation of throat muscles at the onset of sleep. Work by William Dement shows that approximately 60 seconds after this over-relaxation occurs, the sleep apnea victim wakes up, the muscle tone returns, and the person takes a few choking gasps of air before falling asleep again, only to have the cycle repeat itself (Dement & Villablanca, 1974).

Dement's discovery would explain why people who suffer from sleep apnea often snore very loudly. It would also explain why a surgical procedure known as a *tracheotomy* (i.e., putting a permanent hole in the trachea so that the air to the lungs is not blocked during sleep) has proven effective in the treatment of some insomniacs who suffer from sleep apnea.

Sudden Infant Death Syndrome

Sleep apnea has been implicated in the disorder known as *sudden infant death syndrome*, or crib death. Approximately 7000 infants die (annually in the United States) mysteriously in their cribs, without any apparent sign of illness, and some researchers now believe that these infants may lack the neural development to respond when oxygen levels in their blood drop during sleep (Zollar, 1993). Rather than waking and gasping for air as adult insomniacs do, they die of suffocation.

Insomnia and Sleep Medications

One of the ways in which many insomniacs (particularly those who are excessively anxious) try to cope with their condition is to take sleep medications, such as barbiturates. Such medications are undoubtedly capable of inducing sleep, but an increasing number of studies suggest that the sleep they produce is not normal. Most barbiturates, including the most commonly used, suppress REM sleep at first. With repeated use, however, REM sleep reappears, albeit with some differences, especially a loss in the vividness of dreams (Oswald, 1968). When the medications are discontinued, there is a so-called rebound effect. That is, REM sleep and accompanying nightmares return with such intensity that the person is often forced to resume medication simply to avoid these frightening experiences.

Benzodiazepines, most notably flurazepam and triazolam, have fewer side effects and have thus become the drugs of choice in treating insomnia (Mendelson et al., 1982). The problem with these drugs, however, is that they achieve their effect not by increasing the amount of time people sleep—in fact they actually suppress stage 4 sleep—but rather by increasing the quality of sleep: people seem to experience fewer spontaneous awakenings.

Benzodiazepines, because they suppress stage 4 sleep, have also been used effectively to treat a sleep abnormality in children known as *night terrors*. Night terrors occur during stage 4 sleep and are distinguished by their sheer intensity—a terrorized child may sit up in bed screaming, perspiring, breathing rapidly, and staring at some imaginary image. The episode may last for 1 or 2 minutes, and the next morning there is no recollection (Kelly, 1991). (See Chapter 5 for details of how benzodiazepines act in the synapse.)

Narcolepsy

Most of us take for granted that sleep occurs gradually. We feel drowsy. We get ready for bed. We lie down. We fall asleep. A feeling of drowsiness almost always precedes sleep.

But what if the feeling of drowsiness did not occur—or what if drowsiness occurred with such intensity that we could not fight it off—and we simply fell asleep without any warning regardless of where we were or what we were doing? A surprisingly high number of people, perhaps as many as 3 in every 1000, suffer from this very problem (Webb, 1975). It is known as *narcolepsy*.

Narcolepsy can best be described as an "attack" of sleep. Suddenly, in the midst of such routine activities as eating a meal, driving a car, or standing in front of a group of people talking, a narcoleptic will be seized by an overwhelming need to sleep and will remain asleep for anywhere from 5 minutes to $\frac{1}{2}$ hour.

Apart from these sudden attacks of sleep, narcoleptics are also subject to brief episodes of muscle weakness or paralysis that are usually elicited by a strong emotional experience and that occur with such suddenness that the stricken person often simply crumbles to the ground. These attacks, known as *cataplexy*, are *not* accompanied by sleep but nonetheless are thought to be related to a sleep component—namely, the motor inhibition that normally occurs during REM sleep (Dement & Villablanca, 1974). For some reason as yet unknown, the narcoleptic sometimes experiences this inhibition while still awake.

Narcoleptics suffer from yet two other symptoms, both of which, however, occur much less frequently than the sleep attacks and cataplexy. Occasionally, during the normal transition period between wakefulness and sleep, a narcoleptic becomes briefly paralyzed and remains so for several seconds. Occasionally, too, at the onset of sleep narcoleptics experience unusually vivid dreams known as *hypnagogic hallucinations*.

The causes of narcolepsy are unknown. At one time many researchers believed it to be closely associated with epilepsy, but EEG findings indicate no such relationship. There is evidence, however, that narcolepsy tends to run in families and therefore may have a strong genetic component (Dement & Villablanca, 1974).

Most of what we know about narcolepsy comes from drug and EEG research. Several studies have indicated a strong link between narcoleptic attacks and REM sleep (Kruyger, Roth, & Dement, 1989). Drugs that inhibit REM sleep—e.g., amphetamine and imipramine,—are also effective in treating narcolepsy, prompting some researchers to speculate that narcolepsy is the result of REM sleep spilling into wakefulness. And EEG studies indicate that narcoleptics show REM sleep immediately upon falling asleep; in contrast, the onset of REM sleep in normal people takes roughly 90 minutes. This abrupt entry into REM sleep would account for the sleep paralysis (motor inhibition) and hypnagogic hallucinations (vivid dreams) that narcoleptics occasionally show at the onset of sleep. The narcoleptic thus appears to suffer from a neural dysfunction that causes "premature" and "unpredictable" REM sleep. What this dysfunction is and why it occurs remain to be determined.

But if there is no cure as yet for narcolepsy, there are at least a number of therapies now available that enable narcoleptics to live more safely with their affliction. There are now drugs available that in some cases can reduce the number and the severity of narcoleptic attacks (Honda & Juji, 1988; Billiar & Seignalet, 1985). Narcoleptics are also being trained to recognize the subtle but specific sensation that nearly always precedes an attack. In this way, at least, they can remove themselves from a potentially dangerous situation (pull over to the side of the road if they are driving, for instance) before the attack strikes. Finally, many narcoleptics undergo therapy whose purpose is to minimize the shattering impact that narcoleptic attacks can have on someone's personality. The message behind the therapy is similar to that behind the therapy given to epileptics, namely, that narcoleptics are not "crazy" but simply suffer from a physiological condition that can be controlled.

SUMMARY

1. *Why we sleep.* Despite the fact that most animals have an unrelenting need to sleep, nobody has been able to establish the specific physiological function sleep actually serves. There are two general theories. One theory, the restorative theory of sleep, depicts sleep as a restorative mechanism. The second theory, known as the evolutionary theory of sleep, views sleep as mainly a vestige of our prehistoric past—important for our survival during the course of evolution but not important for our survival today. There is evidence to support both theories, but evidence for the restorative theory is more problematic. The main reason is that sleep deprivation appears to have little effect on most physiological functions and little effect on the overall ability to reason and comprehend.

2. *The nature of sleep.* There are several stages of sleep, each characterized by distinctive EEG activity. The three stages following the onset of sleep—collectively known as slow-wave sleep—are characterized by two distinct wave forms: occasional bursts of 14- to 18-Hz waves, known as sleep spindles, and a sharp high-amplitude spikelike wave, known as the K complex. After deep sleep is reached, the brain-wave pattern reverses, gradually moving from stage 4 back to stage 2 over a similar time span.

3. *REM sleep.* The stage of sleep known as REM sleep (sometimes referred to as paradoxical sleep) occurs periodically during a typical night's sleep. It starts 90 minutes after most people fall asleep, lasts for about 10 minutes, reappears for a slightly longer time frame after a period of slow-wave sleep, disappears again and so forth until the person wakes. During REM sleep cortical activity enters an aroused, desynchronized state, and the EEG pattern becomes far more rapid with less amplitude. Most dreaming takes place during REM sleep, and one theory of dreaming links dreams to the neural arousal that accompanies REM sleep. Among the other differences that distinguish slow-wave sleep from REM sleep are: (1) heart rate and respiration tend to be much more irregular during REM sleep; (2) sex organs are more active; (3) the skeletal muscles—with the exception of the muscles controlling the eyes, respiration, and the ossicles in the middle ear—lose muscle tone.

4. *How sleep is controlled.* Most humans and other animals appear to have built-in biological clocks that control sleeping and waking patterns on a remarkably rhythmic cycle. This cycle is called the circadian rhythm. The cycle varies among species. Most predators tend to sleep during the day and search for food at night. Humans tend to sleep at night and to carry out the active parts of their lives in the daylight. Numerous studies involving both animals and humans have confirmed the existence of circadian rhythms, and recent experimental work has implicated an area of the hypothalamus known as the suprachiasmatic nucleus as the source.

5. *Signals for sleep and wakefulness.* The original theory of what signals underlie sleep and wakefulness pointed to sensory stimulation as the source. Studies that seemed to confirm this hypothesis were carried out in the late 1930s by Fredric Bremer, but were called into question several years later when Donald Lindsley identified the brain stem per se (rather than its sensory connections) as the critical factor in the control of wakefulness. Lindsley's work indicated that wakefulness is controlled by the midbrain reticular formation and its circuits to the upper parts of the brain.

6. *The neural basis of sleep.* Two general theories have been proposed to explain the physiological basis of sleep. The passive theory argues that sleep occurs when the waking center is fatigued. The active theory argues that the waking center is actively turned off by a separate sleep center. Evidence favors the active theory of sleep. Indeed the most recent studies indicate that sleep is not only controlled by specific areas of the brain but that the two types of sleep—slow-wave and REM—are controlled by different areas of the brain.

7. *Identifying sleep areas.* Several areas of the brain loom as likely candidates for sleep control involvement. The preoptic area has been linked to slow-wave sleep through a series of lesion and stimulation studies indicating that lesions to this area produce insomnia and stimulation produces slow-wave sleep. Three areas in the brain stem—the raphe nuclei, the locus coeruleus, and the pontine reticular formation—have been implicated in the control of cortical arousal during REM sleep. Alan Hobson has proposed a model to account for how these areas interact to produce cortical arousal. The model draws support from a number of studies that show, among other things, that drugs that affect neurotransmitter activity in these areas have a direct effect on REM sleep.

8. *The need for REM sleep.* Although the function of REM sleep in adults is a mystery, humans apparently have a strong need for it. When human subjects in sleep studies are awakened night after night as soon as they enter into REM sleep, they become irritable and confused. And when they are finally allowed to sleep normally, their EEG readings show an abnormal amount of REM sleep. These findings, coupled with the fact that infants spend much more of their time in REM sleep than adults (even more so among premature infants), have led Howard Roffwarg to speculate that REM sleep may be related to stimulation of neural growth and development.

9. *Insomnia.* Insomnia—a chronic inability to sleep—is a common problem that takes a number of forms. In one type of insomnia, known as sleep apnea, people stop breathing as soon as they fall asleep and immediately wake up gasping for air. The causes of sleep apnea are not yet fully understood, but the respiratory system is clearly involved to some extent. Sleep apnea has been suggested as a factor in the disorder known as sudden infant death syndrome, or crib death.

10. *Sleep medications.* The most common sleep medications—barbiturates in particular—induce sleep but not necessarily normal sleep. Initially they suppress REM sleep, but when the medications are taken repeatedly, the REM sleep reappears, with a loss in the vividness of dreams. One problem with these medications is that when they are discontinued, people sometimes experience horrifying nightmares. Side effects are less pronounced with the category of sleep medications known as benzodiazepines, which achieve their effect not by increasing the amount of time people sleep—in fact they actually suppress stage 4 sleep—but rather by increasing the quality of sleep.

11. *Narcolepsy.* Narcoleptics are people who, in the midst of their normal daily activities, experience an overwhelming need to sleep. Narcoleptics are also subject to brief episodes of muscle weakness or paralysis, known as cataplexy. Narcoleptic attacks are elicited by a strong emotional experience and occur with such suddenness that the stricken person will often simply crumble to the ground. The causes of narcolepsy are unknown, but some studies suggest a strong link between narcoleptic attacks and the abnormal onset of REM sleep.

KEY TERMS

activation-synthesis theory
alpha waves
autoradiographs
beta waves
cataplexy
cerveau isolé
circadian rhythm
delta waves
electroencephalograph
encéphale isolé
evolutionary theory of sleep
Factor S

flurazepam
free-running conditions
hypnagogic hallucinations
K complex
locus coeruleus
midbrain reticular formation
narcolepsy
night terrors
nucleus of the solitary tract
nucleus reticularis
  magnocellularis
paradoxical sleep

pontine reticular formation
REM rebound
REM sleep
restorative theory of sleep
retinohypothalamic tract
S sleep
serotonin

sleep apnea
sleep spindles
slow-wave sleep
suprachiasmatic nucleus
tracheotomy
triazolam
zeitgebers

SUGGESTED READINGS

Hastings, J. W., Rusack, B., & Boulos, Z. "Circadian Rhythms: The Physiology of Biological Timing." In Prosser, D. L. (Ed.), *Neural and Integrative Animal Physiology, Comparative Animal Physiology*, 4th ed. New York: Wiley-Liss, 1991.

Hobson, J. A. *Sleep*. New York: Scientific American Library, 1989.

Horne, J. *Why We Sleep: The Functions of Sleep in Humans and Other Mammals*. Oxford: Oxford University Press, 1988.

Kruyger, M. H., Roth, T., & Dement, W. C. *Principles and Practices of Sleep Disorders in Medicine*. New York: W. B. Saunders, 1989.

13

SEX

The neural mechanisms that underlie sexual behavior are no more complex or difficult to isolate than the mechanisms that underlie eating, drinking, or sleep, but exploring the dynamics of these mechanisms nonetheless obliges us to take a decidedly different approach. More so than in the other behaviors we have studied so far, there are factors, quite apart from what happens inside the nervous system, that have a strong bearing on human sexual behavior. Cultural mores, personality traits, religious values, moral attitudes, family upbringing—each of these factors has a bearing on how humans conduct the sexual aspect of their lives. And it is rare that such commonly reported sexual problems as impotence and frigidity can be traced exclusively to physiological causes.

As interesting and as important as they may be, however, the non-physiological issues of sexual behavior are not within the domain of physiological psychology. So, as we look into this fascinating and sensitive subject, keep in mind that we are examining only one aspect of sex—its physiological aspect.

DEFINING SEX

Sex is a very broad term, too broad, really, to define in one or two sentences. In the broadest sense, we use the term to differentiate two general groups within nearly every species: the male sex and the female sex. We use the term, too, to describe a wide range of behaviors that include everything from the mating rituals of insects to deviant behaviors—sado-masochism, for instance—that are unique to humans. Finally, we use the term to describe a basic drive, one that may not be as essential to survival of the individual as some other biological drives, such as hunger and thirst, but one that is nonetheless essential to survival of the species. Sexual behavior is the means through which a species passes on life-sustaining capacities to each new generation.

The Basic Dynamics of Sexual Behavior

Except among single-celled organisms, which pass on life-sustaining capacities simply by splitting, sexual behavior in the pure sense of the term is generally a partnership affair: when individuals of any species engage in sex in the strictest and most limited sense of the term, the egg of the female and the sperm of the male—the *gametes*—join to produce a new, fertilized cell, or *zygote*. The repeated divisions and differentiation of the zygote ultimately produce a new individual.

It is true of course that not all aspects of sexual behavior—human sexual behavior, in particular—are reproduction-dependent. But except for special situations (such as artificial insemination), reproduction is itself dependent upon sexual behavior, and how reproduction takes place varies considerably from species to species. Male and female fish, for example, never touch. The female lays eggs, and the male fertilizes them. The entire process takes place outside the body. In mammals, the union of egg and sperm occurs inside the body, but here again, variations abound not only in the physical nature of the sexual act but also in the frequency of the behavior. Elephants, as a rule, engage in sex no more than once every 2 years. Laboratory rats may do so several times a day. Human sexual patterns vary so much that it is next to impossible to establish norms.

The Human Difference

If there is one aspect of sexual behavior that more dramatically separates humans from other animals, it is the degree to which the behavior is controlled by the biological demands of fertilization. The sexual behavior of lower animals is generally confined to periods when the female is ovulating—when the egg is available for fertilization. During this period the sex urge of the female is at its height, and she is said to be "in heat," or in *estrus*. To some extent, human females, too, experience heightened feelings of sexuality around the time of ovulation each month, but a human female's sexual receptivity is not confined to these periods.

Even with this key difference, the general principles that underlie sexual behavior apply to lower animals and humans alike. In each instance, we are concerned with two sets of controls: external and internal. We shall look into the external controls first.

EXTERNAL CONTROL OF SEXUAL BEHAVIOR

Most behavior, as we have seen, depends to some extent on stimuli that originate outside the body, and sex is no exception. For two individuals of any species to engage in sexual behavior, two conditions must be present: the female must be in a receptive state, and the male must be responsive to this state. In most species, the receptivity of the female is controlled by certain internal factors, which we shall examine in a moment. Sexual responsiveness in the male, however, is generally keyed to external cues, such as odors, colors, and body positions assumed by the female. The sexual responsiveness of male dogs, for instance, is keyed to the odor, known as a *pheromone*, emitted by female dogs in heat. Odors, it turns out, can also affect the fertilization process itself in some species. Alan Parkes and H. M. Bruce have reported that odors in mice play so critical a role in determining a successful pregnancy that pregnant mice abort when presented with the odor of a strange male (Parkes & Bruce, 1961).

Social factors are also important in determining sexual responsiveness, even in lower animals. One of the more interesting examples of how social factors affect sexual behavior is known as the "Coolidge effect": the tendency of a male to be more sexually responsive when presented with a variety of sexual partners than when presented with only one. The Coolidge effect occurs among most higher species and draws its name from an incident, almost certainly apocryphal, involving former President Calvin Coolidge and his wife. The Coolidges, it seems, were touring a farm when Mrs. Coolidge asked if it were true that a single rooster could handle the sexual needs of an entire flock of hens. When the farmer replied that it was true, Mrs. Coolidge is reported to have said, "You might point that out to Mr. Coolidge." The president, however, was not to be outdone. "Is a different hen involved each time?" he asked the farmer. When the farmer answered yes, Mr. Coolidge said, "You might point that out to Mrs. Coolidge."

Humorous implications aside, the Coolidge effect does seem to embody certain adaptive advantages, especially among species in which a single male has the job of inseminating a large number of females. Preference, though, is probably not at issue. Given the limited reproductive capability of a single female within a given species, it makes adaptive sense to spread whatever reproductive capability there is among as many receptive females as possible.

External Cues for Human Sexual Behavior

The external cues capable of stimulating sexual activity in humans are many and varied, and no single cue can be said to dominate. We can be sexually aroused by what we see, touch, hear, smell, or even think, and there is evidence that the impact of certain cues varies along gender lines.

But external cues do not work alone, either for lower animals or for humans. What goes on *inside* the body—hormonal and neural activity—is as important to sexual behavior as what goes on *outside* the body. So while it is true that sexual arousal is typically triggered by stimuli associated with the opposite sex, it is also true that for the stimuli to be arousing, the individual must be in a responsive state. We shall now consider the role that internal factors play in controlling sexual responsiveness—first the hormones, then the nervous system.

HORMONES AND SEXUAL BEHAVIOR

Sex hormones can be divided roughly into two groups: *androgens*, the most prominent of which is *testosterone*, and *estrogens*, the most prominent of which is *estradiol*. Androgens predominate in males and are produced chiefly in the testes, or testicles—two glandular bodies located in the scrotum. Estrogens predominate in females and are produced in the ovaries, two glands located in the pelvic region. The important term is "predominate." Androgens and estrogens are also produced by the cortex of the adrenal gland and thus are present in both males and females. This is why it is misleading to describe androgen as a "male sex hormone" and estrogen as a "female sex hormone."

A third group of sex hormones, also produced by the ovaries, are known as *progestins*. The most prominent hormone in this group is *progesterone*, whose function, as its name indicates, is to promote gestation or pregnancy. As we will soon see, however, it also plays an important role in the control of sexual behavior. The glands that produce sex hormones are shown in Figure 13.1.

The degree to which sexual behavior is controlled by hormones varies extensively among animals, but hormonal action is clearly more important among lower animals, where it is indispensable, than it is among

Figure 13.1 *The Glands and the Brain Area (Hypothalamus) That Produce Hormones Involved in Sexual Behavior*

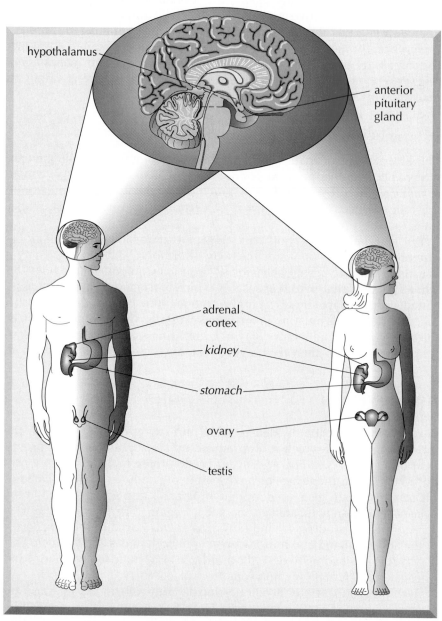

higher animals (Beach, 1949). Our knowledge of sex hormones and their relation to sexual behavior is based mainly on laboratory studies of lower animals and clinical observations of humans whose hormonal levels have been drastically changed through illness, injury, or a procedure such as castration (the removal of the testes) or ovariectomy (the removal of ovaries). Let us now consider some of these studies.

Hormones and Sexual Behavior in Rats

Hormones play a dominant role in the sexual behavior of laboratory rats, although there are significant differences between males and females. The sexual receptivity of female rats appears to be determined almost exclusively by hormones—specifically by the presence of estrogen. A normal female rat ovulates once every 4 or 5 days, and during ovulation three things happen: her ovaries release high levels of estrogen, the egg is released for fertilization, and she becomes sexually receptive.

Sexual receptivity is reflected in several behavioral changes. As estrogen levels rise, females become noticeably more responsive to males and show an increased willingness to approach them. They sniff, groom themselves, wiggle their ears, and begin to dart back and forth. This behavior, known as *proceptive behavior*, induces the male rat to chase and eventually mount the female (Dewsbury, 1979; McClintock, 1987). The receptive female in turn responds by arching her hindquarters and setting her tail to one side. This behavior, known as *lordosis*, enables the male rat to achieve intromission, that is, to insert his penis into the female's vagina.

When estrogen levels drop, either spontaneously or because of an ovariectomy, the female becomes noticeably *unresponsive* to the male. Injections of estrogen, however, restore her responsiveness.

The sexual behavior of male rats, on the other hand, appears to be less hormonally dependent than that of females. After their testes have been removed, male rats do not cease sexual activity immediately. Instead, frequency declines gradually. But as in the case of females, hormonal injections—in this case testosterone—restore the behavior to normal.

Fertilization

Hormonal factors also appear to play a role in the actual fertilization process in rats. Norman Adler and his colleagues have found a relationship between fertilization and the number of times the male rat intromits before ejaculation (Adler, 1969). Normally, a male rat does so 8 to 10 times before ejaculation. The intromissions are dry (without ejaculation), but they appear to be necessary to make the ultimate wet (ejaculatory) intromission "take." Adler has found, interestingly, that if the male wastes a few intromissions without ejaculation on a "secondary" female before being allowed to ejaculate with the primary female, fertilization does not occur. The reason is that repeated intromissions stimulate release of the female sex hormone progesterone, which is necessary for fertilization.

Progesterone and Sexual Behavior

Progesterone, in addition to promoting fertilization, appears to play an important role in regulating sexual receptivity. This role is known as the *biphasic effect of progesterone*, the reason being that progesterone can either facilitate or inhibit sexual behavior depending on the levels of estrogen in the female. When female rats are in estrus and estrogen levels are high, progesterone acts to enhance sexual receptivity. When estrogen levels drop, the condition that occurs after fertilization, progesterone acts to inhibit sexual receptivity (Feder, 1985; Schwartz-Giblin et al., 1989).

Hormones and Sexual Behavior in Monkeys and Humans

The relation between hormones and sexual behavior established for rats applies, in general, to most lower animals. But among higher animals, especially monkeys and humans, sexual responsiveness appears to be more closely related to the nervous system than to hormonal levels, even though the two interact in many respects.

Evidence supporting the notion that hormones become increasingly less important factors in sexual behavior the higher you move up the evolutionary ladder comes from a number of studies and observations. First of all, female humans, and to a lesser extent female monkeys, are sexually responsive even when estrogen levels are *not* notably high. In monkeys, receptivity is somewhat greater during periods of ovulation—when estrogen levels are high—but is not confined to those periods (Beach, 1947). In human females, the differences in sexual receptivity between ovulation periods and nonovulation periods are negligible (Money & Ehrhardt, 1972). Furthermore, while an ovariectomy does not eliminate sexual activity among female monkeys, it does reduce its frequency (Beach, 1947). The effect of an ovariectomy on human sexual activity, on the other hand, is relatively minor.

Similar patterns are found in males. Removal of the testes produces a more gradual decline in sexual behavior among monkeys than it does among rats, and an even more gradual decline among humans, with one exception (Beach, 1947; Sherwin, 1988). If castration (removal of the testes) takes place before a boy reaches puberty, which occurs at about 13 years of age, the effect on behavior is profound. Sexual responsiveness simply does not develop.

Implications of Hormone and Sexual Behavior Studies

It would be wrong to conclude on the basis of the information we have presented so far that hormones play only a negligible role in shaping human sexual behavior. Castrated males show at least some decline in sexual urge—an indication that testosterone is an important factor in human sexuality. And though removal of the ovaries or testes may not have immediate or pronounced effects on human sexual behavior, removal of other glands does. John Money, a leading figure in human sex research, has reported that women who have undergone adrenalectomies (removal of the adrenal cortex glands) show a marked decline in sexual urge. This decline can be reversed, however, through administration of sex hormones normally produced by the adrenal cortex glands (Money, 1961; Sherwin, 1985). Money has also reported that men with underactive testes show increased sexual activity following treatment with adrenal sex hormones but lapse again when treatment is discontinued. Finally, sex offenders who have been treated with drugs (antiandrogens) that prevent the testes from producing testosterone report a decline in sexual urge and activity (Money et al., 1976).

Overall then, the relation of sex hormones to sexual behavior in humans, though not so critical as in other animals, is still important. What's more, it is not only the presence or absence of a hormone that influences sexual behavior, it is also where in the brain the hormone acts.

THE BRAIN AND SEXUAL BEHAVIOR

In all animals with reasonably developed central nervous systems, the chief regulator of sexual behavior is the brain, and the area that is the most involved in this regulation is the hypothalamus.

The hypothalamus, as depicted in Figure 13.1, exerts this control indirectly through the interaction it has with the anterior pituitary gland. What happens, in brief, is that the hypothalamus releases hormones that stimulate the anterior pituitary, which in turn releases hormones that stimulate the sex glands—the ovaries to release estrogen and progesterone, the testes to release testosterone. The sex hormones then feed back to the hypothalamus to stimulate sexual behavior. Let us now take a closer look at this pattern.

The Hypothalamus and Hormone Production

Hormonal release differs between females and males, and the behavioral consequences of this difference are significant. The release of estrogen and progesterone in females is cyclical and in lower animals (but not in humans) parallels the rise and fall of levels of sexual receptivity. There is one exception: if fertilization occurs, progesterone levels remain high, estrogen levels fall, and sexual receptivity is inhibited. In males the relatively constant output of testosterone provides a steady stream of stimulation, which translates into a constant state of "sexual readiness."

Yet it isn't so much the difference in sex glands that accounts for this female-male difference as much as it is the hypothalamic areas that control them. The hypothalamus controls testosterone in a relatively straightforward manner—through a simple feedback system. Low levels of testosterone interact with the hypothalamus to increase testosterone (via the anterior pituitary); high levels of testosterone interact with the hypothalamus to decrease testosterone. The mechanism that controls estrogen in the female is more complex. Commonly referred to as the *menstrual cycle*, this sequence of events is illustrated in Figure 13.2.

Evidence Implicating Hypothalamic Involvement

That the hypothalamus has an impact on the hormonal activity underlying sexual behavior has been established through a number of studies on rats showing that lesions in the hypothalamus abolish secretion of hormones by the anterior pituitary. Denied these hormones, the ovaries and

Figure 13.2 *The Menstrual Cycle*

(a) Low levels of estrogen stimulate the hypothalamus, which in turn stimulates the anterior pituitary to release follicle-stimulating hormone (FSH). (b) FSH initiates maturation of the follicle and egg and promotes production of estrogen. (c) High levels of estrogen feed back to the hypothalamus to inhibit the release of FSH and to promote the release of luteinizing hormone (LH) by the anterior pituitary. (d) The sudden surge of LH triggers ovulation. The empty follicle develops into the corpus luteum, which secretes progesterone and estrogen. (e) The high levels of progesterone and estrogen feed back to the hypothalamus, inducing it to inhibit the release of LH by the anterior pituitary. The high levels of progesterone and estrogen also prepare the lining of the uterus for implantation of the egg. If the egg is fertilized, the corpus luteum remains functional and progesterone and estrogen help maintain the pregnancy. (f) If the egg is not fertilized, the corpus luteum degenerates, estrogen and progesterone decrease, and the lining of the uterus is shed in the form of menstrual discharge. Finally, the low level of estrogen stimulates the release of a new follicle and the cycle begins again.

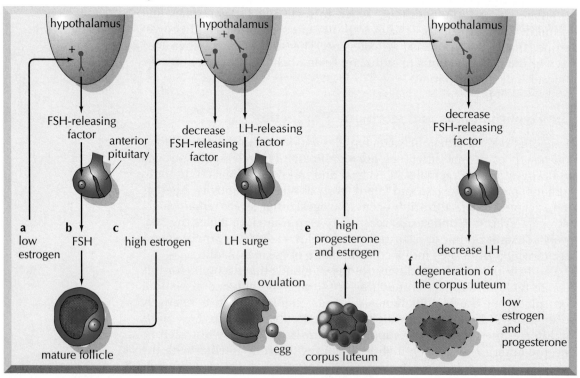

testes atrophy, secretion of estrogen and testosterone declines, and the animal's sexual behavior diminishes. Replacement therapy (injections of estrogen in the female and testosterone in the male), however, restores sexual behavior (Sawyer, 1960).

In summary, the overall relation between the brain and hormones is more or less a circular series of events. It begins when the hypothalamus stimulates the anterior pituitary. It ends when the anterior pituitary stimulates the sex glands to release sex hormones which feed back to the brain to initiate sexual receptivity. Let us now take a closer look at how hormones interact with the brain to produce sexual behavior.

From Hormones to Hypothalamus

As we saw in Chapter 11, the hypothalamus contains neural cells sensitive to water and salt. We can now add to this picture a set of neural cells sensitive to sex hormones.

This sensitivity has been demonstrated in several studies in rats in which the sex glands (ovaries or testes) have been removed and hormones implanted directly in the brain. Sexual behavior in female rats that have undergone this procedure has been induced through implants of estrogen and progesterone in the ventromedial hypothalamus (Rubin & Barfield, 1983). Sexual behavior in similarly prepared males has been induced through preoptic implants not only of testosterone but of estrogen as well (Davidson, 1966; Davis & Barfield, 1979). One especially significant aspect of this work is that it indicates that estrogen implants can activate different types of sexual behavior—male or female—depending on where in the hypothalamus the implant is administered. Estrogen induces female sexual behavior in females when it is implanted in the ventromedial hypothalamus, and it induces male sexual behavior in the male when it is implanted in the medial preoptic area of the hypothalamus. These differences indicate that in rats, at least, sexual behavior is governed more by the area of the hypothalamus stimulated than by the hormone responsible for the stimulation.

Related studies in which brain areas have been lesioned rather than stimulated have generally confirmed the idea that different areas of the hypothalamus are involved in different types of sexual behavior. We would expect, for instance, that if the ventromedial hypothalamus controls female sexual behavior and the medial preoptic area controls male sexual behavior in rats, then lesions in the ventromedial hypothalamus (Pfaff & Modianos, 1985) would abolish female sexual behavior and lesions in the medial preoptic area would abolish male sexual behavior (DeJong et al., 1989; Breedlove, 1992).

This is precisely what has been observed, albeit with one complication. Lesions can interfere with sexual behavior in at least two respects—the animals' *ability* to perform and the animals' *urge* to perform. And there is evidence, at least in the male, that the disruption affects performance ability more than it affects the urge. Male rats lesioned in the medial preoptic area will approach receptive females and will even press a lever to gain access to a receptive female. Once in the presence of the female, they attempt—but cannot perform—the sexual response (Everitt & Stacey, 1987).

Implications

Performance-urge complications notwithstanding, it is clear from anatomical work that some of the long-standing beliefs concerning hormones and sexual behavior are no longer as valid as was once thought. It has long been assumed, for instance, that there is a direct connection between a particular hormone and a particular sexual tendency, with male sexual behavior rooted in testosterone and female sexual behavior rooted in estrogen. Such a connection may exist, but hormonal injections in and of themselves do not necessarily determine the nature of the sexual behavior. When male rats exhibiting female behavior are injected with testosterone, for example, they do not become more "male" in their sexual behavior. They simply increase their "female" behavior (Sodersten & Larsson, 1974). Similarly, homosexual humans (male and female alike) who have been given hormonal injections (estrogen to females, testosterone to males) have not become any less homosexual but have simply increased sexual behavior with their own sex (Money & Ehrhardt, 1972). The question we must now address is what at the neural and hormonal levels finally determines the kind of sexual behavior—male or female—that any given individual will engage in.

Female and Male Brains: A Closer Look

As we've just seen, evidence from both lower animals and humans indicates that how animals actually behave sexually appears to be determined, in rats at least, by which area of the hypothalamus is involved. In females, it is the ventromedial area. In males it is the medial preoptic area.

This pattern, however, raises a troublesome question. Under normal (nonexperimental) conditions, hormones travel to both the ventromedial hypothalamus and medial preoptic area in both females and males. The question then is, Why do hormones activate the ventromedial hypothalamus in the female and the medial preoptic area in the male? The best answer is that there are structural differences between the brain of a female rat and the brain of a male rat—differences that may make the ventromedial hypothalamus more responsive in the female and the medial preoptic area more responsive in the male.

Structural Differences

In 1971 Geoffrey Raisman and Pauline Field reported that the preoptic area in male and female rats exhibited different patterns of synaptic connections (Raisman & Field, 1971). Several years later Roger Gorski and his colleagues went a step further and found that a specific nucleus in the preoptic area, illustrated in Figure 13.3, is roughly five or six times larger in the male brain than in the female brain (Gorski et al., 1978). Gorski and his colleagues have labeled this nucleus the *sexually dimorphic nucleus of the preoptic area.* ("Sexual dimorphism" is a term originally coined by Darwin to refer to bodily characteristics that distinguish males from females.) More recently, Laura Allen and her colleagues have found in humans evidence for a similar but not as large a difference in the preoptic area as well as in the *interstitial nucleus of the anterior hypothalamus* (Allen et al., 1989).

Lesion work on rats has produced results confirming that the sexually dimorphic nucleus of the preoptic area controls male sexual behavior. Lesions in the nucleus abolish male sexual behavior, but with one qualification: the animals must be sexually naive. Sexually experienced animals who receive lesions in this nucleus do not suffer disruptive effects. This finding suggests that male sexual behavior, as a result of experience, can come under control of areas other than the sexually dimorphic nucleus (DeJong et al., 1989).

Figure 13.3 *Tissue Sections Taken from the Preoptic Area of the Male and Female Rat Brain*
Circled areas in the photos designate the sexually dimorphic nuclei, which are larger in the male.

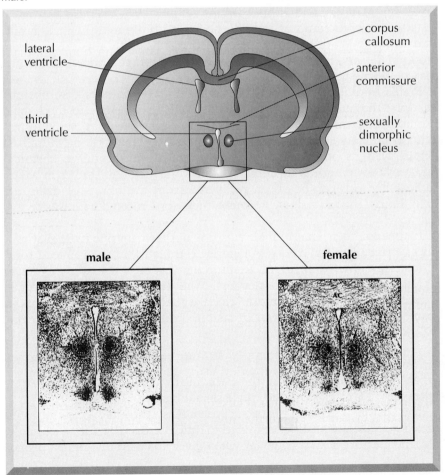

Male and Female Hormones: A Closer Look

While some researchers have been looking at the structural features of the male and female brain, others have been focusing on its hormonal features.

As we saw earlier, estrogen implanted in female and male brains activates both types of sexual behavior, depending on where in the brain the hormone is implanted. It is easy to understand why estrogen, when implanted in the ventromedial hypothalamus (the female area) of ovariectomized females, produces female behavior. But why should estrogen implanted in the preoptic area (the male area) of castrated males produce *male* behavior? The answer to this question requires a closer look at the male brain and its relationship to estrogen.

Odd though it may seem, the male brain (certainly in lower animals) contains receptors sensitive to the female hormone estrogen. This sensitivity has been determined by *autoradiography*, a procedure in which animals are injected with a hormone that has been radioactively labeled in order to track its target site. Through autoradiography, Donald Pfaff and his coworkers have isolated estrogen-sensitive receptors (as shown in Figure 13.4) in four areas: the ventromedial hypothalamus, preoptic area, septal area, and hippocampus (Pfaff, 1971). These estrogen-sensitive receptors appear in both the female brain and the male brain. And because Pfaff has obtained these results with rats, fish, birds, amphibians, and monkeys, it seems safe to assume that the same pattern may hold true for humans.

Pfaff's findings raise an obvious question with some not so obvious answers: the question is, Why should receptors sensitive to the female hormone be found in the male brain? The answer, in short, is that estrogen (specifically estradiol) itself is found in the male brain (Naftolin et al., 1975). It is produced there from testosterone through a chemical process known as *aromatization*. We know this through studies in which radioactive estrogen has been recovered from the brains of male rats even though the radioactive hormone they were injected with was testosterone.

It appears, then, that in male rats it is not testosterone itself that produces male sexual behavior but rather estrogen that is produced from testosterone (McEwen, 1976). Reinforcing this view is a study by Larry Christensen and Linwood Clemens, who have shown that estrogen implants in the brain are more effective than testosterone implants in restoring male sexual behavior to castrated rats (Christensen & Clemens, 1974).

A Cautionary Note

What are the implications of these findings? Should we revise our view of the way hormones produce male sexual behavior?

The answer is no, and for two reasons. First, the effect of estrogen on male sexual behavior may be limited to rats. Estrogen, so far as we know, does not restore sexual behavior when given to castrated guinea pigs or

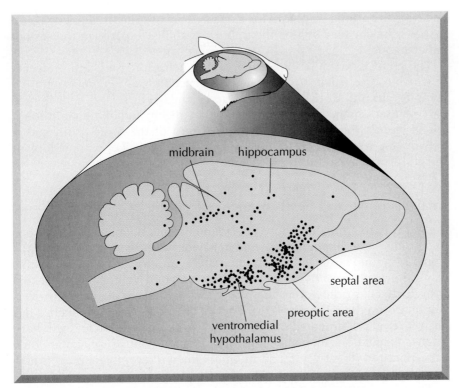

Figure 13.4 *Brain Areas Containing Estrogen-Sensitive Neurons*
The dots indicate the areas that contain the greatest concentration of estrogen-sensitive neurons.

monkeys (Phoenix, 1973). Second, the effect of estrogen in rats is incomplete. Even after estrogen treatment, castrated animals are still deficient in intromission and ejaculatory behavior. Only after they are given both estrogen and dihydrotestosterone (a type of testosterone that is *not* converted into estrogen) does their behavior return to normal (Feder, Naftolin, & Ryan, 1973). These findings strongly suggest that testosterone as well as estrogen is involved in male sexual behavior—a hypothesis that has stimulated much interest and research.

SEARCHING FOR THE PERFORMANCE CIRCUIT

The main circuit that underlies sexual behavior, as we have just seen, runs from the hypothalamus to the anterior pituitary to the gonads (testes or ovaries) and back to the hypothalamus. It is clear, however, that other circuits affect sexual behavior as well. Damage to the spinal cord or the cortex in lower animals, for example, can disrupt sexual behavior in various ways and for various reasons. The urge to engage in sexual behavior may still be there, but the ability to perform the sex act may be gone.

The point is worth emphasizing: sexual behavior is a chain of events in which each element is controlled by a specific neural component in a complex circuit. Motivation (the urge to engage in sexual behavior) is part of that chain, presumably rooted in the hypothalamus-pituitary-gonad circuit. Performance, however, is part of the same chain and is presumably rooted in the spinal cord–cortex circuit. Let us now look at the performance circuit in more detail.

Analysis of Sexual Performance

A good way to appreciate how the brain controls sexual performance is to consider what happens to sexual behavior when the brain is detached from the spinal cord. As you might expect, an animal prepared in this way (known as a *spinal animal*) cannot respond voluntarily to sexual stimuli. Even so, however, there is still a response—in fact, an over-response—on the reflex level. If the penis of a dog whose spinal cord has been severed is stimulated, the dog will develop an erection and will have intense ejaculatory responses. Normal dogs, in contrast, ejaculate only in response to direct genital stimulation when a receptive female is also present (Hart, 1967).

The sexual behavior of spinal animals demonstrates something important about the function of the brain and the influence of higher brain centers on sexual behavior. Unless appropriate environmental cues (a receptive female) are present, reflexive sexual behavior is rarely seen when the brain is intact. We can therefore assume that the brain normally acts to *inhibit* reflex circuits and that the environmental cues act to remove the inhibitory effect.

Brain Areas and Performance

It has not yet been determined what specific areas of the brain evaluate environmental stimuli and exert control over spinal reflexes. But we do have some important clues based on studies in which researchers have been able to elicit various components of the sexual response through electrical stimulation of certain areas of the brain. Stimulation of the anterior dorsolateral hypothalamus in rats produces an erection (Vaughan & Fisher, 1962), stimulation of the medial forebrain bundle produces isolated ejaculation (Herberg, 1963), and stimulation of the posterior hypothalamus produces a full sequence of copulatory behavior, beginning with mounting and ending with ejaculation.

The evaluative aspects of sexual behavior—the decision to approach a particular sex object—on the other hand, seem to be chiefly under the control of the cortex. When the temporal lobes of the cortex in a male cat are surgically removed, the animal becomes noticeably indiscriminate in its choice of sex objects. It mounts furniture, other male cats—even the experimenter. Interestingly, however, female cats who undergo the same procedure do not exhibit the same behavioral tendencies.

This difference in response between males and females is not limited to the temporal lobes of the cortex. In cats, as in most lower animals, cortical damage in general disrupts the sexual behavior of males more than it does the sexual behavior of females. Here again, though, the problems brought on by cortical damage may have more to do with the *ability* to respond than with the *urge* to respond. A receptive female rat can prepare for copulation simply by elevating her hindquarters—the response referred to as lordosis. Male rats, however, face a more difficult challenge. They need to approach and mount. It is thus logical to assume that the male sexual response, because of its greater complexity, depends more on neural intactness (particularly in the motor areas of the cortex) than does the female sexual response.

This difference suggests that cortical damage in male rats affects performance more than it does motivation. Experiments have confirmed this hypothesis, at least as it pertains to cats. When the motor demands of a neurally damaged cat are minimized by placing a male cat directly atop a female, copulatory behavior proceeds unimpeded (Beach, 1949).

Sexual Response: The Human Dimension

To talk about the sexual response purely in terms of erection, mounting, and ejaculation is like talking about eating purely in terms of chewing and swallowing. Sexual responses are not limited to the genitalia. Responses and sensations relating to sex involve the entire body, and there is no better example of this than the human sexual response.

Two scientists whose names have become synonymous with human sex research are William Masters and Virginia Johnson, who have spent most of their careers studying the human sexual response (Masters & Johnson, 1966). On the basis of studies begun in the mid-1960s, they have identified four distinct phases of the sexual response cycle: excitation, plateau, orgasm, and resolution. Each phase is accompanied by its own characteristic physiological response. Here is a closer look at each phase.

Excitation
During excitation, both sexes show a general increase in muscle tension (known as *myotonia*) and in blood flow (known as *vasocongestion*) to areas in and around the genitals. As a result of vasocongestion, men achieve full erection of the penis and women experience nipple erection and lubrication of the vaginal walls. Because the mechanism for erection involves a reflex circuit between the penis and the lower part of the spinal cord, erection calls for neither consciousness nor an intact spinal cord. Unconscious men have been excited to erection by direct stimulation of the penis. So have men who are paralyzed from the waist down by a severed spinal cord (Hart, 1978).

Plateau

During plateau, sexual arousal (vasocongestion and myotonia) gradually increases to a level approaching orgasm and is accompanied in both sexes by a shift in the position of the internal sex organs. In women the uterus becomes enlarged (in some instances as much as double its normal size) and the clitoris rises from its normal position and draws away from the vaginal entrance. In men, the penis continues to swell and the testicles become larger and are drawn upward within the scrotal sac.

Orgasm

The orgasm phase is similar in both sexes—with this difference: female orgasm does not involve ejaculation; it consists of a series of rhythmic contractions of the pelvic muscles accompanied by a sensation of pleasurable release lasting for several seconds.

Resolution

The differences between men and women are the most pronounced in this phase. In men there is a refractory period—it can last a few minutes or much longer—during which they cannot achieve erection. Women, on the other hand, have no refractory period, and if sexual stimulation continues, they can have several orgasms in succession.

What is perhaps most significant about the work of Masters and Johnson is their discovery that individuals may differ in the intensity of their response in each of these phases. And while different kinds of stimulation can evoke different responses in different people, the basic pattern of sexual response, from excitation to resolution, appears to be all but universal. The precise neural events that underlie each of these phases have yet to be determined, but the foundation for their study has been established and we can expect important findings in years to come.

DEVELOPMENTAL ASPECTS OF SEXUAL BEHAVIOR

No one disputes that there are significant differences in the sexual behavior of males and females, and no one disputes that these differences are the result of differences in the brain. The key question, however, is, How do we account for these differences? To ask the same question another way, How does sexual behavior develop within the life span of an individual? Is the development of sexual behavior programmed from birth, or is it controlled by environmental factors? This is the question we will be examining throughout the rest of this chapter.

Genetics and Sex

Sexual behavior actually begins (albeit in a roundabout way) with the sex chromosomes XX in the female and XY in the male. The key chromosome is the Y chromosome. When it is present, the testes develop and androgen is secreted; when it is absent, the ovaries develop and estrogen is secreted.

The section on the Y chromosome that contains the gene or genes for development of the testes is called the *sex-determining region of Y* (SRY for short), and the chemical that is produced by this region and that results in differentiation of the testes is aptly known as the *testes-determining factor* (TDF for short) (Gubbay et al., 1990; Palmer et al., 1989).

Chromosomes affect sexual behavior indirectly through the role they play in determining the presence of ovaries and estrogen, and testes and androgen. There are two critical periods during which the sex hormones establish the blueprint in humans for adult sexual appearance and behavior. The first is during *fetal development*, and the second comes approximately 13 years later, during *puberty*.

Fetal Development and Sex

What is important about the sexual aspects of fetal development is that while the genetic sex of the child (XX or XY) is determined at the time of fertilization, the actual physical differences—differences in the internal reproductive organs and differences in the external reproductive organs—take time to develop. It takes roughly 6 to 7 weeks for the ovaries and uterus to develop in the female fetus and for the vas deferens and seminal ducts to develop in the male. Until this differentiation occurs, the fetus has the potential for developing either reproductive system.

Internal Reproductive Organs

As shown in Figure 13.5, every fetus (whether it eventually develops into a "male" or a "female") has two genital ducts: a male system known as the *Wolffian ducts*, and a female system, known as the *Müllerian ducts*. Which internal system actually develops is determined by the sex hormones.

In the male, the testes secrete two hormones. One is androgen, which results in differentiation of the Wolffian ducts into male internal organs. The other is known as *Müllerian duct-inhibiting substance*, which causes the Müllerian ducts to degenerate, preventing them from differentiating into female internal organs.

In the female, hormones are *not* released and, in the *absence* of hormones, the female system (the Müllerian ducts) develops and the male system (the Wolffian ducts) degenerates. Unless male hormones are present, in other words, the fetus develops female internal organs.

External Reproductive Organs

The external reproductive organs (the penis and scrotum in males and the clitoris and labia in females) appear somewhat later than the internal organs in embryological development, as depicted in Figure 13.5. Here again, as is the case with the internal reproductive organs, the fetus

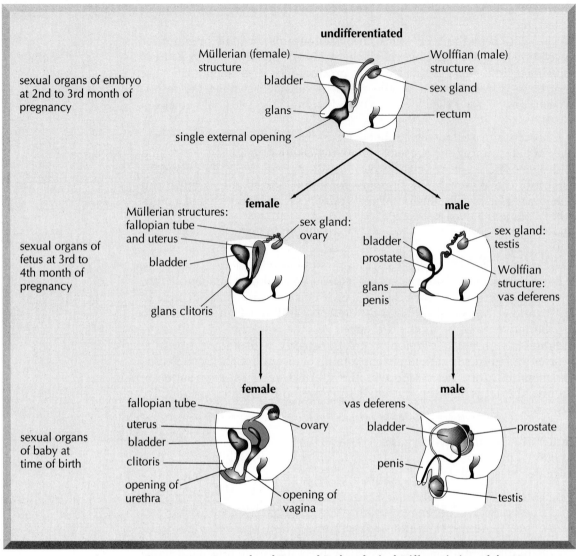

Figure 13.5 *Internal and External Embryological Differentiation of the Human Reproductive System*
Undifferentiated sex organs, which initially are the same in the human male and female, differentiate into the female when androgen is absent and into the male when androgen is present.

has the potential until roughly the twelfth week to develop either external reproductive system. And here again, it is the release of androgen that determines the development of male organs and the absence of androgen that determines the development of female organs. Estrogen is *not* involved in the development of either internal or external female organs. This is because the ovaries do not secrete estrogen until after differentiation of both internal and external organs is completed.

How Anomalies Develop

If the delicate hormonal environment of the fetus is disturbed during differentiation, the result will be sexual anomalies in both appearance and behavior. In both lower animals (such as guinea pigs and monkeys) and humans, excess androgen in a female during embryological development of the external genitalia will give her genitalia a male appearance. The greater the excess, the greater the extent of male characteristics. Figure 13.6a shows an intermediate effect in the human. Notice that the enlarged clitoris resembles a penis and the swollen labia a scrotum.

A person afflicted with this anomaly (i.e., someone who possesses the chromosomes of one sex and the sex organs, either intermediate or complete, of the other) is known as a *pseudohermaphrodite*. In most cases, a pseudohermaphrodite has the chromosomes of a female and the sexual organs of a male. Occasionally, though, as pictured in Figure 13.6b, a male has a deficiency of or an insensitivity to androgen during differentiation and develops the sex organs of a female (Hamburg & Lund, 1966). In this case, though, because the Müllerian duct-inhibiting substance is active, the internal organs of the female do not develop.

Behavioral Patterns of Pseudohermaphrodites

The behavioral patterns that accompany anomalous sexual development are generally consistent with the external sexual appearance. In mon-

Figure 13.6 *A Female and Male Pseudohermaphrodite*
(a) The female pseudohermaphrodite pictured here has the chromosomes of a female (XX), and, because of androgen during fetal development, masculinized external organs. (b) The male pseudohermaphrodite pictured here has the chromosomes of a male (XY) and, because of insensitivity to androgen during fetal development, the sex organs of a female.

a

b

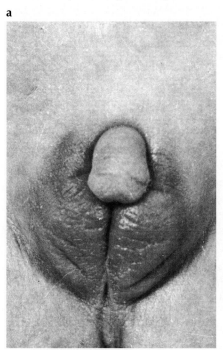
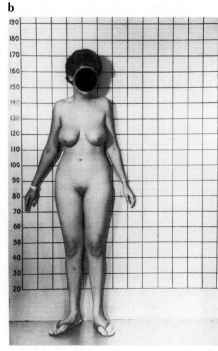

keys, the young female pseudohermaphrodite displays aggressiveness—a trait normally shown by young males. Moreover, as an adult, she tends to show male sexual behavior (Young, 1964). Apparently, then, the sex hormones in the fetus determine the development not only of bodily traits but also of the neural circuits that control sexual behavior. In humans, too, the tendency is for sexual behavior to fall in line with external appearance, but this outcome may be the result of learning and cultural conditioning rather than hormones. We will consider these factors later in the chapter. Now, however, we shall take a closer look at the role that hormones play in the development of sexual behavior.

Development of Sexual Behavior in Lower Animals

Sexual behavior depends on more than the mere development of male or female organs. Neural circuits appropriate to specific kinds of sexual behavior must be present as well. The fetal brain in lower animals has the ability to develop circuits to control either type of sexual behavior, and the specific type that emerges is determined by the sex hormones. If androgen is present during the period of neural differentiation, the male circuit and behavior develop. If androgen is not present, the female circuit and behavior develop (Phoenix et al., 1959).

Some of the most compelling evidence for the relationship between the presence or absence of male hormone and the development of the male or female brain comes from work on the preoptic area in rats. As we saw earlier, a nucleus in the preoptic area—known as the sexually dimorphic nucleus—is as much as five to six times larger in male rats than in female rats. Here again, hormones hold the key. If males are castrated at birth, a smaller sexually dimorphic nucleus develops and so does female behavior. If females are given androgen at birth, a larger sexually dimorphic nucleus develops and so does male behavior (Gorski, 1984). Significantly, though, these developmental changes can be initiated only within a very limited time frame—immediately before or after birth. Altering the androgen levels of male or female rats (castration for males, injections of androgen for females) once the rats become adults has no effect on the sexually dimorphic nucleus.

In summary, then, what holds for development of the body and development of behavior in lower animals holds for development of the brain. When androgen is present, the male brain (i.e., a larger sexually dimorphic nucleus) develops; when androgen is absent, the female brain (i.e., a smaller sexually dimorphic nucleus) develops. Let us take a closer look at the relation between hormones and development of the nervous system.

Role of Hormones in Neural Development

Studies on lower animals have given us a clearer picture of how sex hormones affect the actual development of neural circuits. Although the presence or absence of androgen coincides with the presence or absence of specific neural circuits, androgen, it turns out, is not directly responsible for actual neural differentiation, at least not in rats. Estrogen is. The brain of the fetal male rat (like the brain of the adult male rat) converts androgen (specifically testosterone) into estrogen, and it is estrogen that determines the development of the male neural circuit (McEwen, 1976).

In other words, and as illogical as it may seem, the rule governing sex differentiation in the fetal rat brain is that if estrogen is present, the male circuit develops; if estrogen is not present, the female circuit develops. Given these findings, we are faced with an intriguing question: What protects the female brain from the effects of its own estrogen? That is, if estrogen results in development of the male circuit in the male brain, why does it not also result in development of the male circuit in the female brain? The answer is an enzyme known as *alphafetoprotein*.

Alphafetoprotein
The basic function of alphafetoprotein is to destroy estrogen before it reaches the brain of the female fetus (McEwen, 1976). Alphafetoprotein is produced by the liver in the fetus (not in the adult) and is carried by the bloodstream, as depicted in Figure 13.7*a*. Estrogen in the female fetus is produced in the ovaries and is also carried in the bloodstream, where it is destroyed by alphafetoprotein. The reason alphafetoprotein has no effect on *male* estrogen is that male estrogen is not carried in the bloodstream. It is produced in the brain from testosterone (see Figure 13.7*b*) and is thus unaffected by the destructive effects of alphafetoprotein.

Figure 13.7 *Development of the Fetal Rat Brain*
(a) Estrogen in the female is destroyed by alphafetoprotein in the bloodstream and thus never reaches the fetal brain. (b) Testosterone in the male escapes destruction by alphafetoprotein in the bloodstream and is converted into estrogen (by aromatization) in the fetal brain.

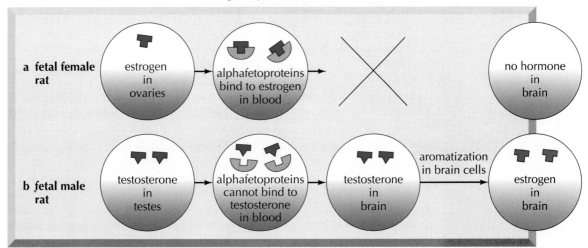

Again we must be careful not to overgeneralize. Our knowledge of human fetal physiology is limited, and it would be premature even to suggest that alphafetoprotein plays a role in sexual differentiation in humans. The possibility, however, has stimulated much interest and research.

Sources of Disruption

Because the hormonal state of the fetal environment is so critical to the development of sexual appearance and behavior, that environment, as you would expect, is well protected. The human fetus is enveloped by a protective membrane, known as the *placenta*, whose function is to regulate the exchange of oxygen, water, and nourishment between mother and fetus. Under normal conditions, the placenta ensures that the baby will be born healthy, but the barrier provided by the placenta is not foolproof. Drugs, for example, can pass from mother to fetus, which explains why women addicted to drugs may give birth to addicted children. Hormones, too, can pass through this barrier. A pregnant woman with a tumor in the adrenal gland will pass excess androgen to the fetus. The result may be a pseudohermaphrodite, with the chromosomes of a female and the sex organs of a male.

Another potential source of hormonal imbalance in the fetus is the mother's external environment. Ingeborg Ward has shown that pregnant rats subjected to stressful conditions (a bright light, for instance) give birth to males that have smaller external genitalia and are not as sexually active as rats born to mothers who were not subjected to the same stress (Ward, 1972). These same rats, when given injections of estrogen, show more "female" behavior than normal males do when given the same injections. Based on these observations, it was assumed that stress decreases the level of testosterone in the male fetus, thereby disrupting normal sexual development, but it took additional work by Ward and her colleague Judith Weisz to supply evidence in support of the notion (Ward & Weisz, 1980). What Ward and Weisz did was to monitor testosterone levels in male rat fetuses during embryological development. Consistent with Ward's hypothesis, they found that in fetuses of mothers undergoing stress, testosterone levels decreased significantly on the eighteenth and nineteenth days following conception. This time period, they postulate, is critical to the sexual differentiation of the rat's brain.

Interesting as the implications of these studies may be, we must again remind you that these studies involve rats, not humans. It is risky to assume on the basis of this work that stressful conditions during pregnancy can affect the sexual development of human offspring. Certainly there is no evidence as yet to establish this pattern in humans.

Puberty

Despite the fact that the sexes have different reproductive systems, human males and females—aside from the obvious differences in sexual organs—are physically similar at birth and remain so until the onset of puberty. With puberty, which usually begins at age 13 (give or take a year or two), differences known as *secondary sexual characteristics* begin to appear. Women develop fuller breasts, wider hips, and a higher voice. Men develop facial hair, a broader build, and a lower voice.

These differences, as far as we know, are triggered by the hypothalamus. Through its connections with the pituitary gland, the hypothalamus causes the anterior pituitary to release two hormones: follicle-stimulating hormone (FSH) and luteinizing hormone (LH). Both hormones act on the sex glands—the testes and ovaries—which in turn release testosterone and estrogen to stimulate the development of secondary sexual characteristics.

As we have already established, testosterone and estrogen are present in both males and females. During puberty, testosterone begins to predominate in males, producing the secondary sexual characteristics normally associated with males. Estrogen, on the other hand, predominates in females, producing the secondary sexual characteristics normally associated with females. Both groups of hormones also affect the reproductive system: testosterone promotes the production of sperm, estrogen the development of eggs.

The fact that even after puberty both testosterone and estrogen (albeit to different degrees) are present in both males and females would explain why some men have physical characteristics normally found in females (such as full breasts and high voices) and why some women have physical characteristics normally found in men (such as facial hair and deep voices). The reason in each case is the balance between testosterone and estrogen. Women with more testosterone than normal take on male characteristics, and men with more estrogen than normal take on female characteristics.

Sometimes these "reversals" are seen in a very mild form in older people, especially in older women. The main reason is that once women go through menopause, they lose their ability to produce estrogen. As a result, the relatively low level of male hormone that normally exists in women can now work unopposed. The reason that changes are not as pronounced among older men is that testosterone production never completely stops in men. It simply declines, thus preventing the relatively low level of female hormone that normally exists in men from producing its "female" effects (Katchadourian & Lunde, 1980).

Summing Up

Although our knowledge of the development of sexual behavior remains limited, we can say with reasonable certainty that men and women differ in their sexual behavior because of basic differences in neural organization. But let us not overstate the case. While each of us may be born with a circuitry that predisposes us to a certain pattern of sexual behavior, these circuits are not necessarily immutable. We saw in earlier chapters that hungry or thirsty as we may be, we may choose not to drink or eat—and may do so for any number of reasons. Sexual behavior is no different. Certain people may indeed be born with a tendency to be either sexually active or sexually underactive, or to be heterosexual or homosexual. What we must never lose sight of, however, is the degree to which social and environmental factors shape sexual behavior. So let us conclude this chapter by considering some of the environmental factors that play so basic a role in determining our sexual behavior.

THE LEARNING AND SOCIAL ASPECTS OF HUMAN SEXUAL BEHAVIOR

In humans, social interaction and learning experiences may be as important as hormonal development when it comes to determining the nature of adult sexual behavior. But where does the balance lie? Which in the end is more important—hormones or early learning? Can learning offset hormonal imbalance?

The definitive answers to these questions have yet to be discovered, although more and more work is being done each year. Many of these studies have involved pseudohermaphrodites. In one famous study, John Money and his colleagues located pseudohermaphrodites who were reared as females despite the presence of male external organs (Money & Ehrhardt, 1972). Of the 25 cases Money and his colleagues studied, 23 had assumed the gender role consistent with their "female" upbringing rather than the role consistent with their external male genitalia.

In another case reported by Money, a 7-month-old boy, one of a pair of identical male twins, lost his entire penis as the result of a doctor's carelessness during circumcision. The family decided to raise the child as a girl, and so the child was castrated and given an artificial vagina. Once the child reached puberty, estrogen was administered to feminize the body. Money reported that this individual, at the age of 12, responded relatively well to her upbringing as a girl, modeling her behavior after that of her mother and taking on what we normally think of as "girlish" characteristics (Money & Ehrhardt, 1972). And his report helped to strengthen the argument that hormonal and genetic factors can be superseded by the learning process.

A year later, however, a group of British psychiatrists examined the girl and offered a judgment that was not at all consistent with Money's description (Diamond, 1986). According to their report, the girl did not behave in a stereotypically "girlish" manner.

The issue, by any measure, is a controversial one. Most of us have grown up with a variety of notions regarding behavioral differences between the sexes, but who is to say whether these differences are the result of genetics or simply a matter of cultural conditioning. Do some young boys gravitate to sports and some young girls to dolls, for instance, because boys are more naturally aggressive and competitive and girls are more naturally maternal? Or is it simply the social pressures of our culture that influence these behaviors? For instance, would men be more like women in their interpersonal relationships if the culture did not identify such behavior as being "female"?

The fact that so many women today are taking part—and succeeding—in sports and in careers that were long considered the domain of men supports the notion that gender roles are more learned then genetically determined. However, data emerging from the growing number of transsexual operations suggest the opposite (Benjamin, 1966). Transsexuals, as you probably already know, are men and women whose desire to become a member of the opposite sex is so strong that they undergo major surgery and/or hormone treatment in order to change their gender. Because many transsexuals report that their identification with the opposite sex began to emerge early in life—too early, it is thought, to have resulted from cultural differences alone—most researchers studying transsexualism contend that while environmental factors are certainly important, heredity cannot be ruled out.

Homosexuality: Genetics or Environment?

The question of whether environment or genetics is the chief motivating force in sexual behavior has obvious implications for theories of sexual orientation—heterosexuality or homosexuality. Are some people programmed to become homosexuals by virtue of inborn traits, or is homosexuality a learned behavior influenced by environmental factors such as childhood experiences, parental relationships, or adolescent sexual encounters?

Conventional wisdom has tended to favor the environmental position. It is well established, for instance, that men and women who have always considered themselves heterosexual often engage in homosexual activity if they are placed in situations—prison, for instance—in which there are no sex partners of the opposite sex. And the fact that most homosexuals have heterosexual parents seems to minimize the role of genes in causing homosexuality.

But these observations by no means rule out genetic factors. Indeed, the results of several recent studies have given considerable support to the genetic side of the debate (LeVay & Hamer, 1994).

The Genetic Factor in Homosexuality

Michael Bailey and Richard Pillard studied a group of male homosexual twins and found that the concordance rate (that is, the tendency for both twins to show homosexuality) was much higher (57 percent) among identical twins (twins with the same genetic makeup) than among fraternal twins (24 percent) (Bailey & Pillard, 1991). Strikingly similar results—approximately 50 percent among identical twins, as opposed to 16 percent among fraternal twins—were found in a recent study of female homosexuals (Bailey et al., 1993). Taken within the genetic framework, these results are to be expected. Identical twins have the same genetic makeup; fraternal twins do not. Therefore, if genes are a factor in homosexual behavior, a higher concordance rate is to be expected in identical than fraternal twins.

Dean Hamer and his colleagues have taken the genetic work one step further (Hamer et al., 1993). Using a family history approach, Hamer has gone so far as to identify the specific chromosome—the X chromosome—that may in fact be the genetic factor in male homosexuality. Hamer bases his contention on the fact that there is a family pattern to homosexuality and that it tends to occur primarily on the mother's side of the family. The mothers of homosexual males have a slightly higher than normal chance of having a homosexual brother or a heterosexual sister who has a homosexual son. Since males receive the X chromosome from their mothers and the Y chromosome from their fathers, Hamer's data would suggest that if there is a "homosexuality" gene, at least in males, it is carried by the X chromosome. Hamer has gone so far as to identify an area on the X chromosome where the gene may, in fact, be located.

Weighing the Genetic Evidence

The results of these studies strongly suggest that homosexuality does indeed have a significant genetic component, but the results in no way rule out the impact of environmental factors as well. A number of questions, even in the face of these results, remain. If homosexuality is indeed genetically determined, for instance, why aren't the family patterns more striking than they are and why are there so many instances in which one of two identical twins is homosexual and the other is heterosexual. And even if it is true that in some cases homosexuality is "inherited," there is yet another question that needs to be addressed: Is there a genetically influenced brain mechanism that actually determines sexual orientation, or do some people who become homosexuals simply inherit a predisposition to a certain personality that, in turn, results in homosexuality (Byne, 1994)? Recent findings, as we are about to see, would seem to favor the brain mechanism side of the argument, but these findings are not without their complications.

Exploring the Neuroanatomical Link

The question of whether homosexuality is an inherited or acquired behavior took on a new—and controversial—dimension in the early 1990s when a prominent neuroscientist named Simon LeVay published a study in which he reported neuroanatomical differences between male homosexuals and heterosexuals (LeVay, 1991).

LeVay performed postmortem examinations on brains from three groups, heterosexual men, homosexual men, and heterosexual women, and his findings confirmed an earlier report by Laura Allen and her colleagues (1989) that the third interstitial nucleus of the anterior hypothalamus (known as the INAH-3) is roughly twice as large in heterosexual men as in women. LeVay also reported—and this is the startling result—that a similar difference in INAH-3 size exists in heterosexual and homosexual men. He found, in fact, that the INAH-3 in homosexual men was the same size as it was in heterosexual women.

Qualifying the Findings

LeVay himself has emphasized that it is far too early to draw definitive conclusions from his work. To begin with, the work is new and is in need of replication. Second, many of the homosexual brains LeVay studied came from AIDS victims, raising the possibility that the reduction in INAH-3 size was related in some way to the disease. (LeVay did, however, find that in a small sample of subjects, INAH-3 was larger in heterosexual men even if they died from AIDS.) Third, LeVay's study was limited to *male* homosexuals, leaving open the critical question of whether INAH-3 differences exist between heterosexual and homosexual women. Finally, and most importantly, even if these problems are resolved and the neuroanatomical differences between heterosexual and homosexual men are found to be "real," the question remains, What conclusions can be drawn?

The problem, and it is a problem inherent in all correlational studies, is what can we conclude from a correlation? Does the neuroanatomical difference between heterosexual and homosexual men play a role in causing homosexuality or does it merely correlate with homosexuality? And what is the source of the neuroanatomical difference? Is it the result of genetics or is it the result of some other factor, such as early childhood experiences?

At best, then, all that we can conclude from LeVay's findings is that there may be a neuroanatomical difference between some homosexual and some heterosexual men. Whether this difference is related to a genetic causal factor of homosexuality or is only a consequence of homosexuality remains to be determined.

Cerebral Lateralization: Female-Male Differences

We would be remiss if we ended this chapter by giving you the impression that sexual dimorphism—the differences between males and females—are limited to physical appearance and sexual behavior only. There is recent evidence suggesting that anatomical differences between the male brain and the female brain may account for behavioral differences not related to sexual behavior and previously thought to be culturally determined. These differences involve a feature of the brain called cerebral lateralization.

As you saw in Chapter 3, the brain is divided into two cerebral hemispheres with a number of interconnections, the most prominent of which is the corpus callosum. Each hemisphere in humans tends to have its own special function. In most people (male or female), the left cerebral hemisphere controls language and the right cerebral hemisphere is involved in nonverbal behavior such as perceiving spatial relations (see Chapter 18 for details).

There is now some evidence suggesting that hemispheric specialization, to a certain extent, may be different in males and females and that these differences in turn may be rooted in neuroanatomical differences. Behavioral evidence comes from the fact that females on average perform better than males on tests that rely on language skills than they do on tests that involve spatial relations. The neuroanatomical evidence comes from studies indicating that the corpus callosum (de Lacoste-Utamsing & Halloway, 1982; Allen et al., 1991), as well as the anterior commissure (another interconnecting tract between the hemispheres) is larger in females than in males (Allen & Gorski, 1992). It is worth noting that differences in the size of the anterior commissure have been found in comparative autopsy studies involving homosexual and heterosexual males, with homosexual males showing the same pattern as heterosexual females—a larger anterior commissure than heterosexual males (Allen & Gorski, 1992). The significance—and indeed the cause—of this difference has yet to be determined. Neither has it been determined if the behavioral differences between heterosexual males and females—differences in language and spatial skills—are paralleled by differences between heterosexual and homosexual males.

What are we to conclude from the cerebral lateralization studies with respect to gender-related behavior in general? Are females on average more skilled in language and males on average more adept in spatial relations because female and male brains have different interconnecting tracts? Or are the interconnecting tracts a result of the differences in female and male behavior? Or are the two merely correlates and unrelated? We'll return to these and related questions in Chapter 18.

Recapitulation

It is now time for us to put the entire matter of the human brain and sexual orientation into some perspective, particularly since differences in brain anatomy and behavior have received considerable publicity in recent years. Table 13.1 presents a summary of the relations between brain anatomy and behavior. We need to make a distinction, however, between the findings themselves and the conclusions we draw from them.

Clearly, we know far more about the human brain and sexual orientation today than we knew as recently as ten years ago. We can now say, with reasonable certainty, that there are neuroanatomical differences between the heterosexual male and female brain. We can also say, with somewhat less certainty, but with increasing empirical support, that

TABLE 13.1

A SUMMARY OF NEUROANATOMICAL DIFFERENCES AMONG HETEROSEXUAL MALES AND FEMALES AND HOMOSEXUAL MALES AND THE BEHAVIORAL DIFFERENCES THAT THEY THEORETICALLY ACCOUNT FOR

	MALE HETEROSEXUAL	FEMALE HETEROSEXUAL	MALE HOMOSEXUAL
Sexual orientation	Large INAH-3	Small INAH-3	Small INAH-3
Cognitive abilities (spatial and verbal)	Small anterior commissure (AC)	Large AC	Large AC

there may also be differences between the male heterosexual and the male homosexual brain. Beyond these observations, however, the picture becomes more speculative especially with respect to the differences between the heterosexual and homosexual brain. We've already stated—but it's worth repeating—that no one can say at this time whether these neuroanatomical differences are genetically determined or the result of environmental factors, nor can anyone state with any real confidence that these neuroanatomical differences necessarily determine or are merely correlates of sexual orientation.

SUMMARY

1. *Sex defined.* In the strictest sense of the term, sexual behavior is inextricably connected to reproduction—to the joining of the egg of the female and the sperm of the male to produce a new, fertilized cell, known as the zygote. The physical means through which sexual behavior takes place varies considerably from species to species, as do other factors, such as the frequency of sexual behavior. Human sexual patterns vary so much it is next to impossible to establish norms.

2. *The human difference.* The principal difference between sexual behavior in lower animals and sexual behavior in humans is that sexual behavior in lower animals, much more so than in humans, is biologically bound—confined to periods when the female is ovulating (that is, when the egg is available for fertilization). Although human females experience heightened feelings of sexuality around the time of ovulation each month, the sexual receptivity of human females is not confined to these periods.

3. *External control.* For two individuals of any species to engage in sexual behavior, two conditions must be present: the female must be in a receptive state and the male must be responsive to this state. In most species, the receptivity of the female is controlled by internal factors whereas sexual responsiveness in the male is generally keyed to external cues, such as odors, colors, and body positions assumed by the female. The external factors capable of influencing sexual activity in humans are many and varied. They include any number of social factors, such as religious beliefs and peer pressure.

4. *Hormones and sexual behavior.* Chief among the controlling mechanisms for sex are hormones, and two hormones in particular—androgen and estrogen—play a central role. Androgen and estrogen are found in both males and females, but androgen predominates in males whereas estrogen predominates in females. A third group of sex hormones, known as the progestins, plays a role in fertilization. The sexual responsiveness of female rats can be manipulated by increasing or decreasing levels of estrogen. And the sexual activity of male rats, albeit to a lesser extent, can be manipulated by increasing or decreasing levels of testosterone.

5. *Hormone influence on human sexual behavior.* The extent to which hormones control sexual behavior diminishes the higher up you move on the evolutionary ladder. Procedures that reduce sex hormone levels in female monkeys reduce sexual behavior but do not eliminate it. The effect of such procedures on human sexual activity is less pronounced, although John Money has found that women who have undergone adrenalectomies—removal of the adrenal glands—show a decline in sexual urge. A similar pattern is seen with male monkeys and male humans, but with one exception. If castration—removal of the testes—takes place before a boy reaches puberty, sexual responsiveness simply does not develop.

6. *Sex and the brain.* The area of the brain most directly involved in sexual behavior is the hypothalamus. This control, however, is exerted indirectly through a more or less circular series of events that begin when the hypothalamus stimulates the anterior pituitary gland. This gland then stimulates the sex glands to release sex hormones, which travel to the hypothalamus and initiate sexual behavior. One of the more significant findings in this area of research is that estrogen can activate both male and female behavior, depending upon where in the hypothalamus it is implanted. Characteristic female sexual behavior is initiated by the ventromedial hypothalamus, while characteristic male sexual behavior is under the control of the medial preoptic area. The suspicion that different areas of the hypothalamus are involved in different types of sexual behavior has been confirmed in a number of studies showing that lesions to either area abolish the normal behavioral pattern. One complication to these findings is the fact that hypothalamic disruption in males appears to have more effect on their ability to perform than on the urge to perform.

7. *Explaining the difference.* The fact that different areas of the hypothalamus initiate different types of behavior suggest there are structural differences between the male rat brain and the female rat brain. Rat studies reported in the late 1970s confirm these differences, showing that the preoptic area of the hypothalamus is roughly five or six times larger in the male rat brain than female brain. Laura Allen, more recently, has found evidence that a similar difference—although not as pronounced—exists in humans. Differences in brain structure that have a bearing on sexual activity are known as dimorphic differences, and studies on these differences have focused, in particular, on an area of the hypothalamus known as the sexually dimorphic nucleus.

8. *Estrogen in male rats.* The discovery by Donald Pfaff that receptors responsive to estrogen appear in both the male brain and female brain of lower animals has clouded what once appeared to be a clear-cut picture of sexual hormone activity in the brain. The source of estrogen, however, differs in the male and female brains. In females it comes from the ovaries. In males it is produced in the brain from testosterone through a chemical process known as aromatization. The effect of estrogen in male sexual behavior, however, may be limited to rats. Although estrogen

given to castrated male rats restores sexual behavior, estrogen given to
guinea pigs and monkeys does not.

9. *The sexual behavioral circuit.* Regardless of how it is initiated, sexual
behavior is a chain of events, each element controlled by a specific neural
component in a complex circuit. The motivational aspect of sexual
behavior is rooted in the hypothalamus–pituitary–gonad circuit.
Performance—the ability to engage in sexual behavior—is part of the
same chain and is rooted in the spinal cord–cortex circuit.

10. *The circuit: a closer look.* It has not yet been determined what specific areas of the brain evaluate environmental stimuli related to sex and
which areas exert control over the spinal circuit that controls performance. But electrical stimulation studies have yielded significant clues.
Areas believed to play a part in various aspects of actual sexual behavior
include the dorsolateral hypothalamus, the medial forebrain bundle
(which produces isolated ejaculation), and the posterior hypothalamus.
The evaluative aspects of sexual behavior—the decision to approach a
particular sex object—seem to be chiefly under the control of the cortex.
Cortical damage in experimental animals disrupts the sexual behavior of
males more than it does the sexual behavior of females, but it is likely
that the cortical damage may have more to do with the *ability* to respond
than it does with the *urge* to respond.

11. *Sexual response: the human dimension.* Much of what is known
about the human sexual response comes from the work of William
Masters and Virginia Johnson, who have identified four distinct phases
of the sexual response cycle: excitation, plateau, orgasm, and resolution,
with each phase accompanied by its own characteristic physiological
response. The precise neural events that underlie each of these phases
have yet to be determined, but the foundation for the study of these
events has been established and we can expect important findings in
years to come.

12. *Developmental aspects of sex.* There are two critical periods during
which sex hormones establish the blueprint in humans for adult sexual
appearance and behavior. The first is during fetal development, the second is during puberty. Whether a fetus develops male or female characteristics during the early stages of development depends on the presence
or absence of androgen. When androgen is present, the male characteristics develop. When androgen is absent, female characteristics develop.
Should this delicate hormonal environment of the fetus be disturbed during differentiation, the result is usually some form of sexual anomalies,
a classic example of which is seen in pseudohermaphrodites—individuals who have the chromosomes of one sex but the sexual organs of the
other.

13. *The role of alphafetoprotein.* Research on the hormonal development
in rats has revealed a critical difference between males and females.
Estrogen is present in both the male and female fetal brain, but the male
brain is capable of converting androgen into estrogen, which, in turn,

determines the development of the male neural circuit. The female fetal brain does not have this capacity, but even so, estrogen never reaches the female brain. The reason is an enzyme known as alphafetoprotein, whose function is to destroy estrogen in the bloodstream. The reason alpha-fetoprotein has no effect on *male* estrogen is that male estrogen is not carried in the bloodstream.

14. *Puberty.* Secondary sexual characteristics—e.g., the development of breasts in women and the growth of facial hair in men—begin to appear during puberty and, as far as we know, are triggered by the hypothalamus and two hormones, FSH and LH, released by the pituitary gland. Both hormones act on the sex glands—the testes and ovaries—which, in turn, release testosterone and estrogen to stimulate the development of secondary sexual characteristics. The two hormones—testosterone and estrogen—are found in both men and women. The difference is the ratio. Estrogen predominates in women; testosterone predominates in men. The balance, however, varies from individual to individual, and is affected by aging. Once women go through menopause, they lose their ability to produce estrogen, which tilts the hormonal balance toward testosterone. In males, testosterone production doesn't stop, but it gradually declines with age.

15. *Learning and sexual development.* Learning and environmental factors play a significant role in shaping individual sexual preferences and habits, and a significant role, too, in determining characteristic behaviors by both sexes. Whether these factors are as important as genetic factors remains an open and highly controversial question, particularly when it comes to homosexuality. Conventional wisdom has tended to attribute homosexuality to environmental factors, and this view draws support from the fact that men and women who have always considered themselves heterosexual often engage in homosexual behavior when they are sent to prison. Some recent and highly publicized studies by Laura Allen and by Simon LeVay, on the other hand, have reported neuroanatomical differences between homosexuals and heterosexuals—a finding that would suggest a genetic basis for homosexuality. These newer studies apart, the question of whether homosexuality—and indeed any specific sexual pattern or behavior—is genetically or environmentally determined remains open.

16. *Comparing the male and female brain.* Recent findings suggest that anatomical differences between the male brain and the female brain may account for behavioral differences that were previously thought to be culturally determined. Anatomical evidence comes from studies showing that the corpus callosum is larger in females than it is in males. Behavioral evidence comes from the fact that females on average perform better than males on tests that rely on language skills, and not as well as males on tests that involve spatial relations.

alphafetoprotein
androgens
aromatization
autoradiography
biphasic effect of progesterone
estradiol
estrogens
estrus
fetal development
gametes
homosexuality
hypothalamus
interstitial nucleus of the anterior hypothalamus (INAH-3)
lordosis
medial preoptic area
menstrual cycle
Müllerian ducts
Müllerian duct–inhibiting substance

myotonia
orgasm
pheromone
proceptive behavior
progesterone
progestins
pseudohermaphrodite
puberty
resolution
sex-determining region of Y
sexual dimorphism
sexually dimorphic nucleus of the preoptic area
spinal animal
testes-determining factor
testosterone
vasocongestion
ventromedial hypothalamus
Wolffian ducts
zygote

SUGGESTED READINGS

Becker, J. B., Breedlove, S. M., & Crews, D. *Behavioral Endocrinology*. Cambridge, MA: MIT Press, 1992.

Kelly, D. D. "Sexual Differentiation of the Nervous System." In Kandel, E. R., Schwartz, J. H., & Jessell, T. M. *Principles of Neural Science*, 3rd ed. New York: Elsevier, 1991.

Kimura, D. "Sex Differences in the Brain." *Scientific American*, 1992, 267, 118–125.

Knobil, E., & Neill, J. *The Physiology of Reproduction*. New York: Raven Press, 1988.

THE NEURAL BASIS OF EMOTION

INTRODUCTION

At first glance, emotions appear to be an almost impossible subject for physiological psychologists to study. It is challenging enough, after all, to study the physiological bases of easily defined and easily observed behaviors, such as eating and drinking. But how do you go about analyzing and quantifying behaviors that are experienced *internally*—and on a purely subjective level? And how do you differentiate the various feelings—love, joy, anger, fear, grief—customarily identified as emotions. Does the joy we experience when we first fall in love have the same physiological basis as the joy we experience when our favorite team wins a championship? Is the momentary flash of anger we feel toward a driver who cuts in front of us on a highway produced by the same internal processes the underlie the hurtful anger that comes when we learn that a close friend has betrayed our confidence?

Equally important (and equally troubling) is how to ascertain whether an observed behavior is in fact an accurate reflection of what is actually being experienced by the person being observed. When we see a friend crying, for instance, we assume that our friend is "sad"; and when we see people with joyful expressions on their faces, we assume that they are "happy," at least for the moment. We all know, however, that people often cry out of joy and that it's possible to conceal rage with a smile.

These complications are by no means easily resolved. Yet the undeniable fact that the internal sensations we identify as emotions are indeed distinguishable from one another—that is, the feelings we experience when we are sad differ from those we experience when we are happy—suggests that there are neural events specific to each experience. And the assumption is that the combination of neural events that produce, for example, the emotion identified as joy is different from the combinations of events that produce the emotions identified as anger, love, and hate.

There is a further assumption, namely, that in humans and probably in other higher animals, the neurochemical events that produce an emotional experience represent not the activity of any *one* particular neural structure but rather a diffusion of input from numerous structures, from the lowest, most primitive levels to the highest levels of the brain.

It is for these reasons, both behavioral and neural, that the study of emotions within the context of physiological psychology is so challenging an undertaking. Precious little is known at present about the physiological nature of such common emotional experiences as love and joy; and even less is known about the so-called secondary emotions, such as guilt and pity.

Overwhelming or not, this particular area of physiological inquiry has produced significant findings over the past 80 years. These studies, as you will see throughout this chapter, represent only the beginnings of our understanding of the neural basis of emotion, but they have established a reasonably solid scientific foundation on which insights and data will build as research moves forward. In this chapter, we will focus on the visceral (i.e., the bodily reactions) and cognitive aspects of emotion and then on the neural circuits involved in processing emotional states. In the following chapter, we will consider the behavioral abnormalities that result when the neural circuits for emotions break down.

ISOLATING THE CHAIN: AN OVERVIEW

Everyone agrees that emotional experiences can be triggered by stimuli originating both inside and outside the body. Watching a small dog being hit by a car on a busy street is a chilling experience. But you do not necessarily have to witness that sight to become emotionally upset. The mere memory of the experience can be chilling. So can simply imagining an event of this nature.

Several theories have been proposed to chart the chain of events that produces the experience (regardless of its source), but for the most part all the theories fall into one of two categories, as illustrated in Figure 14.1. According to one general theory, emotional experiences are initially triggered by external stimuli—the sight of a dog being hit by a car, for instance—that produce impulses which travel directly to the brain. Neural processes then transform these impulses first into the feelings we identify as emotions and then into the bodily reactions—a quickened heartbeat, for instance—that accompany a particular emotion. The nature of the emotion, in other words, governs the bodily response.

A second theory is more complex. It proposes the following: before a stimulus can be transformed into an emotional feeling, the impulses produced by the stimulus travel first to the brain, then to the viscera, where they produce such behavior as a quickened heartbeat, and then back to the brain, where they produce emotion. According to this theory, the bodily reaction (e.g., the rapid rise in heartbeat that accompanies the

Figure 14.1   *Two Theories of Emotion*
According to one theory (a), stimuli produce emotion, which in turn produces behavior. According to the other theory (b), stimuli produce behavior, which in turn produces emotion.

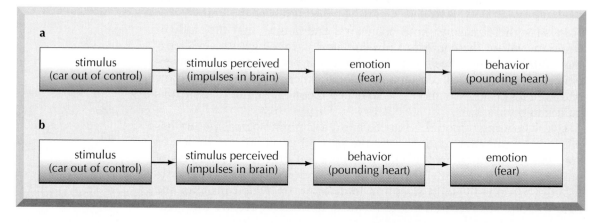

sight of a car going out of control) determines the emotion we feel—in this case fear. We shall consider both theories, but because it is the more complex of the two, let us consider the latter theory first.

The James-Lange Theory

The idea that behavior determines emotion was first formulated in 1884 by William James, and it was reaffirmed shortly thereafter by Carl Lange in Denmark. Known appropriately enough as the *James-Lange theory* of emotion, this view of emotion—that behavior determines emotion and not the other way around—was difficult for most people to accept at the time (James, 1884). Students of behavior had long taken for granted that a stimulus triggers an emotion, which in turn determines behavior. You go to a funeral, and the sight of the dead person makes you sad. You cry. You see a child fall off a swing. You become frightened and you run to help the child. Stimulus, emotion, response.

Neither James nor Lange agreed with this position. In their view, the stimulus itself—the sight of a dead relative or a child in danger—does not, in and of itself, produce the emotional experience. It merely arouses a visceral response (the stirred-up state in your stomach during the funeral, for instance), which in turn produces the emotional feeling. Your stomach does not churn, in other words, because you are sad. You are sad because your stomach churns.

Stated briefly, and detailed in Figure 14.2, the James-Lange theory proposes that the following sequence of events determines an emotional experience:

1. A stimulus, either external or internal, triggers impulses to the sensory cortex, producing ordinary sensations (visual, auditory, etc.).
2. The sensory cortex initiates impulses to the autonomic nervous system, arousing the viscera.
3. The aroused state in the viscera triggers impulses back to the cortex.
4. Depending on where these impulses go and with what frequency they reach the brain, the individual experiences an emotional sensation that has a certain quality and intensity.

Cannon's Attack

When it was first introduced, the James-Lange theory was dismissed by most psychologists on the grounds that it was simply illogical. In the late 1920s, however, Walter Cannon challenged the theory on scientific grounds (Cannon, 1927).

Cannon insisted that the viscera could not possibly be the basis of emotion. His reasoning was based on timing. Emotions, he pointed out, occur very rapidly (as you well know if you have ever been in a car that has suddenly skid). Visceral signals, on the other hand, depend on endocrine function and not on rapid neuroelectrical signals, and so they tend to require relatively long reaction times. How, then, Cannon wanted to know, could a visceral response *precede* and cause an emotion?

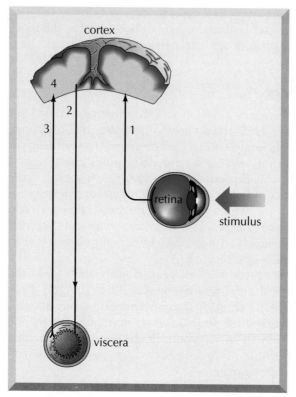

Figure 14.2 *The James-Lange Theory of Emotion*
James and Lange propose that emotion is experienced
when visceral activity is projected to the cortex (shown as
circuit 3).

Cannon also questioned the ability of the viscera to produce the *variety* of emotions we humans are capable of experiencing. He argued that visceral responses are neither versatile nor sensitive enough to provide a cue distinctive enough for each of the vast variety of emotions that humans can experience, let alone for each of the many gradations of individual emotions.

He noted, too, that even after cats were surgically deprived of input from their sympathetic nervous system, they nonetheless displayed emotional-type behaviors, such as hissing and clawing. More recent studies on people with spinal cord damage confirm this view. Even though the patients have diminished feedback from their viscera, they still report experiencing intense emotions (Chwalisz, Diener, & Gallagher, 1988; Bermond et al., 1991). These observations, it should be pointed out, indicate that visceral feedback is not essential for emotion. They do not rule out, as we are about to see, that under normal non-damaged conditions visceral feedback may *contribute* to emotion.

The Cannon-Bard Theory

Like any good scientist, Cannon did not simply criticize the James-Lange theory, but with his colleague Philip Bard he advanced an alternative theory (Bard, 1928; Cannon, 1929). This theory is known today as the *Cannon-Bard*, or *thalamic*, *theory* of emotion, and its focal point is the thalamus, which Cannon believed to be the origin of emotional behavior in the brain.

Cannon and Bard discovered that they could produce emotionally loaded rage behavior by removing the cortex of laboratory animals (Bard, 1934). This discovery led them to propose that the cortex normally *inhibits* the release of emotion by inhibiting the thalamus, and they built their theory around this assumption. The sequence of events is illustrated in Figure 14.3 and can be stated roughly as follows.

Figure 14.3 *The Cannon-Bard Theory of Emotion*
Cannon and Bard submit that emotion is experienced when thalamic activity, which is released from the inhibitory influence of the cortex (denoted by X) when the cortex is stimulated, feeds back to the cortex (circuit 3).

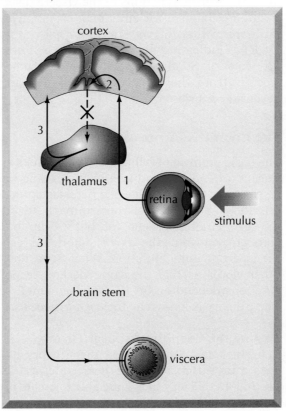

1. Stimuli (internal or external) produce impulses that are projected to the sensory cortex and are accompanied by corresponding sensations (visual, auditory, etc.).
2. Once these impulses reach the cortex (and here, really, is the key to the theory), they block the inhibitory action of the cortex and release activity in the thalamus.
3. The impulses excited in the thalamus then travel concurrently in two directions: to the brain stem, where the autonomic nervous system is triggered to produce visceral responses, and—crucially—back to the cortex, where the sensation of emotion is produced.

The critical difference between the Cannon-Bard theory and the James-Lange theory of emotion, as you can see by comparing Figures 14.2 and 14.3, is that Cannon and Bard did not believe that visceral reactions *produce* emotion; their view was that these reactions simply *accompany* the emotion as a side effect. Emotion has its real source, according to Cannon and Bard, in impulses that originate in the thalamus and travel to the cortex.

Subsequent experiments on the physiology of emotion have suggested that Cannon's dismissal of the visceral argument, as embodied in the James-Lange theory, may not have been entirely warranted. The insensitivity and diffuse reactions of the viscera discount the viscera as the sole coding mechanism for emotional experiences. But this does not necessarily mean that the viscera do not play at least *some* role in emotion. Evidence indicating that emotion has a visceral component comes from the work of Stanley Schachter and Jerome Singer (1962) and more recently from the work of Paul Ekman and his colleagues (Ekman, Levenson, & Friesen, 1987).

The Cognitive-Arousal Theory

The basic premise of Schachter and Singer's view is that emotional experiences are indeed produced by visceral action, but that this action represents only the first stage of a two-stage process. In their view, a visceral sensation—butterflies in your stomach, for instance—serves as a signal to trigger emotional behavior, but it is up to the cognitive powers of the cortex to determine the *kind* of emotional response that is appropriate to the environmental situation. What Schachter and Singer are saying, in other words, is that the same visceral response can produce different emotions depending on the environmental situation (see Figure 14.4). Their theory is known as the *cognitive-arousal theory* of emotion.

Testing the Cognitive-Arousal Theory

Schachter and Singer tested their theory by injecting human subjects with a drug that increases heart rate and creates a general feeling of arousal. In this way they were able to create roughly the same level of visceral arousal in all subjects. Next they gave the subjects different instructions regarding the effects of the drug, thus varying cognitive appraisal of the visceral arousal. One group was accurately informed about the

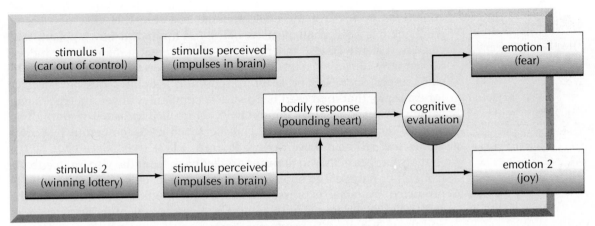

Figure 14.4 *Schachter and Singer's Theory of Emotion*
According to Schachter and Singer, emotion depends on two factors: the bodily response produced by the stimulus and cognitive evaluation of the environmental situation. In this illustration two stimuli result in the same bodily response (pounding heart); the emotion depends on which stimulus (car or lottery) the person attributes the bodily response to.

effects of the drug—that is, they were told exactly what its manifestations are—and therefore did not have to look to the environmental situation to explain the arousal sensations they were experiencing. Another group of subjects was *not* informed about the drug's effects and was in fact misinformed. Presumably, then, these subjects were obliged to look to the environmental situation to explain the source of arousal.

Each subject was then put in a room with a confederate (a person whose role in the experiment is unknown to the subject) of the experimenter. In some cases the confederate acted happy; in others the confederate acted angry. Consistent with their hypothesis, Schachter and Singer found that although the state of visceral arousal remained constant in all subjects, the emotional feelings of the subjects differed according to the mood state of the confederate. Subjects who had been informed of the drug's effect described their emotional reaction to the confederate as "indifferent." Subjects in the uninformed group identified their reaction as "happy" or "angry," depending on the behavior of the confederate. The conclusion: environmental factors shape emotional experiences.

Schachter and Singer's view is not without its critics. For one thing, the Schachter and Singer experiment has proven difficult to replicate (Reisenzein, 1983). The more serious challenge, however, has been made to the cognitive-arousal theory itself.

THE JAMES-LANGE THEORY REVISITED

Schachter and Singer's work strongly suggests that the James-Lange theory is at least partially correct—that visceral responses are important keys to emotional experience, albeit only to the extent that they trigger cognitive appraisal of the environment. But even this view of visceral feedback has been challenged as being too limited. It now appears that certain visceral states, independent of the environment, may indeed accompany and contribute to the quality of certain emotions (specifically, anger, sadness, and fear). Ekman and his colleagues have found, for example, that increased heart rate accompanies anger, increased galvanic skin response (skin conductivity which is a measure of autonomic arousal) accompanies sadness, and increased hand temperature accompanies fear (Ekman, Levenson, & Friesen, 1987).

It also appears that in addition to feedback from the viscera, feedback from other parts of the body—specifically, feedback from muscle activity produced by facial expressions—may contribute to the quality of the emotional experience. Let us now take a closer look at facial expression and the role it plays in producing emotions.

Facial Expression and Emotions

We can usually tell simply by looking at someone's face what emotion that person is experiencing. But why would an emotional experience manifest itself in a facial expression?

One of the first people to explore this issue was Darwin, who in his book *Expression of Emotions in Man and Animals* speculated about facial expressions and their relation to the physiological basis of emotion. Darwin argued that the ability to *express* emotions—either by body position in lower animals or by facial expressions in humans—was an important factor in evolution (Darwin, 1872). Facial expressions in humans and behavioral displays in lower animals (e.g., a dog baring its teeth), in his view, served as a means of communication, informing other humans or animals of the emotional state at that moment and, possibly, of what behavior to expect. Heeding these signals in turn enabled our ancestors to avert confrontation and thus increased the likelihood of survival for both the person expressing the emotion and the person observing it. The implications of this evolutionary view are significant. If the ways in which we express our emotions—the fact that we smile when we are happy and frown when we are sad—are indeed vestiges of our prehistoric past, then we would expect the expression of emotions to be universal among all humans. We would also expect that the behavior is genetically determined. Evidence exists confirming both assumptions.

Evidence for Darwin's Theory of Facial Expression

Look at Figure 14.5. What is so remarkable about the facial expressions and the emotions they signify is that, as Darwin predicted, the connections between the two (the facial expression and the emotion signified) appear to be part of our human heritage—that is, they appear to be both universal and genetically determined.

Evidence that they are universal comes from cross-cultural studies conducted by Paul Ekman and his colleagues (Ekman, 1977; Ekman & Friesen, 1971). In one study, subjects from a number of different coun-

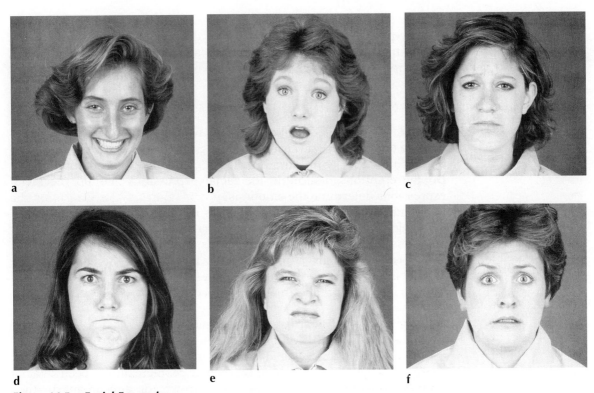

Figure 14.5   Facial Expressions
The photos depict the facial expressions that are regarded as reflecting the six basic human emotions: (a) happiness, (b) surprise, (c) sadness, (d) anger, (e) disgust, and (f) fear.

tries were asked to identify the emotions portrayed in the photographs. Regardless of the culture—whether literate (American, Japanese) or nonliterate (people from an isolated tribe in New Guinea)—the subjects made similar judgments (Ekman, 1992; Ekman et al., 1987). Apparently, then, it doesn't matter if you are an American college student or a tribesman from New Guinea—a smile signifies pleasure and happiness, a frown signifies sadness, and a scowl signifies disgust and scorn.

Evidence that these facial expressions and the emotions they represent are genetically determined and not learned comes from observations of children who have been blind from birth. These children show the same facial expressions—a smile, a frown, a scowl, and so forth—under the same emotional conditions as sighted children even though they clearly have been unable to learn these expressions simply by observing (Eibl-Eibelfelt, 1972).

We must be careful, however, not to overstate the genetic case. To say that facial expressions in response to emotional states are genetically determined is not to say that you cannot deliberately adopt a facial expression that runs counter to the emotion you are feeling. We have all been in situations in which, for any number of reasons, we have not wanted to reveal how we are feeling—that we're afraid, or angry, or secretly pleased. And what we have all done in this situation is to put forth a facial expression that communicates the emotion we would like people to think we are feeling and not what we are actually feeling.

Facial Feedback Hypothesis

The link between the facial expressions we present to the outside world and the emotions we are actually feeling introduces an important question: What does the link between facial expression and emotion mean? Do the emotions determine the facial expressions? Or do the facial expressions determine the emotions?

Surprising as it may sound, there is evidence to suggest that facial expressions, like visceral responses, may contribute to the quality of emotions. You are happy, in other words, because you smile. You do not smile because you are happy. The view is known as the *facial feedback hypothesis* and, apart from emphasis on facial rather than visceral feedback, is identical to the James-Lange theory (Izard, 1977).

Testing the Facial Feedback Hypothesis

Evidence for the facial feedback hypothesis comes from an experiment conducted by Fritz Strack and his colleagues (Strack, Martin, & Stepper, 1988). Their goal was to show that when people exhibit specific facial expressions—that is, when they smile, frown, or appear angry—they eventually begin to feel the emotion that normally accompanies the expression, even without an external stimulus to cause the emotion.

The experimenters in this instance faced a major procedural obstacle. They had to rule out the possibility that cognitive factors might produce the emotional experience. On the one hand, they wanted their subjects to tense their facial muscles in a way that would produce a smile or a nonsmile. On the other hand, they didn't want the subjects to be aware that they were smiling or not smiling. Why? Because the awareness itself (rather than the muscle state per se) might influence the emotional feeling.

To resolve this problem, Strack and his colleagues devised a procedure in which subjects were given a set of instructions that produced either a smile or a nonsmile, but the subjects were never instructed directly to "smile" or "not smile." For example, to produce a simulated smile, subjects were told to clench a felt-tipped pen between their teeth. To produce the simulated nonsmile, they were told to hold the pen between their lips without involving the teeth.

If you try these tasks yourself, you will see that clenching a pen between your teeth does indeed force you to smile, whereas holding the pen between your lips makes a smile impossible. To further ensure that cognitive factors were not influencing the emotional experience, the experimenters gave the subjects misleading instructions. They told the subjects that the purpose of the experiment was to study what happens when people are asked to perform a task with a part of the body that normally is not involved in the task.

Having discounted cognitive factors in this way, the researchers then asked the subjects to indicate how funny they found a series of cartoons. The results supported the facial feedback hypothesis. When subjects were clenching the pen between their teeth (i.e., "smiling") they gave a higher humor rating to a cartoon than they did when they wore the non-smiling expression.

Cognitive-Arousal Theory Revisited

It is safe to conclude on the basis of the studies we have been considering that feedback from viscera and facial muscles may play at least some role in emotion. By the same token, however, the feedback is clearly too crude to account for the vast variety of emotions that humans are capable of experiencing, let alone for each of the many gradations of individual emotions. We mentioned at the beginning of this chapter how the same emotion—joy, for instance—can differ depending on the source of the joy: a victory from your hometown team or a smile from someone you've fallen in love with. These differences of course can be explained only in terms of cognitive factors. So while emotions may be produced by visceral or facial feedback, the precise form of emotions—the variety and gradations—appears to depend, as Schachter and Singer argued, on the environmental context in which the feedback occurs and, even more importantly, how the person perceives and interprets that situation.

The parallels between emotional and sensory processing are striking. As we emphasized earlier in the chapters on sensory processing, there is more to sensing a stimulus then just determining its physical properties. We "sense" lines and colors and clicks and tones but what we actually see and hear—scenes and paintings, voices and music—depends on the environmental context in which it occurs and how we interpret the situation. The same may hold for emotion. There is more to emotion than just its physical properties. We sense visceral and facial feedback, but what we actually experience, the precise form of that emotion—the variety and gradations of it—depends on the environmental context in which it occurs and how we choose to view it at that given moment in time.

THE ANATOMICAL BASIS OF EMOTION

Even if we assume that the cognitive theory of emotion combined with visceral and facial feedback is essentially correct and that emotional experiences result from a *combination* of aroused visceral activity, facial expressions, and cognitive activity, we are still left with a basic question: what, specifically, are the neural structures that transmit and code this information?

Research into this question has been going on for more than 80 years, but because this research characteristically involves manipulating and frequently destroying brain structures, it has been basically confined to lower animals. For this reason, only those behaviors from which emotions can be readily inferred—in particular, rage, fear, and pleasure—have been studied. Let us begin with fear and rage.

The Neural Basis of Fear and Rage

It is reasonable to question whether research that seeks to discover the neural substrates of rage or fear behavior in lower animals can be applied to human behavior, especially since the modulating and overriding role of the cortex in humans has no apparent parallel throughout the animal kingdom. It is, however, common knowledge—and history serves as its own witness—that interaction among humans, even among close and presumably loving family members, can be marked by animal-like violence. It is also a fact that a significant number of people seem to be unable to control these intense feelings (as the rising incidence of violent crime indicates). In light of these facts, a growing number of psychologists and neurologists now believe that certain forms of violent behavior may be specifically related to brain dysfunctions that are under experimental study in lower animals.

THE EARLY STUDIES

For all practical purposes, the search for the neural basis of emotional behavior began in the early 1890s. That was when the German physiologist Friedrich Goltz turned a docile dog into an ill-tempered, growling beast by making a cut at the midbrain level of the dog's brain stem (a technique known as a *decerebrate preparation*). Goltz's procedure produced the first empirical evidence linking specific areas of the brain to violent or aggressive behavior.

Follow-up studies in the early 1920s, most notably by Walter Cannon and his colleagues, narrowed the brain-rage relationship. Cannon's studies showed that detaching only the cortex from the rest of the brain (a technique known as a *decorticate preparation*) produced rage behavior in dogs, but with one interesting difference: the rage behavior was a good deal more organized than the behavior demonstrated by Goltz's decerebrate dogs (Cannon & Britton, 1925).

Philip Bard went several steps further. Using cats and starting at the top of the brain and working systematically downward, Bard detached different sections of the brain and then studied the resultant behavioral effects. Bard's work provided a wealth of information regarding brain-rage relationships, but the key finding pinpointed the hypothalamus as the area that apparently organizes attack behavior and then coordinates this behavior with internal visceral reactions.

Bard's data, summarized in Figure 14.6, stand as one of the first major steps in unraveling the neural basis of emotional behavior. Among the most interesting aspects of his work was the discovery that the type of rage manifested in animals whose cortices have been removed differs from the type of rage shown by normal animals. Normal rage responses

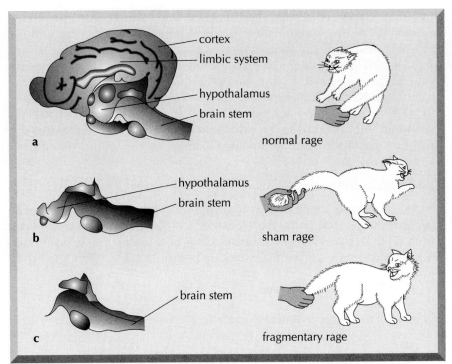

cortex
limbic system
hypothalamus
brain stem

a

normal rage

hypothalamus
brain stem

b

sham rage

brain stem

c

fragmentary rage

Figure 14.6 *Ablation-Rage Relations in Cats*
A cat with an intact brain (a) shows normal rage when its tail is pinched. A cat with only the hypothalamus and lower brain structures (b) shows a hypersensitive "sham rage" response when its tail is touched—normally an unprovocative stimulus. A cat with only lower brain structures (i.e., lacking the hypothalamus and all structures above it), as in (c), shows a disorganized "fragmentary rage" response to tail pinching.

continue even after the provocation stops and are always directed toward the provoker. Bard's neurally damaged animals simply struck out at random, in the air and at the ground. As soon as the provocation stopped, so did the rage. Because the response differed from that of real rage, having neither direction nor durability, Bard referred to it as *sham rage* and concluded that the cortex normally acts to inhibit this rage response (Bard & Mountcastle, 1948).

Bard then proceeded to lower his cut slightly and to disconnect the hypothalamus as well as the cortex, leaving only part of the midbrain and the lower brain stem connected to the spinal cord. Although this procedure erased any recognizable form of rage behavior, bits and pieces of rage, which were inappropriate and nonintegrated, did appear when the animal was provoked (Bard & Macht, 1958). A cat, for instance, would frequently purr while unsheathing its claws, indicating that without the hypothalamus it could not coordinate or organize its emotional response. The conclusion was that the hypothalamus is the area in the brain that organizes overt attack behavior and then synchronizes it with internal visceral reactions.

All told, Bard's data suggested that the key to the control of attack behavior lay in the antagonistic relationship between the cortex and the hypothalamus, with the hypothalamus organizing and releasing attack behavior and the cortex acting to inhibit the release. This conclusion seemed reasonable at the time, but subsequent research has shown the process to be considerably more complex. To understand its complexity, you need to understand something about the specific brain structures that lie in and around the hypothalamus. Most of these structures are part of an area in the brain known collectively as the limbic system.

The Limbic System

The limbic system, pictured in Figure 14.7, includes essentially those brain structures that lie in the oldest part of the cerebral hemispheres, which is known as the *rhinencephalon*, or *nose brain*. Included among these structures are parts of the hypothalamus, the amygdala, the septal

Figure 14.7 *The Principal Structures of the Limbic System*

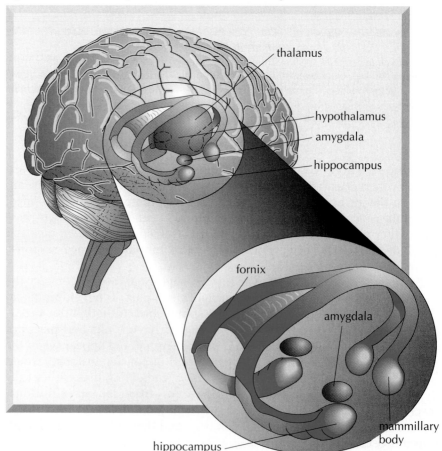

area, the hippocampus, the mammillary bodies, and parts of the cortex. Because they form a crude border around the brain stem, they are known as the *limbic* (meaning "border") system.

The existence of the limbic system was known long before Bard made his observations on rage. More than 100 years ago, the system was dubbed *le grand lobe limbique* by Pierre Broca, a prominent neurosurgeon who played a major role in elucidating the neural basis of language (see Chapter 1) (Broca, 1878). Initially, however, most anatomists assumed that the limbic system, because of its connections with the olfactory receptors, was concerned exclusively with smell. Not until a theoretical paper by James Papez in 1937 (Papez, 1937) and experimental findings reported 2 years later by Heinrich Kluver and Paul Bucy did researchers take seriously the possibility that the limbic system might be involved in emotion (Kluver & Bucy, 1939).

Papez's Circuit

The neural circuit for emotional experience proposed by Papez included, for the most part, structures in the limbic system. In addition to using Bard's observations and his own superb knowledge of neuroanatomy, Papez pieced the circuit together based on observations he had made on emotional behavior in brain-damaged humans and dogs.

The crucial feature of the circuit was the neural distinction Papez made between behavioral expression and the actual feeling of emotion. The neural circuit for behavioral expression, he theorized, was centered in the hypothalamus, which controls visceral reactions, and the motor cortex, which controls skeletal reactions. The neural circuit for the feeling of emotion was somewhat more complex, beginning in the hypothalamus and winding its way (via the mammillary bodies, the posterior hypothalamus, and the anterior nuclear group of the thalamus) to the cingulate cortex where the feeling of emotion is produced.

Paul Maclean has since revised Papez's circuit for emotion to include the amygdala, to emphasize the hippocampus, and to deemphasize the importance of the cingulate cortex. This revision of Papez's circuit has for the most part been confirmed (Maclean, 1949, 1954).

The Kluver-Bucy Syndrome

Not long after Papez's paper appeared, Heinrich Kluver, a psychologist, and Paul Bucy, a neurosurgeon, found that damage to the limbic system did indeed have dramatic effects on emotional behavior (Kluver & Bucy, 1939). After they removed each tip of the bilateral temporal lobes, Kluver and Bucy found that monkeys that were normally irascible and given to attacks of rage became extremely docile. They also found that some curious behaviors accompanied this docility, and these behaviors were eventually grouped into what is now called the *Kluver-Bucy syndrome*.

The chief feature of the Kluver-Bucy syndrome is that the animals express none of their normal fears, such as avoiding snakes, but do show a marked increase in other behaviors. For instance, they exhibit an increase in chewing behavior, attempting to ingest anything that can be taken into their mouths, including screws and bolts. The animals also show an increase in sexual behavior, attempting to copulate with males and females indiscriminately.

Kluver and Bucy's results were compromised to some extent by the crudeness of their procedure. In removing the temporal lobes, they inadvertently damaged several surrounding areas, notably the amygdala, the pyriform lobe, the presubiculum, and the hippocampus. So it was impossible at the time to tell which structures were linked with which behaviors in the syndrome. Hypersexuality, for instance, has since been linked to damage confined to the pyriform lobe. And with more precise analysis it has been discovered that the taming effect is related more to the amygdala than to the temporal lobes per se. Kluver and Bucy found, for instance, that when damage was confined to the amygdala while the temporal lobes were left intact, wild animals still exhibited docility (Kluver & Bucy, 1939). Lesions in the amygdala tamed not only wild monkeys but even a lynx, an animal so wild that it normally has to be handled with gloves and nets. It should be noted, however, that the amygdala was not the *only* area that had a taming effect when it was lesioned. Damage to the cingulate cortex also had a calming effect (Smith, 1944). The amygdala does, however, seem to have the most potent effect (Goddard, 1964).

ANALYZING THE LIMBIC SYSTEM

With Papez's circuit as a theoretical guide and the Kluver-Bucy syndrome as supporting evidence, work began in earnest to identify the role of the limbic system in emotional behavior. As data have accumulated over the past five decades, the neural circuit has turned out to be even more complex than researchers originally suspected. Indeed, one of the major problems researchers have encountered is that in a circuit as elaborate as the limbic system, interactions among the separate areas are far more complex than originally imagined—so complex that no single behavior can be attributed to the action of one, two, or even three areas.

Accordingly, we shall deal mainly with those data that are the least contradictory and most characteristic of a particular limbic area. We will begin with the hypothalamus, the center of emotional output, both internal and external. We will then focus on the amygdala, the hippocampus, and the frontal cortex, the areas that appear to control emotional behavior indirectly by modulating—facilitating or inhibiting—hypothalamic output. Finally, we shall consider the therapeutic implications of our understanding of the neural and chemical bases of emotion, in particular the aggressive and violent behavior of humans as well as fear.

The Hypothalamus: The Center of Emotional Output

Figure 14.7 will give you an idea of the location of the hypothalamus. It is a tiny cluster of nuclei with very broad behavioral involvement. We have already examined the role of the hypothalamus in the control of eating, drinking, sleep, and sexual behavior, all of which can be profoundly altered through either injury or artificial stimulation (electrical or chemical) of the hypothalamus. Now we will examine the role played by the hypothalamus in the control of emotional behavior, both internal (autonomic responses) and external (such as aggression).

The Hypothalamus and Autonomic Responses

At about the same time that Bard was lesioning the hypothalamus and discovering its significance in the control of overt aggressive behavior, Walter Hess, a Swiss physiologist, was applying electrical stimulation to various parts of the hypothalamus (Hess, 1954). Hess discovered that the hypothalamus is organized for the control of autonomic responses: one area (the posterior nucleus) for control of the sympathetic nervous system, and another (the anterior nucleus) for control of the parasympathetic nervous system. By stimulating the posterior hypothalamus, Hess was able to trigger such sympathetic responses as increases in heart rate. When he moved his electrode to the anterior part of the hypothalamus, however, he discovered just the opposite effect. Electrical stimulation now seemed to have a calming effect on both internal and external behaviors. Heart rate slowed and the animal became drowsy: two parasympathetic effects.

Hess's work thus indicates that the hypothalamus, in addition to adjusting the internal state in accord with metabolic needs created by hunger and thirst, has the capacity to adjust the internal state to meet needs created by external threats related to such emotional behavior as fear or rage. Let us now take a closer look at the role of the hypothalamus in the control of emotional behavior.

The Hypothalamus and Aggression

The hypothalamus has been the focal point of many studies designed to uncover the neural processes that underlie fighting and attack behavior (commonly referred to as aggression). Some of the best known of these studies have been performed by John Flynn and his coworkers. Flynn has found that electrical stimulation of different nuclei within the hypothalamus produces two different types of aggressive behavior in cats, depending on which nucleus in the hypothalamus is stimulated (Wasman & Flynn, 1962). Let us look at both.

Affective Behavior

Stimulation of the medial nuclei of the hypothalamus produces behavior that Flynn describes as *affective*. Cats stimulated in the medial nuclei show vicious attack behavior, hissing and unsheathing their claws and lashing out indiscriminately at any object within their reach.

Stalking and Quiet Biting

The situation changes dramatically when the electrode is shifted slightly to the lateral hypothalamus. Now a different sort of aggressive behavior is elicited, described as "stalking and quiet biting." Cats stimulated in the lateral hypothalamus attack but not with the hissing and slashing behavior seen in medial nuclei cats. They go about the attack in a manner suggestive of an unemotional trained killer. Flynn terms this behavior "directed" because the animals are quite selective about what they attack. Given a choice among a number of objects, including an anesthesized rat, a stuffed rat, and a styrofoam block, the stimulated cats almost never direct their attack toward the styrofoam block and almost always attack the stuffed or the anesthetized rat, showing little preference between the two (Levinson & Flynn, 1965).

Flynn compared the quiet-biting attack behavior to hunting, the difference being that the cat does not eat the rat it has attacked and killed. To make certain that the attack produced by electrical stimulation was not related to hunger, Flynn starved cats for 72 hours and then fed them. When stimulated in the lateral hypothalamus, the cats left the food and attacked the rat, indicating that the attack behavior elicited by stimulation could not be due to hunger, as it had overridden the hunger created by the 72 hours of food deprivation (Flynn et al., 1970).

Fine-Tuning the Hypothalamus and Aggression

More recent studies indicate that the areas controlling the two behaviors are not as circumscribed as Flynn originally suggested. Quiet biting can be produced by electrical stimulation in other areas of the hypothalamus (e.g., the perifornical nucleus) as well as areas in the midbrain, and affective behavior can be produced by stimulation in areas in the midbrain and amygdala (Siegel & Pott, 1988; Siegel & Brutus, 1990).

The Amygdala and Aggression

The role of the amygdala in emotional behavior is as complicated as that of the hypothalamus, if not more so. The chief problem is that the findings of numerous studies indicate that removing the amygdala can have diametrically opposite effects on emotional behavior. Some studies have shown that removing the amygdala has a taming effect on animals, while other studies, most notably those by Philip Bard and Vernon Mountcastle, have shown that it produces rage (Bard & Mountcastle, 1948). The conflict remains unresolved, although one plausible explanation is that the amygdala (like the hypothalamus) has overlapping systems, one excitatory and one inhibitory, and that lesions may favor one or the other because of the difficulty of placing lesions precisely.

David Egger and John Flynn have looked further into the amygdala's control of emotional behavior. They have shown not only that it has a dual effect on behavior but also that both effects may control aggressive behavior indirectly by modulating the output of the hypothalamus (Egger & Flynn, 1962, 1963). They have found that attack behavior elicited by stimulation of the hypothalamus can be *inhibited* if the basomedial nucleus of the amygdala is stimulated concurrently and that it can be *facilitated* by stimulation of the posterior portion of the lateral nucleus of the amygdala.

Flynn has also found that the amygdala is not the only structure that has a modulating influence on the output of the hypothalamus. The hippocampus also modulates it. Concurrent stimulation of the dorsal hippocampus and the hypothalamus inhibits attack, whereas concurrent stimulation of the ventral hippocampus and the hypothalamus facilitates attack (Flynn, 1967; Siegel & Flynn, 1968; Siegel & Edinger, 1981).

Temporal Lobe Epilepsy

Evidence for amygdala involvement in violent behavior in humans comes from experiments in "nature." Temporal lobe epilepsy is a type of epilepsy in which abnormal neuroelectrical activity remains confined to the temporal lobes (which include the amygdala). Typically, during these attacks people act in a repetitive manner. They make chewing movements, even though they have nothing in their mouths, and on occasion their behavior turns violent (Mark & Ervin, 1970).

The Amygdala and Social Order

Granting for the moment that the amygdala is in fact one of the principal neural structures controlling violent behavior, should we then conclude that the presence of the amygdala in the brain is maladaptive, perhaps a mutation?

Hardly. As numerous studies have shown, aggressive behavior seems to play an important role in the preservation of most species. Many animal societies are based on dominant-submissive hierarchies, and fighting is the means by which the social hierarchy is established. Moreover, the fighting that establishes this hierarchy (as in the case of the pecking order established among chickens) can be extended to fighting with members of other species (as in the case of a dog dominating a cat).

The means by which this order is achieved varies among species. In some lower animals, the hierarchy is controlled by odor. When the olfactory system is removed from some fish, for instance, many fight one another to the death (Moulton, 1968). Among other animals, social order is controlled by hormones. When injections of testosterone are administered to hens, they begin to behave like roosters. They become fighters, raising their status in the pecking order.

In higher animals, such as monkeys, the dominant-submissive hierarchy is clearly under neural control and involves the amygdala. Karl Pribram and his colleagues have found that the social hierarchy of a monkey colony can be dramatically altered by removing the amygdala from the brain of the dominant monkey (Pribram, 1962). Before surgery, a monkey named Dave was number one in the colony and could bully everyone else without fear of retaliation. Zeke was the number-two monkey, able to bully everyone except Dave. Once Dave's amygdala was removed, however, he slipped to the bottom of the hierarchy. Zeke took over the top spot, and everyone else moved up one rung.

The Amygdala and Fear

Apart from the role it plays in producing aggressive-type behavior, the amygdala also plays a central role in controlling fear. It appears to operate, in effect, like a central coordinating center, some areas in the amygdala receiving fear-related sensory information, other areas issuing fear-related motor instructions. At the hub of all of this activity is one area in particular—the central nucleus of the amygdala (Davis, 1992).

Researchers who study the physiological basis of fear in lower animals use a variety of behaviors to measure fear, chief among them "freezing" (cessation of ongoing behavior) and changes in autonomic activity such as heart rate, blood pressure, and respiration. These behaviors, moreover, are studied in two types of fear situations: unlearned fear that occurs when animals encounter aversive or threatening stimuli for the first time; and learned fear that occurs when animals are presented with stimuli that have previously been associated with an aversive event.

Evidence indicates that the amygdala is involved in both types of fear (see Chapter 16 for details on the amygdala and learned fear). When different areas of the amygdala are stimulated, for instance, behaviors that normally accompany unlearned or learned fears are produced. The animals, for instance, freeze and show a sharp increase in respiration, a prominent symptom of panic disorder seen in humans, described in Chapter 15 (Applegate et al., 1983; Harper et al., 1984). On the other hand, when different areas of the amygdala in lower animals are lesioned, the behaviors that normally accompany unlearned or learned fear are either impaired or abolished (LeDoux et al., 1988; 1990). Work in humans complements the work in lower animals. When the amygdala of humans being prepared for brain surgery is electrically stimulated, the patients not only show changes in autonomic activity, they also report "feelings" of fear (Gloor et al., 1981).

The Amygdala and Fear: A Closer Look

That the amygdala is involved in fear is clear, but how that involvement manifests itself is another matter. The general picture, as illustrated in Figure 14.8, is that the amygdala receives fear-related input from three sources—the sensory areas in the thalamus, the sensory areas in the cortex, and the hippocampus—with input from each accounting for a different aspect of fear. Input from the sensory areas in the thalamus and in the cortex accounts for how stimuli in the external world—the sight of a snake, the sound of thunder, for instance—are able to produce fear. The input from the hippocampus, an area involved in memory (see Chapter 17 for details), would explain why the memory of a frightening experience can often produce fear responses and would explain the familiar statement, "I get chills just thinking about it."

But why, you might ask are there two sensory circuits to the amygdala (as pictured in Figure 14.8), one that carries information from the receptors to the thalamus to the amygdala, and one that takes a more circuitous route, from the receptors to the thalamus and then to the cortex

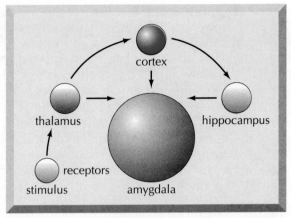

Figure 14.8 *The Amygdala and the Areas (Thalamus, Cortex, and Hippocampus) from Which It Receives Input*

before ending up in the amygdala? What behavioral purpose could be served by such an arrangement? No one as yet has come up with a definitive answer to this question, but one researcher, Joseph LeDoux, has recently advanced a compelling theory (LeDoux, 1994).

As LeDoux sees it, having two sensory circuits—a simple receptor-to-thalamus-to-amygdala circuit and a more complex receptor-to-thalamus-to-sensory cortex-to-amygdala circuit—is adaptive because it endows us with what might best be described (and we are paraphrasing LeDoux's explanation) as a "better safe than sorry reaction" to potentially threatening stimuli. The simple thalamic circuit gives us, in effect, an "early warning" system. It produces a quick but crude fear response on the basis of scant and raw sensory data, never mind that the response may turn out to be unwarranted—that is, the stimulus may ultimately turn out to be relatively harmless. The more sophisticated cortical circuit—more sophisticated because it subjects the sensory stimuli to cognitive processing—gives us a slightly delayed but more accurate perception of the stimulus, enabling us to verify whether the stimulus is indeed threatening enough to maintain the fear response. The presence of this dual-level processing system means that we will sometimes overreact (at least initially) to benign stimuli, but the benefit is that we are less likely to *underreact* to stimuli that could be life-threatening.

To illustrate his point, LeDoux poses a hypothetical situation in which you are walking in the woods and you spy a "slender curved shape" object lying on the path before you. The sight of this object, of course, suggests the presence of a snake, and so your initial reaction—even before you have ascertained that, yes, it *is* a snake—is to react in a defensive manner: to stop and to experience a sharp rise in autonomic activity, in short, to prepare for danger. LeDoux proposes that this initial quick response occurs because the raw sensory information travels directly from the thalamus to the amygdala, without being filtered through the cortex. Your ultimate response, though, depends on what happens when the amygdala receives input from the cortex. The more elaborate sensory processing of the cortex produces a more accurate perception of the object enabling you to verify the appropriateness of your initial response. If the "curved shape" turns out to be a snake, you continue to engage in the defensive behavioral pattern—back up, walk around the snake, pick up a stick to defend yourself—do any number of things to avoid the danger. If, however, the "curved shape" turns out to be nothing but an oddly configured branch, you resume your normal behavior—a little shaken, perhaps, but no worse for wear.

Aggression and Fear: A Behavioral Perspective

Tempting as it is to use the emotion-related studies among lower animals as models for human behavior, we need to exercise restraint, even when the results of animal studies seem relatively clear-cut.

A case in point are studies of how cats behave when presented with mice. The behavior of the cats varies. Some simply kill the mice, others play with them and then kill them, and still others exhibit fear and withdraw.

It is tempting to conclude on the basis of these observations that each of these animals is under the influence of a different emotional or motivational state—aggression, play, or fear. Recent evidence, however, indicates that the emotional state underlying the behavior is far more complex.

First, animals that demonstrate playful behavior before they kill the mice may not be "playing" in the normal sense of the word. Closer analysis of what has now come to be called *predatory play* indicates that what appears to be play behavior is in fact a mix of both aggressive and withdrawal behavior. By vacillating between the two, the animals create the illusion of play (Adamec, 1978; Adamec & Stark-Adamec, 1983).

Second, aggressive animals may not be motivated by pure aggression but rather by two emotional states operating at the same time: aggression and withdrawal (or, equivalently, fear)—with aggression dominating but held in check, at least to some degree, by withdrawal. The same holds for withdrawal animals—two emotions operating at the same time with withdrawal dominating but held in check to some degree by aggression.

Evidence for this view comes from an experiment by Sergio Pellis and his colleagues (Pellis et al., 1988). They gave cats an antianxiety drug, that is, a drug designed to make them less timid and thereby weaken withdrawal. If aggressive behavior is indeed held in check by the counterinfluence of withdrawal, now, with withdrawal weakened, aggression should be intensified. And this is precisely what they observed: aggressive animals became even more aggressive, playful animals (i.e., animals who normally showed a mix of both withdrawal and aggressive behavior) became aggressive, and withdrawal animals became playful. In short, following injection of the drug, aggressive behavior increased in all animals. Depending on their natural inclinations before receiving the drug, the increased aggression was exhibited in a different way.

We mention these findings not to confuse the issue but simply to illustrate how difficult it is to study emotional behavior in lower animals and to emphasize that the complexity of the analysis comes not only from the brain mechanisms that underlie emotion but also from the behavioral states used to infer emotion.

FROM LOWER ANIMALS TO HUMANS

Let us now return to the issue we raised earlier: the degree to which our knowledge of emotional behavior in lower animals can be applied to humans. The question is certainly valid but difficult to answer. The chief problem—and the main reason that applying the findings of animal research to human behavior is so delicate an issue—lies in the fact that however structurally similar the human brain may be to the brain of a rat, a cat, or a monkey, the human brain operates quite differently. Indeed, one of the most notorious examples of what can happen when researchers assume too much too quickly involves animal work on the frontal cortex and its application to the treatment of emotionally disturbed patients.

The Frontal Lobes and Aggression

In 1935 John Fulton and Carlyle Jacobsen observed that damage to the frontal cortex of chimpanzees eliminated emotional responses (Fulton & Jacobsen, 1935). Normally, when animals make errors in a learning task, they show signs of emotion; but Fulton and Jacobsen discovered that if the chimpanzees' frontal lobes were removed, the emotional response to errors tended to drop out. Even the most emotionally excitable animals became docile. These findings gave Egas Moniz, a Nobel Prize–winning neurologist, the idea of treating emotionally disturbed patients with frontal surgery. His procedure, known as *prefrontal lobotomy*, consisted of severing the connections between the frontal lobes and the rest of the brain. The purpose behind the procedure was to relieve some of the extreme emotions seen in human patients. The procedure seemed to work so well, especially in patients who suffered from bouts of extreme rage and aggression, that for a time it became a common practice in the treatment of emotional disorders. If you've ever seen the movie *One Flew over the Cuckoo's Nest*, you may recall that this procedure was performed on the hero of the movie, played by Jack Nicholson.

Prefrontal lobotomies, for the most part, are no longer performed today. That's because the procedure does more than simply calm emotionally disturbed people. It also produces a broad range of behavioral effects devastating to the psychological well-being of the patient.

Lobotomized individuals have difficulty solving problems: they have a marked tendency to repeat incorrect responses and also have difficulty following instructions. And clinical observations reveal that their emotional responses are dampened indiscriminately. The surgery not only corrects emotional overreaction but often produces patients who experience only euphoria or no emotional feelings and tend to have no social inhibitions. They do what they want when they want and rarely concern themselves with the consequences.

Psychosurgery

Prefrontal lobotomies fall into a broad therapeutic category known as *psychosurgery*. In recent years, as the role of the limbic system in violent behavior has come into clearer focus, some neurosurgeons have refined the surgical techniques used in prefrontal lobotomies and have used these techniques to destroy specific areas in the human brain—areas in the amygdala, for example—in an effort to curb the violent behavior seen with temporal lobe epilepsy (Mark and Ervin, 1970). Clinicians who advocate this highly selective type of psychosurgery see in it enormous therapeutic potential in the treatment of violent behavioral disorders that do not lend themselves to other forms of therapy. They also believe that the areas in the brain implicated in the control of violent behavior, notably the amygdala, can often be sacrificed with minimal side effects to the patient.

Psychosurgery itself, not surprisingly, is a highly controversial procedure. Apart from the temporal lobe work, psychosurgery in the United States has been performed primarily on violence-prone inmates in mental institutions, and reports of these operations indicate a relatively high level of success in curbing violent behavior. The problem, though, is this: the condition of the patients to begin with—the fact that nearly all suffered from serious behavioral abnormalities apart from violent behavior—leaves unanswered the question of how psychosurgery affects normal behavior. On the basis of a few reports involving patients who were functioning normally aside from occasional fits of violence, there is reason to believe that psychosurgery, no matter how discrete the physical damage it causes, can impair intellectual capacity (Valenstein, 1980). In any event, the legal and ethical implications of the technique, quite apart from any questions regarding its ultimate effectiveness, make it unlikely that psychosurgery will become a common therapeutic technique for many years to come.

The Case of Phineas Gage: Looking Back to the Future

Clinical studies, as you have just seen, have demonstrated clearly that prefrontal lobotomies in all but extreme cases create more problems than they solve. But long before prefrontal lobotomies were first performed, there was evidence to suggest a strong link between frontal lobe damage and profound changes in personality. The problem was that few people at the time were willing to accept the evidence as valid, as demonstrated in the following account (Damasio et al., 1994).

The source of this evidence was a man named Phineas Gage, who while working as a railroad construction foreman in 1848 suffered a horrifying accident in which a pencil-thin tamping iron used routinely to trigger an explosion tore like a bullet through his face, skull, and brain, exiting the top of his skull and landing many yards away. Miraculously, Gage survived the accident and, according to accounts, regained consciousness within seconds and was able to converse with the men who helped him walk away from the scene. Eventually, too, he was able to recover from his injury physically intact and with little noticeable damage to his sensory or motor or intellectual faculties.

But Gage was never the same man after the accident. Once described by his employers as "the most efficient and capable" employee in the company, Gage seemed to lose all interest in work. He showed no respect for his fellow workers and could not be trusted to carry out any task that involved any responsibility. He simply didn't care any more. He was fired and eventually became a drifter, ending up 12 years later, when he died, under the care of his family.

Given what we know about the impact of prefrontal lobotomies, Gage's behavior is hardly surprising, for the accident produced the kind of brain damage that a prefrontal lobotomy often produces; it severed a part of the frontal lobe from the rest of his brain. And it led to precisely the kind of moral and social indifference that is characteristic of many lobotomy patients.

Some 20 years after the accident, and several years after Gage's death, John Harlow, the physician who originally treated Gage, became interested once again in the particulars of the case and was able to gain the family's permission to exhume Gage's body so that Gage's skull could be examined. Harlow later wrote a paper in which he suggested a link between the frontal-lobe damage that Gage suffered and the personality changes that ensued, but his views didn't find a receptive audience in the scientific community.

It is worth noting that at roughly the same time Harlow was proposing a link between specific areas of the brain and personality traits (emotional and social behavior), Pierre Broca was using data from his brain-damaged patients to demonstrate a link between specific areas of the brain and the ability to speak. Broca's work, as we saw in Chapter 1, was accepted (albeit reluctantly), and so it's reasonable to ask why Harlow's work was all but unilaterally dismissed. There are two reasons. The first was philosophical: as tough as it was for the scientific world in the mid-1800s to accept the notion that language—a higher-order behavior—is under the control of a specific area of the brain, the notion that emotional and social behavior, too, could be traced to a specific area of the brain was well beyond what scientists at the time were prepared to believe. The second reason is that unlike Broca, Harlow had no autopsy data (other than a damaged skull) to document the precise nature of the brain damage. Thus, he had no way of showing that Gage's behavior was linked to specific areas in the frontal lobe, areas distinct from those areas known to be involved in the control of motor behavior and speech.

Today, thanks to computer technology, we know that Harlow's observations were correct. A team of neurologists, led by Hanna Damasio, recently obtained Gage's skull (it was on display at the Warren Anatomical Medical Museum at Harvard) and ran a series of highly sophisticated neuroimaging studies in which, based on the size of the tamping iron and the location of the entry and exit points, they were able to determine with reasonable accuracy which areas of the brain had been damaged (Damascio et al., 1994). Their studies bore out their initial suspicions; that Gage's injury had produced damage to the ventromedial region of frontal lobe. Their data not only confirm that the frontal lobe is involved in the control of emotional and social behavior but it adds to existing evidence, based on brain-damaged cases, that the frontal lobe is divided into two systems: the ventromedial system concerned with emotional and social behavior, and the dorsolateral system, involved with intellect and reasoning (Goldman-Rakic, 1992). Phineas Gage, it now appears, was a classic example of someone with ventromedial damage—that is, his intellectual behavior remained untouched while his emotional and social behavior were profoundly affected.

Chemical Coding for Aggression: Therapies of the Future

Just as the lesion work in rats and monkeys inspired the development of psychosurgical techniques for humans, research on the chemical basis of aggression may provide a basis for the development of drugs. Exactly when such drugs will become a therapeutic reality is difficult to predict, but breakthroughs at the chemical level have made such possibilities more likely.

Acetylcholine and Aggressive Behavior

Much of what we know about acetylcholine and aggressive behavior began with the early work of Bartley Hoebel and his colleagues (King & Hoebel, 1968; Smith, King, & Hoebel, 1970). Hoebel implanted cannulas (tiny hypodermic needles) in the lateral hypothalamus of rats that had been screened for mouse-killing tendencies and categorized as either "killers" or "nonkillers." He then administered chemical stimulation in the form of either carbachol, a drug that acts like acetylcholine, or atropine, a drug that inhibits the action of acetylcholine. Hoebel found that carbachol caused the nonkillers to kill, and atropine caused the killers to stop killing. Thus, in rats at least, it seems that acetylcholine levels in the lateral hypothalamus are critically related to aggressive behavior. It appears, too, that the tendency to kill, controlled as it may be by the lateral hypothalamus, can be shifted from one extreme to the other with injections of acetylcholine-related drugs.

Serotonin and Aggressive Behavior

While Hoebel and his colleagues concentrated much of their early work on the relationship between acetylcholine and aggression, other researchers studied another neurotransmitter, serotonin (Vergnes, 1981). The case for serotonin as a factor in aggression is based mainly on observations that depletion of serotonin produces mouse-killing behavior in rats. Various procedures have been used to deplete serotonin—lesions, drugs, and dietary manipulations—and each procedure has given us a different insight into the problem.

Lesion work, for instance, has centered on the raphe nuclei, an area in the brain stem. The reason is twofold: first, the raphe nuclei are one of the few areas of the brain known to produce serotonin; second, the raphe nuclei give rise to neurons that project to many areas of the midbrain and forebrain, including the limbic system. The rationale behind these studies is that the raphe nuclei, through their connections to the limbic system, may exert control over aggression by inhibiting the output of the limbic system through the release of serotonin. Consistent with this hypothesis, lesions in the raphe nuclei have been shown to produce mouse-killing behavior, and the same results have been obtained by injecting drugs that block the action of serotonin in the limbic system (Vergnes, Mack, & Kemp, 1973). Similarly, dietary work has pointed to a connection between a deficiency in serotonin and aggressive behavior. Rats fed a diet deficient in tryptophan—an amino acid used in the production of serotonin—manifest killing behavior (Vergnes & Kemp, 1981). Conversely, rats given tryptophan show a decrease in aggressive behavior (Broderick & Bridger, 1984).

Humans, Serotonin Deficits, and Aggressive Behavior

Here again, it is logical to ask ourselves whether these findings have any bearing on human behavior. In this particular instance, there is some evidence—albeit preliminary—that serotonin deficiencies may be a factor in aggressive behavior of humans. Studies on people who have a history of aggressive behavior either toward others or toward themselves (i.e., who commit or attempt to commit suicide) show serotonin deficits (Brown et al., 1979, 1982).

The fact that serotonin deficiencies *correlate* with aggressive behavior, however, in no way means that the deficiencies *produce* aggressive behavior. The problem, and it is a problem inherent in all correlational studies, is what we can conclude from a correlation. Does the serotonin deficit cause aggressive behavior in humans or does the aggressive behavior cause the serotonin deficit? Or does a third unknown factor cause both? Unfortunately, no experiment employing a correlational approach can answer these questions. Experiments using a manipulative approach—that is, experiments showing that *altering* serotonin levels also alters aggressive behavior—may do so. But even if it could be shown that serotonin deficits do play a role in aggressive behavior in humans, you must realize that it is one of several factors, one of the others being learning.

The Chemistry of Fear

While some researchers have been looking at the chemical basis of aggression, others have focused on the chemical basis of fear and have begun to gain an understanding of how chemical events within the brain control fear behavior.

A common procedure in these experiments is to inject rats with drugs, such as benzodiazepines (Valium and Librium), known to allay anxiety in humans, and then to observe how the rats behave in fear-provoking situations. One apparatus typically used in these studies is known as the elevated plus maze (Pellow et al., 1985). The maze consists of four narrow alleys, two walled and two unwalled, arranged at right angles to each other in the form of a "plus sign" and elevated 50 cm above the floor. Because rats have an inherent fear of heights, they tend to explore and spend more time, once they are placed in the maze, in the walled (enclosed) than in the unwalled (open) alleys. But as you might expect, when rats are administered benzodiazepines, they appear to lose their fear, as measured by their willingness to explore and spend time in the unwalled alleys of the maze they normally avoid in the nondrugged state.

Based on what we know about how benzodiazepines operate in the synapse (see Chapter 5 for details) and what we know about the brain—specifically the amygdala—and its control of fear, it is possible to piece together a general picture of how benzodiazepines interact with the amygdala and how this interaction relates to the control of fear behavior. Benzodiazepines, to begin with, bind to synaptic receptors (known as benzodiazepine receptors), which, in turn, enhance the action of the inhibitory neurotransmitter GABA. As it turns out, the amygdala has a high density of these receptors (Niehoff & Kuhar, 1983), and it has been shown that injections of benzodiazepines directly into the amygdala can reduce fear behavior (Hodges et al., 1987). It has also been shown that when drugs that block the action of GABA accompany injections of benzodiazepines, the benzodiazepines lose their fear-reducing properties (Scheel-Kruger & Petersen, 1982). Thus, it is reasonable to conclude that the ability of benzodiazepines to reduce fear is tied to the effect they have on the amygdala and, in particular, on their ability to decrease activity in the amygdala by enhancing the inhibitory effects of GABA.

THE NEURAL BASIS OF PLEASURE

Nearly everything we have been talking about in this chapter has focused on what we normally think of as "negative" emotions—aggression and fear, in particular. But as you know from your own experience, some emotions—delight, affection, gratitude, and the like—are highly pleasurable. Furthermore, a great deal of our behavior is motivated by the expectation of these pleasurable feelings. We choose to socialize with certain people because we enjoy their company. We go out of our way to eat certain foods not necessarily to satisfy our hunger but because we find them delicious.

The basic assumption in physiological psychology is that the specific pleasure we experience when we take part in these activities has a neural basis, and this assumption has led to the hypothesis that the nervous system, apart from everything else, has an area or group of areas that operate exclusively as a central mechanism for the control of pleasure or reward. The evidence for such a mechanism first came to light in 1954 through a series of momentous experiments conducted by James Olds and Peter Milner (Olds & Milner, 1954). Briefly, what Olds and Milner found is that under no apparent motivational impetus, animals will press a lever thousands of times for nothing more than a minute electric pulse fed to the septal area of the brain after each press.

Such behavior has since come to be known as *self-stimulation*. The assumption has been that if an animal is willing to work for a stimulus that takes the form of electrical stimulation of the brain, the stimulus must be positively reinforcing and the electrodes must be located in "reward" or "pleasure" areas in the brain. Further analysis has shown, moreover, that reward sites are not confined to the septal area but are scattered throughout the brain. One feature that many of the sites have in common, as you can see in Figure 14.9, is that they lie in and around the *medial forebrain bundle*, a large tract that runs from the brain stem to the cortex. Stimulation of some areas, notably the medial forebrain bundle itself, shows stronger reinforcing properties than stimulation of others, such as the septal area. Indeed, the reinforcing properties of electrical stimulation of the medial forebrain bundle are so strong that a starving rat will neglect food if it is permitted to press a lever to obtain stimulation in this area (Routtenberg & Lindy, 1965).

Brain Stimulation: The Basic Question

The fact that electrical stimulation of the brain produces behavior similar to the behavior produced by natural rewards (lever pressing for food or water) has raised important questions regarding the role of the brain in producing rewards. But before we can address these questions, it is important that you understand and appreciate the problems that arise in general when electrical stimulation of the brain is used to study behavior.

As we explained in Chapter 3, the neural activity produced by electrical stimulation of the brain is not a precise duplication of the activity produced by naturally occurring stimuli. Nonetheless, the similarity between the two types is striking enough to warrant the critical assumption that the neural activity produced by brain stimulation mimics the neural activity produced by naturally occurring stimuli. Keep in mind, however, that this is only an assumption. The possibility always exists that the neural activity produced by brain stimulation is simply a phe-

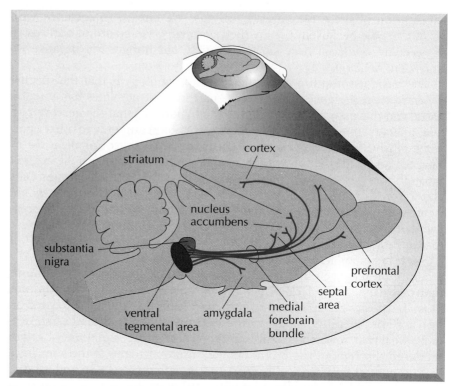

Figure 14.9 *Several of the Major Reward Areas in the Brain*

nomenon unto itself and that its neurophysiological dynamics have little to do with the neural activity produced by the naturally occurring stimuli, aside from a general similarity in their pattern.

If the neural activity produced by self-stimulation were distinct from the neural activity evoked by naturally occurring stimuli, there would be no point in studying it as a means to further understanding of the brain's role in reinforcement. For this reason, most of the early studies involving self-stimulation were designed to determine whether the neural mechanisms underlying reinforcement produced by brain stimulation were the same as or similar to the mechanisms underlying the reinforcement produced by natural rewards.

Natural Reward versus Brain-Stimulation Reward

It is generally agreed that reinforcement produced by natural rewards can result from both need reduction and pleasure. Drinking a cold glass of water when you are thirsty can be a highly reinforcing experience. But if you appreciate fine wine, you do not need to be thirsty in order to enjoy a vintage Lafite-Rothschild. Whether the same principle holds true for lower animals is less certain, but studies suggest that for animals, natural rewards also owe their reinforcing properties not only to the reduction of needs but also to the "pleasurable" experience that directly results from them. It has been found, for instance, that male rats will run to females in heat even though they have been prevented from ejaculating (Sheffield, Wulff, & Backer, 1951; Whalen, 1961) and that rats will drink highly palatable chocolate milk even when they are not deprived (Trowill, Panksepp, & Gandelman, 1969).

Evidence indicates that the reward produced by brain stimulation, too, is characterized by both need reduction and pleasure. Experiments by Olds indicated that self-stimulation behavior could be increased or decreased by manipulating need (hunger, for example), a finding that strongly suggests a need reduction component in self-stimulation (Olds, 1958). But subsequent studies have introduced a pleasure element into the behavior as well. Carl Sem-Jacobsen and his colleagues have used rewarding brain stimulation in humans to treat depression and have received reports from their patients of a general "pleasant" feeling not necessarily related to specific need reduction (Sem-Jacobsen, 1959).

The Idiosyncrasies of Self-Stimulation

The fact that self-stimulation, like natural-reward behavior, is governed by both need reduction and pleasure strengthens the argument that reinforcement produced by brain stimulation is governed by the same neural mechanisms as reinforcement produced by natural rewards. But one factor has proved troublesome from the start. The issue of whether self-stimulation and natural-reward behaviors are governed by the same neural mechanisms has been complicated by the fact that there are several important differences between the behavior of animals in self-stimulation studies and that of animals in natural-reward studies. We will focus on the two most prominent: the so-called satiation effect and the extinction effect.

Animals that press a lever to receive self-stimulation show no signs of satiation and will press hour after hour until they drop from fatigue. Hungry animals that have learned to press a lever for food, in contrast, stop pressing when they become sated (Valenstein & Beer, 1964).

No matter how relentlessly animals respond to obtain brain stimulation, they cease responding almost immediately when the pressing no longer results in reinforcement (i.e., brain stimulation) (Seward, Uyeda, & Olds, 1959). The omission of reinforcement in this case is known as *extinction* and is a routine practice in studies that aim to eliminate a learned behavior. But the extinction pattern differs greatly in hungry animals that have learned to respond for food. These animals continue to respond for a period of time after food is omitted. So whereas the number of lever presses that follow termination of reinforcement in self-stimulation is no more than 5 to 10, the number of lever presses among natural-reward animals can be anywhere from 50 to 500.

These idiosyncrasies do not necessarily refute the notion that brain stimulation and natural rewards are governed by the same mechanisms, but they certainly cloud the issue. The satiation effect and the extinction effect indicate strongly that the positive reinforcing properties of brain stimulation are unique; the question is, Why are they unique?

Explaining the Idiosyncrasies

Today researchers agree that the idiosyncratic behavior may not be idiosyncratic at all. This view is based on evidence indicating that there are important procedural differences between self-stimulation and natural-reward experiments and when these procedural differences are eliminated the behavioral differences are eliminated as well.

In a typical self-stimulation experiment, animals press a lever and receive a reward in the form of electrical stimulation directly to the brain. The reward is immediate. In a typical natural-reward experiment animals press a lever, food is delivered in a dispenser, the animals eat the food, and somewhere along the line, after the first bite of food, reward is signaled to the brain. The reward is *not* immediate.

When the procedures in the self-stimulation and natural-reward experiments are made similar—that is, when the animals in the natural-reward experiment receive the reward (highly palatable chocolate milk squirted directly into their mouths) immediately following the pressing of a lever—the behavioral differences between the two procedures disappear: the animals press a lever for the chocolate milk even though they are apparently not in a state of need, and when the reward is terminated for a brief period of time they show rapid extinction (Panksepp & Trowill, 1967a, b).

THE CHEMICAL NATURE OF REWARD

Electrical stimulation represents one way to activate the reward areas in the brain, and naturally occurring rewards of course represent another. But there is a third way—pleasure-producing drugs such as opiates and stimulants.

In principle, opiates and stimulants are no different from electrical stimulation or naturally occurring stimuli—they produce pleasure because they act in the pleasure areas of the brain. But what are these areas? And how do the drugs affect them? Before we address these questions, we must first take a closer look at the anatomy and chemistry of the reward circuits, specifically, the medial forebrain bundle.

Medial Forebrain Bundle: A Closer Look

As you can see in Figure 14.9, the medial forebrain bundle originates in the substantia nigra and ventral tegmental area and terminates in a number of areas including the amygdala, the septal area, the prefrontal cortex, the striatum, and a very important area, the nucleus accumbens. Added to the complexity is the fact that different circuits within the medial forebrain bundle produce and release different neurotransmitters—specifically, serotonin, norepinephrine, and dopamine.

This complexity poses a problem. When the medial forebrain bundle is stimulated and reward is produced, the stimulation spreads to a number of areas and activates the release of several neurotransmitters. So when we ask the question, How does electrical stimulation of the medial forebrain bundle produce reward? what we are really asking is, What area(s) of the brain and which neurotransmitter(s) are involved? It is too early to say with certainty. What we do know, however, is that the prime candidate among brain areas is the nucleus accumbens, which is located near the hypothalamus, and the prime candidate for the neurotransmitter is dopamine (Wise & Bozarth, 1984).

Dopamine and Reward

Evidence for dopamine involvement comes from two approaches. One involves *histofluorescence*, a procedure that enables researchers to determine the location of monoamine transmitters in the nervous system (see Chapter 5 for details). The second involves drugs known to affect the levels of neurotransmitters in those areas of the brain involved in reward.

The histofluorescence work indicates that the brain areas that produce the strongest reward when electrically stimulated overlap with the areas in the substantia nigra and ventral tegmentum that contain the highest concentration of dopamine-producing neurons (Corbett & Wise, 1979, 1980; Wise & Rompre, 1989). Confirming the dopamine-reward connection are pharmacological studies showing that drugs capable of increasing dopamine activity increase the reinforcing effects of medial forebrain bundle stimulation (Gerhardt & Liebman, 1985); drugs capable of decreasing dopamine activity reduce the reinforcing effects of medial forebrain bundle stimulation (Franklin, 1978).

Nucleus Accumbens and Reward

The evidence for nucleus accumbens involvement in reward behavior also comes from drug work. By injecting drugs known to block dopamine receptors into the nucleus accumbens, researchers have been able to significantly reduce reward produced by medial forebrain bundle stimulation (Stellar & Corbett, 1989). Conversely, injecting drugs that increase dopamine activity into the nucleus accumbens significantly increases reward produced by medial forebrain bundle stimulation (Colle & Wise, 1986). Injections of the same drugs into other areas connected to the medial forebrain bundle—such as the prefrontal cortex or the striatum—had no effect.

It seems clear, then, that dopamine and the nucleus accumbens both play critical roles in reward produced by medial forebrain bundle stimulation. We must be cautious, however, not to overgeneralize from these results. As far as we know, dopamine and the nucleus accumbens are not involved in reward produced by stimulation of other sites. And even in the case of the medial forebrain bundle the involvement of dopamine and the nucleus accumbens does not rule out the involvement of other areas and other neurotransmitters.

Pleasure-Producing Drugs and the Medial Forebrain Bundle

One of the reasons there is so much interest at present in the role that dopamine and the nucleus accumbens play in reward produced by medial forebrain bundle stimulation is that understanding that role more clearly might shed some light on the neurochemical basis of pleasure-producing drugs. As it happens, both the nucleus accumbens and dopamine appear to be involved in the reward produced by morphine, amphetamines, and cocaine.

Evidence of this involvement comes from a procedure similar to self-stimulation, in which researchers have taught animals to press a lever to obtain drugs (e.g., morphine, cocaine, amphetamines) injected either into the body or directly into specific areas of the brain (Yokel, 1987). The assumption has been that if an animal is willing to work for a drug—the term used is *self-administer*—the drug must be positively reinforcing and it must be acting in reward or pleasure areas of the brain. The assumption has also been that if animals *stop* working or slow their rate of pressing to obtain a drug after a specific area of the brain has been damaged or a specific neurotransmitter has been altered, then that brain area or neurotransmitter must be involved in producing the reward.

Dopamine and the nucleus accumbens fit these criteria for two reasons: (1) animals work for drugs—morphine and amphetamine—injected directly into the nucleus accumbens (Goeders, Lane, & Smith, 1984; Hoebel et al., 1983); (2) animals stop working (or slow their rate of lever pressing) for drugs (cocaine, amphetamine, or morphine) after either their nucleus accumbens is lesioned or they are injected with drugs that block the action of dopamine (Goeders, Dworkin, & Smith, 1986; Kelsey, Carlezon, & Falls, 1989).

A point is in need of clarification. We've just seen that amphetamine, cocaine, and morphine work in the same way to produce reward: they increase dopamine activity in the nucleus accumbens. This is not to say, however, that amphetamine, cocaine, and morphine work the same way for the same reason. Amphetamine, for instance, increases dopamine by affecting the synapse in two ways: by displacing it from its storage sites and by blocking its reuptake. Cocaine, on the other hand, apparently has only the second effect, blocking the reuptake of dopamine. And morphine works in an entirely different way. It binds to opiate receptors, which in turn increase the release of dopamine. In any event the effect of the three drugs is the same: dopamine increases in the nucleus accumbens and reward is produced.

Summing Up

The neurochemical work has added an important dimension to our understanding of the physiological basis of emotion. It has provided important links between the behavior of lower animals and that of humans, and it has given us insights into the chemical basis of emotional behavior from two perspectives: normal and abnormal. Indeed much of this work constitutes the experimental basis for the use of certain drugs in the treatment of some forms of mental illness. We will consider this work in detail in the next chapter.

SUMMARY

1. *Problems inherent in the study of emotions.* The experimental analysis of emotions presents problems on two levels: behavioral and neural. The behavioral problem is that the observable behavior is not necessarily a reflection of what emotion a person is experiencing at any given moment. The neural problem is that the neural events that produce emotions involve a number of areas in the brain ranging from the lowest levels of the brain stem to the highest levels of the cortex.

2. *The two main theories.* Several theories have been proposed to explain the chain of events that produces emotions but nearly all of them are versions of two main theories: the James-Lange theory of emotion and the Cannon-Bard theory of emotion. Both theories agree that the cortex is the last link in the chain and that impulses arriving at the cortex produce different emotions. Where they disagree is on the origin of the signal. The James-Lange theory of emotion argues that visceral responses are the signals to the cortex that govern what we experience as emotions. The Cannon-Bard theory argues that visceral responses are neither versatile nor rapid enough to produce emotion and these visceral reactions simply *accompany* the emotion as a side effect. The impulses generated by the stimuli that produce emotional responses, according to this theory, originate in the thalamus.

3. *The cognitive-arousal theory.* Stanley Schachter and Jerome Singer have proposed a theory of emotion that favors the James-Lange view and attempts to resolve the issue of whether visceral responses are varied enough to qualify as the neural signal for emotion. In their view, a visceral sensation—butterflies in your stomach, for instance—serves as a signal to trigger emotional behavior, but it is up to the cognitive powers of the cortex to determine the *kind* of emotional response that is appropriate to the environmental situation. In other words, the same visceral response can produce different emotions depending on how the situation is perceived. In support of the theory Schachter and Singer showed that subjects injected with a viscera-arousing drug (epinephrine) reported experiencing either anger or euphoria depending on the environmental situation they were exposed to immediately after the injection.

4. *Facial expressions and emotions.* Facial expressions and the emotions they signify appear to be both universal and genetically determined. Evidence for universality comes from cross-cultural studies indicating that the type of emotion people infer from facial expressions is the same regardless of the culture. Evidence for genetics comes from observations of children who have been blind from birth indicating that they show the same facial expressions as sighted children. Facial expressions, like visceral responses, may also contribute to the quality of emotion. In one study subjects were given a task that inadvertently produced either a smile or a nonsmile (without the person having been asked to smile or not to smile) and were then instructed to give humor ratings to a set of cartoons. People whose facial task produced a smile consistently gave higher humor ratings to the cartoons they evaluated than people whose facial task resulted in a nonsmile. These findings suggest strongly that feedback from facial expressions may play at least some role in emotion.

5. *Searching for the neural signals.* The search for the neural basis of emotion has been going on for roughly 100 years, but it has been largely confined to lower animals. The first empirical evidence linking violent or aggressive emotional behavior to areas of the brain emerged in the early 1890s when the German physiologist Friedrich Goltz produced violent attack behavior in dogs by making a cut at the midbrain level of the dog's brain stem. Goltz's work indicated that higher brain areas normally act to inhibit rage, but it took the work of Philip Bard many years later to get a clearer fix on the neural circuitry that underlies this inhibitory capacity. Bard found that the key to the control of attack behavior lay in the cortex and its inhibitory relationship with the hypothalamus. His work was instrumental in helping other researchers focus their efforts on a group of areas in and around the hypothalamus known as the limbic system.

6. *The limbic system.* The link between the limbic system and emotion was first suggested in 1937 when James Papez published a paper on the subject, and this link was confirmed by a number of studies using electrical brain stimulation and lesioning techniques. The picture that emerged is this: the hypothalamus is the center for emotional output (internal and external) and the amygdala, the hippocampus, and the frontal cortex are centers for modulating (facilitating or inhibiting) the output.

7. *Emotion and the hypothalamus.* Experiments conducted in the early 1950s by Walter Hess shed new light on how the hypothalamus controls internal responses. His key finding: that different parts of the hypothalamus, when stimulated, produce opposite effects. Stimulating the posterior hypothalamus produced sympathetic responses, such as increases in heart rate. Stimulating the anterior part of the hypothalamus produced calming, parasympathetic responses. Hess's work thus showed that the hypothalamus, in addition to adjusting the internal state in accord with metabolic needs created by hunger and thirst, has the capacity to adjust the internal state to meet needs created by external threats related to such emotional behavior as fear or rage.

8. *The hypothalamus and aggression.* The hypothalamus has been the focal point of many studies designed to uncover the neural processes that underlie fighting and attack behavior (commonly referred to as aggression). Prominent among these studies is the work of John Flynn, who found that electrical stimulation of different nuclei within the hypothalamus produces two different types of aggressive behavior in cats, depending on where the hypothalamus is stimulated. Stimulation to the medial nuclei of the hypothalamus produced vicious, hissing attack behavior. Stimulating the lateral hypothalamus produced a much quieter, more directed and unemotional attack behavior. More recent studies, while confirming Flynn's basic finding of two different kinds of attack behavior, indicate that the areas controlling the two behaviors are not as circumscribed as Flynn originally suggested.

9. *The amygdala and aggression.* The amygdala is clearly involved in emotional behavior, but its precise role is not yet fully understood. Some studies have shown that removal of the amygdala has a taming effect on animals, while other studies, most notably by Philip Bard and Vernon Mountcastle, have shown that removing the amygdala produces rage. The work of David Egger and John Flynn has confirmed that the amygdala has a dual effect on behavior and has also shown that attack behavior normally elicited by the hypothalamus can be either inhibited or facilitated through simultaneous stimulation of different parts of the amygdala and hippocampus. The amygdala also appears to play an important role in the dominant-submissive hierarchical behavior of monkeys. Karl Pribram was able to alter the social hierarchy of a monkey colony by removing the amygdala from the brain of the dominant monkey. Other studies involving lower animals and humans have shown that stimulating the amygdala produces fearlike behavior, learned and unlearned. Evidence also indicates that the amygdala is involved in processing fear-related information at two levels—a quick, crude response based on scant and raw sensory data and a slower, more accurate perception based on more sophisticated cortical processing.

10. *Animal models and human behavior.* Recent experiments involving predatory play behavior in cats have drawn attention to an ongoing problem in emotion research—being able to draw accurate conclusions from the behavior manifested by animals in experimental studies. It is extremely difficult to tell whether animals demonstrating aggressive behavior are operating out of fear or raw aggression. This difficulty, in turn, underscores the danger of using inferred behavior from lower animals as the basis for speculation about human emotional behavior.

11. *The frontal lobes and aggression.* Egas Moniz developed the surgical procedure known as the prefrontal lobotomy to treat emotionally disturbed patients. The procedure consists of severing the connections between the frontal lobes and the rest of the brain, and at first it appeared to work exceptionally well—so much so that for a time prefrontal lobotomies became a common procedure. Lobotomies are rarely performed today because, in addition to calming emotionally disturbed patients, they produce a wide range of devastating behavioral side effects.

12. *Psychosurgery.* Prefrontal lobotomies fall into a broad therapeutic category known as psychosurgery—a form of surgery in which areas deep in the brain are removed from people who are unable to control violent behavior. Psychosurgery in this country has been performed in an effort to curb the violent behavior seen with temporal lobe epilepsy and it has also been performed on violence-prone inmates in mental institutions. The reports of these operations indicate a relatively high level of success in curbing violent behavior. The problem, though, is that the procedure is controversial because no matter how discrete the physical damage it causes, it impairs intellectual capacity.

13. *Chemical coding for aggression.* Killing behavior in rats has been either produced or curtailed through injections of chemicals that alter the level of acetylcholine in the hypothalamus. Killing behavior in rats has also been produced by drugs, lesions (raphe nuclei), or dietary manipulations (a diet deficient in tryptophan) that deplete serotonin.

14. *Serotonin and violent behavior in humans.* Several studies on people who have a history of aggressive behavior, either toward others or toward themselves (that is, who commit or attempt to commit suicide) show serotonin deficits, but the data are purely correlational: they do not tell us whether serotonin deficiencies actually cause aggressive behavior or whether aggressive behavior causes a serotonin deficit.

15. *The chemistry of fear.* Experiments involving rats and drugs known to alleviate anxiety—benzodiazepines, for instance—have yielded invaluable data on the chemical basis of fear. Evidence indicates that the ability of benzodiazepines to reduce fear is linked to the effect they have on the amygdala and, in particular, on their ability to enhance the inhibitory effects of GABA.

16. *The neural basis of pleasure.* In 1954, James Olds and Peter Milner conducted a series of famous experiments in which rats, with no apparent motivational impetus, were trained to press a lever thousands of times for a reward that consisted of nothing but brief electric pulses to certain areas of the brain. The behavior is known as self-stimulation and the areas of the brain that produce the behavior when stimulated lie in around the medial forebrain bundle, a large tract that runs from the brain stem to the cortex. It has been clearly established that these areas do, in fact, have reinforcement properties as strong as natural rewards, but there are significant differences between the way animals behave when the reinforcement comes from brain stimulation and when the reinforcement comes from conventional sources. The current view is that these differences have less to do with differences in the reinforcement properties of each reward source—stimulation or conventional—and more to do with differences in the procedures.

17. *The neuroanatomical and chemical basis of self-stimulation.* The medial forebrain bundle travels to several areas of the brain (including the nucleus accumbens, the septal area, and the frontal cortex) and when stimulated releases several different neurotransmitters (serotonin, norepinephrine, and dopamine). Dopamine appears to be the key neurotransmitter and the nucleus accumbens the key area of the brain. The evidence comes from studies showing that drugs that decrease dopamine or lesions made in the nucleus accumbens decrease the reinforcing effects of medial forebrain bundle stimulation.

18. *The neuroanatomical and chemical basis of cocaine, amphetamine, and morphine.* Both the nucleus accumbens and dopamine appear to be involved in the reward produced by pleasure-producing drugs, such as morphine, amphetamines, and cocaine. The evidence comes from studies showing that animals (a) will work for the drugs when they are injected directly into the nucleus accumbens and (b) will stop working for the drugs if either the nucleus accumbens is lesioned or drugs that block the action of dopamine are administered.

KEY TERMS

acetylcholine
affective behavior
amygdala
benzodiazepines
Cannon-Bard theory of
   emotion
cognitive-arousal theory of
   emotion
decerebrate preparation
decorticate preparation
directed attack behavior
facial feedback hypothesis
frontal cortex
histofluorescence

James-Lange theory of
   emotion
Kluver-Bucy syndrome
limbic system
medial forebrain bundle
nucleus accumbens
Papez's circuit
predatory play
prefrontal lobotomy
psychosurgery
self-stimulation
sham rage
striatum

SUGGESTED READINGS

Aggleton, J. P., (Ed.). *The Amygdala: Neurobiological Aspects of Emotion, Memory, and Mental Dysfunction*. New York: Wiley-Liss, 1992.

LeDoux, J. "Emotion, Memory and the Brain." *Scientific American*, 270, 50–57, 1994.

Liebman, J. M. & Cooper S. J. (Eds.). *The Neuropharmacological Basis of Reward*. Oxford: Clarendon Press, 1989.

Stein, N. L., Leventhal, B., & Trabasso, T. (Eds.). *Psychological and Biological Approaches to Emotion*. Hillsdale, NJ: Lawrence Erlbaum Associates, 1990.

15

THE NEURAL BASIS OF PSYCHO-LOGICAL DISORDER

THE SCHIZOPHRENIC BRAIN
AND BEHAVIOR
Recapitulation

INTRODUCTION

In Chapter 14 we focused on the visceral, affective, and cognitive aspects of emotion and then on the neural circuits involved in processing emotional states. In this chapter we will consider the evidence for neural involvement in certain psychological disorders. We will discuss two types of psychological disorders: those involving primarily the body or viscera and those involving primarily mental experiences. Those involving the body are known as *psychosomatic* or *psychophysiological disorders*. Those involving mental experiences are commonly referred to as *mental illness*. Each of these terms—psychosomatic and mental illness— is used so frequently and in so many different ways that their meanings tend to be confusing. For this reason, it is worthwhile to take a closer look at the terms and to clarify some of the confusion that surrounds them.

A Closer Look at the Terminology

The term "psychosomatic" is generally used to describe any physical condition that has been brought about by—or is being aggravated by— psychological or emotional factors such as worry, excitability, and anxiety. Medical conditions that are thought to be psychosomatic in many instances include stomach ulcers, allergies, headaches, and high blood pressure.

What is important to bear in mind about such conditions is that their symptoms are not imaginary: they are as real and as measurable as the symptoms of illnesses that result from physical factors—injuries or infections. The splitting headache you get because you have been under intense pressure all day is no less painful than the splitting headache you get because of a sinus infection.

The main question surrounding psychosomatic problems—and it is a question we will be looking into later—is whether they are rooted in purely psychological factors. It has long been assumed that psychological factors, such as fear and anxiety, can lead to physical ailments, but until recently there has been little in the way of concrete evidence to verify the link. What's more, even though the evidence for such a link continues to mount, exactly how psychological factors lead to somatic symptoms is still unknown. But more of this later.

Mental Illness

Another set of problems complicates our use of the term "mental illness." When aspects of our psychological experience—emotion, cognition, the ability to plan and carry out actions—break down, the problem is considered mental or psychological. But diagnostic labels in this case, too, need clarification.

At one time mental illness was divided into two broad categories, *neurosis* and *psychosis*, with the principal difference being the extent to which the individual lost contact with reality. Neurosis was used in connection with abnormal conditions—phobias, panic disorder, obsessions, compulsions—that interfered with, but didn't necessarily cripple, a person's ability to function on a day-to-day basis. Psychosis was used in reference to conditions—such as schizophrenia—that involved a loss of contact with reality and made it impossible for someone to live a normal life.

The terms "neurosis" and "psychosis" are no longer commonly used by psychiatrists and psychologists as diagnostic categories. The terms are too vague, and the trend today is to classify disorders not so much in terms of their severity but rather their symptoms. In this chapter we shall consider three of the more prominent types of psychological disorders—anxiety disorders, affective disorders, and schizophrenia.

Stress: An Overview

Regardless of the type of psychological disorder—psychosomatic or mental illness—the underlying cause can be traced to abnormalities in genetics, to conditions in the environment (whether those conditions be physical, social, or interpersonal), or to both. The term psychologists now use to describe the environmental trigger of emotional breakdown is *stress*.

Usually when we use the term "stress," we think of it as a temporary state of mind: that anxious, harried feeling that comes over us when we're under pressure. In this chapter we use the term to describe any situation in which a stimulus—regardless of what psychological effect it has—is sufficiently excessive to require significant adaptation and changes on the part of the individual.

It is important to emphasize that stress itself is a normal and, some would argue, necessary ingredient in our lives. Some varieties of stress are even pleasurable, as evidenced by the millions of people who eagerly take part in such adventurous pastimes as skiing, sky diving, and mountain climbing. And why else do so many people go out of their way to attend horror movies? Then, too, most of us are able to tolerate reasonable amounts of stress for reasonable periods of time. We have all gone through, and gotten over, periods during which we have felt "overworked" or "stressed out." On the other hand, there is a breaking point in this otherwise routine picture—a point at which we no longer respond adaptively to the constant onslaught of stimuli provoking the stress. It is at this point—and the point varies widely from person to person and from situation to situation—that behavior breaks down.

Exactly why this breaking point varies so widely from person to person is unknown at this time. We know that factors such as an individual's repertoire of coping responses and the presence of supportive people in their lives are important. Popular belief has it that some people have the inborn ability to shrug off the petty annoyances that make other people angry and overwrought. But if there are genetic factors in stress tolerance, we do not know what they are. Neither do we know at this time exactly how our upbringing and our learning history affects the way we respond to stress. What we do know is that there are physiological components to the behavioral breakdown—visceral or mental. In this chapter we shall examine these components.

VISCERAL BREAKDOWN: THE EARLY FINDINGS

As we suggested earlier, the idea that our state of mind can affect what goes on in our bodies has existed since antiquity, but it has been only within the past 50 years or so that scientists have been able to establish a clear connection between the two.

The General Adaptation Syndrome

One scientist whose name has long been closely associated with efforts to establish the relationship between stress and physical breakdown is Hans Selye, the late endocrinologist who spent most of his career studying what happens inside the body during periods of stress (Selye, 1950, 1970). Selye proposed a compelling, if not universally accepted, theory to explain the physiological bases of visceral breakdown. His theory was based on the premise that all humans show the same general responses to stress. Selye labeled these reactions the *general adaptation syndrome*, and he contended that no matter what the stressor might be (poison, aberrant temperatures, psychological distress, or whatever), the general reactions of the body and the mechanisms of visceral breakdown are the same. It begins with a generalized alarm response, moves on to resistance, and ultimately ends in "exhaustion"—that is, the cessation of a visceral process or the breakdown of an organ—or even death.

Selye went so far as to identify the physiological basis of the three-stage syndrome, as illustrated in Figure 15.1: the alarm response, in his view, is initiated by the hypothalamus and involves elevated sympathetic activity and the release of adrenocorticotrophic hormone (ACTH) from the anterior pituitary gland; resistance involves the release of steroids, specifically glucocorticoids, from the adrenal cortex gland; and exhaustion and ultimately tissue destruction result from a prolonged overall increase in ACTH, glucocorticoids, and sympathetic nervous system

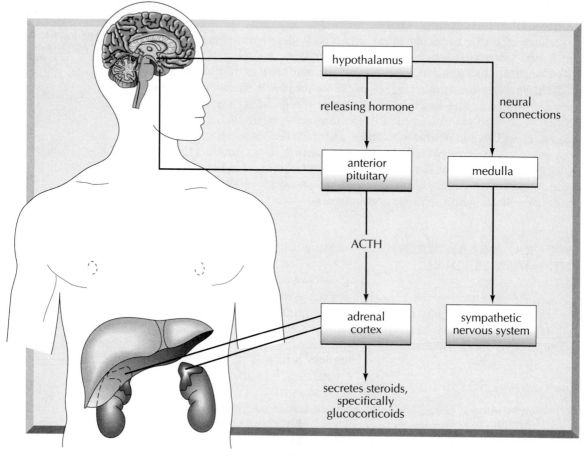

Figure 15.1 *Alarm and Resistance*

The alarm response is initiated by the hypothalamus and involves elevated sympathetic activity (via nuclei in the medulla) and the release of ACTH via the anterior pituitary; resistance involves the release of steroids (specifically glucocorticoids) from the adrenal cortex. The increased glucocorticoids increase blood sugar, the increased sympathetic activity increases blood pressure, and together they increase metabolic activity throughout the body.

activity. The organs that finally break down vary according to individual predisposition. A person born with a vulnerable heart, he argued, may respond by having a heart attack, whereas a person prone to stomach problems may develop ulcers.

Selye's work opened several continuing lines of research on stress and adaptation. This research has uncovered aspects of visceral breakdown that extend beyond his theory. Today we know that visceral breakdown is caused by more than elevated sympathetic activity and release of glucocorticoids. And we know that stress consists of more than exposure to or the threat of an aversive stimulus. Equally important are the psychological as well as the physical aspects of stress. How we perceive an aversive stimulus is every bit as important as what that stimulus is. Let us take a closer look at one line of work that addresses this issue.

Experiments that have established a connection between psychological stress and visceral breakdown have primarily involved rats, monkeys, and dogs, and one of the most common psychological conditions studied in these experiments is a state known as *helplessness*. It is not the only stressful condition whose relationship to visceral breakdown is being studied, but it provides us with a useful focal point.

In a typical helplessness experiment, two groups of animals are subjected to the same physical stress—electric shock. The animals in one of the groups are "in control." That is, they can escape the shock by pressing a lever or running to a safe compartment. The other animals are "helpless"—that is, they themselves have no means of controlling the shock. Whenever the animals in the first group respond, they terminate shock not only for themselves but for the helpless animals as well. In short, then, in the first stage of the experiment both groups of animals are subjected to the same physical stress (the same number and pattern of shocks) but not the same psychological stress (the ability or lack of ability to do something about the shocks) (Seligman, 1975).

In the second stage of the experiment, both groups are again subjected to the physical stress. This time, though, the animals in both groups have the same opportunity to learn to escape the shock in a new situation. What happens, however, is that the "helpless" animals do nothing, even though they now have the opportunity to escape the shock. They appear simply to give up. Researchers have labeled this behavior *learned helplessness*. The explanation for the behavior is that in the first stage of the experiment the helpless animals learn that their behavior has no effect on the presence or absence of shock. That is why in the second stage they continue to behave as if the cessation of the shock is not dependent on their behavior (Seligman & Maier, 1967).

Learned Helplessness: The Human Dimension

Some investigators, chief among them Martin Seligman, have suggested that learned helplessness manifested by animals in laboratory experiments is analogous to behavior often manifested by humans suffering from certain kinds of depression. Their studies have shown, for example, that animals made helpless in the laboratory, like depressed humans, tend to stop eating and become lethargic (Seligman et al., 1976). Helpless animals also have a tendency—again, like depressed humans—to remain passive and indifferent.

Based on these similarities, Seligman has theorized that helplessness in lower animals may be governed by the same underlying mechanism that underlies certain kinds of depression in humans. Like helpless animals, many people become depressed after experiencing a traumatic event (loss or sickness of a loved one, severe financial pressure, etc.) during which they see themselves as powerless to control their environment. So, like the helpless animals, they seem to give up. Seligman's view of course is theoretical, but it has drawn further support from the fact that helpless animals, like depressed humans, are often helped by antidepressant drugs (Porsolt et al., 1977), a treatment that will be discussed in detail later in this chapter.

Learned Helplessness and Visceral Breakdown

Learned helplessness in animals not only produces behavior that resembles depression in humans but also causes visceral breakdown similar to that seen in humans and, in extreme cases, may even result in sudden death.

Sudden Death

In an experiment conducted nearly 40 years ago, when little was known about learned helplessness, a group of wild rats was placed in a water tank. Normally excellent swimmers, the rats in this case stopped swimming after a few minutes and drowned. If, however, the procedure was changed so that before the rats were placed in the tank for a lengthy period, they were placed in the water several times for brief periods and then required to swim under the conditions that normally resulted in death, the rats then survived (Richter, 1957).

Investigators had no way of explaining at the time why the procedural change produced dramatically higher survival rates. Today, though, based on what we know about learned helplessness, there is an explanation. Rats exposed to the water gradually presumably were not as overwhelmed by the final test as those who were simply dumped into the water for the very first time. In other words, the animals learned through the brief exposures that they could "cope" with the situation. Left to swim on their own, in contrast to helpless animals, they did not give up.

The question that concerns us here is, What physiological processes account for this change in perspective? What happens in the body of an experimental rat when it gives up and dies or when it keeps trying? The answer to this question appears to lie in the autonomic nervous system (see Chapter 3 for details)—specifically the delicate balance between the sympathetic and parasympathetic systems and how each system reacts to stress.

During the initial stress, when animals in these "do-or-die" situations are struggling to survive, both systems are operating, but the sympathetic system dominates even though the parasympathetic system may be overreacting to offset the sympathetic activity. Once the animals give up, however, the sympathetic system shuts off. Now, no longer opposed by the sympathetic system, the parasympathetic system, which normally inhibits heart rate, "overshoots" and the animals die. This phenomenon is known as *parasympathetic overshoot* or *rebound*.

The important conclusion to be drawn from this study and others like it is not that the sympathetic system is dominant during stress. That we've known for a long time. What is important is that the sympathetic system reacts not only to the *physical* demands of the stress but to the *psychological* demands as well. The water itself is just as cold and presumably just as physically stressful for animals that have been given brief exposures and eventually dumped into the water as it is for animals dumped into the water for the first time. But the animals' perception of the water as a threat to their survival appears to be different. It is this difference in perception, as opposed to the temperature of the water, that determines the sympathetic response to stress—resist or give up.

Ulcers

Helplessness may also play a role in one of the most common psychosomatic illnesses, gastrointestinal ulcers, with evidence coming from studies using a procedure similar to the learned helplessness procedure. The main variable in this group of studies, however, is the *predictability* of shock.

The method used was to give two groups of animals the same amount of shock—that is, the same intensity and frequency—with one difference in the procedure. One group of animals received a warning signal (e.g., a tone) immediately before the shock, enabling them to, in effect, "predict" the shock; the other group received no warning. The findings: the group receiving the warning signal showed far less gastrointestinal damage than the group for whom the shock came without warning (i.e., was unpredictable) (Guile, 1987; Abbott, Schoen, & Badia, 1984).

The basis for the difference in the gastrointestinal damage suffered by the animals in each group has been traced to the release of excess gastric juices that damage the lining of the stomach and produce ulcers. Rats in the group receiving an unpredictable shock were found to release a greater level of gastric juices than rats in the other group (Weiss, 1971). What is significant about this release, however, is that it occurs not when the animals are receiving the shock but rather during the rest periods, when the shock is turned off (Desiderato, 1974; Garrick et al., 1989).

This pattern may seem unusual, but there is an explanation again having to do with how the sympathetic and parasympathetic systems interact. Gastric secretions are produced by parasympathetic activity, and it is during the rest period, when the sympathetic system is not active, that the parasympathetic system works unopposed and exerts its major effect.

The Immune System

The most recent—and in some ways the most intriguing—studies on the physiological consequences of learned helplessness have focused on the immune system, the body's first line of defense against disease.

A key function of the immune system, as you undoubtedly know, is to produce cells that seek out and destroy disease-producing agents. It has long been suspected that prolonged periods of stress can diminish the capacity of the immune system to produce these cells, but it wasn't until the early 1980s that researchers were able to show that learned helplessness could be one of the major sources of the stress.

Some of the more significant studies conducted in this area have involved so-called killer cells (also known as T cells)—cells that have the power to search out and destroy tumor cells. Working with rats, Steven

Maier and his colleagues found that helpless rats that had no control over shock produced fewer killer cells and, when injected with tumor cells, were less likely to reject the cells than rats that had the opportunity to control shock (Maier, 1985; Visintainer, 1982). These findings of course have important implications for understanding the cause of cancer and its possible relation to stress.

Learned Helplessness and Visceral Breakdown: An Assessment

Laboratory findings that show a direct connection between learned helplessness and visceral breakdown strongly suggest that psychological factors play a much more prominent role in many diseases than anyone dared to suggest as recently as 30 years ago. An increasing number of medical specialists believe that many illnesses—including cancer—have a strong psychological component ultimately tied to the relationship between stress and immune function (Horne & Picard, 1979; Shekelle et al., 1981). In light of what we have begun to see in animal studies, this view seems plausible.

Once again though, we must be careful not to overstate the case. It is one thing to say that prolonged psychological stress can weaken the immune system, but another thing altogether to isolate psychological stress as the principal agent in specific illnesses. There are many vexing questions that must be answered before this link is fully understood, not the least of which is how psychological stress works to impair immune function and how we can control it.

MENTAL ILLNESS: A PHYSIOLOGICAL PERSPECTIVE

Just as disruption of the neural circuits that control visceral responses can trigger visceral breakdown, so too can disruption of the circuits that control the affective (mood or feeling), motivational, perceptual, and cognitive aspects of an experience trigger mental breakdown. Mental disorders involving this category of brain abnormalities generally fall into three groups: affective disorders, anxiety disorders, and schizophrenia.

The differences, in brief, are these. *Affective disorders* are distinguished by extreme shifts in mood. *Anxiety disorders* involve severe and debilitating anxiety or fear in the face of experiences or situations that pose no real danger. *Schizophrenia* is characterized by pronounced disturbances in perception, disordered thought and speech patterns, social withdrawal, and inappropriate emotions.

It wasn't very long ago that people who suffered from these disorders were considered "mad" or possessed by demons. Today, few people take such a view seriously. These disorders are now generally recognized as different forms of mental illness, but the nature of each disorder and its cause is debatable.

There are essentially three views of mental illness today. One view attributes the abnormal behavior largely to brain abnormalities (chemical or structural) often genetically induced. Another view attributes mental illness primarily to environmental factors—an individual's upbringing or the life stresses to which he or she has been subjected. The third attributes the abnormal behavior to a combination of genetics and environmental factors.

The most widely accepted of these views today is the combination view—and for good reason. If we look at depression, for example, we find certain hereditary patterns indicating a genetically induced biochemical basis. But we also find that depression often follows a traumatic event (loss or sickness of a loved one, severe financial pressure, etc.).

We shall focus throughout the remainder of this chapter on the neural and chemical aspects of mental illness, but we do not mean to minimize the importance of environmental and social factors. Indeed, even if we were to unravel the biochemical mysteries of affective disorders, anxiety disorders, and schizophrenia, the riddle of the interrelations among environment, psychological response, and physiological abnormalities would still remain.

Affective Disorders: An Overview

Affective disorders are marked by emotional extremes: depression, on the one hand, mania, on the other hand. The defining emotional symptoms of depression are sadness and despondency. The defining emotional symptoms of mania are exaggerated expansiveness, exuberance, and energy.

Affective disorders are divided into two broad categories: unipolar depression, in which the person suffers exclusively from prolonged periods of sadness and despondency; and bipolar disorder, in which the person undergoes alternating periods of depression and mania. You might expect there to be a third type of affective disorder—one that involves exclusively mania—but this condition is very rare and in fact many question whether indeed it exists at all (APA, 1987).

Unipolar Depression

Of the two categories, *unipolar depression* (also known as major depression) is the more common. It is estimated that roughly 20 percent of the female population in the United States and 10 percent of the male population suffer from unipolar depression at some point in their lives and that, at any given time, the number of people in the United States suffering from the disorder is roughly 8 million (Weissman & Boyd, 1984). Apart from the principal emotional symptoms—sadness and despondency—people suffering from unipolar depression frequently lose their appetites, have difficulty sleeping, and have trouble concentrating. In severe cases, victims of unipolar depression become suicidal.

Bipolar Disorder

The number of people in the United States suffering from *bipolar disorder* (once known as manic-depressive disorder) is estimated at 2 million. The symptoms that occur during a manic episode contrast broadly with those that occur during a depressive episode. During a manic episode an individual is excessively energetic. He or she may talk incessantly, have a diminished need to sleep, and go through periods of vigorous activity. Overconfidence, extraversion, bad judgment, and euphoria may also be observed.

The patterns of depression and mania vary considerably from person to person. In some people the episodes (either depression or mania) may last for as little as 2 or 3 weeks. In others an episode may continue unabated for years. Many people suffering from this disorder experience periods of remission (a return to normal behavior) that can last several months or even years. For others the condition is chronic.

THE MONOAMINE THEORY OF DEPRESSION

As recently as the early 1970s, it was generally thought that both forms of depression—unipolar and bipolar—had their neurophysiological roots in deficits in the neurotransmitters norepinephrine and serotonin. Because these neurotransmitters are monoamines, the theory linking them to depression came to be known as the *monoamine theory of depression*.

This theory is based on the observation that drugs whose effect in the body is to *decrease* the levels of norepinephrine and serotonin tend to *produce* depression, while drugs that *increase* the amounts of these neurotransmitters alleviate the symptoms. Although there are valid elements in the theory, recent studies have uncovered aspects of depression that cannot be explained within the context of the monoamine theory as it stands. As a result, the theory has been modified.

Fine-Tuning the Monoamine Theory

You have probably heard of drugs such as *Prozac* and *Zoloft*, sometimes described as the wonder drugs of depression. They belong to a new class of "second-generation" antidepressant drugs known as *selective serotonin reuptake inhibitors* (SSRIs) (Burrows et al., 1988).

The chief difference between SSRIs and "first-generation" antidepressant drugs is their effect on the neurotransmitters norepinephrine and serotonin. First-generation antidepressant drugs [MAO inhibitors and tricyclic antidepressants (see Chapter 5 for details)] affect both norepinephrine and serotonin, making it impossible to determine the degree to which each of the two neurotransmitters is alleviating the symptoms.

No such ambiguity, however, exists with SSRIs. Their principal action is to *increase serotonin levels* in the brain, and they do so by blocking the reuptake of serotonin. This effect, combined with new evidence indicating that drugs that *decrease* serotonin levels *produce* depression, makes a strong case for a serotonin-depression connection (Delgado, 1990). Whether serotonin is the only neurotransmitter involved in producing depression or whether deficits in norepinephrine or some other neurotransmitter are also involved remains to be determined.

Drug studies have not only helped clarify our view of which neuro-transmitters are involved in depression but have also helped clarify our view of how drugs work to alleviate depression. Originally the critical factor in depression was thought to be the *amount* of neurotransmitter in the brain: when there was a deficit, there was depression; when the deficit was relieved, the depression disappeared. This view has changed. Today we know that there is more to relieving depression than eliminating the neurotransmitter deficit. Let us take a closer look at the evidence.

Accounting for the Time-Lag Factor

It takes only 2 or 3 hours for antidepressant drugs to exert their chemical effects—that is, to increase the amount of serotonin or norepineph-rine and serotonin (Sulser, Vetulani, & Mobley, 1978). Yet when these drugs are administered to patients suffering from depression, it usually takes 2 or 3 weeks of repeated administration of the drug before they experience any relief from the symptoms. What accounts for the time lag? If increased levels of serotonin (or norepinephrine and serotonin) do indeed alleviate depression, why do patients have to take the drugs for 2 to 3 weeks before experiencing any therapeutic benefit?

Logic tells us that administering the drug over a 2- to 3-week period must produce effects that do not occur when the drug is administered for only a brief period of time. What those effects are remains unclear, but recent studies point to two possibilities, each of which involves different features of the synapse. One of these features is autoreceptors; the other is synaptic defense mechanisms.

Autoreceptors
Autoreceptors are located on the presynaptic endings (see Chapter 5 for details), and one of their principal functions is to inhibit the release of neurotransmitter when an excess accumulates in the synaptic gap. Repeated administration of antidepressant drugs over a 2- to 3-week period causes autoreceptors to lose their inhibitory capacity, thus increasing the amount of norepinephrine and serotonin released (Crews, 1978; Sulser, 1984). The conclusion is that if antidepressant drugs are to relieve the symptoms of depression, they must first diminish the inhibitory effect of autoreceptors, and this action requires that the drug be taken for at least 2 to 3 weeks.

Synaptic-Defense Mechanisms
As mentioned in Chapter 5, one of the ways the synapse responds to a neurotransmitter deficit is to increase the number of receptors on the postsynaptic neuron. Presumably then, before depressed patients take an antidepressant drug, they may be suffering from two problems. One is a deficit in neurotransmitters. The other is an abnormally high number of postsynaptic receptors that have formed to offset the deficit, albeit unsuccessfully.

It is also reasonable to assume (although the evidence documenting this assumption is still sketchy) that if an antidepressant drug is to alleviate the symptoms, it must correct both problems. It must *increase* the level of neurotransmitters, and it must also *decrease* the abnormal number of postsynaptic receptors. The increase in neurotransmitters results presumably from the change in autoreceptors. The decrease in postsynaptic receptors (and there is indeed evidence for such a decrease) results from the synaptic defense (Charney et al., 1981; Heninger & Charney, 1987). And each process takes a 2- to 3-week period to develop.

There is, however, one complication. It is easy to understand why an increase in neurotransmitters brought about by a decrease in autoreceptor sensitivity would help relieve the symptoms of depression. Not clear, however, is why the postsynaptic receptors must decrease in number before the drug can alleviate the symptoms. For if depression is indeed the result of a deficit in synaptic activity, an abnormally high number of postsynaptic receptors should be expected to help restore the sensitivity of the synapse and relieve the symptoms. Apparently it does not, but the reason is unclear.

Accounting for the Deficit Factor

Just as our view of the therapeutic action of antidepressant drugs has changed—that is, relief from depression appears to be the result of correcting both deficits in the neurotransmitter and decreasing postsynaptic sensitivity—so has there been a change in our view of how depression is caused.

The assumption has long been that depression is caused by a neurotransmitter deficit, be it serotonin or both serotonin and norepinephrine. On this basis it seems reasonable to surmise that depressed patients who are *not* medicated will show lower than normal levels of these neurotransmitters. As it happens, there is a simple, if crude, method of measuring the level of neurotransmitters in the brain. You can measure the breakdown products of the neurotransmitters in the urine and the cerebrospinal fluid. The reason the level of these breakdown products is used as a measure of neurotransmitters in the brain is that the neurotransmitters themselves are prevented by the blood-brain barrier from passing into body fluids, whereas the breakdown products are not.

Chemical assays of this type performed on depressed patients have yielded a mixed picture. Some patients do indeed show deficits in the amount of breakdown products of norepinephrine and serotonin—an indication that there is a deficit of these neurotransmitters in the brain (Garver & Davis, 1979). Other patients, however, show deficits in only one or the other. Still others—and this is the troublesome finding—show no deficits or even an increase in the amount of norepinephrine (Gold, Goodwin, & Chrousos, 1988).

There are explanations for why a depressed patient might show deficits in only one of the two neurotransmitters thought to underlie depression: a deficit in either one can cause depression. But how do we explain the last finding—the *absence* of deficits in some patients?

Once again, as was the case when we tried to account for the time-lag factor in drug therapy, we must return to the dynamics of synaptic transmission. And once again, given the absence of hard data, we are obliged to speculate. If it is true that deficits in neurotransmitters can cause depression, it follows that a deficit in postsynaptic sensitivity—that is, a decrease in the number of postsynaptic receptors—should also produce depression. Such an absence, according to the monoamine theory, would explain why some depressed patients show no neurotransmitter deficits or even an increase.

To recapitulate, according to the monoamine theory, the important factor in depression is diminished activity in neural circuits involving serotonin and/or norepinephrine. The new assumption is that the diminished activity can be caused in one of two ways: by a deficit in neurotransmitters or by a deficit in postsynaptic receptors. Figure 15.2 illustrates the new assumption and compares it to the original monoamine theory.

Time Lag and Neurotransmitter Deficit: A Point of Clarification

To explain the time-lag data we postulated that before drug therapy, depressed patients have an *elevated* number of postsynaptic receptors combined with a deficit in neurotransmitter. To explain the absence-of-neurotransmitter-deficit data, we postulated that depressed patients, at least in some cases, have a *deficit* in postsynaptic receptors. Which is

Figure 15.2 *The Monoamine Theory of Depression: Original and Revised*
(a) A normal amount of transmitter interacts with a normal number of postsynaptic receptors. (b) The original monoamine theory proposes that a deficit in transmitter interacts with a normal number of receptors. (c and d) The revised monoamine theory proposes that a deficit in transmitter interacts with an abnormally high number of receptors (c) or that a normal amount of transmitter interacts with an abnormally low number of receptors (d).

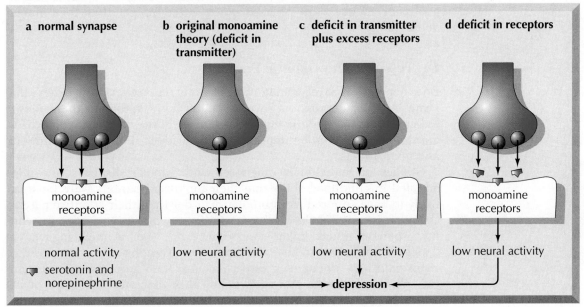

it? Is depression a result of excess receptors combined with a neuro-transmitter deficit? Or is depression the result of a deficit in postsynap-tic receptors? The answer is that it may be the result of both. Depression may be caused by a deficit in postsynaptic receptors, in which case ele-vated neurotransmitter levels restore normal activity, or it may be caused by an increase in receptors (combined with a neurotransmitter deficit), in which case a decrease in receptors (combined with an increase in neu-rotransmitter) restores normal activity. Only future research will tell.

The Symptom Picture

Even if we are able to reconcile such factors as the time lag and the absence of neurotransmitter deficits in depressed patients with the monoamine theory, we must still explain the range of symptomatic behavior that accompanies depression. Why, for instance, do many (though not all) depressed people lose their appetite and suffer from insomnia, to name just two of the more common symptoms?

The answer is fairly clear, particularly when you remember that sero-tonin and norepinephrine are found in several areas of the brain—the hypothalamus, the raphe nuclei, and the limbic system—known to be involved with such behaviors as eating, sleeping, and emotion. Thus deficits of neurotransmitters (combined with excess receptors) or deficits of receptors in these brain areas are very likely to influence these behaviors.

Summing Up

Unipolar depression and bipolar disorder appear to be the result of abnormalities in neurotransmitters, postsynaptic receptors, or both. But a complete understanding of the disorders requires yet another level of analysis. Brain abnormalities may exist, but the question is, Why do they exist? What gives rise to these abnormalities? Evidence points to genet-ics as a critical factor, perhaps more so for bipolar than for unipolar depression.

Depression: The Genetic Factor

Does depression have a genetic basis? Many researchers now believe that some kinds of depression have a genetic basis, although the evidence indicates that the genetic factor is stronger in the case of bipolar disor-der than it is in unipolar depression. The evidence comes from adoption and twin studies.

Studies on individuals diagnosed with bipolar disorder who were adopted in childhood show that their biological parents were far more likely to have suffered from bipolar disorder than their adoptive parents (Mendelwicz, 1977). In addition, studies on bipolar disorder in twins have found a much higher concordance rate (i.e., a much higher ten-dency for both twins to have the same illness) among identical twins (i.e., twins who have the same genetic makeup) than among fraternal twins (i.e., twins who are no more genetically alike than any other pairs of siblings)—roughly 70 percent for identical twins, in contrast to approximately 20 percent for fraternal twins (Bertelsen et al., 1977).

A similar pattern of results—adopted children aligning with their birth parents and pairs of identical twins showing a higher concordance rate than fraternal twins—has been obtained for unipolar depression as well, except that the incidence of depression in family members is not as high and thus the genetic contribution apparently not as strong (Wender et al., 1986).

The Amish Study

One of the most important and highly publicized studies aimed at isolating the genetic factors in depression was published in the late 1980s and focused on a small, tightly knit community of Amish, a Protestant religious sect living in southern Pennsylvania. The study looked at both the genetic and the genealogical history of the community and uncovered two striking findings. It found that nearly all the Amish currently suffering from bipolar disorder had relatives, going back several generations, who had suffered from the same condition. And it found that a large percentage (63 percent) of Amish who suffered from bipolar disorder also had in common a defective gene located on chromosome 11 (Egeland et al., 1987).

A warning is in order. Genealogical and chromosomal studies, such as those on the Amish, do not *prove* that depression is inherited. They merely bring to light a pattern that strongly suggests a genetic link. What's more (as we saw in the discussion in Chapter 13 on homosexuality), to say that there is a genetic component to depression does not automatically rule out environmental factors; nor does it say that children born to depressed parents are irreversibly earmarked for depression. Finally, we must not lose sight of the fact that the role played by genetics in bipolar disorder appears to be stronger than in unipolar depression. And, as we are about to see, the differences between the two surface again when we look at their treatment.

TREATING DEPRESSION: ASSESSING THE OPTIONS

Depression today is treated in a variety of ways. Psychotherapy remains an important component in the treatment of depression, but biologically-based treatments are becoming increasingly common and are often used in concert with psychotherapy. The biological therapies consist of three broad categories: antidepressant drugs, electroconvulsive therapy (ECT), and, in the case of bipolar depression, the drug known as lithium. The effectiveness of the treatments vary: what works for unipolar depression doesn't work for bipolar disorder, and vice versa. This pattern reinforces the view that even though the two disorders (unipolar and bipolar) have some elements in common, they involve different physiological mechanisms.

Unipolar Depression: Drug Therapies and ECT

Drug therapies and ECT have both proven to be effective treatments for unipolar depression. The typical approach has been to use drugs and, if they prove ineffective or their side effects prevent their use, then to use ECT. Drugs produce remission or improvement in roughly 70 percent of patients with unipolar depression. The basic action of these antidepressant drugs, as we have already seen, is to increase the level of neurotransmitter—serotonin in the case of the SSRIs (such as Prozac), and serotonin and norepinephrine in the case of tricyclic antidepressants and MAO inhibitors (see Chapter 5 for a detailed discussion of drug action).

Prozac

The story of Prozac's development (as related by Peter Kramer) stands in sharp contrast to the usual story of a clinician serendipitously stumbling across a psychopharmacologically active agent (Kramer, 1993). Prozac's birth, it turns out, was carefully planned. It took place in a state-of-the-art neurochemistry laboratory, and the research team credited with its development knew exactly what their goal was: to develop a compound that would selectively inhibit serotonin reuptake. Such a compound, they hypothesized, would reduce or alleviate symptoms of depression and, because of its greater chemical specificity (it affects only serotonin), would produce fewer side effects than existing drugs.

The clinical use of Prozac has confirmed both hypotheses. Prozac, like other antidepressants, relieves the common symptoms of depression and clearly produces fewer side effects. Prozac users do not suffer from dizziness, weight gain, and the general sluggishness often produced by other antidepressant drugs. Not that the side effects are entirely absent. Roughly one-third of Prozac users reportedly suffer from insomnia, and some Prozac users report a diminished interest in sex. Then, too, there have been reports that Prozac has, in some cases, produced violent behavior and suicidal impulses, although it has yet to be confirmed that Prozac is the contributing factor in these episodes (Lickey & Gordon, 1991).

Clinical experience with Prozac suggested some unanticipated uses. Because it is so easily tolerated, clinicians are now prescribing it for milder cases of depression, and even in situations where clear-cut depressive symptoms are absent (e.g., shyness, lack of confidence, and unassertiveness). At the same time, as we shall see shortly, Prozac appears to help with obsessive-compulsive disorders. More than a dozen drugs with Prozac's chemical properties are either on the market or awaiting final approval. Because of their chemical specificity, clinical experience with these drugs will likely lead us to new hypotheses about brain function in pathological states.

Electroconvulsive Therapy

In the short term, ECT is even more effective than drug treatment: it produces remission or improvement in an estimated 90 percent of unipolar depressed patients (Fink, 1987). ECT consists of administering a brief electric current of moderate intensity to electrodes attached to the patient's forehead (see Figure 15.3). To minimize the possibility of injuries that might result from the epileptic-like convulsion that occurs during the procedure, several measures are taken. Patients are given an anesthetic and a muscle relaxant, and because their breathing sometimes stops temporarily, they are given oxygen. A typical ECT treatment consists of a total of six to eight exposures over a 2-week period (Silver & Yudofsky, 1988). However, the symptoms usually return if the ECT is discontinued for any length of time.

The reason ECT relieves depression remains unknown. Evidence suggests that like antidepressant drugs, it affects norepinephrine and serotonin synapses. In contrast to antidepressant drugs, however, ECT is thought to act only on postsynaptic receptors, increasing their sensitivity (Heninger & Charney, 1987) and thereby increasing activity in norepinephrine and serotonin synapses.

Like antidepressant drugs, ECT is not without side effects. In the first 12 hours or so after ECT, patients frequently become disoriented, many unable to recall their own addresses or telephone numbers. In addition, ECT disrupts the memory of events that occur both before and after the treatment. Memory loss can extend back to experiences that occurred as long ago as 1 to 3 years before the ECT. Fortunately, the loss is usually temporary and subsides within a few weeks after termination of treat-

Figure 15.3 *Electroconvulsive Therapy (ECT)*
Patients administered ECT are given an anesthetic to promote sleep, a muscle relaxant to prevent convulsive jerks, and oxygen because they often stop breathing.

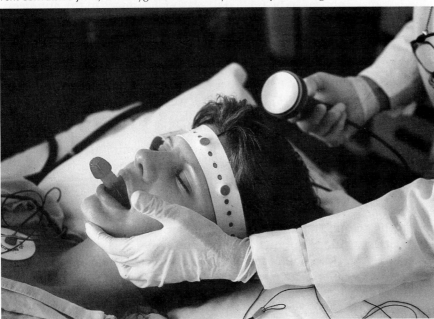

ment (see Chapter 17 for details). Because of these side effects, most psychiatrists agree that ECT should be used as a treatment of last resort only after antidepressant drugs are found to be ineffective.

Bipolar Disorder and Lithium

Often the drug of choice in the treatment of bipolar disorder is lithium. Lithium, in the form of lithium carbonate, is used primarily to prevent or treat the manic phase of the disorder, but it can also prevent depressive episodes. The effect of lithium on mania is rapid: symptoms usually subside within 5 to 10 days after medication.

Understanding exactly how lithium works in the nervous system to alleviate bipolar disorder is still in the experimental stage. Surprisingly, rather than lithium affecting serotonin and norepinephrine, as originally thought, recent evidence indicates that lithium affects acetylcholine, decreasing its ability to produce postsynaptic activity (Drummond, 1987; Avissar & Schreiber, 1989; Worley et al., 1988).

Seasonal Affective Disorder and Light Therapy

One intriguing type of depression that we have not yet covered can be treated effectively by, of all things, prolonged exposure to bright light. People who suffer from this type of depression are affected by the changing of the seasons, and their condition has come to be known as *seasonal affective disorder* (SAD).

People who suffer from SAD typically become depressed in late fall, when the days become shorter. In early spring as the days become longer, the depression lifts and they may feel unusually energized. These mood changes appear to be related to seasonal changes in the number of hours of daylight they are exposed to per day. When people who suffer from SAD go south in the winter, their depression lifts, often in a matter of days. When they come north in the fall, the depression often returns (Rosenthal et al., 1984).

How and why does light affect mood? One theory links SAD in humans to the hibernation patterns of lower animals (Lam et al., 1990). Clinicians have noted that some of the behavioral patterns of people who suffer from SAD are not only atypical of depressed patients in general, they also resemble the behavioral patterns of animals preparing for hibernation. Unlike typical depressed patients, but similar to pre-hibernating animals, people with SAD experience an increase in appetite, a craving for carbohydrates, and an increased need for sleep (Gupta, 1988).

Equally significant is the fact that when SAD patients are exposed to light (either artificial or natural) for several hours a day, their symptoms are frequently relieved, and there is a biochemical explanation that links this light effect with the pre-hibernation patterns of animals. The pre-hibernation patterns appear to be governed—in part, at least—by the hormone *melatonin*, which is secreted by the *pineal gland* (a gland located in the brain). Melatonin is secreted only in the dark. Its secretion ceases when animals are exposed to light. The same pattern holds for humans. It is thus conceivable that the depression—and the accompanying changes in appetite and sleep—experienced by people with SAD is the result of abnormally high levels of melatonin secretion (or sensitivity), and that the relief these people experience when they are exposed to light (natural or artificial) reflects a cessation of the abnormal melatonin-produced activity (Rosenthal et al., 1989).

ANXIETY DISORDERS

Anxiety disorders differ from affective disorders in one key respect: the primary symptom is not a disturbance in mood but rather severe anxiety or fear (manifested by arousal, sweating, dry mouth, and a desire to run or escape). In typical anxiety disorders, the anxiety may be severe and quite limiting, but the individual does not lose contact with reality.

Anxiety disorders are the most common of all psychiatric disorders, affecting 12.6 percent of the general population in the United States in the course of 1 year. These disorders are divided into several subtypes, and we shall consider three: panic attacks, generalized anxiety, and obsessive-compulsive disorders. A fourth is phobia—an irrational fear of specific objects such as snakes or situations such as heights—which may have a biological component but for the most part is seen as a *learned* disorder and is treated effectively by behavioral therapies. These therapies include behavior modification and counterconditioning; all are designed to extinguish the inappropriate behavior and reduce levels of experienced anxiety and muscle tension.

Panic Attacks

Panic attacks are brief, unexpected episodes of extreme anxiety. Their principal symptoms are shortness of breath, heart palpitations, dizziness, nausea, sweating, and an overwhelming sense of terror and dread. These attacks can occur as frequently as three or four times a week and can last as long as 15 minutes or so. They appear spontaneously under circumstances that normally do not evoke fear. People report in fact that panic attacks appear "out of the blue." There is some evidence that panic attacks "run in families," though this pattern has not been studied closely yet.

The Chemical Basis of Panic Attacks

Evidence from both lower-animal work and humans has shown a strong connection between panic attacks and norepinephrine. When the locus coeruleus, the major production site of norepinephrine in the brain, is electrically stimulated in monkeys, the resulting behavior parallels the behavior seen in a typical panic attack suffered by humans (Redmond, 1987). When drugs that increase the level of norepinephrine are given to people predisposed to panic attacks, the attacks increase (Charney, 1986). Drugs (antidepressants) that *decrease* the level of norepinephrine, on the other hand, can decrease or prevent the attacks (Simson & Weiss, 1989; Liebowitz, 1985; Ballenger, 1988). Complicating the neurotransmitter and neuroanatomy picture is evidence indicating that: (a) benzodiazepines (Valium and Librium), drugs that affect the neurotransmitter GABA (not norepinephrine), are also effective treatments for panic attacks, and (b) electrical stimulation of the amygdala in lower animals produces an increase in fear-related behavior as well as an increase in respiration (a prominent symptom in panic attacks) (Noyes et al., 1984).

Panic attacks may be governed by GABA, norepinephrine, or both, but evidence indicates that in addition to these neurotransmitters, chemicals that normally build up in the body during exercise and stress may also be involved (Gorman, 1988). Lactate and elevated carbon dioxide, chemicals in the blood related to exercise and stress, have been administered to panic-prone individuals and with some surprising results. These individuals tend to overreact and exhibit panic responses, while normal control subjects do not. For some reason, they appear to be overly sensitive to lactate and carbon dioxide which in turn may trigger the panic reaction, but we are not certain why.

Generalized Anxiety Disorder

Generalized anxiety disorder is a condition characterized by fear, tension, and anxiety that do not appear to be related to any particular situation or stimulus. The distinguishing feature of generalized anxiety—sometimes referred to as *free-floating anxiety*—and the feature that sets it apart from panic attacks is its duration and intensity. In panic attacks, the anxiety usually lasts for a few minutes and then subsides. In generalized anxiety disorder, the anxiety is a chronic state, persisting for months.

Two types of drugs have been used to alleviate anxiety: benzodiazepines (Valium, Librium, Xanax, and Atavan) and more recently *buspirone*. Benzodiazepines act by enhancing the action of GABA (an inhibitory neurotransmitter), and this effect suggests that the abnormal anxiety is the result of a decrease in GABA activity. Buspirone acts by binding to and activating serotonin receptors, suggesting that the abnormal anxiety is the result of a decrease in serotonin activity (Green, 1991). The conclusion is that a deficit in either GABA or serotonin activity may produce generalized anxiety; restoring either is sufficient to alleviate the symptoms.

Obsessive-Compulsive Disorder

Obsessive-compulsive disorder (OCD) was once considered a rare condition. Today, though, the number of people in the United States who suffer from the condition to one degree or another is thought to be between 4 and 6 million. Does this mean OCD is sharply on the rise? Probably not. The more likely explanation is that because of increased publicity about the disorder and because of newly developed drug therapies, treatment is now being sought by people who, in the past, would have kept their condition a secret (Rapoport, 1989).

Obsessions are recurring thoughts, ideas, wishes, or concerns that take hold of our consciousness and refuse to let go. We all experience mild obsessions from time to time. We sit in a restaurant or movie and keep asking ourselves over and over again, "Did I lock the door?" Or a tune we heard earlier in the morning runs through our heads over and over again.

For people suffering from OCD, however, the familiar obsessions that we all experience now and then are an all but constant force in their lives, and can revolve around any number of focal points. Some OCD patients are so obsessed by the fear of being contaminated by germs that they refuse to venture into public places and refuse to eat in restaurants. Others spend the better part of their waking hours preoccupied by the fear that something terrible (a fire, an accident, murder, etc.) is about to happen at any minute. Still others are constantly haunted by the fear that they themselves will bring harm to people.

Compulsions, on the other hand, are repetitive actions, and here, too, we need to draw a distinction between the quirks we all have and the repetitive actions of OCD patients. You may be a little fussier than your friends are about the way your desk is organized, or you might be in the habit of checking and double checking to see if your doors are locked, but these idiosyncrasies bear little resemblance to full-blown compulsive behavior. A person who suffers from OCD will repeat the same ritualistic act over and over, when there is clearly no practical reason for the behavior. They will wash their hands over and over—sometimes several times an hour. They will check whether a door is locked not just once but hundreds of times.

What is perhaps most striking about the behavior of people who suffer from OCD is that they are usually aware of how senseless and irrational their behavior or thoughts may be but nonetheless powerless to control their behavior. It is generally agreed the more severe forms of OCD are rooted in brain abnormalities. Precisely what those abnormalities are is just now coming to light. Brain-imaging studies using CT and PET scans (see Chapter 3 for details) have revealed structural and metabolic abnormalities in OCD patients. Drug studies have revealed chemical abnormalities.

Structural and Metabolic Abnormalities in OCD

CT scans and PET scans done on OCD patients have uncovered abnormalities in areas of the brain in and around the basal ganglia (a collection of areas involved in motor control). CT scans indicate that the caudate nucleus (one of the structures in the basal ganglia) in OCD patients is smaller than normal (Rapoport & Wise, 1988). PET scans show that in OCD patients both the frontal lobes and the pathways (cingulate tract) that connect the frontal lobes to the basal ganglia have a higher than normal metabolic rate (Baxter et al., 1987, 1988; Rubin et al., 1992). Exactly how these abnormalities relate to the recurrent thoughts and acts that haunt the daily lives of OCD patients remains to be determined. Figure 15.4 depicts the brain areas that have been implicated in OCD.

Chemical Abnormalities in OCD

While some investigators have been focusing their attention on the anatomy of the OCD brain, others have been studying neurotransmitters. Their objective has been to see whether a chemical imbalance may also be involved in the condition. Researchers have studied the effects of certain drugs on OCD patients and have concluded that a deficit in the neurotransmitter serotonin may be involved in producing OCD (Zohar et al., 1988; Charney et al., 1988). Three drugs have been found to be effective in treating OCD: clomipramine, fluvoxamine, and fluvoxetine (Prozac). All act to increase the level of serotonin by blocking its reuptake in the synapse. Although they do not work in every case, each has the capacity to improve the behavior of OCD patients. However, the symptoms usually return if the drug is discontinued.

OCD: Brain and Behavior

Assuming that OCD is caused by a deficit in serotonin, we still must ask ourselves how and why the deficit produces OCD symptoms. Why should a deficit in serotonin produce recurrent thoughts and repetitive acts? And why should the behaviors center around washing and checking? The answer, in Judith Rapoport's view, lies in the behaviors normally controlled by the basal ganglia (the area of the brain apparently involved in OCD) and the role that serotonin plays in controlling these behaviors (Rapoport & Wise, 1988).

Figure 15.4   *Brain Areas Implicated in OCD*
The caudate nucleus is smaller than normal and the frontal lobes have a higher than normal metabolic activity.

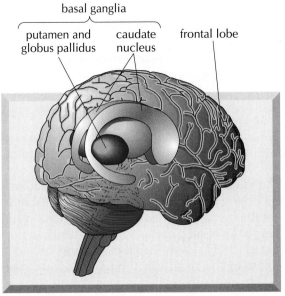

The behaviors produced by the basal ganglia, according to Rapoport, are vestiges of our prehistoric past. During the course of evolution it was—and still is—to our adaptive advantage to protect our territory and to keep ourselves clean. Checking doors and washing hands, suggests Rapoport, may well be aspects of these behaviors that have remained with us, stored in the basal ganglia (Rapoport, 1989).

Rapoport theorizes that the lack of serotonin in OCD patients interferes with the ability of the basal ganglia to control these behaviors. According to her theory, when a sufficient amount of serotonin is present, the behaviors are inhibited. In OCD patients, presumably because of a lack of serotonin, the behaviors are released over and over again. So even though patients recognize that their behaviors serve no purpose, they are unable to stop them. Antiobsessional drugs restore serotonin and in the process restore inhibition of the basal ganglia and reduce the repetitive rituals.

SCHIZOPHRENIA

Schizophrenia is not only the most severe of all the mental disorders we have considered, it is also probably the most difficult to define. The word itself means "split mind" and was originally coined by the Swiss psychiatrist Eugene Bleuler in 1911.

The term "schizophrenia" was intended to describe the symptoms that are characteristic of schizophrenics: a split from reality (they may hear voices no one else hears or they may have beliefs that no one else has) and a split between their own thinking and feeling (they may feel nothing at all or they may feel inappropriate emotions). The term "schizophrenia" is not to be confused with the term "multiple personality disorder." *Multiple personality disorder* refers to a person who exhibits two or more distinct identities—for example, the fictional Dr. Jekyll and Mr. Hyde, or the famous case history of the three faces of Eve.

It is estimated that roughly 1 percent of the population in the United States has schizophrenia. But schizophrenia has proven to be extremely difficult to diagnose because the symptom picture is so varied and complex. Schizophrenic patients have difficulties in many areas of their lives: thought and language, social relationships, emotions. In addition, they may experience hallucinations (false sensory experiences), delusions (false beliefs), and social withdrawal.

In an effort to simplify the systematic study of schizophrenia, some theorists divide the symptoms into two basic categories, positive and negative. *Positive symptoms* are those that are marked by the *presence* of abnormal behavior: hallucinations, delusions, confused thinking (as opposed to absence of thought), and inappropriate emotions (as opposed to absence of emotions). *Negative symptoms* are marked by the *absence* of behavior: poverty of thought or speech, blunting of emotion, and social withdrawal. Some schizophrenics exhibit only positive symptoms, others only negative symptoms, and still others a mixture of the two.

The positive-negative division in symptomatology is more than a mere labeling device used for diagnosis. As we will soon see, the positive-negative division may reflect fundamental differences in the causes of schizophrenia. We'll return later in this chapter to this distinction in symptomatology and to the implications the distinction has for understanding the underlying cause of schizophrenia.

What Causes Schizophrenia?

Whatever its symptoms, schizophrenia is generally thought to have a strong biological component centered in the part of the body that controls behavior—the brain. Something in the neural machinery of schizophrenics causes them to behave in ways that are inconsistent with and unrelated to environmental demands. They see a group of happy children and are convinced that the children are laughing at them. They hear voices that no one else hears.

Nobody knows why people with schizophrenia behave in this way, but there is no shortage of theories, many of which point to an inherited *predisposition* (i.e., a genetic factor that places people at a higher than normal risk). The argument that schizophrenia has a genetic component draws most of its support from two findings. First, adoption studies have shown a high frequency of schizophrenia in children with a schizophrenic birth parent, even when the children are reared by nonschizophrenic adoptive parents (Heston, 1966). Second, studies on schizophrenia in twins have found a much higher concordance rate (i.e., a much higher tendency for cotwins to have the same illness) in identical twins than in fraternal twins—30 to 50 percent for identical twins, in contrast to roughly 15 percent for fraternal twins (Gottesman & Shields, 1966).

Taken within a genetic framework, these differences are to be expected. Identical twins, as we have stressed before, have the same genetic makeup; fraternal twins do not. Therefore, if genes are implicated in the disorder, a higher concordance rate is to be expected in identical than in fraternal twins. We must be careful, however, not to overstate the genetic case. If a genetic abnormality were the sole cause of schizophrenia, we would expect the concordance rate for identical twins to be 100 percent. The fact that this rate is far below 100 percent indicates that environmental factors also play a role.

If genes do indeed play a role in schizophrenia, we can assume that they do so by producing an abnormality in the brain. The question then is, What in the brain is abnormal? A number of hypotheses have been proposed, and studies have been undertaken to answer this question. None, however, has been more influential than work implicating the neurotransmitter dopamine.

The Dopamine Theory

Basing his theory on the effects of certain drugs on humans, Solomon Snyder suggested that an *excess* of the neurotransmitter dopamine produces schizophrenia (Snyder, 1976). Snyder's view was based on the observation that drugs that increase dopamine levels in the nervous system produce behavior that resembles certain (but not all) of the symptoms of schizophrenia, whereas drugs that decrease dopamine levels reduce or alleviate these symptoms (Snyder, 1967, 1972). Let us examine these drug effects in more detail.

Schizophrenia and Amphetamines

The case for dopamine as a factor in schizophrenia is built mainly around the fact that people who take excessive amounts of amphetamine—a drug known to increase dopamine levels in the brain—show certain symptoms (e.g., delusions and hallucinations) similar to those of schizophrenia. This condition is known as *amphetamine psychosis* (Connell, 1967). There is, however, one problem: amphetamine not only increases dopamine levels but also increases norepinephrine levels. So if the chemical effects of amphetamines are to be of any scientific value in understanding schizophrenia, we must first find a way of determining the extent to which each neurotransmitter is involved in producing amphetamine psychosis.

One approach to this problem has been to give human subjects (volunteers) two different types of amphetamines—dextroamphetamine (*d*-amphetamine) and levoamphetamine (*l*-amphetamine). Each type produces increases in both norepinephrine and dopamine levels, but the amount of norepinephrine produced by *d*-amphetamine is 10 times greater than the amount of norepinephrine produced by *l*-amphetamine.

Thus if norepinephrine is indeed the triggering agent for schizophrenic symptoms, subjects given *d*-amphetamine should manifest these symptoms to a much greater degree than subjects given *l*-amphetamine. As it turns out, there is no difference in the degree of schizophrenic symptoms produced by both types of amphetamines (Angrist et al., 1974). The conclusion is that dopamine, not norepinephrine, appears to be the triggering agent in amphetamine psychosis.

Additional evidence for a dopamine-schizophrenia connection comes from studies showing a relation between decreases in dopamine levels and improvement in patients with schizophrenia. Let us look at this evidence more closely.

Antischizophrenic Drugs

Certain drugs have proven effective in reducing schizophrenic symptoms. These drugs are called antischizophrenic drugs and they fall into two classes: *phenothiazines* (notably chlorpromazine) and *butyrophenones* (notably haloperidol). Both can bring a measure of normalcy to the behavior of schizophrenic patients, although once the drugs are discontinued, the symptoms often reemerge. What's more, both types of drugs affect a variety of symptoms, albeit in different ways. Patients who are agitated and excited become calmer when they are treated with antischizophrenic drugs. Patients who are withdrawn become more active. Hallucinations diminish in their intensity, and confused thought and speech may clear up.

The effectiveness of these drugs has spurred a good deal of research into their effect on neurotransmitters in the brain. Research to date indicates that the principal effect of antischizophrenic drugs is to block the action of neurotransmitters by occupying but not activating their receptor sites. Because the most potent antischizophrenic drugs—butyrophenones—selectively block dopamine but not norepinephrine receptors, the evidence for a dopamine link with schizophrenia has become stronger than ever (Seeman & Lee, 1975).

Side Effects of Antischizophrenic Drugs

Antischizophrenic drugs are not without their limitations and side effects. First of all, these drugs are more effective in the treatment of positive symptoms than negative symptoms—an issue we will return to shortly. Second, if taken in very large doses, they can produce the same motor tremors, postural rigidity, and shuffling gait frequently observed in victims of Parkinson's disease (see Chapters 2 and 10 for details). Finally, and perhaps most devastating, prolonged use of antischizophrenic drugs can produce a seemingly irreversible motor disorder known as *tardive dyskinesia* that is characterized by tics of the face and involuntary movements of the legs and arms (see Chapter 5 for details).

That antischizophrenic drugs affect not only cognitive and emotional behavior but motor behavior as well is not surprising when you consider that dopamine receptors are located in both the limbic and extrapyramidal systems. The blocking action of the drugs in the limbic system (the cognitive-emotional areas of the brain) is therapeutic and relieves the symptoms. The blocking action of the drugs in the extrapyramidal system (specifically the basal ganglia), however, produces motor disabilities similar to those seen in Parkinson's disease.

Fine-Tuning the Dopamine Theory

The evidence for a dopamine link to schizophrenia is strong, but the picture is still riddled with questions and contradictions (Seeman & Lee, 1975). Autopsies on the brains of schizophrenic patients, for example, have found no evidence that the schizophrenic brain releases abnormally high levels of dopamine, although some of these studies have uncovered an abnormally high number of dopamine receptors (Lee & Seeman, 1980; Pickar et al., 1990). So, while the original assumption of the dopamine theory—that schizophrenics release abnormally high levels of a neurotransmitter—may not be valid, dopamine may still hold the key to schizophrenia. The reason is that excess dopamine receptors can be just as effective as excess dopamine itself in producing overactive dopamine circuits. Figure 15.5 illustrates how this is possible.

Dopamine Receptors and Schizophrenia

Changing the focus of the dopamine theory from neurotransmitter to receptors solves one problem: it explains the autopsy data. Unfortunately, it introduces a new problem having to do with the nature of the abnormal dopamine receptors.

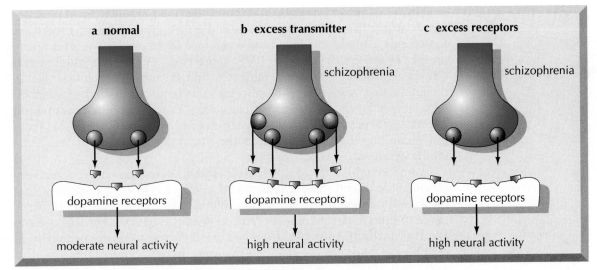

Figure 15.5 *The Two Dopamine Theories of Schizophrenia*
(a) A normal amount of dopamine (DA) interacts with a normal number of postsynaptic receptors. (Note that not all neurotransmitters bind to the receptors.) (b) An abnormal amount of dopamine interacts with a normal number of receptors. The increase in neurotransmitters increases the likelihood that more receptors will be stimulated and more impulses produced. (c) A normal amount of dopamine interacts with an abnormally high number of receptors. The increase in receptors increases the likelihood that more receptors will be stimulated and more impulses produced. Recent autopsy studies on schizophrenics favor model c.

Six different types of dopamine receptors have been identified so far. They are known as D_1, D_{2a}, D_{2b}, D_3, D_4, and D_5, and they differ from one another in their protein structure (Spano, Govoni, & Trabucchi, 1978; Creese, 1982). So if excess dopamine receptors are indeed at the root of schizophrenia, the question now becomes, Which ones are involved? Are they all involved? Are only some involved? Or is only one type of dopamine receptor involved?

To answer these questions, researchers have studied how antischizophrenic drugs affect dopamine receptors. As we have already mentioned, antischizophrenic drugs work by binding to, but not activating, dopamine receptors. As it happens, though, the binding occurs to only certain receptors. Antischizophrenic drugs selectively bind to D_2, D_3, and D_4 receptors but tend not to bind to D_1 and D_5 receptors. This finding has led researchers to conclude that it is the D_2, D_3, and D_4 receptors and not the D_1 and D_5 receptors that are at the root of the problem. Strengthening the link between schizophrenia and D_2 receptors is the fact that the therapeutic effectiveness of the most potent antischizophrenic drugs correlates with their ability to bind to D_2 receptors (Seeman, 1992).

Atypical Antischizophrenic Drugs
Aided by the discovery of a new class of drugs known as *atypical* antischizophrenic drugs (the most notable of which is *clozapine*), researchers have recently been able to take the receptor analysis one step further.

This new category of antischizophrenic drugs is known as atypical for two reasons: they alleviate schizophrenic symptoms without producing motor side effects, and they bind to D_3 and D_4 receptors but tend not to bind to D_2 receptors (Marder, 1988; Kane et al., 1988). This binding pattern is significant because it indicates that D_3 and D_4 receptors, like D_2 receptors, are factors in schizophrenia. The pattern also helps to explain why atypical antischizophrenic drugs affect cognitive and emotional but not motor behavior—D_3 and D_4 receptors are located in the limbic (cognitive-emotional areas) but not in the extrapyramidal (motor area) system (Davis et al., 1991).

Unfortunately atypical antischizophrenic drugs may have other very serious side effects. There is a risk of *agranulocytosis*, a condition that involves a dangerous drop in white blood cells and a lowering of resistance to infections and disease (Krupp & Barnes, 1989). For this reason, atypical antischizophrenic drugs are used very cautiously, primarily in people who have not been helped by other drugs (Meltzer, 1990).

Weaknesses of the Dopamine Theory

It would be misleading to suggest that dopamine is the whole story of the biochemistry of schizophrenia. It is more likely, in fact, that dopamine is only one part (albeit a crucial one) of a much more complex story.

One problem with studies that indicate an abnormally high number of dopamine receptors is that the data are not easily interpreted. Most (but not all) of the autopsied patients have had a long history of medication use, raising the possibility that the excess number of dopamine receptors may be the *result* of the medication and not the *cause* of the schizophrenic symptoms. Then, too, we are again faced with the problem we encountered when we talked about drugs that alleviate depression. Antischizophrenic drugs take only a few hours to block dopamine action but take several weeks to alleviate schizophrenic symptoms (Crow, 1979). It is indeed possible that this time lag is linked, once again, to long-term changes in receptor sensitivity, but this hypothesis has yet to be confirmed.

The Achilles' heel of the dopamine theory of schizophrenia is the fact that patients with predominantly negative symptoms (impoverished thinking, blunted emotions, extreme withdrawal, and underactivity) tend not to respond to antischizophrenic drugs, typical or atypical. The question, then, is that if schizophrenia is caused by excessive dopamine activity, why should some schizophrenics (those suffering from positive symptoms) respond to drugs that decrease dopamine activity and others (those suffering from negative symptoms) not? The answer brings us to another theory of schizophrenia, the so-called *two-syndrome theory of schizophrenia* proposed by Timothy Crow (Crow, 1980; Tyrer, 1986).

Two-Syndrome Theory of Schizophrenia

According to the two-syndrome theory of schizophrenia, the disease is a composite of two disorders. Crow has dubbed the disorders Type I and

Type II, and each disorder, in his view, has its own symptoms and its own underlying pathology. Type I schizophrenia is marked by positive symptoms and, according to Crow's theory, is caused by excess dopamine activity, specifically excess dopamine receptors. Type II schizophrenia is marked by negative symptoms and, according to the theory, is caused by structural brain damage.

There is evidence to support the two-syndrome theory. The positive symptoms of schizophrenia tend to be reduced by drugs, and patients with predominantly positive symptoms tend not to have structural brain damage. By the same token, negative symptoms tend not to be reduced by drugs, and patients with predominantly negative symptoms tend to have structural brain damage.

The connection between negative symptoms and brain damage has been established by autopsy and brain-imaging work (see Chapter 3 for a description of brain-imaging techniques). The results of these studies indicate that some schizophrenics do indeed have enlarged ventricles and atrophy of the brain (specifically, in the frontal cortex) and that patients with these structural abnormalities are more likely to show negative than positive symptoms (Andreasen et al., 1986; Andreasen, 1988; Shelton & Weinberger, 1987).

In summary, then, there may be two types of schizophrenia—Type I and Type II—each with its own symptoms (positive and negative) and each with its own cause (excessive dopamine activity and structural brain damage). The connection between negative symptoms and structural brain damage has been established by the autopsy and brain-imaging work. The link between positive symptoms and excessive dopamine activity has been established by drug work.

The Relationship between Type I and Type II

Given that there are two types of schizophrenia, certain questions arise. Are the two types unrelated, developing independently of each other? Or do they simply represent different stages or forms of the same disease? Evidence points to both types of relationships.

In one study conducted on 52 schizophrenic patients who were hospitalized before the advent of antischizophrenic drugs, it was found that over a 25-year period positive symptoms (hallucinations and delusions, for instance) gradually changed into negative symptoms such as social withdrawal and flat affect (Andreasen, 1985). One explanation for this sequence of events—and this is by no means the only explanation—is as follows: in a genetically predisposed individual an environmental trigger produces abnormal dopamine activity (manifested in positive symptoms), and the abnormal dopamine activity over time in turn produces brain damage (manifested in negative symptoms).

On the other hand, there is also evidence that the two types of schizophrenia develop independently. Nancy Andreasen in her critique of the two-syndrome theory reports that some patients with negative symptoms have no prior history of positive symptoms; they begin with negative symptoms, and they remain in that state for the rest of their lives (Andreasen, 1985). And the question is, Why? What is the source of brain damage in schizophrenic patients who exhibit negative symptoms with no prior history of positive symptoms? Recent evidence points to the environment.

The Environmental Cause of Brain Damage

If you look at Figure 15.6, you will see a photograph of a magnetic resonance imaging scan from a pair of identical twins, one schizophrenic and one normal. Notice that the twin with schizophrenia has larger ventricles than the normal twin. The significance of this pattern—enlarged ventricles in the schizophrenic but not the normal twin—is that it held true for 12 of the 15 twin pairs that were studied (Suddath et al., 1989). Equally significant is that this pattern of brain damage (i.e., brain damage in only one of each twin pair) appears even though the twins are identical, indicating that it is not genetically produced.

If not genetics, then what does cause the brain damage? Until recently we had no answer to this question—and we still don't—but we have some interesting speculations and some intriguing leads. One theory that has recently gained credibility (and you must bear in mind that it is just that, a theory) points to a virus as the culprit.

The Viral Theory of Schizophrenia

Evidence for the viral theory comes from a rather unexpected observation. In the northern United States, schizophrenics are more likely to be born during the winter months (January, February, March) than during any of the other seasons (Kendell, 1989, 1991; Degreef et al., 1988; Kirch, 1993). Moreover, this increase occurs only among patients who do *not* have a family history of the disorder (O'Callaghan et al., 1991).

This observation has led to the following theory. In infants born in the winter, the second trimester of their fetal development (the time during which major developmental changes are occurring in the nervous sys-

Figure 15.6   *The Brains of Identical Twins*
The ventricles are larger in the twin that had schizophrenia (left) than in the twin that did not (right).

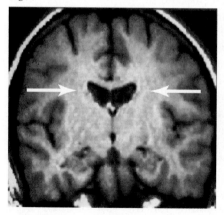
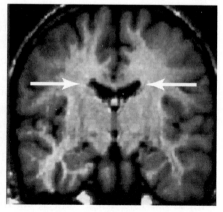

a   b

tem) coincides with the season of the year (the fall) in which viral diseases are most prevalent, especially in northern climates. Thus the reason why people born in the winter are at a higher risk for schizophrenia is that their mothers were more likely to have been exposed to a viral infection during the second trimester of pregnancy. Further support for the viral theory comes from a recent study showing that viral epidemics, regardless of the season in which they occur, are good predictors of a subsequent increase in the incidence of schizophrenia (Barr, Mednick, & Munk-Jorgense, 1990).

Cautionary Note

The viral theory is intriguing, but problems and questions still remain. If a virus causes brain damage, we would expect that schizophrenics born in the winter would be more likely to show brain damage and to exhibit negative symptoms than schizophrenics born during other seasons. This pattern has yet to be established. And if a viral infection during fetal development is the source of brain damage, why in the case of the identical twin study should one twin be affected by the virus and the other twin not? Finally, and perhaps most significant, the human fetus is enveloped by a protective membrane known as the *placenta* that regulates the exchange of nourishment, oxygen, and waste products between mother and fetus. Under normal conditions viruses do not cross the placental barrier from mother to fetus. These are some of the problems that must be resolved before the viral theory becomes generally accepted.

THE SCHIZOPHRENIC BRAIN AND BEHAVIOR

Assuming that schizophrenics have abnormal dopamine activity, structural brain damage, or both, we must ask ourselves how and why these abnormalities produce "schizophrenic" behavior. Why should structural brain damage produce the negative symptoms (the absence of emotion and the absence of thinking) and why should excessive dopamine activity produce the positive symptoms (delusions, hallucinations, inappropriate emotion, and chaotic thinking)? The answers to these questions are far from clear, but they almost assuredly involve those specific areas of the brain, shown in Figure 15.7, in which the structural or chemical abnormalities occur.

The anatomical basis for the negative symptoms—for example, the loss of emotion and the absence of thinking—that dominate the behavior of some schizophrenics seems relatively easy to isolate, at least in theory. The likely candidate is the frontal cortex, and for two reasons: first, the frontal cortex, as you'll recall, is one of the areas found to be damaged in schizophrenics who exhibit negative symptoms; second, the frontal cortex is known to be involved in controlling behaviors that generally are included among the negative symptoms. People who experience frontal cortex damage (from illness, accident, or surgery) typically lose emo-

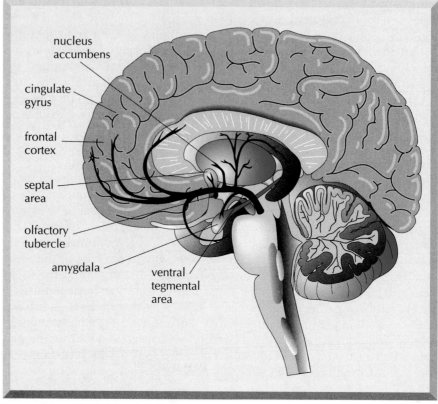

Figure 15.7 *The Schizophrenic Brain*
Negative symptoms may result from damage in the frontal cortex. Positive symptoms may result from dopamine abnormalities in the limbic system (including the amygdala, septal area and nucleus accumbens).

tional responsiveness and social behavior, are poorly motivated, and lose the ability to organize and plan.

Similarly, the anatomical basis of positive symptoms—thought disorder, hallucinations, and inappropriate emotion—is also relatively easy to pinpoint, at least in theory. The likely candidate here is the limbic system, and again for two reasons: first, the limbic system, as you will recall, is one of the areas of the brain that contains dopamine receptors (specifically, D_2, D_3, and D_4 receptors); second, the limbic system is also the area of the brain involved in controlling behaviors that are generally included among positive symptoms.

Recapitulation

Let us now take inventory. Clearly, we know far more about schizophrenia today than we knew as recently as 10 years ago. We can now say, with reasonable certainty, that it is the product of a sequence of events that begins with a genetic or environmental abnormality, takes the form of a brain abnormality, and culminates in a behavioral abnormality. We can also say, with somewhat less certainty but with increasing empirical support, that schizophrenics suffer from two kinds of brain abnormalities: excessive dopamine activity and structural brain damage.

Beyond these observations, the picture becomes more speculative but still has empirical support. There is now reason to believe, although more evidence is needed, that the two different categories of schizophrenic symptoms are rooted in two different kinds of brain abnormalities—excessive dopamine activity producing positive symptoms and structural brain damage producing negative symptoms. Finally, it is reasonable to suggest—although here again the evidence is still sketchy—that excess dopamine activity is rooted in genetic abnormalities, whereas structural brain damage has its roots in environmental factors, perhaps viral.

SUMMARY

1. *Psychological disorders.* Psychological disorders are usually divided into two broad categories: those involving breakdown in the body or viscera and those involving mental experiences. Conditions in the first category are generally referred to as psychosomatic—a term used to describe any physical condition that has been brought on or is aggravated by psychological or emotional factors. The latter category is commonly referred to as mental illness. It, too, at one time was divided into two categories, neurosis and psychosis, with the chief difference being the extent to which the individual suffering from the illness had lost contact with reality. Neurosis and psychosis are rarely used today as diagnostic categories. They are simply too vague. The current practice is to classify mental illnesses not so much in terms of their severity but rather according to their symptoms. The three most common disorders are anxiety disorders, affective disorders, and schizophrenia.

2. *Stress.* The term psychologists use to describe the environmental trigger of emotional breakdown is stress. Stress can best be defined as any form of stimulation that exceeds the norm and requires significant adaptation on the part of the individual. Most people are able to tolerate moderate amounts of stress for reasonable periods of time, but when stress becomes excessive and lasts for too long a period, our coping mechanisms typically begin to break down. No one knows as yet why some people have a greater tolerance to stress than others. Popular belief has it that some people are simply "born" with a disposition that makes them better able to cope with stress, but if there are genetic factors we do not know what they are.

3. *The general adaptation syndrome.* One of the best-known theories on the impact of stress on bodily functions was advanced in the early 1950s by Hans Selye, who argued that the physiological reactions to stress can be broken down into three stages: alarm, resistance, and exhaustion. Selye referred to these reactions as the general adaptation syndrome and maintained that while the reactions vary from individual to individual, each stage is characterized by a distinctive physiological reaction: alarm by the arousal of the sympathetic nervous system and release of ACTH, resistance by elevated levels of glucocorticoids, and exhaustion by prolonged increase in sympathetic activity, ACTH, and glucocorticoids.

4. *Learned helplessness.* It is generally agreed that there is usually a psychological factor to most visceral breakdowns. One such factor that has been studied extensively is learned helplessness. Studies have shown that when animals are placed in situations in which they are unable to control the stimulus producing stress, they are far more likely to suffer behavioral and visceral breakdown than animals who are subject to the same level of stress but have some power to control it. Parallels have been drawn between the behavior of helpless animals in these experiments and the behavior of people suffering from clinical depression. The similarities are striking enough to suggest that helplessness in lower animals and certain kinds of depression in humans may be governed by the same underlying mechanism.

5. *Stress and the autonomic nervous system.* Helplessness may also play a role in producing gastrointestinal ulcers. Predictability of stress (i.e., shock) is the critical factor: a group of rats receiving a warning signal (e.g., a tone) prior to shock showed far less gastrointestinal damage than a group for whom the shock came without warning. The mechanism that underlies the visceral breakdown has been linked to activity in the autonomic nervous system—specifically the interaction between the sympathetic system and the parasympathetic system. Gastric secretions are produced by the parasympathetic system when the sympathetic system is not active and the parasympathetic system works unopposed. More recent work has uncovered evidence suggesting that prolonged psychological stress can ultimately affect the functioning of the immune system—discoveries that have obvious implications for humans and cancer.

6. *Classifying mental illness.* Mental disorders involving brain abnormalities generally fall into three categories: affective disorders, distinguished by extreme shifts in mood; anxiety disorders, characterized by severe and debilitating anxiety and fear; and schizophrenia, characterized by pronounced disturbances in cognitive, emotional, and social behavior.

7. *Affective disorders.* Affective disorders are usually divided into two broad categories: unipolar, which is characterized by extreme feelings of despondency and lethargy; and bipolar, in which episodes of depression are interspersed with periods of manic activity. One of the more widely held theories of depression is known as the monoamine theory of depression and attributes the symptoms of depression to deficits in two neurotransmitters: norepinephrine and serotonin. A new class of antidepressant drugs, known as selective serotonin reuptake inhibitors (SSRIs), relieve depression yet increase only serotonin. This effect, combined with evidence indicating that drugs that decrease serotonin produce depression, makes a strong case for a serotonin-depression connection.

8. *Accounting for the time-lag factor.* It usually takes between 2 and 3 weeks for antidepressant drugs to take effect, and this time lag has begun to shed light on the mechanisms that underlie the therapeutic effects of these drugs. One theory holds that depression is the result of two factors, a deficit in neurotransmitter and an increase in postsynaptic receptors to compensate for the deficit, and that antidepressant drugs taken over a 2- to 3-week period alleviate both problems. The antidepressant drugs increase neurotransmitter by blocking the inhibitory action of autoreceptors and they decrease postsynaptic receptors by enlisting a synaptic defense.

9. *Genetic factors in depression.* Evidence indicates that depression has a strong genetic component, more so for bipolar than unipolar depression. The evidence comes from several sources: (a) adopted children who develop bipolar disorder align with their birth parents, (b) pairs of identical twins who develop bipolar disorder show a higher concordance rate than pairs of fraternal twins, and (c) a large percentage of Amish who suffer from bipolar disorder have relatives who suffer from the same condition.

10. *Treating depression.* Apart from psychotherapy, depression treatments today fall into one of two categories: drug therapy and electroconvulsive shock. One drug that has proven to be particularly effective in the treatment of depression is Prozac, whose principal action is to selectively inhibit the reuptake of serotonin, thereby increasing serotonin levels. The chief advantage of Prozac over earlier antidepressant drugs is that it produces fewer side effects in most people who take it. Prozac also appears to relieve the symptoms of panic attacks and stem the compulsive rituals of obsessive-compulsive disorders. On the negative side, Prozac produces severe insomnia in roughly a third of the people who take it. There have also been reports—highly publicized but not confirmed—that Prozac can produce violent behavior and suicide.

11. *Electroconvulsive therapy (ECT).* ECT consists of briefly administering electric current to electrodes attached to the forehead of patients and has been shown to produce remission or improvement in about 90 percent of unipolar depressed patients. No one knows why ECT relieves depression, although recent evidence suggests that, like antidepressant drugs, ECT affects norepinephrine and serotonin synapses. The problem with ECT (apart from the fact that its effects are temporary) is that it has numerous side effects, including a temporary loss of memory. For this reason, it is used primarily as a treatment of last resort.

12. *Seasonal affective disorder.* Some people suffer from a form of depression known as seasonal affective disorder (SAD)—called so because the symptoms are affected by seasonal changes. The symptoms begin to appear in late fall but usually disappear in early spring, when the days are brighter and longer. A common—and effective—method of treating SAD patients is to expose them to bright light for several hours a day. Because people suffering from SAD show behavior (increased appetite and an increased need to sleep) that resembles the behavioral patterns of animals preparing to hibernate, SAD has been linked to the hormone melatonin, which, in animals, is thought to control hibernation patterns.

13. *Anxiety disorders.* Anxiety disorders—panic attacks, generalized anxiety, obsessive-compulsive disorders, and phobias—are the most common form of psychiatric problem in the U.S., affecting roughly 12.6 percent of the population in any given year. Panic attacks—brief, sudden attacks of extreme anxiety—can often be controlled by drugs that decrease levels of norepinephrine—a connection that implicates norepinephrine as the principal agent in the condition. But other factors—the neurotransmitter GABA, lactate, and carbon dioxide—have also been implicated. Generalized anxiety—free-floating anxiety that can persist for months—has been linked to deficits in both GABA and serotonin, and has been treated with drugs that affect the levels of these neurotransmitters. Obsessive-compulsive disorder—the constant urge to wash one's hands, for instance—has been linked to brain abnormalities (centered in areas in or near the basal ganglia) and also to neurotransmitter deficits (serotonin), but why these abnormalities and deficiencies would produce obsessive-compulsive behavior is still a mystery.

14. *Schizophrenia.* Schizophrenia is not only the most severe of all psychological disorders but the most difficult to define. The term itself means "split mind" and was intended to describe the symptoms characteristic of schizophrenics: a split from reality and a split between their own feelings and thinking. Because the symptoms of schizophrenia are so varied and complex, it has now become customary to divide schizophrenic symptoms into two broad categories: positive—those marked by the presence of abnormal behavior (for example, hallucinations and delusions), and negative—those marked by the absence of behavior (for example, blunting of emotion and social withdrawal).

15. *Causes of schizophrenia.* It is generally believed that schizophrenia in all of its varied forms is *biologically* rooted, but what specific biological malfunction produces schizophrenic symptoms and how the problem originates is a subject of considerable debate. Some studies suggest a genetic basis for the condition. The evidence comes from adoption studies, which show a high frequency of schizophrenia among children with a schizophrenic birth parent even when the children are reared by non-schizophrenic adoptive parents, and twin studies, which have found a higher concordance rate in identical twins than in fraternal twins.

16. *The dopamine theory of schizophrenia.* The dopamine theory of schizophrenia, originally proposed by Solomon Snyder, links schizophrenia to an excess of the neurotransmitter dopamine. Supporting the theory is the fact that people who take excessive amounts of amphetamines—drugs that increase levels of dopamine in the brain—manifest a condition known as amphetamine psychosis that is frequently misdiagnosed as schizophrenia. Other support is found in the fact that some of the newer and most potent antischizophrenic drugs are known to block dopamine. Casting doubt on this theory is the fact that autopsies on schizophrenics reveal no evidence of excess dopamine itself, although they do reveal an abnormally high number of dopamine receptors.

17. *Treating schizophrenia.* Several drugs—known as antischizophrenic drugs—developed within the past two decades have brought a measure of normalcy to the behavior of schizophrenic patients. Some antischizophrenic drugs bind primarily to D_2 receptors, others bind to D_3 and D_4. Those that bind to D_2 receptors—the butyrophenones, for example—produce motor side effects similar to symptoms seen in Parkinson's disease; those that bind to D_3 and D_4 receptors—known as atypical antischizophrenic drugs—do not produce motor side effects.

18. *The two-syndrome theory.* All antischizophrenic drugs have one major shortcoming: they tend not to be effective in the treatment of the negative symptoms of schizophrenia. To address this inconsistency, Timothy Crow has introduced a theory of schizophrenia known as the two-syndrome theory. According to this theory, schizophrenia is a composite of two different disorders, Type I and Type II, each with its own symptoms (positive and negative) and each with its own pathology. Type I schizophrenia, in Crow's view, results from excess dopamine receptors; Type II results from structural brain damage. Crow's theory would explain why antischizophrenic drugs tend to have little effect on patients with negative symptoms. It also draws support from autopsies showing that schizophrenic patients, particularly those who suffered from negative symptoms, have noticeable structural abnormalities, especially in the frontal area of the brain.

19. *Connecting the two types.* The advent of Crow's theory has led researchers to question whether the two types of schizophrenia (assuming there are two types) are related or whether they develop independently. There is evidence to support both views. One study has found that the symptoms experienced by schizophrenics over a lengthy period show a positive to negative pattern, suggesting that the abnormal dopamine activity that presumably characterizes the positive symptoms eventually produces the brain damage that underlies the negative symptoms. Other findings indicate that some patients with negative symptoms have no prior history of positive symptoms.

20. *The viral theory.* One of the newest theories of schizophrenia proposes that the illness (specifically the structural brain damage) might have a viral link. Proponents of this theory point to the fact that schizophrenics are more likely to be born during the winter months than during any of the other seasons and are thus in the second trimester of their fetal development (the time in which major developmental changes are occurring in the nervous system) during those months of the year (the fall) in which viral diseases are the most prevalent.

21. *The schizophrenic brain.* Regardless of what causes schizophrenia, a central question in schizophrenia research today is why the presence of excessive dopamine activity or structural brain damage that presumably underlie the disease produces the specific symptoms that characterize the illness. There is no definitive answer, but evidence suggests that structural damage in the frontal cortex is the principal source of the negative symptoms and that excessive dopamine activity in the limbic system is the likely source of positive symptoms.

KEY TERMS

adrenocorticotrophic hormone (ACTH)
affective disorders
amphetamine psychosis
antischizophrenic drugs
anxiety disorders
atypical antischizophrenic drugs
autoreceptors
bipolar disorder
buspirone
clozapine
compulsions
electroconvulsive therapy (ECT)
free-floating anxiety
general adaptation syndrome
generalized anxiety disorder
glucocorticoids
learned helplessness
lithium
melatonin
mental illness
negative symptoms

neurosis
obsessions
obsessive-compulsive disorder (OCD)
panic attacks
phobias
positive symptoms
Prozac
psychophysiological disorders
psychosis
psychosomatic disorders
schizophrenia
seasonal affective disorder (SAD)
selective serotonin reuptake inhibitors (SSRIs)
stress
tardive dyskinesia
two-syndrome theory of schizophrenia
unipolar depression
viral theory of schizophrenia
Zoloft

SUGGESTED READINGS

Comer, R. J. *Abnormal Psychology*. New York, W. H. Freeman, 1992.

Kramer, P. *Listening to Prozac*. New York: Viking, 1993

Lickey, M. E. & Gordon, B. *Medicine and Mental Illness: The Use of Drugs in Psychiatry*. New York: Freeman, 1991.

16

LEARNING

INTRODUCTION

If you place a parasitic tick on a rock that has recently been occupied by a fat person, the tick will try to draw blood from the rock and will persist in this behavior until it has broken its proboscis. Why does a tick engage in this futile and self-destructive behavior? Mainly because ticks tend to behave reflexively, their responses keyed primarily to two stimuli: one is temperature and the other is the odor of butyric acid, which is characteristic of fats. When a tick detects this odor, it will drop from its perch to the fat body of the host, roam around until it finds an area of the skin about 37°C, and then begin its meal of blood. This pattern would not be a problem if it were not that the tick, as J. V. von Uexkull pointed out in 1909, does this even when the true food source is no longer there and even when the result is a broken proboscis. Ticks have great difficulty altering their reflexive behavior according to the circumstances at hand. They have trouble learning.

Learning is the process through which experience leaves its mark upon behavior. It is the missing faculty that would enable a tick to recognize that though a rock may be warm and odorous, it isn't a food source. Learning is thus the means by which lower animals and humans alter old behaviors and develop new behaviors, the better to adapt to changing environments. There is of course no way to overstate what learning contributes to our ability to survive. On occasion, however, what we learn can be maladaptive. An example of maladaptive learning is phobias—irrational fear of the dark, of heights, of crowds, and so on. Phobias are learned behaviors that are frequently incapacitating.

Learning Defined

Adaptive or maladaptive, the ability to learn is, at root, the ability to make new connections or associations. Psychologists interested in this associative phenomenon have long sought to explain why some experiences can have a profound and permanent impact on future behavior while others have little or no impact. This interest has produced a number of theories, many, though not all, of which relate in one way or another to the same basic notion: that we can make associations—i.e., that we can learn—in at least one of two ways. One way is known as *classical conditioning*: learning to make an association between two different stimuli. The other way is known as *instrumental conditioning*: learning to make an association between a specific response and a consequence produced by that response.

Not all learning, it should be stressed, can be reduced to one or the other of these simple categories. Some forms of learning clearly go well beyond the formation of associations. Monkeys, for instance, can learn to use a stick as a tool to reach a banana—a skill that cannot be readily explained by either classical or instrumental conditioning principles. Then, too, we humans spend a good deal of our lives solving complex mathematical, mechanical, and logistical problems in ways that go beyond the mere formation of associations.

In this chapter, however, we will confine our discussion to the simplest types of learning. We will look first at classical and instrumental conditioning and then at other simple types of learning, such as *habituation* (the decrease in the strength of a response to stimuli that have become familiar through repeated exposure) and *sensitization* (the increase in the strength of a response to a stimulus that follows the introduction of a noxious stimulus). Our reason for excluding higher-order learning is not that this aspect of learning is unimportant but rather because the most recent and dramatic breakthroughs in understanding what is happening in the nervous system when learning occurs have come from studies based on simple learning paradigms.

EARLY LEARNING DISCOVERIES

The pioneering discoveries in learning were made by Ivan Pavlov in a series of classic experiments involving dogs (Pavlov, 1927). Pavlov and his colleagues took one stimulus (food) that on its own could produce a predictable response (salivation) and paired it with another stimulus (the sound of a tone) that under normal circumstances was *not* capable of producing the same predictable response. The initial stimulus in this procedure—the stimulus that already produces a predictable response—is known as the *unconditioned stimulus*. The second stimulus—the one that when paired with the first eventually produces the same response—is known as the *conditioned stimulus*.

The result of Pavlov's procedure, as every psychology student well knows, was that following a number of tone-food pairings, the tone, by itself, produced salivation. The dogs had been "conditioned" to associate the tone with the food. They had learned, in other words, that the tone predicts the imminent appearance of food, and this learning resulted in the anticipatory response of salivation. Indeed, the animals in a typical Pavlovian experiment eventually salivated in response to practically anything associated with the food, including the sight of the person who fed them.

Soon after Pavlov made his discovery, his colleague Vladimir Bekhterev demonstrated that the principles of classical conditioning also apply to *aversive* stimulation. Bekhterev modified Pavlov's procedure by pairing a brief tone (the conditioned stimulus) with a shock (the unconditioned stimulus) to a dog's forepaws. The shock at first produced vigorous leg flexion, while the tone itself elicited no noticeable response other than a slight ear twitch. After the animal had been repeatedly exposed to a tone followed immediately by a shock, however, leg flexion began to occur before the shock—as soon as the tone was presented.

The pioneering work in instrumental conditioning was done with cats by Edward Thorndike and with pigeons and rats by B. F. Skinner and his colleagues. Both scientists found that by following a specific response with reinforcement it was possible to transform random trial-and-error behavior into a well-organized response. The reinforcement, they also discovered, can be either positive (such as food for a food-deprived animal) or negative (such as termination of shock). In either case, and with only rare exceptions, the reinforcement must be delivered immediately and consistently after the desired response if it is to have an impact on learning. What is learned in this case, again, is a relation, not a relation between stimuli—as Pavlov demonstrated—but a relation between a response and the consequence of that response.

Searching for the Association

Whether learning takes place because of classical conditioning or instrumental conditioning, the assumption regarding the association is the same: if the learning is to occur, an association has to be made at some point during the learning experience. Understanding exactly *how* this association is made in the nervous system, *where* it is made, and what *form* it takes are the ultimate goals of physiological psychologists who study learning.

These goals would be difficult enough to achieve on their own, given the complexity of the nervous system. They become all the more difficult in light of one condition that always needs to be addressed in learning experiments: the need to rule out *nonlearning* factors that might influence the results of the experiment.

To illustrate the importance of nonlearning factors in learning experiments, let us consider Pavlov's procedure once again, and let us assume for a moment that the dogs, after receiving the conditioning trials, still do not salivate to the tone. We might conclude from this result that the animals have failed to make an association between the tone and the food. But can we be sure? Is it not possible that an animal in this situation fails to salivate because it has a glandular problem that makes salivation impossible? And how can we know for sure that the animal was able to hear the tone?

By the same token, if a dog in a Pavlovian experiment has undergone a procedure that produces brain damage and now loses the capacity to salivate in response to the tone, can we automatically assume that the brain damage is affecting the dog's ability to form an association? Not really. Could it not be that the brain damage has either deafened the animal or impaired its ability to salivate—that is, compromised its physical ability to *perform* the conditioned response?

These purely performance considerations may seem obvious to you, but they become extremely important in any experimental procedure involving learning. We cannot automatically assume that when damage to a particular area of the brain impairs or prevents the response that we take to be an indication of learning, the impairment is related to the associative learning process itself. We must always be alert to the possibility that an animal's behavior—or lack of behavior—is the result of sensory, motor, or motivational processes and not the result of learning. With this cautionary note in mind, we can now turn to the problem at hand: the search for the neural basis of learning.

Two basic assumptions underlie the search for the neural basis of learning. The first is that learning can take place only in animals that possess a nervous system. The second is that the brain, at least in higher animals, is the true seat of learning.

These assumptions were not always taken for granted. Several investigators throughout the years have tried to demonstrate that single-celled animals—animals that have no nervous system—can learn. In one well-known study, single-celled organisms known as paramecia were placed in a tube that had more light in the center than at the two ends. Whenever the paramecia swam from the center into either end zone, they received a shock. When they returned to the center of the tube, the shock was terminated. After a number of trials using this procedure, the paramecia behaved as if they had learned to avoid the shock. When they reached the boundary between the lighted center and the darker end zones, they immediately turned back to the center zone.

Here, clearly, was a change in behavior—a change that seemed to indicate that paramecia were capable of learning (Jensen, 1965). But did this change in behavior truly indicate learning? Did the animals learn to associate the boundaries defined by the change in illumination with punishment? In this instance, the answer is no. To understand why, we must go back to the training trials and consider what happens when paramecia receive a shock.

When paramecia are shocked, they secrete metabolic droppings. These droppings accumulated along the boundary between the lighted center and the darker end zones and in and of themselves produced an unconditioned escape response. Thus the fact that the paramecia eventually avoided crossing the light boundary and did not enter the shock zone does not necessarily indicate that they had learned to associate the light boundary with impending shock. The more likely explanation is that they simply swam into the metabolic droppings and, because the droppings were aversive, turned around and swam out. Confirming this hypothesis is the fact that when the light boundaries were changed after training, but the droppings were not changed, the paramecia made the turning response to the droppings and seemed oblivious to the new boundaries (Jensen, 1965). The findings in this study illustrate a phenomenon known as *pseudolearning*—a result that appears on the surface to indicate learning but is due instead to nonlearning factors.

Learning and the Brain

While no one has yet demonstrated conclusively that learning can take place *without* a nervous system, studies have indicated that it can take place without a brain, although the implications of these studies are not entirely clear.

Here is an example. If you decapitate an earthworm (which has a group of neural cells thought to be a primitive brain at the anterior end of its body), its learning ability will be severely impaired, but some learning nonetheless can take place. Even when worms are decapitated after training, they show the ability to retain learned information (Ratner, 1962). It appears, then, that in the worm learning is not confined to the primitive brain but occurs in neurons spread throughout the lower regions of the body.

What is true of the earthworm is also true, apparently, of the cockroach. In one classic experiment, G. Adrian Horridge found that headless roaches could be conditioned to control their leg movements sufficiently to avoid a shock they were given whenever one of their legs dropped into water (Horridge, 1962). Here again of course researchers had to make sure that the behavioral change could not be attributed to performance effects, such as motor impairment caused by the repeated shocks.

To find out, Horridge included a control group of headless roaches that received the same number of shocks as the learning group but with one exception: the shocks were delivered randomly, sometimes when a leg dropped into water and sometimes when it did not. When the control group was finally given the opportunity to avoid shock, the roaches showed no signs of avoidance behavior, thus confirming that the avoidance behavior shown by the learning group was not merely the result of motor impairment produced by repeated shocks.

Finally, what holds true for worms and cockroaches holds true for the mammalian nervous system as well. Cats whose spinal cords are experimentally severed are able to learn a classically conditioned response (a hindleg motor reflex) even though the sensory input and motor output that govern the learned response are confined to the isolated section of the spinal cord and never reach the brain (Patterson et al., 1973).

Despite these discoveries, conclusions regarding the role of the brain in learning must be guarded. Some learning may indeed take place without a brain, but it has been clearly established that the higher one goes on the phylogenetic ladder, the more the brain—particularly the cortex—expands and the greater the animal's capacity to learn. On this basis, it is reasonable to assume that most learning in higher animals requires an intact brain and, in particular, an intact cortex.

THE CORTEX AND LEARNING

The notion that the cortex plays a dominant role in learning in higher animals was originally suggested by Ivan Pavlov (Pavlov, 1927). Although most of Pavlov's experiments were behavioral and not physiological (he made the seminal observations on classical conditioning in dogs), he did not hesitate to speculate about the brain and the role it plays in learning. Pavlov's view of what happens in the brain of a dog during classical conditioning, as pictured in Figure 16.1, was roughly as follows.

1. The tone stimulates sensory input that travels to the auditory cortex.
2. The food stimulates sensory input that travels to the food area in the cortex and also stimulates the motor reflex that causes salivation.

So far, nothing in this sequence is new. The circuits that underlie audition, eating, and salivation, as you already know, are built into the nervous system; they are reflexive. But Pavlov maintained that the process of exciting these reflexive circuits creates a *new* connection between the two areas in the cortex activated by each stimulus: the tone area and the food area. This new connection, as pictured in Figure 16.1, is what Pavlov considered the physiological basis of learning. Once an animal has been conditioned, in Pavlov's view, the tone excites impulses that travel not only to the auditory cortex (via the reflex circuit) but also to the food area (via the newly formed associative circuit) and trigger salivation. Pavlov went even further, suggesting where (the cortex) and how (exciting reflexive circuits) the new associative connection is formed. What he couldn't do, however, was offer empirical support for the existence of this circuit. His view was purely theoretical.

Figure 16.1 *A Model of Learning*
Before training, the conditioned stimulus (the tone) and the unconditioned stimulus (the food) produce reflexive behavior—the orienting reflex (e.g., the dog pricks its ears) and salivation, respectively. After training, when the conditioned stimulus is presented alone, conduction along the association circuit is sufficient to produce the response (salivation) previously elicited by the unconditioned stimulus.

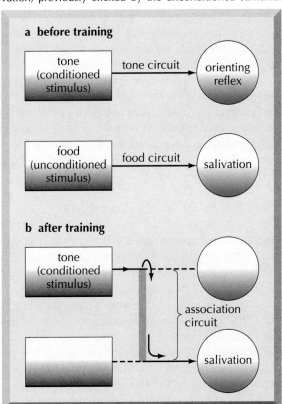

Lashley's Attack

The challenge of finding empirical evidence for Pavlov's theory was taken up with vigor in the 1920s by Karl Lashley, one of the most prominent figures in the history of physiological psychology (Lashley, 1929, 1950). By his own admission, Lashley began his work with a definite bias toward the Pavlovian view, for he fully expected to find empirical evidence that the cortex contained connections formed during conditioning. Lashley's approach—logical at the time—was to prepare rats surgically by destroying various parts of their cortices and then to train them in a variety of maze-learning tasks. His reasoning was that if Pavlov was correct and learning did indeed depend on the formation of new connections in the cortex, disrupting these connections should *prevent* learning.

Lashley's Findings

Much to Lashley's surprise, removing parts of the cortex did not interfere with learning as much as he had expected. He discovered, in fact, that animals with parts of their cortex missing learned as readily as animals with intact cortices. This unexpected finding eventually led Lashley to propose—and to spend three decades of research trying to corroborate—what at the time was a revolutionary idea: that learning does not depend, as Pavlov had suggested, on specific circuits located in specific areas of the brain, but that the circuits that underlie the associative process are distributed homogeneously *throughout* the brain. Thus, according to Lashley, if part of the brain is damaged, the intact remaining tissue will continue to carry on the associative process—an ability Lashley referred to as *equipotentiality*.

Because of Lashley's stature and because of the time and care he devoted to his studies, his theory regarding the physiological basis of learning dominated physiological psychology for nearly 50 years. In recent years, however, it has become increasingly clear that his view of an associative circuit diffused throughout the brain is essentially incorrect and that Lashley, for all his brilliance as a scientist, was simply a victim of technology that was unequal to the task.

The Flaw in Lashley's Procedures

The problem with Lashley's view has to do with his basic procedure and the conclusions he drew as a result. Lashley assumed that because removing portions of the brain did not affect the learning process, those portions—in this case the cortex—were not involved or at least were not involved alone in learning. What he failed to take into account, however, was the plasticity of the nervous system. It apparently never occurred to him that brain areas not ordinarily involved in conditioning might very well assume control of conditioning following damage to the cortex. In other words, Lashley did not recognize the possibility that when the circuits normally involved in learning a maze are damaged, undamaged circuits might take over the learning function.

Given this plasticity—the perplexing possibility that an area of the brain can be related to learning and yet can undergo damage without any consequent disruption of learning—more and more researchers today are not relying on the ablation approach, at least not exclusively, in their analysis of the associative circuits involved in learning. The approach is to combine the ablation technique with other techniques such as the recording of ongoing neural activity from an intact nervous system during the course of learning.

The equipment used in these procedures is remarkably sophisticated, but even so, procedural problems still remain. The primary problem is the ever-present possibility that neural activity in a particular area of the brain is not a reflection of associative or learning processes at work but rather of sensory, motor, or motivational processes involved in performance of the conditioned response.

Meeting the Procedural Challenge

The procedural challenge inherent in recording experiments on learning is to devise a way to isolate neural activity produced by performance processes from neural activity produced by associative processes. Theoretically, the challenge is easy enough to solve. What is needed is some means of observing the development of the conditioned response before, during, and after it is formed and correlating this development with neural activity in the brain. Brain areas that show neural activity on the initial trials, before the conditioned response appears, can safely be presumed to be involved in sensory, motor, or motivational processes. Brain areas that show unique activity during and after the onset of conditioned responding, on the other hand, can safely be presumed to be involved in the associative process. All that is necessary—theoretically at least—is to establish a correlation between the onset of conditioning and the appearance of neural activity in new areas of the brain.

As uncomplicated as this challenge may seem, it has its difficulties. The chief problem lies in the fact that when animals are allowed to move freely, the neural activity being recorded is often distorted by random neural activity produced by the general movement—the running, bar pressing, and leg withdrawal—that normally accompany the training trials. This distortion makes it extremely difficult to isolate neural activity produced by the association.

A training procedure that enables researchers to circumvent this problem is shown in Figure 16.2. Originally developed by Isadore Gormezano, this procedure uses rabbits as subjects and involves classical conditioning of the rabbits' nictitating membrane response—movement of the so-called third eyelid that some mammals possess (Gormezano, Kehoe, & Marshall, 1983).

The rabbit is an ideal subject for neural recording experiments because, with minimal restraints, it will remain virtually motionless (except for its nictitating membrane response) for up to 2 hours. One investigator who has used the nictitating membrane response technique to great advantage has been Richard Thompson, who successfully identified brain areas involved in the formation of the association.

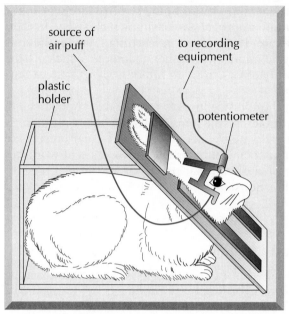

Figure 16.2 *Apparatus for Nictitating Conditioning*
A rabbit is held in a plastic restrainer, a tone serves as the conditioned stimulus, and a puff of air delivered to the eye serves as the unconditioned stimulus. The eyelid is attached to a fine string tied to a potentiometer, which triggers an electric signal to the recording apparatus every time the eye blinks.

THE ROLE OF THE HIPPOCAMPUS IN LEARNING

Much of Thompson's early work on the physiological basis of learning focused on one brain area in particular: the hippocampus (an area located in each cerebral hemisphere beneath the temporal lobe of the cortex). Most of his work has also involved one type of training procedure: classical conditioning of the nictitating membrane response (Thompson et al., 1976).

In this procedure, activity from neurons is recorded in the hippocampus while the animal is being trained. The conditioned stimulus is a brief tone, and the unconditioned stimulus is a puff of air to the eye that immediately follows the tone. The puff of air, predictably, produces the unconditioned nictitating membrane response, but after repeated training trials, Thompson's rabbits eventually make the conditioned nictitating membrane response to the tone alone. The conclusion, logically, is that a new association has been made between the tone and the nictitating membrane response.

The critical question of course is the extent to which hippocampal activity correlates with the appearance of the conditioned response. The answer, in brief, is that the two correlate, though not perfectly. During the first few training trials there is neither hippocampal activity nor a conditioned nictitating membrane response to the tone; instead there is an unconditioned nictitating membrane response to the puff. But once the rabbit has been conditioned to perform the nictitating membrane response to the tone, hippocampal activity also appears in response to the tone. The only inconsistency in this correlation is that hippocampal activity also appears *before* conditioning occurs. It normally takes anywhere from 50 to 200 trials before a rabbit makes the conditioned nictitating membrane response to a tone, but hippocampal activity in Thompson's procedure began to appear early in the training procedure concurrent with the unconditioned nictitating membrane response to the puff, at about the sixth trial.

This inconsistency apart, Thompson's findings present a strong case for a hippocampal connection to learning. The fact that hippocampal activity does *not* appear during the initial training trials, even though the tone, the puff, and the unconditioned nictitating membrane response to the puff are present, rules out the possibility that hippocampal activity is the result of either sensory or motor processes. The fact that hippocampal activity appears on later training trials, during conditioned responding, provides strong evidence that the hippocampus is involved in the associative process. And even the presence of hippocampal activity during the trials before conditioning occurs does not necessarily invalidate the argument. For it is reasonable to assume, as Thompson has done, that this activity represents the association in its rudimentary stage (when it may be too weak to produce the conditioned nictitating membrane response).

Thompson's work doesn't end here. He has also recognized the possibility that there may be an alternative interpretation of his results— the possibility that hippocampal activity may result not from the formation of an association but from the increased arousal produced by the repeated exposure to tones and puffs.

To find out, Thompson included a control group that received the same number of tones and puffs as the learning group, albeit with one exception: the tones and puffs were *not* paired, and thus conditioning did not occur. Thompson reasoned that if hippocampal activity appeared because of the arousal effects produced by repeated tones and puffs, both groups—the control group and the learning group—would show hippocampal activity. This did not happen. The control group showed no increase in hippocampal activity, indicating that the presence of hippocampal activity in the learning group could not be attributed simply to the effects of neural arousal.

The Hippocampal Connection: The Effect of Delay

Convincing as Thompson's evidence may be for a relationship between the hippocampus and conditioning, we have to be careful about the conclusions we draw. Studies in which lesions have been made in the hippocampus indicate that the role of the hippocampus can vary according to the nature of learning and that areas outside the hippocampus may be involved in the associative phase of learning as well.

These studies have employed two different classical conditioning procedures. In one, known as the *delayed procedure*, the tone continues until the puff is delivered (this is the same conditioning procedure originally used by Thompson). In the other procedure, the *trace procedure*, the tone and the puff are separated by the briefest of intervals (a matter of milliseconds). The practical effect of this brief separation is to complicate the conditioning task, and the results are significant. When there is no break between the tone and the puff, animals learn to make the association quickly and lesions in the hippocampus have *no* effect on the learning (Schmaltz & Theios, 1972). With an interval, however, normal animals have great difficulty learning, and animals that have been lesioned do not learn at all (Thompson et al., 1983; Weisz, Solomon, & Thompson, 1980). Figure 16.3 presents an illustration of the two procedures along with a summary of the results.

How do we explain this phenomenon? Why would hippocampal lesions have no apparent impact on learning during an easy task and yet profoundly affect learning when the task becomes complicated? The apparent answer is that the degree of hippocampal involvement in learning varies according to the difficulty of the task. The more difficult the conditioning, the more important the hippocampus appears to become. When conditioning is easier, the hippocampus may still be involved (as evidenced by Thompson's recording results), but other areas appear to assume the essential role. What are these areas? This is the question we shall address next.

Figure 16.3   *Delayed and Trace Conditioning Experiments*
(a) The training procedures. In the delayed procedure the tone (the conditioned stimulus) continues until the puff is delivered; in the trace procedure the tone and the puff are separated by a brief interval. (b) Normal (nonlesioned) animals have more difficulty learning the trace than the delayed procedure. (c) Lesions in the hippocampus have no effect on the learning of the delayed task but impair the learning of the trace task.

a procedure		b normal	c lesions in hippocampus
delayed conditioning (overlap)	CS (tone) ⎍ US (puff) ▉	few trials (easy learning)	no effect
trace conditioning (no overlap)	CS (tone) ⎍ US (puff) ▉	many trials (difficult learning)	learning impaired

Evidence of an "associative" area outside the hippocampus has come to light through some of Thompson's more recent work (Thompson et al., 1983). He has recorded from areas other than the hippocampus during classical conditioning trials and has found activity during the onset of conditioning in an area of the cerebellum known as the *interpositus nucleus*. Even more significant has been his discovery that lesions in the interpositus nucleus of the cerebellum prevent learning in the delayed procedure—the one in which lesions in the hippocampus had no effect.

These findings suggest strongly that the cerebellum is involved in forming the association in the easier task. We must not forget, however, that the cerebellum is also involved in sensory processes and motor movement (including the control of eye movement). So we must ask ourselves if lesions in the cerebellum might impair learning not because the lesions impair the associative process but because they interfere with the animal's ability to hear the tone or blink its eyes.

Thompson discounts this possibility on the basis of studies in which lesions in only one lobe of the cerebellum (the cerebellum is bilaterally lobed) were shown to disrupt learning in only one eye. When, for example, a lesion was made in the interpositus nucleus in the left lobe of the cerebellum, the rabbit was unable to learn a conditioned response with the left eye but was able to do so with the right eye. Thompson's contention is that if a lesion affected the animal's ability to hear the tone, it would disrupt learning in both eyes. Thompson also showed that the eye that did *not* learn as the result of a lesion was still capable of responding to the puff of air (the unconditioned stimulus), thus ruling out the possibility that the lesion affected motor function.

The Cerebellum: A Closer Look

Studies over the past few years have taken the motor analysis a step further and have suggested that, Thompson's results notwithstanding, the possibility exists that lesions in the cerebellum may affect motor function—not the motor function governing the unconditioned response (the blink to the air puff) but rather the motor function governing the conditioned response (the blink to the tone). In other words, it is possible that different motor circuits govern conditioned and unconditioned responses, that lesions in the interpositus nucleus affect the motor circuit governing the conditioned response, and that lesioned animals have difficulty learning not because they can't form the association but because they can't perform the conditioned response governed by the association.

But how do you determine whether a lesioned animal is unable to form the association or is unable to perform the conditioned response governed by the association? The approach taken to answer this question has been to use a "reversible" lesion technique. In this procedure animals are trained with the cerebellum (interpositus nucleus) temporarily rendered inactive (by cooling) and then tested after the cerebellum has been restored to normal (with the cooling discontinued) (Clark, Zhang, & Lavond, 1992).

The reasoning behind this procedure is as follows: if the reversible lesion during training disrupts the animal's ability to perform the conditioned response but not its ability to learn the conditioned response, the animal should show retention of the conditioned response during testing, when the brain has been restored to normal. If, on the other hand, the reversible lesion during training disrupts the animal's ability to learn the conditioned response (i.e., disrupts its ability to make the association), there should be no retention during testing even though the animal, its brain normal, can now perform the conditioned response.

The result: the animals show *no* retention. The conclusion: the cerebellum (specifically, the interpositus nucleus) governs the *associative process*, not the motor process, in classical conditioning of the nictitating membrane response in rabbits.

MAPPING THE ANATOMICAL SITE

To be considered part of the associative circuit, an area of the brain must obviously meet certain criteria, two above all: (1) its neural activity must correlate with conditioning, and (2) its presence in the brain must be essential for conditioning. The cerebellum clearly meets these criteria, but so does the hippocampus in certain cases. It is also reasonably clear, on the basis of Thompson's work and that of others who have used his general procedure, that the easier the task, the less the hippocampal involvement. This is not to say that the hippocampus is not involved at all in easier learning, only that its involvement is less essential than in more difficult tasks.

These findings are significant not only for what they indicate about the neural basis of classical conditioning but also for what they imply about learning in general. The discovery that a learning process as simple as classical conditioning of the nictitating membrane response is mediated by different areas of the brain (the hippocampus and cerebellum), depending on the difficulty of the conditioning task, underscores how complex and diverse the circuitry for learning in general may be.

However, to limit our discussion of associative processes to the hippocampus and cerebellum and to eyelid conditioning and difficulty of task would be misleading, for recent studies have made it increasingly apparent that the relationship between the brain and learning is far more complex. Seemingly minor changes in the learning task are accompanied by major changes in the brain circuits that contribute to associative processes. Let us take a closer look at two of these studies, one concerned with heart rate conditioning and the other with maze learning.

The Amygdala and Heart Rate Conditioning

An important series of studies on the associative circuits involved in learning was carried out in the early 1980s by Bruce Kapp and his colleagues, who used rabbits in a classical conditioning training procedure similar to that of Thompson's. Their focal point, however, was the amygdala and not the hippocampus, and their goal was to study how the amygdala functions during heart rate conditioning (Kapp et al., 1982; Kapp et al., 1990).

Kapp's procedure was as follows. He gave normal nonlesioned rabbits a series of training trials in which a tone was paired with a mild shock to the eyelid (rather than an air puff as Thompson used). Initially the animals showed a change in heart rate to only the shock—an unconditioned response. But with repeated tone-shock trials they eventually showed a change in heart rate to the tone—a conditioned response. The conclusion, logically, is that a new association was made between the tone and the shock. This is classical conditioning in its most rudimentary and clearest form.

To determine the role that the amygdala plays in the learning process, Kapp gave a second group of rabbits the tone-shock training procedure. In this instance, however, he lesioned the *central nucleus of the amygdala* before training. His results showed that the lesioned animals were unable to learn.

These findings raise some difficult though familiar questions. Do the lesions disrupt the animal's ability to learn because they interfere with the sensory process (hearing the tone) or the motor process (controlling changes in the heart rate)? Or do they disrupt learning because they interfere with the associative process?

Kapp maintains that the disruptive effect of the amygdala lesions is not the result of interference with sensory or motor processes. He bases this view on the following observations. Before he began the tone-shock training trials, Kapp gave the nonlesioned and lesioned rabbits the opportunity to respond to the tone alone (without a shock) for several trials. Exposed to the tone for the first time, rabbits responded in the same way whether they were lesioned or not: both groups showed a heart rate change. Exposed to a repeated tone, they also responded in the same way: the heart rate returned to normal.

Kapp's findings clearly demonstrate that before the conditioning procedure the rabbits had the same sensory and motor abilities whether they had been lesioned or not. The question is, What do lesioned and nonlesioned animals do after conditioning begins? The answer, as we've just seen, is that nonlesioned animals learn, but lesioned animals do not. The conclusion is that the amygdala is involved in the associative process, not the sensory or motor processes, underlying heart rate conditioning.

Again, however, as was the case with lesions in the cerebellum, we must be cautious. Kapp's results notwithstanding, it is conceivable that unconditioned and conditioned heart rate responses are governed by different motor circuits, that lesions in the amygdala affect the motor circuit governing the conditioned response, and that the lesioned animals have difficulty learning not because they can't form the association but because they can't perform the conditioned response governed by the association. In the case of the cerebellum, as we've already seen, the issue was settled by using reversible lesions, and the evidence points to disruption of an associative and not a motor process. In the case of the amygdala the problem remains unresolved.

The Generality of the Amygdala Effect: A Case for Fear Learning

Studies involving other species (rats and pigeons) and other response measures—blood pressure changes and startle response—have shown that the disruptive effects that amygdala lesions can have on classical conditioning are not limited to rabbits and are not confined to heart rate conditioning (LeDoux et al., 1988; Davis, 1986). Moreover, the fact that the disruptive effects are general and occur with response measures (e.g., blood pressure changes) that typically are used as measures of conditioned fear strengthens the case for a relationship between the amygdala and fear learning, a relationship we considered earlier in Chapter 14 (Davis, 1992).

Summing Up

Kapp's results, apart from implicating the central nucleus of the amygdala in heart rate conditioning, underscore the subtle relationship that exists between learning and the brain. His training procedure is identical to Thompson's in nearly every respect: the rabbits, the tone, and the noxious stimulus to the eyelid. The differences are that (1) Kapp was interested in heart rate conditioning rather than eyelid conditioning, and (2) the amygdala, rather than the cerebellum, is involved in the associative process. A seemingly minor change in the type of response learned (a heart rate change rather than an eye blink) resulted in a major change in the brain circuit (amygdala rather than cerebellum) contributing to the associative process. Strengthening this view of specificity is a study showing that although lesions in the amygdala impair heart rate conditioning, lesions in the cerebellum do not (Lavond et al., 1983).

But let us not overstate the case. It is true that different types of learning are controlled by different areas of the brain—eyelid conditioning by the cerebellum, heart rate conditioning by the amygdala. But it is also possible—in fact it is common—for different types of learning to be controlled by different circuits within the *same* area of the brain. There is no better example of this than the hippocampus and its relation to learning.

Reference and Working Memories and the Hippocampus

Studies on the nictitating membrane response of rabbits have established that the hippocampus is involved in classical conditioning. But the work of David Olton and his colleagues has implicated the hippocampus in another form of learning in lower animals (Olton & Samuelson, 1976; Olton et al., 1989). Olton's work has shown that hippocampal lesions interfere with a rat's ability to learn a complex maze. Illustrated in Figure 16.4 is one of the mazes used in Olton's studies. It is known as a *radial-arm maze*, and in this instance consists of 17 arms.

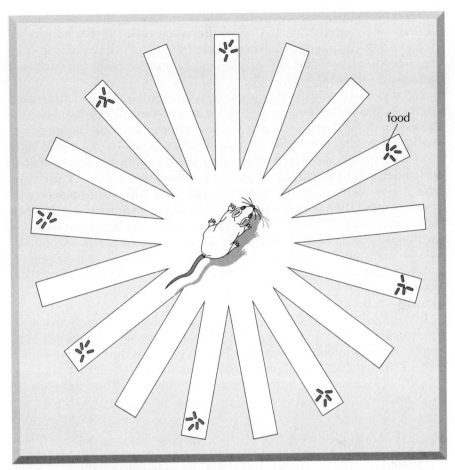

food

Figure 16.4 *Radial-Arm Maze*
Eight arms contain food, nine arms do not. The animal must remember which arms are baited, which of the baited arms it has entered, and which it has not.

Before the beginning of each day's training session, Olton baited eight of the arms—the same ones every day—with food and did nothing with the other nine. This meant that if the animals were to learn where to find food, they had to do two things: (1) they had to remember from day to day which of the 17 arms contained food, and (2) in order to gather food most efficiently they had to remember, within a given training session as they moved from one arm to the next, which of the baited arms they had already entered and which of the baited arms they had not.

In learning terms, Olton's procedure required animals to learn and remember two types of information: (1) information that remained *constant* across sessions (the eight arms that were always baited and the nine arms that were not), and (2) information that changed within a given session (which of the eight baited arms they had just entered and which of the eight arms they had not). Olton referred to the first kind of memory, that of constant information, as *reference memory*. He termed the second kind of memory, that of changing information, *working memory*.

Olton found in his studies that normal nonlesioned animals had no difficulty learning the maze; that is, they were able to form both reference and working memories. They learned to identify the eight arms that contained food, and they also learned *not* to revisit an arm in which they had already received food.

The scenario was different, however, with animals that had undergone lesions in the hippocampus. Unlike their nonlesioned counterparts, the lesioned animals were *unable* to learn the maze, but with an important qualification: they were able to remember from day to day which eight arms were baited and which nine arms were not, but they were unable to remember within any given session which arms they had just visited and which they had not. In other words, they were able to form reference memories, but they were unable to form working memories. And because the memory loss produced by hippocampal damage is specific—that is, the loss is specific to working but not to reference memories—Olton was able to discount performance factors. His reasoning is that if the hippocampal lesions affected the animals' motor or sensory ability, they would disrupt retention of both working and reference memories, and clearly they do not.

In conclusion, then, the hippocampus is involved in more than simply the learning and remembering of a specific type of information (e.g., complex classical conditioning). It is involved as well in a more fundamental learning and memory process—the ability to keep track of and remember short-term information that changes from moment to moment.

Spatial Memories and the Hippocampus

Evidence gathered by John O'Keefe and his colleagues has added a significant wrinkle to the picture of hippocampal involvement in learning and memory (O'Keefe & Dostrovsky, 1971; O'Keefe & Speakman, 1987). What he has discovered, in short, is the capacity of single neurons in the hippocampus to respond selectively to cues that are, on the one hand, independent of the maze itself and yet, on the other hand, vary according to where in the maze an animal happens to be at any given time. What this finding indicates is that the hippocampus, apart from the role it plays in processing a specific type of memory (that is working memories) is also involved in processing a specific type of information: information that depends on spatial cues.

Spatial Processing: A Closer Look

O'Keefe's procedure consisted of recording activity of single neurons in the hippocampus while rats were exploring a radial maze. His key finding was that different neurons—he called them "place" neurons—increased firing depending on where in the maze the animal was exploring. If the animal, for example, was in an area located on the north side of the maze, firing occurred in a particular neuron. When the animal moved to another area of the maze, yet another neuron fired, and so forth.

It is worth bearing in mind that the cues within the radial maze itself are the same regardless of the area the animal is exploring. Thus we can rule out stimuli within the maze as the source of the neural "place" signal. What, then, produces the selective firing? The answer, in brief, is cues outside the maze in the laboratory itself in which the maze is located. These cues would include windows, doors, cabinets, lights, and so on—anything the animal might potentially use as a "landmark." Researchers have determined that these extramaze cues are indeed the source of the selective neural firing by manipulating both the external cues and the maze itself. They found that when they altered the external cues the firing of a particular neuron that previously had been recorded when the animal was in a specific location no longer occurred. On the other hand, they found that altering the maze itself by placing the animal in a new arm of the maze had no impact on the firing of "place" neurons as long as the new arm of the maze remained in the original position with respect to the rest of the room. The conclusion: the hippocampus plays a role in processing spatial information that enables animals to learn—or as some researchers put it, to construct a cognitive map of their environment.

Lesion experiments have confirmed the "cognitive map" view of the hippocampus. When lesions are made in the hippocampus of animals who must rely on spatial (extramaze) cues to learn a maze, the animals' ability to learn is significantly impaired (Morris et al., 1982). For example, normal (non-brain-damaged) rats are excellent swimmers and are able to learn very quickly, using extramaze cues, to find a platform (which they climb on) submerged in cloudy water. Lesion the hippocampus, and the animals can still swim and they can still find the platform but—unable to learn where the platform is located—they swim in a rather haphazard way and appear to find the platform only by accident.

The picture changes significantly if a seemingly minor change in the procedure is made. If the top of the platform is raised above the water so it can be seen and the animals do not have to rely on extramaze cues to find it, the lesioned animals are able to learn to swim to the platform much as normal non-brain-damaged animals do.

The conclusion: damage in the hippocampus does not impair sensory processes (the animal can see the platform) or motor processes (the animal can swim to the platform) or for that matter it does not even completely impair learning (the animal can learn to swim to the platform) as long as the animal can rely on nonspatial cues. What it does impair is the animal's ability to use spatial information in the learning process. Change the information to nonspatial cues—the ability to see the platform itself—and the lesioned animal is now able to learn without any noticeable impairment.

Summing Up

Let us now take inventory. It should be clear to you by now that the hippocampus has multiple, learning-related functions. Thompson's work with rabbits and the nictitating membrane response indicates that the hippocampus is involved in complex classical conditioning. Olton's work with rats and the radial maze has shown that the hippocampus is involved in processing working memory—that is, memory that changes from moment to moment. O'Keefe's recording experiments and lesion work using the water maze indicate that the hippocampus is involved in processing spatial information. All told, what these studies tell us is that the hippocampus confers upon lower animals a unique sense of both their present and their past—an awareness of their surrounding environment informing them as to where they are at any given moment, as well as the ability to remember what has just happened and where they have just been. As we will see in the next chapter, this capacity of the hippocampus is shared by humans as well, but to a far more sophisticated degree.

Sensory and Associative Processes: A Comparison

To complete the picture of the brain and its relation to learning, we need to reexamine one additional element of the process. Just as different areas of the brain or different circuits within the same area are involved in *different* types of learning, evidence indicates that different areas of the brain or different circuits within the same area are involved in the *same* type of learning. The amygdala, as we've just seen, is clearly involved in classical conditioning, but so are the cerebellum and the hippocampus.

We mention these complexities not to confuse you but to impress upon you that the associative process and its relation to brain anatomy simply do not lend themselves to a singular classification. Nor does the implication of one area of the brain in the learning process preclude the inclusion of others. In fact, research has reinforced the view that learned behavior takes many different forms, all vital to adaptive behavior but each mediated by different circuits in the brain.

This description should sound familiar, for it is not unlike the principles of coding we have already encountered in our study of complex sensory experiences. In Chapter 6 we introduced the concept of coding as the mechanism that accounts for the complexity of such sensory experiences as pitch, brightness, and color. Now we must consider the possibility that a coding process of sorts is at work in learning. Conceivably, there may be one circuit or area in the human brain that codes for difficult tasks and another that codes for simple tasks. Likewise, there may be specific circuits for the associative aspects of verbal learning, as well as specific circuits for mathematical learning, emotional learning, and so forth. If this hypothesis is correct, the sensory blind spots that underlie blindness or tone deafness may well have parallels in learning—that is, there may be associative blind spots in the coding for language, mathematics, or emotional experiences.

Keep in mind that the analogy between the sensory process and the associative process is more conceptual than real. And although some researchers may take issue with this analogy, there is one point that none would argue. No matter how numerous associative circuits may be and no matter where they are located in the brain, they must all share one feature. Because they all change as a function of experience, they must all have an element of *plasticity*. And that element, all would agree, resides in the synapse.

THE SYNAPTIC BASIS OF LEARNING

Our focus to this point has been on the neural circuits involved in forming associations—where in the brain learning takes place. We have not yet discussed *how* these associations are actually formed. The question we must now ask ourselves is whether there is something special about the associative circuits that enables them to mediate changes in behavior during the learning process.

To answer this question, we are drawn to the synapse—that juncture point in the nervous system where neurons converge and interact. The possibility that the synapse holds the key to learning was originally raised by Donald Hebb, who suggested that learning does not create new pathways but rather alters the sensitivity of existing pathways (Hebb, 1949). According to Hebb's synaptic theory, learning is a *realization of a potential*. Its effect on synaptic conduction is to alter the sensitivity of existing pathways, thus enhancing the likelihood of a particular response.

Various synaptic changes have been suggested as the source of this phenomenon. Hebb, for example, has contended that presynaptic terminals actually grow or swell as a result of stimulation during learning. In this manner, he theorized, the gap between adjacent neurons is reduced, presumably facilitating the subsequent transmission across the synapse. Hebb's contention seems logical. A smaller gap between neurons, after all, would decrease the amount of neurotransmitter needed to stimulate the adjacent neurons, and indeed there is evidence for such growth.

In the early 1960s David Krech and his colleagues showed that long-term environmental stimulation had effects on both the growth and the overall size of the nervous system, particularly the cortex. They found that laboratory rats reared in an enriched environment (in this case, with toys and with other rats) developed much heavier cortices than rats reared in isolation. These thick-cortex rats also showed faster learning than the thin-cortex rats (Krech, Rosenzweig, & Bennett, 1962).

These findings suggest a general relationship between the number of synapses and neurons packed in the cortex and the potential for learning. More recently, William Greenough and his colleagues confirmed Krech's results and extended the analysis to show that thick cortices contain more dendrites and more synapses per neuron than thin cortices (Greenough & Volkman, 1973; Turner & Greenough, 1983). Thus, Greenough's findings provide further support for a relationship between the number of synapses and neurons packed in the cortex and the potential for learning.

On the surface, the work of Krech and Greenough appears to make a strong case for Hebb's theory linking learning and structural changes in the nervous system. Still we must be careful not to overgeneralize. The growth that occurs in the nervous system as a result of long-term environmental stimulation may be important for learning, but it does not *account* for learning. It merely accounts for the *potential* for learning. It explains why animals reared in certain environments are better prepared to learn than others, but it does not explain *how* they learn. Let us now look at some of the work that addresses the "how" of learning.

KANDEL'S *APLYSIA* WORK

Just as advances in recording technology and work with the rabbit's nictitating membrane helped Richard Thompson identify some of the brain areas involved in learning, so have advances in synaptic chemistry and the use of the *Aplysia*, a large sea snail with a unique gill-withdrawal reflex, enabled another scientist, Eric Kandel, to make an equally valuable contribution to understanding the synaptic changes that underlie learning (Kandel, 1991).

What Kandel has been able to do in effect is to bypass overt behavior altogether and observe learning as it occurs in the synapse. This is no small achievement, particularly when you consider the minuscule size of synapses and the complexity of their interactions. This is why the *Aplysia* is so important in this particular area of research. The invertebrate nervous system of the *Aplysia* is ideally suited for the study of synapses in much the same way as the giant axon in the squid, as we saw in Chapter 4, is ideally suited for study of the electrochemical nature of the neural impulse. The nervous system of the *Aplysia* consists of only 20,000 or so neural cells, a minuscule fraction of the number of cells found in higher animals. This relative simplicity allows for a detailed analysis of individual neurons and their interaction within individual synapses.

Aplysia: A Closer Look

Before we consider the details of Kandel's work, let us first familiarize ourselves with the *Aplysia*. Figure 16.5 depicts an *Aplysia*, whose simplest and most adaptive behavior is its gill-withdrawal reflex.

The gill of the *Aplysia* is covered by a protective membrane known as a mantle shelf, which has at its extremity a flesh spout known as a siphon. When the siphon or the mantle shelf is stimulated, the *Aplysia* withdraws its gill into the mantle cavity. Kandel has used this withdrawal reflex to study two simple forms of learning. One, known as *habituation*, is characterized by a decrease in the strength of the withdrawal response when a stimulus (a jet of water on the siphon, for instance) is presented repeatedly. The other, known as *sensitization*, is characterized by a strengthening of the withdrawal reflex whenever a second, noxious stimulus is presented. If, in the midst of habituation, the repetitive stimulus is preceded by a shock to the head, for instance, the withdrawal reflex is noticeably enhanced.

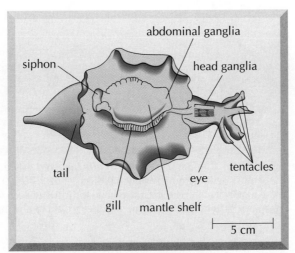

Figure 16.5 *A Top View of the* **Aplysia**
Stimulation of the siphon causes the gill to withdraw, repeated stimulation results in habituation, and repeated stimulation followed by shock to the head results in sensitization. Neural recording is done in the abdominal ganglion, where sensory neurons from the siphon and head converge on and form synapses with motor neurons to the gill.

Despite their simplicity, both habituation and sensitization play a vital role in the learning of most animals, including humans. Habituation enables us to learn to ignore stimuli that are repetitive and have no special significance. Sensitization alerts us to attend to stimuli that occur after an aversive experience.

Why are habituation and sensitization considered forms of learning? The answer, in brief, is that both produce relatively permanent (up to 3 weeks in the *Aplysia*) changes in behavior. Why should both be of interest to Kandel? The answer is that both are mediated by unique neural circuits.

Kandel has discovered that the habituation and sensitization of the gill-withdrawal reflex are ideally suited for neural analysis. The reflex is controlled by a circuit simple enough to allow for detailed analysis of its individual neurons and synapses. The circuit itself, pictured in Figure 16.6, is a monosynaptic circuit consisting of a sensory neuron, a motor neuron, and a synapse between the two. An interneuron is also located between the sensory and motor neurons.

Kandel's Procedures

By placing electrodes in the motor neurons of two groups of *Aplysia*, Kandel was able to observe the synaptic activity produced in the motor circuits by individual sensory neurons. He then stimulated the siphons of

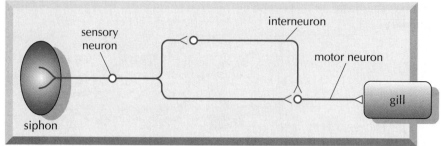

Figure 16.6 *The Basic Neural Circuits Involved in the Gill-Withdrawal Reflex*
The sensory neuron from the siphon projects either directly or indirectly (via an interneuron) to the motor neuron. The diagram shows only one of each type of neuron, but in fact there are approximately 24 sensory neurons that project to a group of 6 motor neurons.

the animals with precisely calculated jets of water, varying the procedure in the two groups. In one group (the habituation group), the stimulus was delivered repeatedly. In the other group (the sensitization group), the stimulus was delivered after a noxious stimulus—a shock to the head.

Kandel discovered that when the stimulus was delivered repeatedly, two things occurred. The withdrawal reflex habituated (i.e., became progressively weaker), and the excitatory postsynaptic potentials (EPSPs) in the motor neurons became progressively smaller. The result was that fewer impulses were produced in the motor neurons.

On the other hand, when Kandel preceded the stimulation of the siphon with a noxious stimulus to the head, both the withdrawal response and the excitatory postsynaptic potential showed sensitization. That is, the withdrawal response increased, the excitatory postsynaptic potentials in the motor neurons became progressively larger, and more impulses were produced. Kandel found, in other words, that for every change in overt behavior (the withdrawal response) there was a corresponding change in synaptic activity—either a decrease (habituation) or an increase (sensitization) in the excitatory postsynaptic potential.

You may be wondering why Kandel's findings are so important. Why go to all the trouble of observing habituation and sensitization at the level of the synapse when it is possible to observe the same phenomena at the level of the behavioral reflex?

The answer to this question is to be found less in what Kandel recorded at the level of the synapse than in what he did *after* this recording. By working with individual synapses, Kandel was able to identify the actual mechanism that underlies habituation and sensitization. Most researchers agree, as we mentioned earlier, that the synapse is the seat of learning. That is to say, the behavioral change we observe during learning is the result of a synaptic change produced by training trials. But how the synapse changes and what causes it to change have long been matters for speculation. Kandel's work represents a significant step toward solving this mystery, at least with respect to the changes that occur in the synapse during habituation and sensitization. Let us now look at this work.

Learning in the Presynapse

What Kandel did was to trace the change in synaptic activity—the change, in other words, in the excitatory postsynaptic potential—to a change in the ability of the presynaptic endings to release a neurotransmitter. Kandel found that the ability of the presynaptic endings to release a neurotransmitter *decreased* during habituation but *increased* during sensitization.

You will recall from Chapter 4 that before a neurotransmitter can be released there needs to be an influx of calcium into the presynaptic terminals. The more calcium entering the presynapse, the more neurotransmitter released by the presynapse. One of Kandel's key findings was that the amount of calcium that entered the presynapse varied according to the kind of training trial. It decreased with habituation and increased with sensitization, as illustrated in Figure 16.7.

His findings show, too, that this variation can be traced to so-called *calcium channels*, pores in the membrane that regulate the movement of calcium into the presynapse. Because these channels are voltage-sensitive (i.e., sensitive to changes in the charge across the membrane), they open when the neural impulse produced in the sensory neurons from the siphon reaches the presynaptic endings, thus allowing calcium to enter. According to Kandel, the repeated stimulation of the siphon that occurs during habituation *inhibits* the opening of these calcium channels, while the noxious stimulus during sensitization *facilitates* the opening.

If you look at Figure 16.8, you can get a clearer picture of this process, particularly as it applies to sensitization. Notice that both sensitization and habituation circuits involve the same sensory neurons (from the

Figure 16.7 *Habituation and Sensitization*
The figure shows calcium (Ca) entering the presynaptic neuron and its effect on the release of the neurotransmitter under normal, habituation, and sensitization conditions. Note that this is a highly schematic diagram designed to show only the relative differences among the three conditions. In reality hundreds of thousands of transmitter units and receptors are involved.

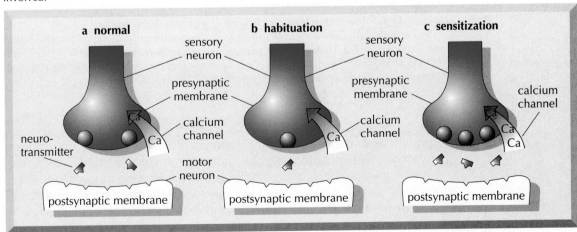

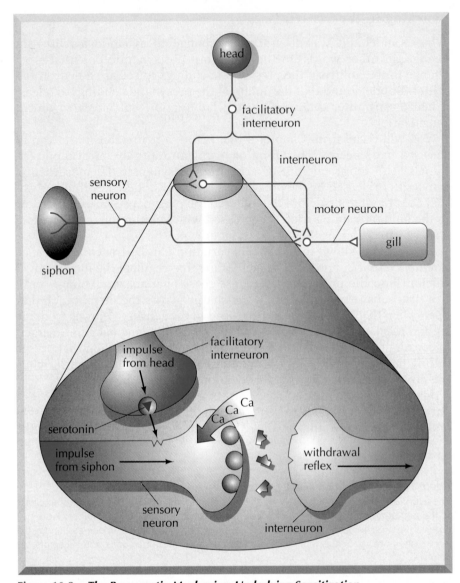

Figure 16.8 *The Presynaptic Mechanism Underlying Sensitization*
This simplified diagram shows how shock may operate to sensitize the withdrawal reflex. Shock to the head activates sensory neurons that release serotonin. Serotonin, in turn, acts on the presynaptic endings of the sensory neurons from the siphon to open their calcium channels and in the process increases their release of neurotransmitters.

siphon) and the same motor neurons (controlling the withdrawal response). Sensitization circuits, however, involve a third set of neurons—a group of *facilitatory* interneurons originating in the head. These neurons, as you can see, form synapses with the presynaptic endings of the sensory neurons from the siphon. What they do there, in effect, is to *prime* the system. When the head is stimulated by shock, the facilitatory neurons release the neurotransmitter serotonin. Serotonin in turn acts on the presynaptic endings of the sensory neurons, making them more responsive to neural impulses from the siphon. The presynaptic endings, which normally release little neurotransmitter, when later stimulated by neural impulses from the siphon, now release a large amount.

Serotonin's effect on the release of neurotransmitter in this case is an example of *synaptic modulation*. Serotonin does not "trigger" the release of the neurotransmitter. That aspect of neurotransmission is reserved for the neural impulse in the sensory neuron itself. What happens instead is that serotonin "modulates" the release, increasing it by increasing the amount of calcium that enters the presynaptic endings of the sensory neuron when the impulse from the siphon finally arrives.

Serotonin's Action: A Closer Look

How does serotonin act on the presynaptic endings to increase the amount of calcium that enters? The answer brings us to the voltage-sensitive calcium channels that regulate the flow of calcium into the presynaptic endings. Serotonin increases the amount of calcium that enters the presynaptic endings by increasing the number of voltage-sensitive channels that open when the impulse in the sensory neuron from the siphon finally arrives. It does so, however, in a circuitous way. Serotonin doesn't act on the voltage-sensitive calcium channels directly. Instead it prolongs the depolarization produced by the neural impulse in the sensory neurons, and the prolonged depolarization in turn increases the number of voltage-sensitive calcium channels that open. Let us take a closer look.

The process begins when stimulation is applied to the siphon and a neural impulse travels down the sensory neuron, causing it to depolarize. Depolarization, as you will recall, is initiated when sodium ions rush into the neuron and is terminated when potassium ions flow out. Normally, potassium ions flow out quickly, which means that depolarization is terminated quickly. In the case of presynaptic endings that have been exposed to serotonin, however, the picture changes. The potassium ions flow out slowly, depolarization is prolonged, calcium channels remain open, neurotransmitter release is increased, and the withdrawal reflex is enhanced.

This brings us to our final question regarding the action of serotonin on the presynaptic endings: if impeding the flow of potassium ions out of the sensory neuron is the means by which serotonin enhances the withdrawal response, it is reasonable to ask how serotonin does this. The answer brings us to another level of analysis, to the structure of the presynaptic membrane itself and the structural changes that occur when the membrane is exposed to serotonin.

Kandel's view is that serotonin impedes the flow of potassium through a series of chemical reactions that change the structure of the potassium channels in the presynaptic endings. The steps are as follows:

1. Serotonin binds to receptors on the presynaptic endings.
2. An enzyme (protein kinase) is activated.
3. A chemical reaction (phosphorylation) is triggered.
4. The structure of the potassium channels is changed.

In summary, then, Kandel proposes a chain of events beginning with the release of serotonin and ending with the enhanced withdrawal response. But the key step in the sequence—the one that, at root, brings this phenomenon into the realm of learning and memory—is the capacity of serotonin to *change* the structure of the potassium channels and in the process to prolong the depolarization produced by the impulses coming from the siphon. The structural change accounts for the change in behavior—the heightened withdrawal reflex. The fact that the structural change *endures* accounts for why the change in behavior endures. In short, the structural change in the potassium channels accounts for both learning (the change in behavior) and memory (the enduring change in behavior), albeit in their most rudimentary forms.

Habituation and Sensitization:
Short-Term versus Long-Term
We've been talking about habituation and sensitization as if there were only one type of each. In fact, there are two types: short-term and long-term. Short-term habituation and sensitization are produced by a single training session and last for minutes. Long-term habituation and sensitization are produced by several training sessions and last up to 3 weeks. Short-term habituation and sensitization are governed by the mechanism that we have just described—structural changes in potassium channels resulting in an increase or decrease in calcium influx and an increase or decrease in the amount of neurotransmitter released. Long-term habituation and sensitization, on the other hand, are different. They involve the structural changes in potassium channels that occur during short-term habituation and sensitization, but they also involve a second mechanism: growth of presynaptic connections. The evidence comes from a series of experiments conducted by Craig Bailey and Mary Chen, whose findings are summarized in Figure 16.9. As you can see, long-term sensitization in their studies produced growth in presynaptic endings (as much as twice as many as in untrained controls), whereas habituation produced regression or pruning of presynaptic endings (as much as one-third fewer as in untrained controls) (Bailey & Chen, 1983, 1988).

Bailey and Chen's results are significant for several reasons. First and foremost, they provide a glimpse (however broad and general) of what might actually be happening at the level of the synapse to produce long-term learning and memory. Second, they provide yet another dimension of empirical evidence to support the basic position of Hebb's theory—that learning is rooted in *structural* changes (i.e., growth) occurring in presynaptic endings. And because their findings show that short- and long-term habituation and sensitization produce different effects on presynaptic endings, the work of Bailey and Chen provides an empirical

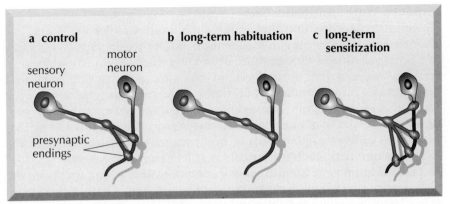

a control

sensory
neuron

motor
neuron

presynaptic
endings

b long-term habituation

c long-term sensitization

Figure 16.9 *Long-Term Habituation and Sensitization*
Presynaptic endings decrease in number with long-term habituation and increase in number with long-term sensitization.

basis for the theories currently being advanced to explain differences between short- and long-term memory, a subject we will consider in detail in the next chapter.

Classical Conditioning in the *Aplysia*

Kandel and his colleagues have found that in addition to habituation and sensitization, the *Aplysia* can also be classically conditioned. A light touch to the siphon *followed* by shock to the tail eventually resulted in a withdrawal response to the light touch (much like Pavlov's tone followed by food in dogs eventually resulted in salivation to the tone).

Kandel's explanation for classical conditioning is similar to the one he proposes for sensitization. Shock to the tail, he theorizes, *facilitates* the opening of calcium channels in the sensory neurons when they are stimulated—with one difference. The key factor—the one that distinguishes classical conditioning from sensitization—is that the sensory neurons from the siphon are active (i.e., the siphon is stimulated by a light touch) just *before* the shock is delivered. This activity, coupled with the neural activity produced by subsequent shock, facilitates the opening of the calcium channels in the sensory neurons. Kandel refers to this feature of presynaptic facilitation as *activity dependence* (Buonomano & Byrne, 1990; Small, Kandel, & Hawkins, 1989).

In summary, the facilitatory effect that Kandel proposes for classical conditioning in principle is no different from the facilitatory effect he proposes to account for sensitization—both are produced by shock and both result from facilitation of the opening of calcium channels in the sensory neurons. There is one difference, however: for sensory neurons to benefit maximally from the facilitatory effect of the shock, they must be active just before the shock. This condition exists during classical conditioning but not during sensitization.

Kandel's Work: An Evaluation

However compelling and interesting such studies as Kandel's may be, their relevance to learning in higher animals, and particularly in humans, has been questioned by a number of investigators—and justifiably so. It could be argued that to understand complex systems you must first understand simple systems, but there is no way as yet of knowing whether simple systems, interesting though they may be in their own right, mirror the dynamics of complex systems. And who is to say that activity in individual neurons and synapses tells us anything about the extensive interactions that normally occur in complex systems?

This question is by no means easy to answer. It is a long way from the *Aplysia* nervous system to the human nervous system. On the other hand, it has been demonstrated time and again that by studying the principles that govern the dynamics of simple systems we can learn a great deal about more complicated systems. Research on the squid has taught us much about the neural impulse. Research on the horseshoe crab has taught us much about vision. Given these precedents, it is not unreasonable to assume that what we learn from *Aplysia* research may prove equally valuable.

LONG-TERM POTENTIATION

Questions about Kandel's *Aplysia* work notwithstanding, recent work on how learning occurs in the mammalian nervous system has begun to yield promising results. One of the most important areas of study involves a phenomenon known as *long-term potentiation* (LTP).

Long-term potentiation refers to the well-documented fact that slices of hippocampal tissue can be taken from a rat brain and, while kept alive outside the brain in a saline medium (as pictured in Figure 16.10), can be stimulated to produce synaptic changes that endure over long periods of time (Lynch & Baudry, 1984). Long-term potentiation has also been produced in the intact hippocampus of both free-moving and anesthetized animals and has also been produced in the amygdala and cortex (Clugnet & LeDoux, 1990).

Researchers involved in this work maintain that understanding the changes in the nervous system that accompany long-term potentiation—how they occur and why they endure—will lead to important insights into understanding the changes in the nervous system that underlie learning and memory. Thus the phenomenon of long-term potentiation has emerged as one of the cornerstones in the analysis of the cellular and molecular basis of learning and memory.

In a typical long-term potentiation experiment (and there are a number of variations of this basic procedure), electrodes are implanted in hippocampal tissue, electrical stimulation is delivered to presynaptic neurons, and neural activity is recorded from postsynaptic neurons. The electrical stimulation itself consists of two stimuli delivered in succession, separated by an interval of as much as several weeks. The first stim-

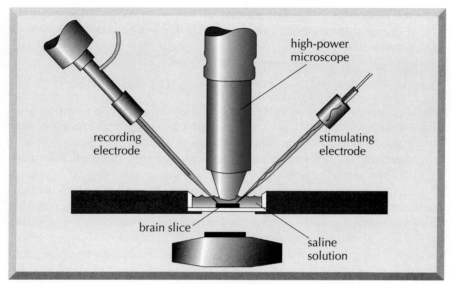

Figure 16.10 *The Stimulating and Recording Procedure in a Long-Term Potentiation Experiment*
A slice of neural tissue is mounted on a stage of a microscope, the tissue is kept alive in a saline solution, and recording and stimulating electrodes are placed in single neurons while the tissue is visualized through a high-powered microscope.

ulus is an intense stimulus delivered in brief pulses (100 per second) that last for roughly 1 second. The second stimulus is much weaker and is delivered at some later time.

Both stimuli produce postsynaptic activity. But the activity produced by the second stimulus, the weaker stimulus, is more significant because of what it tells us about the neural properties of the first stimulus. If the first stimulus produces a change in the nervous system that endures, we might expect an effect on the postsynaptic activity produced by the second stimulus. This is precisely what has been observed. The key discovery is that the first stimulus potentiates postsynaptic activity (i.e., increases the excitatory postsynaptic potentials [EPSPs]) produced by the second stimulus even though the two stimuli are separated by as much as several weeks (Racine & DeJonge, 1988). Thus, the origin of the term "long-term (enduring) potentiation (enhanced EPSPs)."

You may be wondering why long-term potentiation is so important. Why go to all the trouble of observing what at best is a rough approximation of learning and memory (i.e., a change in the nervous system that endures) in isolated hippocampal tissue when it is possible to observe much clearer examples of learning and memory in the overt behavior of intact animals. The answer to this question, as it was in the case of *Aplysia*, is to be found less in what researchers record from the neural tissue than in what they are able to do after this recording. By working with neural tissue outside the animal and directly open to observation and manipulation, researchers have been able to establish a direct link between neural activity that resembles learning and memory and the actual synaptic mechanisms that underlie this activity. Let us now look at this work more closely.

Long-Term Potentiation: The Mechanism

The experiments using long-term potentiation to study the synaptic basis of learning and memory have been shaped by two questions: First, how does the first stimulus, the intense stimulus, change the nervous system and make it more responsive to the second stimulus, the weak stimulus? Second, how does that change endure?

The answers to these questions, as you may have anticipated, bring us to the synapse, specifically to the postsynaptic membrane. Evidence indicates that the long-term potentiation procedure (i.e., the intense stimulus) triggers neural impulses that release a neurotransmitter which through a series of chemical reactions changes the structure of the postsynaptic membrane. This structural change endures over time, making the nervous system more responsive to the weak stimulus and thus qualifies as a possible candidate for the synaptic basis of learning and memory.

The Mechanism: An Overview

The neurotransmitter at the heart of this process is *glutamate*, and its action on the postsynapse is illustrated in Figure 16.11a. Glutamate is released by the intense stimulus, diffuses across the synaptic gap, where it binds to a specific set of glutamate receptors known as *N-methyl-D-aspartate receptors* (NMDA receptors) and non-NMDA receptors. A closer look at the figure reveals that glutamate, after it binds to the receptors, has a unique effect: it opens NMDA channels, allowing calcium ions to enter the postsynaptic neuron (Lynch & Baudry, 1984). (*Note:* This effect is not to be confused with the opening of calcium channels that occurs on the presynapse and results in release of the neurotransmitter.)

The entry of calcium into the neuron marks the beginning of the process in the postsynapse that underlies the actual structural change. After entering the neuron, calcium initiates a chemical reaction that consists of two steps: activation of an enzyme which in turn produces a change in protein structure. As a result of the change in protein, a signal is produced in the postsynapse that is *fed back* to the presynapse. This feedback signal is crucial: it changes the structure of the presynapse (making it more responsive to subsequent weak stimulation), the release of neurotransmitter is increased, and the EPSPs are enhanced (Bashir et al., 1991).

In summary, then, long-term potentiation can be divided into two stages: one is the *initiation* of long-term potentiation, which is produced when calcium ions enter the postsynaptic neuron causing a structural change and the feedback signal; the other is the *expression* of long-term potentiation, which is produced when the weak stimulus results in an increase in the release of the neurotransmitter and enhanced EPSPs. Let's now take a closer look at each stage.

Initiating Long-Term Potentiation: A Closer Look

Figure 16.11*b* presents a more detailed view of the processes that under-lie the initiation of long-term potentiation.

Initiation of long-term potentiation begins, as we've just seen, when glutamate binds to NMDA receptors and calcium ions enter the post-

Figure 16.11 *Long-Term Potentiation*
(a) (1) An intense stimulus is delivered; (2) glutamate (Glu) is released; (3) glutamate binds to NMDA and non-NMDA receptors; (4) calcium (Ca^{2+}) enters through NMDA channels; (5) protein structure changes and a signal is fed back to the presynapse.
(b) (1) Glutamate binds to NMDA and non-NMDA receptors; (2) non-NMDA receptors depo-larize; (3) magnesium (Mg^{2+}) blockade is undone and calcium (Ca^{2+}) enters through NMDA channels; (4) protein structure changes; (5) a signal is fed back to the presynapse; (6) protein structure on the presynaptic membrane is changed and the release of transmitter is enhanced.

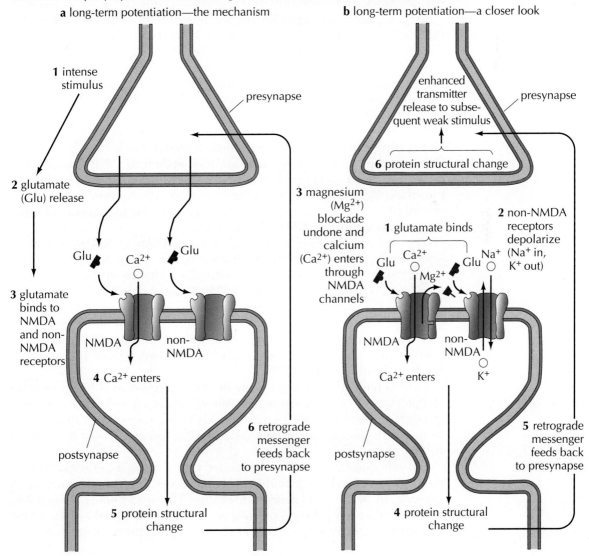

synapse. Entry occurs through NMDA channels. What is unique about NMDA channels, as shown in Figure 16.11*b*, is that they are normally blocked by magnesium ions. For the magnesium blockade to be removed and calcium ions to enter, two conditions must be satisfied: glutamate must bind to the NMDA receptors, and depolarization must occur across the postsynaptic membrane.

Glutamate binding is easily explained: glutamate is released by the presynaptic neurons (when they are stimulated by the intense electrical stimulation) and binds to NMDA receptors as well as to non-NMDA receptors. Depolarization is another matter. Glutamate binding to NMDA receptors normally does not produce depolarization, at least not immediately; glutamate binding to non-NMDA receptors, however, does. And it is the depolarization produced by non-NMDA receptors, combined with glutamate binding to NMDA receptors, that undoes the magnesium block and, as Figure 16.11*b* shows, opens the NMDA channels.

In short, then, although NMDA receptors are directly responsible for calcium entry, without help from non-NMDA receptors (specifically, the depolarization) long-term potentiation would not occur. But it works the other way as well. Just as non-NMDA receptors influence NMDA receptors to initiate long-term potentiation (entry of calcium), NMDA receptors influence non-NMDA receptors to express long-term potentiation (enhanced EPSPs).

Expressing Long-Term Potentiation: A Closer Look

Expression of long-term potentiation (i.e., enhanced EPSPs) is not produced in NMDA receptors but in non-NMDA receptors. So we must ask ourselves, How do we get from the initiation of long-term potentiation, produced in NMDA receptors, to the expression of long-term potentiation, produced in non-NMDA receptors?

The answer, at least theoretically, is as follows: NMDA receptors (specifically, the calcium entry) initiate a change in the postsynaptic membrane that feeds back to and results in a change in the presynaptic membrane (Bekkers & Stevens, 1990; Tsien & Malinow, 1990). The change in the presynaptic membrane in turn produces an increase in the release of neurotransmitter (when later stimulated by the weak stimulus). The increase in the amount of neurotransmitter then acts on the postsynaptic membrane (specifically, on the non-NMDA receptors) to produce the enhanced EPSPs.

In summary, then, we go from the postsynaptic membrane (NMDA receptors)—entry of calcium and release of enzyme—back to the presynaptic membrane—an increase in release of neurotransmitter—back to the postsynaptic membrane (non-NMDA receptors)—an increase in EPSPs.

But one question remains. We stated that a change in the postsynaptic membrane feeds back to the presynaptic membrane and results in an increase in release of neurotransmitter. The question is, How? The answer is that the postsynapse releases a chemical signal known as the *retrograde plasticity factor* that travels back to the presynapse, causing it to change and in the process to release more neurotransmitter when stimulated by the weak stimulus. Recent evidence points to two chemicals—*nitric oxide* and *arachidonic acid*—as the retrograde factors (Bon et al., 1994; Williams et al., 1989).

Reflections on the Long-Term Potentiation Mechanism

It would be misleading to suggest that the picture we have painted of long-term potentiation is as well-defined as has just been described. The research is ongoing, and a number of questions remain unanswered. One of the major points of controversy centers on the initiation of long-term potentiation. We have portrayed the process as one involving a feedback signal from postsynapse to presynapse, resulting in an increase in the release of neurotransmitter. But at least one other possibility has been raised. There is evidence that the postsynapse itself (specifically, an increase in the number of postsynaptic receptors) could be the source of the enhanced EPSPs (Lynch & Baudry, 1984). At this point, the safest conclusion may be a middle-of-the-road position. It is possible that initiation of long-term potentiation may involve both processes—an increase in receptors and an increase in neurotransmitter—and the combination may produce the enhanced EPSPs.

Long-Term Potentiation as a Model for Learning and Memory

One question remains with respect to long-term potentiation, and in some ways it is the most important one. What do the experiments on slices of hippocampal tissue from rats tell us about learning and memory produced by naturally occurring stimuli in an intact animal? No one has shown (or even suggested) that the neural activity produced by long-term potentiation is the same as neural activity produced by naturally occurring stimuli. Even so, however, the fact that both produce a relatively permanent change in the nervous system has led to the assumption that the mechanisms that govern one, long-term potentiation, also govern the other, learning and memory.

Validating Long-Term Potentiation

To validate long-term potentiation as a legitimate model for studying the synaptic basis of naturally occurring learning and memory, researchers have used an approach built around one basic premise: if the neural mechanisms that govern the two are the same or similar, then manipulations that disrupt one should disrupt the other. *Aminophosphonovalerate* (AP5) is a drug known to disrupt long-term potentiation. So, if long-term potentiation and naturally occurring learning are mediated by a common mechanism, AP5 should also disrupt naturally occurring learning.

Experiments using rats have confirmed this hypothesis. Rats are excellent swimmers. When put in a water maze, they can readily learn to find a platform hidden under the water. They are able to do this even when the water is cloudy and the only cues they can use to locate the platform are those in the room in which the maze is located. Richard Morris and his colleagues discovered that injections of AP5 into the hippocampus (the same AP5 that prevents long-term potentiation) impaired the animals' ability to learn the water maze (Morris et al., 1986). If the procedure, however, was changed and the platform was made visible above the water, so that the rats did not have to depend on spatial cues to learn where the platform was located, the rats, even though they were again injected with AP5, could readily swim to the platform without any signs of sensory or motor impairment. The conclusion was that AP5 disrupts associative (not sensory or motor) processes, and that the mechanism that underlies the associative process may be the same mechanism that underlies long-term potentiation.

Recent evidence indicates that the AP5 effect holds not only for maze learning and the hippocampus but also for fear learning and the amygdala as well. Michael Davis and his colleagues have found that injections of AP5 into the amygdala before conditioning impair fear learning in the same way that injections of AP5 into the hippocampus impair maze learning (Davis, 1992).

Learning in the *Aplysia* versus Long-Term Potentiation in Rats: A Comparison

The *Aplysia* studies, coupled with the hippocampal long-term potentiation work just discussed, give us two general views of how learning takes place in the nervous system. Both views agree that learning is mediated by a change in the synapse, and both agree that the change is structural in nature. But that is where the similarity ends. The *Aplysia* work suggests that the change occurs in the presynapse, either in the structure of potassium channels or in the actual growth of presynaptic endings. The hippocampal long-term potentiation work suggests that the change occurs in the postsynapse, in the structure of the membrane, which in turn may either increase the number of postsynaptic receptors or, via feedback to the presynapse, increase the release of neurotransmitter.

How do we resolve these differences? Is it possible that the *Aplysia* nervous system operates differently from the nervous system of the rat? Or is it that presynaptic changes mediate one type of learning and postsynaptic changes another and that with further analysis we will discover that both occur in the mammalian nervous system? We have no answer to these questions, and only time and future research will tell.

There remains, however, one key area of agreement. No matter how numerous the mechanisms for learning and memory may be and no matter where in the brain they occur, they all share one feature: they all appear to involve the synapse. And this brings us to our final question. If a change in the synapse is the means by which learning and memory occur, we can then reasonably ask ourselves, What happens normally in the animal's natural environment to initiate that change?

Until now, the impression we have conveyed is that associative circuits are passive and that once they are stimulated, learning and memory automatically occur. Not quite. Remarkably, the brain itself plays a far more active role in the process. The brain appears to have the ability to actually select the experiences that it comes to learn and remember. Let us take a closer look at this ability.

The Brain as an Active "Learner"

Earlier in the chapter we raised the possibility that learning and memory may be physiologically rooted in principles similar to those we have already encountered in our study of complex sensory experiences. We introduced the possibility that, as in sensory processing, different circuits or areas in the brain may be keyed to different associative features of a task.

Let us now take the sensory analogy one step further. Just as we saw in Chapter 6, some stimuli, even though they meet the physical demands of the sensory system, go unattended and are ignored, so is it the case that some learning experiences, even though they meet the physical demands of the associative system, are neither learned nor remembered.

All of which underscores the importance of screening: the brain's ability to block out extraneous information, be it sensory or associative, and to focus on relevant stimuli, be it in our present environment (sensory) or our past environment (associative). For obvious reasons, we don't want or need to remember *every* learning experience that we have ever had, just as we don't want to sense every stimulus that we encounter. If we did, we would be so overwhelmed by information that we could not possibly respond adaptively.

Entry into our consciousness first at the sensory level and then, in a more enduring way, at the associative level is privileged. Entry is contingent not only on the physical properties, the intensity, and the repetitiveness of a stimulus but also on how we *interpret* these physical properties—in short, their psychological significance. The neural mechanisms at the root of this associative process—remembering the significant and discarding the insignificant—is the subject of the next chapter.

SUMMARY

1. *Learning defined.* Learning is the means by which animals and humans alter old behaviors and develop new behaviors, the better to adapt to changing environments. Learning can best be defined as a change in behavior that endures.

2. *Two types of learning.* A number of theories, but not all, are related in one way or another to the same basic premise—that we can make associations, that is, we can learn in at least one of two ways. The first way is through classical conditioning—learning to make an association between two different stimuli. The other is through instrumental conditioning—learning to make an association between a specific response and a consequence produced by that response.

3. *Forming the association.* One of the fundamental questions regarding the physiological basis of learning is whether learning, that is, forming an association, can occur without the nervous system. In general, the answer is no, although studies have shown that some animals—worms, for instance—can learn certain tasks even when their brains are detached from the rest of their bodies. Even in these cases, however, the learning ability is but a fraction of what it is under normal conditions. All of which has led to the basic assumption that most learning in higher animals requires an intact brain and, in particular, an intact cortex.

4. *Pavlov and the cortex.* The Russian psychologist Ivan Pavlov was one of the first to argue that the cortex is important in learning. He theorized that during classical conditioning a new connection is formed in the cortex, and this new connection, in his view, was the physiological basis of learning. Early data, mainly the work of Karl Lashley in the 1930s, suggested that Pavlov was wrong and that learning is not governed by specific circuits in the cortex but by circuits that are distributed diffusely throughout the brain. More recent studies, though, indicate that specific connections are indeed formed during learning, but not in the cortex.

5. *The hippocampus and learning.* In recent years the ablation (lesion) technique used by Lashley has been complemented by recording techniques. Richard Thompson, working with the nictitating membrane response in rabbits, has found that neural activity appears in the hippocampus during learning—that is, it appears before and during the formation of the conditioned response. Thompson's findings as a whole suggest strongly that the hippocampus is involved in an associative process, but other studies using different classical conditioning procedures indicate that areas outside the hippocampus may be involved in the associative phase of learning as well.

6. *Other brain areas and learning.* Evidence indicates that different types of learning are controlled by different areas of the brain. Learning easy tasks, such as delayed conditioning, involves the cerebellum; learning more difficult tasks, such as trace conditioning, involves the hippocampus. Heart rate conditioning and the conditioning of other fear-related behaviors such as blood pressure changes involve the amygdala, and learning spatial tasks such as the radial-arm maze involves the hippocampus.

7. *Spatial learning.* The work of David Olton indicates that the hippocampus is involved in more than classical conditioning. Using a radial-arm maze which requires that animals learn and remember two types of information, reference memories (information that remains constant) and working memories (information that changes from moment to moment), Olton found that damage to the hippocampus interfered with the animals' ability to form working memories but not reference memories. Taking Olton's work one step further, John O'Keefe has found evidence that the hippocampus is involved not only in processing a specific type of memory but also a specific type of information—spatial information related to the animals' surrounding environment.

8. *The synapse and learning.* No matter how numerous associative circuits may be, they must all have an element of plasticity. It is generally agreed that this plasticity can be mediated by only one neural component: the synapse. A theory, proposed by Donald Hebb, contended that learning doesn't create new pathways but simply alters the sensitivity of existing pathways through the growth and swelling of synaptic terminals. Experiments on the *Aplysia* have confirmed that learning does indeed affect synaptic terminals, promoting growth of terminals during long-term sensitization and pruning terminals during long-term habituation.

9. *Kandel's* Aplysia *work.* Some researchers in studying the synaptic basis of learning have bypassed overt behavior altogether and attempted to observe learning directly in the nervous system—and, in particular, at the level of the synapse. One of the principal researchers in this area is Eric Kandel, who has focused his studies on the *Aplysia*, a large marine snail whose most adaptive and simplest behavior is its gill-withdrawal reflex. Kandel has found that the *Aplysia* shows two very simple forms of learning. The first, known as habituation, represents a decrease in the strength of the withdrawal response when a stimulus is presented repeatedly. The second, known as sensitization, represents a strengthening of the withdrawal reflex whenever a second, noxious stimulus is presented.

10. *Neurotransmitter activity.* Kandel has traced the change in synaptic activity to a change in the presynaptic endings of the sensory neuron and, more specifically, to the presynaptic endings' ability to release the neurotransmitter. He has also found that the amount of neurotransmitter released by the presynapse is determined largely by the concentration of calcium in the presynaptic terminals. He has traced this variation to so-called calcium channels—pores in the membrane that regulate the movement of calcium into the presynapse. According to Kandel, the repeated stimulation that occurs during habituation *inhibits* the opening of these calcium channels, while the noxious stimulus during sensitization *facilitates* their opening.

11. *Classical conditioning in the* Aplysia. Kandel's most recent *Aplysia* work has involved classical conditioning. He has been able to train the *Aplysia* to associate a light touch to its siphon followed by a shock to its tail and, by doing so, has been able to elicit the withdrawal response with the light touch. He has explained his findings in terms of the same dynamics that underlie the findings he has reported with sensitization.

12. *Evaluating Kandel's work.* Although Kandel's studies are compelling, their relevance to human learning has been questioned by some investigators. At issue is whether activity in simple nervous systems can tell us anything about the extensive interactions that occur normally in complex systems. And even if Kandel's work on the *Aplysia* can be applied to higher animals and learning does indeed involve a change in the calcium influx in the presynaptic endings, a basic question still remains: What, specifically, are the neural mechanisms that transform these short-term changes that occur in the synapse during learning to the long-term changes that underlie memory?

13. *Long-term potentiation.* A great deal of the current work in learning has focused on a phenomenon known as long-term potentiation (LTP)—the well-documented fact that an intense stimulus applied to presynaptic neurons in the hippocampus can affect neural activity in a way that influences how a subsequent weak stimulus to the same area will be processed. The experiments using LTP to study the synaptic basis of learning and memory have been shaped by two questions: First, how does the first stimulus, the intense stimulus, change the nervous system making it more responsive to the second stimulus, the weak stimulus? Second, how does that change endure? Evidence points to changes in the structure of the postsynaptic membrane (initiated by the neurotransmitter glutamate) as the structural change that underlies the synaptic basis of learning and memory.

14. *The role of glutamate.* Glutamate (after it is released by the intense stimulus) has the unique ability, once it diffuses across the synaptic gap, to open calcium channels, allowing calcium ions to enter the postsynaptic neuron. The entry of calcium ions triggers a two-stage process, the ultimate result of which is a change in the structure of the postsynaptic membrane—a change that would appear to feed back to the presynapse and enhance the release of neurotransmitter (when the presynapse is later stimulated by the weak stimulus). Underlying this activity are two types of receptors in the postsynaptic membrane—NMDA and non-NMDA, both of which are capable of binding with glutamate.

15. *Validating LTP as a measure of learning.* Evidence indicates that drugs (AP5) that disrupt naturally occurring learning (such as learning a water maze) also disrupt long-term potentiation, indicating that both may be governed by a common mechanism.

16. Aplysia *versus LTP.* The *Aplysia* studies coupled with the LTP work give us two views of the changes in the synapse that may govern how learning takes place in the nervous system. The *Aplysia* work suggests that the change occurs in the presynapse, either in the structure of potassium channels or in the actual growth of presynaptic endings. The LTP work suggests that the change occurs in the postsynapse, in the structure of the membrane.

aminophosphonovalerate (AP5)
amygdala
Aplysia
arachodonic acid
calcium channels
central nucleus of the amygdala
cerebellum
classical conditioning
conditioned stimulus
facilitatory interneurons
glutamate
habituation
hippocampus
instrumental conditioning

interpositus nucleus
long-term potentiation (LTP)
N-methyl-D-aspartate (NMDA)
 receptors
nictitating membrane response
nitric oxide
pseudolearning
radial-arm maze
reference memory
retrograde plasticity factor
sensitization
unconditioned stimulus
working memory

SUGGESTED READINGS

Dudai, Y. *The Neurobiology of Memory: Concepts, Findings, Trends*. Oxford: Oxford University Press, 1989.

Kandel E. R. "Cellular Mechanisms of Learning and the Biological Basis of Individuality." In Kandel, E. R., Schwartz, J. H., & Jessell, T. M. *Principles of Neural Science*, 3rd ed. New York: Elsevier, 1991.

Schwartz, B., & Reisberg, D. *Learning and Memory*. New York: Norton, 1991.

Shaw, J. L., McGaugh, J. L., & Rose, S. P. R. *Neurobiology of Learning and Memory*. World Scientific, 1990.

Teyler, T. J. & DiScenna, P. "Long-term Potentiation." *Annual Review of Neuroscience*, 10, 131–161, 1987.

CHAPTER

17

MEMORY

STRENGTHENING RETRIEVED
MEMORIES

MEMORY: A PSYCHOLOGICAL
PERSPECTIVE

INTRODUCTION

The fact that we are able to make behavioral decisions on the basis of previously learned information indicates that the nervous system is capable of storing information and then retrieving that information at the appropriate time. This capacity of course is what we normally refer to as *memory*, and our study of it is based on a critical assumption: that memory involves structural changes in the nervous system that endure. The presumption is that these structural changes take place during learning and leave a physical residue in the nervous system. Presumably, too, this residue remains in a static, dormant state until it is ready to be retrieved.

In the last chapter we looked at the structural change that underlies learning—*where* it occurs in the brain and *what* form it takes. In this chapter we will be concerned with the physiological dynamics that initiate and regulate the change: *how*, in other words, an enduring memory is formed.

We will be concerned above all in this chapter with the physiological processes that account for one of the most curious aspects of memory: our ability to recall events we first experienced years ago and yet forget events that we first became aware of only seconds before.

This paradox has puzzled philosophers and psychologists for centuries, and it has led researchers to conclude that humans have not one but two distinct memory systems. One is a *short-term memory* system, which comprises the memories that are present and active in the brain at any given moment (the meaning of the words in this sentence, for instance). The other is a *long-term memory* system, which comprises memories stored for long periods (a lifetime, perhaps), some of which are as familiar to you as your own name and others that can be recalled only with great difficulty—the name of your kindergarten teacher, for instance.

If we accept the notion that there are two distinct memory systems, each holding information for different lengths of time, we must also assume the existence of a process that governs the transfer of information from one system to the other. We must assume, too, that the transfer process is highly selective and that most information that enters short-term memory is never transferred. While you are reading these words, for instance, you may also be listening to the radio or there might be some noise in the hallway outside your room. Tomorrow, if you have studied well, you will remember some of the facts you have read in this chapter (thus indicating that the information has been transferred from short-term to long-term memory), but you will probably have forgotten what music was playing while you were reading or what the noise was about, indicating that this information has not made it to long-term memory.

There is a logical reason for this selectivity. We humans are complex organisms, endowed with the ability to learn an enormous amount of information. Were it not for our ability to distinguish relevant from irrelevant information *before* that information is stored in any permanent way, our lives would be chaotic. So nobody questions the existence of a selection process. The question is how the selection occurs: What determines which information passes into long-term storage and which information is discarded?

To be sure, there is no one answer to this question. The content of the information (how important or memorable it is) is obviously one factor. So are cognitive and mental processes—the ability to organize the information into a meaningful framework and then to think about it, mull it over, and use it at a later time. But these factors, as important as they are, will not command our attention in this chapter. Our concern in this chapter lies with the neural structures and chemicals involved in the transformation process itself.

We cannot emphasize enough the fact that no one has yet solved the mystery of precisely how neural activity during learning is transformed into its enduring structural counterpart. The issue, as you can imagine, is monumentally complex. What makes it even more complex—and more fascinating—is the fact that the transformation, when it does occur, is not immediate but gradual. Still, if we lack a definitive answer to the question, we have gained some intriguing insights, and these insights will occupy much of our attention throughout this chapter.

THE THEORY OF MEMORY CONSOLIDATION: A HISTORICAL PERSPECTIVE

Much of the work being done in memory research today can be traced to a theory that was proposed over 40 years ago and that is known as *memory consolidation* (Hebb, 1949). According to this theory, illustrated in Figure 17.1, the transformation of short-term memory into long-term memory is a gradual process. In its early stages, memory appears to be highly vulnerable to interference. As the transformation occurs, however, the memory becomes increasingly resistant to interference. According to the memory consolidation theory, there comes a point at which the memory is *consolidated*—that is, assumes a fixed form. Once it has been consolidated, memory has presumably moved from the vulnerable short-term memory state to the more resistant long-term memory state.

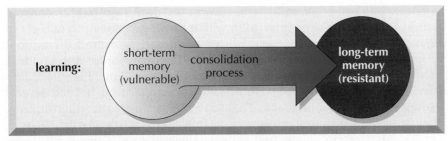

Figure 17.1 *A Consolidation Model of Memory Storage*
The gradations of shading illustrate the fact that consolidation is a gradual process and may
never be totally complete.

Some of the best evidence for the theory of memory consolidation comes from observations of humans who have suffered traumatic head injuries (Russell, 1959). Many such people can recall almost nothing that happened immediately before the trauma, but they are still able to recall long-term memories. A typical pattern among victims of automobile accidents, for instance, is that they remember conversations that took place earlier on the day of the accident but forget how or why the accident itself occurred. This inability—the inability to recall events that occurred immediately before the onset of the neural trauma—is called *retrograde* (in a backward direction) *amnesia*.

The theory of memory consolidation has a good deal of logic going for it. Apart from the fact that it explains the phenomenon of retrograde amnesia (i.e., memories of events that occur immediately before the trauma do not have time to consolidate and thus are destroyed), it offers a theoretical basis for the brain's ability to store relevant information and discard irrelevant information. What we still do not know, however, is what neural and chemical properties account for this ability.

Most of the studies on the physiological basis of memory consolidation have been done in lower animals, mainly rats and monkeys. But studies have also been done on humans, particularly people whose nervous systems have been altered by disease, accident, or surgery. We shall consider both types of studies.

Memory Consolidation in Lower Animals:
The Early Work

The basic problem facing researchers seeking the physiological basis of memory consolidation in lower animals is methodological: How do you go about studying the process in animals?

One approach to this methodological challenge has been to train animals to perform a particular task, to disrupt neural activity in their brain at varying time intervals after training, and to observe what impact each disruption has on the animals' ability to remember what they have learned. By varying the period between training and neural disruption, it is possible to establish, at least in theory, the time required for consolidation—that is, the time interval in which memory is the most subject to disruption and the time interval in which it can withstand disruption.

A prototype of the consolidation experiment in lower animals is a study conducted on rats by Stephan Chorover and Peter Schiller (Chorover & Schiller, 1965). Chorover and Schiller first trained several groups of rats to avoid shock. Then, at various times after the training, they subjected different groups of animals to electroconvulsive shock (ECS)—an electric shock that when delivered to the brain produces convulsions and, more pertinent to the Chorover and Schiller study, amnesia.

Chorover and Schiller's findings appear to confirm the consolidation theory. They found that the briefer the interval between training and ECS, the greater the amnesic effects of the ECS. Animals subjected to ECS 0.5 seconds after training exhibited the most amnesia when tested the next day. Animals subjected to ECS 10 seconds after training exhibited less amnesia. And animals given ECS 30 seconds after training exhibited no amnesia.

This type of time-dependent effect of ECS has come to be known as the *retrograde amnesia gradient* and is precisely what might be expected if ECS does in fact disrupt memory consolidation. The 0.5-second-old memory presumably is in a short-term, highly vulnerable state. This explains why ECS, in this instance, can produce total amnesia. The 10-second-old memory is presumably less vulnerable, thus accounting for less amnesia. The 30-second-old memory, brief though it may seem, is highly resistant: it presumably has been consolidated.

The Time Span of Consolidation: Fact or Illusion?

Hundreds of studies using a variety of amnesic agents, ranging from convulsants (such as ECS) to depressants (such as anesthetics), have produced essentially the same results as Chorover and Schiller's: a retrograde amnesia gradient. The gradient, however, has varied from seconds to as long as hours or even days, depending on the type and amount of agent used. If the duration of the ECS itself is increased from 0.2 to 0.8 seconds, for instance, the time in which it can be delivered after training and still produce retrograde amnesia is increased from 10 seconds to 3 hours (Alpern & McGaugh, 1969).

These variations raise a nettlesome question: If the retrograde amnesia gradient reflects the consolidation process, why should the same memory appear to take different amounts of time to consolidate depending upon the strength of the amnesic agent?

To resolve this issue, most memory researchers today maintain that consolidation is a gradual rather than an all-or-none process (McGaugh & Gold, 1976). The general opinion is that even after 3 hours, consolidation in the rat brain may not be entirely completed but may be nearly so—at least to the extent that only an intense disruption such as a 0.8-second ECS can interfere with the process. Some researchers have even gone so far as to suggest that consolidation may never be fully completed, and that if you used amnesic agents that were intense enough, you would discover retrograde amnesia gradients that spanned years rather than minutes or hours. Later we shall consider human data that confirm this hypothesis.

For now, however, it is important to recognize that the retrograde amnesia gradient, as established in the lower-animal studies, does not reflect a specific time frame for consolidation in general. No one can say on the basis of these studies that a memory consolidates after a certain number of seconds in rats. And we certainly cannot use these studies to establish a time frame with respect to humans.

These limitations notwithstanding, however, the studies show clearly that the more severe the disruption, the more protracted the retrograde amnesia gradient. The gradient in turn indicates that memory consolidation in lower animals does occur and that short-term memories are more vulnerable to disruption than long-term memories. The retrograde amnesia gradient also gives us a procedure, as we will shortly see, for determining the physiological basis—the neural and chemical aspects—of the consolidation process.

Mapping the Anatomical Site: The Early Work

One ongoing problem with using such disruptive agents as ECS and anesthetics to study memory consolidation is the indiscriminate manner in which they spread through the brain. It is all but impossible when using these disruptive agents to implicate any one, or for that matter any group, of anatomical sites in the consolidation process.

To circumvent this problem, experimenters have tried a number of techniques—the use of electrical stimulation through implanted electrodes, for instance—that confine disruption to specific sites in the brain. The reasoning is that if a specific area of the brain is involved in the consolidation process, then the disruption of neural activity in that area at various times after training should disrupt recent but not long-term memory.

The early work has shown that several brain areas fit this description. They include the amygdala, the midbrain reticular formation, and the hippocampus (Kesner & Doty, 1968; Stein & Chorover, 1968). Figure 17.2 shows where these areas are located. If any of these areas are stimulated shortly after training, retrograde amnesia occurs. If stimulation to these areas is delayed, however, there is no effect. The retrograde amnesia gradient is of course the key feature in all these findings. Its presence signals which areas are involved in the consolidation process and which are not.

We must be especially cautious, however, not to draw too hasty a conclusion. To say that specific brain areas are involved in consolidation is

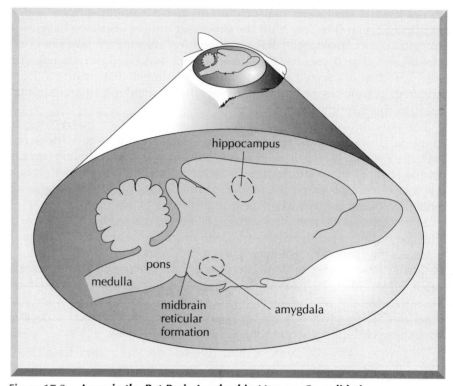

Figure 17.2 *Areas in the Rat Brain Involved in Memory Consolidation*
Stimulation of each of these areas delivered shortly after training produces retrograde amnesia, whereas delayed stimulation has no effect.

not to say that consolidation *resides* in these areas. There are at least two interpretations of the data: the first is that the brain areas could indeed be the actual sites of consolidation; the second is that the areas could be connected to and could serve to *modulate* (facilitate or inhibit) the sites of consolidation (McGaugh & Gold, 1976). The two interpretations are compared in Figure 17.3.

It is too early to make a case for either the direct or the modulatory interpretation of the consolidation areas. In fact, since every area of the brain is related either directly or indirectly to virtually every other area, it is likely that both interpretations will ultimately prove correct.

Consolidation: A Closer Look

It may seem to you at this point, based on what you have read so far in this chapter, that the consolidation process serves a single function: to transform short-term memories into long-term memories. Consolidation, however, serves another function as well. It determines the *strength* of long-term memory—that is, how likely that memory is to be recalled at a future time.

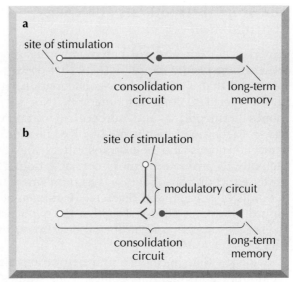

Figure 17.3 *Consolidation versus Modulation*
There are two interpretations of the retrograde amnesia produced by stimulation of a specific area in the brain. Consolidation may reside in the area (a) or may be modulated by the area (b).

That consolidation should do more than simply transform a short-term memory into a long-term memory but also play a role in determining the strength of a memory is hardly surprising. We all know from our own experience, after all, that certain events in our lives—the day we got our driver's license, for instance—stand out in our memory much more vividly than others, and so it is reasonable to assume that something must have occurred during the consolidation process to make these memories so much more vivid. The critical component in this strength-related aspect of consolidation appears to be the perceived importance (at the time) of any event—that is, the emotional impact of the event and the degree of arousal engendered by the event. The more significant an event (significant, that is, as we see it at the time), the greater the arousal and, presumably, the greater the *degree* of consolidation (Kety, 1975; Gold & McGaugh, 1975; McGaugh, 1984).

As you will see later, however, there comes a point at which arousal increases to such a level that it no longer promotes consolidation but actually begins to impede it. But the principle we would like you to bear in mind at this point is that all memories do not have equal value and that, for the most part, the strength of memory correlates, more or less, with the level of arousal. Let us now take a closer look at the evidence that supports this hypothesis and, more specifically, at the physiological mechanisms that account for the relationship between level of arousal and strength of consolidation.

The Arousal Hypothesis of Memory Consolidation

Experiences that are worth remembering produce arousal—a general level of nonspecific neural activity that occurs diffusely throughout the brain and that is essential for consolidation, that is, the transformation of short-term to long-term memory. Not surprisingly, then, the hormones (epinephrine and adrenocorticotrophic hormone) and neurotransmitters (norepinephrine) involved in neural arousal are some of the same hormones and neurotransmitters that have been shown experimentally to promote memory consolidation. The hormone-neurotransmitter effect on consolidation is a complementary one. Neurotransmitter action is fast, brief, and discrete. Hormonal action, in contrast, is prolonged, slow, and diffuse. Together the two work to maximize arousal of the nervous system and, in the process, to maximize memory consolidation.

Evidence that hormones and neurotransmitters both play a role in facilitating consolidation comes from studies in which hormones or neurotransmitters are used to increase neural activity immediately after training. We know that if neural activity is decreased or is disrupted immediately after training, memory is disrupted, that is, retrograde amnesia is produced. It is logical to wonder, then, if *increasing* activity in the brain immediately after training can produce *retrograde facilitation*—the actual strengthening of memories. Evidence suggests that it does.

THE CHEMICAL BASIS OF MEMORY CONSOLIDATION

Numerous experiments involving retrograde facilitation have shown that certain drugs, certain hormones, and certain neurotransmitters can enhance the memory capacities of animals. When a drug known to stimulate the nervous system (amphetamine, for instance) is administered shortly after training, the retention of memories the next day is enhanced. When administration of the same drug is delayed, there is no effect (McGaugh, 1973). The same pattern is produced by injections of drugs that increase levels of norepinephrine (Stein, Belluzzi, & Wise, 1975), a neurotransmitter associated with neural arousal, and also by injections of adrenocorticotrophic hormone (ACTH) (Flood et al., 1976), vasopressin (DeWied, 1974), and epinephrine (Gold & McGaugh, 1977), hormones associated with arousal, that is, hormones that are released during important events and may ultimately be fed back to the brain (directly or indirectly) to enhance neural activity in various areas (McGaugh et al., 1975). By the same token, drugs that deplete norepinephrine impair retention (Randt, Quartermain, & Goldstein, 1971). The same pattern holds true for opiates, such as morphine. Let's take a closer look.

The Opiate Effect

The opiate effect is particularly interesting because it, too, may reflect a decrease in the level of norepinephrine—albeit indirectly. There are two classes of drugs related to the opiate effect. One is the opiates themselves (such as morphine), which produce retrograde amnesia and, as we saw in Chapter 5, *mimic* the action of the neurotransmitter endorphin (Izquierdo, 1979). The other drug is *naloxone,* an opiate antagonist—that is, a drug that *blocks* the action of endorphins. Naloxone, in contrast to morphine, doesn't impair retention, it facilitates it (Messing et al., 1979).

Why should retrograde amnesia be produced by drugs (the opiates) that mimic endorphins, and why should retrograde facilitation be produced by drugs (naloxone) that block the action of endorphins? The answer lies in their effects on norepinephrine: opiates (by mimicking endorphins) decrease the release of norepinephrine; naloxone (by blocking endorphins) increases the release of norepinephrine (Gallagher, Rapp, & Fanelli, 1985; McGaugh et al., 1992).

Epinephrine and Memory Consolidation

Of all the hormones or neurotransmitters that affect memory consolidation (i.e., play a role in regulating memory storage), none has drawn more attention than epinephrine (Gold, 1987; McGaugh, 1984). Of particular interest to memory researchers is the fact that epinephrine is able to improve memory under a variety of conditions. It strengthens the characteristically weak memory capacities of very young and very old laboratory animals. And, even more surprisingly, it can be used to enhance the ability of animals to learn information while they are anesthetized.

Age and Memory

Depending upon how old they are, laboratory rats manifest different memory patterns—a result that suggests a direct link between age and memory. Very young rats (i.e., 16 days old) and very old rats (i.e., 2 years old) have difficulty remembering newly learned information (e.g., learned avoidance behavior). Young rats lose the information after a day—a phenomenon known as *infantile amnesia.* Old rats show significant impairment of memory after a week.

Epinephrine changes the pattern. If the animals, young or old, are given a single injection of epinephrine shortly after training, while memory is still in the process of consolidating, the forgetting in both cases is significantly reduced (Gold et al., 1981; Sternberg et al., 1985). Apparently, then, memory consolidation is related to age, developing slowly in the very young and deteriorating in the very old. Apparently, too, injections of epinephrine during consolidation compensate for these deficits and strengthen retention.

Learning under Anesthesia

Perhaps the most intriguing example of how epinephrine can improve memory in lower animals comes from a study on learning under anesthesia. Animals under deep anesthesia are ordinarily unable to learn even though their sensory systems (as judged by neurophysiological recordings) receive and process information. Exactly why they are unable to learn is unclear. It might be that the physiological processes for learning and memory, including those that mediate memory consolidation, are inactive during anesthesia. It might also be that these processes are active but that they are so weak that later, when the animal is conscious, the experience is forgotten.

One way to find out why animals under anesthesia are unable to learn is to combine a learning experience with an injection of epinephrine while the animals are anesthetized. If the absence of learning during anesthesia is a matter of weak consolidation (i.e., weak regulation of memory storage), a boost in epinephrine during anesthesia should strengthen consolidation and produce learning. The hypothesis is logical. Testing it is another matter.

Norman Weinberger and his colleagues anesthetized rats and then gave them classical conditioning training trials (Weinberger, Gold, & Sternberg, 1984). The training trials consisted of white noise followed by a shock delivered directly to the animal's hindlimb (a procedure that ordinarily produces learned fear). Several groups of animals were used in this study, but we will consider only the two most important: (1) a group that was given an injection of saline before training and (2) a group that was given an injection of epinephrine before training. (The epinephrine group consisted of three subgroups, each given a different dosage of epinephrine but all showing basically the same results.) The animals in both groups, after they recovered from anesthetic, were given a retention test 10 days after training. The test consisted of presenting the white noise (the conditioned stimulus) in the absence of the shock and determining if the noise would suppress water intake (a procedure commonly used to measure retention of conditioned fear). The expectation was that if learning occurred while animals were being trained under anesthesia and if epinephrine administered during that training strengthened consolidation, the epinephrine animals should show conditioned fear in response to the white noise while the saline animals should not. This is precisely what happened.

There are two possible explanations for why the epinephrine animals showed retention and the saline animals did not. One is that epinephrine does indeed affect memory consolidation, promoting consolidation during anesthesia. The other is that epinephrine merely affects the depth of anesthesia, weakening the effects of the anesthetic and thereby making it easier for the epinephrine animals to learn.

Weinberger and his colleagues discount the latter possibility, and they do so on the basis of physiological measures that they took while the animals were anesthetized. They monitored two reactions—heart beat and motor reflex—as a measure of depth of anesthesia, and they found that neither reaction was affected by epinephrine during anesthesia; they thus concluded that the epinephrine did not improve retention by merely counteracting the effect of the anesthetic.

The Mechanism

As simple and straightforward as the epinephrine effect on memory consolidation appears, it is not without complications. The brain, you will recall, is protected from certain chemical substances by the so-called blood-brain barrier (see Chapter 3 for details). This barrier poses no problem for norepinephrine, a neurotransmitter that is produced in the brain and thus does not have to cross the blood-brain barrier to stimulate the brain. Nor is it a problem for ACTH, a hormone that, although manufactured outside the brain by the adrenal cortex gland, is able to pass the blood-brain barrier. This barrier, however, does pose a problem for epinephrine. Epinephrine, as far as we know, is unable to pass the blood-brain barrier. How then do injections of epinephrine into the body enhance memory consolidation produced in the brain?

The answer lies in the capacity of epinephrine to promote consolidation without acting directly in the brain. It does so in two ways: (1) by acting on the peripheral nerves—the vagus nerve, for instance—that ultimately project to the brain; and (2) by promoting the production of glucose, which, unlike epinephrine, is able to pass the blood-brain barrier. Evidence that epinephrine's effect on peripheral nerves can facilitate consolidation comes from studies in which the facilitatory effect has been impeded by drugs that block the ability of epinephrine to affect peripheral nerves (Introini-Collison & McGaugh, 1991). Evidence that epinephrine's effect on glucose production can influence consolidation comes from a series of studies by Paul Gold and his colleagues. We will now look at these studies.

Testing the Glucose Hypothesis

The glucose hypothesis is simple enough to test. If epinephrine's ability to facilitate consolidation depends on glucose, then administering glucose alone, in the absence of epinephrine, should facilitate consolidation. By the same token, administering epinephrine alone, in the absence of glucose, should not.

This is precisely what Gold and his colleagues have observed (Gold, Vogt, & Hall, 1986). In one key experiment injections of epinephrine normally given to rats immediately after training were replaced by an injection of glucose. The result was that retention was facilitated. In a second experiment, the injection of epinephrine was accompanied by the injection of a drug known to block epinephrine's ability to produce glucose. In this case, epinephrine lost its ability to facilitate retention.

It is too early to say exactly how glucose acts in the brain to facilitate memory consolidation, but these findings may have important implications for human memory. Glucose, in contrast to epinephrine, has few if any side effects and thus has far more potential than epinephrine as a treatment for humans with memory disorders. In fact, glucose has already been used in some situations, and with apparent success (Gold, 1987). Working with elderly patients who experience mild forms of memory loss, Gold and his colleagues have found that administering glucose shortly after a learning experience enhances the patients' memory. Whether glucose will prove useful in the treatment of people with more severe memory loss remains to be determined.

Brain-Stimulation Studies and the Arousal Hypothesis

Other studies designed to examine arousal and its relation to memory consolidation have relied on discrete electrical stimulation in various areas of the brain. These studies have generally confirmed the findings of the chemical studies. When electrical stimulation is delivered to the amygdala, or the reticular formation (areas known to be involved in neural arousal) immediately after training, retention is facilitated. When the stimulation is delayed, there is no effect (McGaugh & Gold, 1976; Bloch & Laroche, 1984).

These brain areas should sound familiar to you, for they are among the same areas we considered earlier, except that in the earlier cases we found that stimulating them produced retrograde amnesia. This similarity raises a rather perplexing question: How can stimulation of the same area of the brain produce retrograde amnesia in some studies and retrograde facilitation in others?

There are two explanations. The more obvious has to do with the intensity of the electrical brain stimulation used in some of the studies. When the intensity of the stimulation to the reticular formation, for example, is high, retention is impaired. Lower the intensity, and retention is facilitated (Bloch, 1970). Another explanation for the difference lies in the nature of the training procedure. Paul Gold and his colleagues, using shock-avoidance training to study the effect that stimulation of the amygdala has on retention, have found that amygdala stimulation facilitates retention in animals trained to avoid a weak shock but disrupts retention in animals trained to avoid strong shock (Gold et al., 1975). Apparently, then, the training procedure (shock in this case) is just as important in determining the level of neural activity in the brain as the brain stimulation itself. If either is intense, neural activity becomes excessively high, and the result is amnesia.

Finally, to complete the picture, the same rule holds for neurotransmitters and hormones. When the levels of norepinephrine or epinephrine injected immediately after training are high, retention is impaired. Lower the dose, and retention is facilitated (Gold & van Buskirk, 1975).

In summary, the electrical brain-stimulation and the neurotransmitter-hormone studies have added two new insights regarding the consolidation picture:

1. The level of activity in the brain following training is crucial, but the highest levels are not necessarily the optimal ones; in fact, when neural activity is too high, it becomes disruptive.
2. Several factors appear to be involved in determining the level of neural activity in the brain: the intensity of the electrical brain stimulation, the level of neurotransmitter or hormone, and the arousal consequences of the learning experience itself.

What these insights suggest, all told, is that while there is indeed a relationship between neural activity and the strength of retention, the behavioral implications are not as straightforward as they may have originally seemed. Yes, the level of neural activity does directly influence how strong a memory will become, but only to a certain point, beyond which increases in neural activity can actually decrease the strength of memory. This effect—the fact that beyond a certain threshold neural stimulation impedes consolidation—goes a long way to explain why amnesia sometimes strikes people who have gone through horrifically stressful situations in which the level of neural activity presumably far exceeds the point of optimal stimulation.

Bridging between Chemistry and the Brain
Let us now put into perspective what is known about the chemistry and the brain areas involved in memory consolidation.

To begin with, both the chemical and brain stimulation work have found similar effects. When either epinephrine or norepinephrine is administered immediately after training, the strength of retention is facilitated. The same pattern holds for the brain stimulation: when the amygdala or the reticular formation is stimulated immediately after training, retention is strengthened.

Given this similarity in effect, James McGaugh and his colleagues conducted a series of studies, the purpose of which was to determine whether there is a link between the effects of epinephrine and norepinephrine and the effects of amygdala stimulation. They began with the hypothesis that epinephrine and norepinephrine activate the amygdala and that the amygdala, in turn, modulates the strength of memory. They thus reasoned that the facilitating effects of epinephrine and norepinephrine on memory should be disrupted if the amygdala is lesioned, and this is precisely what McGaugh and his colleagues have found. In one study, they placed lesions in the stria terminalis of the amygdala and found that injections of epinephrine or norepinephrine immediately after training lost their ability to facilitate consolidation (Liang & McGaugh, 1983; Liang et al., 1990).

On the basis of these and related studies, McGaugh has concluded that the amygdala is one of the centers of neuromodulation: it receives input from norepinephrine and epinephrine circuits (the vagus nerve that originates outside the brain) and it, in turn, determines the level of neural arousal and in the process the strength of memory consolidation (McGaugh et al., 1992).

Triggering Memory Consolidation: REM Sleep

If arousal of neural activity is the means by which the nervous system consolidates memory, it is reasonable to ask what happens normally in the animal's natural environment to produce arousal. In other words, What normally stimulates the release of epinephrine and norepinephrine to activate the amygdala?

The answer to these questions appears to be twofold. On the one hand, arousal is almost certainly affected by the learning experience itself, a proposition for which Gold's study on shock intensity has made a strong case (Gold et al., 1975). On the other hand, there is increasing evidence that sleep may also play a role in this process and that arousal may well be produced from within the brain during sleep (Bloch, Hennevin, & Leconte, 1979).

We know from Chapter 12 that sleep is cyclical, consisting of REM and slow-wave stages. Studies indicate that deprivation of REM sleep, apart from its other effects, interferes with memory consolidation. Animals deprived of REM sleep almost immediately after training show retrograde amnesia, whereas those deprived of REM sleep 2 hours after training show no effect (Pearlman & Becker, 1973).

An experiment by Avi Karni and his colleagues has extended the study of REM sleep in memory consolidation to humans and has produced results similar to the animal work (Karni et al., 1994). The subjects in this study were trained to recognize the orientation of an object appearing in their visual field for a brief period of time. Given the opportunity to practice the task over several days, the subjects became progressively more proficient. Having established that practice does indeed improve performance, the researchers divided another group of subjects into two groups, putting both groups through the same practice sessions but with one key exception: The subjects in one group were awakened each night as soon as they entered REM sleep, thus depriving them of REM sleep. The subjects in the other group were awakened during slow-wave sleep.

The results revealed a significant pattern. Subjects awakened during slow-wave sleep, like the subjects in the nondeprived group, showed a distinct improvement in their ability to perform the task—an indication that the training had taken hold. Subjects in the REM-deprived group, however, showed no improvement during the course of the experiment—despite the repeated practice sessions.

Clearly, then, REM deprivation has an impact on learning. The question, though, is why? Two possibilities have been suggested, one related to the inability of REM-deprived subjects to *perform* a previously-learned task and the other relating to the inability of REM-deprived subjects to *remember* (that is, to consolidate) the skill required to perform the task. The more likely of the two possibilities is the latter—and for the following reason. When REM-deprived subjects are tested on a task they have long since mastered (and presumably consolidated), the deprivation appears to have no impact on their ability to perform that task proficiently. It is only when REM-deprived subjects are called upon to learn and recall new and presumably unconsolidated tasks that the difficulty arises. If REM deprivation affected performance, all memories—new and old—should be affected.

Although these findings indicate that REM sleep is required to complete memory consolidation, the exact role that it plays in consolidation remains to be determined. It is important to note, however, that during REM sleep the brain is highly active and norepinephrine is released—two conditions that are consistent with the arousal hypothesis of memory consolidation.

MEMORY CONSOLIDATION: THE ROLE OF SPECIFIC CIRCUITS

It is safe to conclude on the basis of the studies we have been considering that arousal plays an indispensible role in memory consolidation. It determines the transformation of short-term into long-term memory and it determines the strength of that long-term memory.

But there is more to memory consolidation than arousal. We sense arousal but what we actually experience, the precise form of the memory (that is, the content of the experience to be remembered) is keyed to specific areas of the brain. We know this primarily from a series of studies conducted on monkeys in which damage to specific areas of the brain results in loss of specific types of short-term memories.

The reasoning behind these studies was as follows: if a specific area of the brain is involved in consolidation of a specific memory, then lesioning that area should disrupt consolidation or at least disrupt the short-term memory stage required for consolidation of that memory to occur. The lesioned animal may be able to learn and may even be able to recall the short-term memory for a brief period of time, but the short-term memory should quickly slip away.

Several brain areas fit this description. They include the medial temporal lobe, the frontal lobe, and the hippocampus. Let's take a closer look at each.

Medial Temporal Lobe and Short-Term Memory

One of the more common behavioral procedures used to study the effect of lesions on short-term memory is illustrated in Figure 17.4 and is known as *delayed non-matching to sample*. The procedure consists of three stages: a learning stage, a delay interval to measure short-term memory, and a test stage. During the learning stage, the monkeys are presented with a distinctly shaped object (the sample) and are trained to move the object in order to uncover a reward (a peanut) hidden beneath it. During the delay interval, an opaque screen is placed between the monkeys and the object and is kept there for intervals that vary, from as brief as a few seconds to as long as several minutes, from one trial to the

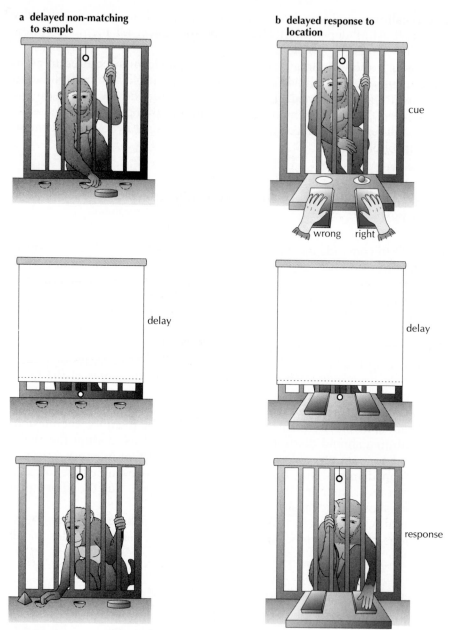

Figure 17.4
(a) Delayed non-matching to sample. A monkey is presented with an object of a distinct shape which it learns to move to uncover a reward. A brief delay is introduced after which the monkey is presented with the original object and a new object. The monkey must respond to the new object to receive the reward. (b) Delayed response to location. A monkey is shown where the reward is located and, after a delay, is allowed to make a choice.

next. During the test stage the monkeys are presented with two objects—the original object and a new differently shaped object. To receive the reward during the test the monkeys must respond to the new object. The three-stage procedure is then repeated over and over again, but each time with different objects and with a different delay interval.

To perform this task correctly on the test stage, the monkeys have to remember two things. First of all they must remember "what" the stimulus is—that is, the shape of the original object. Otherwise they would not know which object *not* to choose during the test stage. Second, the monkeys must remember the "rule" implicit in the experiment—namely, that when there is a choice between the new object and the original object, the correct choice is always the new object.

The critical variable in this experiment is the delay interval between training (that is, seeing the original object) and testing (remembering what the object looked like and choosing the new one). The delay interval provides a measure of short-term memory—how long the animal can hold information from training to testing—and by doing so, it provides a way of gauging the impact of brain damage on short-term memory. Normal (non-brain-damaged) monkeys, as it happens, have little difficulty performing the test behavior, even when the delay interval extends to several minutes. But monkeys with damage in the medial temporal lobe are able to perform the task only when the interval between training and the testing is very brief—ten seconds or less (Mishkin & Manning, 1978; Mishkin, 1982; Mishkin & Appenzeller, 1987).

The time-related difference is critical. The fact that the monkeys with medial temporal lobe damage can perform the task correctly when the interval is short indicates that even with the damage, they can learn and remember both the "what" and the "rule." The fact that errors begin to increase once the interval increases beyond ten seconds indicates that what they can't do is remember—that is, hold what they have learned—for more than a few seconds.

Medial Temporal Lobe: A Closer Look

Studies such as the one we have just described leave little question that damage to the medial temporal lobe affects short-term memory of "what" an animal sees. The studies, however, do not indicate the specific area of the brain responsible for the short-term memory loss. As you can see in Figure 17.5, damage to the medial temporal lobe destroys a number of areas, any one or combination of which may qualify as the source of the short-term memory loss.

To identify which of the areas are involved, researchers have conducted experiments in which damage has been confined to one area at a time. The results of these studies have presented a mixed picture. Damage localized in the hippocampus (an extremely difficult area to study because of its location) produces memory impairment, as does damage to the surrounding cortical areas (specifically, the perirhinal and parahippocampal cortex) (Squire & Zola-Morgan, 1991; Zola-Morgan et al., 1989). Damage localized in the amygdala, however, has no detrimental effects (Zola-Morgan, Squire, & Amaral, 1989). Significantly, a similar pattern—memory impairment linked to hippocampal or surrounding cortex damage but not amygdala damage—has been found in humans, as we will see shortly.

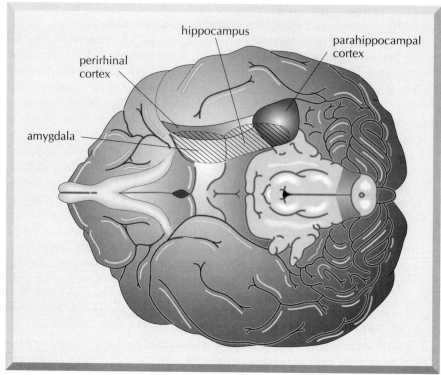

Figure 17.5 *A Ventral View of the Monkey Brain*
Damage to the medial temporal lobe encompasses several areas, including the hippocampus and amygdala (indicated by diagonal lines) and the surrounding cortex (indicated in color—perirhinal in light blue and parahippocampal in darker blue).

Frontal Lobe and Memory of Location

A different picture of short-term memory loss and its relation to brain damage emerges when the task is changed and the monkey is required to remember *where* a stimulus is located rather than *what* that stimulus is. The procedure as illustrated in Figure 17.4*b*, in this instance, consists of showing a monkey *where* food is located under one of two objects, introducing a brief delay by inserting an opaque screen between the monkey and the objects, and then allowing the animal to make a choice. The procedure is then repeated, but each time with the reward in a new location. Thus to perform correctly on a given trial the animal must remember where the object is located.

Monkeys with damage to the frontal lobe (specifically the sulcus principalis) have difficulty performing the location task, which indicates that they are impaired in remembering *where* the stimulus is. The impairment in this case is particularly severe and occurs with a delay interval as brief as 5 seconds. Significantly, however, these monkeys have no difficulty performing the delayed nonmatching-to-sample task, which indicates that they remember *what* the stimulus is (Goldman-Rakic, 1987).

On the basis of these observations we can safely conclude that in monkeys different types of short-term memory are under the control of different areas of the brain, and we can conclude as well that areas in the medial temporal and frontal lobes have separate specialties. Beyond this broad generalization, however, we have to be careful about the specific conclusions we draw (Squire & Zola-Morgan, 1991).

The Animal Studies: A Caveat

To divide short-term memory into two distinct categories "what" and "where," each linked to a specific area of the brain, is a tidy way of explaining brain function and short-term memory, but it is also a simplification that requires some elaboration.

For one thing, it is important to bear in mind that the relationship between brain areas and specific content of memories is a good deal more complex than a simple "what" and "where" distinction suggests. That's because information itself falls into several categories, each with its own relationship to certain areas. Emotional information, for instance, is processed largely in the amygdala (LeDoux, 1994), as we saw in Chapter 14, whereas spatial information, as we saw in Chapter 16, is processed by the hippocampus (Morris et al., 1982).

Second, it is also possible—in fact it is common—for different types of short-term memory to be controlled by different circuits within the same area of the brain. For example, as we've just seen, the medial temporal lobe (specifically, the hippocampus) in monkeys is involved in processing the short-term memory of the "what" of a stimulus, but a recent experiment indicates that the hippocampus in monkeys is involved in processing the short-term memory of the "where" of the stimulus as well (Parkinson, Murray, & Mishkin, 1988). Animals with damage in the hippocampus are so impaired, in fact, that they cannot even *learn*, let alone remember, where an object just appeared.

Finally, it is important to stress that the behavior of lower animals in memory experiments varies considerably from species to species, giving rise to different conclusions of how different features of memory are related to specific brain areas. For example, the monkey studies we have just described link the hippocampus with the ability to recall the "what" of the stimulus, but hippocampal damage in rats produces a different picture. Rats whose hippocampus has been damaged show little or no loss in the ability to recall the "what" of a stimulus, that is, show little or no impairment in a delayed nonmatching-to-sample task modified to accommodate rats (Aggleton, Hunt, & Rawlins, 1986; Mumby, Wood, & Pinel, 1992). Yet, as we saw in Chapter 16, hippocampal damage in rats produces a profound effect on their ability to recall the "where" of the stimulus.

We mention these complexities not to confuse you but to impress upon you that memory processing and its relation to brain anatomy simply do not lend themselves to a singular classification nor to simple experimental analysis. Despite these reservations, however, the anatomical work on short-term memory in animals has added an important dimension to our understanding of the physiological basis of memory and, as we shall see shortly, it has provided important links between the behavior of lower animals and humans.

Reconstructing the Circuit

Let us see where we have been and where we are going. We began by observing that there are two types of memories—short-term and long-term. We then examined the phenomenon of consolidation—the transformation of short-term memory into long-term memory. Finally, we theorized that the transformation is the result of an interaction between two processes: an arousal process related to the significance of the experience and a short-term memory process related to the nature (i.e., the content) of the experience.

Evidence for the arousal process, as we have seen, comes from studies indicating a relationship between the level of neural activity in the brain after training and the strength of long-term memory. Contributing to this process are hormones (epinephrine and ACTH), neurotransmitters (norepinephrine), several brain areas (including the amygdala and the reticular formation), the arousal consequences of the learning experience itself, and perhaps even REM sleep.

Evidence for a short-term memory process related to the nature of the experience comes from studies showing that damage in specific areas of the brain (e.g., the sulcus principalis) impairs short-term memory of some information while leaving other information intact.

This brings us to the final question concerning the consolidation process: What is the physiological substrate of the long-term memory produced by the process? Most researchers today agree that since long-term, established memories survive electroconvulsive shocks, concussions, anesthesia, and other disruptions of electrical activity in the brain, long-term memory must be stored in a durable form that is relatively resistant to interference.

The theory—and it is only a theory—is that long-term memory involves an enduring *structural* change in the nervous system. But what is that structural change and how does it work? As we saw in the last chapter, there are two views. The *Aplysia* experiments link long-term memory to structural changes (synthesis of new protein and growth of new synaptic endings) in the presynapse—enhancing the release of neurotransmitter (Kandel, 1991). The long-term potentiation work in the hippocampus links long-term memory to protein changes in the postsynapse—changes that, in turn, either increase the sensitivity of the postsynapse or feed back to the presynapse to enhance the release of neurotransmitter (Lynch & Baudry, 1984). As it happens, both theories may turn out to be essentially correct. For it is possible that there is not one but several types of long-term memory storage, each produced by a different type of learning and each encoded in a different structural change in the synapse.

On the surface we have evidence for the physiological basis of the two major components of memory—the structural change that underlies long-term storage and the consolidation process that produces it. But there is one complication. Each of these components has been studied by itself—with different methods and in different animals. The work concerned with long-term memory storage has focused on simple systems: the *Aplysia* and slices of hippocampal tissue. The work concerned with the consolidation process that initiates long-term memory storage has been done mainly on rats and monkeys. The question is, Can the results be combined? Is the structural change seen in the simple systems related to, indeed a result of, the consolidation mechanism observed in the more complex systems?

Gold has addressed this question with respect to consolidation and long-term potentiation in a very interesting experiment (Gold, Delanoy, & Merrin, 1984). His reasoning is as follows: if the structural change seen in long-term potentiation in hippocampal tissue is related to a consolidation process similar to the one seen in rats, then the mechanisms that govern one should also govern the other.

The procedure he has devised to test this hypothesis involves epinephrine, the hormone known to enhance memory consolidation in rats. If long-term potentiation is related to a process similar to memory consolidation, argues Gold, then long-term potentiation should be enhanced by epinephrine. Gold's findings confirm this hypothesis (Gold, Delanoy, & Merrin, 1984). Injections of epinephrine do indeed strengthen long-term potentiation in the same way that injections of epinephrine strengthen the consolidation of long-term memory.

In a sense, then, we have come full circle. We began, in Chapter 16, with memory storage—the long-lasting structural changes that are triggered by learning and that endure over time. We then examined, in this chapter, the process that initiates and regulates the change: the neurochemical events that mediate memory consolidation and ensure that we store important information. Now, to complete the picture, we have returned to the long-lasting change and its relation to the process that produces it and we have shown that indeed one (the long-lasting change) may derive from the other (consolidation).

From Animal Memory to Human Memory

We have seen that the animal experiments, be they simple or complex, have provided us with a wealth of information about the physiological basis of memory: the neural and chemical processes involved in the formation of memories, the modulatory circuit and the role it plays in promoting consolidation, and the hormones and neurotransmitters that someday may be used to treat memory disorders in humans.

One of the goals of this research is not only to understand the physiological basis of memory in lower animals but also to be able to use this knowledge to help people afflicted with memory disorders. And this brings us to the final question concerning memory consolidation: Can we assume that the same neural circuits, hormones, and neurotransmitters that control memory in lower animals control memory in humans?

This question is extremely difficult to answer. Like other forms of behavior, memory is far more complex in humans than in lower animals. Human memories are influenced by a variety of factors ranging from social pressures to fear and anxiety. Still, regardless of external influences, the ultimate control of human memory is internal. And just as disruption of the internal circuits of lower animals can disrupt memory, so too can disruption of the internal circuitry of humans have similar consequences. We shall now examine some of these consequences.

HUMAN MEMORY

Because of ethical considerations, memory experiments involving humans have been limited to purely external (i.e., nonphysiological) behavioral considerations, albeit with several important exceptions: individuals who have been given electroconvulsive shock therapy or who have suffered either a concussion from a head injury or brain damage through disease, surgery, or accident.

A number of studies involving such individuals have been carried out, and the data obtained from these studies have been valuable. They have indicated, among other things, that memory disorders experienced by such people have pathological roots in, and are specifically related to, brain structures that have been studied in lower animals. Thus the study of these individuals not only has established the basic ties between human and lower-animal memory but has also enabled psychologists and neurologists to uncover features of human memory that are simply not detectable in lower animals. Let us consider this human work.

Retrograde Amnesia in Humans: The Long Temporal Gradient

It is a matter of medical record that head injuries in humans often produce retrograde amnesia—a form of memory loss in which the victim has difficulty recalling memories of events that happened before the injury. Depending on the severity of the injury, the amnesia may extend to periods ranging from seconds to years.

In most instances, the amnesia is temporary and the memories gradually return, but in reverse order: older memories first and then newer memories. Eventually, nearly everything that happened before the injury might be recalled except the events that occurred immediately before the injury. For some reason, the memory of these events is often permanently lost (Russell, 1959). Figure 17.6 shows the extent of the amnesia and recovery that typically occurs.

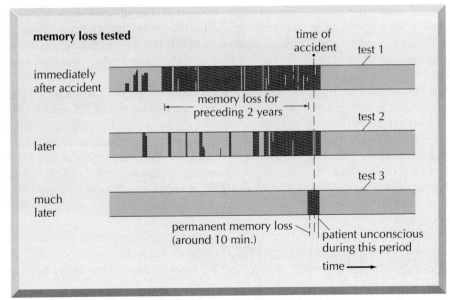

Figure 17.6 *Temporal Course of Amnesia in Humans*
Immediately after an accident a hypothetical patient shows memory loss extending back two years. In time the memories gradually return (the first to come back are the oldest), but recovery is not complete (loss of the most recent memories is permanent).

Clinical reports of this nature, however interesting, must be interpreted with care, for the data are usually based on rather general impressions culled from interviews and there is no way to determine their validity—no way, that is, to document the memory state of the subject, especially the state of distant memories, before or after the accident. For this reason, an experiment conducted by Larry Squire and his colleagues is of particular significance.

Squire's experiment was designed to examine the amnesic effects of electroconvulsive shock on relatively long-term human memories of events ranging from 1 to 17 years in the past (Squire, Slater, & Chase, 1975). To justify the use of human subjects in an electroconvulsive shock experiment, Squire used psychiatric patients who were about to undergo electroconvulsive therapy (ECT—see Chapter 15 for details) anyway to treat their depression. Tangential to the treatment for depression, but as an integral part of his experiment, Squire gave the subjects two retention tests: one 15 to 18 hours before and one 1 hour after the ECT treatments. He also gave the subjects a retention test 2 weeks later to check on the long-term amnesic effects.

The critical aspect of Squire's experiment was the test material he used. He asked his subjects to recall the names of specific television programs presented in a multiple-choice format. The programs he selected had been broadcast for only one season during the years from 1957 to 1972 (the experiment was conducted in 1974). By asking his subjects to recall verifiable events known to have occurred at specific times in the past, Squire was able to establish with some precision the age of each memory. And by asking the subjects to recall the memories twice, once before and once after ECT, he was able to determine exactly which memories were affected by ECT and which were not.

The results of Squire's study are shown in Figure 17.7, and two of the results are particularly noteworthy. First, he found that ECT selectively impaired retention of the more recent memories, even though these memories were at least a year old. His subjects, when tested after ECT, had difficulty recalling programs broadcast 1 to 3 years before the ECT treatment but had no difficulty (other than normal forgetting) recalling programs 4 to 17 years before the ECT treatment. In other words, the subjects showed retrograde amnesia that extended back 3 years but not beyond.

Second, Squire found that the retrograde amnesia was temporary. Patients tested 2 weeks after ECT treatment showed recovery of retention, recalling the more recent (1- to 3-year-old) as well as long-term (4- to 17-year-old) memories.

Squire's experiment thus introduces us to a second feature of retrograde amnesia—its temporary nature—although this feature does not oblige us to change our basic view of memory consolidation. Recovery notwithstanding, the more recent memories (the 1- to 3-year-old memories) were still more vulnerable to interference than the older memories (the 4- to 17-year-old memories). It is just that the interference in this case was temporary.

Why should the 1- to 3-year-old memories be temporarily disrupted and the 4- to 17-year-old memories not? The answer calls for two assumptions:

1. The 1- to 3-year-old memories were weaker than the 4- to 17-year-old memories because they were not as fully consolidated.
2. ECT produces neurological aftereffects that interfere with the ability to recall the weaker (1- to 3-year-old) but not the stronger memories, and within 2 weeks the aftereffects wear off and retention returns.

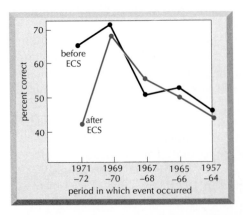

Figure 17.7 _Retrograde Amnesia in Humans_
Subjects received two retention tests, one before electroconvulsive therapy (ECT) and one after. (Data for a third test given 2 weeks later are not shown.) ECT impaired recall of programs broadcast 1 to 3 years before the treatment but had no effect on recall of programs broadcast 4 to 17 years before the treatment.

Squire's findings have confirmed what clinical observations have suggested all along: the time scale for retrograde amnesia in humans spans years, and as the victims recover from the trauma, distant memories tend to return. Squire's experiment, however, does not speak to the issue of very recent memories (i.e., memories of events immediately preceding the trauma), although clinical reports seem to indicate that such memories are lost forever. Thus we must assume that their consolidation has been permanently disrupted.

Summing Up

On the basis of Squire's results, we can begin to draw some general conclusions about how human memory changes over time. At first, immediately after learning, memory storage is vulnerable, and neural trauma can cause a permanent loss of memory. As time passes, however, memory storage becomes more and more resistant to interference. Even if the trauma disrupts some of the memories being stored, retention can still take place once the aftereffects of the trauma wear off. Finally, as more time passes, memory storage presumably reaches a point at which the trauma is unable to produce even a temporary loss.

Notice that as in the lower-animal work, we have avoided putting a time limit on consolidation. The time span for consolidation in humans is very long, but there is no way of determining just how long. Squire's findings indicate that retrograde amnesia reaches back 1 to 3 years. But his findings do not rule out the possibility that with more intense neural trauma retrograde amnesia may reach back still further. This aspect of the consolidation process remains indeterminate.

MEMORY IN BRAIN-DAMAGED HUMANS

Studies on lower animals, as we have seen, have implicated a number of brain areas in memory consolidation, chief among them the hippocampus and the surrounding temporal cortex. Some striking parallels have been discovered in brain-damaged humans. Let us consider the work that has brought these parallels to light.

Links between brain damage and human memory have been established on the basis of studies of individuals who have experienced brain damage in the temporal lobes of the cortex and neighboring areas, such as the thalamus, the hippocampus, the mammillary body, and the fornix. Such damage has been found to occur in chronic alcoholics who suffer from a condition known as *Korsakoff's psychosis* (Victor, Adams, & Collins, 1971) and in people suffering from Alzheimer's disease (see Chapter 2) and brain tumors (Ignelzi & Squire, 1976).

The best case studied by far, however, involves an individual known in the neurological literature only by his initials, H.M., who underwent brain surgery to alleviate epilepsy. It is of course risky to draw conclusions from one subject, but in this instance studies on other brain-damaged humans indicate similar behavioral patterns (Seltzer & Benson, 1974).

The reason H.M. underwent such drastic surgery to begin with was that his epileptic seizures became so severe that they could no longer be controlled through medication. In 1953 William Scoville, a renowned neurosurgeon, performed brain surgery in an attempt to stop the seizures (Scoville & Milner, 1957; Milner, 1970). The surgery consisted of excising parts of both temporal lobes, including two-thirds of the hippocampus, portions of the amygdala, and the surrounding temporal cortex.

The surgery had mixed results. On the one hand, it diminished the intensity of the seizures such that H.M. could control them with medication. On the other hand, it created a serious memory problem—so serious that H.M. was condemned to live the rest of his life virtually devoid of memories of recent events.

Anatomical Fine-Tuning: H.M. versus R.B.

The diffuse nature of H.M.'s damage—and this is a common problem when using human brain-damaged subjects in general—makes it difficult to pinpoint the precise area or areas of damage responsible for H.M.'s memory loss. The suspicion is that damage in the hippocampus is one of the main factors, and a recent study on another brain-damaged patient (known by the initials R.B.) supports this view (Zola-Morgan, Squire, & Amaral, 1986). Because of complications following heart surgery (there was a disruption of blood flow to R.B.'s brain caused by an atrial tear), R.B. suffered damage limited almost exclusively to the hippocampus (specifically to the CA 1 subfield in both hippocampi) and yet he showed memory loss similar to although milder than that of H.M.

But we must also introduce a word of caution. Although H.M.'s and R.B.'s behavior indicates that an intact hippocampus is important for normal memory, recent animal work, as mentioned earlier, points to the surrounding temporal cortex as being equally if not more important. Damage in the medial temporal cortex in monkeys, in the absence of hippocampal damage, results in severe memory loss measured in a non-matching-to-sample task (Zola-Morgan et al., 1989; Squire & Zola-Morgan, 1991). On the other hand, damage in the hippocampus, in the absence of medial temporal cortex damage, results in only a modest memory loss (Clower et al., 1991)—more in keeping with R.B.'s behavior. At this point the safest conclusion is that both the medial temporal cortex and the hippocampus are involved in memory processing and that H.M.'s memory loss may be the result of damage to both.

H.M.: A Closer Look at the Symptoms

At first glance, H.M. shows no apparent physical or personality disorders. His IQ is above normal (118), and he appears normal in conversation. Problems begin, though, as soon as he is asked to recall anything that has happened to him or has been said to him since the surgery. It then becomes apparent that H.M. has added very little to his memory for the past 40 years. If you introduce yourself to H.M., leave the room for a few minutes, and then return, he will act as if he has never seen you before.

H.M.'s primary problem is that he has great difficulty recalling any events that have happened since his surgery. Several months after the surgery, for example, his family moved, but H.M. was unable to recall the location of the new house and kept returning to the old one. H.M. can read the same book or do the same crossword puzzle over and over as if it were one he had never seen before. H.M.'s condition—his inability to remember events that happened *after* the surgery—is known as *antero-grade* (in a forward direction) *amnesia* (Rozin, 1976).

Memories after Surgery

It should be pointed out that H.M. is not totally amnesic with respect to new memories. He can retain very short-term memories, which enables him to carry on a normal conversation; he can remember what he has just said and what has been said to him. Soon, though, the memory slips away. Surprisingly, too, H.M. is able to recall more permanent, long-term memories (although this ability is very limited) of experiences that happened after his surgery. For example, he can learn and recall the mirror-tracing task, shown in Figure 17.8*a*, with the same speed and alacrity as normal subjects. And he can even learn to solve the puzzle known as the tower of Hanoi, shown in Figure 17.8*b*, which requires for-mulating and then recalling a rather higher-order cognitive strategy.

Even in these instances, however, his retention is not completely nor-mal. He can remember *how* to perform the task, but he cannot remem-ber ever having learned to do it. He denies, in fact, that he has ever learned it. In short, H.M. can learn and remember skills, be it perceptual-motor (mirror-tracing) or cognitive (tower of Hanoi), but he does not remember the specific learning experience—when, where, or how he came to acquire these skills. The question is, Why? Why are some long-term memories spared in H.M. and others not?

The answer, most researchers now agree, is that long-term memories fall into two categories which differ not only in content but also in the brain areas in which they are processed (Squire, 1986). Let us take a closer look.

Procedural and Declarative Memories:
A Comparison

The two types of memories we are referring to are known as procedural and declarative memories. *Procedural* memories are memories that occur automatically, outside conscious awareness. They are memories that relate to skills or procedures that involve certain motor or mental opera-tions. We use them when we drive a car or ride a bike. These are the memories that are preserved in H.M.

Declarative memories, on the other hand, are memories that do not occur automatically. These memories reside presumably in conscious awareness, and they must be actively recalled to have an impact on

a

b

Figure 17.8 *Procedural Memories*
(a) Mirror-drawing task. A subject traces the outline of a figure (in this case a star) viewed not directly but through a mirror. (b) The tower of Hanoi puzzle. A subject is required to move all the disks to another peg, one at a time, without placing a larger disk on top of a smaller disk.

behavior. If someone asks you what movie you saw last night, you can answer. The memory is there. You simply have to recall it and declare it. H.M. can't do this.

That one category of long-term memories is spared in H.M. and the other lost should come as no surprise. It suggests that the two types of memories—procedural and declarative—differ not only in content but also in the brain areas that process them. Declarative memories require the integrity of the medial temporal area, the brain area that is damaged in H.M. Procedural memories do not.

Procedural memories such as classical conditioning of an eyeblink, on the other hand, appear to require an intact cerebellum. Patients with damage to the cerebellum, like rabbits in the nictitating membrane experiment described in Chapter 16, can blink their eyes and hear a tone, but they cannot learn to associate the two (a procedural memory). Patients with damage to the medial temporal lobe, on the other hand, can learn the conditioned eyeblink response, but, like H.M., they cannot remember ever having learned the task (a declarative memory) (Weiskrantz & Warrington, 1979).

Memories before Surgery

While H.M.'s memories of most events—specifically declarative memories—never survive more than a few seconds, his memories of events *before* surgery remain relatively unaffected. He has difficulty remembering events that occurred within a 3-year period before surgery, and this retrograde amnesia is patchy and unpredictable. He cannot remember that his uncle died, for example, but he can remember other things. Furthermore, his ability to recall events that occurred more than 3 years before the surgery is excellent. For example, he can recount in detail experiences that he had during his early schooldays.

How do we explain this pattern? Why is H.M. able to recall events that took place long ago in his life yet is unable to recall events that occurred only seconds before? One plausible explanation is that the role of the medial temporal cortex—the brain area in which H.M. has sustained damage—is not to *hold* memory in long-term storage but rather is to *put* (that is, consolidate) memory into long-term storage (Squire, 1992). This explanation would account for why H.M. can recall long-term memories—they are held in sites outside the damage—and it would also account for why H.M. cannot recall recent events for more than a few seconds. Without an intact medial temporal cortex, H.M. is unable to consolidate these memories, and they are simply lost.

In summary, as illustrated in Figure 17.9, H.M.'s memory disorder has three characteristics. The major symptom is anterograde amnesia—loss of memory for events that occurred after surgery. A second symptom is retrograde amnesia—loss of memory for events that occurred within 3 years before surgery. His ability to retain distant events, however, is normal. By any measure, H.M.'s condition is horrific. He has expressed himself as follows:

> Every day is alone in itself. Whatever enjoyment I've had, whatever sorrow I've had. . . . Right now, I'm wondering, have I done or said anything amiss? You see, at this moment everything looks clear to me, but what happened just before? That's what worries me. It's like waking from a dream. I just don't remember (Rozin, 1976, p. 6; Milner, 1970).

H.M.: A Final Look

The prevailing view among memory researchers today is that the memory problems manifested by H.M. and other amnesic patients suffering from anterograde amnesia are the result of a consolidation deficit trig-

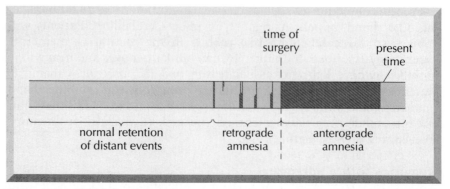

Figure 17.9 *H.M.'s Symptoms*
The most serious symptom is anterograde amnesia—loss of memory for events after surgery. Less serious is retrograde amnesia—loss of memory for events that occur within 3 years before surgery. Retention of distant events is normal.

gered by damage to those brain areas that control consolidation. It is generally assumed, too, as we saw earlier, that the brain damage interferes with declarative memories, not procedural memories. It is worth emphasizing, however, that this view is still very much evolving and one of the factors that has figured prominently in this evolution is a phenomenon referred to as the *priming effect*.

The Impact of the Priming Effect

In the mid-1970s researchers working with H.M. and other brain-damaged patients suffering from anterograde amnesia made a discovery that appeared at first to call into question the declarative-procedural dichotomy. They found that if amnesic patients taking a simple word recall test were "primed"—that is, were given a fragment of a word that they saw earlier as a hint and then told to say the first word that came into their minds—they were able to recall words that they weren't able to remember during a normal free-recall test (i.e., when they were asked to recall the words, but without hints).

These results—the fact that brain-damaged people with anterograde amnesia were able, under certain circumstances, to recall memories (specifically memories that appeared to fall into the declarative category)—called into question the basic notion that H.M. and other anterograde amnesic patients were unable to store (that is, to consolidate) declarative memories.

The results also led some researchers to revise their thinking on the source of anterograde amnesia. One of the early assumptions among researchers working with H.M. and other amnesic patients was that the anterograde amnesia they were observing was the result of a consolidation failure, triggered by damage in those brain areas that control consolidation. The priming effect results, however, led some researchers to suggest that the capacity of H.M. and other amnesic patients to consolidate declarative memories might not be as diminished as had originally been thought. This view, known as the *weak-consolidation theory*, proposed that the brain damage found in H.M. and in other amnesic patients didn't necessarily destroy the brain's ability to consolidate memory but may have simply weakened this ability. It was possible, in other words, that memories originally thought to be lost could be recovered if the recall efforts could somehow compensate for the weaker storage. Priming was thought to represent this compensating factor (Warrington & Weiskrantz, 1970; Rozin, 1976b).

The implications of the weak-consolidation theory were profound. They raised the possibility that selective prompting could recover weakly stored memories and, by doing so, minimize the behavioral effects of amnesia. More recently, however, a newer theory has come to supplant the weak-consolidation theory as the explanation behind the priming effect. This newer theory, which began to emerge in the early 1980s and has continued to evolve since then reaffirms the earlier belief that H.M. and amnesics with similar brain damage do indeed suffer from a serious disruption in their ability to consolidate, and it maintains the dichotomy between the two types of memories: procedural and declarative (Graf et al., 1984; Squire, 1992). Where it differs from the weak-consolidation theory is in its explanation of the priming effect. According to this newer view, the memories that are recalled through priming are not declarative memories that have been weakly stored but are, in fact, a unique category of procedural memories that have come to be referred to as *implicit memory* (Schacter, 1987).

Priming Effect: A Closer Look

To understand this theory—why primed memories fall into the procedural and not the declarative category—you first need to understand the nature of the two types of recall tasks used in the priming experiments: priming and free-recall.

In the priming task, a brain-damaged subject is presented with a fragment of a word he or she has seen before and is instructed to say the *first* thing that comes to mind. The response is automatic and unconscious—not unlike a reflex response. During the free-recall task, a correct response requires a different mode. The subject is not given the fragment of a word to respond to but instead is asked to picture the word that he or she has seen before. Here the response is not automatic but rather the subject must search for the memory and must somehow bring it into conscious awareness.

Given this difference between the two recall tasks, we are now able to understand why primed memories are considered procedural memories: they are automatic and unconscious. And we are also able to answer the question why H.M. and other brain-damaged patients are able to recall memories during priming but not during free recall: primed memories (as is with all procedural memories) do not depend for recall on the brain areas that are damaged.

Evidence for the theory. The view that primed memories are spared in brain-damaged patients and free-recall memories are not is based on one key assumption. That primed memories (because they are procedural memories) and recalled memories (because they are declarative memories) are stored in different areas of the brain. Until recently there was no direct evidence for this assumption. Now thanks to the work of Larry Squire and his colleagues, there is (Squire et al., 1992).

Using a PET-scan procedure, Squire and his colleagues monitored brain activity in normal (non-brain-damaged) subjects while the subjects engaged in priming and free-recall tasks and they found significant differences in the brain areas activated during each task. When the subjects were asked simply to recall the words (that is, to consciously remember the words they had seen on a list) the PET scan revealed that the two most active areas were the hippocampus and the prefrontal cortex—the areas that are often damaged in anterograde amnesia patients. When the subjects were primed and asked to respond with the first word that came to mind, without conscious thought, changes in activity were noted in the visual cortex—areas that are not damaged in anterograde amnesia patients. Squire's work thus goes a long way to confirm the notion that there are indeed two memory systems, one for procedural and one for declarative. And Squire's work also provides added evidence that H.M. and other brain-damaged people experiencing anterograde amnesia suffer from the same deficit: an inability to consolidate and store declarative memories that are rooted in brain areas outside those that control procedural memories.

MEMORY RETRIEVAL

Until now we have been treating the subject of amnesia as if the inability to remember were tied to one deficit—the consolidation of memory into long-term storage. The matter is not quite that simple. It is possible that when individuals are unable to remember, memory storage remains but the ability to retrieve it is lost. Evidence for this hypothesis comes not only from the laboratory but also from everyday experience.

We all know what it is like to experience memory blocks at one time or another. Unable to recall a familiar event, we often give up. Later, for no apparent reason, the missing memory suddenly returns. Since we have no opportunity between the time of the block and the time of recall to relearn the information, it is reasonable to conclude that the memory storage has been present all along but that the ability to retrieve it is not.

You might wonder why scientists are concerned about this matter. Why is it so important to know that retention may depend on an interaction between memory storage and memory retrieval? The reason is that many researchers now believe that once we are better able to understand this interaction—particularly the retrieval process—we will come to better understand the mystery behind more common memory problems such as forgetting.

Forgetting

One of the first clear demonstrations of the retrieval process at work in controlling forgetting came about fortuitously, from observations made by the great neurosurgeon Wilder Penfield (Penfield, 1958). Neurosurgeons routinely prepare patients for surgery by first administering electrical stimulation to the brain while the patients are still awake. This stimulation, which enables the surgeon to map the behavioral function of the tissue lying in and around the diseased area of the brain, produces discrete movements of the limbs as well as sensations. But much to Penfield's surprise (and to the surprise of the scientific world), electrical stimulation of the temporal lobes also induced patients to verbalize vivid memories of past experiences, memories that were simply not accessible to recall in the normal course of events. Some of Penfield's patients found themselves recalling, for example, songs they had learned in their childhood, indicating that although information may be forgotten, much of it remains stored and can be retrieved by electrical stimulation.

Penfield's work, interesting though it is, has not been universally accepted. The problem—and it is a serious problem—is that the recollections of his patients have never been verified (Loftus & Loftus, 1980). It is conceivable, in other words, that the memories elicited by the electrical stimulation were not memories at all but hallucinations or fabrications: there is no practical way of telling. The animal work on retrieval of course carries with it no such problems. Let us now consider the most important examples of this work.

Chemical Control of Retrieval

J. Anthony Deutsch has done as much as anyone else to bring the analysis of the retrieval process into the animal laboratory (Deutsch, 1983). Deutsch's general approach has consisted of producing a clear-cut case of forgetting in laboratory rats and then determining what chemicals are capable of "restoring" the seemingly lost memory.

The Role of Acetylcholine

One of Deutsch's most significant findings to date has been that "lost" memories can be "recovered" by means of a neurotransmitter-sensitive drug injected into the hippocampus. The drug he used—diisopropyl fluorophosphate (DFP)—increased the level of acetylcholine in the nervous system by reducing the levels of acetylcholinesterase, the enzyme that destroys acetylcholine. Deutsch found that animals trained to avoid shock by choosing the correct path in a maze tended to forget the discrimination when tested 28 days later. But other animals injected with DFP just before the test on day 28 tended to show retention.

The Paradox

Although an increase in acetylcholine levels appears to boost retrieval of forgotten memories, it also has a curious effect on normal memories.

Deutsch found that retention in normally trained rats reached its maximum about 14 days after training. When the animals were injected with the acetylcholine booster at this time, they became amnesic (Deutsch & Leibowitz, 1966).

A paradox? Indeed. But Deutsch explains it in a convincing way. Synaptic function, he points out, can be inactivated in one of two ways: a deficiency of acetylcholine or an excess of acetylcholine. An acetylcholine deficiency impedes proper depolarization. An excess triggers prolonged depolarization and puts the synapse into a prolonged refractory period.

Operating on this basic assumption, Deutsch contends that 14 days after training animals were normally under optimal levels of acetylcholine. This would explain why they retained so well, and it also would explain why additional boosts of acetylcholine at this time produced amnesia. Additional acetylcholine added to the optimal level, thus producing an excess that resulted in a synaptic block. Twenty-eight days after the training, when the animals normally had forgotten, acetylcholine levels presumably showed a substantial deficiency. An injection of acetylcholine at this time boosted the acetylcholine to an optimal level.

Central to the acetylcholine explanation of retrieval advanced by Deutsch is the idea that the retrieval process calls for sensitive synapses and that, as time passes, sensitivity diminishes. This change in sensitivity would presumably explain why acetylcholine restores retention: it restores synaptic sensitivity.

STRENGTHENING RETRIEVED MEMORIES

We would be remiss if we ended this chapter without mentioning one of the more puzzling yet fascinating features of the retrieval process. We may have conveyed the impression that the retrieval process serves only one function—the recall of specific memories. Evidence, however, indicates that retrieval may serve still another function: it not only produces recall of a particular memory but also strengthens the storage of that memory. Let us look more closely at the evidence for this phenomenon.

Experiments on lower animals indicate that memories that have just been retrieved during a retention test are subject to the same type of interference (retrograde amnesia) and the same type of facilitation (retrograde facilitation) as newly learned memories. If, for example, electroconvulsive shock is given shortly after a retention test (just as when it is given shortly after a training trial), amnesia occurs the next day. If electroconvulsive shock is delayed, however, it has no effect on the animal (Lewis, 1979). The same pattern prevails with brain stimulation and with drugs that produce neural arousal, except that the effect of these treatments is to facilitate rather than to impair retention (DeVietti & Kirkpatrick, 1976). These findings indicate that consolidation is not limited to strengthening newly learned memories; it also applies to strengthening newly retrieved memories (Gordon, 1977).

This brings us to the final question regarding retrieval: What function, if any, is served by memories being strengthened during the retrieval process? The theory—and it is still highly speculative—is that it makes a certain amount of adaptive sense for a memory to be strengthened every time it is recalled, and a consolidation process during retrieval would serve such a function.

MEMORY: A PSYCHOLOGICAL PERSPECTIVE

Now that you have a basic idea of how information is stored and retrieved in the nervous system, let us consider the behavioral advantages inherent in having two processes. More specifically, we want to look at how adaptive behavior is enhanced by having information pass through a *series* of psychological filters, beginning with short-term memory and ending with retrieval (see Figure 17.10).

The answer to this question is directly related to the sheer volume of stimuli to which we are exposed each day and to the corresponding need to screen out extraneous stimuli and focus on those stimuli relevant to our needs and wants. If we were to store in memory every experience, we would be so overwhelmed by information that we could not possibly respond selectively. This is why consolidation is so important. The fact that information must be consolidated—that is, the nervous system must be aroused—before it is put into long-term storage helps ensure that only significant information will be stored.

Retrieval also serves a regulatory purpose: it establishes a sense of priority for memories in long-term storage. As information stored in long-term memory—childhood memories, for instance—loses its significance to our everyday lives, our ability to retrieve it diminishes (i.e., we forget). Should the information become important again, we would be able to relearn it with relative ease simply because it is still stored.

Thus a fail-safe system of sorts is built into the nervous system. Whether information enters our consciousness as a long-term memory depends primarily on its significance. Information that is significant is stored and remembered. Once information becomes insignificant, it is forgotten.

SUMMARY

1. *Memory defined.* Memory is the process by which we are able to make behavioral use of previously learned information. The assumption that underlies the study of this process is that memory involves structural changes that take place in the nervous system *during* learning and that endure. Another basic assumption is that there are two distinct memory systems: short-term memory and long-term memory. Essential to our understanding of memory is an understanding of how information moves from short-term to long-term memory storage.

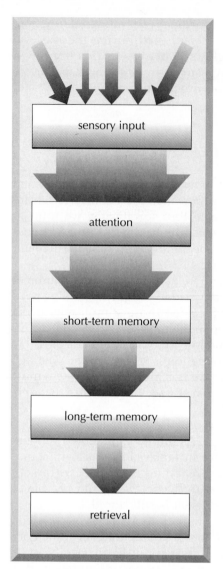

Figure 17.10 *Entry into Long-Term Memory*
The funneling of information begins at the sensory level and ends with long-term memory storage and retrieval. The width of the arrows represents the amount of information and the boxes represent the filters through which the information must pass. Presumably the more significant the information is, the more likely it is to reach long-term memory storage and retrieval.

2. *Memory consolidation.* Memory research today is based on the theory—known as memory consolidation—that the transformation of short-term memory to long-term memory is gradual, and that memory is more vulnerable to interference in the early stages than in later stages. Evidence for this theory comes from observations of victims of head injuries, who can recall long-ago events but cannot recall anything that happened immediately before the trauma. This memory deficiency is known as retrograde amnesia. Animal work seeking to study the physiological basis of memory consolidation generally involves training animals and then disrupting neural activity at various times after the learning. Studies have shown that varying the time between learning and electroconvulsive shock influences an animal's ability to remember, but other studies show that the so-called retrograde amnesia gradient can vary according to the type and amount of disruptive agent used. These findings indicate that memory consolidation is a gradual rather than a fixed process.

3. *Isolating brain areas.* Studies designed to isolate the areas of the brain in which consolidation takes place make it necessary to confine disruption to specific sites. These studies have singled out several areas, among them the amygdala, the midbrain reticular formation, and the hippocampus. Disruption in these areas produces retrograde amnesia. What remains to be resolved is whether these areas are themselves the site of consolidation or simply parts of a circuit that serves to modulate (facilitate or inhibit) the process.

4. *The arousal hypothesis.* The arousal hypothesis of memory consolidation holds that the strength of memory consolidation depends on the level of neural activity in the brain during the consolidation process. Drug studies have confirmed this theory by showing that when stimulants are given immediately after training, they facilitate retention but have no effect when delayed. The same pattern has been produced by injections of norepinephrine, of hormones such as ACTH, epinephrine, and vasopressin, and by electrical stimulation to certain areas of the brain, in particular the amygdala and reticular formation. The fact that stimulation of some of these areas has also been shown to produce retrograde amnesia indicates that the level of stimulation is important. Higher intensities produce disruption. Lower intensities produce facilitation.

5. *Focusing on epinephrine.* The one chemical substance whose effect on memory has been studied the most extensively is epinephrine, a hormone released during behavioral arousal. Injections of epinephrine have been shown to enhance memory in very young and very old rats. Epinephrine has also been shown in some studies to enhance learning under anesthesia.

6. *How epinephrine works.* The ability of epinephrine to enhance memory has been linked to its ability to stimulate the vagus nerve and to promote the production of glucose. Supporting this notion is the fact that glucose itself has been shown to facilitate memory in a way that parallels the action of epinephrine.

7. *REM sleep and memory consolidation.* There is growing evidence that the arousal properties of REM sleep may play a key role in consolidation. Animals deprived of REM sleep show retrograde amnesia, and the same pattern holds for humans. The precise role that REM sleep plays in consolidation is not yet known, but two conditions that occur during REM sleep—an active brain and the release of norepinephrine—are consistent with the arousal hypothesis of memory consolidation.

8. *The where and the what of memory.* A series of experiments on monkeys has suggested that different aspects of memory are under the control of different areas of the brain. The studies make a distinction between the ability of the monkeys to remember *what* stimulus was involved in the initial learning and *where* the stimulus has been placed. Monkeys with damage to the medial temporal cortex do not perform well on tasks designed to measure their ability to remember the stimulus involved in the initial learning. Monkeys with damage to the frontal lobe (specifically the sulcus principalis) are impaired in remembering where the stimulus is located.

9. *Combining the processes.* Research into the physiological basis of memory can be divided into two areas: *Aplysia* and long-term potentiation work (designed to uncover the structural basis of long-term memory), and rat and monkey work (designed to uncover the neural and chemical processes that underlie memory consolidation). There have been attempts to bridge the two areas and the findings suggest that the two processes—long-term potentiation and memory consolidation—are indeed related.

10. *Human implications.* Much of what we know about the physiology of human memory is based on studies of people who have suffered brain damage or neural trauma. Memory research involving such individuals has paralleled the findings involving lower animals. Observations of human amnesia victims, for instance, reveal a pattern similar to the retrograde amnesia produced in animals subjected to neural disruption. A study on psychiatric patients receiving electroconvulsive therapy found that the shock selectively impairs retention of recent memories (1- to 3-year-old memories) but not long-term memories, and that the retrograde amnesia is temporary.

11. *The case of H.M.* One individual whose memory deficits have been studied extensively is known in the neurological literature as H.M., an epileptic who underwent surgery to excise parts of both temporal lobes. H.M. has an above-normal IQ and appears normal in conversation, but has great difficulty recalling anything that has happened to him since the surgery—a condition known as anterograde amnesia. Observations on H.M., coupled with other studies, have raised the possibility that there are two different types of memories, each involving different areas of the brain. One type, known as procedural memories, occurs automatically, outside of conscious awareness, and appears to require, among other areas, an intact cerebellum. The other type, known as declarative memories, must be actively recalled and require an intact temporal lobe. This view draws support from studies showing that people with damage to the cerebellum suffer from deficits in procedural memory whereas people with damage to the temporal lobe (like H.M.) can learn to perform a certain task but have no recollection of having learned it.

12. *The priming effect.* When H.M. and other brain-damaged patients suffering from anterograde amnesia are given hints in a word-recall test—that is, fragments of the word they are being asked to recall—they show retention. This ability—generally referred to as the priming effect—was originally explained in terms of weak consolidation, the view being that priming facilitated the recall of weakly consolidated memories. Newer work, however, suggests that primed memories are a special kind of procedural memory, known as implicit memory, and are recalled automatically outside of consciousness. According to this view, H.M. and other brain-damaged patients who are helped by priming are able to do so because of brain areas outside of those that are damaged. Evidence gathered using PET scans confirms this view.

13. *Why we forget.* Evidence that forgetting is a retrieval problem comes from observations of both humans and lower animals. Wilder Penfield found that electrical stimulation of the temporal lobes in humans elicits recall of otherwise forgotten memories, but his findings left open the question of whether the memories were actual or hallucinations. J. Anthony Deutsch has extended the analysis by showing that in rats, forgotten memories can be restored by injections of diisopropyl fluorophosphate, a drug that increases acetylcholine.

14. *Strengthening retrieved memories.* Memories that are in the process of being retrieved appear to be governed by the same consolidation process that governs newly-learned memories, that is, they are subject to the same type of interference (retrograde amnesia) and the same type of facilitation (retrograde facilitation).

KEY TERMS

adrenocorticotrophic hormone
  (ACTH)
amygdala
anterograde amnesia
declarative memories
electroconvulsive shock (ECS)
hippocampus
implicit memory
infantile amnesia
Korsakoff's psychosis
long-term memory
long-term potentiation
medial temporal cortex
memory consolidation

midbrain reticular formation
morphine
naloxone
norepinephrine
priming effect
procedural memories
REM sleep
retrieval
retrograde amnesia
retrograde facilitation
short-term memory
stria terminalis
sulcus principalis
vasopressin

SUGGESTED READINGS

Martinez, J. L., & Kesner, R. P. (Eds.) *Learning and Memory: A Biological View*. San Diego, CA: Academic Press, 1991.

Squire, L. R., *Memory and Brain*. Oxford: Oxford University Press, 1987.

18

LOCALIZATION OF HIGHER-ORDER FUNCTION

INTRODUCTION

We began this book by pointing out that the basic purpose of physiological psychology is to understand the relationship between the brain and behavior. Now that you have reached this final chapter, you should well appreciate the complexity of this relationship. You know by now that when we talk about the brain, we are talking about two things: how it is structured and how it works—that is, the electrochemical activity that takes place within it. You also know that the relationship between specific behaviors and these two aspects of the brain—structure and function—is rarely clear-cut.

It is possible of course to draw connections between specific areas of the brain and specific behaviors—the hypothalamus with feeding and drinking, the amygdala with emotion, the hippocampus with learning and memory, and so on. But as we have stressed all along, these areas do not exercise *exclusive* control of these behaviors: they are simply some of the areas that are most extensively involved.

Similarly, you know by now that chemistry is involved in one way or another in all behaviors, but that no one chemical—that is, no single neurotransmitter—controls a single behavior. Neurotransmitters have multiple effects. No single neurotransmitter, as far as we know, works in only one area of the brain, and different areas of the brain are involved in different behaviors.

Our concern in this final chapter is with the one area of the brain that we have yet to consider in any great detail—the cortex. We will focus on three areas of the cortex: the frontal, the temporal, and the parietal lobes. As Figure 18.1 indicates, these three areas contain what are known as the *association areas*, and it is safe to say that these association areas, more than any others, underlie the behavioral capacities that distinguish humans from other higher animals.

CORTICAL LOCALIZATION: A HISTORICAL PERSPECTIVE

The idea that higher-order behaviors are rooted in specific areas of the cortex is known as *cortical localization*, and it has its basis in a theory (briefly discussed in Chapter 1) proposed more than a century ago by Franz Gall and popularized by Kasper Spurzheim. Until then the brain had been thought to act as a whole: to be a single organ without differential function. Gall and Spurzheim were among the first to propose that different areas of the brain control different behaviors. That theory has since become known as the *localization-of-function* theory.

That Gall and Spurzheim were essentially correct in the broad outline but not in the details of their theory is now taken for granted. Different areas of the brain, as we have seen, do indeed exert control over different behaviors. As we pointed out in Chapter 1, however, Gall and Spurzheim submitted as "proof" of their position a theory that has long

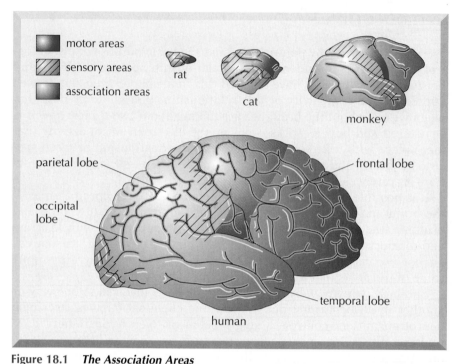

Figure 18.1 *The Association Areas*
The cerebral hemispheres of four mammals. Note the relative increase in the amount of cortex devoted to the association areas.

since been discredited. Known as *phrenology*, this theory held that the size and position of bumps on the skull reflected the size of underlying brain areas and could be used to determine the strength of specific personality traits.

The fact that phrenology was attacked from the beginning as having no scientific basis is significant because it served to discredit the localization-of-function theory in general, never mind that clinical evidence from brain-damaged people clearly indicated a connection between various areas of the brain and specific behaviors. Indeed, it is one of the supreme ironies of physiological psychology that one of the most celebrated figures in the science, Karl Lashley, was in many ways responsible for perpetuating a line of thinking that argued *against* a theory that has since proven itself to be essentially correct—at least where higher animals are concerned.

Lashley, as we mentioned in Chapter 16, began his experimental work with the idea of confirming Pavlov's theory of association circuits in the cortex. He spent the rest of his career advancing the notion that the brain operates by and large as a whole. Lashley had good reason to believe this, for his studies showed that destroying specific areas of the cortex in rats does not necessarily disrupt specific behaviors other than sensory or motor functions. What Lashley did not know (and could not have known, given the limitations of his approach) was that what holds true for cortical function in lower animals (rats, for example) does not often hold true for higher animals, in particular monkeys and humans.

The Cortex: Cataloging the Behavioral Effects

Today we know from experiments involving monkeys that the cortex of monkeys reflects far more localization of function than the cortex of rats. These studies clearly show that various areas in the frontal, temporal, and parietal cortex of the monkey have direct influence on a variety of behaviors. Damage to the frontal cortex, for example, produces abnormal emotional and aggressive behavior as well as deficits in short-term memory for the location of a stimulus (see Chapters 14 and 17) (Zola-Morgan, 1989; Rosenkilde, 1979). Damage to the temporal cortex produces selective deficits in short-term memory for the identity of a stimulus (see Chapter 17) (Zola-Morgan, 1989). And damage to the parietal cortex affects not only memory, but a specific type of visual memory, and attention (Mishkin, Ungerleider, & Macko, 1983; Wurtz & Goldman, 1989).

Localization in the Human Cortex

Studies on brain-damaged humans have roughly paralleled those on monkeys. When specific areas of the cortex are damaged, through illness or injury, specific behaviors are lost. Humans who have undergone the procedure known as prefrontal lobotomy, discussed in Chapter 14, manifest a calm and a loss of short-term memory that is similar to that of monkeys whose frontal lobes have been ablated (Goldman-Rakic, 1987). H.M. and other brain-damaged patients whose temporal lobes have been removed or damaged show memory deficits that parallel those of monkeys who have undergone a similar procedure (see Chapter 17).

There is, however, one important difference between the behavior of brain-damaged monkeys and brain-damaged humans, and this difference represents the theme of this chapter. We know from Chapter 3 that the brain of all higher animals is bilaterally symmetrical, consisting of two hemispheres. Each hemisphere has its own motor, sensory, and association cortex, its own hypothalamus, thalamus, basal ganglia, and so forth. Given this redundancy, it is not surprising that with only a handful of exceptions [the singing ability of birds (Nottenbohm, 1980), for instance], damage to one side of the brain has relatively minimal effects on the behavior of experimental animals and is usually confined to sensory or motor processes.

Humans are different. When damage is confined to one side of the human brain, the resulting behavioral loss can be devastating, especially when damage occurs in the cortex. Damage to the right parietal lobe, for instance, in humans produces an attentional deficit so bizarre (as we will see later) that patients ignore the left side of their environment including their own body. Damage to the left temporal lobe severely disrupts the ability to learn verbal material but doesn't disrupt the ability to recall pictures of faces. Damage to the right temporal lobe, on the other hand, produces just the opposite effect—disruption of perceptual but not of verbal learning (Milner, 1968, 1972).

We will not attempt to elaborate at this point on the differences between humans and other higher animals other than to say that hemispheric division obviously plays a much greater role in humans than it does in other animals. One of the primary goals of this chapter is to identify the behavioral differences between the right and left sides of the human brain.

LANGUAGE AND THE CORTEX: LEANING TO THE LEFT

Most behaviors are under the control of both cerebral hemispheres. Language is one of the notable exceptions. In an estimated 97 percent of all human beings, language is controlled by the left hemisphere. For this reason, language affords a useful starting point for our exploration of the differences between the left and right sides of the human brain.

The discovery that only one hemisphere controls language was made, rather by accident, in the 1860s, by the French physician Pierre Broca. Broca performed autopsies on several patients who had suffered from a speech disorder known as *aphasia* (the inability to speak) and found a consistent pattern of damage to a small area in the left hemisphere— the *third frontal gyrus of the left cerebral cortex*. Before this discovery, researchers had long speculated on the relationship between the brain and speech, but Broca was one of the first to document it clinically. The area Broca isolated is now commonly referred to as *Broca's area*. A few years later he observed (again in postmortem studies) that some of his patients whose speech had been normal had comparable damage in the right hemisphere but no damage in the left hemisphere. This difference provided the initial evidence that speech is a left-hemisphere function.

Not long after Broca made his discoveries, Carl Wernicke found that damage to an area outside Broca's area was also capable of producing a speech disorder, albeit one that had a curious nature. Wernicke found that patients with damage to the *posterior part of the first temporal convolution* spoke rapidly and grammatically but tended to mix up words and the sounds that make up words. This problem was accompanied by a severe loss of comprehension. Patients could hear words but could not understand them. The area Wernicke isolated is now commonly referred to as *Wernicke's area*.

Figure 18.2 shows the location of both Broca's and Wernicke's areas. Not shown in Figure 18.2 but important to note is that a region of the temporal lobe that is contained in Wernicke's area—an area known as the *planum temporale*—is larger in the left hemisphere than in the right in roughly 65 percent of the human brains examined. The larger area in the left hemisphere has generally been assumed to reflect the more elaborate neural connections involved in the control of language (Geschwind & Levitsky, 1968).

The Wernicke Model

On the basis of his own and Broca's observations, Wernicke proposed a neural model for language that, for all intents and purposes, has held up to this day. The key to this model lies in the way he divided the control of language between neural structures in Broca's area and those in the area he had discovered.

Wernicke proposed two language centers: one controlling articulation (the ability to speak) and the other controlling comprehension. Because Broca's area is next to cortical areas controlling the muscles that produce speech (see Figure 18.2), Wernicke theorized that Broca's area is the *articulation center*, controlling the muscle movement necessary for speech. He viewed his own area as a *comprehension center*. Its function, in Wernicke's view, is to draw input from both the auditory cortex and the visual cortex and, by doing so, to control the comprehension of spoken and written language, respectively. But why would damage to a comprehension center produce garbled speech? Wernicke answered that this was due to the loss of the ability to monitor speech for errors, a function normally accomplished through the comprehension system.

The test of any good model, as you should appreciate by now, is how well it accounts for the existing data. By this measure, Wernicke's model fares well (Geschwind, 1967). Indeed it accounts for data involving con-

Figure 18.2 *The Language Areas*
Confined usually to the left hemisphere are Broca's area, which is thought to be involved in the production but not the comprehension of language, and Wernicke's area, which is thought to be involved in the comprehension but not the production of language.

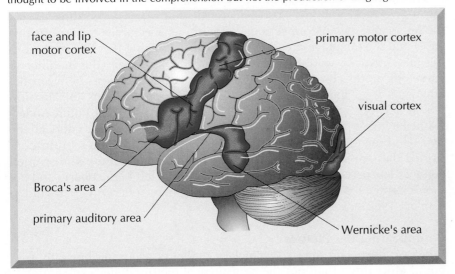

ditions that were not even known in his day. Let us now consider some of these disorders.

Alexia: Writing, Yes; Reading, No

Some brain-damaged people are able to write yet are unable to read. This inability to read is known as *alexia*, and people who suffer from it are known as *alexics*. What is unusual about alexics is that they are able to copy the very letters and words that they are unable to read.

Wernicke's model provides a possible explanation for this apparent paradox. The model makes two predictions. The first is that the alexic's visual cortex and language centers are intact but that the connections between them are disrupted. The disruption would explain how visual stimuli—such as written words—can be seen but not read. Second, the model predicts that the connections between the visual and motor cortices (areas that control hand movement) are *not* disrupted, which would explain how visual stimuli can be traced or copied.

Postmortem analysis tends to confirm these predictions. Alexics often, but not always, have lesions in pathways between the visual cortex and language centers but not between the visual cortex and motor centers.

Apraxia: Responding, Yes; Obeying, No

Apraxia has been defined as a disorder characterized by the inability to carry out a simple motor response to a verbal command (Geschwind, 1975). In the early 1960s Norman Geschwind and Edith Kaplan reported on a patient who had no apparent problems with motor coordination or hearing yet could not respond to a verbal command that required him to use his left hand (Geschwind & Kaplan, 1962). If the patient had to do nothing but simply imitate a certain motion, such as combing his hair with his left hand, there was no problem, ruling out the possibility that he was physically unable to carry out the motor response. Moreover, he was able to follow instructions involving the right hand.

This disorder can be explained—theoretically, at any rate—by returning to Wernicke's model. You will recall that alexia, according to this model, occurs when connections between sensory areas (vision, in this case) and the language area are disrupted. Following this line of reasoning (as Wernicke would have probably done), apraxia (the inability to carry out motor commands) occurs when the connections between the language area and the motor cortex are damaged. This explanation would account for why Geschwind and Kaplan's patient could understand language and make motor responses but could not connect the two. Here again, postmortem examination of the patient's brain confirmed these predictions. The lesion in the patient's brain had disrupted connections between the language center (in the left hemisphere) and the motor center for the left hand (in the right hemisphere) (Geschwind & Kaplan, 1962).

Complicating the Picture

What we have said about Wernicke's model is accurate, but only to a point. More often than not the neurological picture defies explanation—

by Wernicke's model or any other (Gardner, 1975). Many people with apraxia fail to imitate movements, a fact which is not explained by the disconnection from language centers. Some people with alexia can read some types of words but not others (for example, the noun "bee" but not the verb "be"). And some people who suffer injuries to the parietal and occipital lobes of the left hemisphere are often able to understand certain types of sentences but not others (Luria, 1973).

Wernicke's model does not account for these behaviors. Nor does it explain one of the most curious aspects of brain damage to language areas: the fact that the effect of brain damage on language is sometimes temporary.

The Plasticity of Language Control

To say that language is under the control of the left hemisphere in an estimated 97 percent of all people is accurate but perhaps misleading. The overall picture is not quite that simple.

To begin with, the relationship between language and hemisphere control varies with age. Although the left hemisphere preferentially controls speech and language processing from birth, the right hemisphere is able to take over in cases where the left hemisphere is damaged, at least during childhood. This is because of the relative plasticity of the cerebral cortex during the first 10 years of life. It is worth emphasizing, however, that even though the right hemisphere can assume some language functions when the left hemisphere is damaged, it doesn't process language nearly as well as an intact left hemisphere (Dennis, Lovett & Wiegel-Crump, 1981). The older the child is when left-hemisphere damage occurs, the harder it becomes for the undamaged hemisphere to assume control of language. And beyond a certain point, damage to the left hemisphere (and, in rare cases, to the right) produces irreversible aphasia.

This pattern, interestingly, differs in left-handed people. Left-handers are far more likely than right-handers to have language centers in their right hemispheres. Even more interesting is the fact that damage to the hemisphere that controls language in left-handed adults often produces only *temporary* aphasia, indicating that the plasticity present during childhood has remained (Kertesz, 1979).

LOCALIZATION OF PERCEPTION: LEANING TO THE RIGHT

Now that you know something about the left hemisphere and the role it plays in language, let us consider the behavioral specializations of the right hemisphere. Because of the relatively minor role it plays in the control of speech behavior, the right hemisphere is sometimes referred to as the "minor" hemisphere, but don't let the term "minor" mislead you.

The right hemisphere plays a vital role in perception: it controls a particular type of perceptual process involving spatial relations and patterns. It is the right hemisphere, much more so than the left, that enables us to recognize the jumble of lines and angles of a structure as a "house" and to recognize the hodgepodge of facial features—the eyes, the nose, the mouth, the chin, and so on—as a "face," and, more importantly, the face belonging to someone we know. The right hemisphere does this, presumably, through its ability to process the separate and distinct features of a stimulus as a single image.

Evidence for the right hemisphere exerting control over perceptual processes comes chiefly from observations of people with damage to their right hemispheres. These people can recognize the individual parts of a pattern but have difficulty seeing the "whole." They also have trouble gauging the depth and size of objects (Levy & Trevarthen, 1977).

Auditory Perception

Perceptual processing by the right hemisphere applies not only to visual input but to auditory input as well. Not surprisingly, it has been discovered, initially through a series of studies by Brenda Milner, that damage to the auditory cortex in the right hemisphere affects a person's ability to detect familiar melodies (Milner, 1962). Doreen Kimura confirmed this relationship between the right hemisphere and the ability to recognize melodies by using a dichotic-listening technique (Kimura, 1964). Kimura found that if two melodies are presented simultaneously to normal (non-brain-damaged) subjects, one melody to each ear, the melody directed to the left ear dominates. The reason left-ear dominance can be taken as evidence that the right hemisphere processes the melody is that each ear has more connections to the hemisphere on the opposite side than to the hemisphere on the same side.

The Impact of the Neglect Syndrome

What we have said about the right hemisphere and its involvement in perception is not the whole story. Some people who suffer damage to the right hemisphere, for instance, show perceptual abnormalities that cannot be explained in terms of the disruption of specific circuits involved in assembling an image.

One such perceptual abnormality is known as the *neglect syndrome*. The condition occurs in stroke and accident victims who have suffered extensive damage to the parietal areas of the right hemisphere. (It is sometimes seen, too, in patients who suffer parietal damage to the left hemisphere, but the impact is far milder.)

The behavior of patients suffering from the neglect syndrome is by any measure bizarre. They behave as though the left side of their environment—including the left side of their body—does not exist. They eat food from the right side of their plate but not from the left. A male patient shaves the right side of his face but not the left. When asked to draw a picture of a clock, these patients draw a circle but, as shown in Figure 18.3, they group all the numerals of the clock on the right side of the circle.

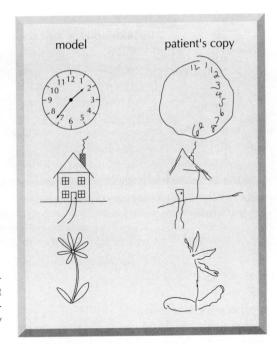

model   patient's copy

Figure 18.3   *Drawings by a Sensory-Neglect Patient*
When a patient with extensive damage to the parietal area of the right hemisphere is asked to draw a picture of a model, he or she will draw only the right side.

Even more bizarre, patients who suffer from this disorder are not aware of their problem: if questioned about their behavior or about the pictures they have drawn, they report that nothing is wrong (Kolb & Whishaw, 1990).

The "Attention" Factor

What is wrong with parietal patients? What psychological defect makes them oblivious to half of their environment? The logical assumption would be a form of blindness, except for one thing: people who are blind in half their visual field (a disorder known as *hemianopia*) do not neglect their blind side. On the contrary, they take great pains to compensate for the blindness by constantly moving their eyes and head.

One clue to the parietal patients' problem comes from the fact that some of them are able to perceive the left side of their environment (the side they normally neglect) under a special set of laboratory conditions: when no visual stimuli are present in the right visual field. Under these special conditions, as Figure 18.4 shows, they are able to perceive stimuli in their left visual field. But once a visual stimulus is introduced to the right visual field, sensory neglect returns and the perceived image of the stimulus in the left visual field is "extinguished." Understanding this extinction effect may hold the key to understanding what is psychologically wrong with parietal patients. Are the stimuli truly extinguished, or are the patients simply unable to report what they see? Bruce Volpe and his colleagues have examined this question (Volpe, LeDoux, & Gazzaniga, 1979).

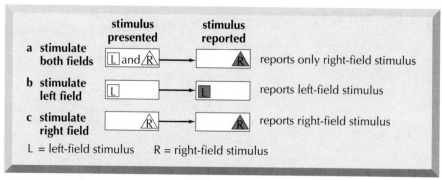

Figure 18.4 *The Visual Extinction Experiment*
A parietal patient is presented with stimuli in both visual fields either at the same time (a) or in sequence (b) and (c). When the stimuli are presented together, the patient reports seeing only the stimulus in the right visual field. When the stimuli are presented one at a time the patient reports seeing each stimulus.

Volpe's Experiment

Volpe's experimental procedure was to present parietal patients with two stimuli simultaneously, one in the left visual field and one in the right visual field, and to ask questions designed to yield insights into their ability to register and process the information.

The results revealed a curious—but telling—pattern. Presented with the two stimuli and asked if the stimuli were the same or different, parietal patients, surprisingly, were able to answer correctly—an indication that they had the ability to register stimuli from the left visual field even when there was a stimulus in the right visual field. What they could not do, however, was to verbally identify the stimulus in the left visual field as long as there was a stimulus in the right visual field. Two of his patients, for instance, complained that the task asked of them was silly, since as far as they could tell, there was no stimulus in the left visual field. Yet when these same patients were asked to guess whether the stimuli were the same or different, they responded correctly.

Clearly, then, parietal patients are able to *register* sensory information from the left visual field. But as long as there is a stimulus in the right visual field, they cannot bring the information to the level of verbal or conscious awareness. This finding brings us to a second question: What does the stimulus in the right visual field do to block the conscious awareness of the stimulus in the left visual field?

To answer this question, it might help to consider what normal (non-brain-damaged) people do in similar situations. When normal subjects are presented with information from both sides of their environment (such as different words presented to the two ears), they can freely shift their attention from one side to the other. Interestingly, however, when normal subjects are asked to focus their attention on one side of their environment (such as to words presented to their left ear), they are still able to register information from the unattended side. What they cannot do is bring that information to conscious awareness and identify verbally what that information is (see Chapter 6 for details) (McKay, 1973).

Patients with right parietal lesions are different. When they are presented with information from both sides of their body, they cannot freely shift their attention. Their attention is drawn automatically to the stimulus on the right side of their body. Once they have focused attention on the right side of their body, however, their behavior is similiar to that of normal people. They appear to register information from the unattended side (enabling them to make accurate same-different judgments), but they are unable to identify verbally what that information is or to use it to control their actions.

The logical conclusion is that the parietal area of the right hemisphere, when intact, controls attention (Heilman & Watson, 1977; Posner et al., 1984, 1987). Certain questions, though, remain unanswered. If, in fact, attention is controlled by the right hemisphere, why isn't there a more generalized disruption of attention to both the right and left sides of the environment? And, equally puzzling, why aren't parietal patients aware of the problem? So the issue is far from resolved, although one thing is clear: the role of the right hemisphere in perception is not limited to assembling images. Other perceptual processes—attention, for one— must also be incorporated into the picture.

COORDINATING THE TWO HEMISPHERES

Regardless of the questions that remain to be answered with respect to hemispheric function and behavior, our exploration into this subject thus far allows us to reach at least one general conclusion: the left hemisphere is dominant for language, and the right hemisphere is dominant for synthesizing perceptual detail and perhaps attention.

These "specialties" aside, however, the brain still operates as a unit. Information channeled to the left hemisphere, for instance, can be processed in a way that leads to behavior appropriate for the right hemisphere, and vice versa. We pick up a seashell on the beach with our left hand (which means that the somesthetic information is being channeled to the right hemisphere), and purely on the basis of touch we are able to describe to a friend what we have found, thus using the verbal capacities of the left hemisphere.

How is this possible? How do the two hemispheres coordinate their specialties to produce integrated behavior? The answer to this question brings us to the neural tract whose sole function appears to be to connect the two hemispheres. This tract, pictured in Figure 18.5, is known as the *corpus callosum.*

The Corpus Callosum: A Closer Look

Until the early 1950s the function of the corpus callosum was one of the great mysteries of the brain. No one understood, for instance, why

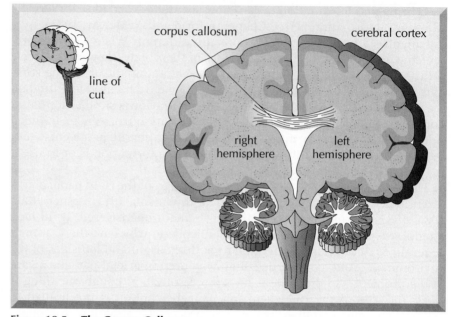

Figure 18.5 *The Corpus Callosum*
In the normal brain the two hemispheres are connected by the corpus callosum. In a split-brain patient the corpus callosum is severed.

epileptics whose corpus callosums had been cut to impede the spread of seizures showed no obvious disruption of normal behavior.

People who undergo this procedure—whose brains, in fact, have been split into two distinct parts—have since become known as *split-brain patients*, and at first glance they seem reasonably normal. They are not. Careful behavioral analysis of such patients by Roger Sperry and his colleagues revealed that there were impairments, and it was the discovery of these impairments that has provided the clues that show how the behavioral specialities of the two hemispheres are coordinated by the corpus callosum in normal individuals (Sperry, 1974).

Studying Split-Brain Humans

By studying the behavior of split-brain patients, researchers are able to do something that is all but impossible with normal humans: they can study the two hemispheres independently. Even so, they are faced with a major procedural problem: how to channel sensory information to one hemisphere at a time.

Two strategies have been used. In one, split-brain patients are blindfolded and asked to identify objects that they sometimes hold in their right hand and sometimes hold in their left hand. The rationale behind this strategy is that in humans, the somesthetic pathways (for pressure, pain, and touch) tend to cross completely from one side of the body to the opposite side of the brain. This is why blindfolded split-brain patients who hold an object in their right hand (with sensory information projected to the left—language-dominant—hemisphere) are able to identify that object verbally but cannot do so when the same object is held in the left hand (with sensory information projected to the right hemisphere).

A second procedure takes advantage of the fact that visual input can be channeled to one hemisphere of the split-brain patient at a time, albeit with more difficulty than somesthetic input. The rationale here is that although visual input from each eye goes to both hemispheres, the input is neatly divided within each eye. Neurons from the right side of each eye travel to the right hemisphere, and neurons from the left side travel to the left hemisphere, as shown in Figure 18.6. Therefore, by carefully projecting visual stimuli to one side of each eye, it is possible to channel visual information to one hemisphere at a time.

Here again though, we face procedural difficulties. If this procedure is to work, the eyes must not move while the stimulus is being projected to the eye. If there is eye movement, the stimulus will move to the other side of the eye and the neural message will travel to the other hemisphere.

To solve this problem, researchers have used a device known as a *tachistoscope*. This instrument allows the experimenter to flash a stimulus for a fraction of a second (for instance, 150 milliseconds) to the right

Figure 18.6 *Visual Pathways from Retina to Cortex*
When the eyes fixate on a point in the middle of the visual field, each eye sees both visual fields, but because of the neural connections between retina and cortex, the right visual field (which stimulates the left half of each retina) is projected to the left hemisphere and the left visual field (which stimulates the right half of each retina) is projected to the right hemisphere.

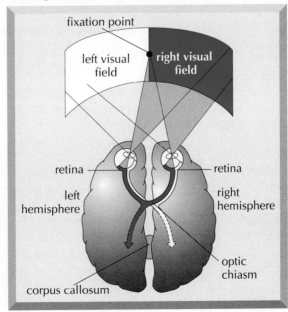

or left half of the eye. This procedure gives the subject enough time to recognize the stimulus, but because the exposure time is so brief, the stimulus is gone before the eye moves. Using this procedure, researchers have found that visual input, as shown in Figure 18.6, to the left side of each eye (projected to the left hemisphere) can be identified verbally by a split-brain patient, but that visual input to the right side of each eye (projected to the right hemisphere) cannot.

Implications

At least two explanations have been advanced to account for why the right hemisphere cannot identify objects verbally. The first is that the right hemisphere is able to recognize objects but simply cannot produce language. The second is that the right hemisphere simply cannot identify objects, verbally or by any other means.

Indications are that the problem lies mainly with language production. Studies have shown that if a picture of a nude figure is projected to the right hemisphere, the subject cannot identify the picture verbally but may blush and show various signs of embarrassment, clearly indicating recognition. Other studies have shown that if a picture of a pair of scissors is projected to the right hemisphere and the subject is asked to pick out (by touch alone) the scissors from among other items placed in a bag, he or she can easily do so. Apparently, then, the right hemisphere clearly recognizes the object but cannot verbally identify it (Sperry, 1974; Sperry & Gazzaniga, 1967).

The Right Hemisphere and Language

Although it seems safe to say that the right hemisphere is unable to produce language, it does not necessarily follow that the right hemisphere is unable to *understand* language. The experiments we have just described and others like them suggest that the right hemisphere does have the capacity to comprehend: How else could it respond to such instructions as "Pick out the scissors from the bag"? How adept the right hemisphere is in comprehending language, however, is another matter.

Early studies suggested that the right hemisphere played a relatively minor role in language comprehension. Today, thanks to improved methodology, we know that the right hemisphere has a greater capacity to comprehend language than was originally thought, although it should be noted that this view is not universally accepted (Gazzaniga, 1983).

The methodological problem that researchers needed to overcome to gain a better understanding of the right hemisphere and language comprehension involves the fact that when studying the function of a given hemisphere, right or left, researchers must be sure that neural messages reach only one hemisphere. This assurance in split-brain patients, as we mentioned earlier, is gained by projecting a stimulus on either the right or the left half of the retina. As you can see in Figure 18.6, a stimulus projected on the right half produces a neural message to the right hemisphere. Projected on the left half of the retina, the stimulus produces a neural message to the left hemisphere. Because the corpus callosum in split-brain patients is cut, the neural message is unable to cross from one hemisphere to the other and remains confined to either the right or the left hemisphere.

The original studies on split-brain patients, using the tachistoscopic procedure, found that the right hemisphere has a rudimentary comprehension of nouns and virtually no comprehension of verbs. When the right half of the retina (i.e., the right hemisphere) of a split-brain patient was presented with the *noun* "scissors," the patient was able to pick out the scissors from among other items with his or her left hand (controlled by the right hemisphere) even though all the items were hidden from view. When the *verb* "smile" was presented to the right half of the retina (i.e., to the right hemisphere), the same patient showed no response. The patient, however, smiled when the word was projected to the left half of the retina (i.e., to the left hemisphere). The conclusion: the right hemisphere has an understanding of nouns but not verbs.

More recent studies using a device known as a *Z lens* (named after its inventor, Eran Zaidel) have added new information to this picture. Zaidel found that the right hemisphere could comprehend not only nouns but also verbs, albeit only at the level of an average 10-year-old (Zaidel, 1983, 1990).

The key difference between the tachistoscopic and the Z-lens procedures is the length of time the subject is allowed to view the stimulus. In the tachistoscopic procedure, eye movement is minimized because the stimulus is projected to the eye for only a fraction of a second. In the Z-lens procedure, a stimulus is fixed on a contact lens that moves as the eye moves. (The other eye is covered with a patch.) Subjects are thus able to move their eyes freely and to view the stimulus indefinitely, and yet the stimulus affects only one part of the retina. When split-brain patients undergoing this procedure receive input to the right hemisphere, they respond correctly to both nouns and verbs.

The Impact of Emotional Tone

Yet another indication that the role of the right hemisphere in the control of language appears to be broader than originally thought comes from observations linking right-hemisphere function to the emotional tone of language.

We all know that we communicate not only through *what* we say but also through *how* we say it. Simply by making slight vocal adjustments, we can change the meaning of a sentence from a statement to a question, and we can make a simple declarative sentence sound like a menacing command. We can also make a compliment ("You look really nice today") sound genuine or, with the right inflection, turn the same words into a sarcastic insult.

The ability to make these adjustments is noticeably limited in people who have suffered damage to the right hemisphere. Interestingly, the way in which the right hemisphere processes the emotional properties of speech, known as *prosody*, may parallel the way the left hemisphere processes language. Elliot Ross has found that individuals with damage to the equivalent of Broca's area in the right hemisphere lose the ability to *produce* prosody, whereas those with damage to the equivalent of Wernicke's area in the right hemisphere lose some of their ability to *comprehend* the prosodic aspects of speech (Ross, 1984). In both cases, they can speak and they can understand, but their speech is either devoid of emotional tone (in the former case) or their understanding of emotional tone is impaired (in the latter case).

In conclusion, then, when it comes to language, it is misleading to depict the right hemisphere as merely a weak version of the left. It is true that the left hemisphere gives us our ability to speak and to understand, but it is also true that the right hemisphere complements and enriches those abilities with subtle but indispensable skills related to the emotional quality of language.

Coordinating Perceptions

A cut corpus callosum may not affect the right hemisphere's perceptual ability in general, but it does affect its capacity to use the language facilities of the left hemisphere. But what about the reverse situation? What happens to the left hemisphere when it is deprived of callosal communication with the right hemisphere?

Jerre Levy and Roger Sperry examined this question in studies that allowed split-brain patients to touch (hold in their hand) but not to see wooden blocks of various shapes (Levy & Sperry, 1972). This procedure meant that the sensory information from the right hand traveled to the left hemisphere and that the sensory information from the left hand traveled to the right hemisphere. Each patient was then given a series of pictures and asked to point to the one that represented the object he or she was holding. (By having the patient point to a picture of a block rather than verbally describe it, the experimenter was assured that each hemisphere was capable of responding.)

The results of these studies show that when a patient holds an object in his left hand (projected to the right hemisphere), his ability to choose the correct picture is significantly better than when he holds a block in his right hand (projected to the left hemisphere). The implication is that without the corpus callosum, the left hemisphere is deprived of such higher-order perceptual processes as spatial relations.

Beyond the Verbal-Perceptual Differences

Evidence gathered by Jerre Levy and her colleagues reveals yet another difference between the hemispheres (Levy & Trevarthen, 1977). When Levy gave split-brain patients different problems to solve with the right hand (left hemisphere) and the left hand (right hemisphere), she found that the right hand was superior in solving problems that called for an analytical approach and that the left hand was superior in solving problems that called for a more spatial approach—in her terms, a "holistic" approach. She has concluded that the left hemisphere processes information analytically (on a step-by-step sequential basis), whereas the right hemisphere deals with information holistically (combining elements simultaneously). These differences, Levy suggests, may help to explain why the left hemisphere controls language (language, after all, is a sequential process) and the right hemisphere controls visual-spatial ability—a more holistic capacity. It should be noted, however, that this view has not gone unchallenged (Trope et al., 1992).

THE FUNCTION OF THE CORPUS CALLOSUM

Observations of split-brain patients, coupled with studies involving stroke victims, enable us to draw certain conclusions about the function of the corpus callosum. If the corpus callosum is intact, the right and left hemispheres are coordinated and are able to share, to some extent, one another's specialty. If the corpus callosum is damaged, however, the one brain becomes, in effect, two brains, with each hemisphere having its own specialization, inaccessible to the other. As Roger Sperry has observed:

> Each hemisphere has its own private sensations, perceptions, thoughts, and ideas, all of which are cut off from the corresponding experiences in the opposite hemisphere. Each left and right hemisphere has its own private chain of memories and learning experiences that are inaccessible to recall by the other hemisphere. In many respects each disconnected hemisphere appears to have a separate "mind of its own."(Sperry, 1974)

The Unified Brain

Sperry's comments notwithstanding, it would be wrong to characterize the corpus callosum as indispensable for normal behavior. Even with a severed or damaged corpus callosum, split-brain patients are able to handle everyday situations rather normally. It is only when they are brought into the laboratory and given special tests that their behavioral abnormalities become manifest. With or without the corpus callosum, the brain is capable of working in a unified, unconflicted way. Presumably, there are mechanisms that compensate for the missing corpus callosum. Let us look now at these mechanisms.

Compensating for the Missing Corpus Callosum

One of the keys to the ability of the brain to compensate for a missing corpus callosum lies in the sensory arrangement of the visual system. As you already know, each hemisphere receives input from both eyes and thus has access to the same visual information. True, the right half of each eye connects to the right hemisphere and the left half of each eye to the left hemisphere, as pictured in Figure 18.6. Remember, though, that our eyes are constantly moving, so that the image that falls on the right half of each eye one moment falls on the left half of each eye the next moment. As a result, the same image is projected to both the right and left hemispheres.

A second compensating mechanism seems to lie in the hemispheres themselves—specifically in the fact that each hemisphere in split-brain patients can assume some control of behavior. If a task demands perceptual skills, for instance, the right hemisphere becomes dominant. If a task demands verbal or analytical skills, the left hemisphere takes over. The separated hemispheres, in other words, do not appear to *vie* for control of behavior (as some early reports suggested) as much as they work together, assuming responsibility for control according to their specialty. How do we know this? Primarily from the work of Jerre Levy (Levy & Trevarthen, 1977; Levy, Trevarthen, & Sperry, 1972).

Dominance Studies in Split-Brain Patients

The Levy experiment we will now consider was designed to answer two questions: Can one hemisphere dominate and control behavior in a split-brain subject? And if such dominance exists, what determines it?

Levy used an ingenious procedure to answer these questions. As detailed in Figure 18.7, she presented different visual information simultaneously to each of the two hemispheres of a split-brain patient. One hemisphere, for example, saw the face of a child, while the other hemisphere saw the face of a woman, as pictured in Figure 18.7b. Levy then turned off both stimuli and instructed her subjects to report which face they had seen by pointing with either hand to one of several photographs projected on a screen, as depicted in Figure 18.7c. Levy found that regardless of which hand the subject used to point, the choice was usually the same: the photograph selected was the one presented to the right hemisphere. In short, then, in a split-brain patient when the two hemispheres are given different faces to recognize, the right hemisphere is dominant.

To understand why these results are important, we need to look at one particular aspect of brain function: motor control. When it comes to controlling certain movements, like those involved in pointing the hand, the motor areas in the right hemisphere tend to control the left hand, and the motor areas in the left hemisphere tend to control the right hand (see Figure 18.8). True, the right hemisphere can also exert control over the right hand, and the left hemisphere can exert control over the left hand, but the control is not as strong. Only by bearing this relationship in mind will you be able to appreciate Levy's findings.

That the subject in this experiment pointed to the face presented to the right hemisphere is not surprising. The right hemisphere, remember, specializes in face recognition. What *is* surprising, however, is that the subject made the same choice regardless of which hand was doing the pointing. This finding indicates that the right hemisphere is so dominant that it exerts control not only over the left hand (the hand it normally

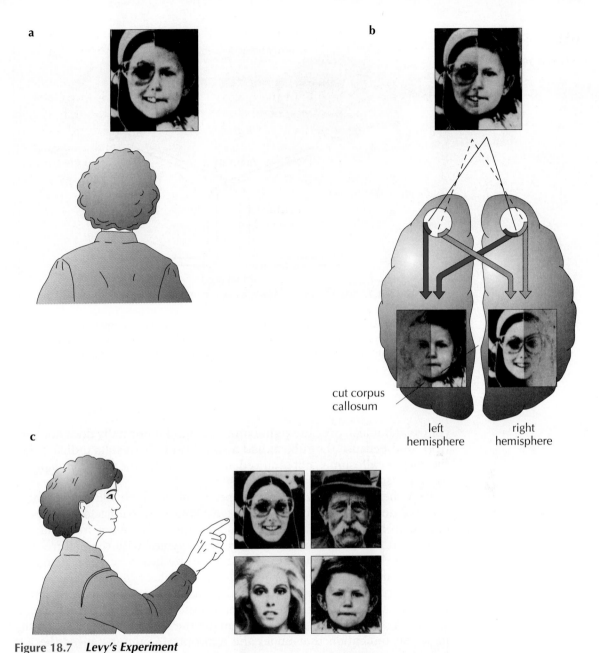

Figure 18.7 *Levy's Experiment*

(a) The split-brain subject fixates on a picture consisting of the left half of one face and the right half of another. (b) Even though each eye sees both faces, the face in the right visual field is projected to the left hemisphere and the face in the left visual field is projected to the right hemisphere. (c) When the subject is asked to point to the picture she saw, she chooses the picture projected to the right hemisphere. It should be noted that even though half a face is projected to each hemisphere, the subject is unaware of the incompleteness of the pictures and behaves as though both hemispheres see one normal face.

651

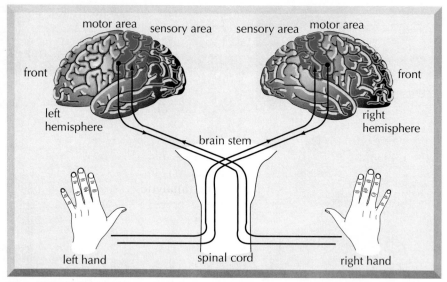

Figure 18.8 *Bilateral Symmetry*
The figure shows the complementary relationships between the two hemispheres. The left hemisphere receives sensory information and issues motor instructions to the right side of the body. The right hemisphere receives sensory information and issues motor instructions to the left side of the body.

controls) but also over the right hand (the hand it normally does not control). And because the subject had a split brain, the results indicate that the corpus callosum is not required, in this case, for the right hemisphere to exert its dominance.

Levy then conducted a second experiment in which she incorporated a verbal demand into the task. She gave split-brain subjects pictures of objects (a bee to one hemisphere and a rose to the other, for instance) and asked them to point to a picture that *rhymed* with the picture they saw. The rhyming element of course gave the task a verbal dimension, thus introducing the need for more left-hemisphere involvement.

Not surprisingly, the subject in this instance pointed to the picture that rhymed with the picture that had been projected to the left hemisphere. Again, however, the subject made the response regardless of the hand, an indication that under the appropriate circumstances the left hemisphere can become just as dominant as the right hemisphere in exerting control over either hand. And again, it does so even though the corpus callosum has been cut.

What these findings tell us essentially is that the two hemispheres have different capacities, one more suited for perceptual tasks and the other more suited for verbal tasks. The findings also tell us that the hemisphere that dominates behavior in a particular situation is the one that has the appropriate capacity. Most importantly, perhaps, the hemisphere exerts this dominance even though the corpus callosum has been cut.

What then is the function of the corpus callosum besides simply sharing information? If it is true that a split-brain patient can behave competently, what could the corpus callosum add to the behavior?

There is no definitive answer to this question, but there is at least one interesting theory (Springer & Deutsch, 1993). This theory is based on the assumption that it may, in fact, be to our *disadvantage* to make decisions as split-brain patients apparently do—on the basis of the physical features of a task, its analytical-verbal or perceptual demands. It is easy to imagine situations in which even though the physical features of a task may indicate one approach, the psychological demands of the task may call for a different approach. An architect may look at a blueprint—a perceptual task—from both an engineering (analytic) and an aesthetic (perceptual) point of view. A scientist uses a perceptual metaphor (e.g., the DNA helix in the gene looks like a ladder) to solve a seemingly analytical problem.

It remains for future research to test this hypothesis, but the corpus callosum may well be the circuit that allows us to use mixed strategies. It may serve, in other words, as the vehicle by which the brain can override the built-in specialties of each hemisphere, allowing us to switch from one hemisphere to the other depending on which specialty is needed at a particular moment. The corpus callosum, in short, may give us the freedom and flexibility to look at problems in new ways. Some scientists, in fact, believe that differences in this ability may account for differences in cognitive style—the way a person approaches (analytical or perceptual or both) life situations in general.

WHY ARE THE HEMISPHERES SPECIALIZED?

Up to now we have been concerned with the question of what characterizes the differences between the two hemispheres. Equally important—and even more puzzling—is the question of *why* the differences exist.

What makes this latter question so difficult to answer is that hemispheric specialization, at first glance, seems to be a disadvantage. From a mere protective point of view, for instance, it would make sense to have such important behaviors as language and spatial-perceptual skills under the redundant control of both hemispheres. We are therefore led to conclude that something quite important—more important, even, than redundant protection—is gained by having language and perception controlled by different hemispheres. What that advantage actually is remains a mystery, but there are some intriguing clues.

Jerre Levy has attempted to solve this mystery by differentiating between the kind of processing needed for language and perception. So incompatible are the two types of information processing, according to Levy, that if they were controlled by the same hemisphere, they would conflict and interfere with one another (Levy & Trevarthen, 1977). If this hypothesis is true, we would expect individuals in whom the two types of information processing are not divided between the hemispheres to show cognitive abnormalities. Support for this hypothesis is sketchy, but there is at least some evidence to back it up.

This evidence comes primarily from experimental observations of children suffering from a disorder known as dyslexia. *Dyslexia* is a term used to describe people who have difficulty learning how to read (Rumsey, 1992). Like most behavioral disorders, it has no single cause. Children reared in environments that discourage the learning of language skills are just as likely to be dyslexic as children who suffer from subtle brain malformations but grow up in intellectually stimulating environments (Gibson & Levin, 1975). So, although our concern in the remainder of this chapter will be with the neural basis of dyslexia, we do not minimize the importance of environmental factors.

Dyslexia: A Closer Look

Many people who suffer from dyslexia are believed to have subtle anomalies in brain organization that are not caused by major brain damage. This dysfunction manifests itself chiefly in reading difficulties affecting an estimated 2 to 8 percent of school-aged children. Dyslexics have normal IQs and appear to have no marked emotional problems. Still, they do not process language the way nondyslexics do.

To find out whether dyslexia is related to hemispheric dysfunction, Sandra Witelson conducted a series of tests on dyslexic boys aged 6 to 14 years (Witelson, 1977). The tests showed very little difference between dyslexic and normal boys in tasks that involved left-hemisphere specialization. The left hemisphere was shown to be specialized for language in both groups of children.

In tests calling for right-hemisphere specialization, however, the performance of the dyslexic boys differed noticeably from that of normal children. In normal children, the right hemisphere was clearly superior to the left on spatial tasks. In dyslexic children, there was no difference between the two hemispheres. The dyslexics showed no hemispheric specialization when it came to spatial relations.

One test, as pictured in Figure 18.9, consisted of giving normal and dyslexic children the opportunity to identify by touch alone two differently shaped objects, one in each hand. Dyslexic children administered this test showed no difference in their ability to recognize the shapes presented to the left or right hand; that is, the two hemispheres seemed to be equally capable of making the identification. Normal children, in contrast, show greater accuracy with their left hand (right hemisphere) than their right hand (left hemisphere).

It would be misleading to stop here and limit our discussion of dyslexia to one cause and to one line of research. Dyslexia is a complex, baffling disorder. The theories that have been proposed to explain it are just as complex and just as bewildering. In all of this complexity and puzzlement one theory stands out above all others, not because it is necessarily correct but because it is broad and comprehensive.

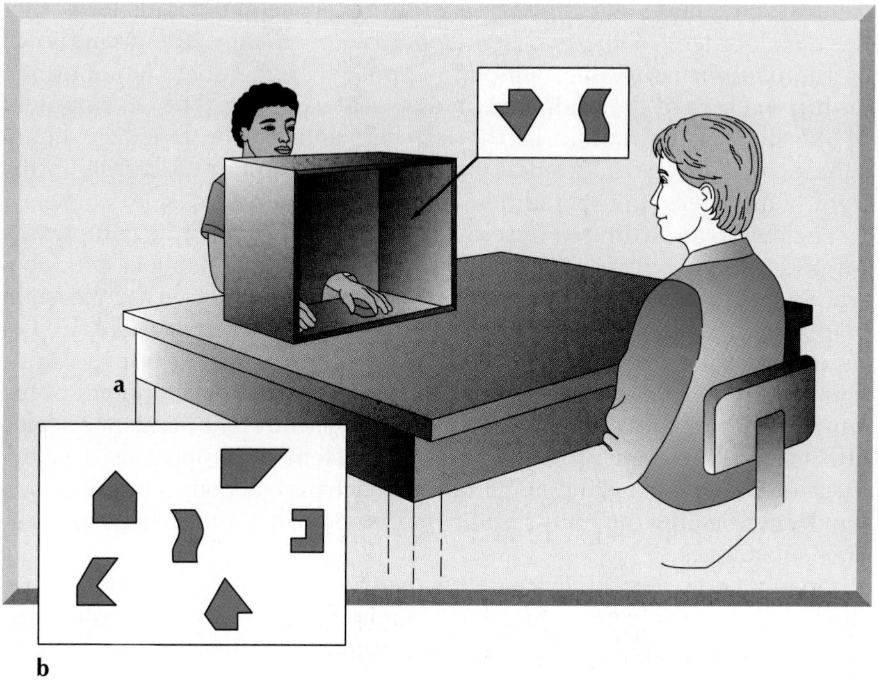

Figure 18.9 *Dichaptic Test*
(a) The subject is allowed to touch (but not see) two objects, one with each hand. (b) The subject is then given six objects (visually displayed) from which he chooses the two that he touched.

The theory was proposed by Norman Geschwind shortly before his death in 1984. Most theories of dyslexia focus on one and only one symptom: the dyslexic's reading disability. Geschwind's concerns were more far-reaching (Geschwind, 1984). He believed that dyslexia could be associated with other, seemingly unrelated, behavioral and biological conditions. After years of gathering anecdotal information from dyslexics and their families, he hypothesized that there is an association among males, left-handedness (left handers and males are more likely to show dyslexia than right handers and females), autoimmune diseases—diseases (such as allergies and ulcerative colitis) in which the body mistakenly attacks its own tissue—and dyslexia (Geschwind & Behan, 1982; Geschwind & Galburda, 1987). Let's take a closer look at the theory.

Geschwind's Theory of Dyslexia
In broad terms, Geschwind's theory of dyslexia proposes that all conditions associated with dyslexia, including the susceptibility to autoimmune diseases and left-handedness, can be traced to one factor: an abnormally high level of the male sex hormone, testosterone, during fetal development.

In Geschwind's view, high levels of testosterone in the male fetus alter the development of the two hemispheres, specifically, the area known as the *planum temporale*, which, as you will remember, is contained within the area of the brain known as Wernicke's area. The development of the planum temporale in the left hemisphere, the language hemisphere, is suppressed. The development of the planum temporale in the right hemisphere, the spatial hemisphere, is enhanced.

The result, according to Geschwind, is dyslexia in all of its complexity. An underdeveloped planum temporale in the left hemisphere produces reading difficulties. An overdeveloped planum temporale in the right hemisphere produces left-handedness. And why is there a susceptibility to autoimmune diseases? Because, according to Geschwind, the same abnormally high level of testosterone that suppresses development of the left hemisphere and enhances development of the right hemisphere also affects the development of the immune system. It suppresses development of the thymus gland, a gland that controls the body's immune system by controlling the body's ability to distinguish between itself and foreign substances.

On what does Geschwind base his theory? He bases it, in part, on intuition, but he also cites some hard data—the fact that autopsies performed on some dyslexics show predominantly left hemisphere damage that appears to have occurred prior to or around the time of birth (Galaburda et al., 1985; Humphreys, Kaufmann, & Galaburda, 1990). The presence of this damage strengthens Geschwind's argument that an underdeveloped left hemisphere is the principal factor in dyslexia, but the problem with the data is that the autopsies were performed only on a handful of subjects. And while there is evidence for the assumption that testosterone affects development of both the nervous and immune systems, this evidence comes from studies involving lower animals, not humans.

On the other hand, in view of what Geschwind has proposed, arguments are unavoidable. He has taken one of the most complex and perplexing behavioral disorders and has attempted to explain it by a single neurological problem (an underdeveloped left hemisphere) and a single developmental cause (abnormally high levels of testosterone during fetal development). Despite the controversy surrounding it, the theory has provoked new ideas and research. Even if Geschwind is ultimately proven wrong, his thinking represents a seminal contribution to the field.

Reading Deficits: The Timing Theory of Dyslexia

It is now generally assumed that dyslexics suffer from some sort of brain anomaly and the suspicion continues to grow that this anomaly is, at root, the cause of a sensory problem. Dyslexics, according to this theory, are able to receive sensory information much as a normal person does—they can see and they can hear—but what they cannot do is process this sensory information in ways consistent with the demands of reading.

Identifying the specific sensory deficit that impairs the ability of dyslexics to read is one of the primary goals of current dyslexia research, and one theory that has gained increasing credibility since it was introduced in the 1970s is based on the notion that dyslexia, along with a number of other language disabilities, results from the inability to process a very important component of speech—fast-changing sounds that characterize certain syllables (Tallal & Piercy, 1973; Tallal, 1980). Central to the theory, whose chief proponent is Paula Tallal, is the fact that some sounds, such as vowels, continue for more than 100 milliseconds while other sounds (certain consonants) continue for only 40 milliseconds.

Tallal theorizes that during early development, when language is being acquired, dyslexics are able to process the long-lasting sounds but are unable to process the brief, rapid-changing sounds. Deprived of this ability to distinguish among the subtle sounds of language, dyslexics ultimately run into a problem when the time comes for them to learn to read. Reading calls for the ability to process a steady and rapid flow of sounds, long and short alike, and dyslexics, if Tallal is correct, lack this ability (Tallal, Miller, & Fitch, 1993).

Evidence for the Timing Theory of Dyslexia

The timing element of the theory draws support from Tallal's own experimental work. In the early 1970s she conducted a study in which two different groups of children—one language-impaired (including children who would now be categorized as dyslexic), the other unaffected by language problems—were presented two tones at varying intervals and were asked to indicate (by pushing one of two response panels) whether the second tone was the same as the first. As long as the interval between the two tones was relatively long—150 milliseconds or more—both groups made accurate judgments. Once the interval dropped below 150 milliseconds and obliged the children to process information much more rapidly, however, the accuracy of the children in the language-impaired group (but not in the unaffected group) began to drop noticeably as well (Tallal & Piercy, 1973). More recently, similar timing problems have been identified in processing visual information, indicating that the timing problem is more general and not linked only to the auditory system (Lovegrove, Garzia, & Nicholson, 1990; Slaghuis, Lovegrove, & Davidson, 1993).

The chief reason the timing theory of dyslexia is gaining broader acceptance these days is that postmortem examinations of the brains of dyslexic people reveal abnormalities that point to timing as a critical factor in the condition. Albert Galburda and his colleagues, for instance, have found evidence indicating that dyslexics are deficient in certain neural cells—large cells in both the lateral geniculate nucleus (visual) and medial geniculate nucleus (auditory)—known to be involved in coding rapid changes in sensory input (Livingstone et al., 1991; Galburda, Mennard, & Rosen, in press).

The combination of behavioral data—the tone experiments of Tallal—coupled with the neural data—the autopsy work of Galburda—makes a strong case for the notion that dyslexics have a neural deficiency that

interferes with their ability to process rapidly changing sensory information. Once again, however, we are faced with the problem we have
encountered time and time again throughout this book—the qualifications whenever the evidence is correlational. Assuming that there are
indeed brain abnormalities and timing problems in dyslexics, we need to
ask ourselves whether these factors are merely correlates of dyslexia (the
inability to read) or are causes of dyslexia.

Unfortunately no experiment employing a correlational approach can
answer these questions. Ideally what is needed is a manipulative
approach—one that would experimentally damage the neural areas
thought to be involved with dyslexia and observe the behavioral effects.
There is animal work to indicate that lesions to those brain areas that are
damaged in dyslexics impair the animal's ability to perform tasks that
require the ability to process rapidly changing sensory stimuli, but similar experiments involving humans are obviously out of the question
(Fitch et al., 1994). On the other hand, if there is indeed a link between
a person's ability to process rapidly changing sensory information and
that person's ability to read, then any steps that can be taken to treat the
timing problem should have a beneficial impact on reading. This possibility is the focus of current work.

Recapping the Theories of Dyslexia

The theories and research seeking to explain the physiological basis of
dyslexia are obviously among the most important now being reported in
physiological psychology. We have considered three of the more prominent theories—Witelson's, Geschwind's, and Tallal's—but by no means
the only ones. The theories agree on one point: that dyslexia stems from
a neurological dysfunction. Where the theories differ is in the nature and
site of the dysfunction. Witelson links dyslexia to an undifferentiated left
hemisphere. Geschwind cites an underdeveloped left hemisphere as the
culprit. And Tallal maintains that the dysfunction is sensory in nature.
The evidence to date favors Tallel's view, but you must keep in mind that
dyslexia research is still in its early stages, and the evidence is neither
solid nor extensive enough to allow definitive conclusions.

Hemispheric Differences: A Sobering Overview

It is now time for us to put the entire matter of hemispheric specialization into some perspective, particularly since differences in left- and
right-brain functions have received considerable publicity in recent
years. If you look at Table 18.1, you will see descriptions of hemispheric
functions. But as Sally Springer and Georg Deutsch point out, we cannot
move from the top to the bottom of the table with undiminished confidence (Springer & Deutsch, 1993).

The first, and safest, conclusion we can draw with respect to hemispheric differences relates to verbal and nonverbal competence. That the
right hemisphere is largely nonverbal and the left hemisphere is largely
verbal is by now a generally accepted fact. The second conclusion, that
the two hemispheres differ in the way they process information, is more

TABLE 18.1

**KNOWN AND SUSPECTED CHARACTERISTICS
OF RIGHT AND LEFT HEMISPHERES**

The verbal-nonverbal and sequential-simultaneous characteristics are based on
experimental evidence; the other characteristics are hypothetical.

Left hemisphere	Right hemisphere
Verbal	Nonverbal, visuospatial
Sequential, temporal, digital	Simultaneous, spatial, analogical
Logical analytic	Gestalt, synthetic
Rational	Intuitive
Western thought	Eastern thought

Adapted from S.P. Springer and G. Deutsch, *Left Brain, Right Brain*, 4th Ed. (San Francisco: Freeman, 1993).

speculative. Jerre Levy's work indicates that there are differences, but that distinction is not yet universally accepted.

As we move down the rest of the list, agreement becomes progressively less universal. It is tempting to make a sharp distinction between the left brain and the right brain, as Robert Ornstein did when he observed that Western society is dominated by a "rational" left-brain approach to life as opposed to the more "intuitive" right-brain approach to life that predominates in the East (Ornstein, 1972). The problem with this notion is that there is no concrete experimental evidence to document it. Yes, there are differences in left-brain and right-brain functions, but to say that the two hemispheres are specialized for different types of thought—the left brain for rational thought and the right brain for intuitive thought—is merely an interesting speculation, not a scientific fact.

HEMISPHERIC DIFFERENCES
BETWEEN THE SEXES

These misconceptions about hemispheric differences and their relation to behavior notwithstanding, there is one popular view that is gradually gaining empirical support. It has to do with behavioral differences between the sexes and the degree to which these differences reflect differences in the hemispheres (Kimura, 1992).

Evidence continues to grow that females, on average, are better than males in verbal skills, and that males, on the whole, fare better than females on tests of spatial and mathematical ability. There are, to be sure, many exceptions to the pattern. Even so, however, certain patterns of behavior are striking. When males and females are given the mental rotation task shown in Figure 18.10, males are more likely to solve it. And when males and females are given the same questions involving grammar or vocabulary, females are more likely to give the correct answer (Halpern, 1992).

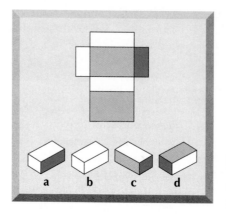

Figure 18.10 *A Spatial Relations Task*
The subject is asked to choose the figure (A, B, C, or D) that can be constructed by folding the pattern shown above.

These differences, to repeat, are purely statistical. There are females who do as well if not better than males on spatial tasks and males who do as well if not better than females on verbal tasks. But taken as a whole, males on average are better at spatial tasks and females, on average, are better at verbal tasks. The question is, Why?

Gender Differences and Brain Function

Are there fundamental differences in the male brain and female brain that would account for the documented difference in test results involving spatial relationships and language skills? This is a difficult question to answer, by any measure. Most of us have grown up with a variety of notions regarding behavioral differences between males and females, but who is to say whether these differences are the result of genetics and its influence on the development of the hemispheres or simply a matter of cultural conditioning? Do young boys exhibit superior spatial ability and young girls superior verbal skills because males and females are born with hemispheric differences? Or is it simply the social pressures of our culture that influence these behaviors? For instance, would men and women be more alike if our culture did not view higher mathematics as a man's field? As recently as 2 or 3 years ago, we had no answer to these questions.

Today we have begun to formulate answers, but the answers are far from complete and are almost certain to change as we learn more and more about the differences between the male and female brain.

Hemispheric Differences: An Anatomical View

Let us begin with the most basic question: Are there hemispheric differences between the sexes? As a first step in answering this question, researchers have sought to identify differences in anatomical structures between male and female brains that may account for the differences in verbal-spatial abilities.

Autopsies have revealed that there are indeed hemispheric differences between the sexes, not in the hemispheres per se but in the corpus callosum, the neural tract that interconnects the hemispheres. A specific region of the corpus callosum, the *splenium*, tends to be larger in females than in males (Lacoste & Holloway, 1982; Allen et al., 1991). These data are new, and more evidence is needed. But even if it is true that women have a larger splenium than men, what can we conclude?

One seemingly logical conclusion is that the larger splenium in women accounts for their superior verbal skills. It may. But it is also possible—and this is the critical point—that there is no relationship between the large splenium and superior verbal skills, and even if there were, the large splenium may be a *result* of superior verbal skills rather than the other way around. For example, women, because of their superior verbal skills, may simply spend more time reading than men. Thus if we assume that the circuits involved in reading are the same circuits that make up the splenium, the increase in the *use* of the circuits could account for the increase in the *size* of the circuits.

Second, it would be a mistake to conclude that the anatomical differences between men and women are the result of genetic differences. As we saw in Chapter 2, environmental factors may be just as important as genetics in shaping the development of the nervous system. And since the environmental experiences of males and females, beginning at birth, are so vastly different, it is not unreasonable to expect that the brain areas affected by these experiences might come to differ as well.

Finally, and perhaps most important, we must view the behavioral differences between the sexes, be they genetic or environmental, for what they really are. They are neither biological deficiencies nor biological constraints. Rather they are merely statistical quirks of nature which at one time may have been adaptive—females as child rearers imbued with superior verbal skills, males as hunters equipped with superior spatial skills—but today in our society serve no purpose (Levy, 1978). So even though it may be true that each sex is born with circuitry that predisposes it to a certain intellectual style—verbal or spatial—it is also true that the circuits and the behaviors they control are not immutable. Males may indeed be born with a predisposition to be spatial and females with a predisposition to be verbal, but what we must never lose sight of is that these predispositions are just that—predispositions. Just as we are born with certain behavioral inclinations, so are we born with the ability to learn to change these inclinations.

A FINAL LOOK

We have seen in this chapter that there is a great deal more to localization of function in the brain of higher animals than of lower animals. We have seen, too, that no animal shows more localization of function than humans and that humans are the only animals (with rare exceptions) in which hemispheric division of the brain has major behavioral implications.

But where does this leave us on the question of localization? The answer, as far as we know, is as follows: there are indeed areas in the brain that are more involved in the control of specific behaviors than other areas, but this involvement in no way allows us to say that a particular behavioral function *resides* in a particular area. Indeed, if we have learned anything at all about how the brain functions to control behavior, it is that every area of the brain is related to virtually every other area, either directly or indirectly.

Thus we can safely say that we will probably never completely understand the physiological basis of any single behavior until we understand not only the area primarily involved in that behavior but also how that area relates to other areas in the brain. It would be difficult to name any task in science more challenging.

SUMMARY

1. *Localization of function.* Specific behaviors can be traced to specific areas in the cortex. This idea, known as cortical localization, has only recently gained widespread acceptance. One reason the idea has taken so long to gain support is that it has its roots in the discredited theory known as phrenology, which sought to establish a direct connection between mental functions and the size and position of bumps on the skull. Another—and perhaps more important—reason is that Karl Lashley, one of the most influential figures in physiological psychology, argued for decades that the brain operates by and large as a whole. Lashley based his view on lower-animal studies in which destruction of various areas of the cortex did not necessarily disrupt behaviors other than sensory or motor functions. What Lashley did not know is that cortical function differs dramatically between lower and higher animals.

2. *Evidence for the theory.* The most compelling evidence for the localization-of-function theory comes from both monkey and human studies showing that damage to specific areas of the cortices produces specific behavioral deficits. The studies also indicate that hemispheric division plays a much greater role in controlling behavior in humans than it does in other higher animals.

3. *Hemispheric division.* Most behavior in humans is under the control of both hemispheres, but one notable exception is language, which is controlled by the left hemisphere in an estimated 97 percent of human beings. The discovery that the left hemisphere controls language was initially made in the 1860s by Pierre Broca, who identified an area—now known as Broca's area—that controls the ability to speak. Carl Wernicke later found that damage to an area outside Broca's area also created a speech disorder (a severe loss in comprehension), and he proposed a neural model for language that has since been borne out by many—but not all—clinical observations.

4. *Exceptions to the pattern.* There are several exceptions to the general principle that the left hemisphere controls language. When damage to areas in the left hemisphere controlling speech occurs during childhood or in left-handed adults, the right hemisphere is often able to assume control, although it doesn't process language nearly as well as the left hemisphere.

5. *The role of the right hemisphere.* From all indications, the hemisphere that does not control speech—the right hemisphere, in most people— controls a particular type of perceptual process: the ability to recognize the separate features of a stimulus as a "whole." Evidence for this function comes from observations of people with damage to their right hemispheres, who can recognize the individual parts of a visual pattern or individual notes of a melody but have difficulty seeing or hearing the "whole."

6. *The neglect syndrome.* Some people who have suffered damage to the parietal area in the right hemisphere show a pattern of perceptual abnormalities known as the neglect syndrome. These people are able to *register* sensory information from the left visual field but, under most circumstances, are unable to bring that information to the level of verbal or conscious awareness. Because this abnormality disappears under conditions in which stimuli are absent in the right visual field, it has been theorized that the parietal area of the right hemisphere, when intact, controls attention.

7. *The corpus callosum.* Because the brain, despite its hemispheric divisions, operates as a whole, research has focused on how the hemispheres coordinate information. The chief focus of this research has been the corpus callosum, a large tract that connects the two hemispheres. Nearly everything we know about the corpus callosum in humans is the result of experimental work on so-called split-brain patients—epileptics whose corpus callosums have been severed to impede the spread of seizures. The typical strategy in this work has been to channel sensory information to one hemisphere at a time and observe the behavioral results.

8. *Working with split-brain patients: early results.* When split-brain patients are given sensory input (visual or somesthetic) to the right hemisphere, they are able to recognize it (for instance, they blush when shown a nude figure) but cannot respond to it verbally. When given sensory input to the left hemisphere, split-brain patients can respond to it verbally but have difficulty making perceptual judgments (identifying the form or shape of the stimulus).

9. *The right hemisphere and language.* Recent findings have revealed that the right hemisphere has a broader role in language than originally suspected. The right hemisphere, it now appears, can understand nouns and has a limited ability to understand verbs. It has also been found that the right hemisphere plays an important role in producing and comprehending the emotional tone that is used in speech. People who suffer damage to the right hemisphere tend to speak in a manner devoid of emotional tone or their understanding of emotional tone is impaired.

10. *Hemispheric specialties.* The work of Jerre Levy has helped to clarify some of the ways the two hemispheres may work together to control higher-order behaviors. Levy's work suggests that the left hemisphere processes information analytically—on a step-by-step sequential basis—whereas the right hemisphere deals with information holistically—combining elements simultaneously. Levy cites these differences as the main reason the left hemisphere controls language and the right hemisphere controls visual-spatial ability—a more holistic capacity.

11. *What the corpus callosum does.* Studies have shown that the two hemispheres of split-brain patients do not vie for control of behavior as much as they assume responsibility in accordance with their specialty. In other words, the hemisphere that controls behavior in a particular situation is the hemisphere that has the appropriate capacity: verbal or perceptual. The fact that split-brain patients can function reasonably well has raised the question of what function is served by the corpus callosum other than to allow the hemispheres to share their specialties. There is no definitive answer to this question, but one theory holds that the corpus callosum imbues us with the ability to use a mixture of strategies when making decisions.

12. *Why hemispheric specialization?* One theory, advanced by Jerre Levy, is that once the left hemisphere gained control of language, it was to our adaptive advantage for the right hemisphere to assume control of perception. Without this separation of power, in her view, the processing of the two types of information—language and perception—in the same hemisphere would create conflicts and interfere with behavior. Studies on children who suffer from a perceptual abnormality known as dyslexia lend some support to this view, indicating that the source of the problem that dyslexics have is hemispheric dysfunction. Normal children, when asked to identify objects by touch, show greater accuracy with their left hand (right hemisphere) than their right hand (left hemisphere)—a finding consistent with the general view of hemispheric specialization. Dyslexic children, however, show no difference.

13. *Geschwind's theory of dyslexia.* Norman Geschwind has proposed that dyslexia (which is far more common among boys and left-handers than girls or right-handers) is caused by high levels of testosterone in the male fetus, which, in turn, alter the development of the two hemispheres, specifically, the area known as the planum temporale. An underdeveloped planum temporale in the left hemisphere, according to Geschwind, produces reading difficulties. An overdeveloped right hemisphere produces left-handedness. More recent studies have linked dyslexia (specifically, impaired reading) to an impairment in processing rapidly changing information caused by damage in the lateral and medial geniculate nuclei.

14. *Hemispheric differences: an overview.* There is a growing body of evidence to suggest that there are hemispheric-related differences in the brain structure of males and females and that these differences might account for the well-documented fact that women, as a rule, tend to do better than men on tests involving verbal skills whereas men tend to do better on tests involving spatial skills. Recent work has identified an area in the corpus callosum that is larger in females than in males, but there is no telling at present whether the difference is the *reason* that women do better on verbal tests or simply the *result* of superior verbal skills that have been gained through environmental experience. And even if it were true that each sex is born with circuitry that predisposes it to a certain intellectual style—verbal or spatial—this is not to say that the circuits and the behaviors they control are immutable. Just as we are born with certain behavioral inclinations, so we are born with the ability to learn to change these inclinations.

KEY TERMS

alexia
aphasia
apraxia
association areas
bilateral symmetry
Broca's area
corpus callosum
cortical localization
dyslexia
hemianopia

localization of function
neglect syndrome
phrenology
planum temporale
prosody
splenium
split-brain patients
tachistoscope
third frontal gyrus of the left
   cerebral cortex

SUGGESTED READINGS

Damasio, A. R. & Damasio, H. "Brain and Language." *Scientific American*, 267, 60–67, 1992

Kolb, B., & Whishaw, I. Q. *Fundamentals of Human Neuropsychology* (3rd ed.). New York: W. H. Freeman, 1990.

Geschwind, N., & Galburda, A. M. *Cerebral Lateralization: Biological Mechanisms, Associations, and Pathology*. Cambridge, MA: MIT Press, 1987.

Springer, S., & Deutsch, G. *Left Brain Right Brain* (4th ed.). New York: W.H. Freeman, 1993.

A-beta fibers   Fast-conducting (30 to 75 meters per second) *sensory neurons* that code for pressure and touch.

A-delta fibers   Moderate-conducting (5 to 30 meters per second) *sensory neurons* that code for temperature.

abducens nerve   The *motor nerve* that controls eye movement.

ablation   A surgical technique that involves the damaging or removal of neural tissue.

absolute refractory period   A stage in the *neural impulse* that occurs immediately after an *axon* fires, during which it is incapable of being excited.

accommodation   The process by which the *lens* changes in shape to focus on near objects.

acetylcholine   A *neurotransmitter* produced in both the *peripheral nervous system* and the *brain*. It is involved in the control of a wide variety of behavior including motor, cognitive, and emotional.

acetylcholinesterase (AChE)   An enzyme that destroys *acetylcholine*.

achromatic   A term used to describe visual sensations in black and white. See also *chromatic*.

ACTH   The abbreviation for *adrenocorticotrophic hormone*.

action potential   The abrupt change in *polarization* when a stimulus exceeds *threshold* in the *axon*. It is caused by sodium rushing into the *neuron*, which initiates *depolarization*, followed by potassium exiting the neuron, which produces *recovery*.

activation-synthesis theory   A theory stating that dreaming is triggered by the neural arousal that accompanies *REM sleep*. Dream content is determined by two other factors: memories that are activated and the *brain's* attempt to make sense of these memories.

active channels   Microscopic pores in the *neural membrane* having "gates" which allow the movement of *ions* only when the *neuron* is stimulated.

actomyosin   A chemical in *myofibrils* that produces muscle contraction.

acupuncture   A Chinese therapeutic technique during which the body is punctured at various points with long needles. It is used to relieve pain and for anesthesia.

addiction   Extreme dependence, measured by the severity of *withdrawal symptoms*.

adenyl cyclase   The enzyme that is activated when a *neurotransmitter* occupies a *receptor* on the *postsynaptic membrane*. It promotes the conversion of adenosine triphosphate into *cyclic adenosine monophosphate*.

adipocyte cells   Cells in the body that specialize in storing fat. Evidence indicates that these cells are more numerous in obese people than in people of normal weight.

adipsia   The condition of animals that refuse to drink even when they have a serious water deficit.

adrenal cortex   The outer layer of the adrenal *gland*, involved in the production of at least 40 types of *hormones* known as *steroids*.

adrenal medulla   The inner part of the adrenal *gland*, where *epinephrine* and *norepinephrine* are produced.

adrenergic receptors   Areas on the *postsynaptic membrane* selectively sensitive to *norepinephrine*. There are two types of adrenergic receptors, *alpha* and *beta receptors*.

adrenocorticotrophic hormone (ACTH)   A *hormone* that originates in the anterior *pituitary gland* and regulates the release of hormones by the *adrenal cortex*. It increases the adrenal cortex's output of *steroids* during *stress*.

affective disorders   Disorders distinguished by extreme shifts in mood.

afferent   Pertaining to *neurons* carrying impulses toward the *central nervous system*. (Compare *efferent*.)

agnosia   A neural disorder in which a brain-damaged patient can sense an object but does not know what that object is (from the Latin, meaning "without knowledge").

agonists   Drugs that enhance activity by mimicking the action of *neurotransmitters* at the synaptic receptor level.

agranulocytosis   A side effect of *atypical antischizophrenic drugs*. It consists of a drop in white blood cells and a lowering of resistance to infections and disease.

alcohol   The most widely known and widely used drug in the *depressant* category.

alexia   A neurological disorder characterized by the inability to read.

all-or-none law   A law stating that an *axon* will fire only when a stimulus reaches a particular intensity and that any intensity beyond this *threshold* will have no further effect on the magnitude of the *neural impulse*.

alpha motor neuron   A *neuron* that connects with and excites a *skeletal muscle*.

alpha receptors   *Adrenergic receptors* located on blood vessels.

alpha rhythm   The frequency of brain waves measuring between 9 and 12 Hz, generally found when a person is relaxing.

alpha-fetoprotein   An enzyme produced by the liver. It destroys *estrogen* but not *testosterone* in newborn rats.

Alzheimer's disease   A neurodegenerative disorder that is characterized by profound personality changes and intellectual impairment, including memory loss.

amacrine cells   Cells in the *retina* that interconnect *bipolar neurons*.

amblyopia   A visual abnormality in which children who have a tendency to squint fall into the habit of relying on only one eye for their visual stimulation, depriving the other eye of input. Also called lazy eye.

amino acid autoradiography   A technique in which radioactively labeled amino acids are injected in the vicinity of *cell bodies* and are transported to *axonal endings*. It is used to establish connections between cell bodies and axonal endings.

aminophosphonovalerate (AP5)   A drug that disrupts both *long-term potentiation* and the ability to learn a water maze.

amnesia   Loss of memory, either partial or total, following a *trauma*.

amphetamine   A drug that causes an initial elevation in mood and energy through an increase in *norepinephrine* and *dopamine*.

amphetamine psychosis   A syndrome shown by people who use excessive amounts of *amphetamine*. It resembles *schizophrenia* and includes *hallucinations* and *delusions*.

amplitude   In *sound*, the degree of pressure (the number of molecules compressed into a given area) in a sound wave or the force a vibrating object exerts on the molecules. (See also *loudness*.)

ampullae   Cavities at the base of each *semicircular canal*, each of which contains *receptors* (the *cristae*) that are sensitive to head movements.

amygdala   An area of the *brain*, within the *temporal lobe*, believed to play a role in aggressive and fear-related behavior.

analgesics   Drugs—*morphine*, for instance—that relieve pain.

anandamide   A newly discovered *neurotransmitter* isolated in the pig *brain* whose action is similar to that of *THC*.

anatomical coding   The concept that relates specific sensations to neural activity in specific areas of the *brain*.

androgens   Male sex *hormones*, the most prominent of which is *testosterone*.

angiogram   A procedure that makes it possible to visualize blood vessels in the *brain*. An x-ray is taken after dyes have been injected into the blood vessels connecting to the brain.

angiotensin II   A *hormone*, released by the kidneys, that regulates drinking behavior.

angstrom unit (Å)   A unit of measurement equal to 10^{-4} micrometers (μ).

annulospiral endings   *Stretch receptors* that wrap around the *nuclear bag* of *intrafusal fibers*. Their firing initiates the *stretch reflex*.

anorexia nervosa   An eating disorder that chiefly affects women in their teens and early twenties, who suddenly manifest an intense fear of becoming fat and develop so distorted an image of themselves that they see themselves as overweight even though they are emaciated.

antagonistic muscles   Muscles that work in opposition to each other, such as *flexors* and *extensors*.

antagonists   Drugs that impede the action of *neurotransmitters* by blocking the effects of neurotransmitters at the synaptic receptor level.

anterior   Toward the front (similar to *ventral*). Opposite of *posterior*.

anterior commissure   An interconnecting *tract* between the hemispheres that is larger in homosexual men and heterosexual women than in heterosexual men.

anterior pituitary gland   See *pituitary gland*.

anterograde amnesia   The inability to recall events that occur after neural *trauma*.

anterolateral system   Ascending neural *tracts* from the *spinal cord* to the *brain* that carry information related to temperature and pain.

antianxiety drugs   Drugs capable of relieving anxiety. *Librium* and *Valium* are examples.

antidepressants   Drugs used in the treatment of *depression*. Imipramine is an example.

antidiuretic   Drug used to decrease the amount of water lost in urine. One of the chief functions of the *hormone vasopressin*.

antiobsessional drugs   Drugs that relieve the extreme symptoms of *obsessive-compulsive* disorder. *Clomipramine* is an example.

antipsychotics   The term used to describe a number of drugs that have proven effective in the treatment of *affective disorders* and *schizophrenia*.

antischizophrenic drugs   Drugs used in the treatment of *schizophrenia*. *Phenothiazines* and *butyrophenones* are examples.

anxiety disorders   Disorders that involve severe and debilitating anxiety or fear in the face of situations that pose no real danger.

aphasia   A loss of language, either partial or complete, produced by brain damage.

Aplysia   A sea snail with a unique gill-withdrawal *reflex*. Its relatively simple *nervous system* makes it ideally suited for studying the synaptic changes that underlie *learning*.

apraxia   A neurological disorder characterized by the inability to carry out motor responses to verbal instructions.

aqueous humor   A fluid in the space between the *cornea* and the *lens*, both of which it nourishes.

arachidonic acid   A chemical that acts as one of the retrograde plasticity factors in *long-term potentiation*.

arachnoid layer   A thin membrane surrounding the *brain* and the *spinal cord*, located between the *dura mater* and the *pia mater*.

area postrema   An area of the *brain* left unprotected by the *blood-brain barrier* and involved in the control of vomiting.

aromatization   A chemical process by which *testosterone* is converted into *estrogen*.

aspartate   An amino acid thought to be one of the chief excitatory transmitters in the brain.

associative tolerance   See *environmental tolerance*.

astrocytes   Nonneural cells found in the *brain* and *spinal cord*. As part of the *blood-brain barrier* they are involved in transporting nutrients from the capillaries to *neurons* in the brain and cord.

atypical antischizophrenic drugs   A new class of *antischizophrenic drugs* that do not produce motor side effects. These drugs work by blocking *dopamine receptors* in the *limbic system* but not in the *extrapyramidal system*.

auditory nerve A *nerve* whose *dendrites* synapse with the *hair cells* in the *cochlea* and whose *cell bodies* collect in the *spiral ganglion* located just outside the walls of the *cochlea*.

auricle The external portion of the ear. Also known as the *pinna*.

autonomic nervous system The subdivision of the *peripheral nervous system* that controls the activity of the *viscera*. It is divided into the *sympathetic nervous system* and the *parasympathetic nervous system*.

autoreceptors *Receptors* on the presynapse which keep the *presynaptic neuron* "informed" about the amount of *neurotransmitter* in the synaptic gap.

axoaxonic synapse A *synapse* between the *axonal endings* of one *neuron* and the *axon* of another.

axodendritic synapse A *synapse* between the *axonal ending* of one *neuron* and the *dendrites* of another *axon*.

axon The generally long, single extension of the *neuron*.

axon hillock A slight elevation on a *neuron* where the *cell body* connects to the *axon*. It marks the point where the *graded potential* in the cell body is converted into the *all-or-none action potential* of the axon.

axonal endings Multibranching fibers at the end of *axons* that form *synapses* with the *dendrites*, the *cell bodies*, and, in some cases, the axons of other *neurons*.

axonal transport Process by which the *microtubules* transport life-sustaining chemicals from the *cell body* to the *axon endings*.

axosomatic synapse A *synapse* between the *axonal endings* of one *neuron* and the *cell body* (soma) of another.

barbiturate A *depressant* that works by enhancing the action of *GABA*.

basal ganglia The collective term for the *substantia nigra*, *caudate nucleus*, *putamen*, *globus pallidus*, and sub-thalamic nuclei, all of which are involved in motor control.

basilar membrane The membrane, crucial to hearing, that is located on the floor of the *cochlear canal* and supports the *organ of Corti*.

behaviorism The doctrine holding that only observable responses—the measurable features of overt behavior—are suitable for psychological study.

benzodiazepines A group of *depressants*, chiefly *Librium* and *Valium*, that are widely prescribed for the treatment of anxiety. They are thought to work by enhancing the action of *GABA*, one of the major inhibitory transmitters in the *brain*.

benzotropine A drug that inhibits the enzymes that normally break down *dopamine*. Used in the early stages of *Parkinson's disease*.

beta receptors *Adrenergic receptors* located in the intestines, lungs, and heart.

beta-amyloid protein A chemical that accumulates in the fluid between *neurons*, in the blood vessels that fuel neurons, and in the membranes (the *meninges*) that surround the *brain*.

binaural Pertaining to the detection of *sound* by two ears. The ability to hear binaurally is believed to account in part for the ability to localize sound.

binding The process by which a *neurotransmitter* couples with a *postsynaptic receptor site*.

biphasic effect of progesterone The fact that *progesterone* either facilitates or inhibits sexual behavior depending on the level of *estrogen*, high or low, respectively.

bipolar cell layer The layer of *bipolar neurons* in the *retina* that connects *rods* and *cones* to *ganglion cells*.

bipolar depression An *affective disorder* in which people undergo alternating periods of *depression* and *mania*.

bipolar neuron A *neuron* that has two extensions issuing from its *cell body*.

blind spot The area where the *optic nerve* leaves the *retina* of each eye. Since there are neither *rods* nor *cones* in the area, a stimulus projected there cannot be seen. Also known as the *optic disk*.

blindsight Disorder in which patients with damage to the *visual cortex* are able to point to objects yet are unaware of them.

blood-brain barrier A mechanism that prevents potentially harmful chemicals in the blood from reaching the *brain*. (See *astrocytes*.)

bottom-up processing The sensing stage of sensory processing, that is, the stage determined by the physical properties of the stimulus.

brain The mass of nerve tissue and supporting structures within the skull.

brain atlas A reference system showing different areas of the *brain* coordinated with bone sutures on the skull.

brain stem The part of the *brain* that contains the areas between the *medulla* and the *thalamus*.

bregma A reference point in *stereotaxic surgery* denoting the junction of two *skull sutures* toward the front of the skull. (From the Greek, meaning "front of the head.")

brightness A visual sensation related to the intensity of a light wave.

brightness contrast An enhanced ability to see objects as distinct from their background.

Broca's area An area in the *cortex* (the third frontal *gyrus*, usually of the left hemisphere) involved in the production of language.

"bug detectors" *Neurons* in the *optic nerve* of the frog's eye sensitive to small, dark, moving objects and unresponsive to stationary objects.

buspirone Drug used to alleviate anxiety that acts by binding to and activating *serotonin receptors*.

butyrophenones A class of *antipsychotic* drugs.

C fibers Slow-conducting (0.5 to 2 meters per second) *sensory neurons* that code for temperature and pain.

caffeine A *stimulant* that accelerates cellular metabolism, temporarily increasing energy.

calcium channels *Voltage-sensitive channels* in the *neural membrane* that open to allow positively charged calcium ions lying outside the *neuron* to move into the *axonal endings*.

cannula Thin hypodermic tubing used to inject chemicals into the *brain*. It is usually implanted with a *stereotaxic instrument*.

cardiac muscle The heart muscle. Unlike striated muscle, which it resembles, it is controlled by the *autonomic nervous system*.

castration The removal of *testes* from the male.

cataplexy Profound muscle weakness seen in *narcolepsy*.

cataracts Clouded *lens* which can lead to blindness if untreated.

catechol-*O*-methyltransferase (COMT) An enzyme that inactivates *monoamines* at the *synapse*. (Compare *monoamine oxidase*.)

caudate nucleus   An area in the *basal ganglia* involved in the inhibition of spontaneous motor activity.

causalgia   A persistent, burning pain that is associated with bullet wounds.

cell body   The part of the *neuron* that contains the *nucleus*; also called the soma.

cellular tolerance   Process whereby cells become less sensitive to drugs as administration continues.

central nervous system   All the neural and supportive tissue inside the *brain* and the *spinal cord*.

central nucleus of the amygdala   An area in the *amygdala* involved in the control of fear, learned and unlearned.

central sulcus   The groove that separates the motor *cortex* from the *somatosensory areas*.

centrifugal influence   The capacity of the *reticular formation* to control sensory input by inhibiting synaptic conduction in sensory pathways.

cerebellum   A large, convoluted structure mushrooming out from the *pons*. On the basis of information from the *somatosensory areas* and the *vestibular system*, it regulates movement and balance.

cerebral hemispheres   The identical halves of the *forebrain* connected by the *corpus callosum*.

cerebrospinal fluid   A colorless liquid that circulates through the *central nervous system*. It nourishes the *brain* and buffers it against blows to the head.

cerebrum   The largest part of the *brain*, divided into two hemispheres linked by *commissures*. Involved in the control of virtually all sensory, motor, and cognitive processes.

chemical-sensitive channels   *Active channels* in the *neural membrane* responsive to *neurotransmitters*.

chemoreceptors   *Receptors*, such as those for taste and smell, that specialize in the *transduction* of chemicals into *neural impulses*.

chlorolabe   A type of *iodopsin*.

chlorpromazine   An *antischizophrenic drug* that works by blocking the synaptic action of *dopamine*.

cholecystokinin   A *neuropeptide* that functions as both a *hormone* and a *neurotransmitter*. As a hormone it is involved in the digestion of fat and may be one of the signals for satiation. As a neurotransmitter it is produced in the *cortex* and *hypothalamus*.

choline   A nutrient found in egg yolks and liver and involved in the production of *acetylcholine*.

choline acetyltransferase   Enzyme involved in the production of *acetylcholine*.

cholinergic receptors   *Receptors* on the *postsynaptic membrane* selectively sensitive to *acetylcholine*. There are two types of cholinergic receptors, *muscarinic* and *nicotinic*.

choroid coat   A darkly pigmented layer of tissue, adjacent to the *cornea*, that supports the blood vessels supplying fuel to the *retina* and absorbs light waves scattered after corneal *refraction*.

choroid plexus   A highly vascular region in the *brain* involved in the production of *cerebrospinal fluid*.

chromatic   Pertaining to color or *hue*.

chromatolysis   The disappearance of *Nissl substance* and the migration of the *nucleus* to the periphery of the *cell body* following damage to the *neuron*.

chromosomes   Threadlike structures, consisting mainly of protein and DNA, found in the *nucleus* of every plant and animal cell. They are the genetic material that perpetuates traits from one generation to the next.

ciliary muscles   Muscles whose contraction and relaxation produce changes in the curvature of the *lens*, allowing focusing.

cingulate cortex   An area immediately above the *corpus callosum* involved in motor function via the *extrapyramidal system* and in emotion via the *hypothalamus*.

classical conditioning   The pairing of a *conditioned stimulus* (e.g., a tone) with an *unconditioned stimulus* (e.g., food) until an organism learns to respond (e.g., salivate) to the conditioned stimulus whether or not the unconditioned stimulus occurs.

clomipramine   A drug used to treat *obsessive-compulsive disorder*. It increases the level of *serotonin* by blocking its reuptake.

clozapine   An *atypical antischizophrenic drug* that alleviates schizophrenic symptoms without producing motor side effects.

cocaine   A *stimulant* that works by increasing *norepinephrine* and *dopamine* levels in the *synapse*.

cochlea   A bony, tubular organ in the *inner ear* consisting of three fluid-filled canals—the *vestibular canal*, the *tympanic canal*, and the *cochlear canal*—that are collectively responsible for the *transduction* of sound into *neural impulses*.

cochlear canal   The fluid-filled canal that lies between the *vestibular canal* and the *tympanic canal*.

cochlear nucleus   An area in the *medulla* where the *auditory nerve* synapses. There are two such areas, one on each side of the *brain stem* (for each auditory nerve).

cocktail-party effect   A selective-attention phenomenon whereby one is able to attend to one voice while shutting out other noise or conversations, and by which a person is able to take notice of significant information (his or her name, for example) though not specifically attending to it.

cognitive   Pertaining to the use of symbols, concepts, and language.

cognitive-arousal theory of emotion   The theory that the intensity of an emotion is related to *visceral* arousal, whereas the quality of an emotion is related to *cognitive* reactions to, or interpretations of, the environment.

cold turkey   The term used to describe overcoming an *addiction* suddenly and on one's own—without the aid of drugs.

collateral sprouting   Process by which neighboring *neurons* respond to damaged neurons by undergoing new growth.

commissure   A bundle of nerve fibers, such as the *corpus callosum*, that connects the *cerebral hemispheres* or the opposite sides of the *spinal cord*.

compensatory response   Response produced by the *synaptic defense* opposing and offsetting the effect of a drug. When the response is present, drug *tolerance* is produced, and when it is absent, tolerance is lost.

complementary colors   Colors that when mixed will produce gray.

complex cells   Cells in the visual *cortex* of the cat that are selectively responsive to lines. In contrast to *simple cells*, they respond to moving as well as stationary lines, and they respond no matter where on the *retina* the lines are projected.

complex tone   *Sound* produced by a complex wave, in which simultaneous sound waves interact. (Compare *simple tone*.)

component view   Wernicke's view of localization of function theorizing that what is localized to specific areas of the *brain* are not abstract psychological functions but rather component behaviors which collectively make up complex psychological functions.

computerized axial tomography (CAT scan)   A procedure that makes it possible to visualize abnormal tissue in the *brain*. The procedure consists of taking a series of x-rays from different positions around the subject's head and then processing them into a picture by using a computer.

concentration gradient   The tendency of *ions* to move until the regions they occupy are equal in concentration.

conditioned response   A response elicited by a *conditioned stimulus* after that stimulus has been paired with an *unconditioned stimulus* (e.g., salivation in response to a tone after the tone has been paired with food).

conditioned stimulus   The stimulus that elicits a *conditioned response* after training.

conduction deafness   Deafness caused by disease in the *middle ear*, where either the *eardrum* or the *ossicles* are rendered inoperative.

cones   Cone-shaped *receptors* in the *retina* whose sensitivity to differences in the length of light waves helps produce the sensation of color. See also *rods*.

consolidation   A theoretical concept to account for the transformation of *short-term memory* into *long-term memory*.

cornea   The transparent tissue covering the front of the eyeball, through which light enters. With the *lens*, it focuses light on the *retina*.

corpus callosum   A large bundle of *neurons* connecting the two *cerebral hemispheres*.

cortex   The outer layer of the *cerebrum*, consisting of gray neural *cell bodies*.

cortical localization   A theory of brain function that links specific behaviors to specific areas of the *cortex*.

cranial nerves   The 12 pairs of *nerves* that enter the *brain* directly, as opposed to the 31 pairs of *spinal nerves* that enter the *central nervous system* below the neck.

cretinism   Marked physical and mental retardation caused by a deficit of *thyroxine* during fetal development.

cristae   A category of *hair cells* that sense changes in the speed of rotating head movement.

cupula   A part of the *cristae*, involved in sensing head movement. (See also *ampullae*.)

curare   A drug that paralyzes *skeletal muscles* by blocking neuromuscular transmission.

cutaneous senses   A general term used to describe a number of sensations produced when substances come in contact with the skin.

cyanolabe   A type of *iodopsin*.

cyclic adenosine monophosphate (cyclic AMP)   The chemical produced when a *neurotransmitter* occupies a *receptor site* on the *postsynaptic membrane* and that acts on the membrane to open *ion* channels.

cytoplasm   All the protoplasmic material in a cell outside the *nucleus*.

Dale's law   The long-standing belief, recently called into question, that a *neuron* is capable of producing and releasing only one *neurotransmitter*.

decerebrate preparation   A surgical procedure in which a cut is made at the level of the *medulla*, detaching most of the *brain* from the *spinal cord*.

decibel (db)   The unit of intensity by which *sound* is measured.

declarative memory   Memories that reside in conscious awareness and require active recall to have an impact on behavior.

decorticate preparation   A surgical preparation in which the *cortex* is detached from the rest of the *brain*.

decremental conduction   The steadily decreasing *amplitude* of the electrochemical signal as it travels along the *dendrites* and the *cell body* up to the point of the *axon hillock*.

delayed conditioning   A *classical conditioning* procedure in which the *conditioned stimulus* (tone, for example) continues until the *unconditioned stimulus* (air puff to the eye, for example) is delivered. (Compare *trace conditioning*.)

delayed non-matching to sample   A behavioral procedure used to study the effects of lesions on *short-term memory*.

delta-9-tetrahydrocannabinol (THC)   The active ingredient in *marijuana*. In low doses, it produces feelings of euphoria and well-being but in large doses can cause paranoia and *hallucinations*.

delusions   Symptoms characterized by false beliefs, often centering on persecution.

dendrites   One of two categories of branching protoplasm that extend from *neurons*. They specialize in receiving neural information. (See also *axons*.)

depolarization   The state a *neuron* enters once the *action potential* has occurred and the neuron has fired, thereby losing its *polarization*.

deprenyl   A drug whose principal function is to inhibit the destructive effects of *MPTP*. Used to treat Parkinson's disease.

depressant   A class of drugs whose principal action is to retard neural activity. *Barbiturates* and *alcohol* are two examples.

depression   An *affective disorder* characterized by sadness, lethargy, difficulty in concentrating, and loss of appetite.

dermatome   An area of skin innervated by one of the *spinal nerves*.

deuteranopia   A type of color blindness characterized by the inability to see red and green. Wavelengths that normally produce the sensation of red are seen as yellow; wavelengths that normally produce the sensation of green are seen as gray.

diabetes insipidus   A disease caused by a deficit in *vasopressin* and marked by loss of water through excessive urination, and an increase in thirst and drinking behavior.

diabetes mellitus   A disease marked by the inability of the pancreas to secrete *insulin*.

dichaptic test   An experimental procedure in which subjects are allowed to touch (but not to see) two objects, one with each hand, and then are given a set of objects (visually displayed) from which they choose the ones they touched.

dichotic listening procedure   An experimental procedure in which subjects are given two different auditory messages at the same time through earphones—one to each ear—and are asked to attend to the words in one ear but not the other.

diisopropyl fluorophosphate (DFP)   A drug that reduces the level of *acetylcholinesterase*, thereby enabling *acetylcholine* to work in the *synapse* for a longer period of time.

distal   Away from. Opposite of proximal.

distance receptors   *Receptors* (auditory, visual, and olfactory) that can detect stimuli from a distance without direct contact with the source.

dopamine   A *neurotransmitter* produced in three areas, the *substantia nigra*, the *ventral tegmental area*, and the *hypothalamus*, and involved in a broad range of behaviors including motor behavior, arousal, and feelings of pleasure.

dopamine theory of schizophrenia   A theory that originally linked *schizophrenia* to an excess of the *neurotransmitter dopamine* but that now attributes the disease to excess *dopamine receptors*.

dorsal   Toward the top of the *brain* or the back of an animal. Opposite of *ventral*.

dorsal column–medial lemniscal system   An ascending neural *tract* from the *spinal cord* to the *brain* that carries information related to touch and pressure.

dorsal root   The area of the *spinal cord* where *sensory neurons* enter.

dorsal root ganglion   A group of *cell bodies* from *sensory neurons* outside the *spinal cord*.

Down's syndrome   A form of mental retardation whose neurological abnormalities are also seen in *Alzheimer's disease*.

drug disposition   The type of *tolerance* that develops to nonpsychoactive drugs, occurring because the more frequently these drugs are taken, the more actively the body acts to eliminate them from the system. Also called *metabolic tolerance*.

dualism   A philosophical view, commonly accepted by early philosophers, that the physical world is an entity separate from the "mind." It holds that since the mind has a "spiritual" nature, it is both superior to the physical body and beyond understanding.

duct glands   See *exocrine glands*.

dura mater   The outermost layer of the *meninges* that surrounds the *brain* and the *spinal cord*.

dyslexia   A learning disability that interferes with a person's ability to read.

eardrum   An extremely sensitive, elastic membrane that covers the opening of the *auditory canal* and vibrates in response to incoming *sound* (changes in air pressure). Also called the tympanic membrane.

efferent   Pertaining to *neurons* carrying impulses away from the *central nervous system*. (Compare *afferent*.)

electroconvulsive shock (ECS)   An electric shock delivered across the *brain* in lower animals, producing a convulsion. It is used experimentally to produce *amnesia*.

electroconvulsive therapy (ECT)   Procedure consisting of administering a brief electric current of moderate intensity to *electrodes* attached to a patient's forehead. Used to treat *unipolar disorder*.

electrode   A thin wire that delivers current to tissue.

electroencephalograph (EEG)   A machine that records neural activity through *electrodes* affixed to the scalp of a subject. Its record is an electroencephalogram.

electron   A negatively charged atomic particle.

electron microscope   A microscope that magnifies submicroscopic structures using beams of *electrons* instead of rays of light.

end organs   Microscopic structures in the skin related to specific stimuli such as pressure, warmth, and cold. They aid in the transmission of the stimulus to the *receptor* but do not transduce it into the *neural impulse*.

endocrine glands   Internal organs, such as the pancreas and the *pituitary gland*, that produce and release *hormones* into the bloodstream, which delivers them to target organs.

endolymph   Fluid in the *semicircular canals*, the *vestibular sacs*, and the *cochlear canal* that nourishes the *receptors* in the *inner ear*.

endorphins   A group of *neurotransmitters* found in the *limbic system*. *Opiates* such as *morphine* and *heroin* mimic their action, and they are involved in the control of a variety of behaviors including pain suppression, feelings of reward and pleasure, and the formation of *long-term memory*.

end plate   The slight elevation on the surface of a muscle fiber where the fiber synapses with a *motor neuron*.

end plate potential (EPP)   The *depolarization* produced by a *neurotransmitter* at the *end plate* of a muscle fiber. Much like the *generator potential* and the *synaptic potential*, the end plate potential is graded and decremental.

enkephalin   A term used to describe the two most prevalent *endorphins* in the *brain* and *spinal cord*—methionine enkephalin and leucine enkephalin.

environmental tolerance   *Tolerance* that occurs with long *interdrug intervals* and that is under the control of the environment in which the drug is taken.

epinephrine   A chemical that acts primarily as a *hormone* but also as a *neurotransmitter*. As a hormone it is produced by the *adrenal medulla* and is released during *stress*, raising blood pressure and glucose levels and facilitating memory consolidation.

epithelium   A square inch of tissue in the upper nasal passage where the *receptors* for smell are located.

equipotentiality, law of   A law stating that intact areas of the *brain* have the capacity to assume the function of damaged areas.

erythrolabe   A type of *iodopsin*.

estrogen   Female sex *hormones*, the most prominent of which is estradiol.

estrus   A recurring time during which female mammals ovulate and experience a higher than normal sexual urge.

Eustachian tube   A narrow passage, leading from the *middle ear* to the back of the mouth, that maintains equal pressure between the inside and outside of the middle ear.

excitatory postsynaptic potential (EPSP)   The depolarization induced in the *postsynaptic membrane* by an excitatory *neurotransmitter*.

exocrine glands   So-called *duct glands*—the salivary glands, for instance—whose *hormones* do not enter the bloodstream but rather are carried to target organs by ducts.

exocytosis   The process by which synaptic vesicles move to the *neural membrane* and discharge *neurotransmitters* into the synaptic gap.

extensors   Muscles that straighten or extend the limbs. (Compare *flexors*.)

external auditory meatus   A narrow passage connecting the *pinna* to the *eardrum*.

exteroceptive stimuli   Stimuli originating outside the body and sensed by *receptors* located on or near the body surface, as distinguished from *interoceptive stimuli* which originate in the *viscera*.

extinction   A procedure by which learned behavior is eliminated through the omission of reinforcement.

extracellular fluid   The medium that surrounds all cells.

extrafusal fibers Fibers that, along with *intrafusal fibers*, make up *skeletal muscles*.

extrapyramidal system The motor system by which the *brain* exerts control over *muscle tone*. It originates in the *cortex* and synapses in a number of areas (the *basal ganglia*, the *cerebellum*, the *reticular formation*) as it descends to the *spinal cord*.

facial-feedback hypothesis The hypothesis that facial expressions, specifically the feedback from facial muscles, contribute to the quality of emotions.

Factor S A chemical in *cerebrospinal fluid* that when extracted from sleep-deprived goats and injected into normal animals produces an increase in *slow-wave sleep* but not in *REM sleep*.

fasciculus cuneatus An ascending spinal *tract* that collects pressure information from the upper part of the body and synapses in the *medulla*. (See also *fasciculus gracilis*.)

fasciculus gracilis An ascending spinal *tract* that collects pressure information from the lower part of the body and synapses in the *medulla*. (See also *fasciculus cuneatus*.)

fetal alcohol syndrome A syndrome caused by the ingestion of *alcohol* during pregnancy that results in a variety of birth abnormalities, including mental retardation, hyperactivity, and heart defects.

final common pathway The *alpha motor neuron* that is the final link between the *central nervous system* and *skeletal muscles*.

firing state The stage of the *action potential* in which a sudden rush of sodium *ions* into the *neural membrane* initiates the electrochemical signal.

fissure A narrow groove that separates brain areas. Also known as the *sulcus*.

flexors Muscles that flex or bend the limbs, such as the biceps. (Compare *extensors*.)

flower-spray endings *Stretch receptors* wrapped around the *nuclear bag*. Impulses initiated in these endings inhibit the contraction of *antagonistic muscles*.

fluoxetine A type of *SSRI*. Also known as *Prozac*.

flurazepam A *benzodiazepine* used to treat *insomnia*. It does not increase the amount of time people sleep but rather the quality of sleep.

follicle-stimulating hormone (FSH) A *hormone* that is produced by the *anterior pituitary gland*. It stimulates the production of sperm in the male and the development of the egg and the release of *estrogen* in the female.

forebrain One of three major subdivisions of the *brain*, including the *cortex*, the *thalamus*, and the *hypothalamus*.

fovea The central part of the *retina*, characterized by a dense concentration of *cones* and no *rods*.

free fatty acids The breakdown product of fat that provides energy once food is metabolized.

free nerve endings The endings of *neurons* that can act as *receptors* as well as conduct impulses. They are found in the skin, the muscles, and the *viscera*.

free-floating anxiety See *generalized anxiety disorder*.

frequency In *sound*, the number of periodic compressions and *rarefactions* per unit of time or the rate of vibration, commonly measured in cycles per second (Hz). Frequency produces the sensation of *pitch*.

frequency theory of pitch The theory that the *basilar membrane* mimics incoming sounds in a way that enables the various *pitches* to be coded as frequencies of *neural impulses*.

Fröhlich's syndrome A condition of obesity and genital atrophy, once thought to be caused by a tumor in the *pituitary gland* but later linked to damage in the *ventromedial hypothalamus*.

frontal cortex Area of the *brain* thought to be responsible for the negative symptoms that dominate the behavior of some *schizophrenics*.

frontal lobe One of four main subdivisions of each *cerebral hemisphere*. Involved in motor control and emotional behavior.

functional coding The concept that relates specific sensations to specific frequencies or patterns of neural activity.

fundamental frequency In a *complex tone*, the wave with the lowest *frequency* and the greatest *amplitude*.

GABA (gamma-aminobutyric acid) An inhibitory *neurotransmitter* that exerts its effects by hyperpolarizing the *postsynaptic membrane*.

gamete A mature sexual reproductive cell (sperm or egg) that unites with another cell, forming a *zygote*.

gamma motor system The system by which the *brain* controls *muscle tone* via the *extrapyramidal system* and the *intrafusal fibers*.

ganglia Groups of neural *cell bodies* and *dendrites* outside the *brain* and the *spinal cord*.

ganglion cells *Neurons* in the *retina*. Their *axons* make up the *optic nerve*, and their *dendrites* synapse with *bipolar neurons*, which in turn synapse with *rods* and *cones*.

general adaptation syndrome A theorized sequence of reactions to prolonged *stress*, consisting of alarm, resistance, and exhaustion.

generalized anxiety disorder A condition that persists for long periods and is characterized by fear, tension, and anxiety that do not appear to be related to any particular situation or stimulus. Also known as *free-floating anxiety*.

generator potential The condition of a *receptor* after it has been excited and partially depolarized. If *depolarization* exceeds the axonal *threshold*, the generator potential produces a *neural impulse*.

gland An organ that manufactures and secretes *hormones* that affect the activity of other organs. The two types are *endocrine glands* and *exocrine glands*.

globus pallidus An area in the *basal ganglia* involved in spontaneous movement.

glomeruli Groups of *dendrites* and *cell bodies* in the *olfactory bulb* that synapse with the *olfactory nerve*.

glucagon A *hormone* produced by the pancreas. It promotes the breakdown of fat into usable nutrients.

glucocorticoids Type of *steroids* released by the *adrenal cortex gland* in response to *stress*.

glucostatic theory A theory of food regulation stating that eating behavior is controlled by the level of glucose in the body.

glutamate An amino acid thought to be one of the chief excitatory transmitters in the *brain*. Abnormal glutamate (and *GABA*) levels have been linked to *Huntington's disease*.

glycine A *neurotransmitter* found in the *spinal cord* and lower portions of the *brain*.

Golgi tendon organ A *receptor* in the tendon. An intense pull on the tendon causes it to fire, which in turn inhibits muscle contraction. The receptor thus protects the tendon from tearing.

672

gonads The term that refers to sex organs: *testes* in males and *ovaries* in females.

graded potential The electrochemical signal in a *receptor*, a neural *cell body*, or a *dendrite*. It is graded because the magnitude of the electrochemical signal depends directly on the intensity of the stimulus.

"grandmother" cells The term used to describe individual *neurons* that are thought to serve a single function, such as recognizing another person.

gray commissure A bundle of *interneurons* in the *spinal cord*, connecting opposite sides of the cord.

gray matter Masses of *cell bodies* and *dendrites* in various parts of the *central nervous system*, which appear gray because they are not *myelinated*.

growth cone The specialized structure, on the tip of the *axon*, responsible for the growth of axons during embryological development.

gustation The sensation of taste.

gyrus The surface area between one *sulcus* and another.

habituation A form of simple *learning* manifested by a decrease in the strength of a response when a stimulus is presented repeatedly.

hair cells *Receptors* in the *organ of Corti*, the *vestibular sacs*, the *semicircular canals*, and the *taste buds*. In the organ of Corti, they are supported by the *basilar membrane* and connect with *neurons* making up the *auditory nerve*.

hallucination A sensory experience in the absence of related stimuli.

hallucinogen A substance that produces *hallucinations*.

harmonics The science of musical *sounds*.

helicotrema A small opening that connects the *vestibular canal* with the *tympanic canal* in the *cochlea*.

helplessness A state in which one has no means of escaping or controlling a psychological stressor.

heroin An *opiate* drug that works by mimicking the action of *enkephalins* and *endorphins*.

hertz (Hz) One hertz is equal to one cycle per second. Sound wave *frequencies* are commonly measured in hertz.

hindbrain One of three main subdivisions of the *brain*. It includes the *medulla* and the *pons*.

hippocampus An area in the *temporal lobe* of each *cerebral hemisphere*, thought to be involved in the processing of *short-term memory* and spatial information.

histofluorescence A procedure for visualizing *monoamine* transmitters. It consists of viewing the tissue under a fluorescent microscope. Different brain areas take on different colors depending on the monoamines they contain.

homeostasis The balanced state of the internal environment, which must remain relatively constant for optimal production of energy.

homosexual A person who has a sexual preference for individuals of his or her own sex.

horizontal cells Cells in the *retina* that interconnect *bipolar cells*.

hormones Chemical substances secreted by *endocrine glands* into the bloodstream or by *exocrine glands* into special ducts.

horseradish peroxidase An enzyme that is used to trace neural pathways in the *brain*.

hue The sensation of color produced by differences in the length of light waves. The human eye is capable of detecting light waves ranging in length from about 380 nm (a violet hue) to 760 nm (a red hue).

Huntington's disease A rare, fatal genetic disease whose symptoms include involuntary motor movements and severe mental deterioration culminating in death.

hydrocephalus A pathological condition in the *brain* resulting from blockage of circulation of *cerebrospinal fluid*. The excessive pressure created by the block results in brain damage and mental retardation.

6-hydroxydopamine A chemical capable of producing irreversible neural damage. It is taken up by the *axonal endings* of *neurons* that produce *norepinephrine* or *dopamine*.

hypercomplex cells *Neurons* in the visual *cortex* of the cat that are selectively sensitive to lines of certain lengths and angles.

hyperglycemia A condition characterized by a high level of glucose in the blood. A symptom of *diabetes mellitus*.

hyperopia Farsightedness, the condition that arises when light waves entering the eye are not bent enough so that they hit the *retina* while still partially scattered.

hyperphagia A condition characterized by constant hunger.

hyperpolarization State of a *neuron* in which the inside of the neuron is more negative than normal in relation to the outside of the neuron.

hypnagogic hallucinations Bizarre and vivid dreams that occur at the onset of sleep in *narcolepsy*.

hypnosis A trancelike state in which a person is highly suggestible.

hypoglossal nerve *Motor nerve* in the *peripheral nervous system* controlling tongue movement.

hypothalamus An area of the *brain* next to the third *ventricle*, often referred to as the guardian of the body because of its dominant role in regulating the internal environment.

hypothyroidism Undersecretion of *thyroxine* by the *thyroid gland*, which in adults results in lethargy and in the fetus produces mental retardation (*cretinism*).

implicit memory Memories recalled through priming at the automatic unconscious level.

incus An anvil-shaped bone of the *middle ear* whose movement sets into motion two other bones—the *malleus* and the *stapes*.

inferior colliculus An area in the *midbrain* involved in control of reflexive reactions to *sound*.

infratemporal cortex The area of the *cortex* which when damaged in monkeys results in loss of the ability to identify visually familiar objects.

inhibitory postsynaptic potential (IPSP) The decrease in excitability of a *neuron*, produced by the *hyperpolarizing* effects of an inhibitory *neurotransmitter* such as *GABA*.

inner ear The innermost part of the ear, consisting of the *semicircular canals*, the *vestibular sacs*, and the *cochlea*.

innervation ratio The number of muscle fibers per nerve fiber. As the ratio increases, precision in motor control decreases.

insomnia A sleep disorder characterized by the inability to fall asleep.

instrumental conditioning The procedure by which behavior is reinforced, transforming trial-and-error behavior into a well-organized learned response. (See also *classical conditioning*.)

insulin   A *hormone* produced by the pancreas. It promotes the uptake of glucose by the cells and the buildup of fat.

intentional tremor   A jerkiness of limbs shown by people with *cerebellar* damage. The jerkiness appears when the limb is moving but not when it is at rest.

interdrug interval   The interval between administrations of a drug.

intermediate colors   Colors that result from the mixing of different wavelengths.

interneuron   A *neuron* that lies between and forms *synapses* with other neurons.

interoceptive stimuli   Stimuli originating in the *viscera*, as distinguished from *exteroceptive stimuli*, which originate outside the body.

interpositus nucleus   An area in the *cerebellum* that when lesioned prevents a rabbit from learning in a *delayed classical conditioning* procedure.

interstitial cells   Cells in the *testes* that produce *testosterone*.

interstitial-cell-stimulating hormone (ICSH)   A *hormone* that is produced by the anterior *pituitary gland*. It stimulates the *testes* to produce and release *testosterone*.

intrafusal fibers   Fibers that, along with *extrafusal fibers*, make up *skeletal muscles*. The combined action of the two kinds of fibers produces muscle tension, which is regulated by the *stretch reflex*.

intragastric feeding   A procedure in which animals are trained to press a lever to obtain injections of a liquid diet administered through a tube connected to the stomach. The procedure allows them to regulate food intake without the benefit of neural feedback related to taste and smell.

intralaminar nuclei   An area in the *thalamus* involved in coding dull, burning pain.

iodopsin   A chemical substance in the *cones* that breaks down into *retinene* and photopsin when exposed to sufficiently bright light. The three types are *cyanolabe* (blue-sensitive), *chlorolabe* (green-sensitive), and *erythrolabe* (red-sensitive).

ion channels   Microscopic pores that penetrate the membrane and govern the flow of *ions* into and out of the *neuron* during the *resting* and *action potentials*. There are two types: *active channels* and *passive channels*.

ions   Electrically charged atoms.

iris   A pigmented membrane behind the *cornea*. It contains muscle fibers that control the amount of light entering the eye by regulating the size of the *pupil*.

juxtallocortex   Layer of neural tissue in the human *cortex* just beneath the *neocortex*.

kainic acid   A neurotoxin which destroys *cell bodies* but not neural *tracts*.

kinesthetic   Pertaining to sensations produced by the position and movement of the muscles.

Kluver-Bucy syndrome   Abnormal behavior in monkeys—including hypersexuality, an increase in chewing, and an absence of characteristic fears—that results from bilateral removal of the *temporal lobes* and damage to the *amygdala* and neighboring areas.

Korsakoff's psychosis   A condition in which neural damage results from alcoholism. Symptoms are loss of recent memories, tremors, and *hallucinations*.

Krause's end bulbs   *End organs* in skin areas receptive to cold.

L-dopa   A drug that promotes the production of *dopamine*. Used to treat *Parkinson's disease*.

labyrinthine organs   The collective term for the *semicircular canals* and *vestibular sacs* in the *inner ear*.

labyrinthine sensitivity   The capacity to regulate *muscle tone* and posture, resulting from stimulation of *receptors* in the *vestibular sacs* and the *semicircular canals*.

laminae   Layers of neural cells found in the *spinal cord*.

lateral   Away from the midline or median plane. Opposite of *medial*.

lateral fissure   A groove on the surface of the *cortex* separating the *temporal lobe* from the *frontal lobe* and the *parietal lobe*.

lateral geniculate nucleus   An area in the *thalamus* where the *optic nerve* synapses with *neurons* that project to the visual area in the *occipital lobe* of the *cortex*.

lateral hypothalamus   An area in the *hypothalamus* that plays a role in the control of eating, drinking, and nonaffective attack behavior.

lateral inhibition   The phenomenon in which stimulation of one *ommatidium* in the *Limulus* eye inhibits spontaneous firing in the *ganglion cell* of its neighbors.

lateral lemniscus   A *tract* that transmits auditory information from the *superior olive* to the *inferior colliculus*.

lateral tegmental area   An area in the *pons* involved in the production of *norepinephrine*.

learned helplessness   A term used to describe the state of animals that have been subjected to inescapable shock for long periods of time and will later do nothing to control the shock even though they have the opportunity to do so.

learning   A change in behavior that results from experience and endures over time.

lens   A transparent structure in the eye located behind the *pupil*. Its function is to complete the focusing begun at the *cornea*.

lesion   Circumscribed damage to tissue due to surgery, injury, or disease.

Librium   A *depressant* drug that is widely prescribed for the treatment of anxiety and whose neural effects have been linked to *GABA*. (See *benzodiazepines*.)

limbic system   A group of brain areas forming a crude border around the *brain stem*. It includes the *amygdala*, the *hippocampus*, the *septal area*, and parts of the *hypothalamus*. Involved in the control of emotional behavior.

Limulus   The horseshoe crab, whose eye is well suited for experimental analysis because of its relatively few and large photosensitive *cells* called *ommatidia*.

lipostatic theory   A theory proposing that fat deposits or fat-related chemicals regulate eating behavior.

lithium   One of the most effective drugs in the treatment of *bipolar disorder*.

local theory of motivation   The theory that there are *receptors* located in the periphery of the body, in such places as the stomach and the mouth, and that these receptors are sensitive to stimuli produced by deprivation of food and water.

local-circuit neuron   An *interneuron* whose *axons* as well as *dendrites* are short and multibranching, a structure that makes it ideally suited for interacting with other *neurons*.

localization of function A theory that proposes that different areas of the *brain* control different behaviors.

locus coeruleus A group of neural *cell bodies* located in the *pons*, involved in the production of *norepinephrine* and believed to play a role in maintaining emotion and regulating *REM sleep*.

long-term memory The storage of learned information in a form that is resistant to *amnesia*.

long-term potentiation (LTP) The phenomenon in which an intense stimulus delivered directly to neural tissue enhances postsynaptic activity produced by a second, weaker stimulus. LTP has been used as a model for studying the physiological basis of *learning* and memory.

lordosis The behavioral response made by sexually receptive female rats (four-legged mammals in general) in preparation for copulation. It consists of elevating the hindquarters.

loudness An auditory sensation related to changes in the *amplitude* of a sound wave, measured in *decibels*. It is neurally coded by the number of impulses reaching the auditory *cortex* per unit of time; as the number increases, loudness increases.

luteinizing hormone (LH) A hormone, also known as *interstitial-cell-stimulating hormone*, that is produced by the *anterior pituitary gland*. Its release is triggered by the *hypothalamus*, and its target organs are the sex *glands*.

lysergic acid diethylamide (LSD) A *psychedelic* drug whose neural effects have been linked to *serotonin*.

M cells *Ganglion cells* in the *retina* that project to the magnocellular layers of the *lateral geniculate nucleus*. Involved in the coding of motion.

Mach bands The perceptual phenomenon in which the contrast between a white area and a black area is sharpest at the border between the two.

macula Walls of the *vestibular sacs*, containing *otoliths* and *hair cells*. As the head moves (accelerates or decelerates), the otoliths bend various hair cells, thereby initiating the neural code for head position.

magnetic resonance imaging (MRI) A technique that makes it possible to monitor differences in chemical composition (e.g., the concentration of hydrogen) in tissue. Because different tissues contain different concentrations of hydrogen, images can be generated to reflect these differences.

malleus A hammer-shaped bone of the *middle ear*. Along with the two other bones in the middle ear, it amplifies sound waves.

mammillary bodies An area in the *limbic system*, damage to which has been implicated in memory loss shown by *Korsakoff* patients.

mania An *affective disorder* characterized by hyperactivity, rapid speech, and extreme expansiveness and elation.

marijuana The most commonly used *psychedelic* drug. Made from the dried leaves and flowers of the plant *Cannabis sativa*, whose active ingredient is *THC*. (See *delta-9-tetrahydrocannabinol*.)

mass action, theory of The theory that the behavioral effects of brain damage are related more to the amount of damage than to the specific area of damage.

medial Toward the midline. Opposite of *lateral*.

medial forebrain bundle A *tract* that originates in the *substantia nigra* and *ventral tegmental area* and terminates in a number of areas including the *amygdala*, the *septal area*, and the *nucleus accumbens*. Referred to as one of the pleasure centers because of the strong reinforcing properties it has when electrically stimulated.

medial geniculate nucleus The area in the *thalamus* to which most of the auditory circuits in the *lateral lemniscus* project, either directly or indirectly.

medial lemniscus A neural *tract* that carries *somatosensory* information from the *medulla* to the *thalamus*.

medulla The part of the *hindbrain* that connects to the *spinal cord*. It contains *nuclei* associated with most of the *cranial nerves* and with vital autonomic functions such as respiration and heart rate.

Meissner's corpuscles *End organs* in the pressure-sensitive areas in the skin.

melatonin A *hormone* secreted by the *pineal gland*, whose release is stimulated in the dark and ceases when individuals are exposed to light. *Depression* experienced by people with *SAD* may be the result of abnormally high levels of melatonin.

membrane theory Bernstein's theory of neural conduction. The theory states that the *neuron* has two electrical states: the resting state, in which charges are separated across the *neural membrane*, and the excitation state, in which charges move in and out of the neuron across the membrane to produce the neuroelectric signal.

meninges Protective membranes (the *dura mater*, the *arachnoid layer*, and the *pia mater*) that surround the brain and the *spinal cord*.

meningitis A disease produced by inflammation of the *meninges*, potentially leading to paralysis and death.

mental illness A psychological disorder characterized by the breakdown of emotion, cognition, and the ability to plan and carry out actions. Mental illnesses are classified by their symptoms.

mescaline A *psychedelic*, whose principal effects are visual *hallucinations* and disorientation in time and space.

metabolic tolerance See *drug disposition*.

methadone A drug that stops the desire for *opiates* and at the same time prevents the *stress* that normally accompanies opiate withdrawal.

N-methyl-D-aspartate (NMDA) receptors *Receptors* to which *glutamate* binds and through which calcium ions enter to initiate *long-term potentiation*.

microglia Nonneural cells found in the *central nervous system* which, along with *oligodendrocytes* and *astrocytes*, provide support and nourishment for *neurons*.

microspikes Fingerlike projections on the *growth cones* of developing *neurons* that reach out and test the surface of the surrounding tissue.

microtubules Cylindrical structures in the *axon* that carry life-sustaining chemicals from the *cell body* to the *axonal endings* by *axonal transport*.

microvilli The hairlike projections that extend from taste *receptors* to the surface of the tongue.

midbrain One of the three main subdivisions of the *brain*. It lies between the *hindbrain* and the *forebrain* and contains such areas as the *red nucleus*, the *superior* and *inferior colliculi*, and the *substantia nigra*.

middle ear An air-filled cavity between the *eardrum* and the *oval window*, in which lie three bones (the *malleus*, the *incus*, and the *stapes*) and two muscles (the *tensor muscle* and the *stapedius muscle*).

midline suture The bony ridge that runs the length of the skull, used as a coordinate in *stereotaxic surgery*.

mitral cells   *Neurons* whose *cell bodies* are in the *olfactory bulb* and whose *axons* make up the *olfactory tract*. They receive information from the *olfactory nerve* and relay it to other areas in the *cortex*.

mixed nerve   Any *nerve* containing both *sensory neurons* and *motor neurons*.

modulation neuron   *Neuron* which forms a *synapse* with a *presynaptic neuron* and releases a *neurotransmitter* that controls the amount of neurotransmitter released by the presynaptic neuron.

monism   Philosophical view that the laws governing the workings of the mind are no different from the laws that govern physical events.

monoamine oxidase (MAO)   An enzyme that deactivates *monoamines* after they act on the *postsynaptic membrane* and are drawn back into the *axonal endings*.

monoamine oxidase inhibitors   *Antidepressant drugs* that increase *monoamines* by inhibiting *monoamine oxidase*.

monoamine theory of depression   A theory that links *depression* to deficits in the *neurotransmitters norepinephrine* and *serotonin*. The theory is based on the fact that drugs that decrease norepinephrine and serotonin in the *brain* produce depression, while drugs that increase the neurotransmitters alleviate the symptoms.

monoamines   The generic term for four *neurotransmitters: norepinephrine, serotonin, dopamine,* and *epinephrine*.

monosynaptic reflex   Neural circuit in which a single *synapse* links the *sensory* and *motor neurons*, as in the knee-jerk reflex.

morphine   An *opiate* which has been used in the treatment of pain. It enhances synaptic activity by occupying *receptor sites* normally occupied by *endorphins*.

motor neuron   A *neuron* that connects the *central nervous system* with muscles and *glands*.

motor unit   A single *motor neuron* and the muscle fibers it controls.

MPTP   Chemical which selectively destroys *neurons* in the *substantia nigra*, causing *Parkinson's*-like symptoms.

Müllerian ducts   The reproductive system that develops into the female organs if *androgen* is not present.

multiple personality disorder   Term referring to a person who exhibits two or more distinct identities. Should not be confused with *schizophrenia*.

multiple sclerosis   Disease which attacks areas of the *brain* related to motor control, producing tremors and postural rigidity.

multipolar neuron   A *neuron* with a single *axon* and many *dendrites* issuing from the *cell body*. It functions as a *motor neuron* or an *interneuron*.

muscarinic receptors   *Receptors* found in the central nervous system on smooth muscles and *glands*. They selectively bind to *acetylcholine*.

muscle spindle   A structure in *skeletal muscles* that contains *intrafusal fibers* and *stretch receptors*. When stimulated, it initiates the *stretch reflex* and controls *muscle tone*.

muscle tone   An ongoing postural response that provides tension or support in muscles, establishing a basis for body position and providing a behavioral backdrop within which discrete motor movements can take place.

mutual inhibition   In vision, a phenomenon in which simultaneous stimulation of several *receptor* cells results in less firing of each cell than occurs when the cells are stimulated individually.

myasthenia gravis   A disease characterized by severe muscle weakness and often paralysis that results from a deficiency of *acetylcholine* receptors in the *neuromuscular junctions*.

myelin   The fatty sheath around an *axon*, formed in the *peripheral nervous system* by *Schwann cells* and in the *central nervous system* by *oligodendrocytes*.

myofibrils   Threadlike contractile fibers in *skeletal muscles* that give rise to a striated appearance.

myopia   Nearsightedness, the condition that arises when light waves entering the eye overbend, focusing in front of the *retina*.

myotonia   Muscle tension that occurs during the excitation phase of the *sexual response cycle*.

naloxone   A drug that blocks the action of *endorphins* and *enkephalins*.

naltrexone   A drug that blocks the action of *endorphins* and *enkephalins*.

nanometer (nm)   A unit of measure equal to one-billionth of a meter or to 10 Å.

narcolepsy   A sleep disorder characterized by sudden attacks of sleep. Other symptoms include *cataplexy*, sleep paralysis, and *hypnagogic hallucinations*.

negative symptoms   Symptoms in *schizophrenia* marked by the absence of behavior. Examples include poverty of thought or speech, and social withdrawal. (Compare with *positive symptoms*.)

neglect syndrome   A condition that occurs in stroke and accident victims who have suffered extensive damage to the *parietal* area of the *cortex* usually of the right hemisphere. The victims behave as though the left side of their environment—including the left side of their body—does not exist.

neocortex   Neural tissue of the human *cortex* consisting of six layers and located on the surface of the *brain*.

nerve   A bundle of *neurons* in the *peripheral nervous system*.

nerve deafness   Deafness caused by degeneration of the *auditory nerve* or the *hair cells* connected to that nerve.

nerve growth factor   Chemical which promotes the growth of *neurons* during neural development and following peripheral nerve damage.

nervous system   The system of cells (*neurons*) specialized in conducting electrochemical information. Divided into the *central nervous system* and the *peripheral nervous system*.

neural crest cells   Cells that migrate from the *neural tube* and develop into the *peripheral nervous system* during embryonic development.

neural impulse   The electrochemical process by which *neurons* transmit information.

neural membrane   Membrane of the *neuron*. Its chief function is exerting control over the movement of *ions* in and out of the neuron.

neural tube   Part of the embryo from which most cells destined to become *neurons* originate.

neuralgia   Persistent pain produced by infection in the *peripheral nervous system*.

neuroblasts   Cells that migrate from the *neural tube* and develop into the *central nervous system* during embryonic development.

676

neurofibrillary tangles Protein filaments which appear in neural *cell bodies* during the aging process.

neuroglial cells Nonneural cells that provide support and nourishment for *neurons*. There are two groups: those in the *central nervous system*—the *oligodendrocytes*, the *astrocytes*, and the *microglia*—and those in the *peripheral nervous system*—the *Schwann cells* and the *satellite cells*.

neuromuscular junction The gap between a *motor neuron* and the muscle fiber *innervated* by it.

neuron A cell distinguished from other cells by its ability to conduct electrochemical signals.

neuropeptide Y A *neurotransmitter* which elicits eating when injected in minuscule amounts into different areas of the *hypothalamus*.

neuropeptides A group of *neurotransmitters* including *cholecystokinin, substance P, endorphins,* and *enkephalins.* Neuropeptides consist of short chains of amino acids, ranging from 2 to 39 amino acids in length.

neurosis Term once used by psychiatrists and psychologists in connection with abnormal mental conditions that interfered with, but didn't necessarily cripple, a person's ability to function on a day-to-day basis.

neurotransmitter A chemical substance, usually produced in the *axonal endings* and released at the *synapse,* that alters the permeability of the *postsynaptic membrane.*

nicotine A mild *stimulant* that produces an effect similar to that of *caffeine* by activating excitatory *synapses.*

nicotinic receptors *Receptors* found on *skeletal muscles* and autonomic *postganglionic fibers.* They selectively bind to *acetylcholine.*

nictitating membrane The so-called third eyelid that some mammals possess. In rabbits the nictitating membrane response has been *classically conditioned* and has been used to study the role played by various brain areas in *learning.*

nigrostriatal tract A *tract* that originates in the *substantia nigra* and terminates in the striatum (the *caudate nucleus* and *putamen*).

Nissl substance The collective term for the endoplasmic reticulum, the ribosomes, and the RNA in the *cell body* of a *neuron.*

nitric oxide A chemical that acts as one of the retrograde plasticity factors in *long-term potentiation.*

nodes of Ranvier Areas along *myelinated axons* that mark unmyelinated gaps. Together with *myelin*, the nodes speed neural conduction through a process called *saltatory conduction,* characterized by *depolarization* skipping from node to node.

nonaromatizable A term used to describe *androgens* such as dihydrotestosterone that cannot be converted into *estrogen.* (Compare *aromatization.*)

nonassociative tolerance A type of *tolerance* that occurs with short *interdrug intervals.* It is produced by a compensatory response that lingers from one drug administration to the next, and it does not depend on the environment. Also known as *physiological tolerance.*

nondecremental conduction Conduction of the electrochemical signal in the *axon* that does not diminish regardless of the distance the signal travels. (Compare with *decremental conduction.*)

norepinephrine (NE) A *neurotransmitter* that is produced in both the *peripheral nervous system* and the *brain,* specifically the *locus coeruleus.* Its behavioral effects are diverse, involving *learning,* memory, wakefulness, and emotion.

nuclear bag An elastic membrane that makes up the middle region of *intrafusal fibers.*

nucleus A group of *cell bodies* found in the *central nervous system.* Not to be confused with the nucleus within each cell body.

nucleus accumbens An area in the *brain* involved in the reward produced by *medial forebrain bundle* stimulation as well as by *cocaine, amphetamine,* and *morphine.*

nucleus basalis One of the areas in the *brain* primarily responsible for the production of *acetylcholine.*

nucleus gracilis An area in the *medulla* that receives pressure and *kinesthetic* information from the lower limbs and the trunk.

nucleus raphe magnus An area in the *medulla* that when electrically stimulated results in the suppression of pain.

nucleus reticularis magnocellularis An area in the *medulla* that receives input from the *locus coeruleus* and in turn gives rise to *tracts* that travel to and inhibit activity in the *spinal cord* during *REM sleep.*

nystagmus reflex Involuntary oscillation of the eye ball.

obsessions Recurring thoughts, ideas, wishes, or concerns that take hold of one's consciousness and refuse to let go.

obsessive-compulsive disorder (OCD) A behavioral disorder characterized by recurring thoughts or acts that are so intrusive and overbearing that they come to dominate the person's life and disrupt normal everyday behavior.

occipital lobe One of four main subdivisions of each *cerebral hemisphere,* located behind the *temporal lobe* and the *parietal lobe* and involved in vision.

oculomotor nerve *Motor nerve* involved in controlling eye movement.

off-center cells *Ganglion cells* in the cat *retina* that fire when a light is focused on the perimeter of their *receptive field* and that cease to fire when a light is focused on the center of their receptive field. (Compare *on-center cells.*)

olfaction The sensation of smell.

olfactory bulb The area at the base of each *cerebral hemisphere* where the *olfactory nerve* synapses.

olfactory nerve Unique among *cranial nerves,* it does not synapse in lower areas of the *brain*; it travels directly from the olfactory *receptors* to the *olfactory bulb* at the base of each *cerebral hemisphere.*

olfactory tract A bundle of *axons* that travels from the *olfactory bulb* to various areas in the *cortex.* (See also *mitral cells.*)

oligodendrocytes Special nonneural cells whose membranes wrap around the *axon* in layers to form *myelin* in the *central nervous system.* (Compare *Schwann cells.*)

olivary nucleus An auditory area of the *brain* giving rise to circuits that exit from the brain and form *synapses* directly with the auditory *receptors,* elevating their *threshold.*

ommatidium A photosensitive cell in the eye of *Limulus.* Each eye has only about 800 such cells, which are large enough to be examined in detail.

on-center cells *Ganglion cells* in the cat *retina* that fire when a light is focused on the center of their *receptive field* and that cease to fire when a light is focused on the perimeter of their receptive field. (Compare *off-center cells.*)

opiates   A term used to describe drugs derived from the opium poppy. Drugs that fall into this category relieve pain, produce euphoria, and are addictive. They act by mimicking *endorphins* and *enkephalins*.

opponent-process theory of vision   A theory of color vision stating that a single chemical can code two primary colors, the buildup of the chemical coding one color and the breakdown coding the other. According to the theory, there are four primary colors: red, green, blue, and yellow.

opsin   A protein, found only in *photoreceptors*, that combines with *retinene* to form *rhodopsin*, the photochemical in *rods*.

optic chiasm   An area at the base of the *brain* where, in humans, half the *neurons* cross to the opposite side of the brain and the other half travel to the same side of the brain.

optic disk   The *blind spot* of each eye.

optic nerve   A *nerve* composed of *axons* that issue from the *ganglion cells* in the *retina* and travel to the *lateral geniculate nucleus*.

organ of Corti   A structure resting on the floor of the *cochlear canal* and supported by the *basilar membrane*. It contains *hair cells* that bend to incoming sound waves, transducing them into *neural impulses*.

organum vasculasum of the lamina terminalis (OVLT)   An area of the *brain* that borders on the *ventricles* and that produces drinking when injected with *angiotensin II*.

oscilloscope   An electronic instrument that uses a cathode ray tube to produce a visual trace of neuroelectrical activity.

osmotic pressure   Movement of fluid from areas of low concentration to areas of high concentration.

osmotic thirst   A condition characterized by drinking in response to a deficit in intracellular fluid. The deficit is thought to be sensed by *receptors* in the *preoptic nucleus*. (Compare *volemic thirst*.)

ossicles   Bones (the *malleus*, the *incus*, and the *stapes*) in the *middle ear* that amplify sound pressure exerted against the *oval window*.

otolithic membrane   The part of the *macula* in the *utricle* and *saccule* containing *otoliths*. Involved in sensing head position.

otoliths   Crystals of calcium carbonate suspended above *hair cells* in the *vestibular sacs*. Linear movement of the head causes them to move and, by bending the hair cells, to produce *neural impulses*.

outer ear   The part of the ear that collects *sound*, including the *pinna*, the *external auditory meatus*, and the *eardrum* (tympanic membrane).

oval window   The opening into the *cochlea* of the *inner ear*, covered by a membrane that receives vibrations from *ossicles* and promotes movement of the fluid in the inner ear.

ovariectomy   The removal of *ovaries* from the female.

ovaries   The female *gonads*, or sex *glands*.

overtones   *Frequencies* of *complex tones* that are characteristically simple multiples of the *fundamental frequency*.

oviducts   The tubes in which the ovum is released and fertilized.

ovulation   The release of an ovum by the *ovaries* into the *uterus* where it can be fertilized.

oxytocin   A *hormone*, manufactured in the *hypothalamus* and stored in the *posterior pituitary gland*, that stimulates contraction of the *uterus* during birth and ejection of milk after birth.

P cells   *Ganglion cells* in the *retina* that project to the parvocellular layers of the *lateral geniculate nucleus*. Involved in the coding of color.

Pacinian corpuscles   Pressure *end organs* in the skin, in the joints, in the *viscera*, and in subcutaneous fat.

paleocortex   Layer of neural tissue in the *cortex* just below the *juxtallocortex*.

panic attacks   Brief, unexpected episodes of extreme anxiety, the principal symptoms of which are shortness of breath, heart palpitations, dizziness, nausea, sweating, and an overwhelming feeling of terror and dread.

papillae   The elevations on the tongue, the palate, and the larynx that contain the *taste buds*.

parachlorophenylalanine (PCPA)   A drug which decreases the production of *serotonin*.

paradoxical cold   An experiential phenomenon in which a physically warm stimulus, when applied to cold *receptors*, results in a cold sensation.

paradoxical warmth   An experiential phenomenon in which a physically cold stimulus, when applied to warmth *receptors*, results in a warm sensation.

paraplegic   A person with a severed *spinal cord* who loses motor control and sensations from below the level of the cut.

parasympathetic nervous system   A subdivision of the *autonomic nervous system* that operates during relaxed behavioral states, conserving energy. For example, it promotes digestion (i.e., increases stomach activity) while inhibiting the heart rate. It exerts its effects by the *neurotransmitter acetylcholine*.

parasympathetic overshoot   Phenomenon that occurs in a "do-or-die" *stress* situation after an animal gives up struggling and the *sympathetic system* shuts off. Also known as parasympathetic rebound.

parietal lobe   One of four main subdivisions of each *cerebral hemisphere*, located behind and above the lateral *sulcus* and involved in the somatic senses and in language.

Parkinson's disease   A disorder characterized by muscle tremors and rigidity, caused by degeneration of the *substantia nigra*. (See also *L-dopa*.)

passive channels   Microscopic pores in the *neural membrane* that are always open.

periaqueductal gray   An area in the *midbrain* that when stimulated electrically suppresses pain.

perifornical area   An area in the *lateral hypothalamus* that elicits eating when injected with *neuropeptide Y*.

perilymph   A fluid in the *vestibular canal* and the *tympanic canal* that provides nourishment.

peripheral nervous system   The neural material outside the *brain* and the *spinal cord*, including *motor neurons* and *sensory neurons*.

phantom limb   Phenomenon observed by amputees in which they report that they still experience sensation in their lost limbs.

phenothiazines   A class of *antischizophrenic drugs*.

phobia   An irrational fear of a specific object or situation. Phobias are viewed largely as learned disorders and are treated effectively by behavioral therapies.

phosphodiesterase   The enzyme that destroys *cyclic adenosine monophosphate* after it acts on the *postsynaptic membrane* to open *ion channels*.

photons   Units of light energy.

photopic vision   Daytime vision characterized by sensations of color.

photoreceptors   *Receptors* that specialize in the *transduction* of light waves into *neural impulses*.

phototropic response   A very rudimentary response to light (e.g., approach or avoidance) by single-celled organisms and insects.

phrenology   An ill-conceived theory that the size and position of bumps on the skull correspond to various brain areas and therefore serve to indicate specific mental functions.

physiological psychology   A branch of psychology that seeks to explain behavior in physiological terms—that is, in terms of the electrochemical events that take place inside the body whenever behavior occurs.

physiological tolerance   See *nonassociative tolerance*.

physiological zero   The skin temperature at which neither warmth nor cold can be experienced.

pia mater   The innermost layer of the three *meninges*, which contains blood vessels and supplies nourishment to the *brain* and the *spinal cord*.

pineal gland   Small *gland* in the center of the *brain* that produces the *hormone melatonin*.

pinna   The flap, normally thought of as the "ear," that in humans plays a minor role in the auditory process, possibly helping to distinguish the direction of *sound*. Also known as the *auricle*.

pitch   The sensation of *sound* produced by sound wave *frequencies* ranging, in humans, from about 16 to 20,000 Hz. Frequencies above or below these limits are not detectable by the human ear.

pituitary gland   A small *gland* at the base of the *brain*, frequently called the master gland because it regulates other *endocrine glands*. It is divided into two lobes: *anterior* and *posterior*.

place theory of pitch   The theory that the coding for *pitch* is primarily a matter of "place," with different *frequencies* of *sound* stimulating different areas on the *basilar membrane*. Also called the *resonance theory*.

placebo   An inert drug that patients believe will help them.

placenta   A protective membrane enveloping the human fetus. It functions to regulate the exchange of nourishment, oxygen, and waste products between fetus and mother.

planum temporale   A region of the temporal *cortex* located in *Wernicke's area*. It is larger in the left hemisphere than in the right in roughly 65 percent of the human *brains* examined and is involved in the control of language.

pneuma theory   A theory of how the mind operates, introduced during the era of the Athenian Empire and based on the belief that the mind is controlled by invisible spirits known as pneuma.

polarization   The difference in charge, positive relative to negative, on the outside and inside of the *neural membrane*. (See also *depolarization*.)

polydipsia   An increase in thirst and drinking behavior characteristic of *diabetes insipidus*, a disorder caused by a deficiency of the *antidiuretic hormone vasopressin*.

polyuria   Loss of water from excessive urination, characteristic of *diabetes insipidus*. (See also *vasopressin*.)

pons   A section of the *hindbrain* consisting primarily of sensory and motor *tracts* traveling to and from the *cortex*.

It also contains a section of the *reticular formation* involved in *REM sleep*.

pontine reticular formation   An area of the *reticular formation* located in the *pons*. Involved in producing cortical arousal during *REM sleep*.

portal system   The group of blood vessels through which *releasing hormones* travel from the *hypothalamus* to the *pituitary gland*.

positive symptoms   Symptoms in *schizophrenia* marked by the presence of abnormal behavior such as *hallucinations* and confused thinking. (Compare with *negative symptoms*.)

positron emission tomography (PET scan)   A procedure that makes it possible to visualize energy metabolism in the neural cells of both normal and abnormal *brains*.

posterior   Toward the hindquarters of a four-legged animal or the back of a two-legged animal. Opposite of *anterior*.

posterior nuclear group   An area in the *thalamus* involved in coding for pain.

posterior pituitary gland   A *gland* that releases two hormones, *oxytocin* and *vasopressin*. (See also *pituitary gland*.)

postganglionic neurons   Neural circuits in the *autonomic nervous system* that originate in *ganglia* outside the *central nervous system* and run to smooth muscles. (Compare *preganglionic neurons*.)

postsynaptic membrane   The *neural membrane* that is stimulated by *neurotransmitters*.

postsynaptic receptor sites   Protein structures on the *postsynaptic membrane* keyed to the molecular shapes of *neurotransmitters* much as a lock is related to the shape of a key.

postsynaptic subsensitivity   The ability of the postsynaptic neuron to decrease the number of *receptors* (i.e., to decrease its sensitivity) when there is an excess of *neurotransmitter*.

postsynaptic supersensitivity   The ability of the postsynaptic neuron to increase the number of *receptors* (i.e., to increase its sensitivity) when there is a deficiency in *neurotransmitter*.

postural reflexes   Reflexive alterations in muscle tension that occur with abrupt changes in body position.

predatory play   Playful behavior exhibited by cats before they kill mice.

prefrontal lobotomy   *Psychosurgery*, no longer practiced, in which *tracts* connecting the prefrontal areas of the *cortex* to the *thalamus* are severed.

preganglionic neurons   Neural circuits in the *autonomic nervous system* that originate in the *brain* and the *spinal cord* and run to *ganglia* outside the *central nervous system*. (Compare *postganglionic neurons*.)

preoptic nucleus   A group of *cell bodies* in the *hypothalamus*, involved in the control of water regulation and male sexual behavior.

presynaptic facilitation   An increase in the amount of *neurotransmitter* released once the *action potential* occurs in the *presynaptic neuron*.

presynaptic inhibition   A decrease in the amount of *neurotransmitter* released once the *action potential* occurs in the *presynaptic neuron*.

presynaptic neuron   The *neuron* that releases *neurotransmitter*.

priming effect   Memories that are recalled when subjects are given a fragment of a word they have seen before and are instructed to say the first thing that comes to mind.

procedural memory   Memories that occur automatically, outside conscious awareness.

proceptive behavior   Behavior exhibited by female rats, including sniffing, grooming, and darting back and forth, that induces the male rat to chase and eventually mount.

progesterone   A female sex *hormone* whose function is to promote gestation.

progestin   A group of sex *hormones* produced by the *ovaries*, the most prominent of which is *progesterone*.

projection neuron   An *interneuron* that has short, multibranching *dendrites* and a long *axon*, a structure that makes it ideally suited for transmitting information over long distances.

proprioceptive   Pertaining to sensations of body position and movement.

proprioceptors   The *receptors* in joints and muscles, which are involved in the *kinesthetic* senses, and in the *semicircular canals* and the *vestibular sacs*, which are involved in *labyrinthine sensitivity*.

prosody   The emotional properties of speech conveyed by changes in intonation and inflection.

prosopagnosia   A perceptual disorder produced by damage usually in the right hemisphere. A person suffering from this condition, although capable of seeing and responding normally to most visual input, loses the ability to recognize familiar faces.

protanopia   Color blindness in which long wavelengths (650 nm) that normally produce the sensation of red cannot be seen and intermediate wavelengths (500 nm) that normally produce the sensation of green are seen as yellow.

Prozac   An *antidepressant* drug which relieves the common symptoms of *depression* and, because of its greater chemical specificity (it affects only *serotonin*), produces fewer side effects than existing drugs. (See *SSRIs* and *fluoxetine*.)

pseudohermaphrodite   An individual who because of a hormonal imbalance during embryonic development has the sex organs of one sex and the *chromosomes* of the other.

psychedelics   A term used to describe drugs that alter states of consciousness. Their primary effects are *hallucinations* and disorientation in time and space.

psychoactive drugs   Drugs that affect behavior.

psychopharmacology   A discipline concerned mainly with studying the effects of drugs on neural function and behavior.

psychosis   Term once commonly used by psychiatrists and psychologists to describe behavioral disorders characterized by loss of contact with commonly perceived reality.

psychosomatic   Pertaining to any bodily illness related to or induced by *stress* or other psychological factors. (Also known as psychophysiological disorders.)

psychosurgery   Brain surgery, such as *prefrontal lobotomy*, to treat mental disorders.

pulvinar nucleus   Area in the *thalamus* involved in attention.

pupil   The opening in the *iris* that controls the amount of light reaching the back of the eye.

putamen   See *basal ganglia*.

pyloric noose   A surgical preparation in which the stomach is tied off from the small intestine.

pylorus   The opening between the stomach and the small intestine.

pyramidal system   The system of motor *tracts* in the *central nervous system* that controls discrete movement.

pyramidal tract   *Tract* of descending pathways from the *brain* to spinal *motor neurons* that, along with the spinothalamic tract, links the *sensory* and *motor neurons* in the *spinal cord* to the *brain*.

radial-arm maze   A maze, used in memory experiments, that consists of a number of arms some of which are baited with food and others not.

raphe nuclei   A group of *nuclei* that lie along the midline of the *reticular formation* in the *medulla*, *pons*, and *midbrain* and are involved in the production of *serotonin*.

rapid eye movement (REM) sleep   A stage in the sleep cycle in which there is movement of the eyeballs and *EEG* activity is similar to that of the waking state. Dreaming usually occurs during this stage.

rarefaction (sound)   The movement of vibrating molecules back into the vacuum created by compression, which forces the molecules to move further apart than normal.

receptive field   The relationship between *neurons* and *receptors*: The more receptors a neuron receives information from, the larger its receptive field.

receptor   A structure that specializes in the *transduction* of stimuli.

receptor sites   Special protein molecules embedded in the *postsynaptic membrane* that serve as structural slots with which *neurotransmitters bind*.

reciprocal innervation   The manner in which two sets of *neurons* relate to each other in regulating movement. For movement to occur, one muscle must contract while the other relaxes.

recording   A research technique that monitors electrical activity in the *brain* during ongoing behavior.

recovery state   The state of the *action potential* occurring after the *firing stage* when the sodium channels close and the potassium channels open, allowing potassium ions to move out of the *neuron*.

red nucleus   An area in the *midbrain* that receives motor information from upper portions of the *brain* and is involved in muscle control.

reference memory   Memory of information that remains constant over time. In the *radial-arm maze*, memory of the arms that are baited from day to day.

reflex   An automatic response to a *stimulus*, such as the knee jerk.

refraction   The bending of light waves.

refractory period   The period of time after a *neuron* fires during which it recovers its *resting potential*.

regional cerebral blood flow (rCBF)   Variant of the *PET scan* procedure that uses cerebral blood flow to measure activity in the *brain*.

reinforcer   Any event or stimulus that strengthens a response. A positive reinforcer strengthens the response that produces it, and a negative reinforcer strengthens the response that terminates it.

relative refractory period   The stage that follows the *absolute refractory period* and precedes the resting state and the restoration of the *resting potential*.

releasing hormones   Chemicals secreted by the *hypothalamus* and transported via the *portal system* to the *anterior pituitary*, which in turn releases *hormones* which regulate the *thyroid*, the *adrenal cortex*, and the *gonads*.

REM rebound   A phenomenon in which human subjects denied *REM sleep* for a time show increased dreaming when finally allowed to sleep normally.

Renshaw cells   *Interneurons* that protect muscles from overcontraction by inhibiting firing in the *alpha motor neurons*.

resonance   The vibrating properties of all objects.

resonance theory   See *place theory of pitch*.

resting potential   The state in which the *neural membrane* is more negative inside with respect to the outside by −70 mV.

reticular formation   A network of *neurons* running through the core of the *brain stem* from the *medulla* to the *thalamus*. It arouses the *cortex* (affecting wakefulness), inhibits sensory input (affecting *attention*), and controls muscle tone.

retina   A membrane located in the innermost part of the eye, composed of three layers of cells: the *photoreceptors* (*rods* and *cones*) the two layers of neural cells (*bipolar cells* and *ganglion cells*).

retinene   A pigment in the *retina* which, when combined with *opsin*, forms *rhodopsin*.

retrieval   The process by which memory becomes accessible or is recalled.

retrograde amnesia   Loss of memory of events prior to a neural *trauma*. *Long-term memory* remains unaffected.

retrograde amnesia gradient   As the interval between training and neural *trauma* (e.g., *electroconvulsive shock*) increases, the amnesic effects of the trauma decrease.

retrograde degeneration   The breakdown of the *axon* (after it is cut) between the severed end and the *cell body*.

retrograde facilitation   The facilitating effect on recall of drugs or brain stimulation administered shortly after training.

retrograde plasticity factor   During *long-term potentiation*, the chemical signal that the postsynapse releases and that travels back to the presynapse.

retrograde transport   The process by which the *neuron* transports life-sustaining chemicals from the *axonal endings* to the *cell body*.

reuptake   The process by which the *neurotransmitter* is drawn back into the vesicles of the *presynaptic neuron*.

rhinencephalon   The oldest part of the *cerebral hemispheres*. It contains structures involved chiefly in emotion. Also known as the nose *brain*.

rhodopsin   A chemical composed of *opsin* and *retinene*, found only in the *rods*. The *transduction* process in rods depends on light's breaking down rhodopsin into *opsin* and *retinene*.

rods   Slender, cylindrical *receptors* in the *retina* that transduce light waves into *neural impulses*. Rods have low thresholds of excitation and show an *achromatic* capacity.

Romberg's sign   A clinical test for damage to *labyrinthine receptors*, in which patients are tested for their ability to maintain balance with closed eyes.

round window   An elastic membrane-covered opening at the end of the *tympanic canal*. It relieves the changes in pressure that are caused by the movement of cochlear fluid.

Ruffini endings   *End organs* in skin areas that are receptive to warmth.

saccule   One of the *vestibular sacs*, containing *receptors* sensitive to stationary and upright positions of the body. (Compare *utricle*.)

SAD   See *seasonal affective disorder*.

saltatory conduction   The process by which neural conduction occurs in *myelinated axons*. It consists of *depolarization* skipping from one *node* of *Ranvier* to the next.

satellite cells   Nonneural cells in the *peripheral nervous system* involved in mechanical support and insulation of *neurons*.

saturation   The purity of a color sensation, which is related to the homogeneity of light waves.

schizophrenia   A *mental illness* characterized by pronounced *cognitive* breakdown that manifests itself in *hallucinations* and incoherent patterns of thought and speech.

Schwann cells   Nonneural cells whose membranes wrap around *axons* in layers to form *myelin* in the *peripheral nervous system*. (Compare *oligodendrocytes*.)

sclera   The "white" of the eye, an opaque, white, fibrous layer that covers about five-sixths of the surface of the eyeball.

scotopic vision   Vision without the sensation of color, such as occurs in darkness.

screening   A testing procedure for drugs, used to determine dose and side effects.

seasonal affective disorder (SAD)   A type of *depression* linked to a decrease in exposure to bright light and an increase in *melatonin* secretion. Persons suffering from SAD are affected by the changing of the seasons.

second-messenger system   One of the ways in which *neurotransmitters* act on the *postsynaptic membrane* to open *ion channels*.

selective inhibition of sensory input   The ability of people to block out all but relevant stimuli (i.e., to pay attention).

selective permeability   A property of the *cell membrane* that enables certain chemical substances to enter the cell and prevents certain others from entering.

selective serotonin reuptake inhibitors (SSRIs)   A new class of *antidepressant drugs* that relieve *depression* by blocking the reuptake of *serotonin* (thus increasing it).

self-stimulation   The term used to describe experimental procedures in which the "reward" consists of self-administered electrical stimulation to so-called "pleasure" areas of the *brain*.

semicircular canals   Three semicircular, tubelike structures in the nonauditory portion of the *inner ear*. Each canal contains fluid that moves and stimulates *receptors* when the head rotates.

senile plaques   Deposits of *beta-amyloid protein* scattered throughout the *brain*.

sensitization   A simple form of *learning* manifested by an increase in the strength of a response following a noxious stimulus. (Compare *habituation*.)

sensory codes   Features of the *neural impulse*—where it travels and how it travels—that correlate with certain sensory experiences. The correlates are referred to as sensory codes.

sensory neuron   A *neuron* that carries impulses from *receptors* toward the *central nervous system*.

septal area   An area in the *limbic system* believed to play a role in the control of fear and rage.

serotonin   A *neurotransmitter* derived from the amino acid *tryptophan* and produced by *neurons* originating in the *raphe nuclei*. Serotonin has been implicated in sleeping behavior and suppression of pain, and deficits have been linked to clinical *depression*.

sertraline A type of *SSRI* also known as *Zoloft*.

sex-determining region of Y (SRY) The section on the Y *chromosome* that contains the gene or genes for development of the *testes*.

sexual dimorphism A term originally coined by Darwin to refer to bodily characteristics that distinguish males from females.

sexual response cycle The sequence of responses that occur when humans engage in sex. It consists of four phases: excitation, plateau, orgasm, and resolution.

sexually dimorphic nucleus of the preoptic area A *nucleus* in the preoptic area of the *hypothalamus* in rats that is roughly five to six times larger in the male than in the female.

sham rage Violent behavior shown by *decorticated* animals, which differs from normal rage in several respects: It occurs with the slightest provocation, it lasts only as long as the provoking stimulus, and it is not directed at the provoker.

short-term memory Recently acquired information, the storage of which is vulnerable.

simple cells Cells in the visual *cortex* of the cat that respond to simple linear stimuli depending on the position of the stimuli within the *receptive field*.

simple tone A tone produced by pressure variations of a simple sound wave, such as a sine wave.

skeletal muscles Muscles attached to the skeleton, involved in voluntary movement.

skeletal nervous system The subdivision of the *peripheral nervous system* that excites *skeletal muscles*. Also called the somatic nervous system.

skull sutures Bony ridges on the skull used as reference points in *stereotaxic surgery*. Two examples are the *bregma* and the *midline suture*.

sleep apnea The inability to breathe during sleep. It results in *insomnia* and may produce *sudden infant death syndrome*.

slow-wave sleep A state of sleep during which brain waves decrease from 9 to 12 Hz as the person relaxes to 1 to 3 Hz as the person falls into deep sleep.

sodium-potassium pump An energy-driven mechanism that works in a pumplike fashion to maintain the *resting potential*.

solitary nucleus An area in the *medulla* that forms *synapses* with sensory *nerves* from the tongue and pharynx and in turn gives rise to *tracts* to the *thalamus*.

soma The *cell body* of the *neuron*. Place where the neuron metabolizes nutrients into energy.

somatosensory areas Primary and secondary areas of the *cortex* that receive pressure and touch information from the skin.

somatosensory system The sensory system that receives and processes information from the skin and *viscera*, such as pressure, temperature, and pain. Its *receptors* fall into two categories: *cutaneous* and *proprioceptive*.

sound Periodic compressions and *rarefications* of molecules produced by vibrating objects and resulting in the sensation of sound when hitting the ear. Depicted as sound waves, the movements of molecules vary in *frequency* (*pitch*), *amplitude* (*loudness*), and purity (*timbre*).

spatial summation See *summation*.

specific hunger A need that, unlike general hunger, is related to a specific food or food group, generally caused by a nutritional deficiency.

specific nerve energies, doctrine of The theory that sensations differ according to which *nerves* are being stimulated and which part of the *brain* these nerves are stimulating.

spinal cord The bundle of *neurons* and supportive tissue that runs through the spinal column and, with the *brain*, makes up the *central nervous system*.

spinal nerves The 31 pairs of *mixed nerves* that originate in the *spinal cord*.

spinal reflex A stimulus-bound behavior, such as the knee jerk, rooted in simple neural circuits called spinal reflex arcs.

spindle organs See *stretch receptors*.

spinothalamic tract The *tract* carrying *somatosensory* information from the *spinal cord* to the *thalamus*.

spiral ganglion A group of *cell bodies* belonging to the *bipolar neurons* that make up the *auditory nerve*.

splenium A specific region of the *corpus callosum* that tends to be larger in females than in males.

split-brain patients Humans whose *corpus callosum* has been surgically cut, thereby severing communication between the two hemispheres.

spontaneous activity Ongoing neural activity that occurs in the absence of stimulation.

staining Chemical technique in which *neurons* are stained with a certain chemical so that their parts stand out in bold relief when viewed under the microscope.

stapedius muscle A muscle whose contraction dampens the movement of the *stapes*, reducing the pressure exerted against the *oval window*. Like the *tensor muscle*, it protects the *inner ear* from intense *sound*.

stapes One of the *ossicles* of the *middle ear*. It transmits vibrations from the *incus* to the *oval window*.

stereochemical theory The theory that explains *transduction* in taste and smell by linking *receptors* to the shape of the stimulating molecules.

stereotaxic instrument An instrument for implanting *electrodes* or *cannulae* in the *brain*. It holds the subject's head in a fixed position and has an arm that can be adjusted to allow for precise implantation when used with coordinates from a *brain atlas*.

stereotaxic surgery Surgical technique in which either *electrodes* or *cannulae* are inserted into specific areas of the *brain* using a *stereotaxic instrument*.

steroids *Hormones* produced in the *adrenal cortex* and *gonads* that regulate *metabolism*, maintain blood pressure, and control sexual appearance and behavior.

stimulants A term used to describe drugs that increase behavioral activity. *Amphetamine* and *cocaine* are two examples.

stimulation A research technique in which the *brain* is stimulated by weak pulses of electric current and the behavioral consequences are noted.

stress Any potentially injurious stimulus, whether physical (e.g., prolonged exposure to noise or freezing temperature) or psychological (e.g., a death in the family).

stretch receptors *Neurons* whose *dendrites*, when stretched, act as *receptors* and initiate neural firing. *Annulospiral endings* and *flower-spray endings* are receptors involved in the *stretch reflex*. Also called *spindle organs*.

stretch reflex   One of the processes by which muscle tension is regulated to withstand strain on a muscle.

stria terminalis   An area in the *amygdala* that when lesioned prevents injections of *epinephrine* or *norepinephrine* from facilitating *consolidation*.

strychnine   *Stimulant* that blocks inhibitory effects of *glycine* on its *receptors* to such a degree that the unleashed excitatory activity in the *brain* can lead to convulsions and death.

subarachnoid space   A spongy layer between the *pia mater* and *arachnoid* containing *cerebrospinal fluid*.

subfornical organ   An area of the *brain* that borders on the *ventricles* and that produces drinking behavior when injected with *angiotensin II*.

substance P   A *neurotransmitter* found in the *peripheral* and *central nervous systems*, where it plays a role in transmitting pain-related information.

substantia gelatinosa   An area of the *spinal cord* in which *interneurons* synapse with *neurons* conducting pain and pressure information. These interneurons play a role in blocking pain.

substantia nigra   An area in the *midbrain* that contains *dopamine* and that has been linked to *Parkinson's disease*. (See *basal ganglia*.)

sudden infant death syndrome   Also known as crib death, the mysterious death of an infant in the crib without apparent signs of illness. (See *sleep apnea*.)

sulcus   (plural: sulci) A fold or groove in the *cortex*. (See also *fissure*.)

sulcus principalis   An area in the *frontal lobe* which when lesioned impairs a monkey's ability to remember the location of a stimulus.

summation   A cumulative effect of several stimuli acting together that is greater than could be produced by any of them acting alone. *Neural impulses* arriving together (*spatial summation*) or one after another (*temporal summation*) produce this type of effect in the *synapse*.

superior colliculus   An area in the *midbrain* where some of the fibers of the *optic nerve* synapse with *motor nerves* that control eye movements.

superior olives   *Nuclei* on each side of the *brain stem* that receive input from the *cochlear nuclei* and give rise to axons that form the *lateral lemniscus*. Thought to be involved in coding the direction of *sound*.

suprachiasmatic nucleus   An area located in the *hypothalamus* immediately above the *optic chiasm*, believed to be the source of the circadian rhythm for the sleep-wake cycle.

supraoptic nucleus   A set of neurosecretory cells in the *hypothalamus* that synthesizes the *hormone vasopressin*.

sympathetic cord   A vertical chain of *ganglia* on each side of the *spinal cord*, from which *neurons* travel to the *viscera*.

sympathetic nervous system   The subdivision of the *autonomic nervous system* that operates during *stress* to expend energy.

synapse   The microscopic gap between the *axonal endings* of one *neuron* and the *cell body* or *dendrites* or, in some cases, the *axon* of another neuron, at which transmission between the two neurons occurs.

synaptic compensatory response   The response, either increasing synaptic activity or decreasing synaptic activity, enlisted by the *synapse* to restore normality when abnormal (excessive or deficient) postsynaptic activity occurs.

synaptic defense   The response of *synapses* to restore optimal activity either by regulating their sensitivity or regulating the production of *neurotransmitters*. This defense mechanism is responsible for drug *tolerance*.

synaptic modulation   The process by which one *neuron* (a *modulation neuron*) regulates the amount of *neurotransmitter* released by a second neuron (a *presynaptic neuron*).

synaptic potential   Neural activity initiated by *neurotransmitters* at the *postsynaptic membrane*. The activity can be either excitatory or inhibitory.

T cells   So-called killer cells that have the power to search out and destroy disease-producing agents such as tumor cells.

tabes dorsalis   A motor disorder caused by selective degeneration of the *nerves* from the *kinesthetic receptors*.

tachistoscope   An apparatus that flashes a visual stimulus for a fraction of a second. It is used in the study of cerebral lateralization, allowing the experimenter to project a stimulus to either the left or right hemisphere.

tapetum   In nocturnal animals, a luminescent layer of cells adjacent to the *cornea* that increases sensitivity to light.

tardive dyskinesia   A ticlike movement disorder produced by prolonged use of *antischizophrenic drugs*.

taste blindness   A deficiency in detecting certain tastes.

taste buds   *Receptors* involved in taste. They are located on the top and sides of the tongue and throughout the oral cavity.

tectorial membrane   A gelatinous structure in the *organ of Corti*. Positioned above the *hair cells*, it is the membrane against which the hair cells bend.

telodendria   *Axonal endings*.

temporal lobe   One of four main subdivisions of each *cerebral hemisphere*, located below the *lateral fissure*. Involved in audition and memory.

temporal summation   See *summation*.

tensor muscle   A muscle attached to the *malleus*. When stimulated by intense *sound*, it contracts, causing the *eardrum* to tighten, thus protecting the *inner ear*. (See also *stapedius muscle*.)

testes   The male *gonads* or sex glands.

testosterone   A *hormone* produced by the *testes* that stimulates the development of male secondary sexual characteristics and behavior.

thalamus   An area in the *forebrain* made up of *nuclei* that relay sensory information from peripheral *receptors* to the *cortex*.

third interstitial nucleus of the anterior hypothalamus (INAH-3)   A *nucleus* in the *hypothalamus* that has been found to be roughly twice as large in heterosexual men as in heterosexual women and homosexual men.

thoracolumbar region   The collective term for the thoracic and lumbar regions of the *spinal cord*.

threshold   The lowest level of stimulation or the least amount of *depolarization* necessary to produce the firing of an *axon*.

thyroid gland   An *endocrine gland* in the neck. It secretes *thyroxine* and plays a major role in regulating metabolism.

thyroxine   A *hormone*, secreted by the *thyroid gland*, that regulates metabolism. A deficiency causes lethargy in adults and *cretinism*.

timbre   The quality or purity of *sound* produced by *overtones*. It allows one to distinguish among different musical instruments producing the same fundamental tone.

time-lag effect   Term referring to the 2- or 3-week lag between the time that *antidepressant drugs* increase the amount of *serotonin* or *norepinephrine* and *serotonin* in the *brain* and the time that patients actually experience relief from their depressive symptoms.

timing theory of dyslexia   A theory of dyslexia based on the belief that dyslexics are able to process long-lasting *sounds* but are unable to process brief, rapid-changing sounds.

tolerance   A decrease in a drug's effectiveness that occurs with repeated use.

tonotopic representation   The anatomical relationship between neighboring regions on the *basilar membrane* and neighboring regions in the *cortex*.

top-down processing   The interpretive stage of sensory processing, governed by past experience, knowledge, and expectation.

trace conditioning   A *classical conditioning* procedure in which the *conditioned stimulus* (tone, for example) and the *unconditioned stimulus* (puff, for example) are separated by the briefest of intervals (a matter of milliseconds). (Compare *delayed conditioning*.)

tract   A bundle of *neurons*—specifically, their *axons*—in the *central nervous system*.

transduction   The transformation of one form of energy into another, as in the transduction of light waves into *neural impulses*.

transneuronal degeneration   Process by which *neurons* that form *synapses* with a dying neuron die as well. Also called transynaptic degeneration.

transplant therapy   An experimental technique in which neural tissue from a healthy animal is transplanted into the *brain* of a brain-damaged animal.

transsexual   A person who strongly desires to be of the opposite sex.

trauma   An emotional shock or physical injury that has a disruptive effect on behavior.

traveling wave   The term used to refer to the bulge in the *basilar membrane* that is produced by *sound* and that moves in a wavelike manner from the *oval window* to the apex of the *cochlea*.

trichromatic theory   A theory of color vision stating that the *retina* contains three groups of *cones* and that each group when stimulated alone will produce one of three primary color sensations (red, green, or blue) and when stimulated simultaneously to different degrees will produce all the other color sensations.

tricyclic antidepressants   *Antidepressant* drugs that increase *monoamine* transmitters by blocking their reuptake in the *synapse*.

trigeminal nerve   A *cranial nerve* that contains *motor neurons* controlling chewing and *sensory neurons* for touch and pain from the face, the scalp, the *cornea*, and the mouth.

tritanopia   A rare kind of color blindness characterized by an inability to discriminate yellow from blue.

trochlear nerve   One of three motor *cranial nerves* involved in eye movement.

tryptophan   The amino acid from which *serotonin* is produced.

two-syndrome theory of schizophrenia   Theory that *schizophrenia* is a composite of two disorders: type I, marked by *positive symptoms*, and type II, marked by *negative symptoms*.

tympanic canal   A fluid-filled canal of the *cochlea* that connects with the *vestibular canal* at the *helicotrema* and ends at the *round window*.

tyrosine   The amino acid from which *norepinephrine* is produced.

unconditioned response   A response elicited automatically by an *unconditioned stimulus* (e.g., salivation in response to food).

unconditioned stimulus   The stimulus that elicits an *unconditioned response* without previous training (e.g., food when it elicits salivation).

unipolar depression   *Depression* in which a person suffers exclusively from prolonged periods of sadness and despondency.

unipolar neuron   A *neuron* that has a single projection from its *cell body*.

uterus   The organ where the fertilized ovum develops.

utricle   One of the *vestibular sacs* involved in sensing changes in head position caused by linear motion. (Compare *saccule*.)

Valium   A *depressant* drug that is widely prescribed for the treatment of anxiety and whose neural effects have been linked to *GABA*. (See *benzodiazepines*.)

vasocongestion   Blood flow to areas in and around the genitals, resulting in penis erection in the male and nipple erection and lubrication of the vaginal walls in the female.

vasopressin   A *hormone* manufactured by the *supraoptic nucleus* in the *hypothalamus* and stored in the *posterior pituitary gland*. It promotes reabsorption of water by the kidney and increases blood pressure.

ventral   Toward the base of the *brain* or the bellyside of an animal. Opposite of *dorsal*.

ventral root   The area of the *spinal cord* from which *motor neurons* leave en route to a muscle.

ventral tegmental area   Area of the *brain* which connects with the *limbic system* and *cortex* and produces *dopamine*.

ventricles   Three fluid-filled cavities in the *brain*, called the lateral, third, and fourth ventricles.

ventrobasal complex   An area in the *thalamus* involved in coding sharp, pricking pain.

ventromedial hypothalamus   An area in the *hypothalamus* believed to play a role in regulation of eating behavior.

vesicles   Tiny, globe-shaped structures in *axonal endings* that contain the chemical transmitter released during synaptic transmission.

vestibular canal   A fluid-filled canal in the *cochlea*, beginning at the *oval window* and tapering to an end at the *helicotrema*.

vestibular nerve   The *nerve* that carries impulses from the sensory cells of the *vestibular system* to the *brain stem*.

vestibular nuclei   *Cell bodies* belonging to *neurons* in the vestibular branch of the *auditory nerve*, located in the *medulla*.

vestibular sacs   Two cavities, the *utricle* and the *saccule*, in the nonauditory part of the *inner ear*, both of which contain *receptors* involved in maintaining posture.

vestibular system   The nonauditory part of the *inner ear*, involved in sensing movement and maintaining posture.

viral theory of schizophrenia   Theory that *schizophrenia* may result from a viral infection during the second trimester of pregnancy, during which major developmental changes occur in the nervous system of the fetus.

viscera   The collective term for the internal organs, which are controlled chiefly by the *autonomic nervous system*.

visible spectrum   Light waves that can be transduced by the eye. In humans, they fall in the 380-to-750-nm range.

visual acuity   The capacity to discern visual detail.

vitreous humor   A viscous substance that fills the space between the back of the *lens* and the *retina*, both of which it nourishes.

vocalization cells   Cells in the auditory *cortex* of the squirrel monkey that process higher-order information by responding only to species-specific vocalizations (i.e., sounds that are unique to squirrel monkeys).

volatility   The capacity to give off a smell (i.e., to release molecules into the air).

volemic thirst   A condition characterized by drinking in response to a deficit in *extracellular fluid*. The deficit is thought to be sensed by *receptors* in the kidneys and vena cava. (Compare *osmotic thirst*.)

volley theory   The theory that *neurons* fire alternately in groups (in volleys) rather than in unison. This would explain how a bundle of neurons can fire at 4000 Hz even though individual neurons can fire only at 1000 Hz.

voltage gradient   The tendency of *ions* to move until the regions they occupy are equal in electric charge.

voltage-sensitive channels   A type of *active channel* in the *neural membrane* that opens as a result of changes in the electric charge across the membrane.

vomeronasal organs   Olfactory *receptors* that are selectively sensitive to scents of prey or of mates. They are found in some reptiles and mammals but not in monkeys or humans.

Wallerian degeneration   Breakdown of the *distal* part of an *axon* following an axonal cut.

Wernicke's area   An area in the *cortex* (the *posterior* part of the first temporal convolution) involved in the comprehension of language. (See *planum temporale*.)

white matter   Tissue consisting mainly of *myelinated* nerve fibers (*axons*) that make up the *central nervous system*. *Myelin* gives axons their whitish appearance.

withdrawal symptoms   The illness that ensues when an individual stops taking a drug to which he or she is addicted. The reaction is both physical (vomiting, fever, tremors) and psychological (*depression* or *mania*).

Wolffian ducts   The reproductive system that develops into the male organs if *androgen* is present.

working memory   Memory of information that varies. In the *radial-arm maze* it takes the form of the arms of the maze the animal has just entered.

zeitgebers   Time-related cues such as light and dark which reset the biological clock (German for "time giver").

Zoloft   See *sertraline*.

Abbott, B. B., Schoen, L. S., and Badia, P. "Predictable and Unpredictable Shock: Behavioral Measures of Aversion and Physiological Measures of Stress." *Psychological Bulletin* 96 (1984): 45–71.

Adamec, R. "Normal and Abnormal Limbic System Mechanisms of Emotive Biasing." In *Limbic Mechanisms*, ed. K. E. Livingston and O. Horynkiewicz. New York: Plenum Press, 1978, pp. 405–55.

Adamec, R., and Stark-Adamec, C. "Limbic Control of Aggression in the Cat." *Progress in Neuro-Psychopharmacology and Biological Psychiatry* 7 (1983): 505–12.

Adler, N. T. "Effects of the Male's Copulatory Behavior on Successful Pregnancy in the Female Rat." *Journal of Comparative and Physiological Psychology* 69 (1969): 613–23.

Adolph, E. F. "Thirst and Its Inhibition in the Stomach." *American Journal of Physiology* 161 (1950): 374–86.

Aggleton, J. P., Hunt, P. R., and Rawlins, J. N. P. "The Effects of Hippocampal Lesions upon Spatial and Non-Spatial Tests of Working Memory." *Behavioral Brain Research* 19 (1986): 133–46.

Alberts, B., Bray, D., Lewis, J., Raff, M., Roberts, K., and Watson, J. D., eds. *Molecular Biology of the Cell*, 3rd ed. New York: Garland, 1994.

Allen, L., Richey, M., Chai, Y., and Gorski, R. "Sex Differences in the Corpus Callosum of the Living Human Being." *Journal of Neuroscience* 11 (1991): 933–42.

Allen, L. S., and Gorski, R. A. "Sexual Dimorphism of the Human Anterior Commissure." *Anatomical Record* 214 (1986): 3A.

Allen, L. S., and Gorski, R. A. "Sexual Orientation and the Size of the Anterior Commissure in the Human Brain." *Proceedings of the National Academy of Sciences (USA)* 89 (1992): 7199–7202.

Allen, L. S., Hines, M., Shryne, J. E., and Gorski, R. A. "Two Sexually Dimorphic Cell Groups in the Human Brain." *Journal of Neuroscience* 9 (1989): 497–506.

Alpern, H. P., and McGaugh, J. L. "Retrograde Amnesia as a Function of Duration of Electroshock Stimulation." *Journal of Comparative and Physiological Psychology* 65 (1969): 265–69.

American Psychological Association. "Ethical Principles of Psychologists." *American Psychologist* 45 (1987): 390–95.

Amoore, J. E. "The Stereochemical Theory of Olfaction." *Nature* 198 (1963): 271–72.

Amoore, J. E., Palmieri, G., and Warke, E. "Molecular Shape and Odour: Pattern Analysis by PAPA." *Nature* 216 (1967): 1084–87.

Andersson, B. "The Effect of Injections of Hypertonic NaCI Solutions into Different Parts of the Hypothalamus of Goats." *Acta Physiologica Scandinavica* 28 (1953): 188–201.

Andersson, B., and McCann, S. M. "A Further Study of Polydipsia Evoked by Hypothalamic Stimulation in the Goat." *Acta Physiologica Scandinavica* 33 (1955): 333–46.

Andreasen, N. C. "Positive vs. Negative Schizophrenia: A Critical Evaluation." *Schizophrenia Bulletin* 11 (1985): 380–89.

Andreasen, N. C. "Brain Imaging: Applications in Psychiatry." *Science* 239 (1988): 1381–88.

Andreasen, N. C., Nasrallah, H. A., Dunn, V., Olson, S. C., Grove, W. M., Ehrhardt, J. C., Coffman, J. A., and Crossert, J. H. W. "Structural Abnormalities in the Frontal System in Schizophrenia." *Archives of General Psychiatry* 43 (1986): 136–44.

Angrist, B., Sathananthan, G., Wild, S., and Gershon, S. "Amphetamine Psychosis: Behavioural and Biochemical Aspects." *Journal of Psychiatric Research* 11 (1974): 13–24.

Applegate, C. D., Kapp, B. S., Underwood, M. D., and McNall, C. L. "Autonomic and Somatomotor Effects of Amygdala Central Nerve Stimulation on Awake Rabbits." *Physiological Behavior* 31 (1983): 353–60.

Arbour, K. W., and Wilkie, D. M. "Rodents' (*Rattus, Mesocricetus*, and *Meriones*) Use of Learned Caloric Information in Diet Source." *Journal of Comparative Psychology* 102 (1988): 177–81.

Avissar, S., and Schreiber, G. "Muscarinic Receptor Subclassification and G-Proteins: Significance for Lithium Action in Affective Disorders and for the Treatment of the Extrapyramidal Side Effects of Neuroleptics." *Biological Psychiatry* 26 (1989): 113–30.

Backlund, E. O., Granberg, P. O., Hamberger, B., Sedvall, G., Seiger, A., and Olson, L. "Transplantation of Adrenal Medullary Tissue to Striatum in Parkinsonism."

In *Neural Grafting in the Mammalian CNS*, ed. A. Bjorklund and U. Stenevi. Amsterdam: Elsevier, 1985, pp. 551–56.

Bailey, C. H., and Chen, M. "Morphological Basis of Long-Term Habituation and Sensitization in *Aplysia*." *Science* 220 (1983): 91–93.

Bailey, C. H., and Chen. M. C. "Long-Term Memory in *Aplysia* Modulates the Total Number of Varicosities of Single Identified Sensory Neurons." *Proceedings of the National Academy of Sciences (USA)* 85 (1988): 2373–77.

Bailey, M. J., and Pillard, R. C. "A Genetic Study of Male Sexual Orientation." *Archives of General Psychiatry* 48 (1991): 1089–96.

Bailey, M. J., and Pillard, R. C. "Heritable Factors Influence Sexual Orientation in Women." *Archives of General Psychiatry* 50 (1993): 217–23.

Baker, T. B., and Tiffany, S. T. "Morphine Tolerance as Habituation." *Psychological Review* 92 (1985): 78–108.

Baldessarini, R. J., and Tarsy, D. "Dopamine and the Pathophysiology of Dyskinesias Induced by Antipsychotic Drugs." *Annual Review of Neuroscience* 3 (1980): 23–41.

Ballard, P. A., Tetrud, J. W., and Langston, J. W. "Permanent Human Parkinsonism Due to 1-Methyl-4-phenyl-1,2,3,6-tetrahydropyridine, (MPTP): Seven Cases." *Neurology* 35 (1985): 949–56.

Ballenger, J. C., Burrows, G. D., DuPont, R. L., Jr., Lesser, I. M., Noyes, R., Jr., Pecknold, J. C., Rifkin, A., and Swinson, R. P. "Alprazolam in Panic Disorder and Agoraphobia: Results from a Multicenter Trial." *Archives of General Psychiatry* 45 (1988): 413–22.

Barbaccia, M. L., Guarneri, P., Berkovich, A., Wambebe, A., Guidotti, A., and Costa, E. "Studies on the Endogenous Modulator of $GABA_A$ Receptors in Human Brain and CSF." In *Allosteric Modulation of Amino Acid Receptors: Therapeutic Implications*, ed. E. A. Barnard and E. Costa. New York: Raven Press, 1989, pp. 125–38.

Barbaro, N. M. "Studies of PAG/PVG Stimulation for Pain Relief in Humans." In *Progress in Brain Research*, vol. 77, ed. H. L. Fields and J.-M. Besson. Amsterdam: Elsevier, 1988, pp. 163–75.

Bard, P., "A Diencephalic Mechanism for the Expression of Rage, with Special Reference to the Sympathetic Nervous System." *American Journal of Physiology* 84 (1928): 490–515.

Bard, P. "On Emotional Expression after Decortication, with Some Remarks on Certain Theoretical Views," pts. 1 and 2. *Psychological Review* 41 (1934): 309–29, 424–49.

Bard, P., and Macht, M. B. "The Behavior of Chronically Decerebrate Cats." In *The Neurological Basis of Behavior*, ed. G. E. W. Wolstenholme and M. O'Connor. London: Churchill, 1958.

Bard, P., and Mountcastle, V. B. "Some Forebrain Mechanisms Involved in the Expression of Rage, with Special Reference to Suppression of Angry Behavior." In *The Frontal Lobes*, ed. J. F. Fulton. Baltimore: Williams & Wilkins, 1948.

Barr, C. E., Mednick, S. A., and Munk-Jorgensen, P. "Exposure to Influenza Epidemics during Gestation and Adult Schizophrenia". *Archives of General Psychiatry* 47 (1990): 869–74.

Bartoshuk, L. M. "Gustatory System." In *Handbook of Behavioral Neurobiology*, vol. 1: *Sensory Integration*,

ed. R. B. Masterton. New York: Plenum Press, 1978, pp. 503–67.

Bashir, Z. I., Alford, S., Davies, S. N., Randall, A. D., and Collingridge, G. L. "Long-Term Potentiation of NMDA Receptor-Mediated Synaptic Transmission in the Hippocampus." *Nature* 349 (1991): 156–58.

Baxter, L. R., Phelps, M. E., Mazziotta, J. C., Guze, B. H., Schwartz, J. M., and Selin, C. E. "Local Cerebral Glucose Metabolic Rates in Obsessive-Compulsive Disorder: A Comparison with Rates in Unipolar Depression and in Normal Controls." *Archives of General Psychiatry* 44 (1987): 211–18.

Beach, F. A. "A Review of Physiological and Psychological Studies of Sexual Behavior in Mammals." *Physiological Review* 27 (1947): 240–307.

Beach, F. A. "A Cross-Species Survey of Mammalian Sexual Behavior." In *Psychosexual Development in Health and Disease*, ed. P. H. Hoch and J. Zubin. New York: Grune & Stratton, 1949.

Bekesy, G. von. *Experiments in Hearing*. New York: McGraw-Hill, 1960.

Bekkers, J. M., and Stevens, C. F. "Presynaptic Mechanism for Long-Term Potentiation in the Hippocampus." *Nature* 346 (1990): 724–28.

Benefy, M., and Aguayo, A. J. "Extensive Elongation of Axons from Rat Brain into Peripheral Nerve Grafts." *Nature* 296 (1982): 150–52.

Benjamin, J. *The Transsexual Phenomenon*. New York: Ace, 1966.

Bermond, B., Nieuwenhuyse, B., Fasotti, L., and Schuerman, J. "Spinal Cord Lesions, Peripheral Feedback, and Intensities of Emotional Feelings." *Cognition and Emotion* 5 (1991): 201–20.

Berridge, K. C., Venier, I. L., and Robinson, T. E. "Taste Reactivity Analysis of 6-Hydroxydopamine-Induced Aphagia: Implications for Arousal and Anhedonia Hypothesis of Dopamine Function." *Behavioral Neuroscience* 103 (1989): 36–45.

Bertelsen, A., Harvald, B., and Hauge, M. "A Danish Twin Study of Manic Depressive Disorders." *British Journal of Psychiatry* 130 (1977): 330–51.

Billiard, M., and Seignalet, J. "Extraordinary Association between HLA-DR2 and Narcolepsy." *Lancet* 1 (1985): 226–27.

Björklund, A., Stenevi, U., Dunnett, S. B., and Gage, F. H. "Cross-Species Neural Grafting in a Rat Model of Parkinson's Disease." *Nature*, 298 (1982): 652–54.

Björklund, A., Stenevi, U., Schmidt, R. H., Dunnett, S. B., and Gage, F. H. "Intracerebral Grafting of Neuronal Suspension. I. Introduction and General Methods Preparation." *Acta Physiologica Scandinavica Supplement* 522 (1983): 1–8.

Blakemore, C., and Cooper, G. F. "Development of the Brain Depends on the Visual Environment." *Nature* 228 (1970): 477–78.

Blass, E., and Epstein, A. N. "A Lateral Preoptic Osmosensitive Zone for Thirst in the Rat." *Journal of Comparative Physiological Psychology* 76 (1971): 378–94.

Blass, E., and Hall, W. G. "Drinking Termination: Interactions among Hydrational, Orogastric, and Behavioral Controls in Rats." *Psychological Review* 83 (1976): 356–74.

Blass, E., and Hanson, D. G. "Primary Hyperdipsia in the Rat Following Septal Lesions." *Journal of Comparative and Physiological Psychology* 70 (1970): 87–93.

Bloch, V. "Facts and Hypotheses Concerning Memory Consolidation." *Brain Research* 24 (1970): 561–75.

Bloch, V., Hennevin, E., and Leconte, P. "Relationship between Paradoxical Sleep and Memory Processes." In *Brain Mechanisms and Learning*, ed. M. A. B. Brazier. New York: Raven, 1979.

Bon, C., Lemaire, M., Piot, O., Reibaud, M., Stutzmann, J.-M., Doble, A., and Bohme, G. A. "Nitric Oxide as a Physiological Messenger in Long-Term Potentiation and Memory Formation: Electrophysiological and Behavioral Evidence." In *Long-Term Potentiation: A Debate of Current Issues*, vol. 2, ed. M. Baurdry and J. L. Davis. Cambridge, Mass: MIT Press, 1994, pp. 3–17.

Bouchard, C., Tremblay, A., Després, J., Nadeau, A., Lupien, P. J., Thériault, G., Dussault, J., Moorjani, S., Pinault, S., and Fournier, G. "The Response to Long-Term Overfeeding in Identical Twins." *New England Journal of Medicine* 322(21) (1990): 1477–82.

Breedlove, S. M. "Sexual Differentiation of the Brain and Behavior." In *Behavioral Endocrinology*, ed. Becker, J. B., Breedlove, S. M., and Crews, D. Cambridge, Mass.: MIT Press, 1992.

Bremer, F. "L'Activite Cérébrale au Cours du Sommeil et de la Narcose: Contribution 3 l'Etude de Mecanisme du Sommeil." *Bulletin de l'Academie Royale de Medecine de Belgique* 2 (1937): 68–86.

Brobeck, J. R. "Mechanisms of the Development of Obesity in Animals with Hypothalamic Lesions." *Physiological Review* 26 (1946): 541–59.

Broca, P. "Anatomie Comparée des Circonvolutions Cérébrales: Le Grand Lobe Limbique et la Scissure Limbique dans la Série des Mammifères." *Revue d' Anthropologie* 1 (1878): 385–498.

Broderick, P. A., and Bridger, W. H. "A Comparative Study of the Effect of L-Tryptophan and Its Acetylated Derivative N-Acetyl-L-tryptophan on Rat Muricidal Behavior." *Biological Psychiatry* 19 (1984): 89–94.

Brown, G. L., Ebert, M. H., Goyer, P. F., Jimerson, D. C., Klein, W. J., Bunney, W. E., and Goodwin, F. K. "Aggression, Suicide, and Serotonin: Relationships of CSF Amine Metabolites." *American Journal of Psychiatry* 139 (1982): 741–46.

Brown, G. L., Goodwin, F. K., Ballenger, J. C., Goyer, P. F., and Major, L. F. "Aggression in Humans Correlates with Cerebrospinal Fluid Amine Metabolites." *Psychiatry Research* 1 (1979): 131–39.

Buonomano, D. V., and Byrne, J. H. "Long-Term Synaptic Changes Produced by a Cellular Analog of Classical Conditioning in Aplysia." *Science* 249 (1990): 420–23.

Burrows, G. D., McIntyre, I. M., Judd, F. K., and Norman, T. R. "Clinical Effects of Serotonin Reuptake Inhibitors in the Treatment of Depressive Illness." *Journal of Clinical Psychiatry* 49 (Suppl. 8) (1988): 18–22.

Byne, W. "The Biological Evidence Challenged." *Scientific American* 270(5) (1994): 50–55.

Campbell, J. N., Raja, S. N., Cohen, R. H., Manning, D. C., Khan, A. A., and Mayer, R. A. "Peripheral Neural Mechanisms of Nociception." In *Textbook of Pain*, 2nd ed., ed. P. D. Wall and R. Melzack. Edinburgh: Churchill Livingstone, 1989, pp. 22–45.

Campion, J., Latto, R., and Smith, Y. M. "Is Blindsight an Effect of Scattered Light, Spared Cortex, and Near-Threshold Vision?" *Behavioral and Brain Science* 6 (1983): 423–86.

Cannon, W. B. "The James-Lange Theory of Emotions: A Critical Examination and an Alternative." *American Journal of Physiology* 39 (1927): 106–24.

Cannon, W. B. *Bodily Changes in Pain, Hunger, Fear, and Rage*, 2d ed. New York: Appleton-Century-Crofts, 1929.

Cannon, W. B. "Hunger and Thirst." In *A Handbook of General Experimental Psychology*, ed. C. Murchison. Worcester, Mass.: Clark University Press, 1934.

Cannon, W. B., and Britton, S. W. "Studies on the Conditions of Activity in Endocrine Glands. XV. Pseudoaffective Medulliadrenal Secretion." *American Journal of Physiology* 72 (1925): 283–94.

Carbonetto, S. "Facilitatory and Inhibitory Effects of Glial Cells and Extracellular Matrix in Axonal Regeneration." *Current Opinion in Neurobiology* 1 (1991): 407–13.

Carskadon, M. A., and Dement, W. C. "Normal Human Sleep: An Overview." In *Principles of Sleep Medicine*, ed. M. H. Kryger, T. Roth, and W. C. Dement. Philadelphia: Saunders, 1989, pp. 3–13.

Charney, D. C., Goodman, W. K., Price, L. H., Woods, S. W., Rasmussen, S. A., and Heninger, G. R. "Serotonin Function in Obsessive-Compulsive Disorder." *Archives of General Psychiatry* 45 (1988): 177–85.

Charney, D. S., and Heninger, G. R. "Regulation of Noradrenergic Function in Panic Disorders: Effects of Clonidine in Healthy Subjects and Patients with Agoraphobia and Panic Disorders." *Archives of General Psychiatry* 43 (1986): 1042–54.

Charney, D. S., Menkes, D. B., and Heninger, G. R. "Receptor Sensitivity and the Mechanism of Action of Antidepressant Treatment." *Archives of General Psychiatry* 38 (1981): 1160–80.

Chase, T. N., Wexler, N. S., and Barbeau, A., eds. "Huntington's Disease." *Advances in Neurology*, vol. 23. New York: Raven Press, 1979.

Cherry, E. C. "Some Experiments upon the Recognition of Speech, with One and with Two Ears." *Journal of Acoustical Society of America* 25 (1953): 975–79.

Choi, D. W. "Glutamate Neurotoxicity and Diseases of the Nervous System." *Neuron* 1 (1988): 623–34.

Chorover, S. L., and Schiller, P. H. "Short-Term Retrograde Amnesia in Rats." *Journal of Comparative and Physiological Psychology* 59 (1965): 73–78.

Christensen, L. W., and Clemens, L. G. "Intrahypothalamic Implants of Testosterone or Estradiol and Resumption of Masculine Sexual Behavior in Long-Term Castrated Male Rats." *Endocrinology* 95 (1974): 984–90.

Chwalisz, K., Diener, E., and Gallagher, D. "Autonomic Arousal Feedback and Emotional Experience: Evidence from the Spinal Cord-Injured." *Journal of Personality and Social Psychology* 54 (1988): 820–28.

Clark, R. E., Zhang, A. A., and Lavond, D. G. "Reversible Lesions of the Cerebellar Interpositus Nucleus during Acquisition and Retention of a Classically Conditioned Behavior." *Behavioral Neuroscience* 106(6) (1992): 879–88.

Clark, S. A., Allard, T., Jenkins, W. M., and Merzenich, M. M. "Receptive Fields in the Body-Surface Map in Adult Cortex Defined by Temporally Correlated Inputs." *Nature* 332 (1988): 444–45.

Cloninger, C. R. "Neurogenetic Adaptive Mechanisms in Alcoholism." *Science* 236 (1987): 410–16.

Clower, R., Alvarez-Royo, P., Zola-Morgan, P., and Squire, L. R. "Recognition Memory Impairment in Monkeys with Selective Hippocampal Lesions." *Society for Neuroscience Abstracts* 17 (1991): 338.

Clugnet, M. C., and LeDoux, J. E. "Synaptic Plasticity in Fear Conditioning Circuits: Induction of LTP in the Lateral Nucleus of the Amygdala by Stimulation of the Medial Geniculate Body." *Journal of Neuroscience* 10 (1990): 2818–24.

Coleman, R. M. "Wide Awake at 3 A.M." New York: W. H. Freeman, 1986.

Colle, L. M., and Wise, R. A. "Facilitation of Lateral Hypothalamic Self-Stimulation by Amphetamine Microinjections into Nucleus Accumbens." *Society for Neuroscience Abstracts* 12 (1986): 930.

Connell, T. H. "Amphetamine Psychosis, a Description of the Individuals and Process." *Journal of Nervous and Mental Diseases* 144 (1967): 27–83.

Cooper, J. R., Bloom, F. E., and Roth, R. H. *The Biochemical Basis of Neuropharmacology*, 6th ed. New York: Oxford University Press, 1991.

Corbett, D., and Wise, R. A. "Intracranial Self-Stimulation in Relation to the Ascending Noradrenergic Fibre Systems of the Pontine Tegmentum and Caudal Midbrain: A Moveable Electrode Mapping Study." *Brain Research* 177 (1979): 423–36.

Corbett, D., and Wise, R. A. "Intracranial Self-Stimulation in Relation to the Ascending Dopaminergic Systems of the Midbrain: A Moveable Electrode Mapping Study." *Brain Research* 185 (1980): 1–15.

Costa, E. "The Allosteric Modulation of $GABA_A$ Receptors: Seventeen Years of Research." *Neuropsychopharmacology* 4 (1991): 225–35.

Cote, L. and Crutcher, M. D. "The Basal Ganglia." In *Principles of Neural Science*, 3rd ed., ed. E. R. Kandel, J. H. Schwartz, and T. M. Jessell. New York: Elsevier, 1991.

Cotman, C. W., and Nieto-Sampredo, M. "Cell Biology of Synaptic Plasticity." *Science* 225 (1984): 1287–94.

Creese, I. "Dopamine Receptors Explained." *Trends in Neurosciences* 5 (1982): 40–43.

Crews, F., and Smith, C. B. "Presynaptic Alpha-Receptor Subsensitivity after Long-Term Antidepressant Treatment." *Science* 202 (1978): 322–24.

Crow, T. J. "What Is Wrong with Dopaminergic Transmission in Schizophrenia?" *Trends in Neurosciences* 2 (1979): 52–55.

Crow, T. J. "Molecular Pathology of Schizophrenia: More Than One Disease Process?" *British Medical Journal*, 280 (1980): 66–68.

Czeisler, C. A., Johnson, M. P., Duffy, J. F., Brown, E. N., Ronda, J. M., and Kronauer, R. E. "Exposure to Bright Light and Darkness to Treat Physiologic Maladaptation to Night Work." *New England Journal of Medicine* 322(18) (1990): 1253–59.

Czeisler, C. A., Kronauer, R. E., Allan, J. S., Duffy, J. F., Jewett, M. E., Brown, E. N., and Ronda, J. M. "Bright Light Induction of Strong (Type O) Resetting of the Human Circadian Pace-maker." *Science* 244 (1989): 1328–33.

Dabak, A. G., and Johnson, D. H. "Function-Based Modeling of Binaural Processing: Interaural Phase." *Hearing Research* 58 (1992): 200–12.

Damasio, A. R. "Prosopagnosia." *Trends in Neurosciences* 8 (1985): 132–35.

Damasio, H., Grabowski, T., Frank, R., Galaburda, A. M., and Damasio, A. R. "The Return of Phineas Gage: Clues about the Brain from the Skull of a Famous Patient." *Science* 264 (1994): 1102–6.

Damasio, A. R., Tranel, D., and Damasio, H. "Face Agnosia and the Neural Substrates of Memory." *Annual Review of Neuroscience* 13 (1990): 89–109.

Dannenbaum, R. M., and Dykes, R. W. "Sensory Loss in the Hand after Sensory Stroke: Therapeutic Rationale." *Archives of Physical Medicine and Rehabilitation* 69 (1988): 833–39.

Darwin, C. *The Expression of the Emotions in Man and Animals*. London: Appleton, 1872.

Davidson, J. M. "Activation of Male Rat's Sexual Behavior by Intracerebral Implantation of Androgen." *Endocrinology* 79 (1966): 783–94.

Davis, J. D., Gallagher, R. J., Ladove, R. F., and Turausky, A. J. "Inhibition of Food Intake by a Humoral Factor." *Journal of Comparative and Physiological Psychology* 67 (1969): 407–14.

Davis, K. L., Kahn, R. S., Ko, G., and Davidson, M. "Dopamine in Schizophrenia: A Review and Reconceptualization." *American Journal of Psychiatry* 148 (1991): 1474–86.

Davis, M. D. "Pharmacological and Anatomical Analysis of Fear Conditioning Using the Fear-Potentiated Startle Paradigm." *Behavioral Neuroscience* 100 (1986): 814–24.

Davis, M. D. "The Role of the Amygdala in Conditioned Fear." In *The Amygdala: Neurobiological Aspects of Emotion, Memory, and Mental Dysfunction*, ed. J. P. Aggleton. New York: Wiley-Liss, 1992.

Davis, P. G., and Barfield, R. J. "Activation of Masculine Sexual Behavior by Intracranial Estradiol Benzoate Implants in Male Rats." *Neuroendocrinology* 28 (1979): 217–27.

De Jonge, F. H., Louwerse, A. L., Ooms, M. P., Evers, P., Endert, E., and van de Poll, N. E. "Lesions of the SDN-POA Inhibit Sexual Behavior of Male Wistar Rats" *Brain Research Bulletin* 23 (1989): 483–92.

De Valois, R. L. "Color Vision Mechanisms in the Monkey." *Journal of General Physiology* 43 (1960): 115–28.

De Valois, R. L., and De Valois, K. K. "Neural Coding of Color." In *Handbook of Perception*, ed. E. C. Carterette and M. P. Friedman, vol. 5. New York: Academic Press, 1975, pp. 117–62.

De Vietti, T. L., and Kirkpatrick, B. R. "The Amnesia Gradient: Inadequate as Evidence for a Memory Consolidation Process." *Science* 194 (1976): 438–39.

De Wied, D. "Pituitary-Adrenal System Hormones and Behavior." In *The Neurosciences: Third Study Program*, ed. F. O. Schmitt and F. G. Worden. Cambridge, Mass.: MIT Press, 1974.

Debons, A. F., Krimsky, I., and From, A. "A Direct Action of Insulin on the Hypothalamus Satiety Center." *American Journal of Physiology* 219 (1970): 938–42.

Degreef, G., and Mukherjee, S. "Season of Birth and CT Scan Findings in Schizophrenic Patients." *Biological Psychiatry* 24 (1988): 461–64.

de Lacoste-Utamsing, C., and Holloway, R. L. "Sexual Dimorphism in the Human Corpus Callosum." *Science* 216 (1982): 1431–32.

Delgado, J. M. R., and Anand, B. K. "Increased Food Intake Induced by Electrical Stimulation of the Lateral Hypothalamus." *American Journal of Physiology* 172 (1953): 162–68.

Delgado, P. L., Charney, D. S., Price, L. H., Aghajanian, G. K., Landis, H., and Heninger, G. R. "Serotonin Function and the Mechanism of Antidepressant Action." *Archives of General Psychiatry* 47 (1990): 411–18.

DeLong, M. R. "Motor Functions of the Basal Ganglia: Single-Unit Activity during Movement." In *Neurosciences: Third Study Program*, ed. F. O. Schmitt and F. G. Worden. Cambridge, Mass.: MIT Press, 1974.

DeLong, M. R. "Primate Models of Movement Disorders of Basal Ganglia Origin." *Trends in Neurosciences* 13 (1990): 281–86.

Dement, W. "The Effect of Dream Deprivation." *Science* 131 (1960): 1705–7.

Dement, W., and Kleitman, N. "The Relation of Eye Movements during Sleep to Dream Activity: An Objective Method for the Study of Dreaming." *Journal of Experimental Psychology* 53 (1957): 339–46.

Dement, W., and Mitler, M. M. "An Introduction to Sleep." In *Basic Sleep Mechanisms*, ed. O. Petre-Quadens and J. D. Schlag. New York: Academic Press, 1974.

Dement, W., and Villablanca, J. "Clinical Disorders in Man and Animal Model Experiments." In *Basic Sleep Mechanisms*, ed. O. Petre-Quadens and J. D. Schlag. New York: Academic Press, 1974.

Dennis, M., Lovett, M. and Wiegel-Crump, C. A. "Written Language Acquisition after Left or Right Hemidecortication in Infancy." *Brain and Language* 12 (1981): 54–91.

Desiderato, O., MacKinnon, J. R., and Hissom, H. "Development of Gastric Ulcers in Rats Following Stress Termination." *Journal of Comparative and Physiological Psychology* 87 (1974): 208–14.

Desimone, R. "Face-Selective Cells in the Temporal Cortex of Monkeys." *Journal of Cognitive Neuroscience* 3 (1991): 1–8.

Desimone, R., Wessinger, M., Thomas, L., and Schneider, W. "Attentional Control of Visual Perception: Cortical and Subcortical Mechanisms." *Cold Spring Harbor Symposium on Quantitative Biology* 55 (1990): 963–71.

Deutsch, J. A. "Dietary Control and the Stomach." *Progress in Neurobiology* 20 (1983a): 313–32.

Deutsch, J. A. "The Cholinergic Synapse and the Site of Memory." In *The Physiological Basis of Memory*, ed. J. A. Deutsch. New York: Academic Press, 1983b.

Deutsch, J. A., and Gonzalez, M. F. "Gastric Nutrient Content Signals Satiety." *Behavior Neural Biology* 30 (1980): 113.

Deutsch, J. A., and Hardy, W. T. "Cholecystokinin Produces Bait Shyness in Rats." *Nature* 266 (1977): 196.

Deutsch, J. A., and Leibowitz, S. F. "Amnesia or Reversal of Forgetting by Anticholinesterase, Depending Simply on Time of Injection." *Science* 153 (1966): 1017.

Deutsch, J. A., Puerto, A., and Wang, M.-L. "The Pyloric Sphincter and Differential Food Preference." *Behavioral Biology* 19 (1977): 543–47.

Deutsch, J. A., Young, W. G., and Kalogeris, T. J. "The Stomach Signals Satiety." *Science* 201 (1978): 165–67.

Dewsbury, D. A. "Description of Sexual Behavior in Research on Hormone-Behavior Interactions." In *Endocrine Control of Sexual Behavior*, ed. C. Beyer. New York: Raven Press, 1979, pp. 3–32.

Dewson, J. H., III. "Efferent Olivocochlear Bundle: Some Relationships to Noise Masking and to Stimulus Attention." *Journal of Neurophysiology* 30 (1967): 817–32.

Di Lorenzo, P. M. "Across Unit Patterns in the Neural Response to Taste: Vector Space Analysis." *Journal of Neurophysiology* 62 (1989): 823–33.

Diamond, J. "I Want a Girl Just Like the Girl. . . ." *Discover* 7 (1986): 65–68.

DiFiglia, M. "Excitotoxic Injury of the Neostriatum: A Model for Huntington's Disease. *Trends in Neurosciences* 13 (1990): 286–89.

Drewnowski, A., Bellisle F., Aimez, P., and Remy B. "Taste and Bulimia." *Physiology & Behavior* 41 (1987): 621–26.

Drummond, A. H. "Lithium and Inositol Lipid-Linked Signaling Mechanisms." *Trends in Pharmacological Sciences* 8 (1987): 129–33.

Duggan, J. P., and Booth, D. A. "Obesity, Overeating, and Rapid Gastric Emptying in Rats with Ventromedial Hypothalamic Lesions." *Science* 231 (1986): 609–11.

Dunleavy, D. L., Brezinova, V., Oswald, I., MacLean, A. W., and Tinker, M. "Changes during Weeks in Effects of Tricycle Drugs on the Human Sleeping Brain." *British Journal of Psychiatry* 120 (1972): 663–72.

Dunnett, S. B., Ryan, C. N., Levin, P. D., Reynolds, M., and Bunch, S. T. "Functional Consequences of Embryonic Neocortex Transplanted to Rats with Prefrontal Cortex Lesions." *Behavioral Neuroscience* 101 (1987): 489–503.

Egeland, J. A., Gerhard, D. S., Pauls, D. L., Sussex, J. N., Kidd, K. K., Allen, C. R., Hostetter, A. M., and Housman, D. "Bipolar Affective Disorders Linked to DNA Markers on Chromosome 11." *Nature* 325 (1987): 783–87.

Egger, M. D., and Flynn, J. P. "Amygdaloid Suppression of Hypothalamically Elicited Attack Behavior." *Science* 136 (1962): 43–44.

Egger, M. D., and Flynn, J. P. "Effect of Electrical Stimulation of the Amygdala on Hypothalamically Elicited Attack Behavior in Cats." *Journal of Neurophysiology* 26 (1963): 705–20.

Eibl-Eibelfelt, I. *Love and Hate: The Natural History of Behavior Patterns* (G. Strachan, trans.). New York: Holt, Rinehart & Winston, 1972.

Ekman, P. "Biological and Cultural Contributions to Body and Facial Movement." In *The Anthropology of the Body*, A.S.A. Monograph 15, ed. J. Blacking. London: Academic Press, 1977.

Ekman, P. "Facial Expressions of Emotion: New Findings, New Questions." *Psychological Science* 3 (1992): 34–38.

Ekman, P., and Friesen, W. V. "Constants across Cultures in the Face and Emotion." *Journal of Personality and Social Psychology* 17 (1971): 124–29.

Ekman, P., Friesen, W. V., O'Sullivan, M., Chan, A., Diacoyanni-Tarlatzis, I., Heider, K., Krause, R., LeCompte, W., Pitcairn, T., Ricci-Bitti, P., Scherer, K., Tomita, M., and Tzavaras, A. "Universals and Cultural Differences in the Judgments of Facial Expressions of Emotion." *Journal of Personality and Social Psychology* 53 (1987): 712–17.

Ekman, P., Levenson, R. W., and Friesen, W. V. "Autonomic Nervous System Activity Distinguishes among Emotions." *Science* 221 (1983): 1208–10.

Epstein, A. N. "Drinking Behavior." In *Encyclopedia of Neuroscience*, ed. G. Adelman. Boston: Birkhauser, 1987, pp. 340–42.

Epstein, A. N., Fitzsimons, I. T., and Rolls, B. J. "Drinking Induced by Injections of Angiotensin into the Brain of the Rat." *Journal of Physiology* 210 (1970): 457–74.

Epstein, A. N., and Teitelbaum, P. "Regulation of Food Intake in the Absence of Taste, Smell, and Other Oropharyngeal Sensations." *Journal of Comparative and Physiological Psychology* 55 (1962): 753–59.

Epstein, A. N., and Teitelbaum, T. "Severe and Persistent Deficits in Thirst Produced by Lateral Hypothalamic Damage." In *Thirst in the Regulation of Body Water*, ed. M. J. Wayner. New York: Macmillan, 1964.

Everitt B. J., and Stacey, P. "Studies of Instrumental Behavior with Sexual Reinforcement in Male Rats. II. Effects of Preoptic Area Lesions, Castration and Testosterone." *Journal of Comparative Psychology* 101 (1987): 407–19.

Fackelmann, K. A. "Marijuana and the Brain." *Science News*, 143 (1993): 88–94.

Fawcett, J. W., and Keynes, R. J. "Peripheral Nerve Regeneration." *Annual Review of Neuroscience* 13 (1990): 43–60.

Feder, H. "Peripheral Plasma Levels of Gonadal Steroids in Adult Male and Adult, Nonpregnant Female Mammals." In *Handbook of Behavioral Neurobiology*, vol. 7: *Reproduction*, ed. N. Adler, D. Pfaff, and R. W. Goy. Plenum Press, New York, 1985, pp. 299–370.

Feder, H., Naftolin, F., and Ryan, K. J. "Male and Female Sexual Responses in Male Rats Given Estradiol Benzoate and 5-α Androstan-17-β-01-3-one Proprionate." *Endocrinology* 94 (1973): 13641.

Fields, H. L. *Pain*. New York: McGraw-Hill, 1987.

Fields, H. L., and Basbaum, A. I. "Brain Stem Modulation of Spinal Pain Transmission Neurons." *Annual Review of Physiology* 40 (1978): 217–48.

Fields, H. L., and Basbaum, A. L. "Anatomy and Physiology of a Descending Pain Control System." In *Advances in Pain Research and Treatment*, vol. 3, ed. J. J. Bonica, J. C. Liebeskind, and D. Albe-Fessard. New York: Raven Press, 1979.

Fields, H. L., Basbaum, A. L., Clanton, C. H., and Anderson, S. D. "Nucleus Raphe Magnus Inhibition of Spinal Cord Dorsal Horn Neurons." *Brain Research* 126 (1977): 441–53.

Fink, M. "Convulsive Therapy in Affective Disorder: A Decade of Understanding and Acceptance." In *Psychopharmacology: The Third Generation of Progress*, ed. H. Y. Meltzer. New York: Raven Press, 1987, pp. 1071–76.

Fitch, R. H., Tallal, P., Brown, C., Galaburda, A. M., and Rosen, G. D. "Induced Microgyria and Auditory Temporal Processing in Rats: A Model for Language Impairment?" *Cerebral Cortex* 4 (1994): 260–70.

Fitzsimons, J. T. "The Physiology of Thirst: A Review of the Extraneural Aspects of the Mechanisms of Drinking." In *Progress in Physiological Psychology*, vol. 4, ed. E. Stellar and J. M. Sprague. New York: Academic Press, 1971.

Flood, J. F., Jarvik, M. E. B., Bennett, E. L., and Orme, A. E. "Effects of ACTH Peptide Fragments on Memory Formation." *Pharmacology, Biochemistry and Behavior* 5 (1976): 41–51.

Flynn, J. P. "The Neural Basis of Aggression in Cats." In *Neurophysiology and Emotion*, ed. D. C. Glass. New York: Rockefeller University Press, 1967.

Flynn, J. P., Vanegas, H., Foote, W., and Edwards, S. "Neural Mechanisms Involved in a Cat's Attack on a Rat." In *The Neural Control of Behavior*, ed. R. E. Whalen, R. F. Thompson, M. Verreano, and N. M. Weinberger. New York: Academic Press, 1970.

Franklin K. B. J. "Catecholamine and Self-stimulation: Reward and Performance Effects Dissociated." *Pharmacology, Biochemistry and Behavior* 9 (1978): 661–71.

Freeman, W. J. The Physiology of Perception. *Scientific American* 264 (1991): 78–85.

Freidman, M. I., and Stricker, E. M. "The Physiological Psychology of Hunger: A Physiological Perspective." *Psychological Review* 83 (1976): 409–31.

Frohman, L. A., and Bernardis, L. L. "Growth Hormone and Insulin Levels in Weanling Rats with Ventromedial Hypothalamic Lesions." *Endocrinology* 82 (1968): 1125–32.

Fulton, J. F., and Jacobsen, C. F. "The Functions of the Frontal Lobes: A Comparative Study in Monkeys, Chimpanzees, and Man." *Advances in Modern Biology* 4 (1935): 113–23. Abstract from the Second International Neurological Congress, London, pp. 70–71.

Fuster, J. M. "The Effects of Stimulation of Brain Stem on Tachistoscopic Perception." *Science* 127 (1958): 150.

Gage, F. H., Dunnett, S. B., Stenevi, U., and Björklund, A. "Aged Rats: Recovery of Motor Impairments by Intrastriatal Nigral Grafts." *Science* 221 (1983): 966–68.

Galaburda, A. M., Menard, M. T., and Rosen, G. D. "Evidence for Aberrant Auditory Anatomy in Developmental Dyslexia." *Proceedings of the National Academy of Sciences (USA)*, 91 (1994): 8010–13.

Galaburda, A. M., Sherman, G. P., Rosen, G. D., Aboitiz, F., and Geschwind, N. "Developmental Dyslexia: Four Consecutive Patients with Cortical Anomalies." *Annals of Neurology* 18 (1985), 222–23.

Gallagher, M., Rapp, P. R., and Fanelli, R. J. "Opiate Antagonist Facilitation of Time-Dependent Memory Processes: Dependence upon Intact Norepinephrine Function." *Brain Research* 347 (1985): 284–90.

Gardner, H. The Shattered Mind: The Person after Brain Damage. New York: Knopf, 1975.

Garrick, T., Minor, T. R., Bauck, S., Weiner, H., and Guth P. (1989). "Predictable and Unpredictable Shock Stimulates Gastric Contractility and Causes Mucosal Injury in Rats." *Behavioral Neuroscience* 103 (1989): 124–30.

Garver, D. L., and Davis, J. M. "Biogenic Amine Hypothesis of Affective Disorder." *Life Sciences* 24 (1979): 383–94.

Gawin, F. H. "Cocaine Addiction: Psychology and Neurophysiology." *Science* 251 (1991): 1580–86.

Gazzaniga, M. S. "Right Hemisphere Language Following Brain Bisection: A 20-Year Perspective." *American Psychologist* (1983) 38: 525–37.

Gerhardt, S., and Liebman, J. M. "Self-Regulation of ICSS Duration: Effects of Anxiogenic Substances, Benzodiazepine Antagonists and Antidepressants." *Pharmacology, Biochemistry and Behavior* 22 (1985): 71–76.

Geschwind, N. "Wernicke's Contribution to the Study of Aphasia." *Cortex* 3 (1967): 449–63.

Geschwind, N. "The Apraxias: Neural Mechanisms of Disorders of Learned Movement." *American Scientist* 63 (1975): 188–95.

Geschwind, N. "The Biology of Cerebral Dominance: Implications for Cognition." *Cognition* 17 (1984) 193–208.

Geschwind, N., and Behan, P. O. "Left-Handedness: Association with Immune Disease, Migraine, and Developmental Disorder." *Proceedings of the National Academy of Science (USA)* 79 (1982): 5097–5100.

Geschwind, N., and Galaburda, A. M. *Cerebral Lateralization: Biological Mechanisms, Associations, and Pathology.* Cambridge, Mass.: MIT Press/Bradford Books, 1987.

Geschwind, N., and Kaplan, E. "A Human Cerebral Deconnection Syndrome." *Neurology* 12 (1962): 675–85.

Geschwind, N., and Levitsky, W. "Human Brain: Left-Right Asymmetries in Temporal Speech Region," *Science* 161 (1968): 186–87.

Gibbs J., Young, R. C., and Smith, G. P. "Cholecystokinin Decreases Food Intake in Rats." *Journal of Comparative and Physiological Psychology* 84 (1973): 488–95.

Gibson, E. J., and Levin, H. *The Psychology of Reading.* Cambridge, Mass.: MIT Press, 1975.

Gleitman, H. *Psychology.* New York: Norton, 1991, p. 11.

Gloor, P., Olivier, A., and Quesney, L. F. "The Role of the Amygdala in the Expression of Psychic Phenomenon in Temporal Lobe Seizures." In *The Amygdaloid Complex*, ed. Y. Ben-Ari. New York: Elsevier/North-Holland, 1981.

Goate, A., Chartier-Harlin, M.-C., Mullan, M., Brown, J., Crawford, F., Fidani, L., Giuffra, L., Haynes, A., Irving, N., James, L., Mant, R., Newton, P., Rooke, K., Roques, P., Talbot, C., Pericak-Vance, M., Roses, A., Williamson, R., Rossor, M., Wen, M., and Hardy, J. "Segregation of a Missense Mutation in the Amyloid Precursor Protein Gene with Familial Alzheimer's Disease." *Nature* 349 (1991): 704–6.

Goddard, G. V. "Functions of the Amygdala." *Psychological Bulletin* 62 (1964): 89–109.

Goeders, N. E., Dworkin, S. L., and Smith, J. E. "Neuropharmacological Assessment of Cocaine Self-administration into the Medical Prefrontal Cortex." *Pharmacology, Biochemistry and Behavior* 24 (1986): 1429–40.

Goeders, N. E., Lane, J. D., and Smith, J. E. "Self-administration of Methionine Enkephalin into the Nucleus Accumbens." *Pharmacology, Biochemistry and Behavior* 20 (1984): 451–55.

Gold, P. E. "Memory Modulation." In *Neurobiology of Learning and Memory*, ed. G. Lynch, J. L. McGaugh, and N. M. Weinberger. New York: Guilford Press, 1984, pp. 374–82.

Gold, P. E. "Sweet Memories." *American Scientist* 75 (1987): 151–55.

Gold, P. E., Delanoy, R. L., and Merrin, J. "Modulation of Long-Term Potentation by Peripherally Administered Amphetamine and Epinephrine." *Brain Research* 305 (1985): 103–8.

Gold, P. E., Hankins, L., Edwards, R. M., Chester, J., and McGaugh, J. L. "Memory Interference and Facilitation with Posttrial Amygdala Stimulation: Effect on Memory Varies with Foot Shock Level." *Brain Research* 86 (1975): 509–13.

Gold, P. E., and McGaugh, J. L. "A Single-Trace, Two Process View of Memory Storage Processes." In *Short-Term Memory*, ed. D. Deutsch and J. A. Deutsch. New York: Academic Press, 1975, pp. 355–78.

Gold, P. E., and McGaugh, J. L. "Hormones and Memory." In *Neuropeptide Influences on the Brain and Behavior*, ed. L. H. Miller, C. A. Sandman, and A. J. Kastin. New York: Raven Press, 1977.

Gold, P. E., McGaugh, J. L., Hankins, L. L., Rose, R. P., and Vasquez, B. J. "Age-Dependent Changes in Retention in Rats." *Experimental Aging Research* 8 (1981): 53–58.

Gold, P. E., and van Buskirk, R. B. "Facilitation of Time-Dependent Memory Processes with Posttrial Epinephrine Injections." *Behavioral Biology* 13 (1975): 145–53.

Gold, P. E., Vogt, J., and Hall, J. L. "Posttraining Glucose Effects on Memory: Behavioral and Pharmacological Characteristics. *Behavioral Neural Biology* 46 (1986): 145–55.

Gold, P. W., Goodwin, F. K., and Chrousos, G. P. "Clinical and Biochemical Manifestations of Depression: Relation to the Neurobiology of Stress." *New England Journal of Medicine* 319 (1988): 343–53.

Gold, R. M. "Hypothalamic Hyperphagia Produced by Parasagittal Knife Cuts." *Physiology and Behavior* 5 (1970): 23–26.

Gold, R. M. "Hypothalamic Obesity: The Myth of the Ventromedial Nucleus." *Science* 182 (1973): 488–90.

Gold, R. M., Jones, A. P., Sawchenko, P. E., and Kapatos, G. "Paraventricular Area: Critical Focus of a Longitudinal Neurocircuitry Mediating Food Intake." *Physiology and Behavior* 18 (1977): 1111–19.

Goldman-Rakic, P. S. "Circuitry of Primate Prefrontal Cortex and Regulation of Behavior by Representational Memory." In *Handbook of Physiology*, sect. 1: *The Nervous System*, vol. V: *Higher Functions of the Brain*, pt. I, ed. F. Plum and V. B. Mountcastle. Bethesda, Md.: American Physiological Society, 1987, pp. 373–417.

Goldman-Rakic, P. S. "Working Memory and the Mind." *Scientific American* 262 (1992): 110–17.

Goldstein, A., and Hilgard, E. R. "Failure of the Opiate Antagonist Naloxone to Modify Hypnotic Analgesia." *Proceedings of the National Academy of Sciences (USA)* 72 (1975): 2041–43.

Gonzalez, M. F., and Deutsch, J. A. "Vagotomy Abolishes Cues of Satiety Produced by Gastric Distension." *Science* 212 (1981): 1283–84.

Goodlett, C. R., Marcussen, B. L., and West, J. R. "A Single Day of Alcohol Exposure during the Brain Growth Spurt Induces Brain Weight Restriction and Cerebellar Purkinje Cell Loss." *Alcohol* (1990): 107–14.

Gordon, W. C. "Similarities between Recently Acquired and Reactivated Memories with Production of Memory

Interference." *American Journal of Psychology* 90 (1977): 231–42.

Gorman, J. M., Fyer, M. R., Goetz, R., Askanazi, J., Liebowitz, M. R., Fyer, A. J., Kinney, J., and Klein, D. F. "Ventilatory Physiology of Patients with Panic Disorder." *Archives of General Psychiatry* 45 (1988): 31–39.

Gormezano, I., Kehoe, E. J., and Marshall, B. S. "Twenty Years of Classical Conditioning Research with the Rabbit." In *Progress in Psychobiology and Physiological Psychology*, vol. 10, ed. J. M. Sprague and A. N. Epstein. New York: Academic Press, 1983, pp. 198–275.

Gorski, R. A. "Critical Role for the Medial Preoptic Area in the Sexual Differentiation of the Brain." *Progress in Brain Research* 61 (1984): 129–35.

Gorski, R. A., Gordon, J. H., Shryne, J. E., and Southam, A. M. "Evidence for a Morphological Sex Difference within the Medial Preoptic Area of the Rat Brain." *Brain Research* 148 (1978): 333–46.

Gottesman, I. I., and Shields, F. "Schizophrenia in Twins: Sixteen Years' Consecutive Admissions to a Psychiatric Clinic." *British Journal of Psychiatry* 112 (1966): 809–18.

Graf, P., Squire, L. R., and Mandler, G. "The Information That Amnesic Patients Do Not Forget." *Journal of Experimental Psychology: Learning, Memory, and Cognition* 10 (1984): 164–78.

Grau, J. W., Hyson, R. L., Maier, S. F., Madden, J., and Barchas, J. D. "Long-Term Stress-Induced Analgesia and Activation of the Opiate System." *Science* 213 (1981): 1409–11.

Green, D. J., and Gillette, R. "Circadian Rhythm of Firing Rate Recorded from Single Cells in the Rat Suprachiasmatic Brain Slice." *Brain Research* 245 (1982): 198–200.

Green, S. "Benzodiazepines, Putative Anxiolytics and Animal Models of Anxiety." *Trends in Neurosciences* 14 (1991): 101–3.

Greenough, W. T., and Volkman, F. R. "Pattern of Dendritic Branching in Occipital Cortex of Rats Reared in Complex Environments." *Experimental Neurology* 40 (1973): 491–504.

Grossman, S. P., Dacey, D., Halaris, A. E., Collier, T., and Routtenberg, A. "Aphagia and Adipsia after Preferential Destruction of Nerve Cell Bodies in Hypothalamus." *Science* 202 (1978): 537–39.

Growdon, J. "Treatment for Alzheimer's Disease?" *The New England Journal of Medicine* 327 (1992): 1306–8.

Gubbay, J., Collignon, J., Koopman, P., Capel, B., Economou, A., Munsterberg. A., Vivian, N., Goodfellow, P., and Lovell-Badge, R. "A Gene Mapping to the Sex-Determining Region of the Mouse Y Chromosome Is a Member of a Novel Family of Embryonically Expressed Genes." *Nature* 346 (1990): 245–50.

Guile, M. N. "Differential Gastric Ulceration in Rats Receiving Shocks on Either Fixed-Time or Variable-Time Schedules." *Behavioral Neuroscience* 101 (1987): 139–40.

Gupta, R. "Alternative Patterns of Seasonal Affective Disorder: Three Case Reports from North India." *American Journal of Psychiatry* 145(4) (1988): 515–16.

Hall, W. G. "A Remote Stomach Clamp to Evaluate Oral and Gastric Controls of Drinking in the Rat." *Physiology and Behavior* 11 (1973): 897–901.

Halpern, D. F. *Sex Differences in Cognitive Abilities*. New York: Erlbaum, 1992.

Hamburg, D. A., and Lunde, D. T. "Sex Hormones in the Development of Sex Differences." In *The Development of Sex Differences*, ed. E. E. Maccoby. Stanford: Stanford University Press, 1966.

Hamer, D. H., Hu, S., Magnuson, V. L., Hu, N., and Pattatuci, A. M. "A Linkage between DNA Markers on the X Chromosome and Male Sexual Orientation." *Science* 261 (1993): 321–26.

Han, P. W. "Hypothalamic Obesity in Rats without Hyperphagia." *Transactions of the New York Academy of Sciences* 30 (1967): 229–43.

Harada, S., Agarwal, D. P., Goedde, H. W., Tagaki, S., and Ishikawa, B. "Possible Protective Role against Alcoholism for Aldehyde Dehydrogenase Isozyme Deficiency." *Japanese Lancet* ii 8302 (1982): 827.

Harper, R. M., Frysinger, R. C., Trelease, R. B., and Marks, J. D. "State-Dependent Alteration of Respiratory Cycle Timing by Stimulation of the Central Nucleus of the Amygdala." *Brain Research* 306 (1984): 1–8.

Hart, B. "Sexual Reflexes and Mating Behavior in the Male Dog." *Journal of Comparative and Physiological Psychology* 66 (1967): 388–99.

Hart, B. "Hormones, Spinal Reflexes, and Sexual Behaviour." In *Determinants of Sexual Behavior*, ed. J. B. Hutchinson. Chichester: Wiley, 1978.

Hartmann, E. L. *The Functions of Sleep*. New Haven: Yale University Press, 1974.

Hayflick, L. "The Cell Biology of Human Aging." *Scientific American*, 242 (1980): 54–65.

Hebb, D. O. *The Organization of Behavior*. New York: Wiley, 1949.

Heffner, H. E., and Masterton, R. B. "Sound Localization in Mammals: Brainstem Mechanisms." In *Comparative Perception*, vol. I: *Discrimination*, ed. M. Berkley and W. Stebbins. New York: Wiley, 1990.

Heilman, K., and Watson, S. "The Neglect Syndrome—A Unilateral Defect of the Orienting Response." In *Lateralization in the Nervous System*, ed. S. Harnad, R. Doty, L. Goldstein, J. Jaynes, and G. Krauthamer. New York: Academic Press, 1977.

Helmholtz, H. von. "On the Theory of Compound Colors." *Philosophical Magazine* (1852): 519–34.

Heninger, G. R., and Charney, D. S. "Mechanism of Action of Antidepressant Treatments: Implication for the Etiology and Treatment of Depression Disorders." In *Psychopharmacology: The Third Generation of Progress*, ed. H. Y. Meltzer. New York: Raven Press, 1987, pp. 535–44.

Hentall, I. D., and Fields, H. L. "Segmental and Descending Influences on Intraspinal Thresholds of Single C-Fibers." *Journal of Neurophysiology* 42 (1979): 1527–37.

Herberg, L. "Seminal Ejaculation Following Positively Reinforcing Electrical Stimulation of the Rat Hypothalamus." *Journal of Comparative and Physiological Psychology* 56 (1963): 679–85.

Hess, W. R. *Diencephalon: Autonomic and Extra Pyramidal Functions*. New York: Grune & Stratton, 1954.

Heston, L. L. "Psychiatric Disorders in Foster Home Reared Children of Schizophrenic Mothers." *British Journal of Psychiatry* 112 (1966): 819–25.

Hetherington, A. W., and Ranson, S. W. "Hypothalamic Lesions and Adiposity in the Rat." *Anatomical Record* 78 (1940): 149–72.

Hinson, R. E., Poulos, C. X., and Cappell, H. "Effects of Pentobarbital and Cocaine in Rats Expecting Pentobarbital." *Pharmacology, Biochemistry and Behavior* 16 (1982): 661–66.

Hirsch, H. V. D., and Spinelli, D. N. "Visual Experience Modifies Distribution of Horizontally and Vertically Oriented Receptive Fields." *Science* 168 (1970): 869.

Hirsch, J., and Knittle, J. L. "Cellularity of Obese and Nonobese Human Adipose Tissue." *Federation of American Societies for Experimental Biology: Federation Proceedings* 29 (1970): 1516–21.

Hobson, J. A. "The Reciprocal Interaction Model of Sleep Cycle Control: Implications for PGO Wave Generation and Dream Amnesia." In *Neurobiology of Sleep and Memory*, ed. R. R. Drucker-Colin and J. L. McGaugh. New York: Academic Press, 1977, pp. 159–83.

Hobson, J. A. *Sleep.* New York: Scientific American Library, 1989.

Hobson, J. A., and McCarley, R. W. "The Brain as a Dream State Generator: An Activation-Synthesis Hypothesis of the Dream Process." *American Journal of Psychiatry* 134 (1977): 1335–48.

Hobson, J. A., McCarley, R. W., and Wyzinski, P. W. "Sleep Cycle Oscillation: Reciprocal Discharge by Two Brainstem Neuronal Groups." *Science* 189 (1975): 55–58.

Hodges, H., Green, S., and Glenn, B. "Evidence That the Amygdala Is Involved in Benzodiazepine and Serotonergic Effects on Punished Responding But Not on Discrimination." *Psychopharmacology* 92 (1987): 491–504.

Hodgson, E. S., and Roeder, K. D. "Electrophysiological Studies of Arthropod Chemoreception: General Properties of the Labellar Chemoreceptors of *Diptera.*" *Journal of Cellular and Comparative Physiology* 48 (1956): 51–76.

Hoebel, B. G., Monaco, A. P., Hernandez, L., Aulisi, E. F., Stanley, B. G., and Lenard, L. "Self-injection of Amphetamine Directly into the Brain." *Psychopharmacology* 81 (1983): 158–63.

Hoebel, B. G., and Teitelbaum, P. "Weight Regulation in Normal and Hypothalamic Hyperphagic Rats." *Journal of Comparative and Physiological Psychology* 61 (1966): 189–93.

Honda, Y., and Juju, T., eds. *HLA in Narcolepsy.* Heidelberg: Springer, 1988.

Horne, J. A. "Mammalian Sleep Function with Particular Reference to Man." In *Sleep Mechanisms and Functions in Humans and Animals*, ed. A. R. Mayes. Wokingham, England: Van Nostrand Reinhold, 1982, pp. 262–312.

Horne, J. A. *Why We Sleep.* Oxford, England: Oxford University Press, 1988.

Horne, R. L., and Picard, R. S. "Psychosocial Risk Factors for Lung Cancer." *Psychosomatic Medicine* 41 (1979): 503–14.

Horridge, G. A. "Learning of Leg Position by the Ventral Nerve Cord in Headless Insects." *Proceedings of the Royal Society B* 157 (1962): 33–52.

Hosobuchi, Y. "Subcortical Electrical Stimulation for Control of Intractable Pain in Humans: Report of 122 Cases (1970–1984)." *Journal of Neurosurgery* 64 (1986): 543–53.

Hosobuchi, Y., Adams, J. E., and Linchitz, R. "Pain Relief by Electrical Stimulation of the Central Gray Matter in Humans and Its Reversal by Naloxone." *Science* 197 (1977): 183–86.

Howlett, A. C., Bidaut-Russell, M., Devane, W. A., Laurence, S. M., Johnson, M. R., and Herkenham, M. "The Cannabinoid Receptor: Biochemical, Anatomical and Behavioral Characterization." *Trends in Neurosciences* 13 (1990): 420–24.

Hubel, D. H., and Wiesel, T. N. "Receptive Fields of Single Neurons in the Cat's Striate Cortex." *Journal of Physiology* 148 (1959): 574–91.

Hubel, D. H., and Wiesel, T. N. "Single-Cell Responses in Striate Cortex of Kittens Deprived of Vision in One Eye." *Journal of Neurophysiology* 26 (1963): 1003–17.

Hubel, D. H., and Wiesel, T. N. "Receptive Fields and Functional Architecture in Two Nonstriate Visual Areas (18 and 19) of the Cat." *Journal of Neurophysiology* 28 (1965): 229–89.

Hubel, D. H., Wiesel, T. N., and LeVay, S. "Plasticity of Ocular Dominance Columns in the Monkey Striate Cortex." *Philosophical Transactions of the Royal Society of London* 278 (1977): 377–409.

Hubel, D. H., Wiesel, T. N., and Stryker, M. P. "Anatomical Demonstration of Orientation Columns in Macaque Monkeys." *Journal of Comparative Neurology* 177 (1978): 361–80.

Humphreys, P., Kaufmann, W. E., and Galaburda, A. M. "Developmental Dyslexia in Women: Neuropathological Findings in Three Cases." *Annals of Neurology* 28 (1990): 727–38.

Hurvich, L. M. and Jameson, D. "An Opponent-Process Theory of Color Vision." *Psychological Review* 64 (1957): 383–404.

Iggo, A. "Cutaneous Heat and Cold Receptors with C Afferent Fibers." *Quarterly Journal of Experimental Physiology* 44 (1959): 362–70.

Ignelzi, R., and Squire, L. R. "Recovery from Anterograde and Retrograde Amnesia Following Percutaneous Drainage of a Cystic Craniopharyngioma." *Journal of Neurology, Neurosurgery and Psychiatry* 39 (1976): 1231–35.

Introini-Collison, I. B., and McGaugh, J. L. "Interaction of Hormones and Neurotransmitter Systems in the Modulation of Memory Storage." In *Peripheral Signaling of the Brain: Role in Neural-Immune Interactions, Learning and Memory*, ed. R. C. A. Frederickson, J. L. McGaugh, and D. L. Felton. Toronto: Hogrefe & Huber, 1991, pp. 205–302.

Izard, C. E. *Human Emotions.* New York: Plenum, 1977.

Izquierdo, I. "Effect of Naloxone and Morphine on Various Forms of Memory in the Rat: Possible Role of Endogenous Opiate Mechanisms in Memory Consolidation." *Psychopharmacology* 66 (1979): 199–203.

Jacobs, J. L. "How Hallucinogenic Drugs Work." *American Scientist* 75 (1987): 386–92.

Jaffe, J. H. "Drug Addiction and Drug Abuse." In *The Pharmacological Basis of Therapeutics*, ed. A. G. Gilman, L. S. Goodman, T. W. Rall, and F. Murad. New York: Macmillan, 1985.

James, W. "What Is Emotion?" *Mind* 9 (1884): 188–205.

Jensen, D. D. "Paramecia, Planaria, and Pseudolearning." *Animal Behaviour* 13 (Suppl.) (1965): 9–20.

Jessell, T. M. "Neuronal Survival and Synapse Formation." In *Principles of Neural Science*, 3rd ed., ed. E. R. Kandel, J. H. Schwartz, and T. M. Jessell. New York: Elsevier, 1991, pp. 929–44.

Jessell, T. M., and Iversen, L. L. "Opiate Analgesics Inhibit Substance P Release from Rat Trigeminal Nucleus." *Nature* 268 (1979): 549–51.

Jessell, T. M., and Kelly, D. D. "Pain and Analgesia." In *Principles of Neural Science*, 3rd ed., ed. E. R. Kandel, J. H. Schwartz, and T. M. Jessell. New York: Elsevier, 1991, pp. 385–99.

Johnson, C. H., and Hastings, J. W. "The Elusive Mechanism of the Circadian Clock." *American Scientist* 74 (1986): 29–36.

Jordan, H. A. "Voluntary Intragastric Feeding: Oral and Gastric Contributions to Food Intake and Hunger in Man." *Journal of Comparative and Physiological Psychology* 68 (1969): 498–506.

Jouvet, M. "Biologic Amines and the States of Sleep." *Science* 163 (1969): 32–41.

Jouvet, M., and Delorme, J. "Locus Coeruleus et Someil Paradoxical." *Compte Rendus de la Societe de Biologie* 159 (1965): 895–99.

Kanamori, N., Sakai, K., and Jouvet, M. "Neuronal Activity Specific to Paradoxical Sleep in the Ventromedial Medullary Reticular Formation of Unrestrained Cats." *Brain Research* 189 (1980): 251–55.

Kandel, E. R. "Visual System III: Physiology of the Central Visual Pathways." In *Principles of Neural Science*, ed. E. R. Kandel and J. H. Schwartz. New York: Elsevier/North-Holland, 1981, 247.

Kandel, E. R. "Cellular Mechanisms of Learning and the Biological Basis of Individuality." In *Principles of Neural Science*, 3rd ed., ed. E. R. Kandel, J. H. Schwartz, and T. M. Jessell. New York: Elsevier, 1991a.

Kandel, E. R. "Perception of Motion, Depth, and Form." In *Principles of Neural Science*, 3rd ed., ed. E. R. Kandel, J. H. Schwartz, and T. M. Jessell. New York: Elsevier, 1991b.

Kane, J. Honigfield, G., Singer, J., and Meltzer, H. "Clozapine for the Treatment-Resistant Schizophrenic." *Archives of General Psychiatry* 45 (1988): 789–96.

Kapp, B. S., Gallagher, M., Underwood, M. D., McNall, C. L., Whitehorn, D. "Cardiovascular Responses Elicited by Electrical Stimulation of the Amygdala Central Nucleus in the Rabbit." *Brain Research* 234 (1982): 251–62.

Kapp, B. S., Wilson, A., Pascoe, J. P., Supple, W. F., and Whalen, P. J. "A Neuroanatomical Systems Analysis of Conditioned Bradycardia in the Rabbit." In *Neurocomputation and Learning: Foundations of Adaptive Networks*, ed. M. Gabriel and J. Moore. Cambridge, Mass.: MIT Press, 1990, pp. 53–90.

Karni, A., Tanne, D., Rubenstein, B. S., Askenasy, J. J. M., and Sagi, D. "Dependence on REM Sleep of Overnight Improvement of Perceptual Skill." *Science* 265 (1994): 679–82.

Katchadourian, H. A., and D. T. Lunde. *Fundamentals of Human Sexuality*, 3d ed. New York: Holt, Rinehart and Winston, 1980.

Kauer, J. S. "Contributions of Topography and Parallel Processing to Odor Coding in the Vertebrate Olfactory Pathway." *Trends in Neuroscience* 14 (1991): 79–85.

Kelly, D. D. "Sleep and Dreaming." In *Principles of Neural Science*, ed. E. R. Kandel, J. H. Schwartz and T. M. Jessell. New York: Elsevier/North-Holland, 792–804, 1991a.

Kelly, D. D. "Disorders of Sleep and Consciousness." In *Principles of Neural Sciences*, ed. E. R. Kandel, T. M. Jessell, and J. H. Schwartz. New York: Elsevier/North-Holland, 1991b, pp. 805–19.

Kelly, J. "The Neural Basis of Perception and Movement." In *Principles of Neural Science* 3rd ed., ed. E. R. Kandel, J. H. Schwartz, and T. M. Jessell. New York: Elsevier, 1991c, pp. 283–95.

Kelsey, J. E., Carlezon, W. A., Jr., and Falls, W. A. "Lesions of the Nucleus Accumbens in Rats Reduce Opiate Reward But Do Not Alter Context-Specific Opiate Tolerance." *Behavioral Neuroscience* 103 (1989): 1327–34.

Kendell, R. E., and Adams, W. "Unexplained Fluctuations in the Risk of Schizophrenia by Month and Year of Birth." *British Journal of Psychiatry* 158 (1991): 758–63.

Kendell, R. E., and Kemp, I. W. "Maternal Influenza in the Etiology of Schizophrenia." *Archives of General Psychiatry* 46 (1989): 878–82.

Kennedy, G. C. "The Role of Depot Fat in the Hypothalamic Control of Food Intake in the Rat." *Proceedings of the Royal Society B*, 140 (1953): 578–92.

Kertesz, A. "Recovery and Treatment." In *Clinical Neuropsychology*, ed. K. M. Heilman and E. Valenstein. New York: Oxford University Press, 1979.

Kesner, R. P., and Baker, T. B. "A Two-Process Model of Opiate Tolerance." In *Endogenous Peptides and Learning and Memory Processes*, ed. J. L. McGaugh. San Diego, Calif.: Academic Press, 1981, p. 479–518.

Kesner, R. P., and Doty, R. W. "Amnesia Produced in Cats by Local Seizure Activity Initiated from the Amygdala." *Experimental Neurology* 21 (1968): 58–68.

Kety, S. S. "Biological Concomitants of Affective States and Their Possible Role in Memory Processes." In *Neural Mechanisms of Learning and Memory*, ed. M. R. Rosenzweig and E. L. Bennett. Cambridge, Mass.: MIT Press, 1976, pp. 321–28.

Keverne, E. B. "Olfaction and Taste Dual Systems for Sensory Processing." *Trends in Neurosciences* (1978): 32–34.

Kimble, D. P. "Functional Effects of Neural Grafting in the Mammalian Central Nervous System." *Psychological Bulletin* 108 (1990): 462–79.

Kimura, D. "Left-Right Differences in the Perception of Melodies." *Quarterly Journal of Experimental Psychology* 16 (1964): 355–58.

Kimura, D. "Sex Differences in the Brain." *Scientific American* 267 (1992): 118–25.

King, A. J., and Moore, D. R. "Plasticity of Auditory Maps in the Brain." *Trends in Neurosciences* 14 (1991): 31–37.

King, B. M., Smith, R. L., and Frohman, L. A. "Hyperinsulinemia in Rats with Ventromedial Hypothalamic Lesions: Role of Hyperphagia." *Behavioral Neuroscience* 98 (1984): 152–55.

King, M. B., and Hoebel, B. "Killing Elicited by Brain Stimulation in Rats." *Communications in Behavioral Biology* 2 (1968): 173–77.

Kirch, D. G. "Infection and Autoimmunity as Etiologic Factors in Schizophrenia: A Review and Reappraisal." *Schizophrenia Bulletin* 19 (1993): 355–70.

Kleitman, N. *Sleep and Wakefulness*, 2nd ed. Chicago: University of Chicago Press, 1963.

Kluver, H., and Bucy, P. " 'Psychic Blindness' and Other Symptoms Following Bilateral Temporal Lobectomy in Rhesus Monkeys." *Amencan Journal of Physiology* 119 (1937): 352–53.

Kluver, H., and Bucy, P. "Preliminary Analysis of Functions of the Four Temporal Lobes in Monkeys." *Archives of Neurology and Psychiatry* 42 (1939): 979–1000.

Knittle, J. L., and Hirsch, J. "Effect of Early Nutrition on the Development of Rat Epididymal Fat Pads: Cellularity and Metabolism." *Journal of Clinical Investigation* 47 (1968): 2091.

Knudsen, E. I. "The Hearing of the Barn Owl." *Scientific American* 245 (1981): 113–25.

Knudsen, E. I., and Konishi, M. "Mechanisms of Sound Localization in the Barn Owl." *Journal of Comparative Physiology* 133 (1979): 13–21.

Kolata, G. "Food Affects Human Behavior." *Science* 218 (1982): 1209–10.

Kolb, B., and Whishaw, I. Q. *Fundamentals of Human Neuropsychology*, New York: Freeman, 1990.

Koopmans, H. S. "The Role of the Gastrointestinal Tract in the Satiation of Hunger." In *The Body Weight Regulatory System: Normal and Disturbed Mechanisms*, ed. L. A. Cioffi, W. B. T. James, and T. B. Van Italie. New York: Raven Press, 1981, pp. 45–55.

Kopin, I. J., and Markey, S. P. "MPTP Toxicity: Implications for Research in Parkinson's Disease." *Annual Review of Neuroscience* 11 (1988): 81–96.

Kornhuber, H. H. "Cerebral Cortex, Cerebellum, and Basal Ganglia: An Introduction to Their Motor Functions." In *Neurosciences: Third Study Program*, ed. F. O. Schmitt and F. G. Worden. Cambridge, Mass.: MIT Press, 1974.

Kramer, P. *Listening to Prozac*. New York: Viking, 1993.

Krauthammer, C., and Klerman, G. L. "The Epidemiology of Mania." In *Manic Illness*, ed. B. Shopsin. New York: Raven Press, 1979.

Krech, D., Rosenzweig, M. R., and Bennett, E. L. "Relations between Brain Chemistry and Problem Solving among Rats Raised in Enriched and Impoverished Environments." *Journal of Comparative and Physiological Psychology* 55 (1962): 801–7.

Krupp, P., and Barnes, P. "Leponex-Associated Granulocytopenia: A Review of the Situation." *Psychopharmacology* 99 (1989): S118–21.

Kryger, M. H., Roth, T., and Dement, W. C. *Principles and Practice of Sleep Medicine*. Philadelphia: Saunders, 1989.

Kuffler, S. W. "Discharge Patterns and Functional Organization of Mammalian Retina." *Journal of Neurophysiology* 16 (1953): 37–68.

Kyrkouli, S. E., Stanley, B. G., and Leibowitz, S. F. "Galanin Stimulation of Feeding Induced by Medial Hypothalamic Injection of This Novel Peptide." *European Journal of Pharmacology* 122 (1986): 159–60.

LaBerge, D., and Buchsbaum, M. S. "Positron Emission Tomographic Measurements of Pulvinar Activity during an Attention Task." *Journal of Neuroscience* 10 (1990): 613–19.

Lader, M. "Fluoxetine Efficiency vs. Comparative Drugs: An Overview." *British Journal of Psychiatry* 153(Suppl. 3) (1988): 51–58.

Lam, R. W., Berkowitz, A. L., Berga, S. L., and Clark, C. M. "Melatonin Supression in Bipolar and Unipolar Mood Disorders." *Psychiatric Research* 33(2) (1990): 129–34.

LaMotte, R. H., and Campbell, J. N. "Comparison of Responses of Warm and Nociceptive C-Fiber Afferents in Monkeys with Human Judgments of Thermal Pain." *Journal of Neurophysiology* 4 (1978): 509–28.

Lancker, D. R. V., Kreiman, F., and Cummings, J. "Voice Perception Deficits: Neuroanatomical Correlates of Phonagnosia." *Journal of Clinical and Experimental Neuropsychology* 11 (1989): 665–74.

Langston, J. W. "MPTP-Induced Parkinsonism: How Good a Model Is It?" In *Recent Developments in Parkinson's Disease*, ed. S. Fahn, C. P. Marsden, P. Jenner, and P. Teychenne. New York: Raven Press, 1986, pp. 119–26.

Langston, J. W., Irwin, I., Langston, E. B., and Forno, L. S. "Pargyline Prevents MPTP-Induced Parkinsonism in Primates." *Science* 225 (1984): 1480–82.

Lashley, K. S. *Brain Mechanisms and Intelligence*. Chicago: University of Chicago Press, 1929.

Lashley, K. S. "In Search of the Engram." *Symposium of the Society for Experimental Biology* 4 (1950): 454–82.

Laursen, A. M. "Corpus Striatum." *Acta Physiologica Scandinavica* 59(Suppl. 211) (1963): 106.

Lavond, D. G., Lincoln, J. S., McCormick, D. A., and Thompson, R. F. "Effects of Bilateral Lesions of the Dentate and Interpositus Cerebellar Nuclei on Conditioning of Heart Rate and Nictitating Membrane/Eyelid Responses in the Rabbit." *Brain Research* 305 (1983): 323–30.

LeDoux, J. E. "Emotion, Memory, and the Brain." *Scientific American* 270(6) (1994): 50–57.

LeDoux, J. E., Cicchetti, P., Xagoraris, A., and Romanski, L. M. "The Lateral Amygdaloid Nucleus: Sensory Interface of the Amygdala in Fear Conditioning." *Journal of Neuroscience* 10 (1990) 1062–69.

LeDoux, J. E., Iwata, J., Cicchetti, P., and Reis, D. J. "Different Projections of the Central Amygdala Nucleus Mediate Autonomic and Behavioral Correlates of Conditioned Fear." *Journal of Neuroscience* 9 (1988): 2517–29.

Lee, T., and Seeman, P. "Elevation of Brain Neuroleptic/Dopamine Receptors in Schizophrenia." *American Journal of Psychiatry* 127 (1980): 191–97.

Lehman, M. N., and Winans, S. S. "Vomeronasal and Olfactory Pathways to the Amygdala Controlling Male Hamster Sexual Behavior: Autoradiographic and Behavioral Analyses." *Brain Research* 240 (1982): 27–42.

Leibowitz, S. F., Hammer, N. G., and Chang, K. "Hypothalamic Paraventricular Nucleus Lesions Produce Overeating and Obesity in the Rat." *Physiology and Behavior* 27 (1981): 1031–40.

Lele, P. P., and Weddell, G. "The Relationship between Neurohistology and Corneal Sensibility." *Brain* 79 (1956): 119–54.

LeMagnen, J. "Advances in Studies of Physiological Control and Regulation of Food Intake." In *Progress in Physi-*

ological Psychology, vol. 4, ed. E. Stellar and J. M. Sprague. New York: Academic Press, 1971, pp. 203–61.

Lettvin, J. Y., Maturanan, H. R., McCulloch, W. S., and Pitts, W. H. "What the Frog's Eye Tells the Frog's Brain." *Proceedings of the Institute of Radio Engineering* 47 (1959): 1940–51.

LeVay, S. "A Difference in Hypothalamic Structure between Heterosexual and Homosexual Men." *Science* 253 (1991): 1034–37.

LeVay, S., and Hamer, D. H. "Evidence for a Biological Influence in Male Homosexuality." *Scientific American* 270(5) (1994): 44–49.

Levine, J. D., Gordon, N. C., and Fields, H. L. "The Role of Endorphins in Placebo Analgesia." In *Advances in Pain Research and Therapy*, vol. 3, ed. J. Bonica, J. C. Liebeskind, and D. Albe-Fessard. New York: Raven Press, 1979.

Levine, J. D., Gordon, N. C., Jones, R. T., and Fields, H. L. "The Narcotic Antagonist Naloxone Enhances Clinical Pain." *Nature* 272 (1978): 826–27.

Levinson, P. K., and Flynn, J. P. "The Objects Attacked by Cats during Stimulation of the Hypothalamus." *Animal Behavior* 13 (1965): 217–20.

Levy, E., Carman, M. D., Fernandez-Madrid, I. J., Power, M. D., Lieberburg, I., van Duinen, S. G., Bots, G. T. A. M., Luyendijk, W., and Frangione, B. "Mutation of the Alzheimer's Disease Amyloid Gene in Hereditary Cerebral Hemorrhage, Dutch Type." *Science* 248 (1990), 1124–26.

Levy, J. "Lateral Differences in the Human Brain in Cognition and Behavioral Control." In *Cerebral Correlates of Conscious Experience*, ed. P. Buser and A. Rougeul-Buser. New York: North Holland, 1978.

Levy, J., and Sperry, R. "Lateral Specialization of the Human Brain: Behavioral Manifestations and Possible Evolutionary Basis." In *The Biology of Behavior: Proceedings of 32nd Annual Biology Colloquium*, ed. J. A. Kiger. Corvallis: Oregon University Press, 1972.

Levy, J., and Trevarthen, C. "Perceptual, Semantic Language Processes in Split-Brain Patients." *Brain* 100 (1977): 105–18.

Levy, J., Trevarthen, C., and Sperry, R. W. "Perception of Bilateral Chimeric Figures Following Hemispheric Deconnexion." *Brain* 95 (1972): 61–78.

Lewin, R. "Trail of Ironies to Parkinson's Disease." *Science* 224 (1984): 1083–85.

Lewis, D. J. "Psychobiology of Active and Inactive Memory." *Psychological Bulletin* 86 (1979): 1054–83.

Lewis, J. W., Cannon, J. T., and Liebeskind, J. C. "Opoid and Nonopoid Mechanisms of Stress Analgesia." *Science* 208 (1980): 623–25.

Liang, K. C., and McGaugh, J. L. "Lesions of the Stria Terminalis Attenuate the Enhancing Effect of Posttraining Epinephrine on Retention of an Inhibitory Avoidance Response." *Behavioral Brain Research* 9 (1983): 49–58.

Liang, K. C., McGaugh, H. L. and Yao, H.-Y. "Involvement of Amygdala Pathways in the Influence of Posttraining Amygdala Norepinephrine and Peripheral Epinephrine on Memory Storage." *Brain Research* 508 (1990): 225–33.

Lickey, M. E., and Gordon, B. *Drugs for Mental Illness.* San Francisco: Freeman, 1991.

Liebelt, R. A., Bordelon, C. B., and Liebelt, A. G. "The Adipose Tissue System and Food Intake." In *Progress in Physiological Psychology*, ed. E. Stellar and J. M. Sprague. New York: Academic Press, 1973.

Liebowitz, M. R., Gorman, J. M., Fyer, Levitt, M., Dillon, D., Levy, G., Appleby, I. L., Anderson, S., and Palij, M. "Lactate Provocation of Panic Attacks. II. Biochemical and Physiological Findings." *Archives of General Psychiatry* 42 (1985): 709–19.

Lindsay, P. H., and Norman, D. A. *Human Information Processing.* New York: Academic Press, 1972.

Lindsay, D. B., Bowden, J., and Magoun, H. W. "Effect upon EEG of Acute Injury to the Brainstem Activating System." *Electroencephalography and Clinical Neurophysiology* 1 (1949): 475–86.

Lindsay, D. B., Schreiner, L. H., Knowles, W. B., and Magoun, H. W. "Behavioral and EEG Changes Following Chronic Brain Stem Lesions in the Cat." *Electroencephalography and Clinical Neurophysiology* 2 (1950): 483–98.

Lindvall, O. "Prospects of Transplantation in Human Neurodegenerative Diseases." *Trends in Neurosciences* 14 (1991): 376–84.

Liuzzi, F. J., and Lasek, R. J. "Astrocytes Block Axonal Regeneration in Mammals by Activating the Physiological Stop Pathway." *Science* 237 (1987), 642–45.

Livingstone, M. S., Rosen, G. D., Drislane, F. W., and Galaburda, A. M. "Physiological and Anatomical Evidence for a Magnocellular Defect in Developmental Dyslexia." *Proceedings of the National Academy of Sciences (USA)* 88 (1991): 7943–47.

Loftus, E. F., and Loftus, G. R. "On the Permanence of Stored Information in the Human Brain." *American Psychologist* 35 (1980): 409–20.

Logue, A. W. *The Psychology of Eating and Drinking.* New York: Freeman, 1986.

Louis-Sylvestre, J., Servant, J., Molimard, R., and Le Magnen, J. "Feeding Pattern of Liver-Transplanted Rats." *Physiology and Behavior* 48 (1990): 321–26.

Lovegrove, W., Garzia, R., and Nicholson, S. "Experimental Evidence for a Transient System Deficit in Specific Reading Disability." *Journal of the American Optometric Association* 2 (1990): 137–46.

Lowenstein, W. R., and Mendelson, M. "Components of Receptors Adaptation in a Pacinian Corpuscle." *Journal of Physiology* 177 (1965): 377–97.

Lu, S. T., Hamalainen, M. S., Hari, R., Ilmoniemi, R. J., Lounasmaa, O. V., Sams, M., and Vilkman, V. "Seeing Faces Activates Three Separate Areas Outside the Occipital Visual Cortex in Man." *Neuroscience* 43 (1991): 287–90.

Lucas, F., and Sclafani, A. "Flavor Preferences Conditioned by Intragastric Fat Infusions in Rats." *Physiology and Behavior* 46 (1989): 403–12.

Luria, A. R. *The Working Brain: An Introduction to Neuropsychology.* New York: Basic Books, 1973.

Lynch, G., and Baudry, M. "The Biochemistry of Memory: A New and Specific Hypothesis." *Science* 224 (1984): 1057–63.

Maclean, P. D. "Psychosomatic Disease and the Visceral Brain: Recent Developments Bearing on the Papez Theory of Emotion." *Psychosomatic Medicine* 11 (1949): 338–53.

Maclean, P. D. "The Limbic System and Its Hippocampal Formation: Studies in Animals and Their Possible Application to Man." *Journal of Neurosurgery* 11 (1954): 29–44.

Magnes, J., Moruzzi, G., and Pompeiano, O. "Synchronization of the EEG Produced by Low-Frequency Electrical Stimulation of the Region of the Solitary Tract." *Archives Italiennes de Biologie* 99 (1961): 33–67.

Magni, F., Moruzzi, G., Rossi, G. F., and Zanchetti, A. "EEG Arousal Following Inactivation of the Lower Brain Stem by Selective Injection of Barbiturate into the Vertebral Circulation." *Archives Italiennes de Biologie* 97 (1959): 33–46.

Maier, S. F., Laudenslager, M. L., and Ryan, S. M. "Stressor Controllability, Immune Function, and Endogenous Opiates." In *Affect, Conditioning, and Cognition.* Hillsdale, N.J.: Erlbaum, 1985.

Marcel, A. J. "Conscious and Unconscious Perception: An Approach to the Relation between Phenomenal Experience and Perceptual Processes." *Cognitive Psychology* 15 (1983): 238–300.

Marder, S. R., and Van Putten, T. "Who Should Receive Clozapine?" *Archives of General Psychiatry* 45 (1988): 865–67.

Mark, V. H., and Ervin, F. R. *Violence and the Brain.* New York: Harper & Row, 1970.

Mark, V. H., Ervin, F. R., and Yakovlev, P. I. "The Treatment of Pain by Stereotaxic Methods." *Confina Neurologica* 22 (1962): 238–45.

Marshall, J. F., Turner, B. H., and Teitelbaum, P. "Sensory Neglect Produced by Lateral Hypothalamic Damage." *Science* 174 (1971): 523–25.

Masters, W. H., and Johnson, V. E. *Human Sexual Response.* Boston: Little, Brown, 1966.

Masterson, R. B. "Adaptation for Sound Localization in the Ear and Brainstem of Mammals." *Federation Proceedings* 33 (1974): 1904–10.

Matthews, D. A., Cotman, C., and Lynch, G. "An Electron Microscopic Study of Lesion-Induced Synaptogenesis in the Dentate Gyrus of the Adult Rat: Reappearance of Morphologically Normal Synaptic Contacts." *Brain Research* 115 (1976): 23–41.

Mattson, S. N., Barron, S., and Riley, E. P. "The Behavioral Effects of Prenatal Alcohol Exposure." In *Biomedical and Social Aspects of Alcohol and Alcoholism*, ed. K. Kuriyama, A. Takada, and H. Ishii. Tokyo: Elsevier, 1988, pp. 851–53.

Mayer, A. *The Crocodile Man.* Boston: Houghton Mifflin, 1982, pp. 1–10.

Mayer, D., Price, D. D., Rafii, A., and Barber, J. "Acupuncture Hypalgesia: Evidence for Activation of a Central Control System as a Mechanism of Action." In *Advances in Pain Research and Therapy*, vol. 1, ed. J. J. Bonica and D. Albe-Fessard. New York: Raven Press, 1976.

Mayer, D. J., Wolfe, T. L., Akil, H., Carder, B., and Liebeskind, J. C. "Analgesia from Electrical Stimulation in the Brainstem of the Rat." *Science* 174 (1971): 1351–54.

Mayer, J. "The Glucostatic Theory of Regulation of Food Intake and the Problem of Obesity." *Bulletin of the New England Medical Center* 14 (1952): 43.

Mayer, J. "Glucostatic Mechanism of Regulation of Food Intake." *New England Journal of Medicine* 249 (1953): 13–16.

McClintock, M. K. "A Functional Approach to the Behavioral Endocrinology of Rodents." In *Psychobiology of Reproductive Behavior*, ed. D. Crews. Englewood Cliffs, N.J.: Prentice Hall, 1987, pp. 176–203.

McEwen, B. S. "Interactions between Hormones and Nerve Tissue." *Scientific American* 235(1) (1976): 48–58.

McGaugh, J. L. "Drug Facilitation of Learning and Memory." *Annual Review of Pharmacology* 13 (1973): 229–41.

McGaugh, J. L., and Gold, P. E. "Modulation of Memory by Electrical Stimulation of the Brain." In *Neural Mechanisms of Learning and Memory*, ed. M. R. Rosenzweig and E. L. Bennet. Cambridge, Mass.: MIT Press, 1976.

McGaugh, J. L., and Gold, P. E., van Buskirk, R. B., and Haycock, J. W. "Modulating Influences of Hormones and Catecholamines on Memory Storage Processes." *Progress in Brain Research* 42 (1975): 151–62.

McGaugh, J. L., Introini-Collison, I. B., Cahill, L., Kim, M., and Liang, K. C. "Involvement of the Amygdala in Neuromodulatory Influences on Memory Storage." In *The Amygdala: Neurobiological Aspects of Emotion, Memory, and Mental Dysfunction*, ed. J. P. Aggleton. New York: Wiley-Liss, 1992.

McGaugh, J. L., Liang, K. C., Bennett, C., and Sternberg, D. B. "Adrenergic Influences on Memory Storage: Interaction of Peripheral and Central Systems." In *Neurobiology of Learning and Memory*, eds. G. Lynch, J. L. McGaugh, and N. M. Weinberger. New York: Guilford Press, 1984, pp. 313–32.

McGinty, D. J., and Sterman, M. B. "Sleep Suppression after Basal Forebrain Lesion in the Cat." *Science* 160 (1968): 1253–55.

McKay, D. G. "Aspects of the Theory of Comprehension, Memory and Attention." *Quarterly Journal of Experimental Psychology* 25 (1973): 22–40.

Meagher, M. W., Grau, J. W., and King, R. A. "Role of Supraspinal Systems in Environmentally Induced Antinociception: Effect of Spinalization and Decerebration on Brief Shock-Induced and Long Shock-Induced Antinociception." *Behavioral Neuroscience* 104 (1990): 328–38.

Meddis, R. *The Sleep Instinct.* London: Routledge & Kegan Paul, 1977.

Meltzer, L. D. "Clinical Efficacy of Clozapine in the Treatment of Schizophrenia." *Clinical Neuropharmacology*, 13 (Suppl. 2) (1990): 259–60.

Melzack, R. "Phantom Limbs." *Scientific American* 266(4) (1992): 120–26.

Melzack, R., and Loeser, J. D. "Phantom Body Pain in Paraplegics: Evidence for a Central 'Pattern Generating Mechanism' for Pain." *Pain* 4 (1978): 195–210.

Melzack, R., and Wall, P. D. "Pain Mechanisms: A New Theory." *Science* 150 (1965): 971–79.

Mendelson, W. B. *Human Sleep: Research and Clinical Care.* New York: Plenum Medical Book Co., 1987.

Mendelson, W. B., Weingartner, H., Greenblatt, D. J., Garnett, D., and Gillin, J. C. "A Clinical Study of Flurazepam." *Sleep* 5 (1982): 350–60.

Mendelwicz, J., and Ranier, J. D. "Adoption Study Supporting Genetic Transmission in Manic-Depressive Illness." *Nature* 268 (1977): 327–29.

Messing, R. B., Jensen, R. A., Martinez, J. L., Jr.,

Spiehler, V. R., Vasquez, B. J., Soumireu-Mourat, B., Liang, K. C., and McGaugh, J. L. "Naloxone Enhancement of Memory." *Behavioral Neural Biology* 27 (1979): 266–75.

Miller, N. E. "Motivational Effects of Brain Stimulation and Drugs." *Federation Proceedings, Federation of American Societies for Experimental Biology* 19 (1960): 846–53.

Miller, N. E. "Learning and Performance Motivated by Direct Stimulation of the Brain." In *Electrical Stimulation of the Brain*, ed. D. E. Sheer. Austin: University of Texas Press, 1961.

Milner, B. "Laterality Effects in Audition." In *Interhemispheric Relations and Cerebral Dominance*, ed. V. B. Mountcastle. Baltimore: John Hopkins Press, 1962.

Milner, B. "Visual Recognition and Recall after Right Temporal-Lobe Excision in Man." *Neuropsychologia* 6 (1968): 191–209.

Milner, B. "Memory and the Temporal Regions of the Brain." In *Biology of Memory*, ed. K. H. Pribram and D. E. Broadbent. New York: Academic Press, 1970.

Milner, B. "Disorders of Learning and Memory after Temporal Lobe Lesions in Man." *Clinical Neurosurgery* 19 (1972): 421–46.

Mishkin, M. "A Memory System in Monkeys." *Philosophical Transactions of the Royal Society of London*, 298 (1982): 85–95.

Mishkin, M., and Appenzeller, T. "The Anatomy of Memory." *Scientific American*, 256 (1987): 80–89.

Mishkin, M., and Manning, F. J. "Non-spatial Memory After Selective Prefrontal Lesions in Monkeys." *Brain Research*, 143 (1978): 313–23.

Mishkin, M., Ungerleider, L. G., and Macko, K. A. "Object Vision and Spatial Vision: Two Cortical Pathways." *Trends in Neurosciences* 6 (1983): 414–17.

Moncrieff, R. W. "The Characterization of Odors." *Journal of Physiology* 125 (1954): 453–65.

Moncrieff, R. W. "The Sorptive Properties of the Olfactory Membrane." *Journal of Physiology* 130 (1955): 543–58.

Money, J. "Sex Hormones and Other Variables in Human Eroticism." In *Sex Internal Secretions*, vol. 2, ed. W. C. Young. Baltimore: Williams & Wilkins, 1961.

Money, J., and Ehrhardt, A. A. *Man and Woman, Boy and Girl*. Baltimore: John Hopkins University Press, 1972.

Money, J., Wiedeking, C., Walker, P. A., and Gain, D. "Combined Antiandrogenic and Counseling Program for Treatment of 46 XY and 47 XYY Sex Offenders." In *Hormones, Behavior, and Psychopathology*, ed. E. J. Sachar. New York: Raven Press, 1976.

Moore, R. Y., and Eichler, V. B. "Loss of a Circadian Adrenal Corticosterone Rhythm Following Suprachiasmatic Lesions in the Rat." *Brain Research* 42 (1972): 201–6.

Moore-Ede, M. C., Czeisler, C. A., and Richardson, G. S. "Circadian Timekeeping in Health and Disease." *New England Journal of Medicine* 309 (1983): 469–76.

Moray, N. "Attention in Dichotic Listening: Affective Cues and the Influence of Instructions." *Quarterly Journal of Experimental Psychology* 11 (1959): 56–60.

Morgane, P. J. "Electrophysiological Studies of Feeding and Satiety Centers in the Rat." *American Journal of Physiology* 201 (1961): 838–44.

Morley, J. E., Bartness, T. J., Gosnell, B. A., and Levine, A. S. "Peptidergic Regulation of Feeding." *International Review of Neurobiology* 27 (1985): 207–98.

Morris, R. G. M., Anderson, E., Lynch, G. S., and Baudry, M. "Selective Impairment of Learning and Blockade of Long-Term Potentiation by an N-Methyl-D-Aspartate Receptor Antagonist, AP5." *Nature* 319 (1986): 774–76.

Morris, R. G. M., Garrud, P., Rawlins, J. N. P., and O'Keefe, J. "Place Navigation Impaired in Rats with Hippocampal Lesions." *Nature* 297 (1982): 681–83.

Moruzzi, G., and H. W. Magoun. "Brainstem Reticular Formation and Activation of the EEG." *Electroencephalography and Clinical Neurophysiology* 1 (1949): 455–73.

Moulton, D. G. "Communication by Chemical Signals." *Science* 162 (1968): 1176–80.

Moulton, D. G. "Dynamics of Cell Population in the Olfactory Epithelium." *Annals of the New York Academy of Science* 237 (1974): 52–61.

Mountcastle, V. B., Andersen, R. A., and Motter, B. C. "The Influence of Attentive Fixation upon the Excitability of the Light-Sensitive Neurons of the Posterior Parietal Cortex." *Journal of Neuroscience* 1 (1981): 218–35.

Mumby, D. G., Wood, E. R., and Pinel, J. P. J. "Object-Recognition Memory Is Only Mildly Impaired in Rats with Lesions of the Hippocampus and Amygdala." *Psychobiology* 20(1) (1992): 18–27.

Muntz, W. R. "Vision in Frogs." *Scientific American* 210(3) (1964): 113.

Naftolin, F., Ryan, K. J., Davies, I. J., Reddy, V. V., Flores, F., and Petro, Z. "The Formation of Estrogen by Central Neuroendocrine Tissue." *Recent Progress in Hormone Research* 31 (1975): 295–315.

Neff, W. D., Fisher, J. F., Diamond, I. T., and Yela, M. "The Role of the Auditory Cortex in Discrimination Requiring Localization of Sound in Space." *Journal of Neurophysiology* 19 (1956): 500–12.

Nicholson, A. N., Pascoe, P. A., Spencer, M. B., Stone, B. M., Roehrs, T., and Roth, T. "Sleep after Transmeridian Flights." *Lancet* 2 (1986): 1205–8.

Niehoff, D. L., and Kuhar, M. J. "Benzodiazepine Receptors: Localization in Rat Amygdala." *Journal of Neuroscience* 3 (1983): 2091–97.

Niijima, A. "Afferent Impulse Discharge from Glucoreceptors in the Liver of the Guinea Pig." *Annals of the New York Academy of Science* 157 (1969): 690–700.

Nottenbohm, F. "Brain Pathways for Vocal Learning in Birds: A Review of the First 10 Years." In *Progress in Psychobiology and Physiological Psychology*, vol. 9, ed. J. M. Sprague and A. N. Epstein. New York: Academic Press, 1980.

Novin, D. "The Relation between Electrical Conductivity of Brain Tissue and Thirst in the Rat." *Journal of Comparative and Physiological Psychology* 55 (1962): 145–54.

Novin, D., Robinson, B. A., Culbreth, L. A., and Tordoff, M. G. "Is There a Role for the Liver in the Control of Food Intake?" *American Journal of Clinical Nutrition* 9 (1983): 233–46.

Noyes, R., Anderson, D. J., Clancy, J., Crowe, R. R., Slyman, D. J., Ghoneim, M. M., and Hinrichs, J. V. "Diazepam and Propranolol in Panic Disorder and Agoraphobia." *Archives of General Psychiatry* 41 (1984): 287–92.

O'Brien, D. P., Chesire, R. M., and Teitelbaum, P. (1985). "Vestibular versus Tail-Pinch Activation in Cats with Lateral Hypothalamic Lesions." *Physiology and Behavior* 34, 811–14.

O'Callaghan, E., Gibson, R., Colohan, H. A., Walshe, D., Buckley, P., Larkin, C., and Waddington, J. L. "Season of Birth in Schizophrenia: Evidence for Confinement of an Excess of Winter Births to Patients without a Family History of Mental Disorder." *British Journal of Psychiatry* 158 (1991): 764–69.

O'Keefe, J., and Dostrovsky, T. "The Hippocampus as a Spatial Map: Preliminary Evidence from Unit Activity in the Freely Moving Rat." *Brain Research* 34 (1971): 171–75.

O'Keefe, J., and Speakman, A. "Single Unit Activity in the Rat Hippocampus during a Spatial Memory Task." *Experimental Brain Research* 68 (1987): 1–27.

Olds, J. "Effects of Hunger and Male Sex Hormone on Self-Stimulation of the Brain." *Journal of Comparative and Physiological Psychology* 51 (1958): 320–24.

Olds, J., and Milner, P. "Positive Reinforcement Produced by Electrical Stimulation of the Septal Area and Other Regions of Rat Brain." *Journal of Comparative and Physiological Psychology* 47 (1954): 419–27.

Oliveras, J. L., Besson, J. M., Guilbaud, G., and Liebeskind, J. C. "Behavioral and Electrophysiological Evidence of Pain Inhibition from Midbrain Stimulation in the Cat." *Experimental Brain Research* 20 (1974): 32–44.

Oliveras, J. L., Hosobuchi, Y., Redjemi, F., Guilbaud, G., and Besson, J. M. "Opiate Antagonist, Naloxone, Strongly Reduces Analgesia Induced by Stimulation of a Raphe Nucleus (Centralis Inferior)." *Brain Research* 120 (1977): 221–29.

Oliveras, J. L., Kedjemi, F., Guilbaud, G., and Besson, J. M. "Analgesia Induced by Electrical Stimulation of the Inferior Centralis Nucleus of the Raphe in the Cat." *Pain* 1 (1975): 139–45.

Olton, D. S., and Samuelson, R. J. "Remembrance of Places Past: Spatial Memory in Rats." *Journal of Experimental Psychology: Animal Behavior Processes* 2 (1976): 97–116.

Ornstein, R. E. *The Psychology of Consciousness.* San Francisco: Freeman, 1972.

Oswald, I. "Drugs and Sleep." *Pharmacological Review* 20 (1968): 272–303.

Palmer, M. S., Sinclair, A. H., Berta, P., Ellis, N. A., Goodfellow, P. N., Abbas, N. E., and Fellous, M. "Genetic Evidence That AFY Is Not the Testis-Determining Factor." *Nature* 342 (1989): 937–39.

Panksepp, J., and Trowill, J. A. "Intraoral Self-Injection. II. Effects of Delay of Reinforcement on Resistance to Extinction and Implications for Self-Stimulation." *Psychonomic Science* 9 (1967a): 405–6.

Panksepp, J., and Trowill, J. A. "Intraoral Self-Injection. II. The Simulation of Self-Stimulation Phenomena with a Conventional Reward." *Psychonomic Science* 9 (1967b): 407–8.

Papez, J. W. "A Proposed Mechanism of Emotion." *AMA Archives of Neurological Psychiatry* 38 (1937): 725–43.

Pappenheimer, J. R., Koski, G., Fenel, V., Karnovsky, M. L., and Krueger, J. "Extraction of Sleep-Promoting Factor S from Cerebrospinal Fluid and from Brains of Sleep-Deprived Animals." *Journal of Neurophysiology* 38 (1975): 1299–1311.

Parkes, A. S., and Bruce, H. M. "Olfactory Stimuli in Mammalian Reproduction." *Science* 134 (1961): 1049–54.

Parkinson, J. K., Murray, E., and Mishkin, M. "A Selective Mnemonic Role for the Hippocampus in Monkeys: Memory for the Location of Objects." *Journal of Neuroscience* 8 (1988): 4159–67.

Patterson, M. M., Cegavske, C. F., and Thompson, R. F. "Effects of a Classical Conditioning Paradigm on Hind-Limb Flexor Nerve Response in Immobilized Spinal Cats." *Journal of Comparative and Physiological Psychology* 84 (1973): 88–97.

Pavlov, I. P. *Conditioned Reflexes.* London: Oxford University Press, 1927.

Pearlman, C., and Becker, M. "Brief Posttrial REM Sleep Deprivation Impairs Discrimination Learning in Rats." *Physiological Psychology* 1 (1973): 373–76.

Pearson, J., Brandeis, L., and Claudio, C. A. "Depletion of Substance P Containing Axons in Substantia Gelatinosa of Patients with Diminished Pain Sensitivity." *Nature* 295 (1982): 61–63.

Pellis, S. M., O'Brien, D. P., Pellis, V. C., Teitelbaum, P., Wolgin, D. L., and Kennedy, S. "Escalation of Feline Predation along a Gradient from Avoidance through 'Play' to Killing." *Behavioral Neuroscience* 102 (1988): 760–77.

Pellow, S., Chopin, P., File, S. E., and Briley, M. "Validation of Open: Closed Arm Entries in an Elevated Plus-Maze as a Measure of Anxiety in the Rat." *Journal of Neuroscience Methods,* 14 (1985): 149–67.

Penfield, W. "Mechanisms of Voluntary Movement." *Brain* 77 (1954): 1–17.

Penfield, W. "Functional Localization in Temporal and Deep Sylvian Areas." *Academy for Research in Nervous and Mental Disease* 36 (1958): 210–26.

Percival, J. E., Horne, J. A., and Tilley, A. J. "Effects of Sleep Deprivation on Test of Higher Cerebral Functioning." *Sleep 1982: 6th European Congress on Sleep Research, Zurich 1982.* Basel: Karger, 1983, pp. 390–91.

Perrett, D. I., Oram, M. W., Harries, M. H., Bevan, R., Hietanen, J. K., Benson, P. J., and Thomas, S. "Viewer-Centered and Object-Centered Coding of Heads in the Macaque Temporal Cortex." *Experimental Brain Research* 86 (1991): 159–73.

Pert, C. B., Kuhar, M. J., and Snyder, S. H. "Opiate Receptor: Autoradiographic Localization in Rat Brain." *Proceedings of the National Academy of Sciences (USA)* 73 (1976): 3729–33.

Pfaff, D. W. "Steroid Sex Hormones in the Rat Brain: Specificity of Uptake and Physiological Effects." In *Steroid Hormones and Brain Function,* ed. C. H. Sawyer and R. A. Gorski. Berkeley: University of California Press, 1971, pp. 103–12.

Pfaff, D., and Modianos, D. "Neural Mechanisms of Female Reproductive Behavior." In *Handbook of Behavioral Neurobiology,* vol. 7: *Reproduction,* ed. N. Adler, D. Pfaff, and R. W. Goy. New York: Plenum Press, 1985, pp. 423–93.

Pfaffmann, C., Frank, M., Bartoshuk, L. M., and Snell, T. C. "Coding Gustatory Information in the Squirrel Monkey Chorda Tympani." In *Progress in Psychobiology and*

Physiological Psychology, ed. J. M. Sprague and A. N. Epstein. New York: Academic Press, 1976, pp. 1–27.

Pfaffmann, C., Frank, M., and Norgen, R. "Neural Mechanisms and Behavioral Aspects of Taste." *Annual Review of Psychology* 30 (1979): 283–325.

Phillips, D. P., and Farmer, M. E. "Acquired Word Deafness and the Temporal Grain of Sound Representation in the Primary Auditory Cortex." *Behavioral Brain Research* 40 (1990): 85–94.

Phoenix, C. H. "The Role of Testosterone in the Sexual Behavior of Laboratory Male Rhesus." *Symposia of the IVth International Congress of Primatology* 2 (1973): 9–122.

Phoenix, C. H., Goy, R. W., Gerell, A. A., and Young, W. C. "Organizing Action of Prenatally Administered Testosterone Propionate on the Tissues Mediating Mating Behavior in the Female Guinea Pig." *Endocrinology* 65 (1959): 369–82.

Pickar, D., Breier, A., Hsiao, J. K., Doran, A. R., Wolkowitz, O. M., Pato, C. N., Konicki, P. E., and Potter, W. Z. "Cerebrospinal Fluid and Plasma Monoamine Metabolites and Their Relation to Psychosis: Implications for Regional Brain Dysfunction in Schizophrenia." *Archives of General Psychiatry* 47 (1990): 641–48.

Porsolt, R. D., LePichon, M., and Jalfre, M. "Depression: A New Animal Model Sensitive to Antidepressant Treatments." *Nature* 266 (1977): 730–32.

Posner, M. I., Inhoff, A. W., Friedrich, F. J., and Cohen, A. "Isolating Attentional Systems: A Cognitive-Anatomical Analysis." *Psychobiology* 15 (1987): 107–121.

Posner, M. I., Walder, J. A., Friedrich, J. J., and Rafal, R. D. "Effects of Parietal Lobe Injury on Covert Orienting of Visual Attention." *Journal of Neuroscience* 4 (1984): 1863–74.

Poulos, C. X., and Cappell, H. "Homeostatic Theory of Drug Tolerance: A General Model of Physiological Adaption." *Psychological Review* 98 (1991): 390–408.

Powley, T. L. "The Ventromedial Hypothalamic Syndrome, Satiety, and a Cephalic Phase Hypothesis" *Psychological Review* 84 (1977): 89–126.

Pribram, K. H. "Interrelations of Psychology and Neurological Disciplines." In *Physiology: A Study of a Science*, vol. 4, ed. S. Koch. New York: McGraw Hill, 1962.

Qualtrochi, J. J., Mamelak, A. N., Madison, R. D., Macklis, J. D., and Hobson, J. A. "Mapping Neuronal Inputs to REM Sleep Induction Sites with Carbachol Fluorescent Microspheres." *Science* 245 (1989): 984–86.

Racine, R. J., and deJonge, M. "Short-Term and Long-Term Potentiation in Projection Pathways and Local Circuits." In *Long-Term Potentiation: From Biophysics to Behavior*, ed. P. W. Landfield and S. A. Deadwyler. New York: Liss, 1988.

Raisman, G., and Field, P. M. "Sexual Dimorphism in the Preoptic Area of the Rat." *Science* 173 (1971): 731–33.

Randt, C. T., Quartermain, D., and Goldstein, M. "Norepinephrine Biosynthesis Inhibition: Effects on Memory in Mice." *Science* 172 (1971): 498–99.

Rapoport, J. L. "The Biology of Obsessions and Compulsions." *Scientific American* 260, (1989): 83–89.

Rapoport, J. L., and Wise, S. P. "Obsessive-Compulsive Disorder: Evidence for Basal Ganglia Dysfunction." *Psychopharmacology Bulletin* 24 (1988): 380–84.

Ratliff, F., and Hartline, H. K. "The Reponse of *Limulus* Optic Nerve Fibers to Patterns of Illumination on the Receptor Mosaic." *Journal of General Physiology* 42 (1959): 1241–55.

Ratner, S. C. "Conditioning of Decerebrate Worms: *Lumbricus terrestris*." *Journal of Comparative and Physiological Psychology* 55 (1962): 174–77.

Ray, O. S. *Drugs, Society, and Human Behavior*. St. Louis: Mosby, 1974, pp. 160, 203.

Recanzone, G. H., Merzenich, M. M., Jenkins, W. M., Grajski, K. A., and Dinse, H. R. "Topographic Reorganization of the Hand Representation in Cortical Area 3b of Owl Monkeys Trained in a Frequency Discrimination Task." *Journal of Neurophysiology* 67 (1992): 1031–56.

Redmond, D. E. "Studies of the Nucleus Locus Coeruleus in Monkeys and Hypotheses for Neuropsychopharmacology." In *Psychopharmacology: The Third Generation of Progress*, ed. J. Y. Meltzer. New York: Raven Press, 1987, 967–75.

Reed, T. E. "Ethnic Differences in Alcohol Use, Abuse, and Sensitivity: A Review with Genetic Interpretation." *Social Biology* 32 (1985): 194–209.

Reeves, T. M., and Smith, D. C. "Reinnervation of the Dentate Gyrus and Recovery of Alternation Behavior Following Entorhinal Cortex Lesions." *Behavioral Neuroscience* 101 (1987): 179–86.

Reisenzein, R. "The Schachter Theory of Emotions: Two Decades Later." *Psychological Bulletin* 94 (1983): 239–64.

Reynolds, D. V. "Surgery in the Rat during Electrical Analgesia Induced by Focal Brain Stimulation." *Science* 164 (1968): 444–45.

Richardson, P. M., McGuinness, U. M., and Aguayo, A. J. "Axons from the CNS Neurones Regenerate into PNS Grafts." *Nature* 284 (1980): 264–65.

Richter, C. P. "On the Phenomenon of Sudden Death in Animals and Man." *Psychosomatic Medicine* 19 (1957): 191–98.

Rizzo, M., Nawrot, M., Blake, R., and Damasio, A. "A Human Visual Disorder Resembling Area V4 Dysfunction in the Monkey." *Neurology* 42 (1992): 1175–80.

Rodgers, W. L. "Specificity of Specific Hungers." *Journal of Comparative and Physiological Psychology* 64 (1967): 49–58.

Rodin, J., Bartoshuk, L., Peterson, C., and Schank, D. "Bulimia and Taste: Possible Interactions." *Journal of Abnormal Psychology* 99 (1990): 32–39.

Roffwarg, H. P., Muzio, J. N., and Dement, W. C. "Ontogenetic Development of the Human Sleep Dream Cycle." *Science* 152 (1966): 604–19.

Rolls, B., Van Duijvenvoorde, P. M., and Rolls, E. T. "Pleasantness Changes and Food Intake in a Varied Four-Course Meal." *Appetite* 5 (1984): 337–48.

Rosenkilde, C. E. "Functional Heterogeneity of the Prefrontal Cortex in the Monkey: A Review." *Behavioral Neural Biology* 25 (1979): 301–45.

Rosenthal, D. *Genetic Theory and Abnormal Behavior*. New York: McGraw-Hill, 1970.

Rosenthal, N. E., Sack, D. A., Carpenter, C. J., Parry, B. L., Mendelson, W. B., and Wehr, T. A. "Antidepressant Effects of Light in Seasonal Affective Disorder." *American Journal of Psychiatry* 142 (1985): 163–70.

Rosenthal, N. E., Sack, D. A., Skwerer, R. G., Jacob-

sen, F. M., and Wehr, T. A. "Phototherapy for Seasonal Affective Disorder." In *Seasonal Affective Disorders and Phototherapy*, ed. N. E. Rosenthal and M. C. Blehar. New York: Guilford Press, 1989.

Rosenzweig, M. R., Krech, D., Bennett, E. L., and Diamond, M. C. "Effects of Environmental Complexity and Training on Brain Chemistry and Anatomy: A Replication and Extension." *Journal of Comparative and Physiological Psychology* 55 (1962): 429–37.

Ross, E. D. "Right Hemisphere's Role in Language, Affective Behavior, and Emotion." *Trends in Neurosciences* 7 (1984) 342–46.

Routtenberg, A., and Lindy, J. "Effects of the Availability of Rewarding Septal and Hypothalamic Stimulation on Bar Pressing for Food under Conditions of Deprivation." *Journal of Comparative and Physiological Psychology* 60 (1965): 158–61.

Rowland, L. P. "Diseases of Chemical Transmission at the Nerve-Muscle Synapse: Myasthenia Gravis and Related Syndromes." In *Principles of Neural Science*, ed. E. R. Kandel and J. H. Schwartz. New York: Elsevier/North-Holland, 1991.

Rowland, N. E. "Sodium Appetite." In *Taste, Experience, and Feeding*, ed. E. D. Capaldi and T. L. Powley. Washington, D.C.: American Psychological Association, 1990, pp. 94–104.

Rozin, P. "Are Carbohydrate and Protein Intakes Separately Regulated?" *Journal of Comparative and Physiological Psychology* 65 (1968): 23–29.

Rozin, P. "The Selection of Foods by Rats, Humans and Other Animals." *Advances in the Study of Behavior*, vol. 6. New York: Academic Press, 1976a, pp. 21–76.

Rozin, P. "The Psychobiological Approach to Human Memory." In. *Neural Mechanisms of Learning and Memory*, ed. M. R. Rosenzweig and E. L. Bennett. Cambridge, Mass.: MIT Press, 1976b.

Rozin, P., and Kalet, J. "Specific Hungers and Poison Avoidance as Adaptive Specializations of Learning." *Psychological Review* 78 (1971): 459–86.

Rubin, B. S., and Barfield, R. J. "Progesterone in the Ventromedial Hypothalamus Facilitates Estrous Behavior in Ovariectomized, Estrogen-Primed Rats." *Endocrinology* 37 (1983): 218–24.

Rubin, R. T., Villanueva-Meyer, J., Ananth, J., Trajmar, P. G., and Mena, I. "Regional Xenon 133 Cerebral Blood Flow and Cerebral Technetium 99m HMPAO Uptake in Unmedicated Patients with Obsessive-Compulsive Disorder and Matched Normal Control Subjects: Determination by High-Resolution Single-Photon Emission Computed Tomography." *Archives of General Psychiatry* 49 (1992): 695–702.

Ruda, M. A. "Opiates and Pain Pathways: Demonstration of Enkephalin Synapses on Dorsal Horn Projection Neurons." *Science* 215 (1982): 1523–25.

Ruda, M. A., Bennett, G. H., and Dubner, R. "Neurochemistry and Neural Circuitry in the Dorsal Horn." *Progress in Brain Research* 66 (1986): 219–68.

Rumsey, J. M. "Biology of Developmental Dyslexia," *Journal of the American Medical Association* 268 (1992): 912–15.

Rusak, B. "The Role of the Suprachiasmatic Nuclei in the Generation of Circadian Rhythms in the Golden Hamster, *Mesocricetus auratus*." *Journal of Comparative Physiology A*, 118 (1977): 145–64.

Russek, M. "Hepatic Receptors and the Neurophysiological Mechanisms Controlling Feeding Behavior." In *Neurosciences Research*, vol. 4, ed. S. Ehrenpreis. New York: Academic Press, 1971.

Russel, M. J. "Human Olfactory Communication." *Nature* 260 (1976): 520–22.

Russell, W. R. *Brain, Memory, Learning: A Neurologist's View*. Oxford: Oxford University Press, 1959.

Sakai, K. "Some Anatomical and Physiological Properties of Pontomescencephalic Tegmental Neurons with Special Reference to the PGO Waves and Postural Atonia during Paradoxical Sleep in the Cat." In *The Reticular Formation Revisited*, ed. J. A. Hobson, and M. A. Brazier. New York: Raven Press, 1980.

Sawyer, C. H. "Reproductive Behavior." In *Handbook of Physiology*, sec. I: *Neurophysiology*, vol. 2, ed. J. Field. Washington, D.C.: American Physiological Society, 1960.

Schachter, S., and Singer, J. E. "Cognitive, Social, and Physiological Determinants of Emotional State." *Psychological Review* 69 (1962): 379–99.

Schacter, D. L. "Implicit Memory: History and Current Status." *Journal of Experimental Psychology: Learning, Memory, and Cognition* 13 (1987): 501–18.

Scheel-Kruger, J. and Petersen, E. N. "Antticonflict Effect of the Benzodiazepines Mediated by a GABAergic Mechanism in the Amygdala." *European Journal of Pharmacology* 82 (1982): 115–16.

Schemmel, R., Mickelsen, O., and Gill, J. L. "Dietary Obesity in Rats: Influence of Diet, Weight, Fat Accretion in Seven Strains of Rats." *Journal of Nutrition* 100 (1970): 1041–48.

Schiffman, S. S. Physiochemical Correlates of Olfactory Quality. *Science* 185 (1974): 112–17.

Schiller, P. H., and Logothetis, N. K. "The Color-Opponent and Broad-Band Channels in the Primate Visual System." *Trends in Neurosciences* 13 (1990): 392–98.

Schmaltz, I. W., and Theios, J. "Acquisition and Extinction of a Classically Conditioned Response in Hippocampectomized Rabbits (*Oryctolagus curriculus*)." *Journal of Comparative and Physiological Psychology* 79 (1972): 328–33.

Schmitt, M. "Influences of Hepatic Portal Receptors on Hypothalamic Feeding and Satiety Centers." *American Journal of Physiology* 225 (1973): 1089–95.

Schwabb, M. E. "Myelin-Associated Inhibitors of Neuritic Growth and Regeneration in the CNS." *Trends in Neurosciences* 13 (1990): 452–56.

Schwartz, W. J., and Gainer, H. "Suprachiasmatic Nucleus: Use of ¹⁴C-Labeled Deoxyglucose Uptake as a Functional Marker." *Science* 197 (1977): 1089–91.

Schwartz-Giblin, S., McEwen, B. S., and Pfaff, D. W. "Mechanisms of Female Reproductive Behavior." In *Psychoendocrinology*, ed. R. Brush and S. Levine. Academic Press, New York, 1989, pp. 41–104.

Scott, E. M., and Verney, E. L. "Self-Selection and Diet. VI. The Nature of Appetites for B Vitamins." *Journal of Nutrition* 34 (1947): 471–80.

Scoville, W. B., and Milner, B. "Loss of Recent Memory after Bilateral Hippocampal Lesions." *Journal of Neurology, Neurosurgery and Psychiatry* 20 (1957): 11–21.

Seeman, P. "Dopamine Receptor Sequences: Therapeutic Levels of Neuroleptics Occupy D2 Receptors, Clozapine Occupies D4." *Neuropsychopharmacology* 7 (1992): 261–84.

Seeman, P., and Lee, T. "Antipsychotic Drugs: Direct Correlation between Clinical Potency and Presynaptic Action of Dopamine Neurons." *Science* 188 (1975): 1217–19.

Sekuler, R., and Blake, R. *Perception,* 3rd ed. New York: McGraw-Hill, 1994.

Seligman, M. E. P. *Helplessness: On Depression, Development, and Death.* San Francisco: Freeman, 1975.

Seligman, M. E. P., Klein, D. C., and Miller, W. R. "Depression." In *Handbook of Behavior Modification and Behavior Therapy,* ed. H. Leitenberg. Englewood Cliffs, N.J.: Prentice Hall, 1976.

Seligman, M. E. P., and Maier, S. F. "Failure to Escape Traumatic Shock." *Journal of Experimental Psychology* 74 (1967): 1–9.

Selkoe, D. J. "The Molecular Pathology of Alzheimer's Disease." *Neuron* 6 (1991): 487–98.

Selkoe, D. J. "Aging Brain, Aging Mind." *Scientific American* 267 (1992): 60–67.

Seltzer, B., and Benson, D. F. "The Temporal Pattern of Retrograde Amnesia in Korsakoff's Disease." *Neurology* 24 (1974): 527–30.

Selye, H. *The Physiology and Pathology of Exposure to Stress.* Montreal: Acta, 1950.

Selye, H. "Adaptive Steroids: Retrospect and Prospect." *Prospective Biological Medicine* 13 (1970): 343.

Sem-Jacobsen, C. W. "Effects of Electrical Stimulation on the Human Brain." *Electroencephalography and Clinical Neurophysiology* 11 (1959): 379.

Sergent, J., and Poncet, M. "From Covert to Overt Recognition of Faces in a Prosopagnostic Patient." *Brain* 113 (1990): 989–1004.

Seward, J. P., Uyeda, A. A., and Olds, J. "Resistance to Extinction Following Cranial Self-Stimulation." *Journal of Comparative and Physiological Psychology* 52 (1959): 294–99.

Sewitch, D. E. "NREM Sleep Continuity and the Sense of Having Slept in Normal Sleepers." *Sleep* 7 (1984): 147–54.

Sewitch, D. E. "Slow Wave Sleep Deficiency Insomnia: A Problem in Thermo-Downregulation at Sleep Onset." *Psychophysiology* 24 (1987): 200–15.

Shapiro, C. M., Bortz, R., Mitchell, D., Bartell, P., and Jooste, P. "Slow Wave Sleep: A Recovery Period after Exercise." *Science* 214 (1981): 1253–54.

Sheffield, F. D., Wulff, J. J., and Backer, R. "Reward Value of Copulation without Sex Drive Reduction." *Journal of Comparative and Physiological Psychology* 44 (1951): 3–8.

Shelton, R. C., and Weinberger, D. R. "Brain Morphology in Schizophrenia." In *Psychopharmacology: The Third Generation of Progress,* ed. H. Y. Meltzer. New York: Raven Press, 1987, pp. 773–81.

Shepherd, G. M. *Neurobiology.* New York: Oxford University Press, 1983, p. 188.

Sherwin, B. B. "Changes in Sexual Behavior as a Function of Plasma Sex Steroid Levels in Post-Menopausal Women." *Maturitas* 7 (1985): 225–33.

Sherwin, B. B. "A Comparative Analysis of the Role of Androgen in Human Male and Female Sexual Behavior: Behavioral Specificity, Critical Thresholds, and Sensitivity." *Psychobiology* 16 (1988): 416–25.

Shimazu, T., Fukuda, A., and Ban, T. "Reciprocal Influences of the Ventromedial and Lateral Hypothalamic Nuclei on Blood Glucose Level and Liver Glycogen Content." *Nature* 210 (1966): 1178–79.

Shor-Posner, G., Grinker, J. A., Marinescu, C., and Leibowitz, S. F. "Role of Hypothalamic Norepinephrine in Control of Meal Patterns." *Physiology and Behavior* 35 (1985): 209–14.

Siegel, A., and Brutus, M. "Neural Substrates of Aggression and Rage in the Cat." *Progress in Psychobiology and Physiological Psychology* 14 (1990): 135–233.

Siegel, A., and Edinger, H. "Neural Control of Aggression and Rage Behavior." In *Handbook of the Hypothalamus,* vol. 3: *Behavioral Studies of the Hypothalamus,* ed. P. J. Morgane and J. Panksepp. New York: Marcel Dekker, 1981, pp. 203–40.

Siegel, A., and Flynn, J. P. "Differential Effects of Electrical Stimulation and Lesions of the Hippocampus and Adjacent Regions upon Attack Behavior in Cats." *Brain Research* 7 (1968): 252–67.

Siegel, A., and Pott, C. B. "Neural Substrates of Aggression and Flight in the Cat." *Progress in Neurobiology* 31 (1988): 261–83.

Siegel, J. M., McGinty, D. J., and Breedlove, S. M. "Sleep and Waking Activity of Pontine Gigantocellular Field Neurons." *Experimental Neurology* 56 (1977): 553–73.

Siegel, S. "Morphine Analgesic Tolerance: Its Situation Specificity Supports a Pavlovian Conditioning Model." *Science* 193 (1976): 323–25.

Siegel, S. "Classical Conditioning, Drug Tolerance, and Drug Dependence." In *Research Advances in Alcohol and Drug Problems,* vol. 7, ed. Y. Israel, F. B. Graser, H. Kalant, W. Popham, W. Schmidt, and R. G. Smart. New York: Plenum Press, 1983, pp. 207–46.

Siegel, S., Hinson, R. E., Krank, M. D., and McCully, J. "Heroin 'Overdose' Death: Contribution of Drug-Associated Environmental Cues." *Science* 216 (1982): 436–37.

Silver, J. M., and Yodofsky, S. C. "Psychopharmacology and Electroconvulsive Therapy." In *The American Psychiatric Press Textbook of Psychiatry,* ed. J. A. Talbott, R. E. Hales, and S. C. Yodofsky. Washington, D.C.: American Psychiatric Press, 1988.

Simpson, J. B., Epstein, A. N., and Camardo, J. S., Jr. "The Localization of Dipsogenic Receptors for Angiotensin II in the Subfornical Organ." *Journal of Comparative and Physiological Psychology* 92 (1978): 581–608.

Simpson, J. B., and Routtenberg, A. "Subfornical Organ: Site of Drinking Elicitation by Angiotensin II." *Science* 181 (1973): 1172–77.

Simson, P. E., and Weiss, J. M. "Peripheral But Not Local or Intracerebral Ventricular Administration of Benzodiazepines Attenuates Evoked Activity of Locus Coeruleus Neurons." *Brain Research* 490 (1989): 236–42.

Skinner, B. F. *Beyond Freedom and Dignity.* New York: Bantam, 1970, p. 3.

Slaghuis, W. L., Lovegrove, W. J., and Davidson, J. A.

"Visual and Language Processing Deficits Are Concurrent in Dyslexia." *Cortex* 29 (1993): 601–15.

Slotnick, B. M., Graham, S., Laing, D. G., and Bell, G. A. "Detection of Propionic Acid Vapor by Rats with Lesions of Olfactory Bulb Areas Associated with High 2-DG Uptake." *Brain Research* 417 (1987): 343–46.

Small, S. A., Kandel, E. R., and Hawkins, R. D. "Activity-Dependent Enhancement of Presynaptic Inhibition in *Aplysia* Sensory Neurons." *Science* 243 (1989): 1603–6.

Smith, D. E., King, M. B., and Hoebel, B. "Lateral Hypothalamic Control of Killing: Evidence for a Cholinoceptive Mechanism." *Science* 167 (1970): 900–7.

Smith, W. K. "The Results of Ablation of the Cingular Region of the Cerebral Cortex." *Federal Proceedings* 3 (1944): 42–43.

Snowdon, C. "Production of Satiety with Small Intraduodenal Infusion in the Rat." *Journal of Comparative and Physiological Psychology* 88 (1975): 231–39.

Snyder, S. H. "New Developments in Brain Chemistry: Catecholamine Metabolism and Its Relationship to the Mechanism of Action of Psychotropic Drugs." *American Journal of Orthopsychiatry* 37 (1967): 864–79.

Snyder, S. H. "Catecholamines in the Brain as Mediators of Amphetamine Psychosis." *Archives of General Psychiatry* 27 (1972): 169–79.

Snyder, S. H. "The Dopamine Hypothesis of Schizophrenia: Focus on the Dopamine Receptor." *American Journal of Psychiatry* 133 (1976): 197–202.

Snyder, S. H., and D'Amato, R. J. "MPTP: A Neurotoxin Relevant to the Pathophysiology of Parkinson's Disease." *Neurology* 36 (1986): 250–58.

Södersten, P., and Larsson, K. "Lordosis Behavior in Castrated Male Rats Treated with Estradiol Benzoate or Testosterone Propionate in Combination with an Estrogen Antagonist MER-25 in Intact Male Rats." *Hormones and Behavior* 5 (1974): 13–18.

Spano, P. F., Govoni, S., and Trabucchi, M. "Studies on the Pharmacological Properties of Dopamine Receptors in Various Areas of the Central Nervous System." In *Advances in Biochemical Psychopharmacology*, vol. 17, ed. P. J. Roberts, G. N. Woodruff, and L. L. Iversen. New York: Raven Press, 1978, pp. 155–65.

Sperry, R. W. "Lateral Specialization in the Surgically Separated Hemispheres." In *The Neurosciences Third Study Program*, ed. F. O. Schmitt and F. G. Worden. Cambridge, Mass.: MIT Press, 1974, p. 7.

Sperry, R. W., and Gazzaniga, M. S. "Language Following Surgical Disconnection of the Hemispheres." In *Brain Mechanisms Underlying Speech and Language*, ed. F. L. Darley. New York: Grune & Stratton, 1967.

Springer, S. P., and Deutsch, G. *Left Brain, Right Brain.* 4th ed. San Francisco: Freeman, 1993.

Squire, L. R. "Mechanisms of Memory." *Science* 232 (1986): 1612–19.

Squire, L. R. *Memory and Brain.* New York: Oxford University Press, 1987.

Squire, L. R. "Memory and the Hippocampus: A Synthesis from Findings with Rats, Monkeys, and Humans." *Psychological Review* 99 (1992): 195–231.

Squire, L. R., Ojemann, J. G., Miezin, F. M., Petersen, S. E., Videen, T. O., and Raichle, M. E. "Activation of the Hippocampus in Normal Humans: A Functional Anatomical Study of Memory." *Proceedings of the National Academy of Sciences (USA)* 89 (1992): 1837–41.

Squire, L. R., Slater, P. C., and Chase, L. M. "Retrograde Amnesia: Temporal Gradient in Very Long-Term Memory Following Electroconvulsive Therapy." *Science* 187 (1975): 77–79.

Squire, L. R., and Zola-Morgan, S. "The Medial Temporal Lobe Memory System." *Science* 253 (1991): 1380–86.

Stanley, B. G., Magdalin, W., Seirafi, A., Thomas, W. J., and Leibowitz, S. F. "The Perifornical Area: The Major Focus of (a) Patchily Distributed Hypothalamic Neuropeptide Y-Sensitive Feeding System(s)." *Brain Research* 604 (1993): 304–17.

Stein, D. G., and Chorover, S. L. "Effects of Posttrial Stimulation of Hippocampus and Caudate Nucleus on Maze Learning in the Rat." *Physiology and Behavior* 3 (1968): 787–91.

Stein, L., Belluzzi, J. D., and Wise, C. D. "Memory Enhancement by Central Administration of Norepinephrine." *Brain Research* 84 (1975): 329–35.

Stellar, J. R., and Corbett, D. "Microinjections Indicate a Role for Nucleus Accumbens in Lateral Hypothalamic Self-Stimulation Reward." *Brain Research* 477 (1989): 126–43.

Sterman, M. B., and Clemente, C. D. "Forebrain Inhibitory Mechanisms: Sleep Patterns Induced by Basal Forebrain Stimulation in the Behaving Cat." *Experimental Neurology* 6 (1962): 103–17.

Sternberg, D. B., Martinez, J., McGaugh, J. L., and Gold, P. E. "Age-Related Memory Deficits in Rats and Mice: Enhancement with Peripheral Injections of Epinephrine." *Behavioral Neural Biology* 44 (1985): 213–20.

Stone, J. "Morphology and Physiology of the Geniculo-Cortical Synapse in the Cat: The Question of Parallel Input into the Striate Cortex." *Investigative Ophthalmology* 11 (1972): 338–46.

Strack, F., Martin, L. L., and Stepper, S. "Inhibiting and Facilitating Conditions of the Human Smile: A Nonobtrusive Test of the Facial Feedback Hypothesis." *Journal of Personality and Social Psychology* 54 (1988): 768–77.

Straile, W. E. "Vertical Cutaneous Organization." *Journal of Theoretical Biology* 24 (1969): 203–15.

Stricker, E. M. "Thirst, Sodium Appetite, and Complementary Physiological Contributions to the Regulation of Intravascular Fluid Volume." In *The Neuropsychology of Thirst: New Findings and Advances in Concepts*, ed. A. N. Epstein, H. R. Kissileff, and E. Stellar. Washington, D.C.: Winston, 1973.

Stricker, E. M. "Brain Neurochemistry and the Control of Food Intake." In *Handbook of Behavioral Neurobiology*, vol. 6: *Motivation*, ed. E. Satinoff and P. Teitelbaum. New York: Plenum Press, 1983.

Stunkard, A. J., Sorensen, T. I. A., Hanis, C., Teasdale, T. W., Chakraborty, R., Schull, W. J., and Schulsinger, F. "An Adoption Study of Human Obesity." *New England Journal of Medicine* 314 (1986): 193–98.

Suddath, R. L., Christison, G. W., Torrey, E. F., Casanova, M. F., and Weinberger, D. R. "Anatomical Abnormalities in the Brains of Monozygotic Twins Discordant for Schizophrenia." *New England Journal of Medicine* 322 (1990): 789–94.

Sulser, F., Gillespie, D. D., Mishra, R., and Manier, D. H. "Desensitization by Antidepressants of Central Norepinephrine Receptor Systems Coupled to Adenylate Cyclase." *Annals of the New York Academy of Sciences* 430 (1984): 91–101.

Sulser, F., Vetulani, J., and Mobley, P. L. "Mode of Action of Antidepressant Drugs." *Biochemical Pharmacology* 27 (1978): 257–61.

Suzdak, P. D., Schwartz, R. D., Skolnick, P., and Paul, S. M. "Ethanol Stimulates Gamma-Amino-Butyric Acid Receptor-Mediated Choline Transport in Rat Brain Synaptoneurosomes." *Proceedings of the National Academy of Science (USA)* 83 (1986): 4071–75.

Takagi, S. F. "Dual Systems for Sensory Olfactory Processing in Higher Primates." *Trends in Neurosciences* 2 (1979): 313–15.

Takahashi, Y. "Growth Hormone Secretion Related to the Sleep Waking Rhythm." In *The Functions of Sleep*, ed. R. Drucker-Colin, M. Shkurovich, and M. B. Sterman. New York: Academic Press, 1979.

Tallal, P. "Auditory Temporal Perception, Phonics and Reading Disabilities in Children." *Brain and Language* 9 (1980): 182–98.

Tallal, P., Miller, S., and Fitch, R. H. "Neurobiological Basis of Speech: A Case for the Preeminence of Temporal Processing." In *Proceedings of the New York Academy of Sciences Conference on Temporal Processing, with Special Reference to Dyslexia and Dysphasia*, ed. P. Tallal, A. M. Galaburda, R. Llinas, and C. von Euler. New York: New York Academy of Sciences, 1993.

Tallal, P., and Piercy, M. "Defects of Non-Verbal Auditory Perception in Children with Developmental Aphasia." *Nature* 241 (1973): 468–69.

Tanaka, Y., Kamo, T., Yoshida, M., and Yamadori, A. "So-called Cortical Deafness." *Brain*, 114 (1991): 2385–2401.

Teitelbaum, P. "Sensory Control of Hypothalamic Hyperphagia." *Journal of Comparative and Physiological Psychology* 48 (1955): 156–63.

Teitelbaum, P. *Physiological Psychology*. Englewood Cliffs, N.J.: Prentice-Hall, 1967, p. 11.

Teitelbaum, P., and Epstein, A. N. "The Lateral Hypothalamic Syndrome: Recovery of Feeding and Drinking after Lateral Hypothalamic Lesions." *Psychological Review* 69 (1962): 74–90.

Terman, G. W., and Liebeskind, J. C. "Relation of Stress-Induced Analgesia to Stimulation-Produced Analgesia." *Annals of the New York Academy of Sciences* 467 (1986): 300–8.

Tetrud, J. W., and Langston, J. W. "The Effect of Deprenyl (Selegiline) on the Natural History of Parkinson's Disease." *Science* 245 (1989): 519–22.

Teuber, H. L., Corkin, S. H., and Twitchell, T. E. "Study of Cingulotomy in Man: A Summary." In *Neurosurgical Treatment in Psychiatry, Pain, and Epilepsy*, ed. W. H. Sweet, S. Obrador, and J. G. Martin-Rodriguez. Baltimore: University Park Press, 1977.

Thomas, L. *The Lives of a Cell*. New York: Bantam, 1974, p. 78.

Thompson, R. F., Berger, T. W., Cegavske, C. F., Patterson, M. M., Roper, R. A., Teyler, T. J., and Young, R. A. "The Search for the Engram." *American Psychologist* 31 (1976): 209–27.

Thompson, R. F., in collaboration with McCormick, D. A., Lavoid, D. G., Clark, G. A., Kettner, R. E., and Mauk, M. D. "The Engram Found? Initial Localization of the Memory Trace for a Basic Form of Associative Learning." In *Progress in Psychobiology and Physiological Psychology*, vol. 10, ed. J. M. Sprague and A. N. Epstein. New York: Academic Press, 1983, pp. 167–96.

Tordoff, M. G., and Friedman, M. I. "Hepatic Control of Feeding: Effect of Glucose, Fructose, and Mannitol." *American Journal of Physiology* 254 (1988): R969–R976.

Tranel, D., and Damasio, A. R. "Knowledge Without Awareness: An Autonomic Index of Facial Recognition by Prosopagnosics." *Science* 228 (1985): 1453–54.

Trope, I., Kemler Nelson, D., and Gur, R. C. "Information Processing in the Separated Hemispheres of Callosotomy Patients: Does the Analytic-Holistic Dichotomy Hold?" *Brain and Cognition* 19 (1992): 123–47.

Trowill, Y. A., Panksepp, J., and Gandelman, R. "An Incentive Model of Rewarding Brain Stimulation." *Psychological Review* 76 (1969): 264–81.

Tsien, R. W., and Malinow, R. "Long-Term Potentiation: Pre-synaptic Enhancement Following Postsynaptic Activation of Ca-Dependent Protein Kinases." *Cold Spring Harbor Symposium on Quantitative Biology* 55 (1990): 147–59.

Turek, F. W. "Circadian Neural Rhythms in Mammals." *Annual Review of Physiology*, 47 (1985): 49–64.

Turner, A. M., and Greenough, W. T. "Synapses per Neuron and Synaptic Dimensions in Occipital Cortex of Rats Reared in Complex, Social, or Isolation Housing." *Acta Stereologica*, 2 (Supl. 1) (1983): 239–44.

Tuszynski, M. H., Sang, H., Yoshida, K., and Gage, F. H. "Recombinant Human Nerve Growth Factor Infusions Prevent Cholinergic Neuronal Degeneration in the Adult Primate Brain." *Annals of Neurology* 30 (1991): 625–36.

Tyrer, P. and MacKay, A. "Schizophrenia: No Longer a Functional Psychosis," *Trends in Neurosciences* 9 (1986): 537–38.

Vaillant, G. E., and Milofsky, E. S. "The Etiology of Alcoholism." *American Psychologist* 37 (1982): 494–503.

Valenstein, E. S. *The Psychosurgery Debate: Scientific, Legal, and Ethical Perspectives*. San Francisco: W. H. Freeman, 1980.

Valenstein, E. S., and Beer, B. "Continuous Opportunity for Reinforcing Brain Stimulation." *Journal of the Experimental Analysis of Behavior* 77 (1964): 183–84.

Valenstein, E. S., Cox, V. C., and Kakolewski, J. W. "Modification of Motivated Behavior by Electrical Stimulation of the Hypothalamus." *Science* 159 (1968): 1119–21.

Valenstein, E. S., Cox, V. C., and Kakolewski, J. W. "Reexamination of the Role of the Hypothalamus in Motivation." *Psychological Review* 77 (1970): 16–24.

Van Broeckhoven, C., Haan, J., Bakker, E., Hardy, J. A., Van Hul, W., Wehner, A., Vegter-Van der Vlis, M., and Roos, R. A. C. "Amyloid Protein Precursor Gene and Hereditary Cerebral Hemorrhage with Amyloidosis (Dutch)." *Science* 248 (1990): 1120–12.

Vaughan, E., and Fisher, A. E. "Male Sexual Behavior Induced by Intracranial Electrical Stimulation." *Science* 137 (1962): 758–60.

Vaughan, T., Wyatt, R. J., and Green, R. "Changes in REM Sleep of Chronically Anxious Depressed Patients Given Alpha-methyl-paratyrosine (AMPT)." *Psychophysiology* 9 (1972): 96.

Vergnes, M. "Effect of Prior Familiarization with Mice on Excitation of Mouse-Killing in Rats: Role of the Amygdala." In *The Amygdaloid Complex*, ed. Y. Ben-Ari. New York: Elsevier/North-Holland, 1981.

Vergnes, M., and Kempf, E. "Tryptophan Deprivation: Effects on Mouse-Killing and Reactivity in the Rat." *Pharmacology, Biochemistry, and Behavior* 14 (1981): 19–23.

Vergnes, M., Mack, G., and Kempf, E. "Behavioral and Biochemical Effects of Lesion of the Raphe on the Rat-Mouse Interspecific Aggressive Behavior," *Brain Research* 57 (1973): 67–71.

Victor, H., Adams, R. D., and Collins, G. H. *The Wernicke Korsakoff Syndrome*. Philadelphia: Davis, 1971.

Visintainer, M. A., Volpicelli, J. R., and Seligman, M. E. P. "Tumor Rejection in Rats after Inescapable or Escapable Shock." *Science* 218 (1982): 437–39.

Volpe, B. T., LeDoux, J. F., and Gazzaniga, M. S. "Information Processing of Visual Stimuli in an 'Extinguished' Field." *Nature* 292 (1979): 722–24.

Wald, G. "The Receptors of Human Color Vision." *Science* 145 (1964): 1007–17.

Wald, G., Brown, P. K., and Smith, P. H. "Iodopsin." *Journal of General Physiology* 38 (1954): 623–81.

Wall, P. D. "The Substantia Gelatinosa: A Gate Control Mechanism Set across a Sensory Pathway." *Trends in Neurosciences* 3 (1980): 221–24.

Waller, W. H. "Progression Movements Elicited by Subthalamic Stimulation." *Journal of Neurophysiology* 3 (1940): 300–7.

Ward, I. L. "Prenatal Stress Feminizes and Demasculinizes the Behavior of Males." *Science* 175 (1972): 82–94.

Ward, I. L., and Weisz, J. "Maternal Stress Alters Plasma Testosterone in Fetal Males." *Science* 207 (1980): 328–29.

Warrington, E. K., and Weiskrantz, L. "The Amnesic Syndrome: Consolidation or Retrieval?" *Nature* 228 (1970): 628–30.

Wasman, G., and Flynn, J. P. "Directed Attack Elicited from Hypothalamus." *Archives of Neurology* 6 (1962): 220–27.

Watkins, L. R., and Mayer, D. J. "Organization of Endogenous Opiate and Nonopiate Pain Control Systems." *Science* 216 (1982): 1185–92.

Webb, W. B. *Sleep: The Gentle Tyrant*. Englewood Cliffs, N.J.: Prentice-Hall, 1975.

Weinberger, N. M., Gold, P. E., and Sternberg, D. B. "Epinephrine Enables Pavlovian Fear Conditioning under General Anesthetic." *Science* 233 (1984): 605–7.

Weiskrantz, L. "Blindsight: A Case Study and Implications." Oxford: Oxford University Press, 1986.

Weiskrantz, L., and Warrington, E. K. "Conditioning in Amnesic Patients." *Neuropsychologia* 17 (1979): 187–94.

Weiss, G. F., Papadakos, P., Knudson, K. and Leibowitz, S. F. "Medial Hypothalamic Serotonin: Effects on Deprivation and Norepinephrine-Induced Eating." *Pharmacology, Biochemistry, and Behavior* 25 (1986): 1223–30.

Weiss, J. M. "Effects of Coping Behavior in Different Warning Signal Conditions on Stress Pathology in Rats." *Journal of Comparative and Physiological Psychology* 77, (1971a): 1–13.

Weiss, J. M. "Effects of Coping Behavior with and without a Feedback Signal on Stress Pathology in Rats." *Journal of Comparative and Physiological Psychology* 77 (1971b): 22–30.

Weissman, M. M., and Boyd, J. H. "The Epidemiology of Mental Disorders." In *Neurobiology of Mood Disorders*, ed. R. M. Post and J. C. Ballenger. Baltimore: Williams and Wilkins, 1984.

Weisz, D. J., Solomon, P. R., and Thompson, R. F. "The Hippocampus Appears Necessary for Trace Conditioning." *Bulletin of the Psychonomic Society Abstracts* 193 (1980): 244.

Wender, P. H., Kety, S. S., Rosenthal, D., Schulsinger, F., and Ortmann, J. "Psychiatric Disorders in the Biological Relatives of Adopted Individuals with Affective Disorders." *Archives of General Psychiatry* 43 (1986): 923–29.

Wever, E. G. *A Theory of Hearing*. New York: Wiley, 1949.

Whalen, R. E. "Effects of Mounting without Intromission and Intromission without Ejaculation on Sexual Behavior and Maze Learning." *Journal of Comparative and Physiological Psychology* 54 (1961): 409–15.

Whitehorn, D., and Burgess, P. R. "Changes in Polarization of Central Branches of Myelinated Mechanoreceptor and Nociceptor Fibers during Noxious and Innocuous Stimulation of the Skin." *Journal of Neurophysiology* 36 (1973): 226–37.

Williams, J. H., Errington, M. L., Lynch, M. A., and Bliss, T. V. P. "Arachidonic Acid Induces a Long-Term Activity-Dependent Enhancement of Synaptic Transmission in the Hippocampus." *Nature* 341 (1989): 739–42.

Wise, R. A., and Bozarth, M. A. "Brain Reward Circuitry: Four Circuit Elements 'Wired' in Apparent Series," *Brain Research Bulletin* 12 (1984): 203–8.

Wise, R. A., and Rompre, P. P. "Brain Dopamine and Reward." *Annual Review of Psychology* 40 (1989): 191–225.

Witelson, S. F. "Developmental Dyslexia: Two Right Hemispheres and None Left." *Science* 195 (1977): 309–11.

Wolgin, D. L., Cytawa, J., and Teitelbaum, P. "The Role of Activation in the Regulation of Food Intake." In *Hunger: Basic Mechanisms and Clinical Implications*, ed. D. Novin, W. Wyrwicka, and G. Bray. New York: Raven Press, 1976.

Wollberg, Z., and Newman, J. D. "The Auditory Cortex of the Squirrel Monkey: Response Patterns of Single Cells to Species-Specific Vocalizations." *Science* 175 (1971): 212–14.

Worley, P. F., Heller, W. A., Snyder, S. H., and Baraban, J. M. "Lithium Blocks a Phosphoinositide Mediated Cholinergic Response in Hippocampal Slices." *Science* 239 (1988): 1428–29.

Wurtman, R. "Nutrients That Modify Brain Function." *Scientific American* 246 (4) (1982): 50–59.

Wurtman, R. "Alzheimer's Disease." *Scientific American* 252 (1985): 62–74.

Wurtz, R. H., and Goldberg, M. E., eds. *The Neurobiology of Saccadic Eye Movements: Reviews of Oculomotor Research*, vol. 3. Amsterdam: Elsevier, 1989.

Wurtz, R. H., Goldberg, M. E., and Robinson, D. L. "Brain Mechanisms of Visual Attention." *Scientific American* 246(6) (1982): 124–35.

Wyatt, R. J. "The Serotonin-Catecholamine Dream Bicycle: A Clinical Study." *Biological Psychiatry* 5 (1972): 33–64.

Wysocki, C. J., and Beauchamp, G. "Ability to Smell Androstenone Is Genetically Determined." *Proceedings of the National Academy of Science* 81 (1984): 4899–4902.

Yaksh, T. L. "Direct Evidence That Spinal Serotonin and Noradrenaline Terminals Mediate the Spinal Antinociceptive Effects of Morphine in the Periaqueductal Gray." *Brain Research* 160 (1979): 180–85.

Yaksh, T. L., Farb, D. H., Leeman, S. E., and Jessell, T. M. "Intrathecal Capsaicin Depletes Substance P in Rat Spinal Cord and Produces Prolonged Thermal Analgesia." *Science* 206 (1979): 481–83.

Yaksh, T. L., Jessell, T. M., Gamse, R., Mudge, A. W., and Leeman, S. E. "Intrathecal Morphine Inhibits Substance P Release in Vivo." *Nature* 286 (1980): 155–56.

Yaksh, T. L., and Rudy, T. A. "Analgesia Mediated by a Direct Spinal Action of Narcotics." *Science* 192 (1976): 1357–58.

Yankner, B. A., Dawes, L. R., Fisher, S., Villa-Komaroff, L., Oster-Granite, M. L., and Neve, R. L. "Neurotoxicity of a Fragment of the Amyloid Precursor Associated with Alzheimer's Disease." *Science* 245 (1989): 417–20.

Yokel, R. A. "Intravenous Self-Administration: Response Rates, the Effect of Pharmacological Challenges, and Drug Preference." In *Methods of Assessing the Reinforcing Properties of Abused Drugs*, ed. M. A. Bozarth. New York: Springer-Verlag, pp. 1–33.

Young, R. C., Gibbs, J., Antin, J., Holt, J., and Smith, G. P. "Absence of Satiety during Sham Feeding in the Rat." *Journal of Comparative and Physiological Psychology* 87 (1974): 795–800.

Young T. A *Course of Lectures on Natural Philosophy*. London, 1807.

Young, W. C., Goy, R. W., and Phoenix, C. "Hormones and Sexual Behavior." *Science* 143 (1964): 212–18.

Yurek, D. M., and Sladek, J. R., Jr. "Dopamine Cell Replacement: Parkinson's Disease." *Annual Review of Neuroscience* 13 (1990): 415–40.

Zahorik, D. M., Maier, S. F., and Pies, R. W. "Preferences for Tastes Paired with Recovery from Thiamine Deficiency in Rats: Appetitive Conditioning or Learned Safety?" *Journal of Comparative Physiological Psychology* 87 (1974): 1083–91.

Zaidel, E. "A Response to Gazzaniga: Language in the Right Hemisphere." *American Psychologist* 38 (1983): 542–46.

Zaidel, E. A. "Technique for Presenting Lateralized Visual Input with Prolonged Exposure." *Vision Research* 15 (1975): 283–289.

Zaidel, E. A. "Language Function in the Two Hemispheres Following Complete Cerebral Commissurotomy and Hemispherectomy." In *Handbook of Neuropsychology*, vol. 4, ed. F. Boller and J. Grafman. Amsterdam: Elsevier, 1990.

Zeki, S. "The Representation of Colours in the Cerebral Cortex." *Nature* 284 (1980): 412–18.

Zeki, S. "The Visual Image in Mind and Brain." *Scientific American* 262 (1992): 68–76.

Zeki, S., Watson J. D. G., Lueck, C. J., Friston, K. J., Kennard, C., and Frackowiak, R. S. J. "A Direct Demonstration of Functional Specialization in Human Visual Cortex." *Journal of Neuroscience* 11 (1991): 641–49.

Zihl, J., von Cramon, D., Mai, N., and Schmid, C. "Disturbance of Movement Vision after Bilateral Posterior Brain Damage, Further Evidence and Follow-up Observations." *Brain* 114 (1991): 2235–52.

Zohar, J., Insel, T. R., Zohar-Kadouch, R. C., Hill, J. L., and Murphy, D. L. "Serotonergic Responsivity in Obsessive-Compulsive Disorder." *Archives of General Psychiatry* 45 (1988): 167–72.

Zola-Morgan, S., Squire, L. R., and Amaral, D. G. "Human Amnesia and the Medial Temporal Region: Enduring Memory Impairment Following a Bilateral Lesion limited to Field CA1 of the Hippocampus." *Journal of Neuroscience* 6 (1986): 2950–67.

Zola-Morgan S., Squire, L. R., and Amaral, D. G. "Lesions of the Amygdala That Spare Adjacent Cortical Regions Do Not Impair Memory or Exacerbate the Impairment Following Lesions of the Hippocampal Formation." *Journal of Neuroscience* 9 (1989): 1922–36.

Zola-Morgan, S., Squire, L. R., Amaral, D. G., and Suzuki, W. A. "Lesions of Perirhinal and Parahippocampal Cortex That Spare the Amygdala and Hippocampal Formation Produce Severe Memory Impairment." *Journal of Neuroscience* 9 (1989): 4355–70.

Zollar, A. C. *The Social Correlates of Infant Reproductive Mortality in the United States*. New York: Garland, 1993.

PERMISSIONS ACKNOWLEDGMENTS

Fig. 1.1: Adapted from "The Visual Image in Mind and Brain" by Semir Zeki. Copyright © 1992 by Scientific American, Inc. All rights reserved.

Fig. 2.9: Adpated from "Aging Brain, Aging Mind" by Dennis J. Selkoe. Copyright © 1992 by Scientific American, Inc. All rights reserved.

Fig. 2.11: Adapted from A. Björklund, U. Stenevi, R. H. Schmidt, S. B. Dunnett, and F. H. Gage, "Intracerebral Grafting of Neuronal Cell Suspensions. I. Introduction and General Methods of Preparation," *Acta Physiologica Scandinavica*, Supplement 522 (1983), Fig. 1, by permission of the publisher.

Fig. 3.10: From *Biological Psychology*, p. 117, by J. W. Kalat. Copyright © 1992, 1988, 1984, 1981 by Wadsworth, Inc. Adapted by permission of Brooks/Cole Publishing Company, Pacific Grove, CA 93950.

Fig. 3.13: From *Biological Psychology*, p. 274, by J. W. Kalat. Copyright © 1992, 1988, 1984, 1981 by Wadsworth, Inc. Adapted by permission of Brooks/Cole Publishing Company, Pacific Grove, CA 93950.

Fig. 3.16: From F. O. Schmitt and F. G. Worden, *The Neural Sciences: Fourth Study* (Cambridge: MIT Press, 1979). Copyright © 1979 by MIT Press.

Fig. 3.17: From *Brain, Mind and Behavior* 2/e by Bloom and Lazerson. Copyright © 1988 by Educational Broadcasting Group. Used with permission of W. H. Freeman and Company.

Fig. 3.24: From *Left Brain, Right Brain* by Springer and Deutsch. Copyright © 1981 by Sally P. Springer and Georg Deutsch. Used with permission of W. H. Freeman and Company.

Fig. 6.1: Adapted from D. Bodian, "The Generalized Vertebrate Neuron," *Science* 137: 323–326. Copyright 1962 by the AAAS.

Fig. 6.5: Adapted from "Phantom Limbs" by Ronald Melzack. Copyright © 1992 by Scientific American, Inc. All rights reserved.

Fig. 7.6: From P. Lindsay and D. Norman, *Human Information Processing*, 2nd edition (Academic Press, 1977). Adapted by permission.

Fig. 7.10: From E. R. Kandel and J. H. Schwartz, *Principles of Neural Science*, Figure 21.1, p. 237 (1981). Adapted by permission of Appleton & Lange, Norwalk, CT.

Fig. 7.13: From Neil R. Carlson, *Physiology of Behavior*, 2nd edition, p. 232. Copyright © 1981 by Allyn and Bacon. Adapted by permission.

Fig. 7.17: From E. Carterette and M. P. Friedman, *Handbook of Perception: Vol. V—Seeing* (Academic Press, 1975). Adapted by permission.

Fig. 8.5: From G. von Bekesy, *Experiments in Hearing*, trans. and ed. E. G. Wever (New York: McGraw-Hill, 1960). Adapted by permission.

Fig. 9.6: Adapted from R. Melzack and P. D. Wall, "Pain Mechanisms: A New Theory," *Science* 150: 971–979. Copyright 1965 by the AAAS.

Fig. 10.8: From E. R. Kandel, J. H. Schwartz, and T. M. Jessell, *Principles of Neural Science*, 3rd edition, Figure 42-4, p. 651 (1991). Reprinted by permission of Appleton & Lange, Norwalk, CT.

Fig. 10.9: From *Fundamentals of Human Neuropsychology* 3/e by Kolb and Whishaw. Copyright © 1990 by W. H. Freeman and Company. Used with permission.

Fig. 13.3: Illustration from J. P. Pinel, *Biopsychology*, 2nd edition, Fig. 11.13, p. 377. Copyright © 1993 by Allyn and Bacon. Adapted by permission.

Fig. 13.5: Adapted from J. Money and A. Ehrhardt, *Man and Woman, Boy and Girl* (Baltimore: John Hopkins University Press, 1972) by permission of J. Money.

Fig. 14.8: Adapted from "Emotion, Memory and the Brain" by Joseph E. LeDoux. Copyright © 1994 by Scientific American, Inc. All rights reserved.

Fig. 16.2: From *Principles of Learning and Behavior*, by M. Domjan and B. Burkhard. Copyright © 1982 by Wadsworth, Inc. Reprinted by permission of Brooks/Cole Publishing Company, Monterey, California.

Fig. 16.9: From E. R. Kandel, J. H. Schwartz, and T. M. Jessell, *Principles of Neural Science*, 3rd edition, Figure 65–6, p. 1016 (1991). Adapted by permission of Appleton & Lange, Norwalk, CT.

Fig. 16.10: Adapted from Arthur Konnerth, "Patch-clamping in Slices of Mammalian CNS," *Trends in Neuroscience*, 13, No. 8 (1990), Fig. 1, p. 321. © 1990, Elsevier Science Publishers Ltd. (UK). Used with permission.

Fig. 16.11: Adapted from B. Gustafsson and H. Wigstrom, "Physiological Mechanisms Underlying Long-term Potentiation," *Trends in Neuroscience*, 11 (1988), pp. 156–162. © 1988, Elsevier Science Publishers Ltd. (UK). Used with permission.

Fig. 17.4: Adapted from "Working Memory and the Mind" by Patricia S. Goldman-Rakic. Copyright © 1992 by Scientific American, Inc. All rights reserved.

Fig. 17.6: From J. Barbizet, *Human Memory and Its Pathology* (New York: W. H. Freeman, 1970). Redrawn by permission of C. P. Barbizet.

Fig. 17.7: Adapted from L. R. Squire et al., "Retrograde Amnesia: Temporal Gradient in Very Long-Term Memory Following Electroconvulsive Therapy," *Science* 187: 77–79. Copyright 1975 by the AAAS.

Fig. 17.8: Data from B. Milner, "Memory Disturbance after Bilateral Hippocampal Lesions," in P. M. Milner and S. E. Glickman, eds., *Cognitive Processes and the Brain.* © 1965 by Wadsworth, Inc. Reprinted by permission of the publisher.

Fig. 18.3: From *Left Brain, Right Brain* by Springer and Deutsch. Copyright © 1981 by Sally P. Springer and Georg Deutsch. Used with permission of W. H. Freeman and Company.

Fig. 18.9: From *Left Brain, Right Brain* 4/e by Springer and Deutsch. Copyright © 1993 by Sally P. Springer and Georg Deutsch. Used with permission of W. H. Freeman and Company.

Fig. 18.10: From *Essentials of Psychological Testing*, 3rd edition, by Lee J. Cronbach. HarperCollins Publishers. Adapted by permission.

PHOTO CREDITS

Page 7: Bettmann Archive.
Page 9: North Wind Picture Archives.

714

location of, **145**
panic attacks and, 532
in peripheral nervous system,
151–152, 180
serotonin, mental depression
and, 153–154
Nuclear bag, 337
Nuclear magnetic resonance
(NMR), 96
Nucleus accumbens, reward and, 505
Nucleus basalis, 148
Nucleus cuneatus, 298
Nucleus gracilis, 298
Nucleus raphe magnus, 310, 312,
313
Nutrient(s), 31, **32, 133**, 365
in everyday diet, activity of
neurotransmitters in brain
and, 178
level of, in body, 366
Nystagmus reflex, 323

Obesity, 365
genetics, metabolism and, 407
in humans and animals, 388–391
Obsessive-compulsive disorder
(OCD), 86, 144, 532
behavior and, 534–535
brain and, 534–535
chemical abnormalities in, 534
serotonin and, 153
structural and metabolic abnormalities in, 533–534
Obstinate progression, 343
Occipital lobe, 83, 85, 87, **214**
Oculomotor nerve, 62, **63**
Odor, categorization of, 285
Off-center cell, 227, 230, 252
Off signal, 408
drinking behavior and, 401–403
eating and, 366–367
Olfaction, 16, 276, 289
sex and aggression and, 284
stereochemical theory of,
284–285
Olfactory nervous system, 283
Oligodendrocyte, 28, 31, 42, 43,
54, 59
Olivary nucleus, 196, 204
Ommatidium, 223, 224
in *Limulus*, 279
On-center cell, 227, 230, 252
On signal for eating, 366–367
Operational definition, 10
Opiate(s), 136, 157, 165–166, 181,
182, 313, 327
actions of, on neurotransmitters,
160
addictive powers of, 177
Opiate effect, 601
Opponent cell, 248
blue-yellow, 247
color-coded, **246**
four types of, 244

red-green, 246–247
Opponent-process theory of color
vision, 243, 244, 253, 254
combining trichromatic theory
and, 245–246
in explaining color blindness, 249
support for, 244–245
Opsin, 218, 251
Optic chiasm, 213, **214**
Optic disk, 213
Optic nerve, 62, **63**, 213, **214, 217,**
251
Optic radiation, **214**
Optical process of vision, 209, 250
Oral factor, 367–368
Orbitofrontal cortex, 283
Organ of Corti, 264, 287
Organum vasculasum of lamina ter-
minalis (OVLT), 400
Orgasm of human, 454
Oscilloscope, **111**
Osmotic receptor, 399
Osmotic thirst, 396, 397
Ossicle, 263
Otolith, 324
Outer ear, 261–262, 287
structures in, 287
Oval window, 262, 263, 271
Ovary, 83, 358
Overtone, 260
Owl, sound localization and,
274–275
Oxygen, 60
Oxytocin, 83, 355

P cell, 236, 252
Pacinian corpuscle, 294, 298, 319,
325
Pain, 62, 85, 87, 201, 293, 295
acupuncture and, 313–314
chronic, 307–310, 326
code for, 306
definition of, 302–303
gate-control theory of, 310
hypnosis and, 313–314
Melzack and Wall's theory of, **308**
neural pathways for, **304**
neuropeptides and, **157**
opiates and, 313
from phantom limb, 203
placebos and, 313–314
relief of, 165
sensitivity for, 184
substance P and, 157
Pain circuitry in brain, 326
Pain suppression, 160, 181,
313–316, 327
adaptive function of, 327
chemistry of, 312–313
dietary therapy and, 178
endorphins and enkephalins
and, 157
neural and chemical pathways
for, **311**

physiological basis of, 136
raphe nuclei and, 80
Paleocortex, 83
Pancreas, 380, 389
eating behavior and, 389–390
Panic attack(s), 163, 531
chemical basis of, 531–532
Papez's circuit, 487
Parachlorophenylalanine (PCPA),
313
Paradoxical cold, 317
Paradoxical sleep, 414
Parallel processing, 235, 252
evidence for, 236
Paralysis, 43, 72
Paraplegic, 78
Paraquat, 47
Parasympathetic nervous system,
66, 70
chemistry of, 68–69
eye and, 210
structure of, 68–69
Parasympathetic overshoot, 518
Paraventricular nucleus, 378
Parietal lobe(s), 83, 85, 87
damage of, 197
Parkinson's disease, 27, 40, 45, 54,
55, 154, 344
abnormal neurotransmitter
and, 36
damage in basal ganglia and, 86
role of environment in, 47
transplant therapy and, 50–52
treatment of, 48–49, 55
Parvocellularis layer, 229
Passive (nongated) channel, 110,
114, 115, 121
Perception(s):
auditory, 640
coordination of, 648
localization of, 639–643
underlying, mechanisms of,
235–236
Periaqueductal gray, 196, 204, 310,
313
Perifornical area, 385
Perilymph, 268
Peripheral circuit for cutaneous
senses, 295–298
Peripheral nerve, 99
disease in, 307
pain and, 303
Peripheral nervous system, 27, 52,
53, 58–**61**, 90
acetylcholine in, 146–**147**
damaged neurons regenerate
in, **41**
division of, 60
function of, 62
integration of central nervous
system with, 88–90
neural crest cells and, 37
nonneural cells in, 28, 31
norepinephrine in, 151–152, 180

727